AF129896

Fuzzy Modeling and Fuzzy Control Systems

Fuzzy Modeling and Fuzzy Control Systems

Editors

Lijuan Zha
Jian Liu
Jinliang Liu

MDPI

Basel • Beijing • Wuhan • Barcelona • Belgrade • Novi Sad • Cluj • Manchester

Editors

Lijuan Zha
College of Science
Nanjing Forestry University
Nanjing
China

Jian Liu
College of Information Engineering
Nanjing University of Finance and Economics
Nanjing
China

Jinliang Liu
School of Computer Science
Nanjing University of Information Science and Technology
Nanjing
China

Editorial Office
MDPI AG
Grosspeteranlage 5
4052 Basel, Switzerland

This is a reprint of articles from the Special Issue published online in the open access journal *Mathematics* (ISSN 2227-7390) (available at: https://mdpi.com/si/137683).

For citation purposes, cite each article independently as indicated on the article page online and as indicated below:

Lastname, A.A.; Lastname, B.B. Article Title. *Journal Name* **Year**, *Volume Number*, Page Range.

ISBN 978-3-7258-2165-5 (Hbk)
ISBN 978-3-7258-2166-2 (PDF)
doi.org/10.3390/books978-3-7258-2166-2

© 2024 by the authors. Articles in this book are Open Access and distributed under the Creative Commons Attribution (CC BY) license. The book as a whole is distributed by MDPI under the terms and conditions of the Creative Commons Attribution-NonCommercial-NoDerivs (CC BY-NC-ND) license.

Contents

Preface vii

Thanh Binh Nguyen and Hyoung-Kyu Song
Further Results on Robust Output-Feedback Dissipative Control of Markovian Jump Fuzzy Systems with Model Uncertainties
Reprinted from: *Mathematics* **2022**, *10*, 3620, doi:10.3390/math10193620 1

Binshuang Zheng, Zhengqiang Hong, Junyao Tang, Meiling Han, Jiaying Chen and Xiaoming Huang
A Comprehensive Method to Evaluate Ride Comfort of Autonomous Vehicles under Typical Braking Scenarios: Testing, Simulation and Analysis
Reprinted from: *Mathematics* **2023**, *11*, 474, doi:10.3390/math11020474 17

Jie Fu, Jian Liu, Dongkai Xie and Zhe Sun
Application of Fuzzy PID Based on Stray Lion Swarm Optimization Algorithm in Overhead Crane System Control
Reprinted from: *Mathematics* **2023**, *11*, 2170, doi:10.3390/math11092170 40

Wei Zhang, Zhe Sun, Jian Liu and Suisheng Chen
A More Efficient and Practical Modified Nyström Method
Reprinted from: *Mathematics* **2023**, *11*, 2433, doi:10.3390/math11112433 58

Muhammad Bilal Khan, Ali Althobaiti, Cheng-Chi Lee, Mohamed S. Soliman and Chun-Ta Li
Some New Properties of Convex Fuzzy-Number-Valued Mappings on Coordinates Using Up and Down Fuzzy Relations and Related Inequalities
Reprinted from: *Mathematics* **2023**, *11*, 2851, doi:10.3390/math11132851 71

Bo Song, Huiming Wu, Yurong Song, Xu Wang and Guoping Jiang
Epidemic Spreading on Weighted Co-Evolving Multiplex Networks
Reprinted from: *Mathematics* **2023**, *11*, 3109, doi:10.3390/math11143109 94

Muhammad Bilal Khan, Eze R. Nwaeze, Cheng-Chi Lee, Hatim Ghazi Zaini, Der-Chyuan Lou and Khalil Hadi Hakami
Weighted Fractional Hermite–Hadamard Integral Inequalities for up and down Ꭻ-Convex Fuzzy Mappings over Coordinates
Reprinted from: *Mathematics* **2023**, *11*, 4974, doi:10.3390/math11244974 109

Shuxia Jing, Chengming Lu and Zhimin Li
Dissipative Fuzzy Filtering for Nonlinear Networked Systems with Dynamic Quantization and Data Packet Dropouts
Reprinted from: *Mathematics* **2024**, *12*, 203, doi:10.3390/math12020203 139

Yuhua Xu, Yang Liu, Zhixin Sun, Yucheng Xue, Weiliang Liao, Chenlei Liu and Zhe Sun
Key Vulnerable Nodes Discovery Based on Bayesian Attack Subgraphs and Improved Fuzzy C-Means Clustering
Reprinted from: *Mathematics* **2024**, *12*, 1447, doi:10.3390/math12101447 156

Chenlei Liu and Zhixin Sun
A Multi-Agent Reinforcement Learning-Based Task-Offloading Strategy in a Blockchain-Enabled Edge Computing Network
Reprinted from: *Mathematics* **2024**, *12*, 2264, doi:10.3390/math12142264 177

Preface

In recent years, with the rapid development of advanced machine learning, artificial intelligence, robot technology, networked control methods, deep space exploration, and other fields, successful applications in fuzzy control systems or even nonlinear dynamics systems (FCS/NDSs) have emerged. The modeling, analysis, and optimal control of FCS/NDSs have received considerable attention in the last two decades. As usual, the design and analysis of classic dynamics systems rely on deterministic mathematical models. However, dynamical systems are riddled with nonlinearity, complexity and time-delay properties, which make it difficult to ensure system optimization. Certain linearization assumptions are often employed to obtain the optimal theoretical closed-form solution in FCS/NDSs, which are inconsistent with real engineering applications. Therefore, these advanced nonlinear sciences motivate us to explore new solutions of abundant problems in FCS/NDSs.

In this Special Issue, the final 10 accepted papers have been peer-reviewed. These papers can be categorized into nonlinear intelligent control, and the following is a brief description of each paper in this Special Issue.

Thanh Binh Nguyen and Hyoung-Kyu Song, in their paper titled 'Further Results on Robust Output-Feedback Dissipative Control of Markovian Jump Fuzzy Systems with Model Uncertainties', investigate an improved criterion to synthesize dissipative observer-based controllers for Markovian jump fuzzy systems under model uncertainties. They present the first attempt to apply double-fuzzy summation-based Lyapunov functions for the observer-based control scheme of the Markov jump fuzzy system regarding the mismatched phenomenon. The obtained observer-based controller ensures that the closed-loop system is stochastically stable, and the dissipative performances produce less conservative results compared to preceding works via two numerical examples.

Binshuang Zheng et al., in their paper titled 'A Comprehensive Method to Evaluate Ride Comfort of Autonomous Vehicles under Typical Braking Scenarios: Testing, Simulation and Analysis', explore the sensing requirement parameters of the road environment during the vehicle braking process to highlight the advantages of autonomous vehicles (AVs) in modern traffic. Based on the texture information obtained using a field measurement, the braking model of an AV was built in Simulink, and the ride comfort under typical braking scenarios was analyzed using CarSim/Simulink co-simulation. The results showed that the proposed brake system for the AV displayed a better performance than the traditional ABS when considering pavement adhesion characteristics.

Jie Fu et al., in their paper titled 'Application of Fuzzy PID Based on Stray Lion Swarm Optimization Algorithm in Overhead Crane System Control', introduce the LSO algorithm and add the stray operator, which effectively improves its global search performance. By combining SLSO and fuzzy PID and comparing them with other methods, this paper confirms that even without targeted optimization by professionals, the optimization algorithm can find the appropriate parameter configuration for fuzzy PID, which can be effectively used in the crane anti-swing problem.

Wei Zhang et al., in their paper titled 'A More Efficient and Practical Modified Nyström Method', propose an efficient Nyström method with theoretical and empirical guarantees. In parallel computing environments and for sparse input kernel matrices, their algorithm can theoretically have computation efficiency comparable to that ofthe conventional Nyström method,. Additionally, they derive an important theoretical result with a compacter sketching matrix and faster speed, at the cost of some accuracy loss compared to existing state-of-the-art results. Faster randomized SVD and more efficient adaptive sampling methods are also proposed, which have wide application in many machine learning and data mining tasks.

Muhammad Bilal Khan et al., in their paper titled 'Some New Properties of Convex Fuzzy-Number-Valued Mappings on Coordinates Using Up and Down Fuzzy Relations and Related Inequalities', define a novel class of convex mappings on planes using a fuzzy inclusion relation, known as coordinated up and down convex fuzzy-number-valued mapping. Several new definitions are introduced by placing some moderate restrictions on the notion of coordinated up and down convex fuzzy-number-valued mapping. Other uncommon examples are also described using these definitions, which can be viewed as applications of the new outcomes. Moreover, Hermite–Hadamard–Fejér inequalities are acquired via fuzzy double Aumann integrals, and the validation of these outcomes is discussed with the help of nontrivial examples and suitable choices of coordinated up and down convex fuzzy-number-valued mappings.

Bo Song et al., in their paper titled 'Epidemic Spreading on Weighted Co-Evolving Multiplex Networks', propose a novel weighted co-evolving multiplex network model to describe the interaction between information diffusion in online social networks and epidemic spreading in adaptive physical contact networks. Considering the difference in the connections between individuals, the heterogeneous rewiring rate, which is proportional to the strength of the connection, is introduced in the model. The simulation results show that the maximum infection scale decreases as the information acceptance probability grows, and the final infection decreases as the rewiring behaviors increase.

Muhammad Bilal Khan et al., in their paper titled 'Weighted Fractional Hermite–Hadamard Integral Inequalities for up and down $\mathfrak{J}$-Convex Fuzzy Mappings over Coordinates', introduce a new class of convexity, as well as prove several Hermite–Hadamard-type interval-valued integral inequalities in the fractional domain. This produces several known classes of convexity. Additionally, they create some new fractional variations in the Hermite–Hadamard (HH) and Pachpatte types of inequalities using the concepts of coordinated UD-$\mathfrak{J}$-convexity and double Riemann–Liouville fractional operators.

Shuxia Jing et al., in their paper titled 'Dissipative Fuzzy Filtering for Nonlinear Networked Systems with Dynamic Quantization and Data Packet Dropouts', discusse the dissipative filtering problem for discrete-time nonlinear networked systems with dynamic quantization and data packet dropouts. The Takagi–Sugeno (T–S) fuzzy model is employed to approximate the considered nonlinear plant. The purpose of this paper is to design full- and reduced-order filters, such that the stochastic stability and dissipative filtering performance of the filtering error system can be guaranteed. The collaborative design conditions for the desired filter and the dynamic quantizers are expressed in the form of linear matrix inequalities.

Yuhua Xu et al., in their paper titled 'Key Vulnerable Nodes Discovery Based on Bayesian Attack Subgraphs and Improved Fuzzy C-Means Clustering', propose a key vulnerable node discovery method based on Bayesian attack subgraphs and improved fuzzy C-means clustering. The optimal number of clusters is adaptively adjusted according to the variance idea, and fuzzy clustering is performed based on the extracted clustering features. Finally, the key vulnerable nodes are determined by setting the feature priority.

Chenlei Liu and Zhixin Sun, in their paper titled 'A Multi-Agent Reinforcement Learning-Based Task-Offloading Strategy in a Blockchain-Enabled Edge Computing Network', propose a blockchain-enabled mobile edge computing task-offloading strategy based on multi-agent reinforcement learning. They propose a deep reinforcement learning algorithm based on multiple agents sharing a global memory pool using the actor–critic architecture, which enables each agent to acquire the experience of another agent during the training process to enhance the collaborative capability among agents and overall performance. In addition, they integrate attenuatable Gaussian noise into the action space selection process in the actor network to avoid falling into the local optimum.

Lijuan Zha, Jian Liu, and Jinliang Liu
Editors

mathematics

MDPI

Article

Further Results on Robust Output-Feedback Dissipative Control of Markovian Jump Fuzzy Systems with Model Uncertainties

Thanh Binh Nguyen and Hyoung-Kyu Song *

Department of Information and Communication Engineering and Convergence Engineering for Intelligent Drone, Sejong University, Seoul 05006, Korea
* Correspondence: songhk@sejong.ac.kr; Tel.: +82-2-3408-3890

Abstract: This paper investigates an improved criterion to synthesize dissipative observer-based controllers for Markovian jump fuzzy systems under model uncertainties. Since fuzzy-basis functions include some immeasurable state variable or uncertain parameters, there are differences in the fuzzy-basis functions between controller and plant, which is a mismatched phenomenon. This work presents the first attempt for applying double-fuzzy summation-based Lyapunov functions for the observer-based control scheme of the Markov jump fuzzy system regarding the mismatched phenomenon. To be specific, the dissipative conditions are formulated in terms of uncertain parameterized bilinear matrix inequalities. Based on the improved relaxation techniques, a linear-matrix-inequality (LMI)-based algorithm is proposed in the framework of sequence linear programming matrix method. The obtained observer-based controller ensures that the closed-loop system is stochastically stable, and the dissipative performances produce less conservative results compared to preceding works via two numerical examples.

Keywords: markov jump fuzzy systems; dissipative control; mismatched phenomenon; model uncertainties

MSC: 93C42; 93E15

Citation: Nguyen, T.B.; Song, H.-K. Further Results on Robust Output-Feedback Dissipative Control of Markovian Jump Fuzzy Systems with Model Uncertainties. *Mathematics* **2022**, *10*, 3620. https://doi.org/10.3390/math10193620

Academic Editors: Lijuan Zha, Jian Liu and Jinliang Liu

Received: 12 September 2022
Accepted: 29 September 2022
Published: 3 October 2022

Publisher's Note: MDPI stays neutral with regard to jurisdictional claims in published maps and institutional affiliations.

Copyright: © 2022 by the authors. Licensee MDPI, Basel, Switzerland. This article is an open access article distributed under the terms and conditions of the Creative Commons Attribution (CC BY) license (https://creativecommons.org/licenses/by/4.0/).

1. Introduction

The development of control engineering is faced with a class of hybrid systems with probabilistic sudden changes to their behavior, named the stochastic hybrid system. The systems have attracted a huge consideration from many control theorists due to their abilities in showing hybrid dynamics with probabilistic changes. Markov jump systems (MJSs) whose jumping parameters are governed by the Markov process belong to the class of the stochastic hybrid system, and have expressed great potential to represent random abrupt variations such as component fault or failures, sudden environmental changes, and changing subsystem interconnections. In the view of realistic problems, discrete-time MJSs have played important roles to implement digital experiments including network control systems [1–3], power systems [4–6] and communication systems [7,8].

The Takagi–Sugeno (T-S) fuzzy model is well known as an effective tool to describe nonlinear dynamics via an average sum of given linear models. Recent years have witnessed a massive increase of studies related to the systematic control design of nonlinear systems using The T–S fuzzy model [9–11] According to this trend, the T-S fuzzy model has been investigated intensively to cover various nonlinear control problems [12,13]. In many situations, all state variables are not fully measurable. The observer-based fuzzy control scheme needs to estimate FBFs and state variables, then establish fuzzy control laws [13–15]. When the premise variables of the T–S fuzzy system are related to the immeasurable state, that leads to a mismatched phenomenon between fuzzy-basis functions

(FBFs) in the plant and those of the controller, there have been fruitful works devoted to observer-based output-feedback control synthesis, such as stability and stabilization [16,17], $\mathcal{H}_\infty$ and dissipative control [18,19].

Over the past decade, the extensions of the T-S fuzzy model to MJSs has established the framework of Markov jump fuzzy systems (MJFSs), and particularly to the output-feedback control of MJFSs [20,21]. However, So far as we know, in the presence of model uncertainties, there has been little progress toward the output-feedback scheme with consideration to the mismatched phenomenon. Studies on [22] have used interval type 2 fuzzy MJFSs to deal with the mismatched phenomenon, while [21] presenting a sliding mode output-feedback with uncertain transition rates. The authors in [23] present a two-step LMI-based method to design dissipative output-feedback controllers for MJFS. To improve the dissipative performance, the work in [24] develops a single-step LMI-based method regarding sensor failures. Lately, relaxed results for observed-based controllers for discrete-time MJFSs have been investigated in [25] by nonparallel distributed compensation (non-PDC) scheme. However, a common limitation of the above studies is relaxed attempts to overcome the conservatism of the output-feedback scheme by a single-step or two-step LMI solution. As reported in [13], the two-step approach has much conservatism and sensitivity due to the weak selection of decision variables in the first step [23], while the single-step requires excessive use of free weighting matrices [24]. Thus, it is necessary to develop an innovative method based on the progress of relaxation techniques and modified Lyapunov functions.

Motivated by these discussions, this paper presents improved results of the output-feedback dissipative control of MJFSs with model uncertainties. By taking advantage of the mode-fuzzy-dependent Lyapunov functions in terms of a double-fuzzy summation, our work can obtain better computed dissipative performance compared to existing results. In short, besides proposing the dissipative observer-based controller for the discrete-time MJFSs regarding the model uncertainties and mismatched phenomenon, our contributions also contain:

- The model uncertainties and mismatch phenomenon entail difficulties in handling multiple parameterized matrix inequalities when deriving LMI-based dissipative conditions. Thus, a refined relaxation process with the sequence linear programming matrix method (SLPMM) is proposed to solve dissipative conditions by LMI-based algorithm.
- Apart from this, our work takes advantage of the double-fuzzy summation-based mode-fuzzy-dependent Lyapunov functions to relax the dissipative conditions. The Lyapunov function collaborates with the relaxation process to release less conservative LMI-based dissipative conditions compared to [13,23,24,26]. The results are verified through two illustrative examples.

In accordance with the contributions, this work can be applied to stabilize the nonlinear systems with jumping and certainties in system parameters, e.g., tracking control of unmanned ground vehicles over network communications with packet losses and stabilization power grids under sudden load changes.

The notations $X \geq Y$ and $X > Y$ mean that $X - Y$ is positive semi-definite and positive definite, respectively. In symmetric block matrices, the asterisk $(*)$ is used as an ellipsis for terms induced by symmetry. $\mathbf{E}\{\cdot\}$ denotes the mathematical expectation; $\mathcal{L}_2[0,\infty)$ stands for the space of square summable sequences over $[0,\infty)$; $\mathbf{diag}(\cdot)$ stands for a diagonal matrix with diagonal entries; $\mathbf{col}(v_1, v_2, \cdots, v_n) = [v_1^T\ v_2^T\ \cdots\ v_n^T]^T$ for scalar or vector v_i; $\otimes$ denotes the Kronecker product; $\mathbf{He}\{\mathcal{P}\} = \mathcal{P} + \mathcal{P}^T$ for a square matrix $\mathcal{P}$; $\mathbb{N}_1 \setminus \mathbb{N}_2$ indicates the set of elements in the set $\mathbb{N}_1$, but not in the set $\mathbb{N}_2$; and $n(\mathbb{N})$ denotes the number of elements in set $\mathbb{N}$. For $\mathbb{N} = \{a_1, a_2, \cdots, a_s\}$, the following matrix expansion notation is used:

$$[\mathcal{M}_i]^{\mathbf{d}}_{i\in\mathbb{N}} = \mathbf{diag}(\mathcal{M}_{a_1}, \cdots, \mathcal{M}_{a_s}),$$

$$[\mathcal{M}_i]_{i\in\mathbb{N}} = \begin{bmatrix} \mathcal{M}_{a_1} \\ \vdots \\ \mathcal{M}_{a_s} \end{bmatrix}, \; [\mathcal{M}_{ij}]_{i,j\in\mathbb{N}} = \begin{bmatrix} \mathcal{M}_{a_1 a_1} & \cdots & \mathcal{M}_{a_1 a_s} \\ \vdots & \ddots & \vdots \\ \mathcal{M}_{a_s a_1} & \cdots & \mathcal{M}_{a_s a_s} \end{bmatrix}$$

where $\mathcal{M}_i$ and $\mathcal{M}_{ij}$ are real matrices with appropriate dimensions or scalar values.

The rest of the paper is sketched as follows. The next section presents problem statements and fundamental definitions of MJFSs, and the preceding useful results exploited in the paper. Section 3 includes control synthesis for LMI-based dissipative conditions of the concerned observer-based controller. The last section shows two numerical implementations to verify the validity and effectiveness of the proposed method.

2. Preliminaries

For a given complete probability space $(\Omega, \mathcal{F}, \mathcal{P})$, consider a discrete-time homogeneous Markov chain ψ as a sequence of random variables $\psi_0, \psi_1, \ldots$ whose values belong to a finite set of state $\mathbb{N}_\psi = \{1, 2, \cdots, s\}$ and satisfy Markov properties. Let $\pi_{pq} = \mathbf{Pr}(\psi_{k+1} = q | \psi_k = p)$ be a time-invariant one-step probability of jumping from state (or mode) p to q. Accordingly, we have $\pi_{pq} \in [0,1]$ and $\sum_{q=1}^{r} \pi_{pq} = 1$. Based on the definitions, let us consider a class of Markovian jump fuzzy systems (MJFSs) as follows:

$$\begin{cases} x_{k+1} = (A(\psi_k, \xi) + \Delta A(\psi_k, k))x_k + (B(\psi_k, \xi) + \Delta B(\psi_k, k))u_k + E(\psi_k, \xi)d_k, \\ z_k = G(\psi_k, \xi)x_k + H(\psi_k, \xi)u_k + J(\psi_k, \xi)d_k, \\ y_k = C(\psi_k, \xi)x_k + D(\psi_k, \xi)d_k, \end{cases} \tag{1}$$

in which $x_k \in \mathbb{R}^{n_x}$, $u_k \in \mathbb{R}^{n_u}$, $y_k \in \mathbb{R}^{n_y}$, $z_k \in \mathbb{R}^{n_z}$, and $d_k \in \mathbb{R}^{n_d}$ represent for the state variable, the control input, the measured output, the performance output, and the bounded-energy disturbance (belonging to $\mathcal{L}_2[0,\infty)$), respectively. In addition, ψ_k is the discrete-time homogeneous Markov chain standing for sudden changes in system matrices $A_p(\xi), B_p(\xi), E_p(\xi), G_p(\xi), H_p(\xi), J_p(\xi)$ where

$$\begin{bmatrix} A & B & E \\ C & 0 & D \\ G & H & J \end{bmatrix}(\psi_k = p, \xi) = \begin{bmatrix} A_p(\xi) & B_p(\xi) & E_p(\xi) \\ C_p(\xi) & 0 & D_p(\xi) \\ G_p(\xi) & H_p(\xi) & J_p(\xi) \end{bmatrix} = \sum_{i=1}^{r} \xi_i \begin{bmatrix} A_{pi} & B_{pi} & E_{pi} \\ C_{pi} & 0 & D_{pi} \\ G_{pi} & H_{pi} & J_{pi} \end{bmatrix},$$

where $A_{pi}, B_{pi}, C_{pi}, D_{pi}, E_{pi}, G_{pi}, H_{pi}$, and J_{pi} are constant system matrices with appropriate dimensions. To be more specific, r indicates the number of fuzzy rules, and we denote the fuzzy-basis function vector as $\xi = \xi(\varrho(x_k))$ (or simply ξ_k) $= [\xi_1(\varrho(x_k)), \xi_2(\varrho(x_k)), \ldots, \xi_r(\varrho(x_k))]^T \in \mathbb{R}^r$ where $\varrho(x_k) = [\varrho_1(x_k), \varrho_1(x_k), \ldots, \varrho_d(x_k)]^T \in \mathbb{R}^d$ stands for premise variable. Please note that $\xi_i(\varrho(x_k))$ denotes the ith element of fuzzy-basis vector ξ who fulfill $\sum_{i=1}^{r} \xi_i = 1$ and $\xi_i \in [0,1]$ for all $i \in \mathbb{N}_\xi = \{1, 2, \cdots, r\}$.

In this paper, we assume that the model uncertainties $\Delta A(\psi_k, k)$ and $\Delta B(\psi_k, k)$ can be decomposed into matrix multiplications of the following forms:

$$\begin{cases} \Delta A(\psi_k = p, k) = \Delta A_p(k) = T_{a,p} U_a(k) Y_{a,p}, \\ \Delta B(\psi_k = p, k) = \Delta B_p(k) = T_{b,p} U_b(k) Y_{b,p} \end{cases} \tag{2}$$

where $T_{a,p}, T_{b,p}, Y_{a,p}$ and $Y_{b,p}$ are given constant matrices with appropriate dimensions; $U_a(k)$ and $U_b(k)$ are time-varying matrices with $U_a(k)U_a^T(k) \leq I$, $U_b(k)U_b^T(k) \leq I$.

Since the premise variable vector depends on several immeasurable state variables x_k or on uncertain parameters, fuzzy control laws to be designed is impossible to share the same premise variables with the plant (1). In this light, we deal with the mismatched phenomenon by the observer-based fuzzy in the following form:

$$\begin{cases} \hat{x}_{k+1} = A_p(\hat{\xi})\hat{x}_k + B_p(\hat{\xi})u_k + L_p(\hat{\xi})(y_k - C_p(\hat{\xi})\hat{x}_k), \\ u_k = K_p(\hat{\xi})\hat{x}_k, \end{cases} \tag{3}$$

where $\psi_k = p$ and $\hat{x}_k \in \mathbb{R}^{n_x}$ stands for the observed state; $\hat{\xi} = \xi_i(\varrho(\hat{x}_k)) = \mathbf{col}(\xi_1(\varrho(\hat{x}_k)), \xi_2(\varrho(\hat{x}_k)), \cdots, \xi_r(\varrho(\hat{x}_k)))$ represents for the observed fuzzy-basis function vector calculated on the controller side based on observed states at time step k; $L_p(\hat{\xi})$ and $K_p(\hat{\xi})$ are the fuzzy-dependent matrices needed to be designed, respectively; and

$$A_p(\hat{\xi}) = \sum_{i=1}^{r} \hat{\xi}_i A_{pi}, \; B_p(\hat{\xi}) = \sum_{i=1}^{r} \hat{\xi}_i B_{pi}, \; C_p(\hat{\xi}) = \sum_{i=1}^{r} \hat{\xi}_i C_{pi}.$$

Furthermore, let $e_k = x_k - \hat{x}_k$, $\zeta_k = [\hat{x}_k^T, e_k^T]^T \in \mathbb{R}^{2n_x \times 2n_x}$, and $\tilde{\xi} = [\tilde{\xi}_1, \tilde{\xi}_2, \cdots, \tilde{\xi}_r]^T$ with $\tilde{\xi}_i = \xi_i - \hat{\xi}_i$, the closed-loop control system of (1) and (3) is represented as follows:

$$\begin{cases} \zeta_{k+1} = \bar{\mathbf{A}}_p(\tilde{\xi}, \xi, \hat{\xi})\zeta_k + \mathbf{E}_p(\xi, \hat{\xi})d_k, \\ z_k = \mathbf{G}_p(\xi, \hat{\xi})\zeta_k + J_p(\xi)d_k, \end{cases} \tag{4}$$

where $\bar{\mathbf{A}}_p(\tilde{\xi}, \xi, \hat{\xi}) = \mathbf{A}_p(\tilde{\xi}, \xi, \hat{\xi}) + \begin{bmatrix} 0 & 0 \\ \Delta A_p(k) + \Delta B_p(k) K_p(\hat{\xi}) & \Delta A_p(k) \end{bmatrix}$,

$$\begin{aligned} \mathbf{A}_p(\tilde{\xi}, \xi, \hat{\xi}) &= \begin{bmatrix} A_p(\hat{\xi}) + B_p(\hat{\xi})K_p(\hat{\xi}) + L_p(\hat{\xi})C_p(\tilde{\xi}) & L_p(\hat{\xi})C_p(\xi) \\ A_p(\tilde{\xi}) + B_p(\tilde{\xi})K_p(\hat{\xi}) - L_p(\hat{\xi})C_p(\tilde{\xi}) & A_p(\xi) - L_p(\hat{\xi})C_p(\xi) \end{bmatrix}, \\ \mathbf{E}_p(\xi, \hat{\xi}) &= \begin{bmatrix} L_p(\hat{\xi})D_p(\xi) \\ E_p(\xi) - L_p(\hat{\xi})D_p(\xi) \end{bmatrix}, \\ \mathbf{G}_p(\xi, \hat{\xi}) &= \begin{bmatrix} G_p(\xi) + H_p(\xi)K_p(\hat{\xi}) & G_p(\xi) \end{bmatrix}. \end{aligned}$$

Before going ahead, this paper presents the following definitions for stochastic analyses.

Definition 1 ([27,28]). *For $d_k \equiv 0$, the closed-loop system (4) is stochastically stable if for any $\zeta_0 = [\hat{x}_0^T, e_0^T]^T$ and ϕ_0, the following inequality holds*

$$\mathbf{E}\left\{ \sum_{k=0}^{\infty} \|\zeta_k\|^2 \Big| \zeta_0, \phi_0 \right\} < \infty. \tag{5}$$

Definition 2 ([29,30]). *For given real matrices $\mathcal{Z}$, $\mathcal{S}$ and $\mathcal{D}$ such that $\mathcal{Z} = -\mathcal{Z}_1^T\mathcal{Z}_1$, $\mathcal{Z}_1 \in \mathbb{R}^{n_q \times n_z} (n_q \le n_z)$, $\mathcal{S} \in \mathbb{R}^{n_d \times n_z}$, and $\mathcal{D} = \mathcal{D}^T \in \mathbb{R}^{n_d \times n_d}$, let us define a quadratic energy supply rate as follows*

$$\begin{aligned} \mathcal{Q}(z_k, d_k) &= \begin{bmatrix} z_k \\ d_k \end{bmatrix}^T \begin{bmatrix} \mathcal{Z} & (*) \\ \mathcal{S} & \mathcal{D} \end{bmatrix} \begin{bmatrix} z_k \\ d_k \end{bmatrix} \\ &= \begin{bmatrix} z_k \\ d_k \end{bmatrix}^T \begin{bmatrix} \mathcal{Z} & (*) \\ \mathcal{S} & \mathcal{D} \end{bmatrix} \begin{bmatrix} \mathbf{G}_p(\xi, \hat{\xi}) & J_p(\xi) \\ 0 & I \end{bmatrix} \begin{bmatrix} \zeta_k \\ d_k \end{bmatrix}. \end{aligned} \tag{6}$$

Then, for $\zeta_0 \equiv 0$, system (4) is said to be $(\mathcal{Z}, \mathcal{S}, \mathcal{D})$-$\gamma$-dissipative if the following condition holds for $\gamma > 0$ and $T > 0$:

$$\sum_{k=0}^{T} \mathbf{E}\left\{ \mathcal{Q}(z_k, d_k) \right\} \ge \gamma \sum_{k=0}^{T} \mathbf{E}\left\{ d_k^T d_k \right\}, \tag{7}$$

where γ stands for the dissipative performance level.

Remark 1. *It follows [22,31] that there are two particular performances deduced from the $(\mathcal{Z}, \mathcal{S}, \mathcal{D})$-$\gamma$-dissipativity (7): **(i)** $\mathcal{H}_\infty$-performance by $\mathcal{Z} = -I$, $\mathcal{S} = 0$, and $\mathcal{D} = (\gamma^2 + \gamma)I$, **(ii)** passivity performance by $\mathcal{Z} = 0$, $\mathcal{S} = I$, and $\mathcal{D} = 2\gamma I$.*

The mismatch phenomenon here is the difference between fuzzy basic functions in the system model $\xi_i(\varrho(x_k))$ and the observed-based controller $\xi_i(\varrho(\hat{x}_k))$. The difference tends to ruin the stability of the closed-loop system (4) if it is not considered in the controller design. Thus, this paper aims to design the observed-based controller (3) that guarantees the stochastic stability and dissipative performance of the closed-loop system (4) with the following constraint:

$$-1 \leq \underline{\alpha}_i \leq \xi_i(\varrho(x_k)) - \xi_i(\varrho(\hat{x}_k)) \leq \bar{\alpha}_i \leq 1, \; \forall i \in \mathbb{N}_\xi = \{1, 2, \cdots, r\}, \tag{8}$$

where $\bar{\alpha}_i$ and $\underline{\alpha}_i$ are given scalars. Next, the following well-known lemmas are used

Lemma 1 ([32])**.** *For any matrix $\mathcal{M}_{ij} = \mathcal{M}_{ij}^T$, the condition $0 \leq \sum_{i=1}^r \sum_{j=1}^r \varsigma_i \varsigma_j \mathcal{M}_{ij}$ holds if*

$$0 \leq \mathcal{M}_{ii}, \; \forall i \in \mathbb{N}_\xi, \tag{9}$$

$$0 \leq \frac{1}{r-1}\mathcal{M}_{ii} + \frac{1}{2}(\mathcal{M}_{ij} + \mathcal{M}_{ji}), \; \forall (i,j) \in \mathbb{N}_\xi \times \mathbb{N}_\xi \setminus \{j\}. \tag{10}$$

Lemma 2 ([33])**.** *Let real matrices $\mathcal{M} = \mathcal{M}^T$, $\mathcal{N}_1$, $\mathcal{N}_2$ and U with appropriate dimensions and $UU^T \leq I$. The inequality $0 > \mathcal{A} + \mathbf{He}\{\mathcal{N}_1 U \mathcal{N}_2\}$ is true if*

$$0 > \begin{bmatrix} \mathcal{M} + \beta \mathcal{N}_1 \mathcal{N}_1^T & (*) \\ \mathcal{N}_2 & -\beta I \end{bmatrix}. \tag{11}$$

3. Control Synthesis

To establish the dissipative condition of a closed-loop system (4), this paper considers a Lyapunov function in the following form:

$$V_k = V(\zeta_k, \psi_k) = \zeta_k^T P(\hat{\xi}, \psi_k) \zeta_k, \tag{12}$$

where $P(\hat{\xi}_k, \psi_k = p) = P_p(\hat{\xi}_k) = P_p^T(\hat{\xi}) > 0$, the double-fuzzy summation $P_p(\hat{\xi}) = \sum_{i=1}^r \sum_{j=1}^r \hat{\xi}_i \hat{\xi}_j P_{pij}$, and symmetric matrices P_{pij}. The Lyapunov function does not require $P_{pij} > 0$ for all $(p, i, j) \in \mathbb{N}_\psi \times \mathbb{N}_\xi \times \mathbb{N}_\xi \setminus \{i\}$. The conditions can be relaxed by Lemma 1. Then, by letting $\hat{\xi}^+ = \xi(\hat{\varrho}_{k+1})$ and $\mathbf{P}_p(\hat{\xi}^+) = \sum_{q=1}^{s} \pi_{pq} P_h(\hat{\xi}^+)$, we can obtain

$$\begin{aligned} \mathbf{E}\{\Delta V_k\} &= \mathbf{E}\{V(\zeta_{k+1}, \psi_{k+1} = h | \psi_k = p)\} - V(\zeta_k, \psi_k = p) \\ &= \zeta_{k+1}^T \mathbf{P}_p(\hat{\xi}^+)(\mathbf{A}_p(\tilde{\xi}, \xi, \hat{\xi})\zeta_k + \mathbf{E}_p(\xi, \hat{\xi}) d_k) - \zeta_k^T P_p(\hat{\xi}) \zeta_k. \end{aligned} \tag{13}$$

Lemma 3. *Suppose that there exist symmetric matrices $0 < P_p(\hat{\xi}) \in \mathbb{R}^{2n_x \times 2n_x}$ and $0 < P_h(\hat{\xi}^+) \in \mathbb{R}^{2n_x \times 2n_x}$ such that for all $p \in \mathbb{N}_\psi$:*

$$\begin{aligned} 0 > &\left[\begin{array}{c:c|c} -P_p(\hat{\xi}) & (*) & (*) \\ \hdashline -\mathcal{S}\mathbf{G}_p(\xi, \hat{\xi}) & -\mathbf{He}\{\mathcal{S}J_p(\xi)\} + \gamma I - \mathcal{D} & (*) \\ \hline \mathcal{Z}_1 \mathbf{G}_p(\xi, \hat{\xi}) & \mathcal{Z}_1 J_p(\xi) & -I \end{array}\right] \\ &+ \begin{bmatrix} \bar{\mathbf{A}}_p(\tilde{\xi}, \xi, \hat{\xi}) & \mathbf{E}_p(\xi, \hat{\xi}) & 0 \end{bmatrix}^T \mathbf{P}_p(\hat{\xi}^+) \begin{bmatrix} \bar{\mathbf{A}}_p(\tilde{\xi}, \xi, \hat{\xi}) & \mathbf{E}_p(\xi, \hat{\xi}) & 0 \end{bmatrix}. \end{aligned} \tag{14}$$

Then, closed-loop system (4) is stochastically stable and $(\mathcal{Z}, \mathcal{S}, \mathcal{D})$-$\gamma$-dissipative.

Proof. The formulation (6) can be rearranged as follows

$$\mathcal{Q}(z_k,d_k)=\begin{bmatrix}\zeta_k\\ d_k\end{bmatrix}^T\left(\begin{bmatrix}0 & (*)\\ \mathcal{S}\mathbf{G}_p(\xi,\hat{\xi}) & \mathbf{He}\{\mathcal{S}J_p(\xi)\}+\mathcal{D}\end{bmatrix}\right.$$
$$\left.-\begin{bmatrix}\mathbf{G}_p^T(\xi,\hat{\xi})\mathcal{Z}_1^T\\ J_p^T(\xi)\mathcal{Z}_1^T\end{bmatrix}\begin{bmatrix}\mathcal{Z}_1\mathbf{G}_p(\xi,\hat{\xi}) & \mathcal{Z}_1J_p(\xi)\end{bmatrix}\right)\begin{bmatrix}\zeta_k\\ d_k\end{bmatrix}.$$

Following (13), it yields

$$\mathbf{E}\Big\{\Delta V_k+\gamma d_k^Td_k-\mathcal{Q}(z_k,d_k)\Big\}=\bar{\zeta}_k^T\Psi_k\bar{\zeta}_k, \tag{15}$$

where $\bar{\zeta}_k=\mathbf{col}(\zeta_k,d_k)=\mathbf{col}(\hat{x}_k,e_k,d_k)$,

$$\begin{aligned}\Psi_k=&\begin{bmatrix}\bar{\mathbf{A}}_p(\tilde{\xi},\xi,\hat{\xi}) & \mathbf{E}_p(\xi,\hat{\xi})\end{bmatrix}^T\mathbf{P}_p(\hat{\xi}^+)\begin{bmatrix}\bar{\mathbf{A}}_p(\tilde{\xi},\xi,\hat{\xi}) & \mathbf{E}_p(\xi,\hat{\xi})\end{bmatrix}\\ &+\begin{bmatrix}\mathcal{Z}_1\mathbf{G}_p(\xi,\hat{\xi}) & \mathcal{Z}_1J_p(\xi)\end{bmatrix}^T\begin{bmatrix}\mathcal{Z}_1\mathbf{G}_p(\xi,\hat{\xi}) & \mathcal{Z}_1J_p(\xi)\end{bmatrix}\\ &+\begin{bmatrix}-P_p(\hat{\xi}) & (*)\\ -\mathcal{S}\mathbf{G}_p(\xi,\hat{\xi}) & -\mathbf{He}\{\mathcal{S}J_p(\xi)\}+\gamma I-\mathcal{D}\end{bmatrix}.\end{aligned} \tag{16}$$

Furthermore, from (15), it follows that $\sum_{k=0}^T\bar{\zeta}_k^T\Psi_k\bar{\zeta}_k=\sum_{k=0}^T\mathbf{E}\{\Delta V_k\}-\sum_{k=0}^T\mathbf{E}\{\mathcal{Q}(z_k,d_k)-\gamma d_k^Td_k\}=\mathbf{E}\{V_{T+1}-V_0\}-\sum_{k=0}^T\mathbf{E}\{\mathcal{Q}(z_k,d_k)\}-\gamma\sum_{k=0}^T\mathbf{E}\{d_k^Td_k\}$. As a result,

- for $d_k\equiv 0$, it follows from (13) that

$$\mathbf{E}\{\Delta V_k\}=\zeta_k^T(\bar{\mathbf{A}}_p^T(\tilde{\xi},\xi,\hat{\xi})\mathbf{P}_p(\hat{\xi}^+)\bar{\mathbf{A}}_p(\tilde{\xi},\xi,\hat{\xi})-P_p(\hat{\xi}))\zeta_k.$$

  Thus, condition $\Psi_k<0$ guarantees that $\mathbf{E}\{\Delta V_k\}<0$, i.e., $\mathbf{E}\{\Delta V_k\}\le-\varepsilon\|\zeta_k\|^2$ for a small scalar $\varepsilon>0$. Sum up the inequality from 0 to T, it holds that

$$\mathbf{E}\left\{\sum_{k=0}^T\|\zeta_k\|^2\Big|\zeta_0,\phi_0\right\}\le\frac{1}{\varepsilon}\mathbf{E}\{V_0\}<\infty,$$

  for all $T>0$, then, closed-loop system (4) with $d_k\equiv 0$ is stochastically stable by Definition 1.
- for $V_0=0$ (i.e., $x_0\equiv 0$), with the inequality $\Psi_k<0$, it has $\mathbf{E}\{V_{T+1}\}-\sum_{k=0}^T\mathbf{E}\{\mathcal{Q}(z_k,d_k)\}-\gamma\sum_{k=0}^T\mathbf{E}\{d_k^Td_k\}<0$ or $\sum_{k=0}^T\mathbf{E}\{\mathcal{Q}(z_k,d_k)\}-\gamma\sum_{k=0}^T\mathbf{E}\{d_k^Td_k\}>\mathbf{E}\{V_{T+1}\}\ge 0$.

  With the two particular cases, $\Psi_k<0$ implies the stochastic stability and $(\mathcal{Z},\mathcal{S},\mathcal{D})$-$\gamma$-dissipative performance of the closed-loop system (4). Finally, the condition $0>\Psi_k$ can be converted into (14) according to the Schur's complement. □

The following lemma aims to address the encountered relaxation problem for Lemma 3 with fewer dimensions of slack matrix variables and the asymmetric range of mismatch level (8).

Lemma 4. *For given a double-parameterized LMI in the following form:*

$$\begin{aligned}0>\Phi_0&+\sum_{i=1}^r\xi_i\mathbf{He}\Big\{\Gamma_1^T\Phi_{1,i}\Gamma_2\Big\}+\sum_{i=1}^r\hat{\xi}_i\Phi_{2,i}\\ &+\sum_{i=1}^r\sum_{j=1}^r\xi_i\hat{\xi}_j\mathbf{He}\Big\{\Gamma_1^T\Phi_{3,ij}\Gamma_2\Big\}+\sum_{i=1}^r\sum_{j=1}^r\hat{\xi}_i\hat{\xi}_j\Phi_{4,ij}\end{aligned} \tag{17}$$

subject to

$$\underline{\alpha}_\ell\le\tilde{\xi}_\ell=\xi_\ell-\hat{\xi}_\ell\le\bar{\alpha}_\ell, \tag{18}$$

where $\Phi_0 \in \mathbb{R}^{p\times p}$, $\Phi_{1,i} \in \mathbb{R}^{n_1\times n_2}$, $\Phi_{2,i} \in \mathbb{R}^{p\times p}$, $\Phi_{3,ij} \in \mathbb{R}^{n_1\times n_2}$, *and* $\Phi_{4,ij} \in \mathbb{R}^{p\times p}$; $\Gamma_1 \in \mathbb{R}^{n_1\times p}$ *and* $\Gamma_2 \in \mathbb{R}^{n_2\times p}$ *are full rank matrices, the condition (17) subjected to (18) holds if there exist matrices* $S_{ij} = S_{ij}^T \in \mathbb{R}^{n_1\times n_1}$ *and* $N_i \in \mathbb{R}^{n_1\times n_2}$ *such that:*

$$0 > \bar{\Phi}_{ii}, \tag{19}$$

$$0 > \frac{1}{r-1}\bar{\Phi}_{ii} + \frac{1}{2}(\bar{\Phi}_{ij} + \bar{\Phi}_{ji}), \tag{20}$$

for all $(i,j) \in \mathbb{N}_{\xi} \times (\mathbb{N}_{\xi} \setminus \{i\})$, *where*

$$\bar{\Phi}_{ij} = \left[\begin{array}{c|c} \Phi_0 + \mathbf{He}\{\Gamma_1^T(\Phi_{1,i} + \Phi_{3,ij})\Gamma_2\} + \Phi_{2,i} + \Phi_{4,ij} + \sum_{\ell=1}^{r} \underline{\alpha}_\ell \bar{\alpha}_\ell \Omega_1^T S_{\ell i}\Gamma_1 & (*) \\ \hline \left[(\Phi_{1,\ell} + \Phi_{3,\ell i} + N_i)\Gamma_2 - \frac{1}{2}(\underline{\alpha}_\ell + \bar{\alpha}_\ell)S_{\ell i}\Gamma_1\right]_{\ell\in\mathbb{N}_\xi} & \left[S_{\ell i}\right]^{\mathbf{d}}_{\ell\in\mathbb{N}_\xi} \end{array}\right].$$

Proof. Since $\sum_{\ell=1}^{r} \tilde{\xi}_\ell = 0$, it stands that $\sum_{\ell=1}^{r}\sum_{i=1}^{r} \tilde{\xi}_\ell\hat{\xi}_i \mathbf{He}\{\Gamma_1^T N_i \Gamma_2\} = 0$ by which we can rewrite (17) as

$$0 > \Phi_0 + \mathbf{Z}(\hat{\xi}) + \mathbf{He}\left\{\sum_{\ell=1}^{r} \tilde{\xi}_\ell \Gamma_1^T \mathbf{Z}_\ell(\hat{\xi})\Gamma_2\right\}, \tag{21}$$

where $\mathbf{Z}(\hat{\xi}) = \sum_{i=1}^{r}\hat{\xi}_i(\mathbf{He}\{\Gamma_1^T\Phi_{1,i}\Gamma_2\} + \Phi_{2,i}) + \sum_{i=1}^{r}\sum_{j=1}^{r}\hat{\xi}_i\hat{\xi}_j(\mathbf{He}\{\Gamma_1^T\Phi_{3,ij}\Gamma_2\} + \Phi_{4,ij})$, and $\mathbf{Z}_\ell(\hat{\xi}) = \Phi_\ell^{(1)} + \sum_{i=1}^{r}\hat{\xi}_i\Phi_{\ell i}^{(3)} + \sum_{i=1}^{r}\hat{\xi}_i N_i$. In accordance with the above expressions and

$$\mathbf{He}\left\{\sum_{\ell=1}^{r}\tilde{\xi}_\ell\Gamma_1^T\mathbf{Z}_\ell(\hat{\xi})\Gamma_2\right\} = \mathbf{He}\left\{(\tilde{\xi}\otimes\Gamma_1)^T\left[\mathbf{Z}_\ell(\hat{\xi})\Gamma_2\right]_{\ell\in\mathbb{N}_\xi}\right\},$$

the condition (21) is rearranged as

$$0 > \left[\begin{array}{c} I \\ \hline \tilde{\xi}\otimes\Gamma_1 \end{array}\right]^T \left[\begin{array}{c|c} \Phi_0 + \mathbf{Z}(\hat{\xi}) & (*) \\ \hline \left[\mathbf{Z}_\ell(\hat{\xi})\Gamma_2\right]_{\ell\in\mathbb{N}_\xi} & 0 \end{array}\right] \left[\begin{array}{c} I \\ \hline \tilde{\xi}\otimes\Gamma_1 \end{array}\right]. \tag{22}$$

Meanwhile, since (19) implies $S_{\ell i} = S_{\ell i}^T < 0$, it follows from (18) that

$$\begin{aligned} 0 &\le \sum_{i=1}^{r}\hat{\xi}_i\sum_{\ell=1}^{r}(\tilde{\xi}_\ell - \bar{\alpha}_\ell)(\tilde{\xi}_\ell - \underline{\alpha}_\ell)\Gamma_1^T S_{\ell i}\Gamma_1 \\ &= \left[\begin{array}{c} I \\ \hline \tilde{\xi}\otimes\Gamma_1 \end{array}\right]^T \left[\begin{array}{c|c} \sum_{i=1}^{r}\hat{\xi}_i\left(\sum_{\ell=1}^{r}\underline{\alpha}_\ell\bar{\alpha}_\ell\Gamma_1^T S_{\ell i}\Gamma_1\right) & (*) \\ \hline \left[-\frac{1}{2}\sum_{i=1}^{r}\hat{\xi}_i(\underline{\alpha}_\ell + \bar{\alpha}_\ell)S_{\ell i}\Gamma_1\right]_{\ell\in\mathbb{N}_\xi} & \left[\sum_{i=1}^{r}\hat{\xi}_i S_{\ell i}\right]^{\mathbf{d}}_{\ell\in\mathbb{N}_\xi} \end{array}\right] \left[\begin{array}{c} I \\ \hline \tilde{\xi}\otimes\Gamma_1 \end{array}\right]. \end{aligned} \tag{23}$$

Supported by the S-procedure, the combination of (22) with (23) ensures

$$\begin{aligned} 0 &> \left[\begin{array}{c|c} \Phi_0 + \mathbf{Z}(\hat{\xi}) + \sum_{i=1}^{r}\hat{\xi}_i\left(\sum_{\ell=1}^{r}\underline{\alpha}_\ell\bar{\alpha}_\ell\Gamma_1^T S_{\ell i}\Gamma_1\right) & (*) \\ \hline \left[\mathbf{Z}_\ell(\hat{\xi})\Gamma_2 - \frac{1}{2}\sum_{i=1}^{r}\hat{\xi}_i(\underline{\alpha}_\ell + \bar{\alpha}_\ell)S_{\ell i}\Gamma_1\right]_{\ell\in\mathbb{N}_\xi} & \left[\sum_{i=1}^{r}\hat{\xi}_i S_{\ell i}\right]^{\mathbf{d}}_{\ell\in\mathbb{N}_\xi} \end{array}\right] \\ &= \sum_{i=1}^{r}\sum_{j=1}^{r}\hat{\xi}_i\hat{\xi}_j\bar{\Phi}_{ij}, \end{aligned} \tag{24}$$

and by Lemma 1, condition (19) implies (24). □

Remark 2. *To deal with presence of two different types of parameters in (17) induced by the mismatch phenomenon, Lemma 4 presents a relaxation technique based on parameterized-LMIs given in Lemma 1 to avoid the excessive use of free slack matrix variables. Compared to other relaxation techniques for the mismatch phenomenon, our work concerns asymmetric range of mismatch level (18) and reduces dimensions of slack matrix variables by introducing constant matrices* Γ_1 *and* Γ_2*.*

With the help of Lemma 4, the following theorem presents a parameter-independent criteria from Lemma 3

Theorem 1. *Suppose that there exist scalars* $\gamma > 0$ *and* β*, matrices* $0 < P_{pi} = P_{pi}^T \in \mathbb{R}^{2n_x \times 2n_x}$*,* $0 < X = X^T \in \mathbb{R}^{2n_x \times 2n_x}$*,* $0 < \bar{X} = \bar{X}^T \in \mathbb{R}^{2n_x \times 2n_x}$*,* $K_{pi} \in \mathbb{R}^{n_u \times n_x}$*,* $L_{pi} \in \mathbb{R}^{n_x \times n_y}$*,* $N_{pi} \in \mathbb{R}^{(2n_x+n_d)\times(2n_x+n_d+n_q)}$*, and* $S_{p\ell i} = S_{p\ell i}^T \in \mathbb{R}^{(2n_x+n_d)\times(2n_x+n_d)}$ *such that the following inequalities hold for all* $p \in \mathbb{N}_\psi$*,* $(m,i,j) \in \mathbb{N}_\xi \times \mathbb{N}_\xi \times \mathbb{N}_\xi \setminus \{i\}$*:*

$$0 < P_{pii},\ 0 < \frac{1}{r-1}P_{pii} + \frac{1}{2}(P_{pij} + P_{pji}), \tag{25}$$

$$0 < X - \Lambda_{pii},\ 0 < \frac{r}{r-1}X - \frac{1}{r-1}\Lambda_{pii} - \frac{1}{2}(\Lambda_{pij} + \Lambda_{pji}), \tag{26}$$

$$0 > \bar{\Phi}_{pmii},\ 0 > \frac{1}{r-1}\bar{\Phi}_{pii} + \frac{1}{2}(\bar{\Phi}_{pij} + \bar{\Phi}_{pji}),\ \forall j \in \mathbb{N}_\xi \setminus \{i\}, \tag{27}$$

$$X\bar{X} = I, \tag{28}$$

where $\Lambda_{pij} = \sum_{q=1}^{s} \pi_{pq} P_{qij}$*,*

$$\bar{\Phi}_{pmij} = \left[\begin{array}{c:c} \Phi_p^{(0)} + \mathbf{He}\left\{\Gamma_1^T\left(\Phi_{pi}^{(1)} + \Phi_{pij}^{(3)}\right)\Gamma_2\right\} + \Phi_{pi}^{(2)} + \Phi_{pij}^{(4)} + \sum_{\ell=1}^{r} \underline{\alpha}_\ell \bar{\alpha}_\ell \Gamma_1^T S_{p\ell i}\Gamma_1 & (*) \\ \hdashline \left[\ \left(\Phi_{p\ell}^{(1)} + \Phi_{p\ell i}^{(3)} + N_{pi}\right)\Gamma_2 - \frac{1}{2}(\underline{\alpha}_\ell + \bar{\alpha}_\ell)S_{p\ell i}\Gamma_1\ \right]_{\ell \in \mathbb{N}_\xi} & \left[S_{p\ell i}\right]^{\mathbf{d}}_{\ell \in \mathbb{N}_\xi} \end{array}\right],$$

$$\Phi_p^{(0)} = \mathbf{diag}\left(0, \gamma I - \mathcal{D}, -I, -\bar{X} + \beta\,\mathbf{diag}\left(0, T_{a,p}T_{a,p}^T + T_{b,p}T_{b,p}^T\right), -\beta I\right),$$

$$\Phi_{pi}^{(1)} = \left[\begin{array}{c|c:cc} -G_{pi}^T\mathcal{S}^T & G_{pi}^T\mathcal{Z}_1^T & 0 & A_{pi}^T \\ -G_{pi}^T\mathcal{S}^T & G_{pi}^T\mathcal{Z}_1^T & 0 & A_{pi}^T \\ \hdashline -J_{pi}^T\mathcal{S}^T & J_{pi}^T\mathcal{Z}_1^T & 0 & E_{pi}^T \end{array}\right],\ \Phi_{pi}^{(2)} = \left[\begin{array}{c:c|c:c|c} 0 & 0 & 0 & (*) & (*) \\ \hdashline 0 & 0 & 0 & 0 & 0 \\ \hline 0 & 0 & 0 & 0 & 0 \\ \hdashline \begin{bmatrix} A_{pi} & 0 \\ -A_{pi} & 0 \end{bmatrix} & 0 & 0 & 0 & 0 \\ \hline \begin{bmatrix} Y_{a,p} & Y_{a,p} \\ 0 & S_{b,q}K_{pi} \end{bmatrix} & 0 & 0 & 0 & 0 \end{array}\right],$$

$$\Phi_{pij}^{(3)} = \left[\begin{array}{c|c:cc} -K_{pj}^T H_{pi}^T \mathcal{S}^T & K_{pj}^T H_{pi}^T \mathcal{Z}_1^T & C_{pi}^T L_{pj}^T & K_{pj}^T B_{pi}^T - C_{pi}^T L_{pj}^T \\ 0 & 0 & C_{pi}^T L_{pj}^T & -C_{pi}^T L_{pj}^T \\ \hdashline 0 & 0 & D_{pi}^T L_{pj}^T & -D_{pi}^T L_{pj}^T \end{array}\right],$$

$$\Phi_{pij}^{(4)} = \left[\begin{array}{c:c|c:c|c} -P_{pij} & 0 & 0 & (*) & 0 \\ \hdashline 0 & 0 & 0 & 0 & 0 \\ \hline 0 & 0 & 0 & 0 & 0 \\ \hdashline \begin{bmatrix} B_{pi}K_{pj} - L_{pj}C_{pi} & 0 \\ -B_{pi}K_{pj} + L_{pj}C_{pi} & 0 \end{bmatrix} & 0 & 0 & 0 & 0 \\ \hline 0 & 0 & 0 & 0 & 0 \end{array}\right],\ \Gamma_1^T = \left[\begin{array}{cc} I & 0 \\ 0 & I \\ 0 & 0 \\ \hdashline 0 & 0 \end{array}\right] \in \mathbb{R}^{n_1 \times (2n_x+n_d)},$$

$$\Gamma_2 = \left[\begin{array}{ccc:c} 0 & I & 0 & 0 \\ 0 & 0 & I & 0 \\ 0 & 0 & 0 & I \end{array}\right] \in \mathbb{R}^{(n_d+n_q+n_x)\times n_1},\ n_1 = 4n_x + n_d + n_q.$$

The closed-loop system (4) is $(\mathcal{Z},\mathcal{S},\mathcal{D})$-$\gamma$-dissipative with the following observer and control gains

$$K_p(\hat{\xi}) = \sum_{i=1}^{r} \hat{\xi}_i K_{pi},\ L_p(\hat{\xi}) = \sum_{i=1}^{r} \hat{\xi}_i L_{pi}. \tag{29}$$

Proof. Following the definition of the Lyapunov function (12), $P_p(\hat{\xi}^+) = \sum_{i=1}^{r}\sum_{j=1}^{r} \hat{\xi}_i^+ \hat{\xi}_j^+ P_{pij}$ which in turn leads to $\Lambda_p(\hat{\xi}) = \sum_{i=1}^{r}\sum_{j=1}^{r} \hat{\xi}_i\hat{\xi}_j\Lambda_{pij}$. Then, by (25) and Lemma 1, it follows that $\Lambda_p(\hat{\xi}) > 0$ and $P_p(\hat{\xi}^+) > 0$. Furthermore, with the help of (26) and Lemma 1, it has $\sum_{i=1}^{r}\sum_{j=1}^{r} \hat{\xi}_i^+ \hat{\xi}_j^+ (X - \Lambda_{pij}) > 0$ and then

$$\mathbf{P}_p(\hat{\xi}^+) = \sum_{i=1}^{r}\sum_{j=1}^{r} \hat{\xi}_i^+ \hat{\xi}_j^+ \Lambda_{pij} < X = \bar{X}^{-1}.$$

Thus, condition (14) satisfies if

$$\begin{aligned} 0 > &\left[\begin{array}{c:c|c} -P_p(\hat{\xi}) & (*) & (*) \\ \hdashline -\mathcal{S}\mathbf{G}_p(\xi,\hat{\xi}) & -\mathbf{He}\{\mathcal{S}J_p(\xi)\} + \gamma I - \mathcal{D} & (*) \\ \hline \mathcal{Z}_1\mathbf{G}_p(\xi,\hat{\xi}) & \mathcal{Z}_1 J_p(\xi) & -I \end{array}\right] \\ &+ \begin{bmatrix} \bar{\mathbf{A}}_p(\tilde{\xi},\xi,\hat{\xi}) & \mathbf{E}_p(\xi,\hat{\xi}) & 0 \end{bmatrix}^T \bar{X}^{-1} \begin{bmatrix} \bar{\mathbf{A}}_p(\tilde{\xi},\xi,\hat{\xi}) & \mathbf{E}_p(\xi,\hat{\xi}) & 0 \end{bmatrix}. \end{aligned} \tag{30}$$

Moreover, the inequality (30) is guaranteed by Schur's complement

$$\begin{aligned} 0 > &\left[\begin{array}{c:c|c:c} -P_p(\hat{\xi}) & (*) & (*) & (*) \\ \hdashline -\mathcal{S}\mathbf{G}_p(\xi,\hat{\xi}) & -\mathbf{He}\{\mathcal{S}J_p(\xi)\} + \gamma I - \mathcal{D} & (*) & (*) \\ \hline \mathcal{Z}_1\mathbf{G}_p(\xi,\hat{\xi}) & \mathcal{Z}_1 J_p(\xi) & -I & (*) \\ \hdashline \bar{\mathbf{A}}_p(\tilde{\xi},\xi,\hat{\xi}) & \mathbf{E}_p(\xi,\hat{\xi}) & 0 & -\bar{X} \end{array}\right] \\ = &\left[\begin{array}{c:c|c:c} -P_p(\hat{\xi}) & (*) & (*) & (*) \\ \hdashline -\mathcal{S}\mathbf{G}_p(\xi,\hat{\xi}) & -\mathbf{He}\{\mathcal{S}J_p(\xi)\} + \gamma I - \mathcal{D} & (*) & 0 \\ \hline \mathcal{Z}_1\mathbf{G}_p(\xi,\hat{\xi}) & \mathcal{Z}_1 J_p(\xi) & -I & (*) \\ \hdashline \mathbf{A}_p(\tilde{\xi},\xi,\hat{\xi}) & \mathbf{E}_p(\xi,\hat{\xi}) & 0 & -\bar{X} \end{array}\right] \\ &+ \mathbf{He}\left\{ \left[\begin{array}{cc} 0 & 0 \\ \hline 0 & 0 \\ \hdashline 0 & 0 \\ T_{a,p} & T_{b,p} \end{array}\right] \begin{bmatrix} U_a(k) & 0 \\ 0 & U_b(k) \end{bmatrix} \left[\begin{array}{cc} Y_{a,p}^T & 0 \\ Y_{a,p}^T & K_p^T(\hat{\xi})Y_{b,p}^T \\ \hdashline 0 & 0 \\ \hline 0 & 0 \end{array}\right]^T \right\}. \end{aligned}$$

Then, buy using Lemma 2, the above inequality can be deduced from

$$0 > \left[\begin{array}{c:c|c:c|c} -P_p(\hat{\xi}) & (*) & (*) & (*) & (*) \\ \hdashline -\mathcal{S}\mathbf{G}_p(\xi,\hat{\xi}) & -\mathbf{He}\{\mathcal{S}J_p(\xi)\} + \gamma I - \mathcal{D} & (*) & (*) & (*) \\ \hline \mathcal{Z}_1\mathbf{G}_p(\xi,\hat{\xi}) & \mathcal{Z}_1 J_p(\xi) & -I & 0 & 0 \\ \hdashline \mathbf{A}_p(\tilde{\xi},\xi,\hat{\xi}) & \mathbf{E}_p(\xi,\hat{\xi}) & 0 & -\bar{X} + \beta\mathbf{T}_p & 0 \\ \hline \mathbf{U}_p(\hat{\xi}) & 0 & 0 & 0 & -\beta I \end{array}\right]. \tag{31}$$

where $\mathbf{Y}_p(\hat{\xi}) = \begin{bmatrix} Y_{a,p} & Y_{a,p} \\ 0 & Y_{b,p}K_p(\hat{\xi}) \end{bmatrix}$ and $\mathbf{T}_p = \mathbf{diag}\Big(0, T_{a,p}T_{a,p}^T + T_{b,p}T_{b,p}^T\Big)$. It can be rearranged in the form of (17) as follows:

$$\begin{aligned} 0 > \Phi_p^{(0)} &+ \sum_{i=1}^{r} \xi_i \mathbf{He}\Big\{\Gamma_1^T \Phi_{pi}^{(1)} \Gamma_2\Big\} + \sum_{i=1}^{r} \hat{\xi}_i \Phi_{pi}^{(2)} \\ &+ \sum_{i=1}^{r}\sum_{j=1}^{r} \xi_i\hat{\xi}_j \mathbf{He}\Big\{\Gamma_1^T \Phi_{pij}^{(3)} \Gamma_2\Big\} + \sum_{i=1}^{r}\sum_{j=1}^{r} \xi_i\hat{\xi}_j \Phi_{pij}^{(4)}. \end{aligned} \tag{32}$$

In accordance with Lemma 4, the inequality (32) is ensured by (27) and (28). □

The following algorithm based on SLPMM [34] is presented to solve the set of conditions in Theorem 1.

Remark 3. *In contrast with the cone complementarity linearization (CCL) method [35], the SLPMM [34] can provide the non-decreasing sequence $\{\mathcal{J}_i\}_{i\in\mathbb{N}}$ and also point out feasibility of the problem. Consequently, we can define a terminal condition by giving a threshold for decrease of sequence $\{\mathcal{J}_i\}_{i\in\mathbb{N}}$ when the problem is infeasible.*

4. Illustrative Examples

The simulation part is carried out using MATLAB software, MathWorks, Inc., Seoul, Korea. The LMI problem (33) and (34) in Algorithm 1 are numerically solved by LMI solver in Robust Control Toolbox, MATLAB. To use the LMI solver, we program our code using the MATLAB script files in a computer with i7 CPU Intel and 16 GB RAM DDR4. The coding program can be found in https://github.com/thanhbinh91/Ro-OuFe-DissCtrl-MJFSs, accessed on 2 October 2022.

Algorithm 1 SLPMM to solve Theorem 1

1: Initialize matrices X_0 and $\bar{X}_0$ that satisfy

$$\text{LMIs: (25)–(27) and} \begin{bmatrix} X_0 & (*) \\ I & \bar{X}_0 \end{bmatrix} \geq 0. \tag{33}$$

2: Chose a sufficiently small real number $\epsilon > 0$ for the error bound of the solution precision and $i = 0$. For given positive scalars $\beta > 0$ and $\gamma > 0$.

3: **for** $i = i + 1$ **do**

4: Find P_{pij}, K_{pi}, L_{pi}, X^* and $\bar{X}^*$ by solving the optimization problem:

$$\mathcal{J}_i^* = \min \mathbf{Tr}\{X_i\bar{X} + \bar{X}_iX\}$$

$$\text{s.t. } (25), (26), (27) \text{ and } \begin{bmatrix} X & (*) \\ I & \bar{X} \end{bmatrix} \geq 0. \tag{34}$$

5: **if** $|\mathcal{J}_i^* - 4n_x| < \epsilon$ **then**

6: **return** P_{pij}, K_{pi}, L_{pi} as a solution of Theorem 1 with respect to performance γ.

7: **end if**

8: Find $\sigma^* = \min_{\sigma\in[0,1]} \mathbf{Tr}\{(X_i+\sigma(X^*-X_i))(\bar{X}_i+\sigma(\bar{X}^*-\bar{X}_i))\}$.

9: **if** $\sigma^* \neq 0$ **then**

10: $X_{i+1} = (1-\sigma^*)X_i + \sigma^*X^*$, $\bar{X}_{i+1} = (1-\sigma^*)\bar{X}_i + \sigma^*\bar{X}^*$,

11: **else return** set of conditions in Theorem 1 is infeasible.

12: **end if**

13: **end for**

Example 1 (Improved results). *Without jumping parameter (no Markov process), let us consider the truck-trailer system, used in [13,26,36] with the sampling time $T_s = 2.0$ [s], length between center of truck and trailer to connection point and maximum velocity $\ell_1 = 5.5$ [m] and $\ell_2 = 2.8$ [m], and maximum velocity $v = -1.0$ [m/s].*

$$
\begin{aligned}
&A_1 = \begin{bmatrix} 1-\dfrac{vT_s}{\ell_1} & 0 & 0 \\ \dfrac{vT_s}{\ell_1} & 1 & 0 \\ \dfrac{(vT_s)^2}{\ell_1} & vT_s & 1 \end{bmatrix}, A_2 = \begin{bmatrix} 1-\dfrac{vT_s}{\ell_1} & 0 & 0 \\ \dfrac{vT_s}{\ell_1} & 1 & 0 \\ \delta\dfrac{(vT_s)^2}{\ell_1} & \delta vT_s & 1 \end{bmatrix}, B_1 = B_2 = \begin{bmatrix} \dfrac{vT_s}{\ell_2} \\ 0 \\ 0 \end{bmatrix}, \\
&E_1 = E_2 = \begin{bmatrix} 0 \\ 0.2 \\ 0.1 \end{bmatrix}, C_1 = \begin{bmatrix} 1 & 0 & 1 \\ 0 & 2 & 1 \\ 1 & 2 & 2 \end{bmatrix}, C_2 = \begin{bmatrix} 1 & 0 & 1 \\ 0 & 1 & 1 \\ 1 & 1 & 1 \end{bmatrix}, \\
&D_1 = D_2 = 0,\ G_1 = \begin{bmatrix} 0.1 & 0 & 0 \end{bmatrix},\ G_2 = \begin{bmatrix} -0.1 & 0 & 0 \end{bmatrix}, \\
&H_1 = H_2 = -0.1,\ J_1 = 3,\ J_2 = -3,
\end{aligned}
\tag{35}
$$

where $\delta = 0.01/\pi$. *There are two fuzzy-basis functions defined as*

$$
\begin{aligned}
&\xi_1(\varrho_k) = \begin{cases} (\sin(\varrho_k) - \delta\varrho_k)/((1-\delta)\varrho_k), & \varrho_k \neq 0, \\ 1, & \varrho_k = 0, \end{cases} \\
&\xi_2(\varrho_k) = 1 - \xi_1(\varrho_k),
\end{aligned}
\tag{36}
$$

where ϱ_k *is premise variable is established as follows:*

$$\varrho_k = x_{2,k} + \frac{v \cdot T_s}{2\ell_2} x_{1,k}.$$

with $x_{1,k}$ *and* $x_{2,k}$ *stands for sampling at time step k of the angle difference between the truck and trailer, and the angle of trailer, respectively.*

The above setups aim at a particular case where the output-feedback controller is synthesized with the matched fuzzy-basis functions, i.e., no mismatched phenomenon ($\alpha_i \equiv 0$ set in (8)), to asymptotically stabilize the truck-trailer system (36). Accordingly, the comparison of the smallest $\mathcal{H}_\infty$ performance indices obtained by [12,13,26] and Theorem 1 is shown in Table 1. To create the comparison, LMI-based conditions in Theorem 1 are solved by Algorithm 1 with $\beta = 0.02$. It is shown in Table 1 that Theorem 1 provides much improved results (the lower the better) in comparison with preceding works [12,13,26]. For more details, Theorem 1 releases about 98%, 51% and 15% better $\mathcal{H}$-index than that of [12,13,26], respectively. With $\gamma_{\min} = 3.18$, Algorithm 1 provides the following solution

$$
\begin{aligned}
&F_1 = \begin{bmatrix} 2.921 & -1.568 & 0.076 \end{bmatrix},\ F_2 = \begin{bmatrix} 2.152 & -0.510 & 0.034 \end{bmatrix}, \\
&L_1 = \begin{bmatrix} 0.9655 & -1.0692 & 0.2855 \\ -0.8570 & -0.6130 & 0.7821 \\ 0.2938 & -1.1399 & 0.5619 \end{bmatrix},\ L_2 = \begin{bmatrix} 0.9205 & -0.9312 & 0.2135 \\ -0.6855 & -0.1369 & 0.6408 \\ -0.2100 & -0.2520 & 0.4045 \end{bmatrix}.
\end{aligned}
$$

In accordance with the following initial setups

$$\hat{x}_0 = \begin{bmatrix} 0 & 0 & 0 \end{bmatrix}^T,\ x_0 = \begin{bmatrix} 0.2 & -0.3 & 0.1 \end{bmatrix}^T,\ d_k = e^{-0.3k}\sin(k),\ \text{for } k \geq 0,$$

state behavior and control input are shown in Figure 1a–d, in which Figure 1a–c present the asymptotic convergence of $x_{1,k}$, $x_{2,k}$ and $x_{3,k}$. Moreover, the observed states $\hat{x}_{1,k}$, $\hat{x}_{2,k}$ and $\hat{x}_{3,k}$ asymptotically track the real $x_{1,k}$, $x_{2,k}$ and $x_{3,k}$, respectively. In addition, Figure 1d shows the behavior of control input that proves the well-defined control problem. Eventually, Figure 1 shows the availability and validity of the observer and controller gains designed by Theorem 1 for (35),

Table 1. A comparison of minimum $\mathcal{H}_\infty$-performance indices in Example 1 between several studies.

Methods	[12] [Th. 3]	[26] [Th. 1]	[13] [Th. 3.4]	[23] [Th. 9]	[24] [Cor. 1]	Th. 1
$\bar{\alpha}_i = \underline{\alpha}_i = 0$	6.27	4.77	3.63	3.54	Infeasible	3.18

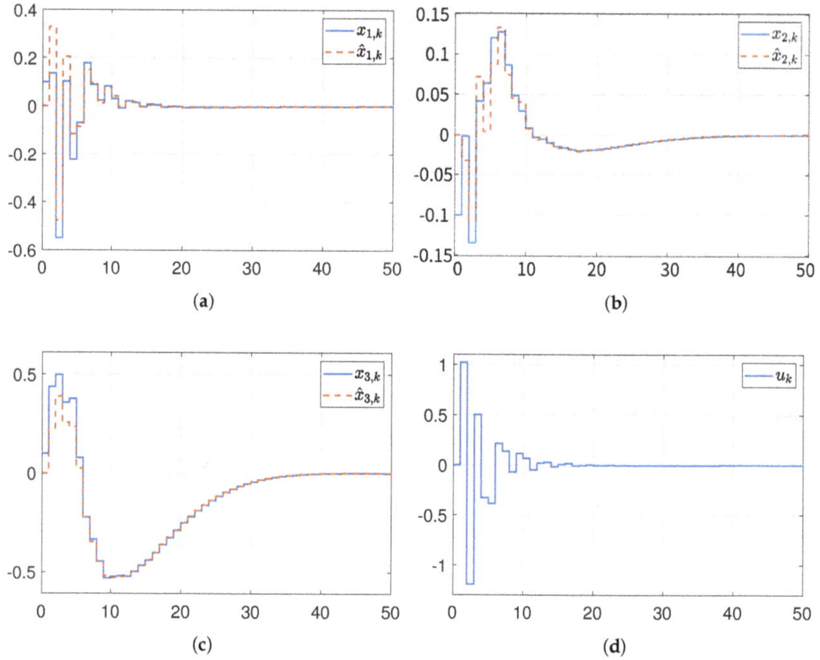

Figure 1. Time evolution of the truck-trailer system (35): (**a**–**c**) real and observed state and (**d**) control input.

Example 2 (Relaxed practical example). *Let us consider the following single-link robot arm system with plant mode $\psi(t) \in \mathbb{N}_\psi = \{1,2,3\}$, adopted in [37]:*

$$\begin{cases} \ddot{\varphi}(t) = -\dfrac{M(\psi(t))g_a\ell}{J(\psi(t))}\sin(\varphi(t)) - \dfrac{c_v\dot{\varphi}(t)}{J(\psi(t))} + \dfrac{1}{J(\psi(t))}u(t) + d(t), \\ y(t) = \varphi(t), \end{cases} \tag{37}$$

where $\varphi(t)$, $\dot{\varphi}(t)$, $y(t)$, $u(t)$, and $d(t)$ stands for the angle, angular velocity, the controlled torque input, the load torque of the arm, and the measurement noise, respectively; and payload mass $M(\psi(t))$, inertia moment $J(\psi(t))$, arm length ℓ = 0.5 [m], the gravity acceleration g_a = 9.81 [m/s^2], and viscous friction coefficient c_v = 2.0 [N.s/m]. Then, by defining $x(t) = [x_1(t)\ x_2(t)]^T = [\varphi(t)\ \dot{\varphi}(t)]^T$ and $d(t)$ and performing the same process with the sampling time $T_s = 0.1$ as in [38,39], we can obtain the following discrete-time T-S fuzzy model for (37) with $p \in \mathbb{N}_\psi = \{1,2,3\}$:

$$A_{p1} = \begin{bmatrix} 1 & T_s \\ -\frac{T_s M_p g_a \ell}{J_p} & 1 - \frac{T_s c_v}{J_p} \end{bmatrix}, A_{p2} = \begin{bmatrix} 1 & T_s \\ -\frac{\delta T_s M_p g_a \ell}{J_p} & 1 - \frac{T_s c_v}{J_p} \end{bmatrix},$$
$$B_{p1} = B_{p2} = \begin{bmatrix} 0 \\ \frac{T_s}{J_p} \end{bmatrix}, E_{p1} = E_{p2} = \begin{bmatrix} 0 \\ T_s \end{bmatrix},$$
$$C_{p1} = C_{p2} = \begin{bmatrix} 1 & 0 \end{bmatrix}, D_{p1} = D_{p2} = \begin{bmatrix} 0 & 0.05 \end{bmatrix},$$
$$G_{p1} = G_{p2} = \begin{bmatrix} 1 & 0 \end{bmatrix}, H_{p1} = H_{p2} = 0.1, J_{p1} = J_{p2} = 0,$$

where $\delta = 0.01/\pi$, $M_1 = M(\psi(t) = 1) = 1.0$ *[kg]*, $M_2 = M(\psi(t) = 2) = 1.5$ *[kg]*, $M_3 = M(\psi(t) = 3) = 2.0$ *[kg]*, $J_1 = J(\psi(t) = 1) = 1.0$ *[kg.m/s²]*, $J_2 = J(\psi(t) = 2) = 2.0$ *[kg.m/s²]*, *and* $J_3 = J(\psi(t) = 3) = 2.5$ *[kg.m/s²]. In addition, for* $x_{1,k} \in (-\pi, \pi)$, *we define FBFs as*

$$\xi_1(x_{1,k}) = \begin{cases} \frac{\sin(x_{1,k}) - \delta x_{1,k}}{(1-\delta)x_{1,k}}, & x_{1,k} \neq 0, \\ 1, & x_{1,k} = 0, \end{cases}$$
$$\xi_2(x_{1,k}) = 1 - \xi_1(x_{1,k}),$$

and the mismatched FBFs were given by $\hat{\xi}_1 = \xi_1(\hat{x}_{1,k})$ *and* $\hat{\xi}_2 = 1 - \hat{\xi}_1$.

Furthermore, the transition probabilities are chosen similarly [23]:

$$[\pi_{pq}]_{p,q \in \mathbb{N}_\psi} = \begin{bmatrix} 0.8 & 0.1 & 0.1 \\ 0.2 & 0.7 & 0.1 \\ 0.5 & 0.2 & 0.3 \end{bmatrix}. \quad (38)$$

Based on the setup as [23], a comparison of ($\mathcal{Z} = -0.01, \mathcal{D} = 5, \mathcal{S} = 0.2$)-dissipative and $\mathcal{H}_\infty$-performance indices obtained by Algorithm 1 and preceding studies, are shown in Table 2. Intuitively, Theorem 1 provides higher dissipative indices (the higher the better) compared to [23] and lower $\mathcal{H}_\infty$-indices compared to [23,24]. In particular, since mismatched level increases $\bar{\alpha}_i = -\underline{\alpha}_i = 0.1, 0.2$, our advantages are shown clearly, i.e., at $\bar{\alpha}_i = -\underline{\alpha}_i = 0.2$ [23] failed to obtain a solution and our result is 18% less than that of [24]. In the case where $\bar{\alpha}_i = -\underline{\alpha}_i = 0.2$, Theorem 1 provides a solution for dissipative performance at $\gamma_{\min} = 3.64$:

$$\left[\begin{array}{c|c|c} F_{11} & F_{21} & F_{31} \\ \hline F_{12} & F_{22} & F_{32} \end{array}\right] = \left[\begin{array}{cc|cc|cc} 0.9701 & -1.5750 & 2.1238 & -6.2871 & 4.0832 & -7.5086 \\ \hline -2.7655 & -2.2250 & -5.4372 & -6.0615 & -7.0027 & -7.5363 \end{array}\right],$$
$$\left[\begin{array}{c|c|c} L_{11} & L_{21} & L_{31} \\ \hline L_{12} & L_{22} & L_{32} \end{array}\right] = \left[\begin{array}{c|c|c} 1.2946 & 1.5475 & 1.8345 \\ -1.3860 & -1.0266 & -0.4478 \\ \hline 1.5122 & 1.4357 & 1.3936 \\ 0.4437 & 1.1962 & 1.2943 \end{array}\right].$$

With $\hat{x}_0 = \begin{bmatrix} 0 & 0 & 0 \end{bmatrix}^T$, $x_0 = \begin{bmatrix} 0.2 & -0.3 & 0.1 \end{bmatrix}^T$, and $d_k = e^{-0.4k}\sin(k)$, the time evolution of the single-link robot arm is shown in Figure 2. As can be seen in the Figure 2a,b, real state variables asymptotically converge, and the observed error converges to zero as time increases. Despite sudden changes in system mode, the closed-looped systems are asymptotic stable.

Table 2. Three performance levels for different mismatch phenomena $\bar{\alpha}_i = -\underline{\alpha}_i$ in (8).

	Dissipativity			$\mathcal{H}_\infty$ Performance		
	Th. 1	**[23]**	**[24]**	**Th. 1**	**[23]**	**[24]**
$\bar{\alpha}_i = -\underline{\alpha}_i = 0$ (matched)	4.65	4.30	-	1.61	1.85	1.71
$\bar{\alpha}_i = -\underline{\alpha}_i = 0.1$	4.38	2.89	-	2.42	5.13	3.64
$\bar{\alpha}_i = -\underline{\alpha}_i = 0.2$	3.64	Infeasible	-	4.78	Infeasible	5.78

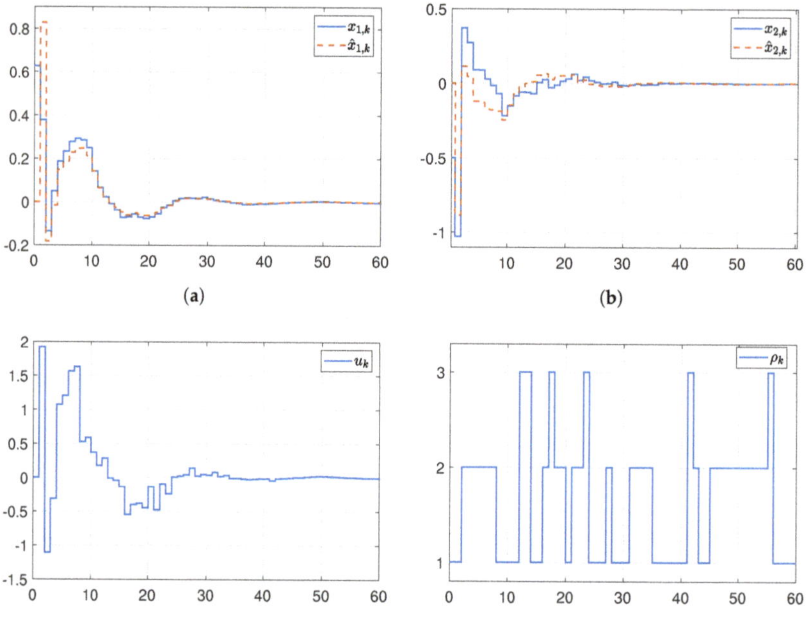

(**a**) (**b**) (**c**) (**d**)

Figure 2. Time evolution of single-link robot arm (37): (**a**,**b**) real and observed state variables and (**c**) control input, (**d**) system mode.

5. Conclusions

This paper addresses the problem of observer-based dissipative control design for MJFSs under model uncertainties and a mismatched phenomenon entailed by the output-feedback scheme of fuzzy systems. The $(\mathcal{Z}, \mathcal{S}, \mathcal{D})$-dissipative conditions first were formulated in terms of multiple parameterized matrix inequalities. In light of proper relaxation techniques, the conditions were cast into parameter-independent bilinear matrix inequalities. Then we proposed an LMI-based algorithm to obtain the observer-based dissipative controller. The key success of our work is an achievement of much less conservative dissipative performance compared to other studies via the refined relaxation process and double-fuzzy summation Lyapunov function. The better results and validity of the LMI-based algorithm were verified via two numerical examples with different mismatch levels. In light of the success, future works should take asynchronous phenomena of operation mode between controller and plant into account to cover more realistic problems.

Author Contributions: Conceptualization, T.B.N.; Formal analysis, T.B.N.; Funding acquisition, H.-K.S.; Methodology, T.B.N.; Project administration, H.-K.S.; Software, T.B.N.; Validation, T.B.N. All authors have read and agreed to the published version of the manuscript.

Funding: This research was supported by the MSIT (Ministry of Science and ICT), Korea, under the ITRC (Information Technology Research Center) support program (IITP-2022-2018-0-01423), supervised by the IITP (Institute for Information & Communications Technology Planning & Evaluation) and in part by the Basic Science Research Program through the National Research Foundation of Korea (NRF) funded by the Ministry of Education (2020R1A6A1A03038540).

Institutional Review Board Statement: Conceptualization, T.B.N.; Formal analysis, T.B.N.; Funding acquisition, H.-K.S.; Methodology, T.B.N.; Project administration, H.-K.S.; Software, T.B.N.; Validation, T.B.N. All authors have read and agreed to the published version of the manuscript.

Informed Consent Statement: Not applicable.

Data Availability Statement: Not applicable.

Conflicts of Interest: The authors declare no conflict of interest.

References

1. Gelabert, X.; Sallent, O.; Pérez-Romero, J.; Agustí, R. Spectrum sharing in cognitive radio networks with imperfect sensing: A discrete-time Markov model. *Comput. Netw.* **2010**, *54*, 2519–2536. [CrossRef]
2. Kim, S.H.; Park, P. Networked-based robust $\mathcal{H}_\infty$ control design using multiple levels of network traffic. *Automatica* **2009**, *45*, 764–770. [CrossRef]
3. Gao, X.; Deng, F.; Zhang, H.; Zeng, P. Reliable $\mathcal{H}_\infty$ filtering of semi-Markov jump systems over a lossy network. *J. Frankl. Inst.* **2021**, *358*, 4528–4545. [CrossRef]
4. Loparo, K.A.; Abdel-Madek, F. A probabilistic mechanism to dynamic power systems security. *IEEE Trans. Circuits Syst.* **1990**, *37*, 787–798. [CrossRef]
5. Arrifano, N.; Oliveira, V.; Ramos, R. Design and application fuzzy PSS for power systems subject to random abrupt variations of the load. In Proceedings of the 2004 American Control Conference, Boston, MA, USA, 30 June–4 July 2004; Volume 2, pp. 1085–1090.
6. Ugrinovskii, V.; Pota, H.R. Decentralized control of power systems via robust control of uncertain Markov jump parameter systems. *Int. J. Control* **2005**, *78*, 662–677. [CrossRef]
7. Dong, H.; Wang, Z.; Gao, H. Distributed $\mathcal{H}_\infty$ filtering for a class of Markovian jump nonlinear time-delay systems over lossy sensor networks. *IEEE Trans. Ind. Electron.* **2013**, *60*, 4665–4672. [CrossRef]
8. do Valle Costa, O.L.; Fragoso, M.D.; Todorov, M.G. *Continuous-Time Markov Jump Linear Systems*; Springer: Berlin/Heidelberg, Germany, 2013.
9. Wang, H.O.; Tanaka, K.; Griffin, M.F. An approach to fuzzy control of nonlinear systems: Stability and design issues. *IEEE Trans. Fuzzy Syst.* **1996**, *4*, 14–23. [CrossRef]
10. Ying, H. An analytical study on structure, stability and design of general nonlinear Takagi–Sugeno fuzzy control systems. *Automatica* **1998**, *34*, 1617–1623. [CrossRef]
11. Chen, B.S.; Tseng, C.S.; Uang, H.J. Robustness design of nonlinear dynamic systems via fuzzy linear control. *IEEE Trans. Fuzzy Syst.* **1999**, *7*, 571–585. [CrossRef]
12. Lo, J.C.; Lin, M.L. Observer-based robust $\mathcal{H}_\infty$ control for fuzzy systems using two-step procedure. *IEEE Trans. Fuzzy Syst.* **2004**, *12*, 350–359. [CrossRef]
13. El Haiek, B.; Hmamed, A.; El Hajjaji, A.; Tissir, E.H. Improved results on observer-based control for discrete-time fuzzy systems. *Int. J. Syst. Sci.* **2017**, *48*, 2544–2553. [CrossRef]
14. Dong, J.; Yang, G.H. Dynamic output feedback control synthesis for continuous-time T–S fuzzy systems via a switched fuzzy control scheme. *IEEE Trans. Syst. Man Cybern. Part B Cybern.* **2008**, *38*, 1166–1175. [CrossRef] [PubMed]
15. Qiu, J.; Feng, G.; Gao, H. Observer-based piecewise affine output feedback controller synthesis of continuous-time T–S fuzzy affine dynamic systems using quantized measurements. *IEEE Trans. Fuzzy Syst.* **2012**, *20*, 1046–1062.
16. Li, H.; Wu, C.; Yin, S.; Lam, H.K. Observer-based fuzzy control for nonlinear networked systems under unmeasurable premise variables. *IEEE Trans. Fuzzy Syst.* **2015**, *24*, 1233–1245. [CrossRef]
17. Vafamand, N.; Asemani, M.H.; Khayatian, A. Robust $\mathcal{L}_1$ Observer-Based Non-PDC Controller Design for Persistent Bounded Disturbed TS Fuzzy Systems. *IEEE Trans. Fuzzy Syst.* **2017**, *26*, 1401–1413. [CrossRef]
18. Kim, S.H.; Park, P. Observer-Based Relaxed $\mathcal{H}_\infty$ Control for Fuzzy Systems Using a Multiple Lyapunov Function. *IEEE Trans. Fuzzy Syst.* **2008**, *17*, 477–484.
19. Aslam, M.S.; Chen, Z. Observer-based dissipative output feedback control for network T–S fuzzy systems under time delays with mismatch premise. *Nonlinear Dyn.* **2019**, *95*, 2923–2941. [CrossRef]

20. Saif, A.W.A.; Mudasar, M.; Mysorewala, M.; Elshafei, M. Observer-based interval type-2 fuzzy logic control for nonlinear networked control systems with delays. *Int. J. Fuzzy Syst.* **2020**, *22*, 380–399. [CrossRef]
21. Jiang, B.; Karimi, H.R.; Yang, S.; Gao, C.; Kao, Y. Observer-based adaptive sliding mode control for nonlinear stochastic Markov jump systems via T–S fuzzy modeling: Applications to robot arm model. *IEEE Trans. Ind. Electron.* **2020**, *68*, 466–477. [CrossRef]
22. Nguyen, T.B.; Kim, S.H. Dissipative control of interval type-2 nonhomogeneous Markovian jump fuzzy systems with incomplete transition descriptions. *Nonlinear Dyn.* **2020**, 100, 1–20. [CrossRef]
23. Kim, S.H. Observer-based control for Markovian jump fuzzy systems under mismatched fuzzy basis functions. *IEEE Access* **2021**, *9*, 122971–122982. [CrossRef]
24. Nguyen, T.B.; Song, H.K. Relaxed observer-based $\mathcal{H}_\infty$-control for Markov jump fuzzy systems with incomplete transition probabilities and sensor failures. *Mathematics* **2022**, *10*, 2055. [CrossRef]
25. Lee, W.I.; Park, B.Y.; Kim, S.H. Relaxed observer-based stabilization and dissipativity conditions of TS fuzzy systems with nonhomogeneous Markov jumps via non-PDC scheme. *Appl. Math. Comput.* **2022**, *434*, 127455.
26. Chang, X.H.; Yang, G.H.; Wang, H. Observer-based $\mathcal{H}_\infty$-control for discrete-time T-S fuzzy systems. *Int. J. Syst. Sci.* **2011**, *42*, 1801–1809. [CrossRef]
27. Mahmoud, M.S.; Shi, P. Robust control for Markovian jump linear discrete-time systems with unknown nonlinearities. *IEEE Trans. Circuits Syst. I-Fundam. Theor. Appl.* **2002**, *49*, 538–542. [CrossRef]
28. Wang, Z.; Lam, J.; Liu, X. Robust filtering for discrete-time Markovian jump delay systems. *IEEE Signal Process. Lett.* **2004**, *11*, 659–662. [CrossRef]
29. Dong, X.Z. Robust strictly dissipative control for discrete singular systems. *IET Control Theory Appl.* **2007**, *1*, 1060–1067. [CrossRef]
30. Tan, Z.; Soh, Y.C.; Xie, L. Dissipative control for linear discrete-time systems. *Automatica* **1999**, *35*, 1557–1564. [CrossRef]
31. Nguyen, T.B.; Kim, S.H. Relaxed dissipative control of nonhomogeneous Markovian jump fuzzy systems via stochastic nonquadratic stabilization approach. *Nonlinear Anal. Hybrid Syst.* **2020**, *38*, 100915. [CrossRef]
32. Tuan, H.D.; Apkarian, P.; Narikiyo, T.; Yamamoto, Y. Parameterized linear matrix inequality techniques in fuzzy control system design. *IEEE Trans. Fuzzy Syst.* **2001**, *9*, 324–332. [CrossRef]
33. Wang, Y.; Xie, L.; De Souza, C.E. Robust control of a class of uncertain nonlinear systems. *Syst. Control Lett.* **1992**, *19*, 139–149. [CrossRef]
34. Leibfritz, F. An LMI-based algorithm for designing suboptimal static $\mathcal{H}_2/\mathcal{H}_\infty$ output feedback controllers. *SIAM J. Control Optim.* **2001**, *39*, 1711–1735. [CrossRef]
35. El Ghaoui, L.; Oustry, F.; AitRami, M. A cone complementarity linearization algorithm for static output-feedback and related problems. *IEEE Trans. Autom. Control* **1997**, *42*, 1171–1176. [CrossRef]
36. Tanaka, K.; Kosaki, T. Design of a stable fuzzy controller for an articulated vehicle. *IEEE Trans. Syst. Man Cybern. Part B Cybern.* **1997**, *27*, 552–558. [CrossRef] [PubMed]
37. Kim, S.H. Dissipative control of Markovian jump fuzzy systems under nonhomogeneity and asynchronism. *Nonlinear Dyn.* **2019**, *97*, 629–646. [CrossRef]
38. Wang, G.; Xie, R.; Zhang, H.; Yu, G.; Dang, C. Robust exponential $\mathcal{H}_\infty$ filtering for discrete-Time switched fuzzy systems with time-varying delay. *Circuits Syst. Signal Process.* **2016**, *35*, 117–138. [CrossRef]
39. Fei, Z.; Shi, S.; Wang, T.; Ahn, C.K. Improved stability criteria for discrete-time switched T–S fuzzy systems. *IEEE Trans. Syst. Man Cybern. Syst.* **2018**, *51*, 712–720. [CrossRef]

mathematics

MDPI

Article

A Comprehensive Method to Evaluate Ride Comfort of Autonomous Vehicles under Typical Braking Scenarios: Testing, Simulation and Analysis

Binshuang Zheng [1], Zhengqiang Hong [2,*], Junyao Tang [3,*], Meiling Han [1], Jiaying Chen [4] and Xiaoming Huang [3,5]

1 School of Modern Posts, Nanjing University of Posts and Telecommunications, Nanjing 210023, China
2 China State Construction Engineering (Hong Kong) Limited, Hong Kong 999077, China
3 School of Transportation, Southeast University, Nanjing 211189, China
4 China Construction America, CCA Headquarters, 525 Washington Blvd., 31st Floor, Jersey City, NJ 07310, USA
5 National Demonstration Center for Experimental Education of Road and Traffic Engineering, Southeast University, Nanjing 211189, China
* Correspondence: zhengqiang.hong@cohl.com (Z.H.); jytang@seu.edu.cn (J.T.); Tel.: +852-63666247 (Z.H.); +86-1879-5888-673 (J.T.)

Abstract: To highlight the advantages of autonomous vehicles (AVs) in modern traffic, it is necessary to investigate the sensing requirement parameters of the road environment during the vehicle braking process. Based on the texture information obtained using a field measurement, the braking model of an AV was built in Simulink and the ride comfort under typical braking scenarios was analyzed using CarSim/Simulink co-simulation. The results showed that the proposed brake system for the AV displayed a better performance than the traditional ABS when considering pavement adhesion characteristics. The braking pressure should be controlled to within the range of 4 MPa~6 MPa on a dry road, while in wet road conditions, the pressure should be within 3 MPa~4 MPa. When steering braking in dry road conditions, the duration of the "curve balance state" increased by about 57.14% compared with wet road conditions and the recommended curve radius was about 100 m. The slope gradient had a significant effect on the initial braking speed and comfort level. Overall, the ride comfort evaluation method was proposed to provide theoretical guidance for AV braking strategies, which can help to complement existing practices for road condition assessment.

Keywords: autonomous vehicles; texture information; ride comfort; multiple logistic regression analysis; braking scenarios

MSC: 9M37; 65K99

Citation: Zheng, B.; Hong, Z.; Tang, J.; Han, M.; Chen, J.; Huang, X. A Comprehensive Method to Evaluate Ride Comfort of Autonomous Vehicles under Typical Braking Scenarios: Testing, Simulation and Analysis. *Mathematics* **2023**, *11*, 474. https://doi.org/10.3390/math11020474

Academic Editors: Lijuan Zha, Jian Liu and Jinliang Liu

Received: 25 November 2022
Revised: 9 January 2023
Accepted: 11 January 2023
Published: 16 January 2023

Copyright: © 2023 by the authors. Licensee MDPI, Basel, Switzerland. This article is an open access article distributed under the terms and conditions of the Creative Commons Attribution (CC BY) license (https://creativecommons.org/licenses/by/4.0/).

1. Introduction

With the significant improvement of intelligent technology, the concept of human-oriented experiences in the field of transportation continues to develop [1]. To highlight the advantages of autonomous vehicles (AVs) in modern traffic under the precondition of driving safety, ride comfort will become a hot topic in the development of AVs in the future [2]. Ride comfort mainly depends on the vehicle body vibration frequency and road condition (e.g., textural properties of road surfaces, road distresses and road geometry features). The emergency braking, steering process, continuous braking and other operation actions, which are influenced by road geometry features, will have an impact on passenger psychology and physiology. Thus, it is impossible to accurately quantify ride comfort.

So far, many researchers have carried out studies on ride comfort from different perspectives, such as CAE simulation, laboratory tests and human physiology [3,4]. In 1935, the ride comfort of a vehicle was first studied from the perspective of an evaluation index, including Janeway's J evaluation standard, Dickman's *K* coefficient method, M. J. Griffin's "total ride value method" and the widely used ISO-2631 standard. A comparative analysis of existing comfort indexes is shown in Table 1. To improve the ride comfort of vehicles, an assisted driving system was developed using a simulation method to appropriately modify the vehicle driving path so that it was better adapted to the driving road environment [5]. With ADAMS/car software, the dynamic simulation analysis of the vehicle was carried out by Tang [6]; then, the root mean square value of the weighted acceleration at various speeds was calculated to analyze the impact of vehicle speed on road comfort for a certain road contour. For a more practical study of human comfort, Kumar recommended evaluating the railway ride comfort index according to the ISO-2631 standard [7]. Genser [8] proposed a methodology that included a high-precision road surface model and accurate virtual chassis acceleration data to detect an AV's ride comfort under different situations (such as preventable, over-, or underestimated) by utilizing the thresholding procedure. According to current research results [9–12], ride comfort is the result of a complex human–vehicle–road–environment system, which is mainly influenced by factors such as the vehicle braking time, vehicle body parameters and road traffic environment. Therefore, there is still no unified evaluation standard for the ride comfort of vehicles, especially for AVs.

Table 1. Comparative analysis of existing comfort indexes.

Index	Content	Drawback
Janeway comfort factor *J*	$J = \frac{1}{6}Af^3; f = 1 \sim 6\,\text{Hz}$ $J = Af^2; f = 6 \sim 20\,\text{Hz}$ $J = 20Af; f = 20 \sim 60\,\text{Hz}$ where A is the vibration amplitude and f is the vibration frequency.	Vibration time is not taken into account.
Dieckmann index *K*	$K = a{\cdot}f^2$, where a is the vibration amplitude and f is the vibration frequency.	Only the case of unidirectional vibration is considered.
Spering index *Wz*	$W_z = 2.7 \times \sqrt[10]{Z^3 f^2 F(f)}$, where Z is the vibration amplitude, f is the vibration frequency and $F(f)$ is the frequency correction factor.	Pavement performance is not considered.
IRI comfort threshold value	Connection between IRI (International Roughness Index) and comfort threshold value is established by considering the human psychological response.	The threshold is statistically based on the probability distribution of the experimental data, which has certain limitations and a singularity.
Braking deceleration	According to ergonomic theory, taking into account the degree of influence of the size of the deceleration on the braking strength, the comfort level is divided into four levels.	This method is used more often in braking and steering control.
ISO 2631-1 driving comfort standard	Comfort is evaluated using the root mean square value of acceleration within a 1~80 Hz vibration frequency range $a_w = \left[\frac{1}{T}\int_0^T a_{wz}^2(t)dt\right]^{1/2} k_{wp} < 9.0$, $VDV = \left[\int_0^T a_{wz}^4(t)dt\right]^{1/4} k_{wp} > 9.0$, where k_{wp} is the vibration waveform peak coefficient and a_w is the weighted acceleration root-mean-square.	The variable influences of vehicle type and its dynamics parameters, dry and wet road conditions, vehicle speed and road type are neglected.
Vehicle-integrated vibration comfort	By combining the vehicle driving scenario, road texture parameters and vehicle dynamics parameters, an integrated vibration comfort was proposed based on the international standard ISO 2361/CD-1991 "Total Ride Value Method".	ISO regulations do not take into account the impact of vibration below 1 Hz on passenger comfort, and a longer period in the vibration environment does not reflect the actual objective feeling.

With the rapid development of driverless technology, the comfort issues caused by the overall vibration of a vehicle body and road unevenness have gradually become hot topics. More and more researchers are focusing on improving aspects of autonomous vehicles, such as the suspension system [13,14], seats [15] and tires [16]. In order to improve ride comfort on a rough road, a genetic algorithm was used to minimize the vibration level of the system and a heuristic vehicle suspension parameter modeling method was proposed [17]. Taking the driving simulator as the test object, Tatsuno [18] studied the application of autonomous functions, such as lane change control, to reduce the vehicle body vibration and discussed the effect of reducing the exposure of the vehicle body vibration on improving the ride comfort. Considering the importance of ride comfort under emergency braking, a vehicle emergency braking system model was established based on CarSim/Simulink co-simulation and a fuzzy control strategy with vehicle safety distance as the index was proposed [19]. Recently, the brake control system design of autonomous vehicles has become quite mature. For an autonomous vehicle, the collision avoidance systems, which contain a longitudinal layered brake controller, slide-mode controller and lane changing/steering controller, can automatically maintain a safe distance and emergency braking behavior [20,21]. European research institutes demonstrated and studied driving stability based on an autonomous vehicle control system and put forward many new concepts, including lane detection and stability discrimination [22,23]. As one of the main influential factors that affect ride comfort, the increased rutting potential because of the AV movement for strictly defined wheel paths can be expected to induce hydroplaning and road safety issues because of water accumulation along the wheel paths [24]. Regarding this problem, related research toward a smarter detection of friction in real-time was recently reviewed [25]. Meanwhile, some recent studies about intelligent tires focused on AVs, which can communicate the road status in real time and provide parameters for adjusting vehicle driving behavior. For example, Matsuzaki [26] designed a scheme for identifying the friction coefficient of tire–road contact surfaces during driving, while Gupta developed an experimental setup to identify the road surface in real time [27].

However, most of the studies ignored problems such as the influence of road adhesion characteristics on ride comfort during the braking process [28]. As is well known, the adhesion characteristics of the road surface directly affect the skid resistance performance, which has become the main objective factor that affects the braking stability of AVs [29–31]. In the braking process of AVs, even though both the anti-skid braking system (ABS) and traction control system (TCS) play a role, phenomena such as speed fluctuation, vehicle rollover and slippage can still occur, which indicates that the braking system of traditional vehicles is not suitable for the ride comfort of AVs. Thus, in order to forecast ride comfort during realistic braking strategies, it is necessary to investigate the sensing characteristics of road information in the braking process of AVs based on the vehicle dynamics theory.

In view of the above research shortcomings, we aimed to propose an evaluation method for ride comfort to provide theoretical guidance for braking strategies and a braking system design for autonomous vehicles according to theoretical analysis and numerical simulation. First, pavement texture information, as the main objective influencing factor of the ride comfort of AVs, was directly obtained using field testing. The braking comfort index in the international standard ISO was applied to evaluate and classify the ride comfort level of AVs under typical braking scenarios in this study. Based on the change rule of comfort level, reasonable strategies to improve the braking comfort of AVs were proposed. The predictive model of an autonomous vehicle comfort index was obtained through multiple logistic regression analysis. An evaluation system for the ride comfort of AVs was established and the sensing requirement parameters of road information based on ride comfort were determined in this study. The chapter structure of this study is shown in Figure 1.

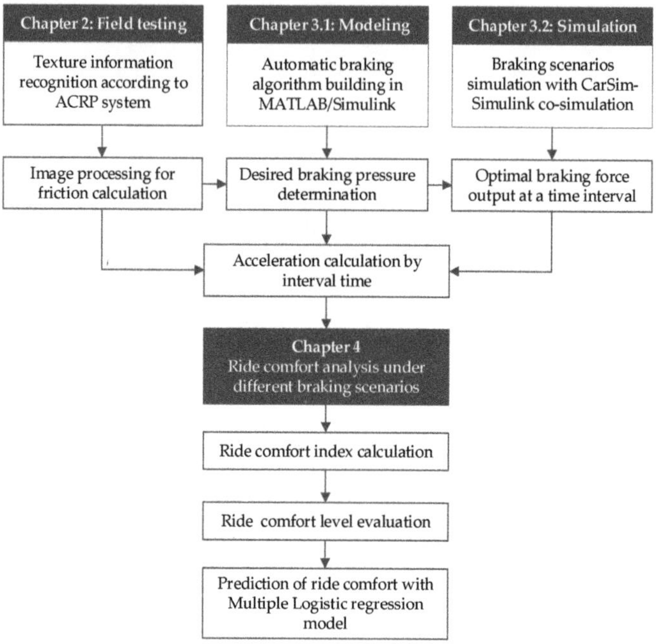

Figure 1. Research framework of this study.

2. Field Testing

2.1. Field Testing of Road Surface Texture Information

Dense-graded asphalt concrete (AC-13) was selected in this study, and the gradation design of asphalt mixtures was shown in Table 2. Then, the AC asphalt pavement (Figure 2a) had its surface textures captured on site using the research team's automated close-range photogrammetry system (ACRP system) [32]. After preprocessing the gathered photos, the reverse reconstruction method was applied to rebuild the three-dimensional (3D) images of the surface texture of the asphalt pavement, and the 3D model of the surface texture of the asphalt pavement was constructed (Figure 2b). After preprocessing the reverse-reconstructed 3D model of the surface texture of the asphalt pavement with GeoMagic and MeshLab, it was possible to extract 3D elevation data for the surface texture of the road from the 3D model, which contained (x, y, z) 3D coordinate values (Figure 2c).

Table 2. Gradations for AC asphalt pavement.

Sieve Size (mm) / Components	Passing Rate of Each Sieve (%)									
	0.075	0.15	0.3	0.6	1.18	2.36	4.75	9.5	13.2	16
AC-13	6	10	13.5	19	26.5	37	53	76.5	95	100

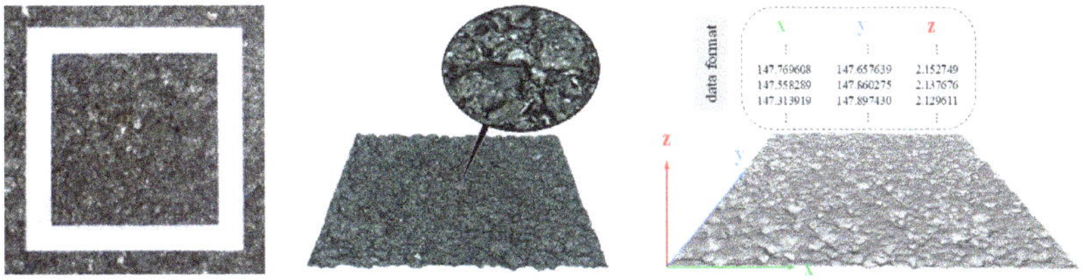

(a) (b) (c)

Figure 2. Acquisition of road surface texture information: (**a**) testing range of the pavement texture; (**b**) reconstructed digital pavement model; (**c**) 3D coordinate values.

2.2. Calculation of the Dynamic Friction Coefficient

A power spectral distribution (PSD) solver was created in MATLAB using the PSD calculation model in the Persson friction theory and the 3D texture data (x, y, z) discussed in Section 2.1 [33–35]. Considering the random variables of the fractal road surface as discrete points, additional filtering, windowing and sampling window compensation of the coordinate values were required in the procedure of resolving the power spectrum [36].

In order to create a wet pavement surface, water was uniformly sprayed on the dry surface until the concave asperities were sealed with water [37,38]. The PSD of the wet and dry pavement surfaces were both calculated, as shown in Figure 3a.

$$C(q) = \frac{1}{(2\pi)^2} \int \langle h(x)h(0) \rangle e^{iqx} dx \tag{1}$$

where x is the wave vector direction; $h(0)$ is the surface elevation of the origin point; $h(x)$ is the surface elevation with the average elevation as the starting point; <...> represents the average across the plane; q is the wave vector, which could be obtained using the wavelength λ; and e is a universal constant.

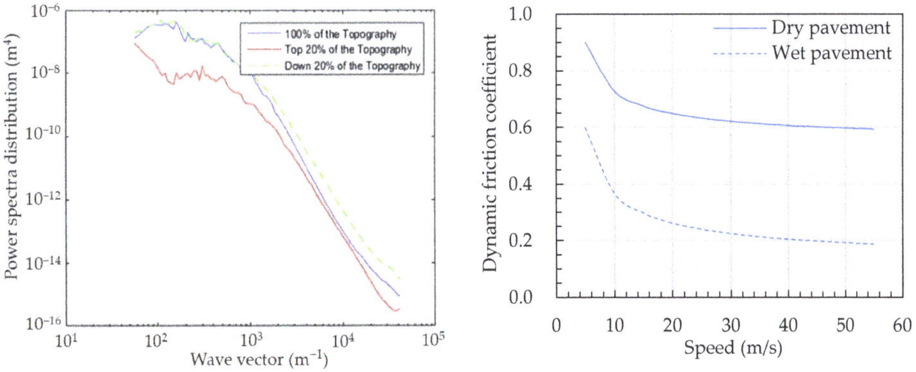

(a) (b)

Figure 3. Acquisition of asphalt pavement texture information: (**a**) 2D-PSD of the pavement texture; (**b**) dynamic friction coefficient curves.

In fact, when there is a water film on the road surface, the traditional method of calculating the PSD is not applicable, and the calculated road surface PSD is already inaccurate. This is because there is a water film barrier between the tire and the road, where the water film has a great lifting effect on the tire when the vehicle is driving at a high speed [39], and thus, there will be a larger untouched area between the vehicle tire rubber and the fractal surface of the asphalt pavement, which is one of the reasons for the significant decrease in the anti-skid performance of a vehicle during rainy weather.

The untouched area between the vehicle tire rubber and the fractal surface of the asphalt pavement is defined as the "anti-skid non-contribution area". The asphalt pavement surface texture morphology and the "anti-skid non-contribution area" under dry and wet conditions were visualized, as shown in Figure 4. It can be seen that during the driving process in the wet condition, there is an unconnected area between the tire and the road due to the water stasis barrier and the water film lifting action, and these areas are called "anti-skid non-contribution areas".

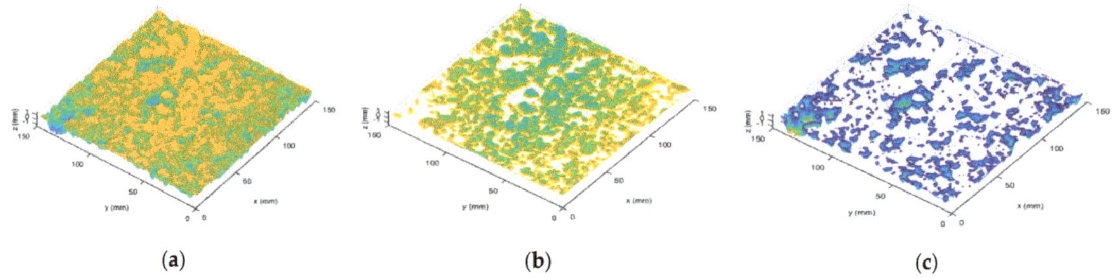

Figure 4. Pavement texture morphology visualization under different conditions: (**a**) dry pavement; (**b**) wet pavement; (**c**) anti-skid non-contribution area.

The friction coefficient curve, which was obtained using the Persson friction coefficient formula, varied with speed under different pavement conditions (dry and wet) (see Figure 2b). The curve tended to be gentler above 40 km/h, indicating that at relatively high speeds, the actual tire–road contact area stabilized. The friction coefficient of the wet state of the road surface was lower than that of the dry state, and the higher the speed, the greater the difference between the two states' friction coefficients (dry and wet pavement).

2.3. Peak adhesion Coefficient of the Asphalt Pavement

Referring to the tire hydroplaning model built by the research group [40,41], the dynamic friction coefficient curves (in Figure 3b) between the tire and pavement under various road conditions were integrated into the built hydroplaning model. We set the tire's internal pressure to 240 kPa and the load to 3.922 kN. We also set the tire slip rate to approximately 15% and changed the rolling speed of the tire model while keeping other parameters constant. After that, the peak adhesion coefficient curve for various road conditions was determined, as shown in Figure 5.

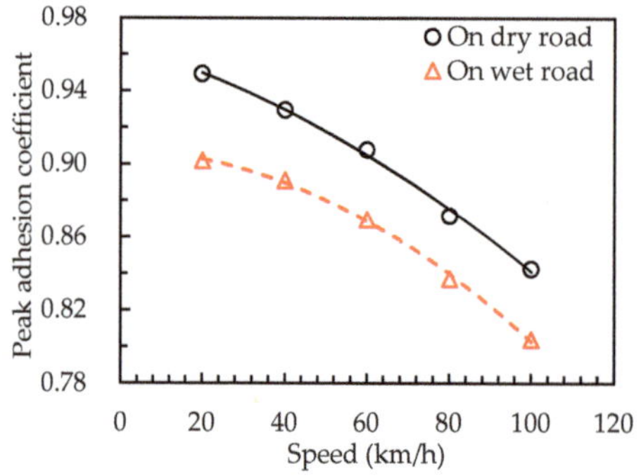

Figure 5. Peak adhesion coefficient curves of asphalt pavement.

The peak adhesion coefficient of the road surface gradually dropped with increasing vehicle speed, and the peak adhesion coefficient of the road surface was distributed as a convex parabola. The fundamental reason for this was that the tire's rolling radius expanded at high speed, which increased the contact area between the tire and the road surface. Therefore, the adhesion force provided by the road surface was reduced. Obviously, the peak adhesion coefficient on a wet road was slightly lower than that on a dry road, which was mainly determined by the contribution rate of the road surface's texture.

3. Braking Model

3.1. Braking Control Model

Based on the various peak adhesion coefficients of the road surface determined in real time, the appropriate braking deceleration was obtained. The required brake deceleration was converted into the desired brake pressure threshold by the anti-brake system model. Through the use of a brake pedal simulator, the electronic control unit (ECU) system of an AV determines the braking pressure. After determining the present brake situation, the brake actuator sends a brake signal to the pressure controller. To complete the vehicle's autonomous braking procedure after a quick response, the brake system on the wheel sends the actual braking force to the tire in real time.

3.1.1. Braking Algorithm

The braking model of an AV was mainly adopted to calculate the wheel cylinder braking force under the condition of safe braking, that is, the calculation of the braking pressure P_{des} of the wheel cylinder. By considering driving straight on a road under good conditions, a mathematical model of forward braking dynamics was established. We set the vehicle deceleration behavior on a horizontal road in the model and ignored ramp resistance F_i. On this basis, air resistance and rolling resistance were considered. However, the slope resistance, a small amount of the acceleration resistance and the internal friction of the system were neglected [42]. Combined with Newton's second law, the inverse braking model for an AV was obtained:

$$P_{des} = \frac{\left| ma_{des} + \frac{1}{2}C_D A\rho v^2 + mgf \right|}{\left(T_{bf} + T_{br}\right)/r_r P_b} \tag{2}$$

where T_{bf} and T_{br} are the braking torques for the front and rear wheels, respectively; r_r is the tire rolling radius; and P_b represents the tire braking pressure.

According to the reverse braking model (Equation (2)) of an AV, the desired brake pressure P_{des} of the wheel cylinder was calculated. Then, the unit module of the reverse braking model was created in MATLAB/Simulink for the following CarSim/Simulink co-simulation, as shown in Figure 6a. The vehicle current speed v and pavement adhesion coefficient μ_h obtained above were integrated into the braking model. Regarding safety braking, the braking pressure P_{des} of the required wheel cylinder could be calculated in real time. The created braking model of an AV was integrated into CarSim to replace the original braking model of a conventional vehicle.

In order to make the automatic steering behavior of an AV closer to the driver's operability, the adaptive braking control approach was implemented by the system to alter the state of the vehicle in real time, which ensured that the vehicle would pass through the curved section at the optimal speed along the optimal travel path (in Figure 6b). During the steering process, the car drove at the ideal speed limit to ensure braking comfort and safety. Under the optimized state of the permitted lateral offset distance, the car drove off the curve with the shortest braking time to achieve the best braking effect according to the ideal braking force based on road surface adhesion characteristics. The steering system calculated the driving speed in real time to avoid exceeding the speed limit so that the autonomous vehicle ran along the intended path.

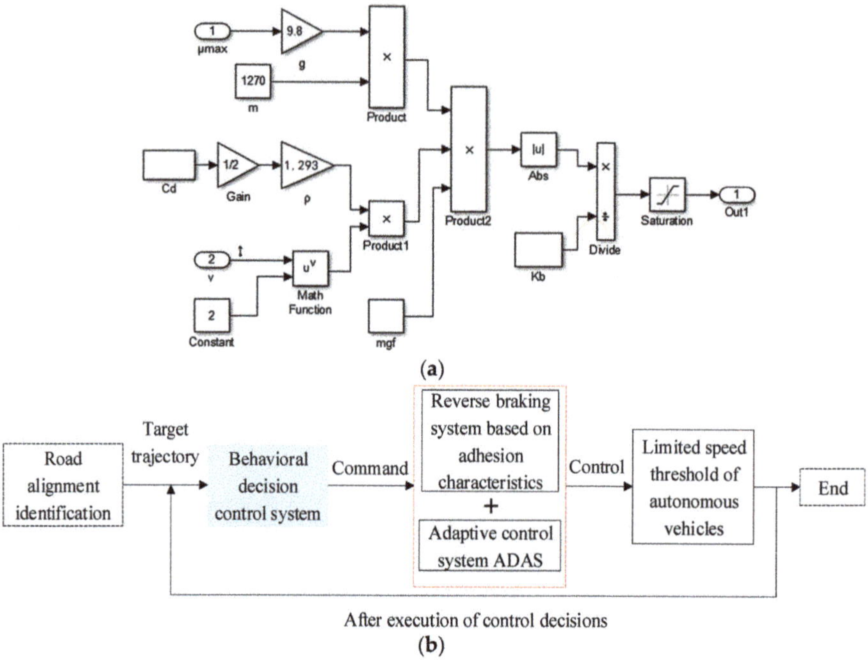

Figure 6. Brake system of the AV: (**a**) reverse brake control algorithm based on MATLAB/Simulink; (**b**) schematic diagram for the steering braking control system.

3.1.2. Validation of the Braking Model

Simulink was used to build a model of the brake control algorithm based on the proposed brake system for the AV. The precision of the brake system in comparison to the conventional ABS brake system was then validated through co-simulation using CarSim. An excellent road condition was used in the simulation, and a peak adhesion coefficient of 0.90 was chosen for the AC-13 asphalt pavement in a dry state. The initial driving speed was set to 120 km/h at the start of braking, the throttle percentage was 0 degrees and the simulation time step was 20 s.

The conventional ABS braking vehicle was subjected to a constant braking pressure of 10 MPa in order to reflect its maximum braking effectiveness. The autonomous car used an adaptive braking control system to brake with the anticipated braking force depending on the characteristics of the adhesion of the road surface. The braking performance curves of the vehicle under two scenarios were determined using the simulation results and are displayed in Figure 7a,b. It is clear that the autonomous vehicle's braking performance surpassed that of the conventional ABS. The braking distance was decreased by 10.92 percent, while the braking time was lowered by 10.95 percent. It can be observed from a comparison of the lateral acceleration–time curves for the two scenarios (in Figure 7c) that the autonomous car had roughly consistent lateral acceleration while braking, whereas a standard ABS vehicle had variable lateral acceleration.

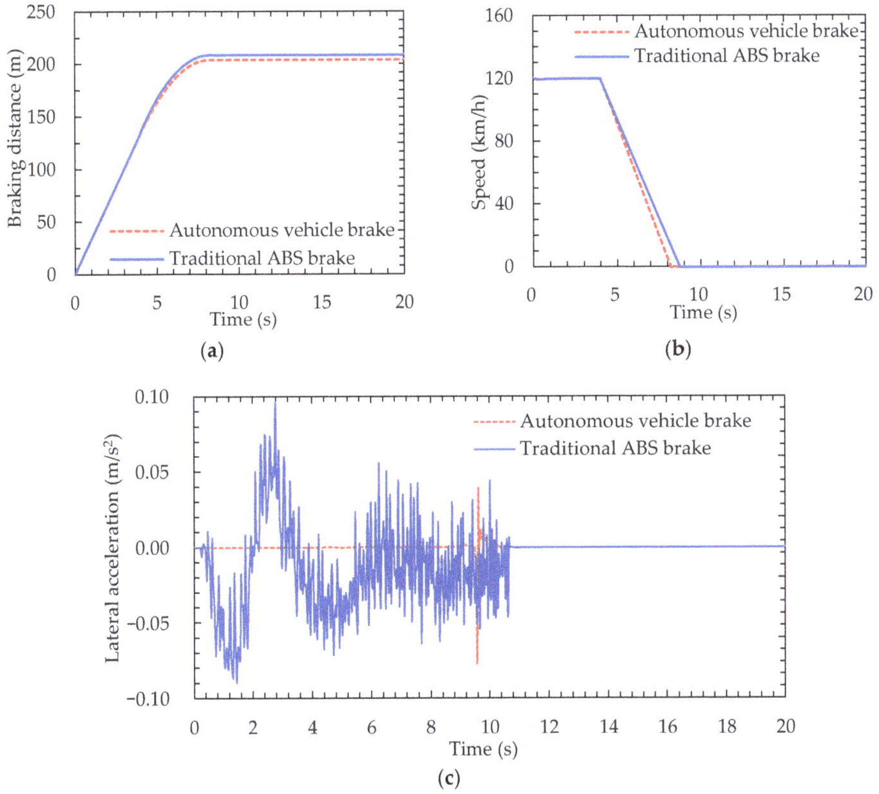

Figure 7. Braking performance analysis compared with a traditional vehicle: (**a**) speed–time curve; (**b**) braking distance–time curve; (**c**) lateral acceleration curve.

The traditional ABS frequently switched between solenoid valves during the braking process to maintain the tire slip rate within the ideal range of 10–20%. As a result, the tire slip rate fluctuated more frequently without consideration of the road characteristics, which led to extremely poor braking performance and a bad passenger experience. Based on the road adhesion characteristics, the braking system of the autonomous vehicle calculated the expected braking pressure at the real-time position and applied it to the tires so that the vehicle drove with the optimal braking deceleration. The tire slip rate of the autonomous vehicle was basically maintained at approximately 12.0% and the fluctuation range was very small.

When the actual tire–road contact characteristics are taken into account in the braking system of an AV, it can better reflect the vehicle braking stability requirements. It was found that the braking system performance of the AV outperformed traditional ABS. The results showed that the proposed braking system is suitable for AVs and has high accuracy.

In accordance with the aforementioned created autonomous vehicle model and pavement model, the simulation analysis under various operating conditions was carried out in CarSim. Meanwhile, the model written in MATLAB/Simulink was integrated into CarSim to replace the original braking model (in Figure 8). In this study, the braking scenarios of emergency braking and braking on curved and slope sections were analyzed in wet or dry road conditions.

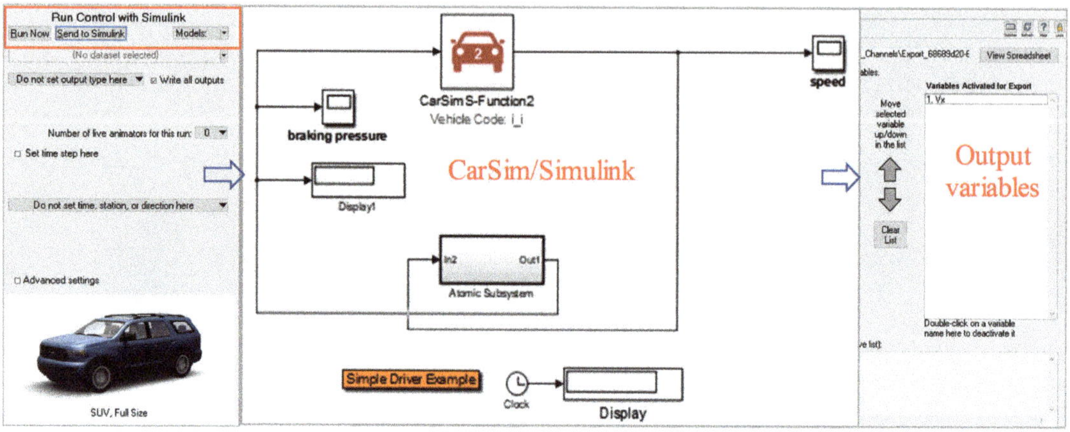

Figure 8. Calculation diagram of the CarSim/Simulink co-simulation.

3.2. Modeling Parameter Settings

(1) Travel path modeling

The reference path, pavement geometry and pavement roughness attributes are key elements of the pavement model in a simulation. As illustrated in Figure 9, the segmentation approach was used to input the pavement's linear key points coordinate data, converting the created reference path into (x, y) coordinates to lessen the workload associated with data entry. The pavement geometry properties (road width, number of lanes, elevation, etc.) were mapped to the matching (x, y) coordinates in the CarSim pavement model database. The adhesion coefficient of the continuous point on the road surface, which was acquired in real time, was also imported.

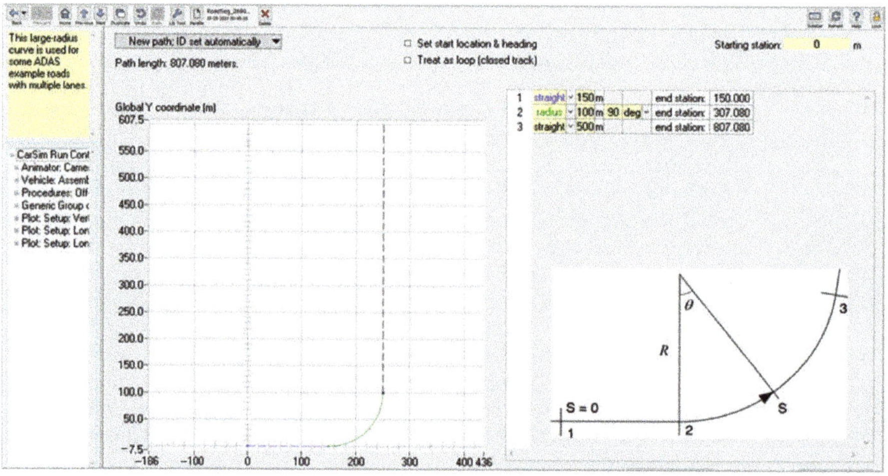

Figure 9. Reference travel route setting.

(2) Vehicle parameters

We selected the common SUV type used in a city as the simulation vehicle model; the vehicle body parameters are shown in Table 3. The specific aerodynamic parameters were set in the simulation, including the vehicle's windward surface area (the SUV vehicle was taken to have an area of 3.3 m^2) and air density (taken as 1.206 kg/m^3). The vehicle tires acted as the only contact parts between the vehicle and the pavement. Theoretically, the force generated from the tire–road interaction ensures the braking safety of the vehicle. To make the vehicle simulation analysis comparable to a real-world situation, the adhesion characteristic curve for the tire–road interaction calculated by our research group was imported into CarSim [43].

Table 3. Parameter settings of the vehicle body.

Items	Value	Items	Values
Vehicle mass	2257 kg	Distance between the centroid and front axis	1330 mm
Vehicle length	4475 mm	Axle spacing	3140 mm
Vehicle width	2029 mm	Roll inertia I_{xx}	846.6 kg·m^2
Vehicle height	1966 mm	Pitch inertia I_{yy}	3524.9 kg·m^2
Centroid height	780 mm	Yaw inertia I_{zz}	3524.9 kg·m^2

Due to the large difference between the autonomous vehicle and the traditional manned vehicle in terms of the braking system, an algorithm for an autonomous vehicle braking model was written using Matlab/Simulink co-simulation to ensure the simulation accuracy. Then, the written model was imported into CarSim to replace the initial braking model.

(3) Sensing parameter settings

The AEB (autonomous emergency brake) system of the autonomous vehicle was simulated. The POP UP Windows subroutine was created using the CarSim interface to display the car driving data using MATLAB. The engine speed, vehicle speed, throttle position and brake percentage were among the selectable statistics. Additionally, the effective maximum brake pressure of the wheel cylinder was divided by the present brake pressure to get the braking percentage. Figure 10a displays a dynamic visualization of the simulation findings.

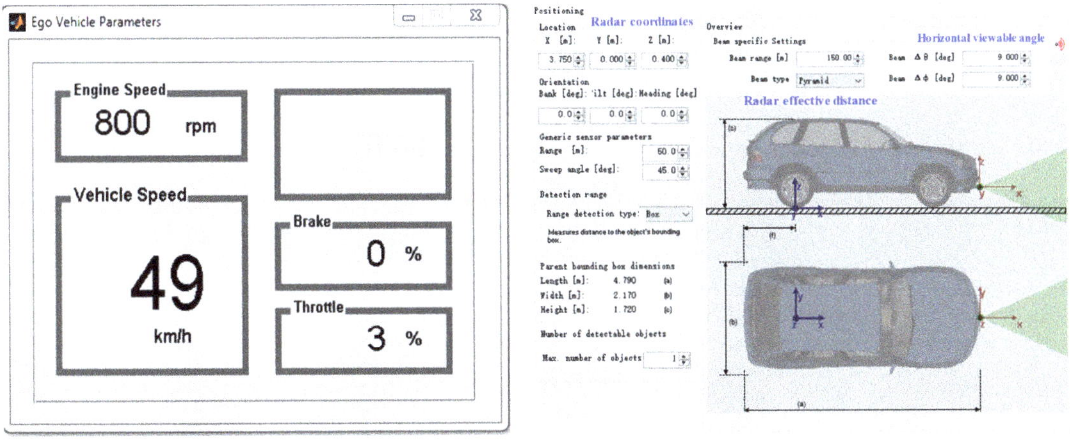

(a) (b)

Figure 10. Simulation results of the dynamic visualization subroutine: (**a**) autonomous vehicle braking parameters; (**b**) vehicle equipped with radar monitoring.

In the simulation, a short-range laser radar was utilized to detect automobiles and pedestrians in proximity to the vehicle, and the long-range laser radar was customized to detect the traffic situation in the distance. The two radars' respective effective ranges were

150 m and 30 m, and their horizontal viewing angles were 9 deg and 80 deg. Additionally, Figure 10b illustrates that both of the two radars' vertical viewing angles were 9 deg.

4. Braking Scenario Simulations

4.1. Emergency Braking on a Straight Road

If an autonomous vehicle is in an emergency during the driving process, in order to avoid a collision, it is necessary to trigger the brake as soon as the vehicle sensor recognizes the danger. Then, the braking force is continuously exerted on the wheel cylinder to stop the vehicle as soon as possible. In the case of emergency braking, only considering safety without passenger comfort, a 500 m long straight road was built in the simulation.

First, the braking effect of an SUV traveling at a speed of 120 km/h on a rainy day was tested. The friction coefficient curve of the road surface calculated using the PSD power spectral density of "anti-skid non-contribution area for skid resistance" on a rainy day was imported. The obstacle ahead was set to be detected in the fourth second. Meanwhile, the vehicle started emergency braking. At the beginning of the fourth second, a braking pressure of 10 MPa was applied instantaneously, as shown in Figure 11.

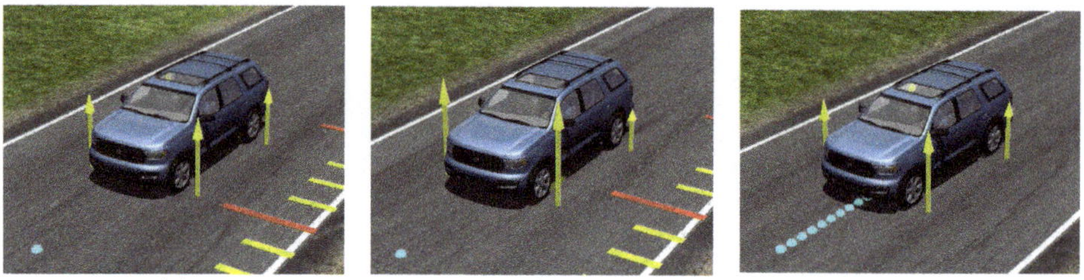

(**a**) (**b**) (**c**)

Figure 11. Emergency brake simulation scene on a straight road: (**a**) constant speed; (**b**) emergency brake; (**c**) stopped.

The vertical force of the front wheel rose suddenly while that of the rear wheel fell suddenly. Meanwhile, the car body leaned forward. When the braking pressure was applied instantaneously, the tires were quickly locked and then began to skid. Then, the ABS of the vehicle began to operate and the vertical force curves of the wheels began to oscillate repeatedly. Similarly, the simulation results with different braking pressure settings of 8 MPa, 6 MPa, 4 MPa, 2 MPa, 1 MPa and 0.5 MPa were also calculated.

4.2. Steering Braking on a Curved Section

In the simulation, a 700 m long road with both straight and curved sections was constructed. A 30 s simulation time was chosen. On both sides of the fictitious road, there were signs indicating the speed limit, safety precautions and lane changes. The model car initially moved at a constant speed of 100 km/h. In addition, the vehicle received a long-range radar, camera and other sensors at the same time. The car could dynamically identify the road surroundings while driving with sensors installed.

The road was identified by the sensors, and an automatic optimal cornering speed was implemented to modify the brake cylinder pressure in real time. At the same time, the lateral acceleration was not more than 0.35 g to ensure the stability of the vehicle when turning. The braking simulation visual interface is shown in Figure 12. Additionally, the adhesion coefficients for wet and dry roads were set to 0.60 and 0.90, respectively.

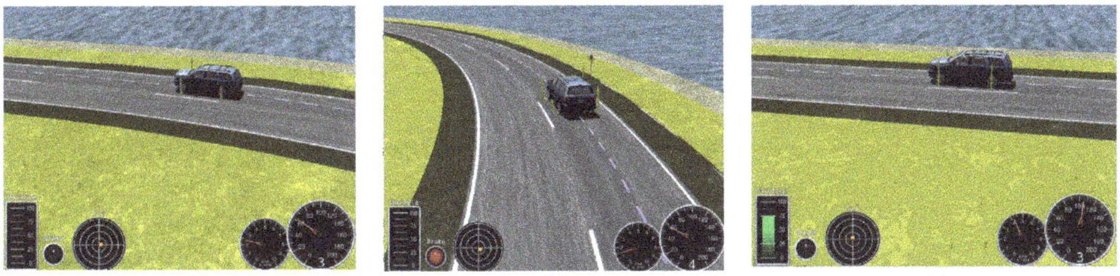

(a) (b) (c)

Figure 12. Brake simulation on a curved section: (**a**) constant speed; (**b**) steering deceleration; (**c**) acceleration driving.

4.3. Braking Simulation on a Sloped Road

It is well known that there is frequent braking when driving uphill and downhill. The vehicle brake can easily fail and there is a blind spot in the onboard camera. In order to maintain a sufficient safety distance and braking comfort, the autonomous vehicle must maintain enough distance in front before starting braking. Braking characteristics on a sloped road were analyzed by considering passenger comfort during the vehicle braking process in this study.

Based on the vehicle dynamics model mentioned above, four slope gradients (5°, 10°, 15° and 20°) were selected in the simulation, taking the dry road condition with good skid resistance as an example (the pavement peak adhesion coefficient was taken as 0.8065). Keeping the other parameters constant, the scene visualization of braking on a sloped road was obtained, as shown in Figure 13.

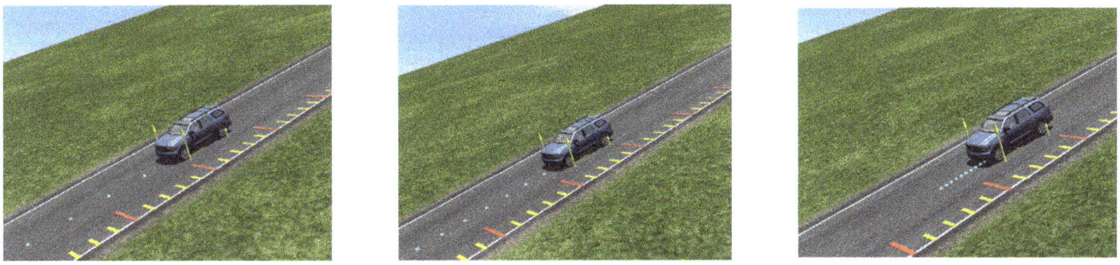

(a) (b) (c)

Figure 13. Brake simulation process on a sloped road: (**a**) uniform acceleration; (**b**) brake with a certain deceleration; (**c**) stopped.

5. Results and Discussion

5.1. Evaluation Index of the Braking Comfort

The comfort index (*CI*) of AVs is specified in International Standard ISO 2631-1 [44]. Without considering the lateral movement, the calculation equation of the comfort index can be simplified to

$$CI = \left[\frac{1}{m} \sum_{i=0}^{m} a_i^2 \right]^{1/2} \tag{3}$$

where a_i is the *i*th statistically determined acceleration value and m is the total number of statistics. In successive simulation trials, the acceleration values were measured at equal time intervals (Δt = 1 s), which is consistent with the statistical frequency of comfort (within 0.5 Hz~80.0 Hz). Six comfort levels were defined in accordance with the comfort index's range and the International Standard ISO 2631-1, as shown in Table 4. The comfort of operating a vehicle lies between two comfort levels when the CI level ranges overlap.

Table 4. Comfort evaluation level for autonomous vehicle braking.

Levels	CI Range (m/s^2)	Description of Vehicle Comfort	Color
0	>2.0000	Extremely uncomfortable	
1	1.2500~2.5000	Very uncomfortable	
2	0.8000~1.6000	Uncomfortable	
3	0.5000~1.0000	Fairly uncomfortable	
4	0.3150~0.6300	A little uncomfortable	
5	<0.5000	Comfortable	

5.1.1. Calculation of Braking Comfort Index

On a dry or wet road, the speed–time relationship was obtained according to the simulation results. Then, the ride comfort level was evaluated for each different braking scenarios according to Equation (3) and Table 4. Taking emergency braking on a straight road as an example, the simulation results are as follows.

The calculation results of the comfort index of the autonomous vehicle during the emergency braking process on dry and wet road conditions are shown in Tables 5 and 6.

Table 5. Comfort level of emergency braking on a dry road.

Time Interval (s)	Comfort Index CI_P with Different Braking Pressures (m/s^2)						
	$CI_{0.5}$	$CI_{1.0}$	$CI_{2.0}$	$CI_{4.0}$	$CI_{6.0}$	$CI_{8.0}$	$CI_{10.0}$
Δt_1	5	5	5	5	5	5	5
Δt_2	5	5	5	5	5	5	5
Δt_3	5	5	5	5	5	5	5
Δt_4	5	5	5	5	5	5	5
Δt_5	5	4	3	2	1~2	1~2	1~2
Δt_6	5	4	3	2	1~2	1~2	1~2
Δt_7	5	4	3	2	1~2	1~2	1~2
Δt_8	5	4	3~4	2	1~2	1~2	1~2
Δt_9	5	4	3~4	2	5	5	5
Δt_{10}	5	4	5	5	5	5	5
Δt_{11}	5	4	3~4	5	5	5	5
Δt_{12}	5	4	3~4	5	5	5	5
Δt_{13}	5	4	3~4	5	5	5	5
Δt_{14}	5	4	4	5	5	5	5
Δt_{15}	5	4	5	5	5	5	5
Δt_{16}	5	4	5	5	5	5	5
Δt_{17}	5	4	5	5	5	5	5
Δt_{18}	5	4	5	5	5	5	5
Δt_{19}	5	4	5	5	5	5	5
Δt_{20}	5	5	5	5	5	5	5
Δt_{21}	5	5	5	5	5	5	5

Table 6. Comfort level of emergency braking on a wet road.

Time Interval (s)	Comfort Index CI_P with Different Braking Pressure (m/s²)						
	$CI_{0.5}$	$CI_{1.0}$	$CI_{2.0}$	$CI_{4.0}$	$CI_{6.0}$	$CI_{8.0}$	$CI_{10.0}$
Δt_1	5	5	5	5	5	5	5
Δt_2	5	5	5	5	5	5	5
Δt_3	5	5	5	5	5	5	5
Δt_4	5	5	5	5	5	5	5
Δt_5	5	4	3	2	2	2	2
Δt_6	5	4	3	2	2	2	2
Δt_7	5	4	3	2	2	2	2
Δt_8	5	4	3~4	2	2	2	2
Δt_9	5	4	3~4	2	2	2	2
Δt_{10}	5	4	3	2	2	2	2
Δt_{11}	5	4	3~4	5	5	5	5
Δt_{12}	5	4	3~4	5	5	5	5
Δt_{13}	5	4	3~4	5	5	5	5
Δt_{14}	5	4	4	5	5	5	5
Δt_{15}	5	4	5	5	5	5	5
Δt_{16}	5	4	5	5	5	5	5
Δt_{17}	5	4	5	5	5	5	5
Δt_{18}	5	4	5	5	5	5	5
Δt_{19}	5	4	5	5	5	5	5
Δt_{20}	5	4	5	5	5	5	5
Δt_{21}	5	4	5	5	5	5	5

5.1.2. Evaluation of Ride Comfort Levels

(1) Emergency Braking on a Straight Road

From Tables 4 and 5, when the braking pressure was 0.5 MPa or 1.0 MPa, the ride comfort was always in a good state within a specific braking time range (ΔT = 20 s), and the comfort level was always 5 or 4. However, the vehicle braking behavior was not completed at the end of 20 s, and its braking comfort was subsequently not evaluated. As the brake pressure changed from 2 MPa to 10 MPa, the following was found:

- The comfort index CI of an autonomous vehicle on a dry road during the period of constant speed (in the time domain of $\Delta t_1 \sim \Delta t_4$) was within the range of 0–0.315, indicating that straight travel at a certain safe speed with real-time perception of the surrounding environment produced ride comfort that was suitable for the passenger's subjective feelings and provided a good riding experience. Due to the low coefficient of adhesion on the wet road, the braking time of the vehicle under the same braking pressure and same initial speed increased, and the braking distance increased in turn. Compared with the dry road condition, braking comfort was poor and the passengers were prone to fatigue.
- When the braking pressure was 2 MPa, the braking time was extended in the case of an initial speed of 120 km/h. During the period of 5–19 s, the comfort level was 4, meaning that the passengers felt slightly uncomfortable but the comfort was within an acceptable range. However, the longer braking time caused the ABS to start frequently and cause passenger fatigue, and there was a high probability of collision and rear-end collision in the emergency braking environment.
- When the braking pressure changed from 4 MPa to 10 MPa, the comfort level was 5 during the constant speed driving phase. During the brake deceleration process, the comfort level appeared in the range of level 2 (brake pressure was equal to 4 MPa) or level 1~level 2 (brake pressure was more than 4 MPa), indicating that the vibration frequency of the vehicle during braking was large, and the uneven distribution of the vertical pressure of the left and right tires resulted in a large fluctuation.

(2) Steering braking on a curved section

As for the sections with different curve radii, the evaluation of ride comfort level in dry and wet road conditions was carried out. The following was found:

- The best curve radius in terms of comfort was 200 m at a speed of 100 km/h, and the CI index was less than 4. This meant that the comfort met the passenger requirement, and the advantage of the AV was demonstrated.
- Compared with the wet road condition, a dry road could provide greater lateral friction because of the good adhesion, which mostly counteracted the centrifugal force generated by the vehicle on the curved section. Thus, the ride comfort during the steering process was greatly improved, and thus, the duration of the "curve balance state" on the dry road lasted longer, i.e., an increase of approximately 57.14% compared with the wet road condition, as shown in Figure 14. In addition, the "curve balance state" was defined as the duration of ride comfort level 5 during the steering braking process.
- As the radius of the curve increased, the braking comfort of the vehicle during cornering was relatively good. This was because the curve length increased with the increased radius of the curved section. The autonomous vehicle used an adaptive control system to navigate the curved segment at the best speed; for curves with a bigger radius, a speed buffering process was in place. Road alignment design might be based on the comfort evaluation results.

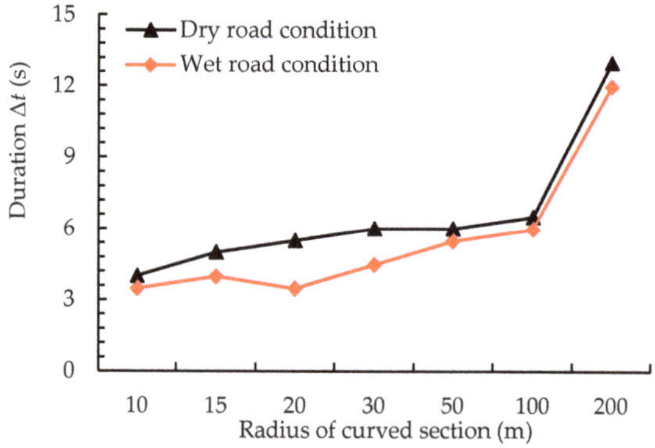

Figure 14. The duration of the "curve balance state" with various radii.

From Figure 14, the "curve balance state" duration slightly increased with the radius increase when the curve radius R was $\leq$100 m, but the variation was not significant. When the radius R was >100 m, the "curve balance state" duration increased significantly. This shows that the curve radius was a significant factor that influenced the ride comfort of AVs during the steering braking process. In order to improve the ride comfort of the vehicle, it is recommended that the curve radius R should be $\geq$100 m and the brake deceleration should start at least 100 m from the entrance of the curved section.

According to Figure 13, when the curve radius R was $\leq$100 m, the "curve balancing state" duration increased somewhat with the radius increase, but the difference was not statistically significant. The "curve balance state" time greatly increased when the radius R was >100 m. This demonstrated how the curve radius had a big impact on how comfortable an AV will ride when steering and stopping. It is advised that the curve radius R should be $\geq$100 m and the brake deceleration should commence at least 100 m from the beginning of the curved segment in order to increase the ride comfort of the vehicle.

(3) Braking on a sloped road

According to the simulation results of the comfort level under different braking speeds and slope gradients, the change law of vehicle comfort was analyzed. The following was found:

- When the slope gradient $i = 10°$ and the initial speed was 80 km/h, or when the slope gradient $i = 20°$ and the initial speed was 60 km/h, the ride comfort level was not greater than 3, indicating that the road slope gradient had a significant effect on the initial braking speed and comfort level. Compared with the slope gradient of 10°, the ride comfort was poor for a slope with a gradient of 20°, which was consistent with the vehicle braking dynamics characteristics.
- Under the conditions of a small slope gradient and low initial speed (such as $i = 10°$ and $v_0 = 60$ km/h) or a large slope gradient and high initial speed (such as $i = 20°$ and $v_0 = 80$ km/h), after perceiving obstacles ahead, because the frictional force on the road surface was insufficient to counteract the inertial force generated by the vehicle body mass, the vehicle started to drive at a uniform acceleration ($a = g*\sin(i)$). Then, the safe braking distance was sensed dynamically and the automatic control mode was activated to adjust the wheel cylinder pressure. Braking deceleration started at the fifth second. In order to prevent the vehicle from rolling over on the sloped road, the vertical pressures of the front and rear tires were automatically controlled to achieve a stable state. At this stage, the vehicle generated a large vibration frequency, and thus, the comfort was poor, with an evaluation level of 2.0.
- As the vehicle mass and the position of the mass center were the same, the braking process on a slope mainly depended on the comprehensive effect of the slope and the initial speed. In a similar braking environment, an AV needs to automatically adjust the wheel cylinder braking pressure according to the initial speed and road slope gradient to adapt to the road alignment to achieve a safe braking behavior.

5.2. Prediction of the Ride Comfort

5.2.1. Multiple Logistic Regression Model

A logistic regression model was used to study the relationship between multiple independent and dependent variables and establish a probabilistic prediction model for discrimination or classification. Logistic regression models are used in a wide range of fields, including machine learning, most medical fields [45] and the social sciences [46]. For a logistic regression model, the most prominent advantage is its simplicity and strong interpretability [47,48].

In order to fit the actual probability of occurrence, there must be a correlation between the selected independent variable and the dependent variable, and each variable is mutually exclusive. Compared with multiple linear regression, logistic regression analysis has the advantages of requiring a low number of assumptions and having a high model accuracy. Therefore, a logistic regression model was applied to build the comfort prediction model of the AV. First, a single-factor analysis was performed for each variable. On this basis, the factors with statistical significance were selected for multivariate unconditional logistic regression analysis, and the optimal model was obtained using the stepwise regression method [49].

Based on the variation range of comfort levels (from level 1 to level 5) under different braking scenarios in Section 5.1.2, level 5 as the highest dependent variable result was selected as the reference group, and the braking comfort of the AV was regarded as a binary dependent variable y_i, where $y_i = 0$ represented level 5 and $y_i = 1$ represented level 1~level 4. In addition, each independent variable $X = (X_1, X_2, \ldots, X_n)$ was regarded as a quantitative or qualitative variable in the logistic regression model, which was applicable to both continuous and discrete variables [50]. Thereby, the probability $P(Y_i)$ that the ith comfort level occurred was denoted as P_i:

$$P_i = P(y_i = 1 | X_1, X_2, \ldots, X_n) \tag{4}$$

The expression of the binary logistic regression model was as follows:

$$\log it(P_i) = \ln\left(\frac{P_i}{1 - P_i}\right) = \alpha + \beta_1 X_{1i} + \ldots + \beta_n X_{ni} \tag{5}$$

Then, the probability for different comfort levels was

$$P_i = \frac{\exp(\alpha + \beta_1 X_{1i} + \ldots + \beta_n X_{ni})}{1 + \exp(\alpha + \beta_1 X_{1i} + \ldots + \beta_n X_{ni})} \tag{6}$$

where α is a constant and the β_i are the regression coefficients representing the correlation between the independent and dependent variables. In addition, $P_i/(1 - P_i) = \exp(\beta)$ is the odds ratio or the relative risk, which is an important index to measure the influence degree of the independent variable on the dependent variable. For each additional unit of the independent variable, the probability of a certain comfort level of the dependent variable will increase by $\exp(\beta_i)$ units.

In this study, the Hosmer–Lemesshow was used to test whether the theoretical frequency distribution predicted by the logistic regression model conformed to the actual theoretical frequency distribution. In addition, the model was globally tested according to the conditional parameter likelihood ratio test and non-significant variables were excluded.

5.2.2. Prediction Model of the Ride Comfort

Based on Section 5.2, the discrete comfort index of each time interval (Δt = 1.0 s) under different braking pressures was acquired. In addition, the braking pressure (X_{1i}) and time (X_{2i}) were the only considered independent variables. Obviously, the tire force during the braking process showed a strong nonlinear characteristic. The binary classification logistic regression analysis was applied to obtain the prediction model of ride comfort for the AV on a straight road during an emergency braking process, which can be expressed as

$$\log it(P_j) = f(P, \Delta t, k_1) \tag{7}$$

where P_j is the probability of the jth comfort level (j represents the four levels of ride comfort, that is level 1~level 4), P is the vehicle braking pressure, Δt is the time interval of acceleration acquisition during the vehicle braking process, and k_1 is the influence coefficient related to the sensor and vehicle type.

The multiple logistic regression model was applied to predict the probability of different ride comfort levels. The regression analysis results are shown in Table 7. Among them, the t-test was the significance test of a single independent variable. The constants and the significance level PL of the independent variables were less than 0.05, indicating that the coefficient of each variable was significant as shown in Table 8.

Table 7. Results of the logistic regression analysis on a dry road.

Prediction Model		Regression Coefficient	Standard Error	t	$P_L > \|t\|$	95% Confidence Interval
Level 2	Constant	−1.5291	0.6514	−2.35	0.019	−2.8060~−0.2523
	P	0.2545	0.0835	3.05	0.002	0.0909~0.4181
	Δt	−0.1429	0.4649	−3.07	0.002	−0.2341~−0.0518
Level 3	Constant	−0.7336	0.8356	−0.88	0.038	−2.3713~−0.9041
	P	−0.3676	0.2001	−1.84	0.015	−0.0542~0.3509
	Δt	−0.0722	0.0708	−1.02	0.031	−0.2110~0.0667
Level 4	Constant	−0.3744	0.7033	−0.53	0.029	−1.7528~1.0039
	P	−0.8316	0.2528	−3.29	0.001	−1.3270~−0.3362
	Δt	0.0571	0.0479	1.19	0.023	−0.0368~0.1510

Table 8. Hausman test result of the prediction model.

Model	Test Coefficient chi^2	*df*	Snell *R*-Squared	P_L > chi^2	Significance
Level 2	−2.561	6	0.2209	1.000	For Ho
Level 3	−2.376	6		1.000	For Ho
Level 4	−1.503	6		1.000	For Ho
Level 5	14.951	3		0.002	Against Ho

Note: d_f is the number of degrees of freedom.

According to the regression analysis results in Table 5, the comfort evaluation model of the AV during emergency braking on a straight road under a dry road condition was obtained as follows:

$$\begin{aligned} \log itP_{j=\text{Level2}} &= -1.5291 + 0.2545P_i - 0.1429\Delta t_i \\ \log itP_{j=\text{Level3}} &= -0.7336 - 0.3676P_i - 0.0722\Delta t_i \\ \log itP_{j=\text{Level4}} &= -0.3744 - 0.8316P_i + 0.0571\Delta t_i \end{aligned} \tag{8}$$

Based on Equation (8), it can be seen that the influence of braking pressure on ride comfort in the level 2 model showed a linear growth trend, while the level 3 and level 4 models showed non-linear decreasing trends with increasing braking pressure. Theoretically, when the brake pressure is too high, the vertical pressure of the tire will be generated instantly, which makes passengers feel highly uncomfortable. However, if the braking pressure is too small to complete the braking process within the effective time, this inevitably leads to a collision and a rear-end accident. Therefore, it is suggested that the braking pressure should be controlled to within the range of 4~6 MPa. Considering the comfort and safety during the vehicle braking process, the braking pressure on a wet road should be within 3~4 MPa. Similarly, the prediction models under other braking scenarios were also obtained as follows:

- Emergency braking on a wet road:

$$\begin{aligned} \log itP_{j=\text{Level1}} &= -3.5729 + 0.3758P_i - 0.2051\Delta t_i \\ \log itP_{j=\text{Level2}} &= -1.6798 + 0.1484P_i - 0.1522\Delta t_i \\ \log itP_{j=\text{Level3}} &= -0.8187 - 0.3722P_i - 0.0872\Delta t_i \\ \log itP_{j=\text{Level4}} &= -0.1853 - 0.7846P_i + 0.0198\Delta t_i \end{aligned} \tag{9}$$

- Steering braking on a curved section:
  (a) On a dry road:

$$\begin{aligned} \log itP_{j=\text{Level3}} &= 1.1966 - 0.0203R_i - 0.1391\Delta t_i \\ \log itP_{j=\text{Level4}} &= 0.7108 - 0.0070R_i - 0.1115\Delta t_i \end{aligned} \tag{10}$$

  (b) On a wet road:

$$\begin{aligned} \log itP_{j=\text{Level3}} &= 1.4319 - 0.0208R_i - 0.1447\Delta t_i \\ \log itP_{j=\text{Level4}} &= 1.0882 - 0.0088R_i - 0.1153\Delta t_i \end{aligned} \tag{11}$$

- Braking on a sloped road:

$$\begin{aligned} \log itP_{j=\text{Level2}} &= -0.9641 + 0.1028i_i + 0.6780v_{0i} - 0.2537\Delta t_i \\ \log itP_{j=\text{Level3}} &= 1.0819 - 0.0228i_i + 0.5295v_{0i} - 0.2454\Delta t_i \\ \log itP_{j=\text{Level4}} &= 0.7255 - 0.0204i_i + 1.1721v_{0i} - 0.2801\Delta t_i \end{aligned} \tag{12}$$

Considering the influence of the road surface adhesion characteristics on the vehicle braking behavior, the sensing parameters of the road environment for vehicle comfort under different braking scenarios were obtained, as shown in Table 9.

Table 9. Sensing parameters of the road environment based on ride comfort.

Braking Scenarios	Road Conditions	Evaluation Function of Comfort Level	Prediction Model	Sensing Parameters of Road Environment
Emergency braking	Dry road	logit $(P_j) = f\ (P, \Delta t, k_1)$	Equation (8)	Brake pressure, adhesion characteristics
	Wet road		Equation (9)	
Steering braking	Dry road	logit $(P_j) = f\ (R, \Delta t, k_2)$	Equation (10)	Radius, travel path and adhesion characteristics
	Wet road		Equation (11)	
Braking on slope section	Dry road	logit $(P_j) = f\ (i, v_0, \Delta t, k_3)$	Equation (12)	Slope gradient, adhesion characteristics and initial speed

Note: k_2 and k_3 are influence coefficients related to traffic environment, road conditions, weather, etc.

6. Conclusions

In this study, based on the braking characteristics of an AV and sensing requirements, the brake model of an AV was built in Simulink. Then, with the consideration of the asphalt pavement adhesion characteristics, the ride comfort during emergency braking on a straight road and steering braking on curved and sloped sections were analyzed using CarSim/Simulink co-simulation. According to multiple logistic regression analysis, the ride comfort prediction models for the AV under different braking scenarios were built in this study. The main research results are as follows:

(1) Based on the Persson friction theory model, the concept of the "anti-skid non-contribution area" was proposed by considering the water stasis barrier and the water film lifting action. When the speed exceeded 40 km/h, the dynamic friction coefficient curve tended to be mild, suggesting that the actual tire–road contact area stabilized when the speed was relatively high. The peak adhesion coefficient of asphalt pavement gradually decreased with increased vehicle speed, which was distributed in a convex parabola. Moreover, the peak adhesion coefficient on a wet road was slightly lower than that on a dry road, which was mainly determined by the contribution rate of the road surface texture.

(2) By considering the road surface adhesion characteristics, the brake control algorithm model was built in Simulink. Compared with the traditional ABS, the proposed brake system of the autonomous vehicle had better performance, where the braking time was shortened by 10.95% and the equivalent braking distance was decreased by 10.92% under the same braking condition.

(3) During the period of constant speed, the comfort index for emergency braking on a dry road was within the range of 0–0.315, that is, level 5, while the comfort level appeared in the range of level 2 (P = 4 MPa) or level 1~level 2 ($P \geq 4$ MPa) during the brake deceleration process. It was suggested that the braking pressure should be controlled within the range of 4 MPa~6 MPa on a dry road, while on a wet road, the pressure should be within 3 MPa~4 MPa.

(4) As for steering braking on a curved section, the comfort level was negatively correlated with the radius R of the curve, indicating that the ride comfort was better as the radius was greater. The "curve balance state" was defined as the duration of ride comfort level 5 during the steering braking process. On a dry road, the duration of the "curve balance state" increased by approximately 57.14% compared with wet road conditions. Considering the passenger comfort requirements and road conditions, the recommended radius of the curved road should be about 100 m.

(5) Compared with the slope gradient of 10°, the ride comfort was poor on a slope with a gradient of 20°, which was consistent with the vehicle braking dynamics characteristics. When the initial speed was constant, the probability of obtaining level 2 gradually

increased with the increase in the slope gradient, while comfort at level 3 and level 4 had a negative correlation.

Further, the sensing system for an AV should be improved to ensure braking comfort by considering the road environment parameters, such as the road surface adhesion characteristics, road alignment and weather. Moreover, the simulation method is suitable for different types of tires and vehicles. Due to the limited paper length, a typical SUV vehicle was selected as the vehicle model. However, the braking principles for different types of autonomous vehicles (such as buses and trucks (especially heavy trucks)) are different. Thus, the specific braking strategies for different types of tires and vehicles under unmanned conditions will be further investigated in the following research. Meanwhile, the proposed model will be integrated with this innovative mobility pattern in the following research. The proposed ride comfort evaluation method can be referred to when building the following AV model, such as the braking model, braking strategies under typical braking scenarios and influence on braking stability of the anti-skid road surface.

Author Contributions: Conceptualization, B.Z. and J.T.; methodology, J.C.; software, Z.H.; validation, B.Z.; formal analysis, J.T.; investigation, J.C.; resources, B.Z.; writing—original draft preparation, B.Z.; writing—review and editing, M.H.; visualization, J.C.; supervision, Z.H. and X.H.; project administration, X.H.; funding acquisition, B.Z. and M.H. All authors have read and agreed to the published version of the manuscript.

Funding: The research was financially supported by the Natural Science Research Start-up Foundation of Recruiting Talents of Nanjing University of Posts and Telecommunications (grant nos. NY221150 and NY219167) and the National Natural Science Foundation of China (grant nos. 51778139 and 62002173).

Informed Consent Statement: Not applicable.

Data Availability Statement: The data used to support the findings of this study are available from the first author upon request. Some models and codes used during the study are proprietary or confidential in nature, such as the PSD calculation code with MATLAB software and the subroutine of the tire–pavement interface in ABAQUS, and may only be provided with restrictions.

Conflicts of Interest: The authors declare no conflict of interest.

References

1. Xiong, Z.; Sheng, H.; Rong, W.; Cooper, D.E. Intelligent Transportation Systems for Smart Cities: A Progress Review. *Sci. China Inf. Sci.* **2012**, *55*, 2908–2914. [CrossRef]
2. Anderson, J.; Kalra, N.; Stanley, K.; Sorensen, P.; Samaras, C.; Oluwatola, T. *Autonomous Vehicle Technology: How to Best Realize Its Social Benefits*; RAND Corporation: Santa Monica, CA, USA, 2014.
3. Karen, İ.; Kaya, N.; Öztürk, F.; Korkmaz, İ.; Yıldızhan, M.; Yurttaş, A. A Design Tool to Evaluate the Vehicle Ride Comfort Characteristics: Modeling, Physical Testing, and Analysis. *Int. J. Adv. Manuf. Technol.* **2012**, *60*, 755–763. [CrossRef]
4. Talebpour, A.; Mahmassani, H.S. Influence of Connected and Autonomous Vehicles on Traffic Flow Stability and Throughput. *Transp. Res. Part C Emerg. Technol.* **2016**, *71*, 143–163. [CrossRef]
5. Wang, F.; Sagawa, K.; Ishihara, T.; Inooka, H. An Automobile Driver Assistance System for Improving Passenger Ride Comfort. *IEEJ Trans. IA* **2002**, *122*, 730–735. [CrossRef]
6. Tang, A.H.; Tian, J.P.; Liao, Y.H. Analysis for Ride Comfort Evaluation of Passenger Car Traveling on Roads with Generalized Road Profiles and Conventional Speeds. *AMR* **2014**, *926–930*, 877–880. [CrossRef]
7. Kumar, V.; Rastogi, V.; Pathak, P. Simulation for Whole-Body Vibration to Assess Ride Comfort of a Low–Medium Speed Railway Vehicle. *Simulation* **2017**, *93*, 225–236. [CrossRef]
8. Genser, A.; Spielhofer, R.; Nitsche, P.; Kouvelas, A. Ride comfort assessment for automated vehicles utilizing a road surface model and Monte Carlo simulations. *Comput.-Aided Civ. Infrastruct. Eng.* **2022**, *37*, 1316–1334. [CrossRef]
9. He, D.; He, W.; Song, X. Efficient predictive cruise control of autonomous vehicles with improving ride comfort and safety. *Meas. Control.* **2020**, *53*, 18–28. [CrossRef]
10. Guo, Y.; Su, Y.; Fu, R.; Yuan, W. Influence of Lane-changing Maneuvers on Passenger Comfort of Intelligent Vehicles. *China J. Highw. Transp.* **2022**, *35*, 221–230.
11. Du, Y.; Chen, J.; Zhao, C.; Liao, F.; Zhu, M. A hierarchical framework for improving ride comfort of autonomous vehicles via deep reinforcement learning with external knowledge. *Comput.-Aided Civ. Infrastruct. Eng.* **2022**, *33*, 79–94. [CrossRef]

12. Winkel, K.N.D.; Irmak, T.; Happee, R.; Shyrokau, B. Standards for passenger comfort in automated vehicles: Acceleration and jerk. *Appl. Ergon.* **2023**, *106*, 103881. [CrossRef] [PubMed]
13. Landersheim, V.; Jurisch, M.; Bartolozzi, R.; Stoll, G.; Möller, R.; Atzrodt, H. Simulation-Based Testing of Subsystems for Autonomous Vehicles at the Example of an Active Suspension Control System. *Electronics* **2022**, *11*, 1469. [CrossRef]
14. Li, N.; Jiang, J.; Sun, F.; Ye, M. Study on the Influence of Suspension Parameters on Longitudinal Impact Comfort. *Secur. Commun. Netw.* **2022**, *2022*, 7749029. [CrossRef]
15. Han, M.Y.; Choi, H.Y.; Hirao, A. Modeling of vehicle seat in lumped network model for ride comfort simulation. *J. Mech. Sci. Technol.* **2021**, *35*, 231–236. [CrossRef]
16. Yordanov, V.; Uszynski, O.; Friederichs, J.; Latfullin, R.; Eckstein, L.; Wiessalla, J. Early Assessment of Tire Related Ride Comfort Based on Component and System Level Measurements. In *12th International Munich Chassis Symposium*; Springer Vieweg: Berlin/Heidelberg, Germany, 2021; pp. 603–623.
17. Jabeen, S.D. Vehicle Vibration and Passengers Comfort. In *Advances in Computational Intelligence*; Sahana, S.K., Saha, S.K., Eds.; Advances in Intelligent Systems and Computing; Springer: Singapore, 2017; Volume 509, pp. 357–372. ISBN 978-981-10-2524-2.
18. Tatsuno, J.; Maeda, S. Driving Simulator Experiment on Ride Comfort Improvement and Low Back Pain Prevention of Autonomous Car Occupants. In *Advances in Human Aspects of Transportation*; Stanton, N.A., Landry, S., Di Bucchianico, G., Vallicelli, A., Eds.; Advances in Intelligent Systems and Computing; Springer International Publishing: Cham, Switzerland, 2017; Volume 484, pp. 511–523. ISBN 978-3-319-41681-6.
19. Liu, S.W.; Zhou, W.K.; Hao, L. The Simulation Research on the Braking Safety and the Ride Comfort of the Vehicle AEB System. *Mod. Manuf. Eng.* **2018**, *10*, 76–81.
20. Guo, J.; Hu, P.; Li, L.; Wang, R. Design of Automatic Steering Controller for Trajectory Tracking of Unmanned Vehicles Using Genetic Algorithms. *IEEE Trans. Veh. Technol.* **2012**, *61*, 2913–2924. [CrossRef]
21. Guo, J.; Hu, P.; Wang, R. Nonlinear Coordinated Steering and Braking Control of Vision-Based Autonomous Vehicles in Emergency Obstacle Avoidance. *IEEE Trans. Intell. Transport. Syst.* **2016**, *17*, 3230–3240. [CrossRef]
22. Zhu, J.; Wang, Z.; Zhang, L.; Dorrell, D.G. Braking/Steering Coordination Control for in-Wheel Motor Drive Electric Vehicles Based on Nonlinear Model Predictive Control. *Mech. Mach. Theory* **2019**, *142*, 103586. [CrossRef]
23. Boopathi, A.M.; Abudhahir, A. Adaptive Fuzzy Sliding Mode Controller for Wheel Slip Control in Antilock Braking System. *J. Engin. Res.* **2016**, *4*, 18. [CrossRef]
24. Zheng, B.; Huang, X.; Zhao, R.; Hong, Z.; Chen, J.; Zhu, S. Study on the rut control threshold of asphalt pavement considering steering stability of autonomous vehicles based on fuzzy control theory. *Adv. Civ. Eng.* **2021**, *2021*, 8879900. [CrossRef]
25. Pomoni, M. Exploring Smart Tires as a Tool to Assist Safe Driving and Monitor Tire–Road Friction. *Vehicles* **2022**, *4*, 744–765. [CrossRef]
26. Matsuzaki, R.; Kamai, K.; Seki, R. Intelligent tires for identifying coefficient of friction of tire/road contact surfaces using three-axis accelerometer. *Smart Mater. Struct.* **2015**, *9435*, 025010. [CrossRef]
27. Gupta, U.; Nouri, A.; Subramanian, C.; Taheri, S.; Kim, M.T.; Lee, H. Developing an experimental setup for real-time road surface identification using intelligent tires. *SAE Int. J. Veh. Dyn. Stab. NVH* **2021**, *5*, 351–367. [CrossRef]
28. Xu, L.; Wang, Y.; Sun, H.; Xin, J.; Zheng, N. Design and Implementation of Driving Control System for Autonomous Vehicle. In Proceedings of the 17th International IEEE Conference on Intelligent Transportation Systems (ITSC), Qingdao, China, 8–11 October 2014; pp. 22–28.
29. Novikov, I.; Lazarev, D. Experimental Installation for Calculation of Road Adhesion Coefficient of Locked Car Wheel. *Transp. Res. Procedia* **2017**, *20*, 463–467. [CrossRef]
30. Ma, B.; Lv, C.; Liu, Y.; Zheng, M.; Yang, Y.; Ji, X. Estimation of Road Adhesion Coefficient Based on Tire Aligning Torque Distribution. *J. Dyn. Syst. Meas. Control.* **2018**, *140*, 051010. [CrossRef]
31. Al-Assi, M.; Kassem, E. Evaluation of Adhesion and Hysteresis Friction of Rubber–Pavement System. *Appl. Sci.* **2017**, *7*, 1029. [CrossRef]
32. Chen, J.; Huang, X.; Zheng, B.; Zhao, R.; Liu, X.; Cao, Q.; Zhu, S. Real-Time Identification System of Asphalt Pavement Texture Based on the Close-Range Photogrammetry. *Constr. Build. Mater.* **2019**, *226*, 910–919. [CrossRef]
33. Persson, B.N.J. Theory of Rubber Friction and Contact Mechanics. *J. Chem. Phys.* **2001**, *115*, 3840–3861. [CrossRef]
34. Persson, B.N.J. On the Fractal Dimension of Rough Surfaces. *Tribol. Lett.* **2014**, *54*, 99–106. [CrossRef]
35. Ciavarella, M. A Simplified Version of Persson's Multiscale Theory for Rubber Friction Due to Viscoelastic Losses. *J. Tribol.* **2018**, *140*, 011403. [CrossRef]
36. Johannesson, P.; Rychlik, I. Laplace Processes for Describing Road Profiles. *Procedia Eng.* **2013**, *66*, 464–473. [CrossRef]
37. Granshaw, S.I. Close Range Photogrammetry: Principles, Methods and Applications: Book Reviews. *Photogramm. Rec.* **2010**, *25*, 203–204. [CrossRef]
38. Tanaka, H.; Yoshimura, K.; Sekoguchi, R.; Aramaki, J.; Hatano, A.; Izumi, S.; Sakai, S.; Kadowaki, H. Prediction of the Friction Coefficient of Filled Rubber Sliding on Dry and Wet Surfaces with Self-Affine Large Roughness. *Mech. Eng. J.* **2016**, *3*, 15-00084. [CrossRef]
39. Scaraggi, M.; Persson, B.N.J. Time-Dependent Fluid Squeeze-Out Between Soft Elastic Solids with Randomly Rough Surfaces. *Tribol. Lett.* **2012**, *47*, 409–416. [CrossRef]

40. Zhu, S.; Liu, X.; Cao, Q.; Huang, X. Numerical Study of Tire Hydroplaning Based on Power Spectrum of Asphalt Pavement and Kinetic Friction Coefficient. *Adv. Mater. Sci. Eng.* **2017**, *2017*, 1–11. [CrossRef]
41. Zheng, B.; Chen, J.; Zhao, R.; Tang, J.; Tian, R.; Zhu, S.; Huang, X. Analysis of Contact Behaviour on Patterned Tire-Asphalt Pavement with 3-D FEM Contact Model. *Int. J. Pavement Eng.* **2022**, *23*, 171–186. [CrossRef]
42. Xu, C.; Wang, W.; Liu, P.; Li, Z. Calibration of Crash Risk Models on Freeways with Limited Real-Time Traffic Data Using Bayesian Meta-Analysis and Bayesian Inference Approach. *Accid. Anal. Prev.* **2015**, *85*, 207–218. [CrossRef]
43. Liu, X.; Cao, Q.; Wang, H.; Chen, J.; Huang, X. Evaluation of Vehicle Braking Performance on Wet Pavement Surface Using an Integrated Tire-Vehicle Modeling Approach. *Transp. Res. Rec.* **2019**, *2673*, 295–307. [CrossRef]
44. Paddan, G.S.; Griffin, M.J. Evaluation of Whole-body Vibration in Vehicles. *J. Sound Vib.* **2002**, *253*, 195–213. [CrossRef]
45. Zabor, E.C.; Reddy, C.A.; Tendulkar, R.D.; Patil, S. Logistic regression in clinical studies. *Int. J. Radiat. Oncol. Biol. Phys.* **2022**, *112*, 271–277. [CrossRef]
46. Ahmadini, A. A novel technique for parameter estimation in intuitionistic fuzzy logistic regression model. *Ain Shams Eng. J.* **2021**, *13*, 101518. [CrossRef]
47. Pisica, D.; Dammers, R.; Boersma, E.; Volovici, V. Tenets of good practice in regression analysis. a brief tutorial. *World Neurosurg.* **2022**, *161*, 230. [CrossRef] [PubMed]
48. Hosmer, F.D.W. A generalized hosmer–lemeshow goodness-of-fit test for multinomial logistic regression models. *Stata J.* **2012**, *12*, 447–453. [CrossRef]
49. Liu, Y.Z. Study on Road Traffic Accident Rate Based on Variance Analysis and Logistic Regression Model. *Technol. Highw. Transp.* **2016**, *32*, 144–147. [CrossRef]
50. Zhang, S.; Peng, Y.; Lu, J.; Chen, Y.; Zhang, H. Examining the Effect of Truck Proportion on Highway Traffic Safety in Free Flow State. *J. Wuhan Univ. Technol.* **2017**, *39*, 42–48. [CrossRef]

Disclaimer/Publisher's Note: The statements, opinions and data contained in all publications are solely those of the individual author(s) and contributor(s) and not of MDPI and/or the editor(s). MDPI and/or the editor(s) disclaim responsibility for any injury to people or property resulting from any ideas, methods, instructions or products referred to in the content.

mathematics

MDPI

Article

Application of Fuzzy PID Based on Stray Lion Swarm Optimization Algorithm in Overhead Crane System Control

Jie Fu [1,*], Jian Liu [2], Dongkai Xie [3] and Zhe Sun [4,5,*]

1 Rail Transit Department, Zhejiang Institute of Communications, Hangzhou 311112, China
2 College of Information Engineering, Nanjing University of Finance and Economics, Nanjing 210023, China; liujian@nufe.edu.cn
3 Alibaba Cloud Intelligence Business Group, Alibaba Co., Ltd., Hangzhou 310024, China; 3039911153@zju.edu.cn
4 Post Industry Technology Research and Development Center of the State Posts Bureau (Internet of Things Technology), Nanjing University of Posts and Telecommunications, Nanjing 210023, China
5 Post Big Data Technology and Application Engineering Research Center of Jiangsu Province, Nanjing University of Posts and Telecommunications, Nanjing 210023, China
* Correspondence: fujie@zjvtit.edu.cn (J.F.); zhesunny@njupt.edu.cn (Z.S.); Tel.: +86-0571-8848-1929 (J.F.); +86-1816-8407-332 (Z.S.)

Abstract: To solve the problem of crane anti-swing, fuzzy PID is a common method. However, the parameter configuration of fuzzy PID requires a lot of time and effort from professionals. Based on this, we introduce the LSO algorithm and add the stray operator, which effectively improves its global search performance. By combining SLSO and fuzzy PID and comparing them with other methods, this paper confirms that even without the targeted optimization by professionals, the optimization algorithm can find the appropriate parameter configuration for fuzzy PID which can be effectively used in the crane anti-swing problem.

Keywords: overhead crane; anti-swing control; fuzzy PID; SLSO algorithm

MSC: 93-10; 93B45; 93C42

Citation: Fu, J.; Liu, J.; Xie, D.; Sun, Z. Application of Fuzzy PID Based on Stray Lion Swarm Optimization Algorithm in Overhead Crane System Control. *Mathematics* **2023**, *11*, 2170. https://doi.org/10.3390/math11092170

Academic Editor: António Lopes

Received: 29 March 2023
Revised: 22 April 2023
Accepted: 23 April 2023
Published: 5 May 2023

Copyright: © 2023 by the authors. Licensee MDPI, Basel, Switzerland. This article is an open access article distributed under the terms and conditions of the Creative Commons Attribution (CC BY) license (https://creativecommons.org/licenses/by/4.0/).

1. Introduction

Fuzzy logic control provides a system theory method for experts to construct language information and convert it into control strategies, which can solve many complex control problems that cannot establish accurate mathematical model systems, so it is an effective method to deal with imprecision and uncertainty in reasoning system and control systems [1–5]. Because of this, the parameter setting of fuzzy control has always depended on the personal ability of experts.

PID control is widely used in various fields because of its advantages of simple structure, strong stability, and convenient adjustment [6–10]. As the core content of control system design, PID parameter tuning is the key factor to determine the control effect. In general, PID parameter tuning can be divided into theoretical calculation tuning and engineering tuning. The former is mainly based on the mathematical model of the system and determines the controller parameters through theoretical calculation, but it still needs to be adjusted and modified on site. The latter mainly adjusts the parameters manually according to field operation experience. Because operator experience is not easy to accurately describe, various semaphores and evaluation indicators in the control process are not easy to quantitatively express, the adjustment process is not controllable, and the optimization effect is extremely dependent on personal ability.

Overhead cranes are indispensable in the construction of bridges, docks, and other buildings. An overhead crane is a typical underactuated system. During the usage, because the sling cannot fully control the load, the swing of the load may collide with other objects.

At present, an overhead crane must be operated by experienced workers. However, due to the inaccuracy of manual operation, it is still impossible to avoid safety accidents. Therefore, the construction industry needs to design a stable and efficient anti-interference controller for the bridge crane system and realize automatic control of the bridge crane system. There are many studies in this field [11–14].

There are many examples of the combination of fuzzy control and PID [15–17], among which Sun et al. applied it to anti-swing control of an overhead crane, and achieved good control results [18]. This avoids the problem of the parameter optimization of PID, but also ushers in new problems. The parameter optimization of fuzzy control is more difficult than PID. This not only requires optimization personnel to have rich practical experience but also requires certain knowledge of fuzzy mathematics, which undoubtedly raises the application threshold of fuzzy control.

In 2016, the lion swarm optimization algorithm was proposed [19]. The lion swarm optimization algorithm is a nature-inspired algorithm based on the special lifestyle of lions and their cooperative behaviors [20]. Compared with some algorithms, the lion swarm optimization algorithm is a new meta-heuristic algorithm, which has the characteristics of simple operation, fast convergence speed, and a small amount of calculation. Subsequently, LSO has been continuously optimized or applied in various fields [21–24]. Although LSO has the characteristics of fast convergence speed and a small amount of calculation, it is still easy to fall into local optimization to a certain extent. Strengthening the algorithm is very important for the optimization performance of complex systems, and there are many papers worthy of reference in this regard [25–29].

PID does not perform well in the control of overhead cranes due to the difficulty in handling the control of nonlinear systems. After the introduction of fuzzy PID, although the x-performance is improved, the dependence of fuzzy PID on expert experience limits its control performance and generalization capability. To improve the performance of the fuzzy PID controller, we proposed an SLSO algorithm-based fuzzy PID controller for overhead crane systems. The contribution can be summarized as follows: (1) a stray operation is introduced to improve the LSO algorithm, which can enhance the population diversity and further reduce the risk of falling into local optimization, to improve the convergence accuracy of the algorithm. (2) Adaptive parameter adjustment based on the SLSO algorithm is designed to eliminate the dependency on experts. In addition, the effectiveness of adaptive fuzzy parameter configuration was verified via anti-swing experiments of the overhead crane.

This paper is divided into six sections. The Section 1 is a general introduction. Section 2 elaborates on the theoretical model and control formulation of an overhead crane. Section 3 introduces the LSO algorithm and our improvement, and conducts a comparison experiment with other algorithms on the test function. Section 4 describes how the SLSO algorithm is combined with fuzzy PID and applied to the control of overhead cranes. Section 5 gives the results and analysis of the simulation experiments. Section 6 provides a summary of this paper and an outlook for future work.

2. Introduction of the Overhead Crane System Model

As shown in Figure 1, the control system controls the horizontal movement of the trolley on the bridge, and the movement and swing of the load can only be indirectly controlled by controlling the movement of the trolley.

According to Euler Lagrange method, the dynamic model of an overhead crane is as follows:

$$(m_l + m_c)\ddot{x} + m_l l(\ddot{\theta}\cos\theta - \dot{\theta}^2 \sin\theta) = u \quad (1)$$

$$m_l \cos\theta + m_l l\ddot{\theta} + m_l g \sin\theta = 0 \quad (2)$$

where x and θ denote the displacement of the trolley and the swing angle of the load, m_l and m_c, respectively, represent the mass of the load and the trolley, l is the length of the sling, u is the control force exerted on the trolley, and g is the acceleration of gravity.

Setting $\dot{x} = x_1, \ddot{x} = x_2, \dot{\theta} = x_3, \ddot{\theta} = x_4$, the following differential equations can be obtained by transformation:

$$\begin{cases} \dot{x}_1 = x_2 \\ \dot{x}_2 = \frac{m_l g \cos x_3 \sin x_3 + m_l l \dot{x}_3^2 \sin x_3 + u}{m_l + m_c - m_l \cos^2 x_3} \\ \dot{x}_3 = x_4 \\ \dot{x}_4 = \frac{m_l l \dot{x}_3^2 \cos x_3 \sin x_3 + (m_l + m_c) g \sin x_3 + u \cos x_3}{l(m_l + m_c - m_l \cos^2 x_3)} \end{cases} \tag{3}$$

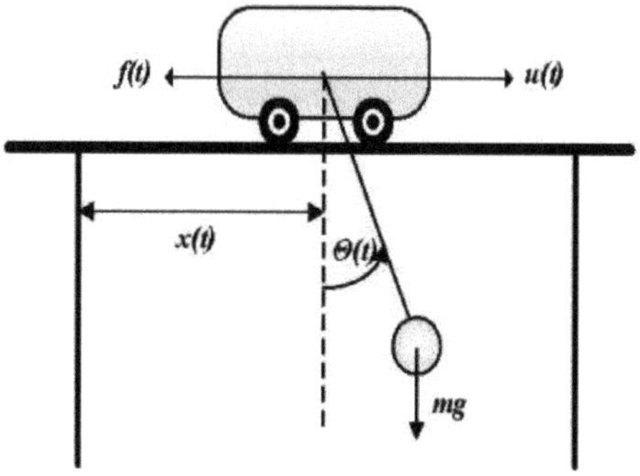

Figure 1. The structure diagram of an overhead crane.

3. The Stray Lion Swarm Optimization Algorithm

This section will employ many symbols, and their meanings are shown in Table 1.

Table 1. The nomenclature list.

Symbols/Abbreviations	Meaning
x_i^k	the i-th individual in the k-th generation population
p_i^k	the historical best position of the i-th individual from the 1st to the k-th generation
g^k	the best position of the k-th generation population
p_c^k	the individual randomly selected from the k-th generation lioness group
p_m^k	the individual randomly selected from the k-th generation lion group
q, γ	random value, $q \sim N(0,1), \gamma \sim U(0,1)$
α_f, α_c	disturbance factor
$f^k[i]$	the value of the stray individual at the i-th dimension in the k-th generation

3.1. Standard Lion Swarm Optimization Algorithm

In order to search for better solutions, the Lion King will conduct a range search based on the historical optimal solution. The formula for updating the position is as follows:

$$x_i^{k+1} = g^k(1 + \gamma \| p_i^k - g^k \|) \tag{4}$$

A lioness randomly selects another lioness to cooperate with, and the formula for updating the position is as follows:

$$x_i^{k+1} = \frac{p_i^k + p_c^k}{2}(1 + \alpha_f \gamma) \tag{5}$$

There are three updating strategies for young lions, namely follow the lioness, follow the lion king, or leave the location of the group to search for the updated location in reverse. The formula is as follows:

$$x_i^{k+1} = \begin{cases} \frac{g^k + p_i^k}{2}(1 + \alpha_c \gamma), 0 \le q \le \frac{1}{3} \\ \frac{p_m^k + p_i^k}{2}(1 + \alpha_c \gamma), \frac{1}{3} < q \le \frac{2}{3} \\ \frac{\overline{g}^k + p_i^k}{2}(1 + \alpha_c \gamma), \frac{2}{3} < q \le 1 \end{cases} \quad (6)$$

where x_i^k refers to the i-th individual in the k-th generation population; γ is a random number generated according to the normal distribution N(0, 1); p_i^k is the historical best position of the i-th individual from the 1st to the k-th generation; g^k is the best position of the k-th generation population; p_c^k is randomly selected from the k-th generation lioness group; p_m^k is randomly selected from the k-th generation lion group; q is the uniform random value generated according to the uniform distribution U [0, 1]; $\overline{g}^k = \overline{low} + \overline{up} - g^k$; $\overline{low}$ and $\overline{up}$ are the minimum value and maximum value of each dimension within the range of lion activity space; α_f and α_c are the disturbance factor. The calculation method is as follows:

$$\alpha_f = 0.1(\overline{up} - \overline{low}) \times \exp\left(-\frac{30t}{T}\right)^{10} \quad (7)$$

$$\alpha_c = 0.1(\overline{up} - \overline{low}) \times \left(\frac{T-t}{T}\right) \quad (8)$$

where t is the current number of iterations and T is the maximum number of iterations.

3.2. *Stray Lion Swarm Optimization Algorithm*

Although LSO has the advantages of high search efficiency and fast convergence speed, it still cannot solve the problem where swarm intelligence can easily fall into local optimization. In the LSO, most individuals will iterate with the lion king as the core, so it is difficult to escape when they fall into the local optimal solution.

In this paper, a stray individual is introduced as optimization interference, which can effectively avoid falling into local optimal solutions and obtain better optimization results on the premise of ensuring the population size.

3.2.1. Stray Operation in SLSO

The stray individual introduced in this paper deviates from the algorithm as far as possible in scope. At the same time, to avoid the individual falling into an extremely bad state, it is necessary to introduce a certain random quantity to ensure the effect. The formula for each generation of the stray individual is as follows:

$$f^k[i] = ((up[i] - low[i]) \times \gamma + 2low[i] + up[i] - g^k[i])/2 \quad (9)$$

where $f^k[i]$ is the value of the stray individual at the i-th dimension in the k-th generation. $up[i]/low[i]$ is the upper/lower limit at the i-th dimension. $g^k[i]$ is the value of the lion king at the i-th dimension in the k-th generation.

3.2.2. Iteration Strategy of the Lion Swarm in SLSO

To avoid the negative impact of dissociated individuals on the population, this paper sets a participation probability. When the probability is met, the cubs and females will be updated according to the new formula. In general, this probability is set to 0.1. Formula (11) is the new iterative strategy of the female lion, and Formula (12) is the new iterative strategy of the young lion.

$$x_i^{k+1} = \frac{p_i^k + f^k}{2} \quad (10)$$

$$x_i^{k+1} = \begin{cases} \frac{g^k+f^k}{2}, 0 \leq q \leq \frac{1}{3} \\ \frac{x_i^k+f^k}{2}, \frac{1}{3} < q \leq \frac{2}{3} \\ \frac{\overline{x}_i^k+f^k}{2}, \frac{2}{3} < q \leq 1 \end{cases} \tag{11}$$

where f^k is the stray individual in the k-th generation. $\overline{x}_i^{k+1} = \overline{low} + \overline{up} - x_i^k$.

3.2.3. Convergence Proof of SLSO

The SLSO algorithm is improved based on the LSO algorithm, and this paper first makes a proof of the convergence of the LSO algorithm. The proof refers to reference [30].

(1) Markov chain model of the LSO algorithm

The position update of each individual is obtained by Gaussian sampling, where the position update distribution of the lion king is $x_i(t+1) \sim N(g, |p_i, g|_2)$.

The position update distribution of the lioness is $x_i(t+1) \sim N(\frac{P_i+P_c}{2}, \alpha_f^2)$.

The position update distribution of the young lion is as follows:

$$x_i(t+1) \sim \begin{cases} N(\frac{g+p_i}{2}, \alpha_c^2), q < 1/3 \\ N(\frac{p_c+p_i}{2}, \alpha_c^2), 1/3 \leq q < 2/3 \\ N(\frac{\overline{g}+p_i}{2}, \alpha_c^2), 2/3 \leq q < 1 \end{cases}$$

In which q = rand [0,1).

To illustrate the Markov chain model of the LSO algorithm, the following definitions and mathematical descriptions are given.

Definition 1. *Lion swarm state and state space. The set of all states in the pride constitutes the state space of the pride, denoted as follows:*

$$|s = (x_1, x_2, \cdots, x_i, \cdots x_N)|x_i = (x_{i1}, x_{i2}, \cdots, x_{id}, \cdots, x_{iD}), 1 \leq i \leq N, 1 \leq d \leq D$$

Definition 2. *State transfer of individuals, For $\forall x_i \in s, x_j \in s$, the lion is transferred from state x_i to state x_j in one step, denoted as $T_s(x_i) = x_j$.*

Theorem 1. *Transfer probability of the LSO algorithm:*

$$P(T_s(x_i) = x_j) = \begin{cases} P_m(T_s(x_i) = x_j), lion-king \\ P_f(T_s(x_i) = x_j), lioness \\ P_c(T_s(x_i) = x_j), young-lion \end{cases}$$

Proof. The corresponding one-step transfer probabilities are different because of the different ways to update the positions of the three lions. The lions' positions can be viewed as a set of points in the hyperspace, and the position update process is a point set transformation in the hyperspace. For computational convenience, let the changed point set obey a uniform distribution U(−1,1) so that the transfer probability of the male lion can be obtained. The transfer probability of the lion king is shown as follows:

$$P_m(T_s(x_i) = x_j) = \begin{cases} \frac{1}{2(|g-p_i|)}, x_j \in [g-|g-p_i|, g+|g-p_i|] \\ 0, esle \end{cases} \tag{12}$$

The transfer probability of the lioness is shown as follows:

$$P_m(T_s(x_i) = x_j) = \begin{cases} \frac{1}{2\alpha_f(|p_c - p_i|)}, x_j \in [\frac{p_i+p_c}{2} - \alpha_f\left|p_c - p_i\right|, \frac{p_i+p_c}{2} + \alpha_f\left|p_c - p_i\right|] \\ 0, esle \end{cases} \quad (13)$$

The transfer probability of the young lion is shown as follows:

$$P_c(T_s(x_i) = x_j) = \begin{cases} \frac{1}{2\alpha_c(|g - p_i|)}, x_j \in [\frac{p_i+g}{2} - \alpha_c\left|g - p_i\right|, \frac{p_i+g}{2} + \alpha_c\left|g - p_i\right|] \\ \frac{1}{2\alpha_c(|p_m - p_i|)}, x_j \in [\frac{p_i+g}{2} - \alpha_c\left|p_m - p_i\right|, \frac{p_i+g}{2} + \alpha_c\left|p_m - p_i\right|] \\ \frac{1}{2(|\bar{g} - p_i|)}, x_j \in [\frac{p_i+\bar{g}}{2} - \left|\bar{g} - p_i\right|, \frac{p_i+\bar{g}}{2} + \left|\bar{g} - p_i\right|] \end{cases} \quad (14)$$

□

Definition 3. *State transfer probabilities of lion swarm. For* $\forall s_i \in S$ *and* $\forall s_j \in S$*, S is the set of lion pride states, and the probability of a lion pride transferring from* s_i *to* s_j *in one step, denoted as* $T_s(s_i) = s_j$*, is* $P(T_s(s_i) = s_j) = \prod_{i=1}^{N} P(T_s(s_i) = x_j^i)$.

where N is the number of individuals in the pride, and x_j^i is the state corresponding to individual x_i. The one-step transfer probability of the pride state in the LSO algorithm is the simultaneous transfer of the states of all lions in the pride.

(2) Convergence analysis of the LSO algorithm

According to the authors in [31], the definitions of Markov chain, finite Markov chain, and chi-square Markov chain are no longer given in this paper; see [31] for details.

Theorem 2. *The population sequence generated by the LSO algorithm* $\{s(t), t \geq 0\}$ *is a finite chi-square Markov chain, where t is the number of iterations.*

Proof.

1. According to Definition 3, in the population sequence $\{s(t), t \geq 0\}$, $\forall s(t) \in S$ and $\forall s(t+1) \in S$, the transfer probability $P(T_s(s(t)) = s(t+1))$ is determined by the transfer probability $P(T_s(x(t)) = x(t+1))$ of all lions.
2. According to Theorem 1, the state transfer probability of any lion in the pride is only related to the state at moment t and other randomly selected individuals in the population at moment t. Therefore, $P(T_s(x(t)) = x(t+1))$ is only related to the state at moment t, but not to t.
3. According to 1 and 2, it can be seen that the population sequence generated by the LSO algorithm has Markov property, and because the state space $\{s(t), t \geq 0\}$ of the lion population is finite, according to the definition of finite Markov chain, the population sequence $\{s(t), t \geq 0\}$ generated by the LSO algorithm constitutes a finite Markov chain.
4. According to Theorem 1, $P(T_s(s(t)) = s(t+1))$ is also only related to the state at moment t of s, but not to t. Therefore, the population sequence produced by the LSO algorithm $\{s(t), t \geq 0\}$ is a finite chi-square Markov chain.

□

According to the authors in [32], it is known that the stochastic algorithm converges globally, and the LSO algorithm is a stochastic search algorithm, so this paper will determine the convergence of the LSO algorithm according to the convergence criterion of the stochastic algorithm.

(3) Convergence proof of LSO algorithm

Definition 4. *The set of optimal states of the lion population is G. Let the optimal solution of the optimization problem* $< A, f >$ *be* g^**, and define the set of optimal states of the lion swarm as follows:* $G = \{s = (x_1, x_2, \cdots x_i, \cdots, x_N) | f(x_i = f(g^*), x_i \in S, s \in S)\}$*. If G = S, then every solution in the feasible space is not only a feasible solution, but also an optimal solution. At this point, the iteration is meaningless, the following discussion of* $G \subset S$*.*

Theorem 3. *The optimal set of lion states G of the lion group algorithm is a closed set on the state space S.*

Proof. $\forall s_i \in G, s_j \notin G, s_j \in S$, the transfer probability of $T_s(s_i) = s_j$ is $P(T_s(s_i) = s_j) = \prod_{i=1}^{N} P(T_s(s_i) = x_j^i)$.

At least one lion state in G is optimal, and let $g^* \sim x_{i_0 k}$ be the optimal state, i.e., at least $\exists x_{i_0 k} \in G$, $P(T_S(x_{i_0 k}) = x_{jk}) = 0$.

At this point, $P(T_s(s_i) = s_j) = 0$, so the set of optimal lion swarm states G is a closed set on the state space S. □

Theorem 4. *There is no nonempty closed set M in the state space S of the lion population such that* $M \cap G = \varphi$*.*

Proof. Suppose there exists a nonempty closed set M in the state space S, and $M \cap G = \varphi$, let $s_i = s(g^*, g^*, \cdots, g^*) \in G$, $s_j = (x_{j1,} x_{j2}, \cdots, x_{jd}) \in M$, and we have $f(x_j) > f(g^*)$.

According to the Chapman–Kolmogorov equation, we can obtain the result as follows:

$$P^l_{s_j, s_i} = \sum_{s_{r1} \in S} \cdots \sum_{s_{rl-1} \in S} P(T_S(s_j) = s_{r1}) P(T_S(s_{r1}) = s_{r2}) \cdots P(T_S(s_{rl-1}) = s_{ri}) \quad (15)$$

The algorithm will satisfy the conditions (12)–(14) in Theorem 1 after finitely many iterations of m. Therefore, the one-step transfer probability of each term of the expansion in Equation (15) satisfies $P(T_s(s_{r_{c+j}}) = s_{r_{c+j+1}}) > 0$ when the step size is large enough.

Therefore, $P^l_{s_j, s_i} > 0$, which yields that M is not a closed set. Thus, the Markov chain of lion group states is not approximately separable, and the z-state space S does not contain closed sets other than G. □

Theorem 5. *Assume that the Markov chain has a nonempty closed set E and there does not exist another nonempty closed set O, such that* $E \cap O = \varphi$*, when* $j \in E$*, there is* $\lim_{k \to \infty} P(x_k = j) = \pi_j$*. When* $j \notin E$*, there is* $\lim_{k \to \infty} P(x_k = j) = 0$*.*

Proof. For the proof process, please refer to [33]. □

Theorem 6. *When the iterations within the lion group tend to infinity, the lion group state must enter the optimal set of states G.*

Proof. From Theorems 3–5, Theorem 6 holds. □

Theorem 7. *The LSO algorithm can converge to the global optimum.*

Proof. The LSO algorithm is stochastic, so the LSO algorithm satisfies the condition of global convergence of stochastic algorithms H1 [33], and we know from Theorem 6 that the probability that the LSO algorithm does not search for the global optimal solution for an infinite number of consecutive times is 0. Then, we have $\prod_{k=0}^{\infty} (1 - u_k[B]) = 0$.

where $u_k[B]$ is the probability measure of the k-th iteration of the LSO algorithm to search for a solution to the set B, which satisfies the global convergence condition of the most taboo algorithm H2 [33]. For the LSO algorithm at each iteration, the update of the individual historical optimum takes the retention mechanism of the optimal individual, when the iteration tends to infinity. $\lim_{k\to\infty} P(x_k \in R_{\varepsilon,M}) = 1$. $\{x_k\}_{k=0}^{\infty}$ is the sequence generated by the iteration of the LSO algorithm, according to the global convergence of the stochastic search algorithm. It can be concluded that the LSO algorithm is globally convergent. □

Theorem 8. *The SLSO algorithm is globally convergent.*

Proof. The dissociation operator only sets up a stray individual outside the population and jointly searches for non-optimal solutions within the population at low probability (probability = 0.1). This means that the population sequence convergence of the SLSO algorithm with size n is equivalent to the population sequence convergence of the LSO algorithm with size 10n/9. The SLSO algorithm proposed in this article still meets the following requirements:

1. The population evolution direction in the SLSO algorithm is monotonic, i.e., $F(X(n+1)) \leq F(X(n))$
2. The population sequence of the SLSO algorithm $\{X(n), n \notin N^+\}$ is a homogeneous Markov chain
3. The Markov chain of the SLSO algorithm $\{X(n), n \notin N^+\}$ converges with probability 1 to a subset of the satisfactory population M $M_0 = M_0^* = \left\{Y = (y_1, \ldots, y_{N_p}) \middle| y_i \in M^*\right\}$ in the solution space, i.e., $\lim_{n\to\infty} P\left(X(n) \in M_0^* \middle| X(0) = X_0\right) = 1$.

Therefore, it can be inferred that the SLSO algorithm in this paper converges.

The relevant symbols are common symbols for the convergence proof of swarm intelligence algorithms, and there will be no expansion explanation here. □

3.3. Numerical Experiments

To verify the performance of the SLSO presented in this paper, six well-known benchmark functions are used. For comparison, the standard LSO, standard GA, and standard PSO algorithms are adopted during the test process.

For a fair comparison, the population = 50, dimension = 10, number of iterations = 100, and each algorithm runs 50 times for each test function. Some of these benchmark functions are lower than 10 dimensions. Since the goal of this paper is to optimize the parameter configuration of ADRC, all benchmark functions have been increased to 10 dimensions for calculation. We take the average of the results of 50 runs as the result to eliminate the uncertain factors in the search process. The final iteration result is compared with the number of iterations used to achieve the optimized iteration result, and the results are shown in Table 2. Information on these benchmark functions is shown in Table 2, too.

Table 2. Comparative results of benchmark functions.

Function Name	SLSO		Standard LSO		GA		PSO		Min Value
	Avg_Result	Std	Avg_Result	Std	Avg_Result	Std	Avg_Result	Std	
Schwefel	3.55×10^3	5.05×10^4	3.66×10^3	6.36×10	3.64×10^3	5.75	3.61×10^3	1.44×10	0
Styblinski Tang	-2.69×10	6.01×10^{-4}	-1.48×10	4.21	−8.58	2.92	-2.68×10	1.02×10^{-10}	−2.903534
Beale	1.01×10^{-5}	1.53×10^{-5}	2.23×10^{-5}	1.58×10^{-1}	2.69×10^{-3}	4.37×10^{-3}	5.69×10^{-5}	2.81×10^{-11}	0
Easom	-9.99×10^{-1}	3.15×10^{-5}	-9.84×10^{-1}	8.89×10^{-2}	-1.07×10^{-2}	7.57×10^{-2}	-2.00×10^{-2}	1.41×10^{-1}	−1
Eggholder	-9.42×10^2	2.66×10	-8.95×10^2	6.58×10	-8.66×10^2	1.12×10^2	-7.12×10^2	9.21×10	−959.6407
Holder_table	-1.85×10	4.74×10^{-1}	-1.82×10	1.13	-1.74×10	1.52	-1.83×10	4.15×10^{-1}	−19.2085

Please note that it is not that there are no more experiments, but that most of the test functions are not difficult to optimize for LSO. Therefore, we only select functions with poor LSO performance to show the improvement effect.

Figure 2 shows the convergence curves of four algorithms with benchmark functions, and shows the performance of the SLSO more intuitively and clearly. From Figures 2–7, we can find that in Function Eason, the LSO obtains a worse result than GA, but the SLSO obtains a better result than the other three methods.

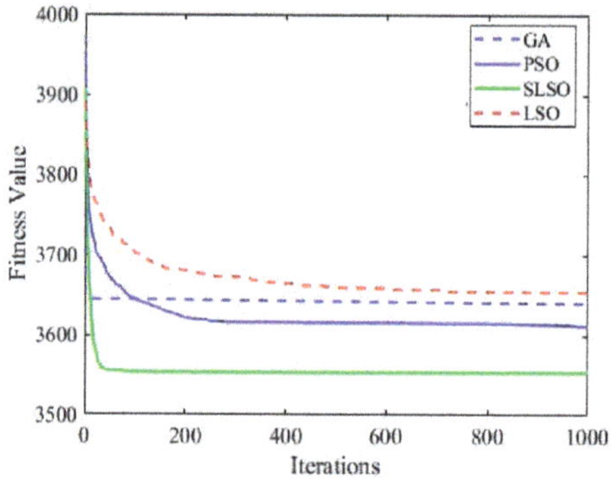

Figure 2. Schwefel.

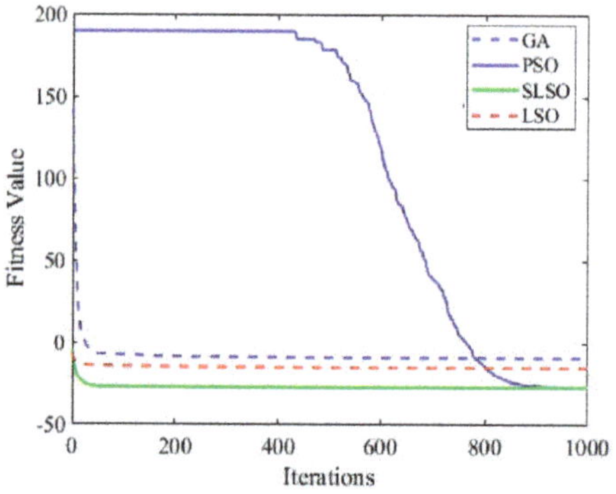

Figure 3. Styblinski-Tang.

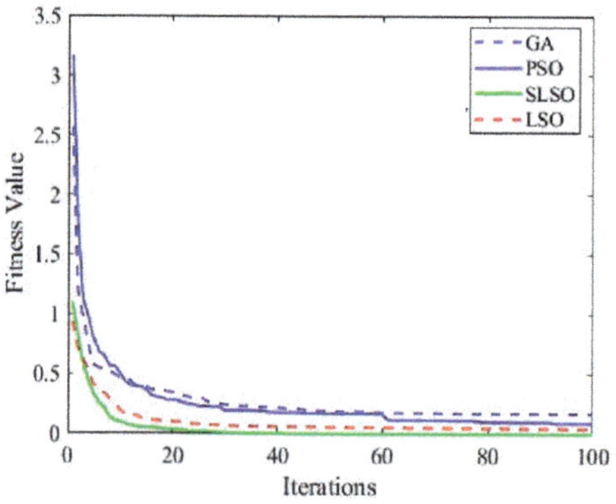

Figure 4. Beale.

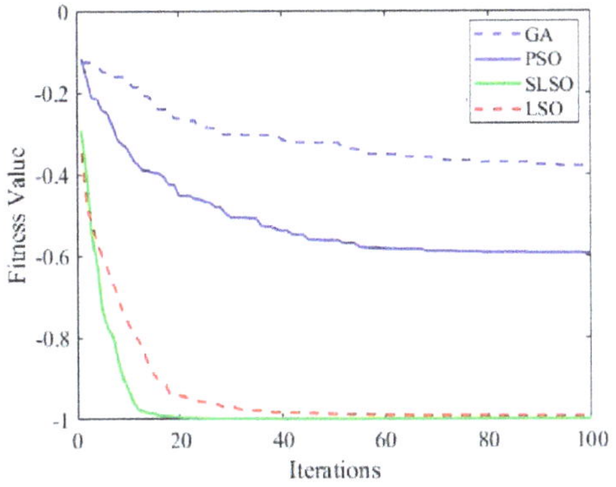

Figure 5. Eason.

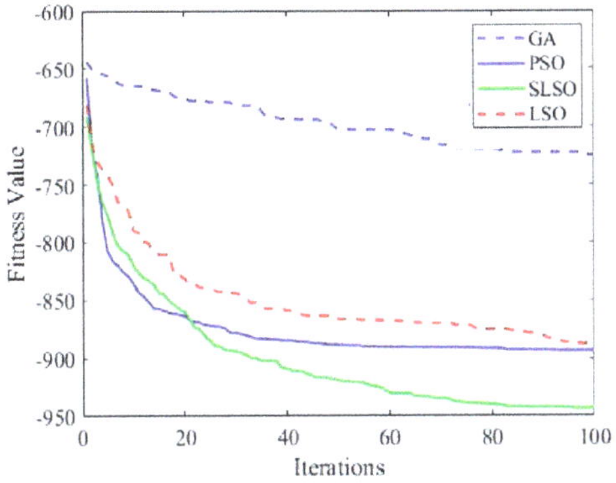

Figure 6. Eggholder.

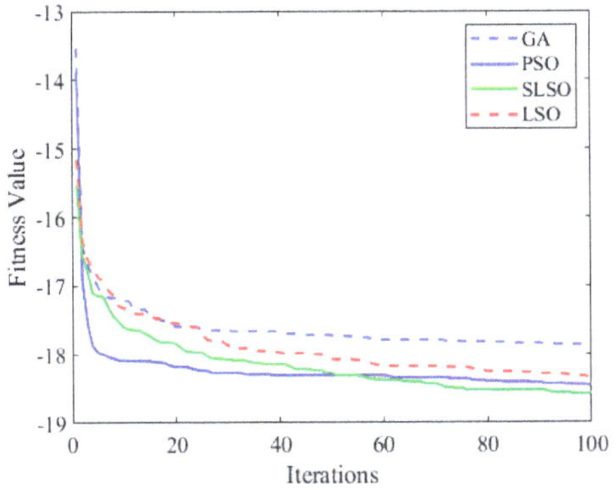

Figure 7. Holder-table.

In Function Styblinski_Tang, Beale, Eggholder, and Holder_table, the LSO works worse than PSO, but better than GA. However, after being improved, it works better than PSO.

In Function Schwefel, we can find that LSO works worst, and the SLSO works best.

We can find that in Table 2, the standard deviation of the results of the function based on the SLSO algorithm for finding the best is smaller than that of the LSO-based, which means that SLSO can find the optimal solution more stably, rather than relying on randomness.

In conclusion, SLSO can not only further improve the optimization results of LSO, but also perform well in the face of functions where LSO is not good at optimizing. Therefore, we can think that the improvement in this paper not only improves the accuracy of the algorithm, but also improves the applicability of the algorithm, and the improvement effect is ideal.

4. Designing of SLSO-Based Fuzzy PID

4.1. Fuzzy PID of Overhead Crane

The structure of fuzzy PID is shown in Figure 8. By calculating the system error $e(t)$ and error change rate $ec(t)$, and combining them with expert experience, the change rates of K_p, K_i and K_d can be deduced through fuzzy rules.

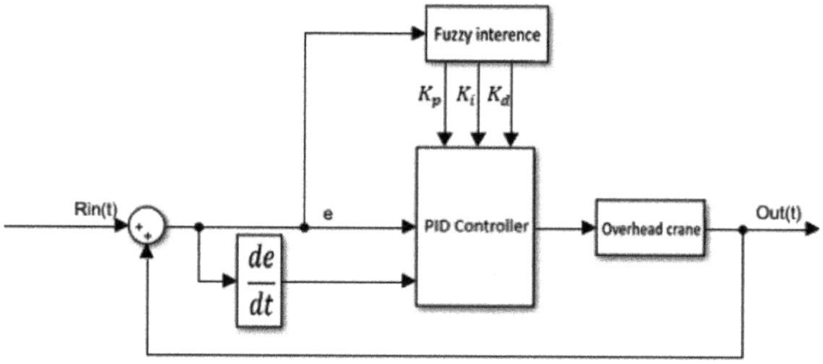

Figure 8. The diagram of fuzzy PID.

The value ranges of $e(t)$, $ec(t)$ and the fuzzy domains of K_p, K_i, and K_d are [−10, 10], [−10, 10], and [−6, 6], respectively. Generally speaking, fuzzy rules include {NB, NM, NS, NZ, ZO, PZ, PS, PM, PB}, and may contain different numbers of fuzzy rules according to different situations. The update method of K_p, K_i, and K_d is shown in Formula (16).

$$K_p = K'_p + \Delta K_p, K_i = K'_i + \Delta K_i, K_d = K'_d + \Delta K_d \tag{16}$$

The fuzzy rules of K_p, K_i, and K_d are shown in Tables 3–5.

Table 3. Fuzzy RULES of Kp.

e(t)() Δkp ec(t)	**NB**	**NM**	**NS**	**Z**	**PS**	**PM**	**PB**
NB	PB	PB	PB	PB	PM	PS	Z
NM	PM	PM	PS	PS	PS	Z	Z
NS	PM	PS	Z	Z	Z	NS	NM
Z	PS	PS	Z	Z	Z	NM	NB
PS	NM	NS	Z	Z	Z	PS	PM
PM	Z	Z	PS	PM	PM	PB	PB
PB	Z	PS	PB	PB	PB	PB	PB

Table 4. Fuzzy RULES of Ki.

e(t)() Δki ec(t)	NB	NM	NS	Z	PS	PM	PB
NB	PB	PB	PB	PB	PM	PS	Z
NM	PB	PB	PB	PM	PS	Z	Z
NS	PB	PM	PS	PS	Z	NS	NM
Z	NM	NS	Z	Z	Z	NS	NM
PS	NM	NS	Z	PS	PS	PM	PB
PM	Z	Z	PS	PM	PM	PB	PB
PB	Z	PS	PB	PB	PB	PB	PB

Table 5. Fuzzy RULES of Kd.

e(t)() Δkd ec(t)	NB	NM	NS	Z	PS	PM	PB
NB	PB	PM	PS	PB	NB	NB	NB
NM	PM	PS	Z	PS	NB	NS	Z
NS	PB	PM	Z	PS	PS	PM	PB
Z	PB	Z	PS	PS	PS	PM	PB
PS	PB	PM	PS	Z	PS	PM	PB
PM	Z	NS	NM	NS	Z	PS	PM
PB	NB	NB	NB	NS	PS	PM	PB

4.2. SLSO-Based Fuzzy PID

The fuzzy rule setting of fuzzy PID can be obtained quickly according to expert experience, but the value setting needs repeated debugging.

In this paper, SLSO is introduced to the interval design of fuzzy numbers.

For PID control, three rules require fuzzy control, each with two input parameters and one output parameter. Each parameter has seven situations and is controlled by seven arrays. Due to the symmetry of the parameters themselves, each parameter requires six numbers to control.

The interval of parameters is determined; therefore, the optimization of fuzzy rules can be transformed into the segmentation of the interval, and the number of segmented nodes is the number we need. Therefore, we patrol through seven numbers, with a range of values in the range (0–100). The ratio of the seven numbers is equivalent to the length ratio between the divided partitions within the interval. In this way, we can obtain the six numbers of the segmentation interval.

In summary, each interval needs 7 parameters, each fuzzy rule needs 3 intervals, this experiment has 3 fuzzy rules, so each individual needs to have 63 dimensions to optimize the parameters of the fuzzy rule. Then, the basic PID parameters also need to be optimized, which means that the length of each individual is 66.

The objective function is set as the product of the actual travel distance and the cumulative swing angle.

The steps are as follows:

Step 1 Establish the overhead crane control system.

Step 2 Set the individual length to 66, where the first and the second mean K_p and K_d, the left mean values of fuzzy rules. The population number to 30, and the number of iterations to 1000 to initialize the population.

Step 3 Analyze individual values, generate FIS files, read them into the base workspace, start Simulink, read the output of the simulation, and calculate individual fitness.

Step 4 Set $i = i + 1$, update individual values according to SLSO.

Step 5 If the obtained parameters meet the termination criteria or i = I_itermax, stop the algorithm and output the result. Otherwise, return to Step 3.

Step 6 Save the best individual as FIS files.

where the FIS file is a file type, which is used to save fuzzy rules and values.

5. Simulation Experiment

Generally speaking, in fuzzy PID, a set of fuzzy rules contains dozens of intervals.

To verify the validity of the proposed method, fuzzy PID control based on SLSO, fuzzy PID control without adjustment, adaptive PID based on the DE algorithm (hereinafter referred to as PID-DE), and the traditional PID control method are simulated under different conditions. The conditions are shown in Table 6.

Table 6. Specific experimental conditions.

Conditions	1	2	3	4	5	6
m_l/kg	7	7	7	12	12	12
x_d	6	12	20	6	12	20

The parameters of the overhead crane are set as M_T = 22 kg, l = 1 m, g = 9.81 m/s^2. The parameters of traditional PID are set to (60, 0, 60), and the parameters of PID-DE refer to the relevant paper [34]. In addition, the relevant parameters of other methods are listed below.

The values of fuzzy PID are based on SLSO and which, without adjustment, are shown in Tables 7–10. In addition, the parameters of fuzzy PID based on SLSO are optimized and set to (31.7, 0, 44.5). The parameters of fuzzy PID without optimization are set to (50, 0, 50) because the up limit is 100 and the low limit is 0 in the process of optimizing the PID parameters using the SLSO algorithm.

Table 7. Values of fuzzy PID rules Kp based on SLSO.

Name	NB	NM	NS	Z
e(t)	[−5.829,−4.457]	[−5.829,−4.457,−4.114,−2.742]	[−4.114,−2.742,−2.4,−1.658]	[−2.4,−1.658,1.658,2.4]
ec(t)	[−5.143,−4.286]	[−5.143,−4.286,−3.429,−2.571]	[−3.429,−2.571,−1.714,−0.857]	[−1.714,−0.857,0.857,1.714]
Δk_p	[−8.571,−7.143]	[−8.571,−7.143,−5.714,−4.286]	[−5.714,−4.286,−2.857,−1.429]	[−2.857,−1.429,1.429,2.857]
Name	PS	PM	PB	
e(t)	[1.658,2.4,2.743,4.114]	[2.742,4.114,4.457,5.829]	[4.457,5.829]	
ec(t)	[0.857,1.714,2.571,3.429]	[2.571,3.429,4.286,5.143]	[4.286,5.143]	
Δk_p,	[1.429,2.857,4.286,5.714]	[4.286,5.714,7.143,8.571]	[7.143,8.571]	

Table 8. Values of fuzzy PID rules Ki based on SLSO.

Name	NB	NM	NS	Z
e(t)	[−5.143,−4.286]	[−5.143,−4.286,−3.429,−2.571]	[−3.429,−2.571,−1.714,−0.857]	[−1.714,−0.857,0.857,1.714]
ec(t)	[−5.073,−4.226]	[−5.073,−4.226,−3.339,−2.54]	[−3.339,−2.54,−1.614,−0.757]	[−1.614,−0.757,0.757,1.614]
Δk_i	[−9.667,−7.0]	[−9.667,−7.0,−6.334,−3.666]	[−6.334,−3.666,−3.0,−0.333]	[−3.0,−0.333,0.333,3.0]
Name	PS	PM	PB	
e(t)	[0.857,1.714,2.571,3.429]	[2.571,3.429,4.286,5.143]	[4.286,5.143]	
ec(t)	[0.757,1.614,2.54,3.339]	[2.54,3.339,4.226,5.073]	[4.226,5.073]	
Δk_i,	[0.333,3.0,3.666,6.334]	[3.666,6.334,7.0,9.667]	[7.0,9.667]	

Table 9. Values of fuzzy PID rules Kd based on SLSO.

Name	NB	NM	NS	Z
e(t)	[−5.8,−4.2]	[−5.8,−4.2,−3.832,−2.232]	[−3.832,−2.232,−1.832,−0.232]	[−1.832,−0.232,0.232,1.832]
ec(t)	[−5.76,−3.84]	[−5.76,−3.84,−3.36,−1.44]	[−3.36,−1.44,−0.96,0.96]	[−1.44,−0.96,0.96,1.44]
Δk_d	[−9.667,−7.0]	[−9.667,−7.0,−6.334,−3.666]	[−6.334,−3.666,−3.0,−0.3333]	[−3.0,−0.333,0.333,3.0]
Name	PS	PM	PB	
e(t)	[0.2,1.832,2.232,3.832]	[2.232,3.832,4.2,5.8]	[4.2,5.8]	
ec(t)	[−0.96,0.96,1.44,3.36]	[1.44,3.36,3.84,5.76]	[3.84,5.76]	
Δk_d,	[0.333,3,3.0,3.666,6.334]	[3.666,6.334,7.0,9.667]	[7.0,9.667]	

Table 10. Values of fuzzy PID rules without optimization.

Name	NB	NM	NS	Z
e(t)	[−5.25,−4.5]	[−5.25,−4.5,−3.75,−3]	[−3.75,−3,−2.25,−1.5]	[−2.25,−0.75,0.75,2.25]
ec(t)	[−5.15,−4.3]	[−5.15,−4.3,−3.44,−2.58]	[−3.44,−2.58,−1.72,−0.86]	[−1.72,−0.86,0.86,1.72]
Δk_p	[−8.58,−7.15]	[−8.58,−7.15,−5.72,−4.28]	[−5.72,−4.29,−2.86,−1.43]	[−2.86,−1.43,1.43,2.86]
Name	PS	PM	PB	
e(t)	[1.5,2.25,3,3.75]	[3,3.75,4.5,5.25]	[4.5,5.25]	
ec(t)	[0.86,1.72,2.58,3.44]	[2.58,3.44,4.3,5.15]	[4.3,5.15]	
Δk_p,	[1.43,2.86,4.29,5.72]	[4.29,5.72,7.15,8.58]	[7.15,8.58]	

The clear values of fuzzy PID rules are shown in Tables 7–9. In addition, the values of fuzzy PID without optimization are shown in Table 10, where parameters are the average points of the interval. Because the values of fuzzy PID without optimization are set by average, we just show the values of Kp; the values of Ki and Kd are the same as Kp.

Introducing the parameters obtained by the SLSO algorithm, the comparative simulation experiment is implemented, and the simulation results are shown below.

From Figures 9–14, we can see that, compared to PID without optimized parameters, fuzzy PID without targeted configuration of fuzzy rules has advantages over ordinary PID in swing-angle control, but its anti-swing performance is worse than the PID-DE. In terms of distance control, its oscillation amplitude is larger than that of ordinary PID. This can prove that fuzzy control lacks usability without parameter optimization.

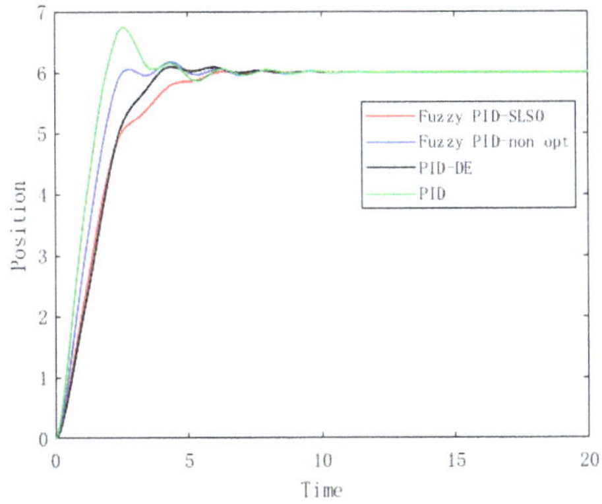

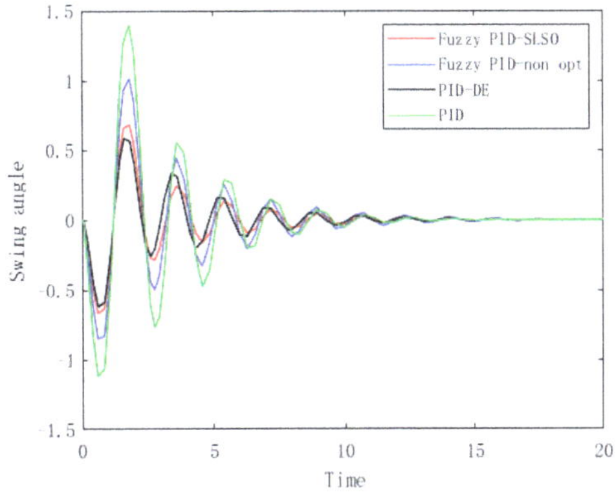

Figure 9. The results of condition 1.

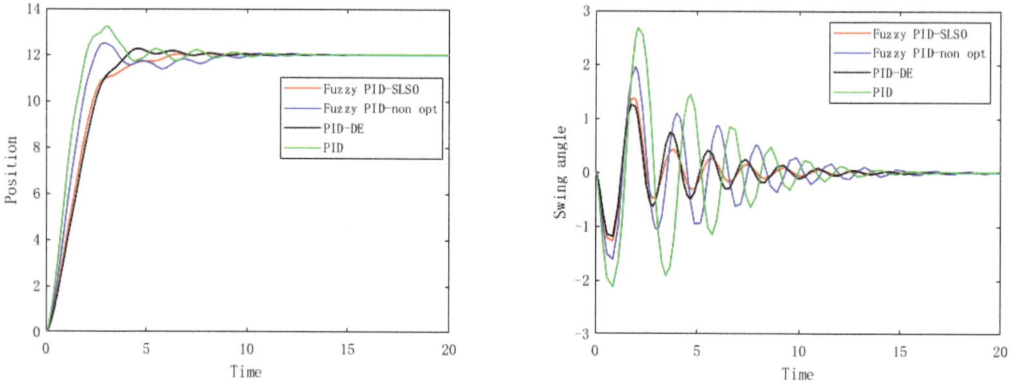

Figure 10. The results of condition 2.

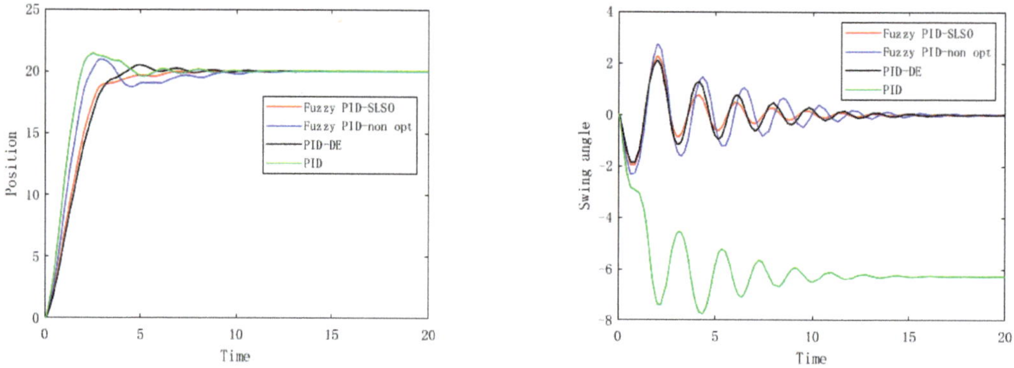

Figure 11. The results of condition 3.

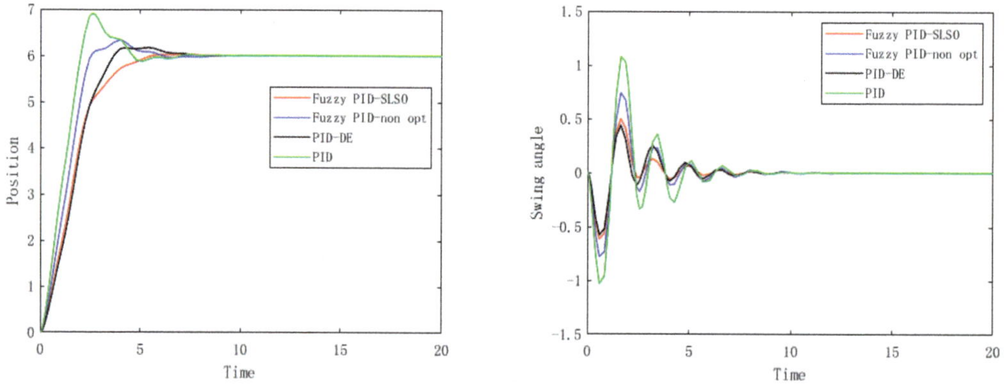

Figure 12. The results of condition 4.

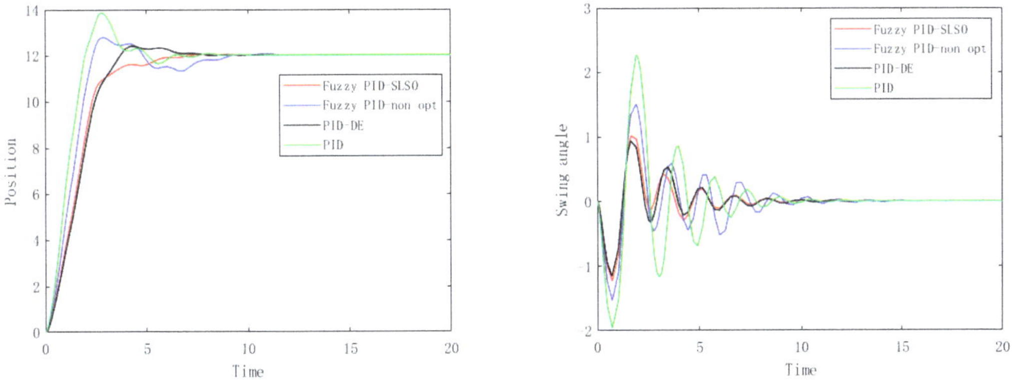

Figure 13. The results of condition 5.

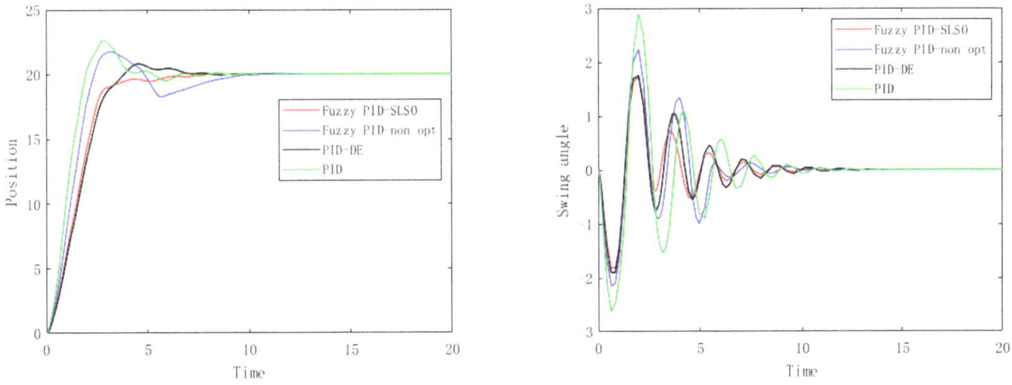

Figure 14. The results of condition 6.

However, in the fuzzy PID, where only basic rules are specified and specific parameters are optimized by the algorithm, its distance control completely exceeds the PID-DE. Most intuitively, the distance of the fuzzy PID almost does not exceed the maximum distance, which is very important in practical applications, meaning that collisions will not occur.

At the same time, the swing angle of the fuzzy PID is also well controlled, which means that the suspended object can reach the endpoint in a very stable attitude.

We conducted comparative experiments on both distance and counterweight dimensions, and the experimental results showed that in both cases, the fuzzy PID control based on SLSO parameter configuration can achieve a good anti-swing effect.

6. Conclusions

In this paper, an SLSO-based fuzzy PID controller is designed to suppress the swing of load during the operation of an overhead crane. To configure the parameter effectively, a modified lion swarm algorithm, which is based on the stray strategy, verifies the effectiveness of the improvement on several functions. By implementing simulation experiments and compared to other adaptive PID methods, the proposed method can dampen the load angle amplitude and residual swing. More precisely, in distance control, the percentages of invalid distance for the four methods of fuzzy PID-SLSO, fuzzy PID-non-optimization, PID-DE, and PID are 3.31%, 35.83%, 10.85%, and 37.03%, respectively. In addition, in the swing control, the swing angle of PID is set to 1, and the swing amplitudes of the four methods are 52.87%, 79.63%, 66.37%, and 100%, respectively. The numerical results show that the fuzzy PID-SLSO algorithm proposed in this paper has an excellent anti-swing control effect in an overhead crane system. This proposed method can also be applied to other under-actuated control systems, such as inverted pendulum systems, pendulum robots, and autonomous surface vehicles.

Author Contributions: Conceptualization, J.F. and Z.S.; methodology, Z.S.; software, D.X.; validation, J.L. and J.F.; formal analysis, Z.S.; investigation, J.F. and J.L.; resources, J.L.; data curation, D.X.; writing—original draft preparation, J.F.; writing—review and editing, Z.S.; visualization, D.X. All authors have read and agreed to the published version of the manuscript.

Funding: This research was funded by the National Natural Science Foundation of China (grant nos. 61972208, 62272239, and 62022044) and the National Natural Science Foundation of Jiangsu Province (grant nos. BK20201043).

Data Availability Statement: The data used to support the findings of this study are available from the corresponding author upon request. Some models and codes used during the study are proprietary or confidential in nature.

Conflicts of Interest: The authors declare no conflict of interest.

References

1. Kuo, K.Y.; Linb, J. Fuzzy logic control for flexible link robot arm by singular perturbation approach. *Appl. Soft Comput.* **2003**, *2*, 24–38. [CrossRef]
2. Lu, Y. Adaptive-Fuzzy Control Compensation Design for Direct Adaptive Fuzzy Control. *IEEE Trans. Fuzzy Syst.* **2018**, *26*, 3222–3231. [CrossRef]
3. Ma, M.; Wang, T.; Qiu, J.; Karimi, H.R. Adaptive Fuzzy Decentralized Tracking Control for Large-Scale Interconnected Nonlinear Networked Control Systems. *IEEE Trans. Fuzzy Syst.* **2021**, *29*, 3186–3191. [CrossRef]
4. Chiou, Y.C.; Lan, L.W. Genetic fuzzy logic controller: An iterative evolution algorithm with new encoding method. *Fuzzy Sets Syst.* **2005**, *152*, 617–635. [CrossRef]
5. Jiang, H.; An, T.; Ma, B.; Li, Y.; Dong, B. Value Iteration-based Decentralized Fuzzy Optimal Control of Modular Reconfigurable Robots via Adaptive Dynamic Programming. In Proceedings of the 2022 5th International Conference on Robotics, Control and Automation Engineering (RCAE), Changchun, China, 28–30 October 2022; pp. 186–190.
6. Sabir, M.M.; Ali, T. Optimal PID controller design through swarm intelligence algorithms for sun tracking system. *Appl. Math. Comput.* **2016**, *274*, 690–699. [CrossRef]
7. Ismayil, C.; Kumar, R.S.; Sindhu, T.K. Optimal fractional order PID controller for automatic generation control of two—Area power systems. *Int. Trans. Electr. Energy Syst.* **2016**, *25*, 3329–3348. [CrossRef]
8. Zamani, A.A.; Tavakoli, S.; Etedali, S. Fractional order PID control design for semi-active control of smart base-isolated structures: A multi-objective cuckoo search approach. *Isa Trans.* **2017**, *67*, 222. [CrossRef]
9. Garrido, J.; VãZquez, F.; Morilla, F. Multivariable PID control by decoupling. *Int. J. Syst. Sci.* **2016**, *47*, 1054–1072. [CrossRef]
10. Xie, M.; Li, X.; Wang, Y.; Liu, Y.; Sun, D. Saturated PID Control for the Optical Manipulation of Biological Cells. *IEEE Trans. Control Syst. Technol.* **2017**, *26*, 1909–1916. [CrossRef]
11. Gao, P.; Wang, Z.; Zhang, Y.; Li, M. Prediction System for Overhead Cranes Based on Digital Twin Technology. *Appl. Sci.* **2023**, *13*, 4696. [CrossRef]
12. Lisperguier, N.; López, Á.; Vielma, J.C. Seismic Performance Assessment of a Moment-Resisting Frame Steel Warehouse Provided with Overhead Crane. *Materials* **2023**, *16*, 2815. [CrossRef] [PubMed]
13. Ungureanu, M.; Medan, N.; Ungureanu, N.S.; Pop, N.; Nadolny, K. Tribological Aspects Concerning the Study of Overhead Crane Brakes. *Materials* **2022**, *15*, 6549. [CrossRef] [PubMed]
14. Mustapää, T.; Tunkkari, H.; Taponen, J.; Immonen, L.; Heeren, W.; Baer, O.; Brown, C.; Viitala, R. Secure Exchange of Digital Metrological Data in a Smart Overhead Crane. *Sensors* **2022**, *22*, 1548. [CrossRef] [PubMed]
15. Shi, Q.; Lam, H.K.; Xuan, C.; Chen, M. Adaptive Neuro-Fuzzy PID Controller based on Twin Delayed Deep Deterministic Policy Gradient Algorithm. *Neurocomputing* **2020**, *402*, 183–194. [CrossRef]
16. Wu, W.; Gong, G.; Chen, Y.; Zhou, X. Performance Analysis of Electro-Hydraulic Thrust System of TBM Based on Fuzzy PID Controller. *Energies* **2022**, *15*, 959. [CrossRef]
17. Sun, L.; Ma, J.; Yang, B. Fuzzy PID Design of Vehicle Attitude Control Systems. In Proceedings of the 2020 Chinese Control and Decision Conference (CCDC), Hefei, China, 22–24 August 2020; pp. 1826–1830.
18. Sun, Z.; Ling, Y.; Sun, Z.; Bi, Y.; Tan, S.; Ding, L. Designing and Application of Fuzzy PID Control for Overhead Crane Systems. In Proceedings of the 2019 2nd International Conference on Information Systems and Computer Aided Education (ICISCAE), Dalian, China, 28–30 September 2019; pp. 411–414.
19. Yazdani, M.; Jolai, F. Lion Optimization Algorithm (LOA): A Nature-Inspired Metaheuristic Algorithm. *J. Comput. Des. Eng.* **2016**, *3*, 24–36. [CrossRef]

20. Almezeini, N.; Hafez, A. Task Scheduling in Cloud Computing using Lion Optimization Algorithm. *Int. J. Adv. Comput. Sci. Appl.* **2017**, *8*, 77–83. [CrossRef]
21. Zhang, D.Q.; Jiang, M.Y. Parallel discrete lion swarm optimization algorithm for solving traveling salesman problem. *J. Syst. Eng. Electron.* **2020**, *31*, 751–760.
22. Qu, S.; Dou, Y.; Wang, Y.; Sun, R.; Liu, J.; Yang, W. Path Planning of Electric Power Inspection Robot Based on Improved Lion Swarm Algorithm. In Proceedings of the 2021 IEEE 5th Conference on Energy Internet and Energy System Integration (EI2), Taiyuan, China, 22–24 October 2021; pp. 3335–3339.
23. Ji, F.; Jiang, M. Tabu Annealing Lion Swarm Optimization Algorithm. In Proceedings of the 2021 International Conference on Computer Engineering and Artificial Intelligence (ICCEAI), Shanghai, China, 27–29 August 2021; pp. 422–426.
24. Wang, Z.; Wang, Q.; He, D.; Liu, Q.; Zhu, X.; Guo, J. An Improved Particle Swarm Optimization Algorithm Based on Fuzzy PID Control. In Proceedings of the 2017 4th International Conference on Information Science and Control Engineering (ICISCE), Changsha, China, 21–23 July 2017; pp. 835–839.
25. Fu, J.; Wang, N.; Zhao, J.H.; Zang, S.C. A Membrane Computing Optimization Algorithm with Multi-Subsystem for Parameter Estimation of Heavy Oil Thermal Cracking Model. *Int. J. Intell. Robot. Appl.* **2022**, *1*, 139–151. [CrossRef]
26. Wang, N.; Wang, D.X.; Xing, Y.Z.; Shao, L.M.; Afzal, S. Application of co-evolution RNA genetic algorithm for obtaining optimal parameters of SOFC model. Renew. *Energy* **2020**, *150*, 221–233.
27. Fu, J.; Zhao, J.H.; Yu, L.D. Self-adaptive membrane computing algorithm and its application in ABS system. *Con. Eng. China* **2019**, *26*, 155–161.
28. Zhu, X.H.; Wang, N. Cuckoo search algorithm with membrane communication mechanism for modeling overhead crane systems using RBF neural networks. *Appl. Soft. Comput.* **2017**, *56*, 458–471. [CrossRef]
29. Debbah, A.; Kherfane, H.; Kelaiaia, R. Gas Turbine Aerodynamics Improvement Via a Design of Intelligent Fractional Control. *Stroj. Časopis J. Mech. Eng.* **2021**, *71*, 85–100.
30. Liu, S.; Yang, Y.; Zhou, Y. A swarm intelligence algorithm-lion swarm optimization. *Pattern Recognit. Artif. Intell.* **2018**, *31*, 431–441.
31. Wu, D.H.; Kong, F.; Ji, Z.C. Convergence Analysis of Chicken Swarm Optimization Algorithm. *J. Cent. South Univ.* **2017**, *48*, 2105–2112. [CrossRef]
32. Solis, F.J.; West, J.B. Minimization by Random Search Techniques. *Math. Oper. Res.* **1981**, *6*, 19–30. [CrossRef]
33. Zhang, W.X.; Liang, Y. *Mathematical Foundation of Genetic Algorithm*; Xi'an Jiaotong University Press: Xi'an, China, 2003.
34. Sun, Z.; Wang, N.; Bi, Y.; Zhao, J. A DE based PID controller for two dimensional overhead crane. In Proceedings of the 2015 34th Chinese Control Conference (CCC), Hangzhou, China, 28–30 July 2015; pp. 2546–2550.

Disclaimer/Publisher's Note: The statements, opinions and data contained in all publications are solely those of the individual author(s) and contributor(s) and not of MDPI and/or the editor(s). MDPI and/or the editor(s) disclaim responsibility for any injury to people or property resulting from any ideas, methods, instructions or products referred to in the content.

mathematics

MDPI

Article

A More Efficient and Practical Modified Nyström Method

Wei Zhang [1,*], Zhe Sun [2,3], Jian Liu [4] and Suisheng Chen [1]

1 Fair Friend Institute of Intelligent Manufacturing, Hangzhou Vocational & Technical College, Hangzhou 310018, China
2 Post Industry Technology Research and Development Center of the State Posts Bureau (Internet of Things Technology), Nanjing University of Posts and Telecommunications, Nanjing 210023, China
3 Post Big Data Technology and Application Engineering Research Center of Jiangsu Province, Nanjing University of Posts and Telecommunications, Nanjing 210023, China
4 College of Information Engineering, Nanjing University of Finance and Economics, Nanjing 210023, China
* Correspondence: zhw618@hzvtc.edu.cn

Abstract: In this paper, we propose an efficient Nyström method with theoretical and empirical guarantees. In parallel computing environments and for sparse input kernel matrices, our algorithm can have computation efficiency comparable to the conventional Nyström method, theoretically. Additionally, we derive an important theoretical result with a compacter sketching matrix and faster speed, at the cost of some accuracy loss compared to the existing state-of-the-art results. Faster randomized SVD and more efficient adaptive sampling methods are also proposed, which have wide application in many machine-learning and data-mining tasks.

Keywords: kernel method; Nyström method; low-rank approximation; machine learning

MSC: 68T05

Citation: Zhang, W.; Sun, Z.; Liu, J.; Chen, S. A More Efficient and Practical Modified Nyström Method. *Mathematics* **2023**, *11*, 2433. https://doi.org/10.3390/math11112433

Academic Editor: Luca Gemignani

Received: 29 March 2023
Revised: 17 May 2023
Accepted: 22 May 2023
Published: 24 May 2023

Copyright: © 2023 by the authors. Licensee MDPI, Basel, Switzerland. This article is an open access article distributed under the terms and conditions of the Creative Commons Attribution (CC BY) license (https://creativecommons.org/licenses/by/4.0/).

1. Introduction

The Nyström method is a widely used technique to speed up kernel machines. Its efficiency in computation has attracted much attention in the past few years [1–8]. Given a kernel matrix $\mathbf{K} \in \mathbb{R}^{n\times n}$, the Nyström method tries to approximate the kernel by random sampling to save computation cost. At the cost of computational efficiency, it suffers from a relatively large matrix approximation error in real applications [9,10]. Given the target rank k and target precision parameter $0 < \epsilon \leq 1$, Wang and Zhang [4] gave a theoretical analysis that, with the Nyström method, it is impossible to obtain a $1+\epsilon$ bound relative to $\|\mathbf{K}-\mathbf{K}_k\|_F^2$ unless the number of sampled columns $c > \Omega(\sqrt{nk/\epsilon})$. Here, $\mathbf{K}_k$ denotes the best rank-k approximation to the kernel matrix $\mathbf{K}$. Several modified Nyström methods were proposed in recent years [3,4,11,12]. In the work of [11], a modified Nyström method just needs k/ϵ columns of the kernel matrix to obtain a $1+\epsilon$ bound relative to $\|\mathbf{K}-\mathbf{K}_k\|_F^2$. To the best of our knowledge, it is the fastest algorithm, costing $O(nk^2) + T_{Multiply}(\text{nnz}(\mathbf{K})\log n)$ to achieve a $1+\epsilon$ relative error of $\|\mathbf{K}-\mathbf{K}_k\|_F^2$, where $\text{nnz}(\mathbf{K})$ means the number of non-zero entries of $\mathbf{K}$. Although these modified Nyström methods are superior in approximation accuracy, it needs a much higher computational burden compared to the conventional Nyström method.

In this paper, we propose a much faster modified Nyström method which runs in $\mathcal{O}(n^{\frac{1}{2}}k^3/\epsilon^{\frac{5}{2}}) + T_{Multiply}(\mathcal{O}(\text{nnz}(\mathbf{K})\log n)$ time to achieve a $1+\epsilon$ bound relative to $\|\mathbf{K}-\mathbf{K}_k\|_F^2$. When $\epsilon > \sqrt{2}-1$, our algorithm will be accelerated to

$$\mathcal{O}(k^3) + T_{Multiply}(\mathcal{O}(\text{nnz}(\mathbf{K})\log n),$$

which is guaranteed by Lemma 3. Our algorithm is given in Algorithm 3. It needs $T_{Multiply}(\mathcal{O}(\text{nnz}(\mathbf{A})\log n))$ times to conduct matrix multiplication which is easily implemented in parallel. The computation complexity of matrix multiplication in Algorithm 3 is near linear in input sparsity. In addition, for the arithmetic operations which are hard to implement in parallel, such as SVD, pseudoinverse and QR decomposition, Algorithm 3 needs $\mathcal{O}(n^{\frac{1}{2}}k^3/\epsilon^{\frac{5}{2}})$ time which is sublinear in the input size n. At the cost of sacrificing a certain accuracy, $\mathcal{O}(k^3)$ can be reached with the same computational complexity as the conventional Nyström method, needing $\mathcal{O}(k^3)$ arithmetic operations when sampling $\mathcal{O}(k)$ columns. Our empirical studies further validate the efficiency of our algorithm.

In this paper, we improve several key algorithms which constitute a faster modified Nyström method. We summarized our contributions as follow.

- First and most importantly, we propose an efficient modified Nyström method with theoretical guarantees.
- Second, a more computationally efficient adaptive sampling method is proposed in Lemma 2. Adaptive sampling is a cornerstone of column selection, CUR decomposition and the Nyström method [4,5,11,13], and it is also very popular in other matrix problems [14].
- Finally, our proposed practical Nyström method can achieve computation efficiency in real applications, as shown by our experiments.

The rest of this paper is structured as follows. In Section 2, we provide the notations used in this study. Section 3, several key algorithms that constitute the modified Nyström are improved. Section 4 gives our modified Nyström method. We conduct empirical analysis and comparison in Section 5, and conclude our work in Section 6. All detailed proofs are omitted except computation complexity analysis.

2. Notation and Preliminaries [15]

Firstly, we introduce the notation and concepts that will be utilized here and hereafter. $\mathbf{I}_m$ is used to represent the identity $m \times m$ matrix. Sometimes we just use $\mathbf{I}$ for simplicity. We also use $\mathbf{0}$ to signify a zero vector or a zero matrix with an appropriate size. The number of non-zero entries in $\mathbf{A}$ is indicated by the notation $\mathrm{nnz}(\mathbf{A})$.

Let $k \leq \rho$ and $\rho = \mathrm{rank}(\mathbf{A}) \leq \min\{m, n\}$. The singular value decomposition (SVD) of $\mathbf{A}$ may be expressed as

$$\mathbf{A} = \sum_{i=1}^{\rho} \sigma_i \mathbf{u}_i \mathbf{v}_i^T = \begin{bmatrix} \mathbf{U}_k & \mathbf{U}_{k\perp} \end{bmatrix} \begin{bmatrix} \mathbf{\Sigma}_k & \mathbf{0} \\ \mathbf{0} & \mathbf{\Sigma}_{k\perp} \end{bmatrix} \begin{bmatrix} \mathbf{V}_k^T \\ \mathbf{V}_{k\perp}^T \end{bmatrix},$$

where the top k singular values are represented by $\mathbf{U}_k$ $(m \times k)$, $\mathbf{V}_k$ $(n \times k)$ and $\mathbf{\Sigma}_k$ $(k \times k)$. The best (or closest) rank-k approximation to $\mathbf{A}$ is denoted by $\mathbf{A}_k = \mathbf{U}_k \mathbf{\Sigma}_k \mathbf{V}_k^T$. The i-th greatest singular value of $\mathbf{A}$ is denoted by $\sigma_i = \sigma_i(\mathbf{A})$. The SVD is the same as the eigenvalue decomposition when $\mathbf{A}$ is symmetric positive semi-definite (SPSD), in which case we obtain $\mathbf{U}_\mathbf{A} = \mathbf{V}_\mathbf{A}$.

Furthermore, let $\mathbf{A}^\dagger$ be the Moore–Penrose inverse of $\mathbf{A}$, defined as $\mathbf{A}^\dagger = \mathbf{V}_\rho \mathbf{\Sigma}_\rho^{-1} \mathbf{U}_\rho^T$. When $\mathbf{A}$ is non-singular, the matrix inverse is the same as the Moore–Penrose inverse.

The matrix norms are defined in the manner as follows. Assume that the spectral norm is $\|\mathbf{A}\|_2 = \max_{\mathbf{x} \in \mathbb{R}^n, \|\mathbf{x}\|_2 = 1}, \|\mathbf{A}\mathbf{x}\|_2 = \sigma_1$ and the Frobenius norm is $\|\mathbf{A}\|_F = (\sum_{i,j} a_{ij}^2)^{1/2} = (\sum_i \sigma_i^2)^{1/2}$.

When given the matrices, $\mathbf{A} \in \mathbb{R}^{m \times n}$ and $\mathbf{C} \in \mathbb{R}^{m \times r}$ with $r > k$, we explicitly define matrix $\Pi_{C,k}^{\zeta}(\mathbf{A})$ as the closest representation of $\mathbf{A}$ in the column space of $\mathbf{C}$ with the rank of the most k. The function $\Pi_{C,k}^{\zeta}(\mathbf{A})$ minimizes the residual $\|\mathbf{A} - \hat{\mathbf{A}}\|_\zeta$ across all $\hat{\mathbf{A}}$ in the column space of C. Here, "ζ" denotes either the spectral norm or the Frobenius norm.

When given three matrices, $\mathbf{A} \in \mathbb{R}^{m \times n}$, $\mathbf{X} \in \mathbb{R}^{m \times p}$, and $\mathbf{Y} \in \mathbb{R}^{q \times n}$, the projection of $\mathbf{A}$ onto $\mathbf{X}$'s column space is represented as $\mathbf{X}\mathbf{X}^\dagger \mathbf{A} = \mathbf{U}_\mathbf{X} \mathbf{U}_\mathbf{X}^T \mathbf{A} \in \mathbb{R}^{m \times n}$, and the one onto $\mathbf{Y}$'s row space is denoted by $\mathbf{A}\mathbf{Y}^\dagger \mathbf{Y} = \mathbf{A}\mathbf{V}_\mathbf{Y} \mathbf{V}_\mathbf{Y}^T \in \mathbb{R}^{m \times n}$.

We now give the definition of leverage score sampling and subspace embedding, which are key tools to construct our Nyström algorithm.

Definition 1 (Leverage score sampling, [13,15]). *Allow* $\mathbf{V} \in \mathbb{R}^{n \times k}$ *to be column orthonormal with* $n > k$*, and* $\mathbf{v}_{i,*}$ *to signify the i-th row of* $\mathbf{V}$*. Allow* $\ell_i = \|\mathbf{v}_{i,*}\|_F^2/k$*. Given that the* ℓ_i *are leverage scores, let r be an integer in the range* $1 \le r \le n$*. Create the sampling matrix* $\mathbf{\Omega} \in \mathbb{R}^{n \times r}$ *and the rescaling matrix* $\mathbf{D} \in \mathbb{R}^{r \times r}$ *as follows. Pick an index i from the set of* $\{1, 2 \ldots, n\}$ *with probability* ℓ_i*, for each column* $j = 1, \ldots, r$ *of* $\mathbf{\Omega}$ *and* $\mathbf{D}$*, separately and with replacements. Let* $\mathbf{\Omega}_{ij} = 1$ *and* $\mathbf{D}_{jj} = 1/\sqrt{\ell_i r}$*. The number of operations required by this procedure is* $\mathcal{O}(nk + n)$*. This procedure is designated as*

$$[\mathbf{\Omega}, \mathbf{D}] = LeverageScoreSampling(\mathbf{V}, r).$$

Definition 2 ([16]). *Assuming* $\varepsilon > 0$ *and* $\delta > 0$*, define a distribution on* $\ell \times n$ *matrix* $\mathbf{S}$ *as* Π*, where* ℓ *depends on n, d,* ε *and* δ*. Assume that, any given* $n \times d$ *matrix* $\mathbf{A}$*, with a probability of at least* $1 - \delta$*, a matrix* $\mathbf{S}$ *chosen from distribution* Π *is a* $(1 + \varepsilon)$ ℓ_2*-subspace embedding for* $\mathbf{A}$*. Meaning that, for every* $\mathbf{x} \in \mathbb{R}^d$*,* $\|\mathbf{SAx}\|_2^2 = (1 \pm \varepsilon)\|\mathbf{Ax}\|_2^2$ *with probability* $1 - \delta$*. After that, we designate* Π *as an* (ε, δ)*-oblivious* ℓ_2*-subspace embedding.*

The sparse subspace embedding matrix $\mathbf{S}$ and subsampled Hadamard matrix $\mathbf{H}$ are the two most popular subspace embedding matrices. For an $n \times k$ matrix $\mathbf{A}$ with k dimension subspace, we can construct a sparse subspace embedding matrix $\mathbf{S}$ for $\mathbf{A}$ with $m = O(k^2/\epsilon^2)$ rows, and the subsampled Hadamard matrix $\mathbf{H}$ with $m = O(k \log k)/\epsilon^2$ [16]. Combining $\mathbf{S}$ with $\mathbf{H}$ still has the property.

Let's discussed the computational costs about the matrix operations mentioned above. Matrix multiplication is an intrinsic parallel operation; hence, it can be easily implemented in parallel efficiently just as many mathematical software do. However, SVD decomposition and QR decomposition are much harder to implement in parallel. Hence, we denote the time complexity of such a matrix multiplication by $T_{Multiply}$. For a general $m \times n$ matrix $\mathbf{A}$ with $m \ge n$, computing the full SVD requires $\mathcal{O}(mn^2)$ flops, whereas computing the truncated SVD of rank k ($k < n$), requires $\mathcal{O}(mnk)$ flops. Additionally, computing $\mathbf{A}^\dagger$ requires $\mathcal{O}(mn^2)$ flops, too. Given a $m \times m$ Hadamard–Walsh transform matrix $\mathbf{H}$, $T_{Multiply}(\tilde{\mathcal{O}}(mn))$ is the cost for the Hadamard–Walsh transform $\mathbf{HA}$, which is substantially quicker than $T_{Multiply}(\mathcal{O}(m^2 n))$ for the typical matrix multiplication. A sparse subspace embedding matrix $\mathbf{S}$ for an $n \times d$ matrix $\mathbf{A}$, $\mathbf{SA}$ needs $T_{Multiply}(\mathcal{O}(\mathrm{nnz}(\mathbf{A})))$ arithmetic operations.

3. Main Lemmas and Theorems

In this part, we will outline our principal theorems and lemmas, which are the key tools to implement Algorithm 3. In addition, these lemmas and theorems are of independent interest and have wide application.

First, we give a fast randomized SVD method which is depicted in Algorithm 1 which is the fastest randomized SVD method as far as we know.

Lemma 1. *Given matrix* $\mathbf{A} \in \mathbb{R}^{m \times n}$*, target rank k and error parameter* $0 < \epsilon \le 1$*,* $\mathbf{Z}$ *is returned from Algorithm 1; then, the following formula holds with high probability.*

$$\|\mathbf{A} - \mathbf{Z}\mathbf{Z}^T\mathbf{A}\|_F^2 \le (1 + \epsilon)\|\mathbf{A} - \mathbf{A}_k\|_F^2$$

In addition, $\mathbf{Z}$ *can be computed in* $\tilde{\mathcal{O}}(k^3/\epsilon^5) + T_{Multiply}(\mathcal{O}(\mathrm{nnz}(\mathbf{A})) + \tilde{\mathcal{O}}(mk^2/\epsilon^4 + k^3/\epsilon^3))$*. We denote Algorithm 1 as*

$$\mathbf{Z} = SparseSVD(\mathbf{A}, k, \epsilon).$$

Algorithm 1 Sparse SVD

1: **Input:** a real matrix $\mathbf{A} \in \mathbb{R}^{m\times n}$, error parameter ϵ and target rank k;
2: Compute $\mathbf{AR}^T$, where $\mathbf{R} = \mathbf{\Pi S} \in \mathbb{R}^{c\times n}$ with $c = \mathcal{O}(k\log k/\epsilon)$. $\mathbf{S} \in \mathbb{R}^{s\times n}$ is a sparse subspace embedding matrix with $s = \mathcal{O}(k^2 + k/\epsilon)$ and $\mathbf{\Pi} \in \mathbb{R}^{c\times s}$ is a subsampled randomized Hadamard matrix with $c = \mathcal{O}(k\log k/\epsilon)$;
3: Compute an orthonormal basis $\mathbf{U}$ for $\mathbf{AR}^T$ by $\mathbf{U} = \mathbf{AR}^T\mathbf{C}^{-1}$, where $\mathbf{C}$ is the Cholesky decomposition of $\mathbf{RA}^T\mathbf{AR}^T$;
4: Compute $\mathbf{\Gamma} = \mathbf{U}^T\mathbf{AW}^T \in \mathbb{R}^{c\times d}$, where $\mathbf{W} = \mathbf{HF} \in \mathbb{R}^{d\times n}$ with $d = \mathcal{O}(k\log k/\epsilon^3)$. $\mathbf{F} \in \mathbb{R}^{n\times t}$ is a sparse subspace embedding matrix with $t = \mathcal{O}(k^2\log^2 k/\epsilon^3)$ and $\mathbf{H} \in \mathbb{R}^{d\times t}$ is a subsampled randomized Hadamard matrix with $d = \mathcal{O}(k\log k/\epsilon^3)$.
5: Compute the SVD of $\mathbf{\Gamma}$ and let $\mathbf{\Delta} \in \mathbb{R}^{c\times k}$ contain the top k left singular vectors of $\mathbf{\Gamma}$;
6: **Output:** $\mathbf{Z} = \mathbf{U\Delta}$.

Proof. Lemma A2 shows that $\|\mathbf{A} - \mathbf{UU}^T\mathbf{A}\|_F^2 \leq (1+\epsilon)\|\mathbf{A} - \mathbf{A}_k\|_F^2$, where $\mathbf{U}$ is of $\mathcal{O}(k\log k/\epsilon)$ columns. Applying Lemma A1 and replacing $\mathbf{V}$ with $\mathbf{U}$, we can obtain the result that

$$\|\mathbf{A} - \mathbf{ZZ}^T\mathbf{A}\|_F^2 \leq (1+\epsilon)\|\mathbf{A} - \mathbf{A}_k\|_F^2$$

For computation time analysis, computing $\mathbf{AR}^T$ takes $T_{Multiply}(\mathcal{O}(\text{nnz}(\mathbf{A}) + \tilde{\mathcal{O}}(mk(k+\epsilon^{-1})))$, and then $T_{Multiply}(\tilde{\mathcal{O}}(mk^2/\epsilon^2 + k^3/\epsilon^3))$ computes the $\mathbf{U} = \mathbf{AC}^{-1}$, where $\mathbf{C}$ is the Cholesky decomposition of $\mathbf{A}^T\mathbf{A}$. Computing $\mathbf{U}^T(\mathbf{AW}^T)$ requires $T_{Multiply}(\mathcal{O}(\text{nnz}(\mathbf{A}) + mk^2/\epsilon^3 + mk^2/\epsilon^4))$. Computing the SVD of $\mathbf{\Gamma}$ requires $\tilde{\mathcal{O}}(k^3/\epsilon^5)$. In addition, computing $\mathbf{Z} = \mathbf{U\Delta}$ requires $T_{Multiply}(\tilde{\mathcal{O}}(mk^2/\epsilon^3))$. Hence, Algorithm 1 takes

$$\tilde{\mathcal{O}}(k^3/\epsilon^5) + T_{Multiply}(\mathcal{O}(\text{nnz}(\mathbf{A})) + \tilde{\mathcal{O}}(mk^2/\epsilon^4 + k^3/\epsilon^3))$$

computation complexity. □

A faster adaptive sampling, Algorithm 2, is developed based on the work of [13]. Boutsidis and Woodruff [13] tried to compute norms of each column of $\mathbf{GB} = \mathbf{GA} - \mathbf{GC}_1\mathbf{C}_1^{\dagger}\mathbf{A}$. To further reduce the computation cost, we introduce the sketched $\mathbf{G\hat{B}} = \mathbf{GA} - \mathbf{GC}_1(\mathbf{RC}_1)^{\dagger}(\mathbf{RA})$ to approximate $\mathbf{GB}$. By such sketching, $\mathbf{GC}_1(\mathbf{RC}_1)^{\dagger}(\mathbf{RA})$ can be computed more efficiently than $\mathbf{GC}_1\mathbf{C}_1^{\dagger}\mathbf{A}$.

Algorithm 2 Adaptive Sampling

1: **Input:** a real matrix $\mathbf{A} \in \mathbb{R}^{m\times n}$, $\mathbf{C}_1 \in \mathbb{R}^{m\times c_1}$ and the number of selected columns c;
2: Construct $\mathbf{\hat{B}} = \mathbf{A} - \mathbf{C}_1(\mathbf{RC}_1)^{\dagger}(\mathbf{RA})$, where $\mathbf{R} = \mathbf{\Pi S} \in \mathbb{R}^{t\times m}$ with $t = 2c_1\log c_1$. $\mathbf{S} \in \mathbb{R}^{s\times m}$ is a sparse subspace embedding matrix with $s = c_1^2 + 2c_1$ and $\mathbf{\Pi} \in \mathbb{R}^{t\times s}$ is a subsampled randomized Hadamard matrix;
3: Construct $\mathbf{\tilde{B}} = \mathbf{G\hat{B}}$ where $\mathbf{G} \in \mathbb{R}^{g\times m}$ is a normalized Gaussian matrix with $g = 9\log n$;
4: Compute sampling probabilities $p_j = \|\mathbf{\tilde{b}}_j\|_F^2/\|\mathbf{\tilde{B}}\|_F^2$ for $j = 1,\ldots,n$, where $\mathbf{\tilde{b}}_j$ is the j−th column of $\mathbf{\tilde{B}}$;
5: **Output:** Obtain $\mathbf{C}_2$ by selecting c columns from $\mathbf{A}$ in c i.i.d. trials; in each trial the index j is chosen with probability p_j.

Lemma 2. *Given $\mathbf{A} \in \mathbb{R}^{m\times n}$, $\mathbf{C}_1 \in \mathbb{R}^{m\times c_1}$ and $\mathbf{V} \in \mathbb{R}^{r\times n}$ such that rank$(\mathbf{V}) =$ rank$(\mathbf{AV}^{\dagger}\mathbf{V}) = \rho$, with $\rho \leq c \leq n$, let $\mathbf{C}_2 \in \mathbb{R}^{m\times c_2}$ be returned from Algorithm 2 containing c_2 columns of $\mathbf{A}$. Then, the matrix $\mathbf{C} = [\mathbf{C}_1, \mathbf{C}_2] \in \mathbb{R}^{m\times(c_1+c_2)}$ satisfies that for any integer $k > 0$, and with a high probability which is at least* 0.9.

$$\|\mathbf{A} - \mathbf{CC}^{\dagger}\mathbf{AV}^{\dagger}\mathbf{V}\|_F^2 \leq \|\mathbf{A} - \mathbf{AV}^{\dagger}\mathbf{V}\|_F^2 + \frac{40\rho}{c_2}\|\mathbf{A} - \mathbf{C}_1\mathbf{C}_1^{\dagger}\mathbf{A}\|_F^2.$$

In addition, this randomized algorithm can be implemented in

$$\tilde{\mathcal{O}}(c_1^3) + T_{Multiply}(\mathcal{O}(\text{nnz}(\mathbf{A})\log n + \tilde{\mathcal{O}}(nc_1^2 + nc_1\log n + c_1^3))$$

computation time. We denote this randomized algorithm as

$$\mathbf{C}_2 = AdaptiveSampling(\mathbf{A}, \mathbf{V}, \mathbf{C}_1, c_2).$$

Proof. Let $\mathbf{B} = \mathbf{A} - \mathbf{C}_1\mathbf{C}_1^{\dagger}\mathbf{A}$ be the residual matrix and $\mathbf{b}_i$ is the i-th column of $\mathbf{B}$. By Theorem A4, with high probability, it holds that

$$\|\mathbf{B}\|_F^2 \le \|\hat{\mathbf{B}}\|_F^2 \le (1+2\epsilon)\|\mathbf{B}\|_F^2 = 2\|\mathbf{B}\|_F^2\|\mathbf{b}_i\|_F^2 \le \|\hat{\mathbf{b}}_i\|_F^2 \le (1+2\epsilon)\|\mathbf{b}_i\|_F^2 = 2\|\mathbf{b}_i\|_F^2$$

Besides, by the JL property of $\mathbf{G}$, we have $\frac{1}{3}\|\hat{\mathbf{b}}_i\|_F \le \|\tilde{\mathbf{b}}_i\|_F \le \frac{4}{3}\|\hat{\mathbf{b}}_i\|_F$. Hence, after utilizing the below distribution for sampling,

$$p_i = \frac{\|\tilde{\mathbf{b}}_i\|_F}{\|\tilde{\mathbf{B}}\|_F} \ge \frac{2}{3}\cdot\frac{3}{4}\cdot\frac{\|\hat{\mathbf{b}}_i\|_F^2}{\|\hat{\mathbf{B}}\|_F^2} \ge \frac{1}{2}\cdot\frac{1}{2}\cdot\frac{\|\mathbf{b}_i\|_F^2}{\|\mathbf{B}\|_F^2} = \frac{1}{4}\frac{\|\mathbf{b}_i\|_F^2}{\|\mathbf{B}\|_F^2}$$

Using Lemma A3, we obtain

$$\mathbb{E}\left[\|\mathbf{A} - \mathbf{C}\mathbf{C}^{\dagger}\mathbf{A}\mathbf{V}^{\dagger}\mathbf{V}\|_F^2\right] \le \|\mathbf{A} - \mathbf{A}\mathbf{V}^{\dagger}\mathbf{V}\|_F^2 + \frac{4k}{c_2}\|\mathbf{A} - \mathbf{C}_1\mathbf{C}_1^{\dagger}\mathbf{A}\|_F^2.$$

Using the Markov inequality, we have that

$$\|\mathbf{A} - \mathbf{C}\mathbf{C}^{\dagger}\mathbf{A}\mathbf{V}^{\dagger}\mathbf{V}\|_F^2 \le \|\mathbf{A} - \mathbf{A}\mathbf{V}^{\dagger}\mathbf{V}\|_F^2 + \frac{40\rho}{c_2}\|\mathbf{A} - \mathbf{C}_1\mathbf{C}_1^{\dagger}\mathbf{A}\|_F^2.$$

holds with a probability of at least 0.9.

As to the running time, it needs $T_{Multiply}(\mathcal{O}(\mathrm{nnz}(\mathbf{A})) + \tilde{\mathcal{O}}(nc_1^2))$ arithmetic operations to compute $\mathbf{RA}$. To compute $\mathbf{RC}_1$ costs $T_{Multiply}(\mathcal{O}(\mathrm{nnz}(\mathbf{C}_1)) + \tilde{\mathcal{O}}(c_1^3))$. To compute $(\mathbf{RC}_1)^{\dagger}$, it requires $\tilde{\mathcal{O}}(c_1^3)$. In addition, computing $\mathbf{GA}$ and $\mathbf{GC}_1$ require $T_{Multiply}$ $(\mathcal{O}(\mathrm{nnz}(\mathbf{A})\log n))$ and $T_{Multiply}(mc_1\log n)$, respectively. In addition, to compute $(\mathbf{GC}_1)(\mathbf{RC}_1)^{\dagger}(\mathbf{RA})$ needs

$$T_{Multiply}(\tilde{\mathcal{O}}(nc_1\log n + c_2\log n))$$

computation. In addition, $\mathbf{GA} - \mathbf{GC}_1(\mathbf{RC}_1)^{\dagger}\mathbf{RA}$ needs another $T_{Multiply}(\mathcal{O}(n\log n))$ arithmetic operations. Thus, all these need $\tilde{\mathcal{O}}(c_1^3) + T_{Multiply}(\mathcal{O}(\mathrm{nnz}(\mathbf{A})\log n + \tilde{\mathcal{O}}$ $(nc_1^2 + nc_1\log n + c_1^3))$ □

Lemma 3 ([15,17]). *Given the matrices* $\mathbf{C} \in \mathbb{R}^{m\times c}$, $\mathbf{A} \in \mathbb{R}^{m\times n}$ *and* $\mathbf{R} \in \mathbb{R}^{n\times r}$, *let's suppose that* $\mathbf{S}$ *is the leverage-score sketching matrix of* $\mathbf{C}$ *with* $s = \mathcal{O}(c/\epsilon + c\log c)$ *rows, and* $\mathbf{T}$ *is the leverage-score sketching matrix of* $\mathbf{R}$ *with* $t = \mathcal{O}(r/\epsilon + r\log r)$ *columns. Let*

$$\mathbf{U}^{\star} = \mathbf{C}^{\dagger}\mathbf{A}\mathbf{R}^{\dagger} = \underset{\mathbf{U}}{\operatorname{argmin}}\|\mathbf{A} - \mathbf{CUR}\|_F$$

and

$$\hat{\mathbf{U}} = (\mathbf{SC})^{\dagger}\mathbf{SAT}(\mathbf{RT})^{\dagger},$$

then we can obtain

$$\|\mathbf{A} - \mathbf{C}\hat{\mathbf{U}}\mathbf{R}\|_F \le (1+\epsilon)\|\mathbf{A} - \mathbf{C}\mathbf{U}^{\star}\mathbf{R}\|_F.$$

The number of sampled rows in Lemma 3 is independent on the input dimension of $\mathbf{A}$ and is linear to c. By losing some accuracy, a much faster algorithm can be implemented.

4. Practical Modified Nyström Method

We use our new lemmas and theorems developed in Section 3 to implement an efficient modified Nyström algorithm.

4.1. Description of The Algorithm

A $n \times n$ real symmetric matrix $\mathbf{A}$, an error parameter $0 < \epsilon < 1$ and a target rank k are the inputs of Algorithm 3. Meanwhile, a matrix $\mathbf{C} \in \mathbb{R}^{n \times c}$ with $c = \mathcal{O}(k/\epsilon + k \log k)$ columns of $\mathbf{A}$, and a matrix $\mathbf{U} \in \mathbb{R}^{c \times c}$ are the results. There are primarily 3 steps in Algorithm 3: (i) using the definition of the leverage score sampling, it samples a number of columns of $\mathbf{A}$ to obtain $\mathbf{C}_1$; and using the adaptive sampling method to obtain $\mathbf{C}_2$ and $\mathbf{R}_2$; (ii) it calculates the leverage scores of $\mathbf{C}$ using the method in [18]; and (iii) it constructs the intersection matrix $\mathbf{U}$. Note that $\widehat{\mathbf{U}}$ in Lemma 3 is asymmetric even when $\mathbf{A}$ is positive semi-definite. Thus, when applied to kernel approximation, we need to construct a positive semi-definite $\mathbf{U}$ shown in Algorithm 3.

Algorithm 3 Practical Nyström

1: **Input:** a real symmetric matrix $\mathbf{A} \in \mathbb{R}^{n \times n}$, error parameter ϵ and target rank k;
2: $\mathbf{Z} = SparseSVD(\mathbf{A}, k, 1)$;
3: $[\mathbf{\Omega}, \Gamma] = LeverageScoreSampling(\mathbf{Z}, \mathcal{O}(k \log k))$ and construct $\mathbf{C}_1 = \mathbf{A}\mathbf{\Omega}$;
4: $\mathbf{C}_2 = AdaptiveSampling(\mathbf{A}, \mathbf{V}_k^T, \mathbf{C}_1, \mathcal{O}(k/\epsilon))$ and $\mathbf{C}_3 = AdaptiveSampling(\mathbf{A}, \mathbf{V}_k^T, \mathbf{C}_1, \mathcal{O}(k/\epsilon))$, constructing $\mathbf{C} = [\mathbf{C}_1, \mathbf{C}_2, \mathbf{C}_3] \in \mathbb{R}^{n \times \mathcal{O}(k/\epsilon + k \log k)}$;
5: Compute approximate leverage scores of $\mathbf{C}$ using the method of [18] and construct the leverage sketch matrix $\mathbf{S}_1$ and $\mathbf{S}_2$ of $n \times s$ size, where $s = \mathcal{O}(\frac{c}{\epsilon} + c \log c)$;
6: Compute $\widehat{\mathbf{U}} = (\mathbf{S}_1\mathbf{C})^{\dagger}\mathbf{S}_1\mathbf{A}\mathbf{S}_2^T(\mathbf{C}^T\mathbf{S}_2^T)^{\dagger}$.
7: Compute $\mathbf{U} = \mathbf{\Pi}_{\mathbb{H}_+^s}(\widehat{\mathbf{U}})$ by conducting eigenvalue decomposition of $\widetilde{\mathbf{U}} = \frac{\widehat{\mathbf{U}} + \widehat{\mathbf{U}}^T}{2}$ and setting the negative eigenvalues of $\widehat{\mathbf{U}}$ to zero.
8: **Output:** $\mathbf{C}$ and $\mathbf{U}$.

4.2. Analysis of Running-Time

Here, we provide a detailed analysis of the Algorithm 3's arithmetic operations.

1. The computation complexity of Algorithm 3 is $\tilde{\mathcal{O}}(k^3) + T_{Multiply}(\mathcal{O}(\text{nnz}(\mathbf{A}) \log n + \tilde{\mathcal{O}}(nk^2 + nk \log n + k^3))$ to find $\mathcal{O}(k/\epsilon + k \log k)$ columns of $\mathbf{A}$ to construct $\mathbf{C}$.
   (a) To obtain $\mathbf{Z} \in \mathbb{R}^{n \times k}$ from Theorem 1, it takes $\tilde{\mathcal{O}}(k^3) + T_{Multiply}(\mathcal{O}(\text{nnz}(\mathbf{A})) + \tilde{\mathcal{O}}(nk^2 + k^3))$.
   (b) To obtain the leverage score and sample $\mathbf{C}_1$ and $\mathbf{C}_2$, it takes $T_{Multiply}(\mathcal{O}(nk))$.
   (c) To construct $\mathbf{C}_3$ and $\mathbf{R}_2$ Lemma 2, it takes $\tilde{\mathcal{O}}(k^3) + T_{Multiply}(\mathcal{O}(\text{nnz}(\mathbf{A}) \log n + \tilde{\mathcal{O}}(nk^2 + nk \log n + k^3))$.
2. The computation complexity of Algorithm 3 is $\mathcal{O}(k^3/\epsilon^4) + T_{Multiply}(\mathcal{O}(nk^2/\epsilon^2) + \tilde{\mathcal{O}}(nk^2 + k^3/\epsilon^5))$ to construct $\mathbf{U}$ when $s = \mathcal{O}(\frac{c}{\epsilon} + c \log c)$ is the row dimension of $\mathbf{S}_1$ and $\mathbf{S}_2$ in Algorithm 3.
   (a) To obtain the leverage scores of $\mathbf{C}$, it takes $\mathcal{O}(k^3/\epsilon^3) + T_{multiply}(\mathcal{O}(n(k/\epsilon)^2 + \tilde{\mathcal{O}}(nk^2))$.
   (b) To compute $(\mathbf{S}_1^T\mathbf{C})^{\dagger}$ and $(\mathbf{S}_2^T\mathbf{C})^{\dagger}$, it takes $\tilde{\mathcal{O}}(k^3/\epsilon^4)$.
   (c) To compute matrix multiplication, it takes $T_{Multiply}(\mathcal{O}(k^3/\epsilon^5))$.
   (d) To compute the eigenvalue decomposition of $\mathbf{U}$, it takes $\tilde{\mathcal{O}}(k^3/\epsilon^3)$.

   The algorithm's overall asymptotic arithmetic operation is

$$T_{Multiply}(\mathcal{O}(\text{nnz}(\mathbf{A}) \log n + nk^2/\epsilon^2 + k^3/\epsilon^5) + \tilde{\mathcal{O}}(nk^2 + nk \log n + k^3/\epsilon^4)).$$

4.3. Error Bound

Primary approximate result regarding Algorithm 3 is shown as the following theorem.

Theorem 1. *Given an error parameter ϵ and a target rank k, run Algorithm 3, then the below inequality holds with high probability.*

$$\|\mathbf{A} - \mathbf{C}\mathbf{U}\mathbf{C}^T\|_F \leq (1+\epsilon)\|\mathbf{A} - \mathbf{A}_k\|_F$$

5. Empirical Study

In this section, we compare our Practical Nyström algorithm with the uniform+adaptive algorithm [11,19], near-optimal+adaptive algorithm [4,11,13] and conventional Nyström using just uniform sampling. All algorithms were implemented in Matlab and experiments were conducted on a workstation with 32 cores of 2G Hz and 24G RAM.

On each data set, we give the approximation error and the execution duration of each algorithm. The approximation error is

$$\text{Approximation Error} = \frac{\|\mathbf{A} - \mathbf{C}\mathbf{U}\mathbf{C}^T\|_F}{\|\mathbf{A}\|_F},$$

where $\mathbf{U}$ is the intersection matrix defined in the Nyström method.

On three data sets we test all three algorithms, and the results are listed in Table 1. We create a RBF kernel matrix $\mathbf{A}$ for each dataset, with $a_{ij} = \exp(\frac{\|\mathbf{x}_i - \mathbf{x}_j\|_2^2}{2\gamma^2})$, where $\mathbf{x}_i$ and $\mathbf{x}_j$ are data instances and γ is the parameter of the RBF kernel function. By the definition of $\mathbf{A}$, the size n of $\mathbf{A}$ is the number of instances of the dataset. Thus, the kernel matrices in our experiments are of large sizes. We set γ different values for each data set as Table 1 describes. However, the effectiveness of our algorithm does not depend on the setting of γ. For each data set, we set $k = 10, 30$ and 50. We sampled $c = ak$ columns from $\mathbf{A}$ and a ranges from 8 to 26. We ran each algorithm 5 times and report the average value of approximation error and running time. All results are illustrated in Figures 1–3.

Table 1. A summary of the datasets for kernel approximation.

Data Set	a9a	USPS	PenDigits
#instance	32,561	11,305	7494
γ	5	4	30
Source	UCI	TKH96a	UCI

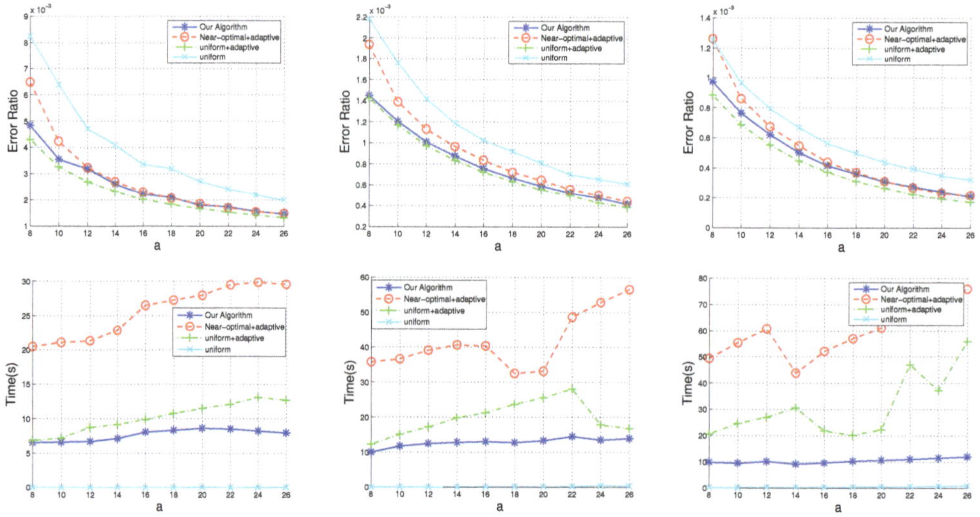

Figure 1. Results of the Nyström algorithms on the a9a dataset. In the first column, we set $k = 10$, and $c = ak$ with $a = 8, \ldots, 26$. In the middle column, we set $k = 30$, and $c = ak$. In the right column, we set $k = 50$, and $c = ak$.

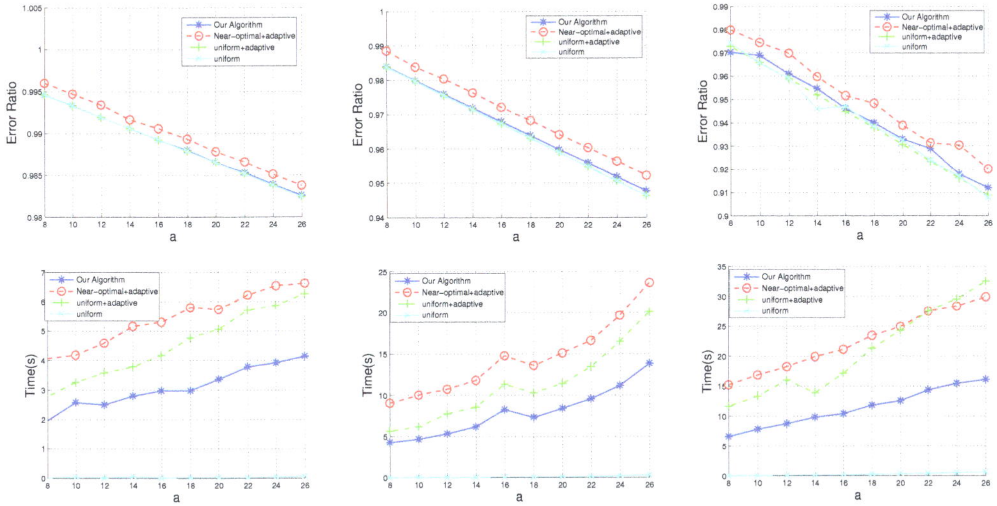

Figure 2. Results of the Nyström algorithms on the pendigit dataset. In the first column, we set $k = 10$, and $c = ak$ with $a = 8, \ldots, 26$. In the middle column, we set $k = 30$, and $c = ak$. In the right column, we set $k = 50$, and $c = ak$.

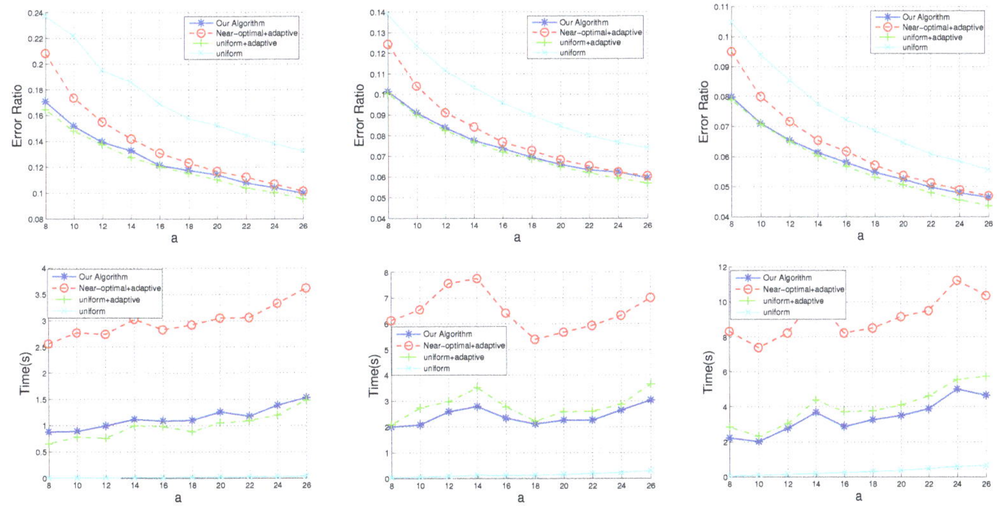

Figure 3. Results of the Nyström algorithms on the usps dataset. In the first column, we set $k = 10$, and $c = ak$ with $a = 8, \ldots, 26$. In the middle column, we set $k = 30$, and $c = ak$. In the right column, we set $k = 50$, and $c = ak$.

As evidenced by the empirical results in the figures, it is clear that our approach is efficient. In terms of accuracy, Our approach is comparable to the state-of-the-art algorithm—the near-optimal+adaptive algorithm [4,11,13]. As to the running time, our approach is much faster than near-optimal+adaptive algorithm and uniform+adaptive algorithm. Our algorithm's running time grows slower than the near-optimal+adaptive algorithm and uniform+adaptive algorithm. The advantage of the running time of our algorithm grows as the dimension of kernel matrix **A** increases. Calculating kernel matrix **A** of size 7494×7494 from the 'PenDigits' data set, our alogrithm is twice as fast as the near-optimal+adaptive algorithm. As to the 'a9a' data set of 32,561 instances, our algorithm is four times faster than near-optimal+adaptive. In addition, as c increases, the running-time superiority of our algorithm also increases. Our algorithm also has similar a advantage over the uniform+adaptive algorithm. Hence, our algorithm is suitable to scale to kernel matrices of high dimensions.

6. Conclusions

In this paper, we proposed an efficient modified Nyström method with a theoretical and emperical guarantee. In a high-level parallel-computation environment with sparse input matrices, our Nyström method can achieve comparable computation efficiency compared to the conventional Nyström method, theoretically. Hence, our Nyström method is suitable for machine-learning algorithms in big-data setting. In addition, we give a sketching generalized matrix approximation which extends the previous work [12]. Faster randomized SVD and more efficient adaptive sampling methods are proposed which have wide application in lots of areas. In addition, our modified Nyström algorithm can be easily extended to CUR decomposition which leads to more efficient CUR decomposition.

Author Contributions: Conceptualization, W.Z. and Z.S.; methodology, W.Z. and J.L.; software, W.Z.; validation, S.C. and Z.S.; writing—original draft preparation, W.Z.; writing—review and editing, S.C.; visualization, J.L.; funding acquisition, Z.S. and S.C. All authors have read and agreed to the published version of the manuscript.

Funding: This research was funded by Hangzhou Key Scientific Research Program of China (No. 20212013B06), Zhejiang Provincial Natural Science Foundation of China (No. LGG21E050005), National Natural Science Foundation of China (No. 61972208, No. 62272239 and No. 62022044) and National Natural Science Foundation of Jiangsu Province (No. BK20201043).

Acknowledgments: The authors would like to thank Professor An Yang, from Hangzhou Vocational & Technical College, for her valuable suggestions and guidance throughout this research.

Conflicts of Interest: The authors declare no conflict of interest.

Appendix A. Key Theorems Used in Our Proofs

Theorem A1 ([15,20])**.** *There is $t = \Theta(\epsilon^{-2})$ for matrix $\mathbf{A} \in \mathbb{R}^{m\times n}$ and orthonormal $\mathbf{U} \in \mathbb{R}^{m\times k}$, thus, for a $t \times m$ leverage-score sketching matrix $\mathbf{S}$ for orthonormal $\mathbf{U}$,*

$$\mathbb{P}\Big[||\mathbf{A}^T\mathbf{S}^T\mathbf{S}\mathbf{U} - \mathbf{A}^T\mathbf{U}||_F^2 < \epsilon^2||\mathbf{A}||_F^2||\mathbf{U}||_F^2\Big] \geq 1-\delta,$$

for any fixed $\delta > 0$.

Theorem A2 ([15,20])**.** *There is $t = \mathcal{O}(k\epsilon^{-2}\log k)$, for any rank k matrix $\mathbf{A} \in \mathbb{R}^{m\times n}$ with row leverage scores, such that leverage-score sketching matrix $\mathbf{S} \in \mathbb{R}^{t\times m}$ is an ϵ-embedding matrix for matrix $\mathbf{A}$, i.e.,*

$$||\mathbf{S}\mathbf{A}\mathbf{x}||_2^2 = (1\pm\epsilon)||\mathbf{A}\mathbf{x}||_2^2$$

Theorem A3 ([15,20])**.** *Given that A is a matrix with m rows and C is a matrix with m rows as well as rank k. $\mathbf{S}$ is a subspace embedding for $\mathbf{C}$ with error parameter $\epsilon_0 \leq 1/\sqrt{2}$, and it is also the $t \times m$ leverage-score sketching matrix of $\mathbf{C}$ with $\mathcal{O}(k/\epsilon)$ rows. Then if $\hat{\mathbf{Y}}$ and $\mathbf{Y}^\star$ are respectively the solutions to*

$$min_{\mathbf{Y}} = ||\mathbf{S}(\mathbf{C}\mathbf{Y} - \mathbf{A})||_F^2$$

and

$$min_{\mathbf{Y}} = ||\mathbf{S}(\mathbf{C}\mathbf{Y} - \mathbf{A})||_F^2$$

then, the below two formulas hold with a probability of at least 0.99.

$$||\mathbf{C}\hat{\mathbf{Y}} - \mathbf{A}||_F \leq (1+\epsilon)||\mathbf{C}\mathbf{Y}^\star - \mathbf{A}||_F$$

$$||\mathbf{C}(\hat{\mathbf{Y}}-\mathbf{Y}^{*})||_F \leq 2\sqrt{\epsilon}||\mathbf{C}\mathbf{Y}^{*}-\mathbf{A}||_F$$

Theorem A4 ([15,20]). *Given that A is a matrix with m rows, and C is a matrix with m rows as well as rank k, where* $\mathbf{R} = \mathbf{\Pi S} \in \mathbb{R}^{t\times n}$ *with* $t = 2k\log k/\epsilon$. $\mathbf{\Pi} \in \mathbb{R}^{t\times s}$ *is a subsampled randomized Hadamard matrix and* $\mathbf{S} \in \mathbb{R}^{s\times m}$ *is a sparse subspace embedding matrix with* $s = k^2 + 2k/\epsilon$. *Then if* $\hat{\mathbf{Y}}$ *and* $\mathbf{Y}^{\star}$ *are respectively the solutions to*

$$min_{\mathbf{Y}} = ||\mathbf{R}(\mathbf{C}\mathbf{Y}-\mathbf{A})||_F^2$$

and

$$min_{\mathbf{Y}} = ||\mathbf{R}(\mathbf{C}\mathbf{Y}-\mathbf{A})||_F^2$$

then, the below two formulas hold with a probability of at least 0.99.

$$||\mathbf{C}\hat{\mathbf{Y}}-\mathbf{A}||_F \leq (1+\epsilon)||\mathbf{C}\mathbf{Y}^{*}-\mathbf{A}||_F$$

$$||\mathbf{C}(\hat{\mathbf{Y}}-\mathbf{Y}^{*})||_F \leq 2\sqrt{\epsilon}||\mathbf{C}\mathbf{Y}^{*}-\mathbf{A}||_F$$

Lemma A1 ([13,15]). *Let* $\mathbf{A} \in \mathbb{R}^{m\times n}$ *and* $\mathbf{V} \in \mathbb{R}^{m\times c}$. *Assume that given a particular rank parameter k and an accuracy parameter* $0 < \epsilon < 1$,

$$||\mathbf{A} - \Pi^F_{V,k}(\mathbf{A})||_F^2 \leq ||\mathbf{A}-\mathbf{A}_k||_F^2.$$

$\mathbf{V}$ *is a QR-decomposition, and let* $\mathbf{V} = \mathbf{QY}$ *where* $\mathbf{Q} \in \mathbb{R}^{m\times c}$ *and* $\mathbf{Y} \in \mathbb{R}^{c\times c}$. *Let* $\Gamma = \mathbf{Q}^T\mathbf{A}\mathbf{W}^T \in \mathbb{R}^{c\times \ell}$, *where* $\mathbf{W}^T \in \mathbb{R}^{n\times \ell}$ *is a sparse subspace embedding matrix, and* $\ell = \mathcal{O}(c^2/\epsilon^2)$. *Let* $\mathbf{\Delta} \in \mathbb{R}^{c\times k}$ *contain the top k left singular vectors of* Γ. *Then, it holds that*

$$||\mathbf{A} - \mathbf{Q}\boldsymbol{\Delta}\boldsymbol{\Delta}^{\mathbf{T}}\mathbf{Q}^{\mathbf{T}}\mathbf{A}||_{\mathbf{F}}^{\mathbf{2}} \leq (\mathbf{1}+\boldsymbol{\epsilon})||\mathbf{A}-\mathbf{A}_{\mathbf{k}}||_{\mathbf{F}}^{\mathbf{2}}.$$

with high probability.

Lemma A2 ([16]). *Given matrix* $\mathbf{R}^{m\times n}$, $\mathbf{R} = \mathbf{\Pi S} \in \mathbb{R}^{c\times n}$ *is a subspace embedding matrix with* $c = \mathcal{O}(k\log k/\epsilon)$. $\mathbf{S} \in \mathbb{R}^{n\times s}$ *is a sparse subspace embedding matrix with* $s = \mathcal{O}(k^2 + k/\epsilon)$ *and* $\mathbf{\Pi} \in \mathbb{R}^{c\times s}$ *is a subsampled randomized Hadamard matrix with* $c = \mathcal{O}(k\log k/\epsilon)$. *Let* $\mathbf{U}$ *be the orthonormal basis of* $\mathbf{A}\mathbf{R}^T$. *Then, it holds that*

$$||\mathbf{A} - \mathbf{U}\mathbf{U}^T\mathbf{A}||_F^2 \leq (1+\epsilon)||\mathbf{A}-\mathbf{A}_k||_F^2.$$

with high probability.

Lemma A3 ([4,15,16]). *Given* $\mathbf{A} \in \mathbb{R}^{m\times n}$, $\mathbf{R}_1 \in \mathbb{R}^{r_1\times n}$ *and* $\mathbf{C} \in \mathbb{R}^{m\times c}$ *such that*

$$rank(\mathbf{C}) = rank(\mathbf{C}\mathbf{C}^{\dagger}\mathbf{A}) = \rho,$$

with $\rho \leq c \leq n$, *given* $\mathbf{R}_1 \in \mathbb{R}^{r_1\times n}$ *and the defined residual*

$$\mathbf{B} = \mathbf{A} - \mathbf{A}\mathbf{R}_1^{\dagger}\mathbf{R}_1 \in \mathbb{R}^{m\times n}.$$

For $i = 1,\ldots,m$, *let* p_i *be the probability distribution such that for each i:*

$$p_i \geq \alpha||\mathbf{b}_i||_F^2/||\mathbf{B}||_F^2,$$

where $\mathbf{b}_i$ *is the i-th row of* $\mathbf{B}$. *Sample* r_2 *rows from* $\mathbf{A}$ *in* c_2 *i.i.d. trials, where in each trial the i-th column is chosen with probability* p_i. *Let* $\mathbf{R}_2 \in \mathbb{R}^{r_2\times n}$ *contain the* r_2 *sampled rows and let* $\mathbf{R} = [\mathbf{R}_1^T, \mathbf{R}_2^T]^T$. *Then*

$$\mathbb{E}||\mathbf{A} - \mathbf{C}\mathbf{C}^{\dagger}\mathbf{A}\mathbf{R}^{\dagger}\mathbf{R}||_F^2 \leq ||\mathbf{A}-\mathbf{C}\mathbf{C}^{\dagger}\mathbf{A}||_F^2 + \frac{\rho}{\alpha r_2}||\mathbf{A}-\mathbf{A}\mathbf{R}^{\dagger}\mathbf{R}||_F^2.$$

Theorem A5 ([13,15]). *Given three matrices* $\mathbf{C} \in \mathbb{R}^{m\times c}$, $\mathbf{A} \in \mathbb{R}^{m\times n}$ *and* $\mathbf{R} \in \mathbb{R}^{r\times n}$, *we have*

$$\mathbf{C}^{\dagger}\mathbf{A}\mathbf{R}^{\dagger} = \operatorname*{argmin}_{\mathbf{U}} \|\mathbf{A} - \mathbf{C}\mathbf{U}\mathbf{R}\|_F$$

Theorem A6 ([15,21]). *Given a matrix* $\mathbf{A} = \mathbf{A}\mathbf{Z}\mathbf{Z}^T + \mathbf{E} \in \mathbb{R}^{m\times n}$, *where* $\mathbf{Z}^T\mathbf{Z} = \mathbf{I}_k$ *and* $\mathbf{Z} \in \mathbb{R}^{n\times k}$, *let* $\mathbf{S} \in \mathbb{R}^{n\times t}$ *be any matrix such that rank* $k = (\mathbf{Z}^T\mathbf{S})$. *Let* $\mathbf{C} = \mathbf{A}\mathbf{S} \in \mathbb{R}^{m\times r}$. *Then*

$$\begin{aligned}&\|\mathbf{A} - \mathbf{C}\mathbf{C}^{\dagger}\mathbf{A}\|_\zeta^2 \le \|\mathbf{A} - \Pi^{\zeta}_{\mathbf{C},k}(\mathbf{A})\|_\zeta^2 \\ \le&\|\mathbf{A} - \mathbf{C}(\mathbf{Z}^T\mathbf{S})^{\dagger}\mathbf{Z}^T\|_\zeta^2 \le \|\mathbf{E}\|_\zeta^2 + \|\mathbf{E}\mathbf{S}(\mathbf{Z}^T\mathbf{S})^{\dagger}\|_\zeta^2.\end{aligned}$$

Appendix B. Theorem 1 Proof

We first provide an essential lemma before proving the theorem.

Lemma A4 ([15]). *Given any* $\mathbf{Z} \in \mathbb{R}^{m\times p}$, $\mathbf{C} \in \mathbb{R}^{m\times q}$ *and* $\mathbf{A} \in \mathbb{R}^{m\times n}$, *assume* $\mathcal{R}(\mathbf{Z}) \subseteq \mathcal{R}(\mathbf{C}) \subseteq \mathcal{R}(\mathbf{A})$. *Let* $\mathbf{X} \in \mathbb{R}^{n\times n}$ *be a projection matrix. Then*

$$\|\mathbf{A} - \mathbf{C}\mathbf{C}^{\dagger}\mathbf{A}\mathbf{X}\|_F \le \|\mathbf{A} - \mathbf{Z}\mathbf{Z}^{\dagger}\mathbf{A}\mathbf{X}\|_F.$$

Now we start to prove Theorem 1.

Proof. According to Theorem A6, we have

$$\|\mathbf{A} - \mathbf{C}_1\mathbf{C}_1^{\dagger}\mathbf{A}\|_F^2 \le \|\mathbf{A} - \Pi^{F}_{\mathbf{C}_1,k}(\mathbf{A})\|_F^2 \le \|\mathbf{E}\|_F^2 + \|\mathbf{E}\mathbf{S}(\mathbf{Z}^T\mathbf{S})^{\dagger}\|_F^2.$$

Let $\mathbf{S} = \mathbf{\Omega}\Gamma$ and $\mathbf{E} = \mathbf{A} - \mathbf{A}\mathbf{Z}\mathbf{Z}^T$, then we have

$$\|\mathbf{E}\|_F^2 \le 2\|\mathbf{A} - \mathbf{A}_k\|_F^2 \tag{A1}$$

because of Lemma A1 with error parameter $\epsilon = 1$. In addition, $\mathbf{S}^T$ is a row leverage score sketching matrix of $\mathbf{Z}$, where Γ, $\mathbf{\Omega}$ and $\mathbf{Z}$ are calculated in Algorithm 3. Additionally, $\mathbf{S}^T$ is also a subspace embedding matrix of $\mathbf{Z}$ with error parameter $\epsilon_0 = 1/2$. Inferring from the fact that $(\mathbf{Z}^T\mathbf{S})^{\dagger} = (\mathbf{Z}^T\mathbf{S})^T(\mathbf{Z}^T\mathbf{S}\mathbf{S}^T\mathbf{Z})^{-1}$, we obtain

$$\begin{aligned}&\|\mathbf{E}\mathbf{S}(\mathbf{Z}^T\mathbf{S})^{\dagger}\|_F^2 = \|\mathbf{E}\mathbf{S}\mathbf{S}^T\mathbf{Z}(\mathbf{Z}^T\mathbf{S}\mathbf{S}^T\mathbf{Z})^{-1}\|_F^2 \\ &\le \|\mathbf{E}\mathbf{S}\mathbf{S}^T\mathbf{Z}\|_F^2\|(\mathbf{Z}^T\mathbf{S}\mathbf{S}^T\mathbf{Z})^{-1}\|_2^2 &\text{(A2)} \\ &\le \frac{1}{4k\log k}\|\mathbf{E}\|_F^2\|\mathbf{Z}\|_F^2\|(\mathbf{Z}^T\mathbf{S}\mathbf{S}^T\mathbf{Z})^{-1}\|_2^2 &\text{(A3)} \\ &\le \frac{1}{\log k}\|\mathbf{E}\|_F^2, &\text{(A4)}\end{aligned}$$

where Equation (A2) follows from the fact that $\|\mathbf{A}\mathbf{B}\|_F \le \|\mathbf{A}\|_2\|\mathbf{B}\|_F$, and Equation (A3) follows from Theorem A1 with error parameter $\varepsilon = 4k\log k$ and $\mathbf{E}\mathbf{Z} = \mathbf{A}(\mathbf{I} - \mathbf{Z}\mathbf{Z}^T)\mathbf{Z} = \mathbf{0}$. Due to Theorem A2 with error parameter $\epsilon_0 = 1/2$, Equation (A4) can be obtained. Because we have

$$\|\mathbf{S}^T\mathbf{Z}\|_2^2 = (1 \pm \epsilon_0)\|\mathbf{Z}\|_2^2 = (1 \pm \epsilon_0).$$

therefore,

$$\|(\mathbf{Z}^T\mathbf{S}\mathbf{S}^T\mathbf{Z})^{-1}\|_2^2 \le (1 - \epsilon_0)^{-2} = 4.$$

Due to Theorem A2, $\mathbf{S}$ needs $t = 4k\log k$ columns as a subspace embedding matrix of $\mathbf{Z}$ with error parameter $\epsilon_0 = 1/2$. Theorem A2 also leads to $\varepsilon = 4k\log k$ in the proof of Equation (A3). Now we have

$$\|\mathbf{A} - \mathbf{C}_1\mathbf{C}_1^{\dagger}\mathbf{A}\|_F^2 \le \|\mathbf{E}\|_F^2 + \frac{1}{\log k}\|\mathbf{E}\|_F^2 \le 4\|\mathbf{A} - \mathbf{A}_k\|_F^2, \tag{A5}$$

where the last inequality follows from Equation (A1) and $1/\log k \leq 1$.

Using Lemma 2, we need to sample $\mathcal{O}(\frac{k}{\epsilon})$ columns from $\mathbf{A}$ such that $\hat{\mathbf{C}} = [\mathbf{C}_1, \mathbf{C}_2]$ has the property

$$\|\mathbf{A} - \hat{\mathbf{C}}\hat{\mathbf{C}}^{\dagger}\mathbf{A}\|_F^2 \leq (1+\epsilon)\|\mathbf{A} - \mathbf{A}_k\|_F^2.$$

Lemma A1 shows that there exists an othonormal matrix $\mathbf{Q}_k$ with rank k in the range of $\hat{\mathbf{C}}$ such that

$$\|\mathbf{A} - \mathbf{Q}_k\mathbf{Q}_k^T\mathbf{A}\|_F^2 \leq (1+\epsilon)\|\mathbf{A} - \hat{\mathbf{C}}\hat{\mathbf{C}}^{\dagger}\mathbf{A}\|_F^2. \tag{A6}$$

$[\mathbf{C}_3] = \mathit{AdptiveSampling}(\mathbf{A}, \mathbf{Q}_k, \mathbf{C}_1, k/\epsilon)$, and we define $\tilde{\mathbf{C}} = [\mathbf{C}_1, \mathbf{C}_3]$, then by Lemma A3, it holds that

$$\begin{aligned}
&\|\mathbf{A} - \tilde{\mathbf{C}}\tilde{\mathbf{C}}^{\dagger}\mathbf{A}\mathbf{Q}_k^T\mathbf{Q}_k\|_F^2 \\
\leq&\|\mathbf{A} - \mathbf{Q}_k\mathbf{Q}_k^T\mathbf{A}\|_F^2 + \epsilon\|\mathbf{A} - \mathbf{C}_1\mathbf{C}_1^{\dagger}\mathbf{A}\|_F^2 \\
\leq&(1+\epsilon)\|\mathbf{A} - \hat{\mathbf{C}}\hat{\mathbf{C}}^{\dagger}\mathbf{A}\|_F^2 + 4\epsilon\|\mathbf{A} - \mathbf{A}_k\|_F^2 \\
\leq&(1+\epsilon)^2\|\mathbf{A} - \mathbf{A}_k\|_F^2 + 4\epsilon\|\mathbf{A} - \mathbf{A}_k\|_F^2 \\
=&(1+6\epsilon)\|\mathbf{A} - \mathbf{A}_k\|_F^2.
\end{aligned}$$

By rescaling the ϵ, we can obtain a $(1+\epsilon)$ relative error bound. Since $\mathcal{R}(\mathbf{Q}_k) \subseteq \mathcal{R}(\hat{\mathbf{C}}) \subseteq \mathcal{R}(\mathbf{A})$, Lemma A4 leads to

$$\|\mathbf{A} - \tilde{\mathbf{C}}\tilde{\mathbf{C}}^{\dagger}\mathbf{A}(\hat{\mathbf{C}}^{\dagger})^T\hat{\mathbf{C}}^T\|_F^2 \leq \|\mathbf{A} - \tilde{\mathbf{C}}\tilde{\mathbf{C}}^{\dagger}\mathbf{A}\mathbf{Q}_k^T\mathbf{Q}_k\|_F^2 \leq (1+\epsilon)\|\mathbf{A} - \mathbf{A}_k\|_F^2.$$

Inferring from the fact that $\mathcal{R}(\hat{\mathbf{C}}) \subseteq \mathcal{R}(\mathbf{C}) \subseteq \mathcal{R}(\mathbf{A})$ and $\mathcal{R}(\tilde{\mathbf{C}}) \subseteq \mathcal{R}(\mathbf{C}) \subseteq \mathcal{R}(\mathbf{A})$, utilizing Lemma A4 twice, we reach the result that

$$\|\mathbf{A} - \mathbf{C}\mathbf{C}^{\dagger}\mathbf{A}(\mathbf{C}^{\dagger})^T\mathbf{C}^T\|_F^2 \leq \|\mathbf{A} - \tilde{\mathbf{C}}\tilde{\mathbf{C}}^{\dagger}\mathbf{A}(\hat{\mathbf{C}}^{\dagger})^T\hat{\mathbf{C}}^T\|_F^2 \leq (1+\epsilon)\|\mathbf{A} - \mathbf{A}_k\|_F^2.$$

$\mathbf{S}$ is a leverage-score sketching matrix of $\mathbf{C}$, when $s = \mathcal{O}(\frac{c}{\epsilon} + c\log c)$ is the row dimension of $\mathbf{S}$; by Theorem 3 of [12], we have,

$$\|\mathbf{A} - \mathbf{C}\mathbf{U}\mathbf{C}^T\|_F^2 \leq \|\mathbf{A} - \mathbf{C}\hat{\mathbf{U}}\mathbf{C}^{\top}\|_F^2 \leq (1+\epsilon)\|\mathbf{A} - \mathbf{C}\mathbf{C}^{\dagger}\mathbf{A}(\mathbf{C}^{\dagger})^T\mathbf{C}^T\|_F^2.$$

By rescaling ϵ, we achieve the final result that

$$\|\mathbf{A} - \mathbf{C}\mathbf{U}\mathbf{C}^T\|_F \leq (1+\epsilon)\|\mathbf{A} - \mathbf{A}_k\|_F.$$

□

References

1. Kumar, S.; Mohri, M.; Talwalkar, A. Sampling methods for the Nyström method. *J. Mach. Learn. Res.* **2012**, *13*, 981–1006.
2. Williams, C.; Seeger, M. Using the Nyström method to speed up kernel machines. In Proceedings of the 14th Annual Conference on Neural Information Processing Systems, Vancouver, BC, Canada, 3–8 December, 2001; Number EPFL-CONF-161322, pp. 682–688.
3. Gittens, A.; Mahoney, M.W. Revisiting the Nyström Method for Improved Large-Scale Machine Learning. *arXiv* **2013**, arXiv:1303.1849.
4. Wang, S.; Zhang, Z. Improving CUR Matrix Decomposition and the Nyström Approximation via Adaptive Sampling. *J. Mach. Learn. Res.* **2013**, *14*, 2729–2769.
5. Anderson, D.G.; Du, S.S.; Mahoney, M.W.; Melgaard, C.; Wu, K.; Gu, M. Spectral Gap Error Bounds for Improving CUR Matrix Decomposition and the Nyström Method. In Proceedings of the AISTATS, San Diego, CA, USA, 9–12 May 2015.
6. Wang, S.; Gittens, A.; Mahoney, M.W. Scalable kernel K-means clustering with Nyström approximation: Relative-error bounds. *J. Mach. Learn. Res.* **2019**, *20*, 431–479.
7. Gao, S.; Dou, S.; Zhang, Q.; Huang, X. Kernel-Whitening: Overcome Dataset Bias with Isotropic Sentence Embedding. *arXiv* **2022**, arXiv:2210.07547.
8. Hamm, K.; Lu, Z.; Ouyang, W.; Zhang, H.H. Boosting Nyström Method. *arXiv* **2023**, arXiv:2302.11032.

9. Hsieh, C.J.; Si, S.; Dhillon, I.S. Fast Prediction for Large-Scale Kernel Machines. In Proceedings of the Advances in Neural Information Processing Systems, Montreal, QC, Canada, 8–13 December 2014; pp. 3689–3697.
10. Si, S.; Hsieh, C.J.; Dhillon, I. Memory efficient kernel approximation. In Proceedings of the 31st International Conference on Machine Learning, Beijing, China, 21–26 June 2014; pp. 701–709.
11. Wang, S.; Luo, L.; Zhang, Z. SPSD Matrix Approximation vis Column Selection: Theories, Algorithms, and Extensions. *J. Mach. Learn. Res.* **2016**, *17*, 1697–1745.
12. Wang, S.; Zhang, Z.; Zhang, T. Towards More Efficient SPSD Matrix Approximation and CUR Matrix Decomposition. *J. Mach. Learn. Res.* **2016**, *17*, 1–49.
13. Boutsidis, C.; Woodruff, D.P. Optimal CUR Matrix Decompositions. *SIAM J. Comput.* **2017**, *46*, 543–589. [CrossRef]
14. Deshpande, A.; Vempala, S. Adaptive sampling and fast low-rank matrix approximation. In *Approximation, Randomization, and Combinatorial Optimization. Algorithms and Techniques*; Springer: Berlin/Heidelberg, Germany, 2006; pp. 292–303.
15. Ye, H.; Li, Y.; Zhang, Z. A simple approach to optimal CUR decomposition. *arXiv* **2015**, arXiv:1511.01598.
16. Woodruff, D.P. Sketching as a tool for numerical linear algebra. *arXiv* **2014**, arXiv:1411.4357.
17. Ye, H.; Wang, S.; Zhang, Z.; Zhang, T. Fast Generalized Matrix Regression with Applications in Machine Learning. *arXiv* **2019**, arXiv:1912.12008.
18. Drineas, P.; Magdon-Ismail, M.; Mahoney, M.W.; Woodruff, D.P. Fast approximation of matrix coherence and statistical leverage. *J. Mach. Learn. Res.* **2012**, *13*, 3475–3506.
19. Wang, S.; Zhang, Z. Efficient Algorithms and Error Analysis for the Modified Nystrom Method. In Proceedings of the Seventeenth International Conference on Artificial Intelligence and Statistics, Reykjavik, Iceland, 22–25 April 2014; pp. 996–1004.
20. Clarkson, K.L.; Woodruff, D.P. Low rank approximation and regression in input sparsity time. In Proceedings of the Forty-Fifth Annual ACM Symposium on Theory of Computing, Palo Alto, CA, USA, 2–4 June 2013; pp. 81–90.
21. Boutsidis, C.; Drineas, P.; Magdon-Ismail, M. Near-optimal column-based matrix reconstruction. *SIAM J. Comput.* **2014**, *43*, 687–717. [CrossRef]

Disclaimer/Publisher's Note: The statements, opinions and data contained in all publications are solely those of the individual author(s) and contributor(s) and not of MDPI and/or the editor(s). MDPI and/or the editor(s) disclaim responsibility for any injury to people or property resulting from any ideas, methods, instructions or products referred to in the content.

mathematics

Article

Some New Properties of Convex Fuzzy-Number-Valued Mappings on Coordinates Using Up and Down Fuzzy Relations and Related Inequalities

Muhammad Bilal Khan [1], Ali Althobaiti [2], Cheng-Chi Lee [3,4,*], Mohamed S. Soliman [5] and Chun-Ta Li [6,*]

1 Department of Mathematics, COMSATS University Islamabad, Islamabad 44000, Pakistan
2 Department of Mathematics, College of Science, Taif University, P.O. Box 11099, Taif 21944, Saudi Arabia
3 Research and Development Center for Physical Education, Health, and Information Technology, Department of Library and Information Science, Fu Jen Catholic University, New Taipei City 24205, Taiwan
4 Department of Computer Science and Information Engineering, Asia University, Taichung 41354, Taiwan
5 Department of Electrical Engineering, College of Engineering, Taif University, P.O. Box 11099, Taif 21944, Saudi Arabia
6 Bachelor's Program of Artificial Intelligence and Information Security, Graduate Institute of Applied Science and Engineering, Fu Jen Catholic University, New Taipei City 24206, Taiwan
* Correspondence: cclee@mail.fju.edu.tw (C.-C.L.); 157278@mail.fju.edu.tw (C.-T.L.)

Abstract: The symmetric function class interacts heavily with other types of functions. One of these is the convex function class, which is strongly related to symmetry theory. In this study, we define a novel class of convex mappings on planes using a fuzzy inclusion relation, known as coordinated up and down convex fuzzy-number-valued mapping. Several new definitions are introduced by placing some moderate restrictions on the notion of coordinated up and down convex fuzzy-number-valued mapping. Other uncommon examples are also described using these definitions, which can be viewed as applications of the new outcomes. Moreover, Hermite–Hadamard–Fejér inequalities are acquired via fuzzy double Aumann integrals, and the validation of these outcomes is discussed with the help of nontrivial examples and suitable choices of coordinated up and down convex fuzzy-number-valued mappings.

Keywords: fuzzy-interval-valued function on coordinates; coordinated up and down convex fuzzy-number-valued mapping; fuzzy double integral; Hermite–Hadamard–Fejér-type inequalities

MSC: 26A33; 26A51; 26D10

Citation: Khan, M.B.; Althobaiti, A.; Lee, C.-C.; Soliman, M.S.; Li, C.-T. Some New Properties of Convex Fuzzy-Number-Valued Mappings on Coordinates Using Up and Down Fuzzy Relations and Related Inequalities. *Mathematics* **2023**, *11*, 2851. https://doi.org/10.3390/math11132851

Academic Editors: Hsien-Chung Wu and Salvatore Sessa

Received: 4 May 2023
Revised: 2 June 2023
Accepted: 23 June 2023
Published: 25 June 2023

Copyright: © 2023 by the authors. Licensee MDPI, Basel, Switzerland. This article is an open access article distributed under the terms and conditions of the Creative Commons Attribution (CC BY) license (https://creativecommons.org/licenses/by/4.0/).

1. Introduction

Convex functions are distinguished from other function classes by their widespread application in mathematics, statistics, optimization theory, and applied sciences. This is due to the analytic inequalities, particularly those of the Hermite–Hadamard, Fejér, Hardy, Simpson, and Ostrowski types, that have been established using this concept [1–17]. The concept of a convex function is one of the core theorems of inequality theory, detailed as follows:

Definition 1. *The real-valued mapping $Y : K \to \mathbb{R}$ is called a convex mapping on convex set K if*

$$Y(\tau\sigma + (1-\tau)s) \leq \tau \odot Y(\sigma) + (1-\tau) \odot Y(s), \tag{1}$$

for all $\sigma, s \in K$, $\tau \in [0, 1]$. If Equation (1) is reversed, then Y is called a concave mapping on K. Y is affine if and only if it is both a convex and concave mapping.

The Hermite–Hadamard inequality, which is a key component of the widespread use and geometrical interpretation of convex functions, has piqued the interest of researchers in fundamental mathematics. This inequality has piqued the interest of multiple scholars from around the world due to its numerous applications, particularly in the domains of numerical analysis, engineering, physical science, and chemistry. The idea of inequality has advanced rapidly in recent years. For convex functions, several inequalities can be found; however, Hermite–Hadamard's inequality is one of the most extensively and intensively studied conclusions. It is worthwhile to consider how closely related the theories of inequality and convexity are. As a result of this reality, the concept of inequality becomes more appealing. Many new expansions, generalizations, and definitions of novel convexity have been given in recent years, as have corresponding advancements in the theory of convexity inequality, particularly integral inequality theory. Formally, the Hermite–Hadamard inequality is as follows:

For a convex mapping $Y : K \to \mathbb{R}$ on convex set K, the HH inequality is written as

$$Y\left(\frac{\rho+\mu}{2}\right) \leq \frac{1}{\mu-\rho}\int_{\rho}^{\mu} Y(\sigma)d\sigma \leq \frac{Y(\rho)+Y(\mu)}{2}, \quad (2)$$

for all $\rho,\ \mu \in K$, with $\rho \leq \mu$. If Y is concave, then Equation (2) is reversed.

If it is a concave function, the inequality in Equation (2) holds in both directions. Based on geometry, the Hermite–Hadamard inequality provides an upper and lower estimate for the integral mean of any convex function defined in a closed and limited domain that encompasses the function's ends and midpoint. Because of the importance of this inequality, multiple modifications of it have been studied in the literature for various classes of convexity, including harmonically convex, exponentially convex, s-convex, h-convex, and co-ordinate convex functions [18–33].

Moore [34] was the first to consider interval analysis. Moore [35] researched interval methods for obtaining the upper and lower bounds of accurate values of the integrals of interval-valued functions and studied the integration of interval-valued functions in 1979. Bhurjee and Panda [36] devised a framework for determining effective solutions to a broad multi-objective fractional programming problem whose parameters in the objective functions and constraints are intervals. Zhang et al. [37] expanded the ideas of invexity and pre-invexity to interval-valued functions, resulting in KKT optimality requirements for LU-pre-invex and invex optimization problems with an interval-valued objective function. Zhao et al. [38] defined the interval double integral and provided Chebyshev-type inequalities for interval-valued functions. Interval analysis has practical applications in economics, chemical engineering, beam physics, control circuit design, global optimization, robotics, error analysis, signal processing, and computer graphics (see [39–58]).

Budak et al. [59] defined the interval-valued right-sided Riemann–Liouville fractional integral and derived H-H-type inequalities for such integrals. Sharma et al. [60] proposed interval-valued pre-invex functions and proved fractional H-H-type inequalities for them. Zhao et al. [61,62] recently developed the concept of interval-valued coordinated convex functions on coordinates and proved H-H-type inequalities for these interval-valued coordinated convex functions. Furthermore, Budak et al. [63] introduced a new concept of interval-valued fractional integrals on coordinates and used these fractional integrals to analyze H-H-type inequalities for interval-valued coordinated convex functions. Kara et al. [64] demonstrated that the product of two interval-valued convex functions on coordinates has H-H–Fejér-type inclusions. We refer to [65–76] and the references therein for more information on the links between the various types of coordinated fuzzy-number-valued mappings, interval-valued functions, and integral inequalities. Similarly, most of the authors work in the field of fuzzy calculus as well as fuzzy fractional calculus. Therefore, we refer the readers to [77–97] and the references therein, which will help in understanding fuzzy theory.

Motivated and inspired by the above ongoing research, this manuscript is divided into four sections. In the second section, we recall some classical and preliminary notions and results which will be helpful in discussing the main outcomes. In the third section, some new estimates of integral inequalities via fuzzy double Aumann integrals and a newly defined coordinated class of convex fuzzy-number mappings on up and down fuzzy relations are presented. Some interesting examples are also given to illustrate the main outcomes. In the final section, some conclusions and future plans are discussed.

2. Preliminaries

First, we will review the fundamental notions of fuzzy mathematics. Additional information can be found in the following references: Anastassiou [77]; Anastassiou and Gal [78]; Gal [79]; Goetschel and Voxman [82]; Gal [83]; and Wu and Zengtai [84].

Let $\Lambda \in \mathbb{E}_0$ be a fuzzy number. Then, this fuzzy number is also represented as q-level sets $[\Lambda]^{\mathfrak{q}}$ defined as

$$\begin{cases} \overline{\{\varsigma \in \mathbb{R} | \Lambda(\varsigma) \geq \mathfrak{q}\}}, \ \mathfrak{q} \in (0,1] \\ \{\varsigma \in \mathbb{R} | \Lambda(\varsigma) > \mathfrak{q}\}, \ \mathfrak{q} = 0, \end{cases} \tag{3}$$

which is a bounded and closed interval of $\mathbb{R}$ and denoted as

$$[\Lambda]^{\mathfrak{q}} = [\Lambda_*(\mathfrak{q}), \ \Lambda^*(\mathfrak{q})].$$

For $\Lambda, \lambda \in \mathbb{E}_0$ and $\varrho \in \mathbb{R}$, the sum $\Lambda \oplus \lambda$, product $\Lambda \otimes \lambda$, scalar product $\varrho \odot \Lambda$, and sum with the scalar are uniquely defined as, for all $\mathfrak{q} \in [0, \ 1]$, we obtain

$$[\Lambda \oplus \lambda]^{\mathfrak{q}} = [\Lambda]^{\mathfrak{q}} + [\lambda]^{\mathfrak{q}}, \tag{4}$$

$$[\Lambda \otimes \lambda]^{\mathfrak{q}} = [\Lambda]^{\mathfrak{q}} \times [\lambda]^{\mathfrak{q}}, \tag{5}$$

$$[\varrho \odot \Lambda]^{\mathfrak{q}} = \varrho \cdot [\Lambda]^{\mathfrak{q}}. \tag{6}$$

$$[\varrho \oplus \Lambda]^{\mathfrak{q}} = \varrho + [\Lambda]^{\mathfrak{q}}. \tag{7}$$

For $\psi \in \mathbb{E}_0$, such that $\Lambda = \lambda \oplus \psi$, via this result, we then determine the existence of Hukuhara difference between Λ and λ, and we can say that ψ is the H-difference between Λ and λ and is denoted as $\Lambda \ominus \lambda$. If H-difference exists, then

$$(\psi)^*(\mathfrak{q}) = (\Lambda \ominus \lambda)^*(\mathfrak{q}) = \Lambda^*(\mathfrak{q}) - \lambda^*(\mathfrak{q}), \ (\psi)_*(\mathfrak{q}) = (\Lambda \ominus \lambda)_*(\mathfrak{q}) = \Lambda_*(\mathfrak{q}) - \lambda_*(\mathfrak{q}). \tag{8}$$

For $[\mathcal{Z}_*, \ \mathcal{Z}^*], \ [\mathcal{Q}_*, \ \mathcal{Q}^*] \in \mathbb{R}_I$, where $\mathbb{R}_I$ is the space of all closed and bounded intervals of real numbers $\mathbb{R}$, the Hausdorff–Pompeiu distance between the intervals $[\mathcal{Z}_*, \ \mathcal{Z}^*]$ and $[\mathcal{Q}_*, \ \mathcal{Q}^*]$ is defined as

$$d_H([\mathcal{Z}_*, \ \mathcal{Z}^*], \ [\mathcal{Q}_*, \ \mathcal{Q}^*]) = max\{|\mathcal{Z}_* - \mathcal{Q}_*|, \ |\mathcal{Z}^* - \mathcal{Q}^*|\}. \tag{9}$$

It is a known fact that $(\mathbb{R}_I, d_H)$ is a complete metric space [82].

Theorem 1 ([82]). *The space* $\mathbb{E}_0$ *dealing with a supremum metric, i.e., for* $\widetilde{\psi}, \ \widetilde{\omega} \in \mathbb{E}_0$

$$d_\infty\left(\widetilde{\psi}, \ \widetilde{\omega}\right) = \sup_{0 \leq \lambda \leq 1} d_H\left(\left[\widetilde{\psi}\right]^{\mathfrak{q}}, \ \left[\widetilde{\omega}\right]^{\mathfrak{q}}\right), \tag{10}$$

is a complete metric space, where H denotes the well-known Hausdorff metric in the space of intervals.

Remark 1 ([86,87]). *Let* $\mathbb{R}_I$ *be the space of all closed and bounded intervals of real numbers* $\mathbb{R}$*. The relation "* $\leq_I$*" is defined in* $\mathbb{R}_I$ as

$$[\Lambda_*, \ \Lambda^*] \leq_I [\lambda_*, \ \lambda^*] \text{ if and only if } \Lambda_* \leq \lambda_*, \ \Lambda^* \leq \lambda^*,$$

for all $[\Lambda_*, \Lambda^*], [\lambda_*, \lambda^*] \in \mathbb{R}_I$, *and it is known as the left and right relation.*

The inclusion " $\subseteq$ " means that

$$\Lambda \subseteq_I \lambda \text{ if and only if } [\Lambda_*, \Lambda^*] \subseteq_I [\lambda_*, \lambda^*], \text{ if and only if } \lambda_* \leq \Lambda_*, \Lambda^* \leq \lambda^*.$$

It is known as the up and down relation.

Proposition 1 ([86]). *If* $\Lambda, \lambda \in \mathbb{E}_0$, *then relation* " $\leq_{\mathbb{F}}$ " *is defined in* $\mathbb{E}_0$ *as*

$$\Lambda \leq_{\mathbb{F}} \lambda \text{ if and only if } [\Lambda]^{\mathrm{q}} \leq_I [\lambda]^{\mathrm{q}} \text{ for all } \mathrm{q} \in [0, 1],$$

and this relation is known as the left and right fuzzy relation.

Proposition 2 ([80]). *If* $\Lambda, \lambda \in \mathbb{E}_0$, *then relation* " $\supseteq_{\mathbb{F}}$ " *is defined in* $\mathbb{E}_0$ *as*

$$\Lambda \supseteq_{\mathbb{F}} \lambda \text{ if and only if } [\Lambda]^{\mathrm{q}} \supseteq_I [\lambda]^{\mathrm{q}} \text{ for all } \mathrm{q} \in [0, 1],$$

and this relation is known as the up and down fuzzy relation.

Definition 2 ([90]). *The IVM* $Y : \Delta = [\mu, \sigma] \times [\varsigma, \nu] \to \mathbb{R}^+$ *is said to be a coordinated convex function on* Δ *if*

$$\begin{aligned} &Y(\tau\mu + (1-\tau)\sigma, s\varsigma + (1-s)\nu) \\ &\leq \tau s Y(\mu,\varsigma) + \tau(1-s)Y(\mu,\nu) + (1-\tau)sY(\sigma,\varsigma) + (1-\tau)(1-s)Y(\sigma,\nu), \end{aligned} \tag{11}$$

for all (μ, σ), $(\varsigma, \nu) \in \Delta$, τ *and* $\tau, s \in [0, 1]$. *If inequality Equation (11) is reversed, then* Y *is called a coordinated concave IVM on* Δ.

Definition 3 ([87]). *The FN-V-M* $\widetilde{Y} : [\varsigma, \nu] \to \mathbb{E}_0$ *is said to be an up and down convex FN-V-M on* $[\varsigma, \nu]$ *if*

$$\widetilde{Y}(\tau\sigma + (1-\tau)\omega) \supseteq_{\mathbb{F}} \tau \odot \widetilde{Y}(\sigma) \oplus (1-\tau) \odot \widetilde{Y}(\omega), \tag{12}$$

for all $\sigma, \omega \in [\varsigma, \nu]$, $\tau \in [0, 1]$, *where* $\widetilde{Y}(\sigma) \geq_{\mathbb{F}} \widetilde{0}$. *If* $\widetilde{Y}$ *is an up and down concave FN-V-M on* $[\varsigma, \nu]$, *then inequality Equation (12) is reversed.*

Theorem 2 ([85]). *Let* $\widetilde{Y}, \widetilde{\mathfrak{S}} : [\varsigma, \nu] \to \mathbb{E}_0$ *be two up and down convex FN-V-Ms. Then, from the* q*-levels, we obtain the collection of IVMs* $Y_{\mathrm{q}}, \mathfrak{S}_{\mathrm{q}} : [\varsigma, \nu] \subset \mathbb{R} \to \mathbb{R}_I^+$ *given as* $Y_{\mathrm{q}}(\sigma) = [Y_*(\sigma, \mathrm{q}), Y^*(\sigma, \mathrm{q})]$ *and* $\mathfrak{S}_{\mathrm{q}}(\sigma) = [\mathfrak{S}_*(\sigma, \mathrm{q}), \mathfrak{S}^*(\sigma, \mathrm{q})]$ *for all* $\sigma \in [\varsigma, \nu]$ *and for all* $\mathrm{q} \in [0, 1]$. *If* $\widetilde{Y} \otimes \widetilde{\mathfrak{S}}$ *is a fuzzy Riemann integrable, then*

$$\frac{1}{\nu-\varsigma} \odot (FR)\int_{\varsigma}^{\nu} \widetilde{Y}(\sigma) \otimes \widetilde{\mathfrak{S}}(\sigma) d\sigma \supseteq_{\mathbb{F}} \frac{1}{3} \odot \widetilde{\mathcal{M}}(\varsigma,\nu) \oplus \frac{1}{6} \odot \widetilde{\mathcal{N}}(\varsigma,\nu), \tag{13}$$

and

$$2 \odot \widetilde{Y}\left(\frac{\varsigma+\nu}{2}\right) \otimes \widetilde{\mathfrak{S}}\left(\frac{\varsigma+\nu}{2}\right) \supseteq_{\mathbb{F}} \frac{1}{\nu-\varsigma} \odot (FR)\int_{\varsigma}^{\nu} \widetilde{Y}(\sigma) \otimes \widetilde{\mathfrak{S}}(\sigma) d\sigma \oplus \frac{1}{6} \odot \widetilde{\mathcal{M}}(\varsigma,\nu) \oplus \frac{1}{3} \odot \widetilde{\mathcal{N}}(\varsigma,\nu). \tag{14}$$

where $\widetilde{\mathcal{M}}(\varsigma,\nu) = \widetilde{Y}(\varsigma) \otimes \widetilde{\mathfrak{S}}(\varsigma) \oplus \widetilde{Y}(\nu) \otimes \widetilde{\mathfrak{S}}(\nu)$, $\widetilde{\mathcal{N}}(\varsigma,\nu) = \widetilde{Y}(\varsigma) \otimes \widetilde{\mathfrak{S}}(\nu) \oplus \widetilde{Y}(\nu) \otimes \widetilde{\mathfrak{S}}(\varsigma)$, *and* $\mathcal{M}_{\mathrm{q}}(\varsigma,\nu) = [\mathcal{M}_*((\varsigma,\nu), \mathrm{q}), \mathcal{M}^*((\varsigma,\nu), \mathrm{q})]$ *and* $\mathcal{N}_{\mathrm{q}}(\varsigma,\nu) = [\mathcal{N}_*((\varsigma,\nu), \mathrm{q}), \mathcal{N}^*((\varsigma,\nu), \mathrm{q})]$.

Theorem 3 ([85]). *Let* $\widetilde{Y} : [\varsigma, \nu] \to \mathbb{E}_0$ *be an up and down convex FN-V-M with* $\varsigma < \nu$. *Then, from the* q*-levels, we obtain the collection of IVMs* $Y_{\mathrm{q}} : [\varsigma, \nu] \subset \mathbb{R} \to \mathbb{R}_I^+$ *given as*

$Y_{\mathfrak{q}}(\sigma) = [Y_*(\sigma, \mathfrak{q}),\ Y^*(\sigma, \mathfrak{q})]$ *for all* $\sigma \in [\varsigma,\ \nu]$ *and for all* $\mathfrak{q} \in [0,\ 1]$. *If* $\widetilde{Y} \in Y\mathcal{R}_{([\varsigma,\ \nu], \mathfrak{q})}$ *and* $\Omega : [\varsigma,\ \nu] \to \mathbb{R}, \Omega(\sigma) \geq 0$, *symmetric with respect to* $\frac{\varsigma+\nu}{2}$, *and* $\int_{\varsigma}^{\nu} \Omega(\sigma)d\sigma > 0$, *then*

$$\widetilde{Y}\left(\frac{\varsigma+\nu}{2}\right) \supseteq_{\mathbb{F}} \frac{1}{\int_{\varsigma}^{\nu} \Omega(\sigma)d\sigma} \odot (FR)\int_{\varsigma}^{\nu} \widetilde{Y}(\sigma)\Omega(\sigma)d\sigma \supseteq_{\mathbb{F}} \frac{\widetilde{Y}(\varsigma) \oplus \widetilde{Y}(\nu)}{2}. \quad (15)$$

If $\widetilde{Y}$ *is an up and down concave FN-V-M, then inequality Equation (15) is reversed.*
If $\Omega(\sigma) = 1$ *, then via Equation (15) we obtain following inequality:*

$$\widetilde{Y}\left(\frac{\varsigma+\nu}{2}\right) \supseteq_{\mathbb{F}} \frac{1}{\nu-\varsigma} \odot (FR)\int_{\varsigma}^{\nu} \widetilde{Y}(\sigma)\Omega(\sigma)d\sigma \supseteq_{\mathbb{F}} \frac{\widetilde{Y}(\varsigma) \oplus \widetilde{Y}(\nu)}{2}. \quad (16)$$

Theorem 4 ([36]). *If* $Y : [\varsigma, \nu] \subset \mathbb{R} \to \mathbb{R}_I$ *is an IVM given as* $(\sigma)\ [Y_*(\sigma), Y^*(\sigma)]$, *then* Y *is Riemann-integrable on* $[\varsigma, \nu]$ *if and only if* Y_* *and* Y^* *are both Riemann-integrable on* $[\varsigma, \nu]$, *such that*

$$(IR)\int_{\varsigma}^{\nu} Y(\sigma)d\sigma = [(R)\int_{\varsigma}^{\nu} Y_*(\sigma)d\sigma,\ (R)\int_{\varsigma}^{\nu} Y^*(\sigma)d\sigma]. \quad (17)$$

The collection of all Riemann-integrable real-valued functions and Riemann-integrable IVMs is denoted as $\mathcal{R}_{[\varsigma,\nu]}$ and $\mathfrak{T}\mathcal{R}_{[\varsigma,\nu]}$, respectively.

Note that Theorem 5 is also true for interval double integrals. The collection of all double-integrable IVMs is denoted as $\mathfrak{T}\mathfrak{O}_{\Delta}$, respectively.

Theorem 5 ([38]). *Let* $\Delta = [\mu,\ \sigma] \times [\varsigma,\ \nu]$. *If* $Y : \Delta \to \mathbb{R}_I$ *is ID-integrable on* Δ, *then we obtain*

$$(ID)\int_{\mu}^{\sigma}\int_{\varsigma}^{\nu} Y(\sigma, \omega)d\omega d\sigma = (IR)\int_{\mu}^{\sigma} (IR)\int_{\varsigma}^{\nu} Y(\sigma, \omega)d\omega d\sigma. \quad (18)$$

Definition 4 ([91]). *A fuzzy-interval-valued map* $\widetilde{Y} : \Delta = [\mu,\ \sigma] \times [\varsigma,\ \nu] \to \mathbb{E}_0$ *is called an FN-V-M on coordinates. Then, from the* $\mathfrak{q}$*-levels, we obtain the collection of IVMs* $Y_{\mathfrak{q}} : \Delta \subset \mathbb{R}^2 \to \mathbb{R}_I$ *on coordinates given as* $Y_{\mathfrak{q}}(\sigma, \omega) = [Y_*((\sigma, \omega), \mathfrak{q}),\ Y^*((\sigma, \omega), \mathfrak{q})]$ *for all* $(\sigma, \omega) \in \Delta$. *Herein, for each* $\mathfrak{q} \in [0,\ 1]$, *the end-point real-valued functions* $Y_*(., \mathfrak{q}),\ Y^*(., \mathfrak{q}) : [\mu,\ \sigma] \times [\varsigma,\ \nu] \to \mathbb{R}$ *are called the lower and upper functions of* $Y_{\mathfrak{q}}$.

Definition 5 ([91]). *Let* $\widetilde{Y} : \Delta = [\mu,\ \sigma] \times [\varsigma,\ \nu] \subset \mathbb{R}^2 \to \mathbb{E}_0$ *be a coordinated FN-V-M. Then,* $\widetilde{Y}(\sigma, \omega)$ *is said to be continuous at* $(\sigma, \omega) \in \Delta = [\mu,\ \sigma] \times [\varsigma,\ \nu]$ *if for each* $\mathfrak{q} \in [0,\ 1]$, *both the end-point functions* $Y_*((\sigma, \omega), \mathfrak{q})$ *and* $Y^*((\sigma, \omega), \mathfrak{q})$ *are continuous at* $(\sigma, \omega) \in \Delta$.

Definition 6 ([91]). *Let* $\widetilde{Y} : \Delta = [\mu,\ \sigma] \times [\varsigma,\ \nu] \subset \mathbb{R}^2 \to \mathbb{E}_0$ *be an FN-V-M on coordinates. Then, the fuzzy double integral of* $\widetilde{Y}$ *on* $\Delta = [\mu,\ \sigma] \times [\varsigma,\ \nu]$, *denoted as* $(FD)\int_{\mu}^{\sigma}\int_{\varsigma}^{\nu} \widetilde{Y}(\sigma, \omega)d\omega d\sigma$, *is defined level-wise as*

$$\begin{aligned}\left[(FD)\textstyle\int_{\mu}^{\sigma}\int_{\varsigma}^{\nu} \widetilde{Y}(\sigma, \omega)d\omega d\sigma\right]^{\mathfrak{q}} &= (ID)\textstyle\int_{\mu}^{\sigma}\int_{\varsigma}^{\nu} Y_{\mathfrak{q}}(\sigma, \omega)d\omega d\sigma \\ &= (IR)\textstyle\int_{\mu}^{\sigma} (IR)\int_{\varsigma}^{\nu} Y_{\mathfrak{q}}(\sigma, \omega)d\omega d\sigma,\end{aligned} \quad (19)$$

for all $\mathfrak{q} \in [0,\ 1]$, *and* $\widetilde{Y}$ *is FD-integrable on* Δ *if* $(FD)\int_{\mu}^{\sigma}\int_{\varsigma}^{\nu} \widetilde{Y}(\sigma, \omega)d\omega d\sigma \in \mathbb{E}_0$. *Note that if the end-point functions are Lebesgue-integrable, then* $\widetilde{Y}$ *is a fuzzy double-Aumann-integrable function on* Δ.

Theorem 6 ([91]). *Let $\widetilde{Y} : \Delta \subset \mathbb{R}^2 \to \mathbb{E}_0$ be an FN-V- M on coordinates. Then, from the q-levels, we obtain the collection of IVMs $Y_q : \Delta \subset \mathbb{R}^2 \to \mathbb{R}_I$ given as $Y_q(\sigma,\omega) = [Y_*((\sigma,\omega),q),\ Y^*((\sigma,\omega),q)]$ for all $(\sigma,\omega) \in \Delta = [\mu,\ \sigma] \times [\varsigma,\ \nu]$ and for all $q \in [0,\ 1]$. Then, $\widetilde{Y}$ is FD-integrable on Δ if and only if $Y_*((\sigma,\omega),q)$ and $Y^*((\sigma,\omega),q)$ are both D-integrable on Δ. Moreover, if $\widetilde{Y}$ is FD-integrable on Δ, then*

$$\begin{aligned}\left[(FD)\int_\mu^\sigma \int_\varsigma^\nu \widetilde{Y}(\sigma,\omega)d\omega d\sigma\right]^q &= \left[(FR)\int_\mu^\sigma (FR)\int_\varsigma^\nu \widetilde{Y}(\sigma,\omega)d\omega d\sigma\right]^q \\ &= (IR)\int_\mu^\sigma (IR)\int_\varsigma^\nu Y_q(\sigma,\omega)d\omega d\sigma \\ &= (ID)\int_\mu^\sigma \int_\varsigma^\nu Y_q(\sigma,\omega)d\omega d\sigma\end{aligned} \tag{20}$$

for all $q \in [0,\ 1]$.

3. Main Results

In this section, we will first propose the new class of coordinated convex functions with the up and down fuzzy relation, which are known as coordinated UD-convex FN-V-Ms. Secondly, we will present *HH*–Fejér inequalities with the help of this new class and double fuzzy integrals as well as verify them with the support of some useful examples.

Definition 7. *The FN-V-M $\widetilde{Y} : \Delta \to \mathbb{E}_0$ is said to be a coordinated UD-convex FN-V-M on Δ if*

$$\begin{aligned}&\widetilde{Y}(\tau\mu + (1-\tau)\sigma,\ s\varsigma + (1-s)\nu) \\ \supseteq_{\mathbb{F}}\ &\tau s \odot \widetilde{Y}(\mu,\varsigma) \supseteq_{\mathbb{F}} \tau(1-s) \odot \widetilde{Y}(\mu,\nu) \oplus (1-\tau)s \odot \widetilde{Y}(\sigma,\varsigma) \oplus (1-\tau)(1-s) \odot \widetilde{Y}(\sigma,\nu),\end{aligned} \tag{21}$$

for all $(\mu,\ \sigma),\ (\varsigma,\nu) \in \Delta$, and $\tau, s \in [0,\ 1]$, where $\widetilde{Y}(\sigma) \geq_{\mathbb{F}} \widetilde{0}$. If inequality Equation (21) is reversed, then $\widetilde{Y}$ is called a coordinated concave FN-V-M on Δ.

The straightforward proof of Lemma 1 will be omitted herein.

Lemma 1. *Let $\widetilde{Y} : \Delta \to \mathbb{E}_0$ be a coordinated FN-V-M on Δ. Then, $\widetilde{Y}$ is a coordinated UD-convex FN-V-M on Δ if and only if two coordinated UD-convex FN-V-Ms exist, $\widetilde{Y}_\sigma : [\varsigma,\nu] \to \mathbb{E}_0$, $\widetilde{Y}_\sigma(\omega) = \widetilde{Y}(\sigma,\omega)$ and $\widetilde{Y}_\omega : [\mu,\sigma] \to \mathbb{E}_0, \widetilde{Y}_\omega(\varsigma) = \widetilde{Y}(\varsigma,\omega)$*

Proof. From the definition of the coordinated FN-V-M, it can be easily proved. □

From Lemma 1, we can easily note that each UD-convex FN-V-M is a coordinated UD-convex FN-V-M. However, the converse is not true (see Example 1).

Theorem 7. *Let $\widetilde{Y} : \Delta \to \mathbb{E}_0$ be an FN-V-M on Δ. Then, from the q-levels, we obtain the collection of IVMs $Y_q : \Delta \to \mathbb{R}_I^+ \subset \mathbb{R}_I$ given as*

$$Y_q(\sigma,\omega) = [Y_*((\sigma,\omega),q),\ Y^*((\sigma,\omega),q)], \tag{22}$$

for all $(\sigma,\omega) \in \Delta$ and for all $q \in [0,\ 1]$. Then, $\widetilde{Y}$ is a coordinated UD-convex FN-V-M on Δ if and only if for all $q \in [0,\ 1]$, $Y_*((\sigma,\omega),\ q)$ and $Y^*((\sigma,\omega),\ q)$ are coordinated UD-convex and concave functions, respectively.

Proof. Assume that for each $q \in [0,\ 1]$, $Y_*(\sigma,q)$ and $Y^*(\sigma,q)$ are coordinated UD-convex on Δ. Then, from Equation (21), for all $(\mu,\ \sigma),\ (\varsigma,\nu) \in \Delta$, τ and $s \in [0,\ 1]$, we obtain

$$\begin{aligned}&Y_*((\tau\mu + (1-\tau)\sigma,\ s\varsigma + (1-s)\nu),\ q) \\ \leq\ &\tau s Y_*((\mu,\varsigma),\ q) + t(1-s)Y_*((\mu,\nu),\ q) + s(1-t)Y_*((\mu,\varsigma),\ q) + (1-\tau)(1-s)Y_*((\mu,\nu),\ q),\end{aligned}$$

and

$$\begin{gathered} Y^*((\tau\mu+(1-\tau)\sigma,\ s\varsigma+(1-s)\nu),\ \mathrm{q}) \\ \geq \tau s Y_*((\mu,\varsigma),\ \mathrm{q})+t(1-s)Y^*((\mu,\nu),\ \mathrm{q})+s(1-t)Y^*((\mu,\varsigma),\ \mathrm{q})+(1-\tau)(1-s)Y^*((\mu,\nu),\ \mathrm{q}), \end{gathered}$$

Then, via Equations (4), (6) and (22), we obtain

$$\begin{gathered} Y_{\mathrm{q}}((\tau\mu+(1-\tau)\sigma,\ s\varsigma+(1-s)\nu)) \\ =[Y_*((\tau\mu+(1-\tau)\sigma,\ s\varsigma+(1-s)\nu),\ \mathrm{q}),\ Y^*((\tau\mu+(1-\tau)\sigma,\ s\varsigma+(1-s)\nu),\ \mathrm{q})], \\ \supseteq_I \tau s[Y_*((\mu,\varsigma),\ \mathrm{q}),\ Y^*((\mu,\varsigma),\ \mathrm{q})]+t(1-s)[Y_*((\mu,\nu),\ \mathrm{q}),\ Y^*((\mu,\nu),\ \mathrm{q})] \\ +s(1-\tau)[Y_*((\mu,\varsigma),\ \mathrm{q}),\ Y^*((\mu,\varsigma),\ \mathrm{q})]+(1-\tau)(1-s)[Y_*((\mu,\nu),\ \mathrm{q}),\ Y^*((\mu,\nu),\ \mathrm{q})]. \end{gathered}$$

That is,

$$\begin{gathered} \widetilde{Y}(\tau\mu+(1-\tau)\sigma,\ s\varsigma+(1-s)\nu) \\ \supseteq_{\mathbb{F}} \tau s\odot\widetilde{Y}(\mu,\varsigma)\oplus\tau(1-s)\odot\widetilde{Y}(\mu,\nu)\oplus(1-\tau)s\odot\widetilde{Y}(\sigma,\varsigma)\oplus(1-\tau)(1-s)\odot\widetilde{Y}(\sigma,\nu), \end{gathered}$$

Hence, $\widetilde{Y}$ is a coordinated UD-convex FN-V-M on Δ.

Conversely, let $\widetilde{Y}$ be a coordinated UD-convex FN-V-M on Δ. Then, for all $(\mu,\ \sigma)$, $(\varsigma,\nu)\in\Delta$, τ and $s\in[0,\ 1]$, we obtain

$$\begin{gathered} \widetilde{Y}(\tau\mu+(1-\tau)\sigma,\ s\varsigma+(1-s)\nu) \\ \supseteq_{\mathbb{F}} \tau s\odot\widetilde{Y}(\mu,\varsigma)\oplus\tau(1-s)\odot\widetilde{Y}(\mu,\nu)\oplus(1-\tau)s\odot\widetilde{Y}(\sigma,\varsigma)\oplus(1-\tau)(1-s)\odot\widetilde{Y}(\sigma,\nu) \end{gathered}$$

Therefore, from Equation (22), for each $\mathrm{q}\in[0,\ 1]$, we obtain

$$\begin{gathered} Y_{\mathrm{q}}((\tau\mu+(1-\tau)\sigma,\ s\varsigma+(1-s)\nu)) \\ =[Y_*((\tau\mu+(1-\tau)\sigma,\ s\varsigma+(1-s)\nu),\ \mathrm{q}),\ Y^*((\tau\mu+(1-\tau)\sigma,\ s\varsigma+(1-s)\nu),\ \mathrm{q})]. \end{gathered}$$

Again, via Equation (22), we obtain

$$\begin{gathered} \tau sY_{\mathrm{q}}(\mu,\varsigma)+\tau(1-s)Y_{\mathrm{q}}(\mu,\nu)+(1-\tau)sY_{\mathrm{q}}(\sigma,\varsigma)+(1-\tau)(1-s)Y_{\mathrm{q}}(\sigma,\nu) \\ =\tau s[Y_*((\mu,\varsigma),\ \mathrm{q}),\ Y^*((\mu,\varsigma),\ \mathrm{q})]+t(1-s)[Y_*((\mu,\nu),\ \mathrm{q}),\ Y^*((\mu,\nu),\ \mathrm{q})] \\ +s(1-\tau)[Y_*((\mu,\varsigma),\ \mathrm{q}),\ Y^*((\mu,\varsigma),\ \mathrm{q})]+(1-\tau)(1-s)[Y_*((\mu,\nu),\ \mathrm{q}),\ Y^*((\mu,\nu),\ \mathrm{q})], \end{gathered}$$

for all $\sigma,\omega\in\Delta$ and $\tau\in[0,\ 1]$. Then, via the coordinated UD-convexity of $\widetilde{Y}$, for all $\sigma,\omega\in\Delta$ and $\tau\in[0,\ 1]$, we obtain

$$\begin{gathered} Y_*((\tau\mu+(1-\tau)\sigma,\ s\varsigma+(1-s)\nu),\ \mathrm{q}) \\ \leq \tau sY_*(\mu,\varsigma)+\tau(1-s)Y_*(\mu,\nu)+(1-\tau)sY_*(\sigma,\varsigma)+(1-\tau)(1-s)Y_*(\sigma,\nu), \end{gathered}$$

and

$$\begin{gathered} Y^*((\tau\mu+(1-\tau)\sigma,\ s\varsigma+(1-s)\nu),\ \mathrm{q}) \\ \geq \tau sY^*(\mu,\varsigma)+\tau(1-s)Y^*(\mu,\nu)+(1-\tau)sY^*(\sigma,\varsigma)+(1-\tau)(1-s)Y^*(\sigma,\nu), \end{gathered}$$

for each $\mathrm{q}\in[0,\ 1]$. Hence, the result follows. □

Example 1. *We consider the FN-V-Ms* $\widetilde{Y}:[0,\ 1]\times[0,\ 1]\to\mathbb{E}_0$ *defined as*

$$\widetilde{Y}(\sigma)(m)=\begin{cases} \frac{m-\sigma\omega}{5-\sigma\omega} & m\in[\sigma\omega,\ 5] \\ \frac{(6+e^{\sigma})(6+e^{\omega})-m}{(6+e^{\sigma})(6+e^{\omega})-5} & m\in\left(5,\ (6+e^{\sigma})(6+e^{\omega})\right] \\ 0 & otherwise, \end{cases} \tag{23}$$

and then, for each $\mathrm{q} \in [0,\ 1]$, *we obtain* $Y_{\mathrm{q}}(\sigma,\omega) = [(1-\mathrm{q})\sigma\omega + 5\mathrm{q}, (1-\mathrm{q})(6+e^{\sigma})(6+e^{\omega}) + 5\mathrm{q}]$. *The end-point functions* $Y_*((\sigma,\omega),\mathrm{q})$ *and* $Y^*((\sigma,\omega),\mathrm{q})$ *are coordinated convex and concave functions for each* $\mathrm{q} \in [0,\ 1]$, *respectively. Hence,* $\widetilde{Y}(\sigma,\omega)$ *is an up and down coordinated convex FN-V-M.*

From Example 1, it can be easily seen that each coordinated UD-convex FN-V-M is not a UD-convex FN-V-M.

Corollary 1. *Let* $\widetilde{Y} : \Delta \to \mathbb{E}_0$ *be an FN-V-M on* Δ. *Then, from the* q*-levels, we obtain the collection of IVMs* $Y_{\mathrm{q}} : \Delta \to \mathbb{R}_I^+ \subset \mathbb{R}_I$ *given as*

$$Y_{\mathrm{q}}(\sigma,\omega) = [Y_*((\sigma,\omega),\mathrm{q}),\ Y^*((\sigma,\omega),\mathrm{q})], \tag{24}$$

for all $(\sigma,\omega) \in \Delta$ *and for all* $\mathrm{q} \in [0,\ 1]$. *Then,* $\widetilde{Y}$ *is a coordinated left-UD-convex (concave) FN-V-M on* Δ *if and only if for all* $\mathrm{q} \in [0,\ 1]$, $Y_*((\sigma,\omega),\ \mathrm{q})$ *and* $Y^*((\sigma,\omega),\ \mathrm{q})$ *are coordinated convex (concave) and affine functions on* Δ, *respectively.*

Corollary 2. *Let* $\widetilde{Y} : \Delta \to \mathbb{E}_0$ *be an FN-V-M on* Δ. *Then, from the* q*-levels, we obtain the collection of IVMs* $Y_{\mathrm{q}} : \Delta \to \mathbb{R}_I^+ \subset \mathbb{R}_I$ *given as*

$$Y_{\mathrm{q}}(\sigma,\omega) = [Y_*((\sigma,\omega),\mathrm{q}),\ Y^*((\sigma,\omega),\mathrm{q})], \tag{25}$$

for all $(\sigma,\omega) \in \Delta$ *and for all* $\mathrm{q} \in [0,\ 1]$. *Then,* $\widetilde{Y}$ *is a coordinated right-UD-convex (concave) FN-V-M on* Δ *if and only if for all* $\mathrm{q} \in [0,\ 1]$, $Y_*((\sigma,\omega),\ \mathrm{q})$ *and* $Y^*((\sigma,\omega),\ \mathrm{q})$ *are coordinated affine and convex (concave) functions on* Δ, *respectively.*

Theorem 8. *Let* Δ *be a coordinated convex set, and let* $\widetilde{Y} : \Delta \to \mathbb{E}_0$ *be an FN-V- M. Then, from the* q*-levels, we obtain the collection of IVMs* $Y_{\mathrm{q}} : \Delta \to \mathbb{R}_I^+ \subset \mathbb{R}_I$ *given as*

$$Y_{\mathrm{q}}(\sigma,\omega) = [Y_*((\sigma,\omega),\mathrm{q}),\ Y^*((\sigma,\omega),\mathrm{q})], \tag{26}$$

for all $(\sigma,\omega) \in \Delta$ *and for all* $\mathrm{q} \in [0,\ 1]$. *Then,* $\widetilde{Y}$ *is a coordinated UD-concave FN-V-M on* Δ *if and only if for all* $\mathrm{q} \in [0,\ 1]$, $Y_*((\sigma,\omega),\ \mathrm{q})$ *and* $Y^*((\sigma,\omega),\ \mathrm{q})$ *are coordinated concave and convex functions, respectively.*

Proof. The demonstration of the proof of Theorem 8 is similar to the demonstration of the proof of Theorem 7. □

Example 2. *We consider the FN-V-Ms* $\widetilde{Y} : [0,\ 1] \times [0,\ 1] \to \mathbb{E}_0$ *defined as*

$$\widetilde{Y}(\sigma)(m) = \begin{cases} \frac{m-\left(6-e^{\sigma}\right)(6-e^{\omega})}{\left(6-e^{\sigma}\right)(6-e^{\omega})-25}, & m \in \left[\left(6-e^{\sigma}\right)(6-e^{\omega}),\ 25\right] \\ \frac{35\sigma\omega-m}{35\sigma\omega-25}, & m \in (25,\ 35\sigma\omega] \\ 0, & otherwise. \end{cases} \tag{27}$$

Then, for each $\mathrm{q} \in [0,1]$, we obtain $Y_{\mathrm{q}}(\sigma,\omega) = [(1-\mathrm{q})(6-e^{\sigma})(6-e^{\omega}) + 25\mathrm{q}, 35(1-\mathrm{q})\sigma\omega + 25\mathrm{q}]$. The end-point functions $Y_*((\sigma,\omega),\mathrm{q})$ and $Y^*((\sigma,\omega),\mathrm{q})$ are coordinated concave and convex functions for each $\mathrm{q} \in [0,1]$. Hence, $\widetilde{Y}(\sigma,\omega)$ is a coordinated up and down concave FN-V-M.

In the next results, to avoid confusion, we will not include the symbols (R), (IR), (FR), (ID), and (FD) before the integral sign.

Theorem 9. *Let $\widetilde{Y} : \Delta \to \mathbb{E}_0$ be a coordinated UD-convex FN-V-M on Δ. Then, from the* q*-levels, we obtain the collection of IVMs $Y_{\mathfrak{q}} : \Delta \to \mathbb{R}_I^+$ given as $Y_{\mathfrak{q}}(\sigma,\omega) = [Y_*((\sigma,\omega),\mathfrak{q}),\ Y^*((\sigma,\omega),\mathfrak{q})]$ for all $(\sigma,\omega) \in \Delta$ and for all $\mathfrak{q} \in [0,\ 1]$. Then, the following inequality holds:*

$$\begin{aligned} \widetilde{Y}\left(\tfrac{\mu+\sigma}{2},\ \tfrac{\varsigma+\nu}{2}\right) &\supseteq_{\mathbb{F}} \tfrac{1}{2} \odot \left[\tfrac{1}{\sigma-\mu} \odot \int_\mu^\sigma \widetilde{Y}\left(\sigma,\ \tfrac{\varsigma+\nu}{2}\right)d\sigma \oplus \tfrac{1}{\nu-\varsigma} \odot \int_\varsigma^\nu \widetilde{Y}\left(\tfrac{\mu+\sigma}{2}, \omega\right)d\omega\right] \\ &\supseteq_{\mathbb{F}} \tfrac{1}{(\sigma-\mu)(\nu-\varsigma)} \odot \int_\mu^\sigma \int_\varsigma^\nu \widetilde{Y}(\sigma,\omega)d\omega d\sigma \\ &\supseteq_{\mathbb{F}} \tfrac{1}{4(\sigma-\mu)} \odot \left[\int_\mu^\sigma \widetilde{Y}(\sigma,\varsigma)d\sigma \oplus \int_\mu^\sigma \widetilde{Y}(\sigma,\nu)d\sigma\right] \oplus \tfrac{1}{4(\nu-\varsigma)} \odot \left[\int_\varsigma^\nu \widetilde{Y}(\mu,\omega)d\omega \oplus \int_\varsigma^\nu \widetilde{Y}(\sigma,\omega)d\omega\right] \\ &\supseteq_{\mathbb{F}} \tfrac{\widetilde{Y}(\mu,\varsigma) \oplus \widetilde{Y}(\sigma,\varsigma) \oplus \widetilde{Y}(\mu,\nu) \oplus \widetilde{Y}(\sigma,\nu)}{4}. \end{aligned} \tag{28}$$

If $Y(\sigma)$ is a concave FN-V-M, then

$$\begin{aligned} \widetilde{Y}\left(\tfrac{\mu+\sigma}{2},\ \tfrac{\varsigma+\nu}{2}\right) &\subseteq_{\mathbb{F}} \tfrac{1}{2} \left[\tfrac{1}{\sigma-\mu} \odot \int_\mu^\sigma \widetilde{Y}\left(\sigma,\ \tfrac{\varsigma+\nu}{2}\right)d\sigma \oplus \tfrac{1}{\nu-\varsigma} \odot \int_\varsigma^\nu \widetilde{Y}\left(\tfrac{\mu+\sigma}{2}, \omega\right)d\omega\right] \\ &\subseteq_{\mathbb{F}} \tfrac{1}{(\sigma-\mu)(\nu-\varsigma)} \odot \int_\mu^\sigma \int_\varsigma^\nu \widetilde{Y}(\sigma,\omega)d\omega d\sigma \\ &\subseteq_{\mathbb{F}} \tfrac{1}{4(\sigma-\mu)} \odot \left[\int_\mu^\sigma \widetilde{Y}(\sigma,\varsigma)d\sigma \oplus \int_\mu^\sigma \widetilde{Y}(\sigma,\nu)d\sigma\right] \oplus \tfrac{1}{4(\nu-\varsigma)} \odot \left[\int_\varsigma^\nu \widetilde{Y}(\mu,\omega)d\omega \oplus \int_\varsigma^\nu \widetilde{Y}(\sigma,\omega)d\omega\right] \\ &\subseteq_{\mathbb{F}} \tfrac{\widetilde{Y}(\mu,\varsigma) \oplus \widetilde{Y}(\sigma,\varsigma) \oplus \widetilde{Y}(\mu,\nu) \oplus \widetilde{Y}(\sigma,\nu)}{4} \end{aligned} \tag{29}$$

Proof. Let $\widetilde{Y} : [\mu,\ \sigma] \to \mathbb{E}_0$ be a coordinated UD-convex FN-V-M. Then, via hypothesis, we obtain

$$4 \odot \widetilde{Y}\left(\frac{\mu+\sigma}{2}, \frac{\varsigma+\nu}{2}\right) \supseteq_{\mathbb{F}} \widetilde{Y}(\tau\mu + (1-\tau)\sigma,\ \tau\varsigma + (1-\tau)\nu) \oplus \widetilde{Y}((1-\tau)\mu + \tau\sigma,\ (1-\tau)\varsigma + \tau\nu).$$

By using Theorem 7, for every $\mathfrak{q} \in [0,\ 1]$, we obtain

$$\begin{gathered} 4Y_*\left(\left(\tfrac{\mu+\sigma}{2}, \tfrac{\varsigma+\nu}{2}\right), \mathfrak{q}\right) \\ \le Y_*((\tau\mu + (1-\tau)\sigma,\ \tau\varsigma + (1-\tau)\nu),\ \mathfrak{q}) + Y_*(((1-\tau)\mu + \tau\sigma,\ (1-\tau)\varsigma + \tau\nu),\ \mathfrak{q}), \\ 4Y^*\left(\left(\tfrac{\mu+\sigma}{2}, \tfrac{\varsigma+\nu}{2}\right), \mathfrak{q}\right) \\ \ge Y^*((\tau\mu + (1-\tau)\sigma,\ \tau\varsigma + (1-\tau)\nu),\ \mathfrak{q}) + Y^*(((1-\tau)\mu + \tau\sigma,\ (1-\tau)\varsigma + \tau\nu), \mathfrak{q}). \end{gathered}$$

By using Lemma 1, we obtain

$$\begin{aligned} 2Y_*\left(\left(\sigma, \tfrac{\varsigma+\nu}{2}\right), \mathfrak{q}\right) &\le Y_*((\sigma, \tau\varsigma + (1-\tau)\nu),\ \mathfrak{q}) + Y_*((\sigma, (1-\tau)\varsigma + \tau\nu),\ \mathfrak{q}), \\ 2Y^*\left(\left(\sigma, \tfrac{\varsigma+\nu}{2}\right), \mathfrak{q}\right) &\ge Y^*((\sigma, \tau\varsigma + (1-\tau)\nu),\ \mathfrak{q}) + Y^*((\sigma, (1-\tau)\varsigma + \tau\nu), \mathfrak{q}), \end{aligned} \tag{30}$$

and

$$\begin{aligned} 2Y_*\left(\left(\tfrac{\mu+\sigma}{2}, \omega\right), \mathfrak{q}\right) &\le Y_*((\tau\mu + (1-\tau)\sigma,\ \omega),\ \mathfrak{q}) + Y_*(((1-\tau)\mu + t\sigma,\ \omega),\ \mathfrak{q}), \\ 2Y^*\left(\left(\tfrac{\mu+\sigma}{2}, \omega\right), \mathfrak{q}\right) &\ge Y^*((\tau\mu + (1-\tau)\sigma,\ \omega),\ \mathfrak{q}) + Y^*(((1-\tau)\mu + t\sigma,\ \omega), \mathfrak{q}). \end{aligned} \tag{31}$$

From Equations (30) and (31), we obtain

$$\begin{gathered} 2\left[Y_*\left(\left(\sigma, \tfrac{\varsigma+\nu}{2}\right), \mathfrak{q}\right), Y^*\left(\left(\sigma, \tfrac{\varsigma+\nu}{2}\right), \mathfrak{q}\right)\right] \\ \supseteq_I [Y_*((\sigma, \tau\varsigma + (1-\tau)\nu),\ \mathfrak{q}), Y^*((\sigma, \tau\varsigma + (1-\tau)\nu),\ \mathfrak{q})] \\ +[Y_*((\sigma, (1-\tau)\varsigma + \tau\nu),\ \mathfrak{q}), Y^*((\sigma, (1-\tau)\varsigma + \tau\nu), \mathfrak{q})], \end{gathered}$$

and

$$\begin{aligned}&2\left[Y_*\left(\left(\tfrac{\mu+\sigma}{2},\omega\right),\mathfrak{q}\right),Y^*\left(\left(\tfrac{\mu+\sigma}{2},\omega\right),\mathfrak{q}\right)\right]\\ &\supseteq_I [Y_*((\tau\mu+(1-\tau)\sigma,\ \omega),\ \mathfrak{q}),Y^*((\tau\mu+(1-\tau)\sigma,\ \omega),\ \mathfrak{q})]\\ &+[Y_*((\tau\mu+(1-\tau)\sigma,\ \omega),\ \mathfrak{q}),Y^*((\tau\mu+(1-\tau)\sigma,\ \omega),\mathfrak{q})],\end{aligned}$$

It follows that

$$Y_{\mathfrak{q}}\left(\sigma,\frac{\varsigma+\nu}{2}\right)\supseteq_I Y_{\mathfrak{q}}(\sigma,\tau\varsigma+(1-\tau)\nu)+Y_{\mathfrak{q}}(\sigma,(1-\tau)\varsigma+\tau\nu) \tag{32}$$

and

$$Y_{\mathfrak{q}}\left(\frac{\mu+\sigma}{2},\omega\right)\supseteq_I Y_{\mathfrak{q}}(\tau\mu+(1-\tau)\sigma,\ \omega)+Y_{\mathfrak{q}}(\tau\mu+(1-\tau)\sigma,\ \omega) \tag{33}$$

Since $Y_{\mathfrak{q}}(\sigma,.)$ and $Y_{\mathfrak{q}}(.,\omega)$ are both coordinated UD-convex-IVMs, from Theorem 7 and inequality Equation (6), for every $\mathfrak{q}\in[0,\ 1]$, and inequality Equations (32) and (33), we then obtain

$$Y_{\mathfrak{q}}\left(\sigma,\frac{\varsigma+\nu}{2}\right)\supseteq_I \frac{1}{\nu-\varsigma}\int_{\varsigma}^{\nu}Y_{\mathfrak{q}}(\sigma,\omega)d\omega\supseteq_I\frac{Y_{\mathfrak{q}}(\sigma,\varsigma)+Y_{\mathfrak{q}}(\sigma,\nu)}{2}. \tag{34}$$

and

$$Y_{\mathfrak{q}}\left(\frac{\mu+\sigma}{2},\omega\right)\supseteq_I \frac{1}{\sigma-\mu}\int_{\mu}^{\sigma}Y_{\mathfrak{q}}(\sigma,\omega)d\sigma\supseteq_I\frac{Y_{\mathfrak{q}}(\mu,\omega)+Y_{\mathfrak{q}}(\sigma,\omega)}{2}. \tag{35}$$

Dividing double inequality Equation (34) by $(\sigma-\mu)$ and integrating with respect to σ on $[\mu,\ \sigma]$, we obtain

$$\frac{1}{\sigma-\mu}\int_{\mu}^{\sigma}Y_{\mathfrak{q}}\left(\sigma,\frac{\varsigma+\nu}{2}\right)d\sigma\supseteq_I\frac{1}{(\sigma-\mu)(\nu-\varsigma)}\int_{\mu}^{\sigma}\int_{\varsigma}^{\nu}Y_{\mathfrak{q}}(\sigma,\omega)d\omega d\sigma\supseteq_I\frac{1}{2(\sigma-\mu)}\left[\int_{\mu}^{\sigma}Y_{\mathfrak{q}}(\sigma,\varsigma)d\sigma+\int_{\mu}^{\sigma}Y_{\mathfrak{q}}(\sigma,\nu)d\sigma\right] \tag{36}$$

Similarly, dividing double inequality Equation (35) by $(\nu-\varsigma)$ and integrating with respect to σ on $[\varsigma,\ \nu]$, we obtain

$$\frac{1}{\nu-\varsigma}\int_{\varsigma}^{\nu}Y_{\mathfrak{q}}\left(\frac{\mu+\sigma}{2},\omega\right)d\omega\supseteq_I\frac{1}{(\sigma-\mu)(\nu-\varsigma)}\int_{\mu}^{\sigma}\int_{\varsigma}^{\nu}Y_{\mathfrak{q}}(\sigma,\omega)d\omega d\sigma\supseteq_I\frac{1}{2(\nu-\varsigma)}\left[\int_{\varsigma}^{\nu}Y_{\mathfrak{q}}(\mu,\omega)d\omega+\int_{\varsigma}^{\nu}Y_{\mathfrak{q}}(\sigma,\omega)d\omega\right] \tag{37}$$

By adding Equations (36) and (37), we obtain

$$\begin{aligned}&\tfrac{1}{2}\left[\tfrac{1}{\sigma-\mu}\int_{\mu}^{\sigma}Y_{\mathfrak{q}}\left(\sigma,\tfrac{\varsigma+\nu}{2}\right)d\sigma+\tfrac{1}{\nu-\varsigma}\int_{\varsigma}^{\nu}Y_{\mathfrak{q}}\left(\tfrac{\mu+\sigma}{2},\omega\right)d\omega\right]\supseteq_I\tfrac{1}{(\sigma-\mu)(\nu-\varsigma)}\int_{\mu}^{\sigma}\int_{\varsigma}^{\nu}Y_{\mathfrak{q}}(\sigma,\omega)d\omega d\sigma\\ &\supseteq_I\tfrac{1}{4(\sigma-\mu)}\left[\int_{\mu}^{\sigma}Y_{\mathfrak{q}}(\sigma,\varsigma)d\sigma+\int_{\mu}^{\sigma}Y_{\mathfrak{q}}(\sigma,\nu)d\sigma\right]+\tfrac{1}{4(\nu-\varsigma)}\left[\int_{\varsigma}^{\nu}Y_{\mathfrak{q}}(\mu,\omega)d\omega+\int_{\varsigma}^{d}Y_{\mathfrak{q}}(\sigma,\omega)d\omega\right]\end{aligned} \tag{38}$$

Since $\widetilde{Y}$ is an FN-V-M, via inequality Equation (38), we then obtain

$$\begin{aligned}&\tfrac{1}{2}\left[\tfrac{1}{\sigma-\mu}\odot\int_{\mu}^{\sigma}\widetilde{Y}\left(\sigma,\tfrac{\varsigma+\nu}{2}\right)d\sigma\oplus\tfrac{1}{\nu-\varsigma}\odot\int_{\varsigma}^{\nu}\widetilde{Y}\left(\tfrac{\mu+\sigma}{2},\omega\right)d\omega\right]\supseteq_{\mathbb{F}}\tfrac{1}{(\sigma-\mu)(\nu-\varsigma)}\odot\int_{\mu}^{\sigma}\int_{\varsigma}^{\nu}\widetilde{Y}(\sigma,\omega)d\omega d\sigma\\ &\supseteq_{\mathbb{F}}\tfrac{1}{4(\sigma-\mu)}\odot\left[\int_{\mu}^{\sigma}\widetilde{Y}(\sigma,\varsigma)d\sigma\oplus\int_{\mu}^{\sigma}\widetilde{Y}(\sigma,\nu)d\sigma\right]\oplus\tfrac{1}{4(\nu-\varsigma)}\odot\left[\int_{\varsigma}^{\nu}\widetilde{Y}(\mu,\omega)d\omega\oplus\int_{\varsigma}^{\nu}\widetilde{Y}(\sigma,\omega)d\omega\right]\end{aligned} \tag{39}$$

From Theorem 7 and the left side of inequality Equation (16), for each $\mathfrak{q}\in[0,\ 1]$, we obtain

$$Y_{\mathfrak{q}}\left(\frac{\mu+\sigma}{2},\ \frac{\varsigma+\nu}{2}\right)\supseteq_I\frac{1}{\sigma-\mu}\int_{\mu}^{\sigma}Y_{\mathfrak{q}}\left(\sigma,\frac{\varsigma+\nu}{2}\right)d\sigma, \tag{40}$$

$$Y_{\mathfrak{q}}\left(\frac{\mu+\sigma}{2},\ \frac{\varsigma+\nu}{2}\right)\supseteq_I\frac{1}{\nu-\varsigma}\int_{\varsigma}^{\nu}Y_{\mathfrak{q}}\left(\frac{\mu+\sigma}{2},\omega\right)d\omega. \tag{41}$$

Adding inequality Equation (40) and inequality Equation (41), we obtain

$$\Upsilon_{\mathrm{q}}\left(\frac{\mu+\sigma}{2}, \frac{\varsigma+\nu}{2}\right) \supseteq_I \frac{1}{2}\left[\frac{1}{\sigma-\mu}\int_{\mu}^{\sigma} \Upsilon_{\mathrm{q}}\left(\sigma, \frac{\varsigma+\nu}{2}\right)d\sigma + \frac{1}{\nu-\varsigma}\int_{\varsigma}^{\nu} \Upsilon_{\mathrm{q}}\left(\frac{\mu+\sigma}{2}, \omega\right)d\omega\right].$$

Since $\widetilde{\Upsilon}$ is an FN-V-M, it follows that

$$\widetilde{\Upsilon}\left(\frac{\mu+\sigma}{2}, \frac{\varsigma+\nu}{2}\right) \supseteq_{\mathbb{F}} \frac{1}{2}\left[\frac{1}{\sigma-\mu}\odot\int_{\mu}^{\sigma} \widetilde{\Upsilon}\left(\sigma, \frac{\varsigma+\nu}{2}\right)d\sigma \oplus \frac{1}{\nu-\varsigma}\odot\int_{\varsigma}^{\nu} \widetilde{\Upsilon}\left(\frac{\mu+\sigma}{2}, \omega\right)d\omega\right] \quad (42)$$

Now, from Theorem 7 and the right side of inequality Equation (16), for every $\mathrm{q} \in [0, 1]$, we obtain

$$\frac{1}{\sigma-\mu}\int_{\mu}^{\sigma} \Upsilon_{\mathrm{q}}(\sigma,\varsigma)d\sigma \supseteq_I \frac{\Upsilon_{\mathrm{q}}(\mu,\varsigma)+\Upsilon_{\mathrm{q}}(\sigma,\varsigma)}{2} \quad (43)$$

$$\frac{1}{\sigma-\mu}\int_{\mu}^{\sigma} \Upsilon_{\mathrm{q}}(\sigma,\nu)d\sigma \supseteq_I \frac{\Upsilon_{\mathrm{q}}(\mu,\nu)+\Upsilon_{\mathrm{q}}(\sigma,\nu)}{2} \quad (44)$$

$$\frac{1}{\nu-\varsigma}\int_{\varsigma}^{\nu} \Upsilon_{\mathrm{q}}(\mu,\omega)d\omega \supseteq_I \frac{\Upsilon_{\mathrm{q}}(\mu,\nu)+\Upsilon_{\mathrm{q}}(\mu,\varsigma)}{2} \quad (45)$$

$$\frac{1}{\nu-\varsigma}\int_{\varsigma}^{\nu} \Upsilon_{\mathrm{q}}(\sigma,\omega)d\omega \supseteq_I \frac{\Upsilon_{\mathrm{q}}(\sigma,\nu)+\Upsilon_{\mathrm{q}}(\sigma,\varsigma)}{2} \quad (46)$$

By adding inequalities Equations (43)–(46), we obtain

$$\begin{aligned}\frac{1}{4(\sigma-\mu)}\left[\int_{\mu}^{\sigma} \Upsilon_{\mathrm{q}}(\sigma,\varsigma)d\sigma + \int_{\mu}^{\sigma} \Upsilon_{\mathrm{q}}(\sigma,\nu)d\sigma\right] + \frac{1}{4(\nu-\varsigma)}\left[\int_{\varsigma}^{\nu} \Upsilon_{\mathrm{q}}(\mu,\omega)d\omega + \int_{\varsigma}^{\nu} \Upsilon_{\mathrm{q}}(\sigma,\omega)d\omega\right] \\ \supseteq_I \frac{\Upsilon_{\mathrm{q}}(\mu,\varsigma)+\Upsilon_{\mathrm{q}}(\sigma,\varsigma)+\Upsilon_{\mathrm{q}}(\mu,\nu)+\Upsilon_{\mathrm{q}}(\sigma,\nu)}{4}\end{aligned}$$

Since Υ is an FN-V-M, it follows that

$$\begin{aligned}\frac{1}{4(\sigma-\mu)}\odot\left[\int_{\mu}^{\sigma} \widetilde{\Upsilon}(\sigma,\varsigma)d\sigma \oplus \int_{\mu}^{\sigma} \widetilde{\Upsilon}(\sigma,\nu)d\sigma\right] \oplus \frac{1}{4(\nu-\varsigma)}\odot\left[\int_{\varsigma}^{\nu} \widetilde{\Upsilon}(\mu,\omega)d\omega \oplus \int_{\varsigma}^{\nu} \widetilde{\Upsilon}(\sigma,\omega)d\omega\right] \\ \supseteq_{\mathbb{F}} \frac{\widetilde{\Upsilon}(\mu,\varsigma)\oplus\widetilde{\Upsilon}(\sigma,\varsigma)\oplus\widetilde{\Upsilon}(\mu,\nu)\oplus\widetilde{\Upsilon}(\sigma,\nu)}{4}\end{aligned} \quad (47)$$

By combining inequalities Equations (41), (42), and (47), we obtain the desired result. □

Remark 2. *From inequality Equation (28), the following exceptional results can be acquired:*

Let $\Upsilon_*((\sigma,\omega),\mathrm{q}) \neq \Upsilon^*((\sigma,\omega),\mathrm{q})$ with $\mathrm{q} = 1$. Then, we can derive the following inclusion (see [61]*):*

$$\begin{aligned}\Upsilon\left(\frac{\mu+\sigma}{2}, \frac{\varsigma+\nu}{2}\right) &\supseteq \frac{1}{2}\left[\frac{1}{\sigma-\mu}\int_{\mu}^{\sigma} \Upsilon\left(\sigma, \frac{\varsigma+\nu}{2}\right)d\sigma + \frac{1}{\nu-\varsigma}\int_{\varsigma}^{\nu} \Upsilon\left(\frac{\mu+\sigma}{2}, \omega\right)d\omega\right] \\ &\supseteq \frac{1}{(\sigma-\mu)(\nu-\varsigma)}\int_{\mu}^{\sigma}\int_{\varsigma}^{\nu} \Upsilon(\sigma,\omega)d\omega d\sigma \\ &\supseteq \frac{1}{4(\sigma-\mu)}\left[\int_{\mu}^{\sigma} \Upsilon(\sigma,\varsigma)d\sigma + \int_{\mu}^{\sigma} \Upsilon(\sigma,\nu)d\sigma\right] + \frac{1}{4(\nu-\varsigma)}\left[\int_{\varsigma}^{\nu} \Upsilon(\mu,\omega)d\omega + \int_{\varsigma}^{\nu} \Upsilon(\sigma,\omega)d\omega\right] \\ &\supseteq \frac{\Upsilon(\mu,\varsigma)+\Upsilon(\sigma,\varsigma)+\Upsilon(\mu,\nu)+\Upsilon(\sigma,\nu)}{4}.\end{aligned} \quad (48)$$

Let $\Upsilon_*((\sigma,\omega),\mathrm{q}) = \Upsilon^*((\sigma,\omega),\mathrm{q})$ with $\mathrm{q} = 1$. Then, we can derive the following inclusion (see [90]*):*

$$\begin{aligned}\Upsilon\left(\frac{\mu+\sigma}{2}, \frac{\varsigma+\nu}{2}\right) &\leq \frac{1}{2}\left[\frac{1}{\sigma-\mu}\int_{\mu}^{\sigma} \Upsilon\left(\sigma, \frac{\varsigma+\nu}{2}\right)d\sigma + \frac{1}{\nu-\varsigma}\int_{\varsigma}^{\nu} \Upsilon\left(\frac{\mu+\sigma}{2}, \omega\right)d\omega\right] \\ &\leq \frac{1}{(\sigma-\mu)(\nu-\varsigma)}\int_{\mu}^{\sigma}\int_{\varsigma}^{\nu} \Upsilon(\sigma,\omega)d\omega d\sigma \\ &\leq \frac{1}{4(\sigma-\mu)}\left[\int_{\mu}^{\sigma} \Upsilon(\sigma,\varsigma)d\sigma + \int_{\mu}^{\sigma} \Upsilon(\sigma,\nu)d\sigma\right] + \frac{1}{4(\nu-\varsigma)}\left[\int_{\varsigma}^{\nu} \Upsilon(\mu,\omega)d\omega + \int_{\varsigma}^{\nu} \Upsilon(\sigma,\omega)d\omega\right] \\ &\leq \frac{\Upsilon(\mu,\varsigma)+\Upsilon(\sigma,\varsigma)+\Upsilon(\mu,\nu)+\Upsilon(\sigma,\nu)}{4}.\end{aligned} \quad (49)$$

Example 3. *We consider the FN-V-Ms* $\widetilde{Y} : [0,\ 2] \times [0,\ 2] \to \mathbb{E}_0$ *defined as*

$$Y(\sigma,\omega)(m) = \begin{cases} \frac{m-\sigma\omega}{5-\sigma\omega},\ m \in [\sigma\omega,\ 5] \\ \frac{(2+\sqrt{\sigma})(2+\sqrt{\omega})-m}{(2+\sqrt{\sigma})(2+\sqrt{\omega})-5},\ m \in \left(5,\ \left(2+\sqrt{\sigma}\right)(2+\sqrt{\omega})\right] \\ 0,\ otherwise, \end{cases} \tag{50}$$

and then, for each $\mathfrak{q} \in [0,\ 1]$, *we obtain* $Y_{\mathfrak{q}}(\sigma,\omega) = \left[(1-\mathfrak{q})\sigma\omega + 5\mathfrak{q}, (1-\mathfrak{q})\left(2+\sqrt{\sigma}\right)(2+\sqrt{\omega}) + 5\mathfrak{q}\right]$. *The end-point functions* $Y_*((\sigma,\omega),\mathfrak{q})$, $Y^*((\sigma,\omega),\mathfrak{q})$ *are coordinated concave functions for each* $\mathfrak{q} \in [0,\ 1]$. *Hence,* $\widetilde{Y}(\sigma,\omega)$ *is a coordinated concave FN-V-M.*

$$Y_{\mathfrak{q}}\left(\frac{\mu+\sigma}{2},\ \frac{\varsigma+\nu}{2}\right) = [1+4\mathfrak{q}, 9-4\mathfrak{q}]$$

$$\begin{aligned} &\tfrac{1}{2}\left[\tfrac{1}{\sigma-\mu}\int_\mu^\sigma Y_{\mathfrak{q}}\left(\sigma, \tfrac{\varsigma+\nu}{2}\right)d\sigma + \tfrac{1}{\nu-\varsigma}\int_\varsigma^\nu Y_{\mathfrak{q}}\left(\tfrac{\mu+\sigma}{2}, \omega\right)d\omega\right] \\ &= \left[1+4\mathfrak{q}, \tfrac{1}{3}\left(\left(9+2\sqrt{2}\right)\mathfrak{q} - 2\sqrt{2}+6\right)\right], \end{aligned}$$

$$\begin{aligned} &\tfrac{1}{(\sigma-\mu)(\nu-\varsigma)}\int_\mu^\sigma\int_\varsigma^\nu Y_{\mathfrak{q}}(\sigma,\omega)d\omega d\sigma = \left[1+4\mathfrak{q}, \tfrac{1}{9}\left(\left(1+24\sqrt{2}\right)\mathfrak{q} - 24\sqrt{2}+44\right)\right] \\ &\tfrac{1}{4(\sigma-\mu)}\left[\int_\mu^\sigma Y_{\mathfrak{q}}(\sigma,\varsigma)d\sigma + \int_\mu^\sigma Y_{\mathfrak{q}}(\sigma,\nu)d\sigma\right] + \tfrac{1}{4(\nu-\varsigma)}\left[\int_\varsigma^\nu Y_{\mathfrak{q}}(\mu,\omega)d\omega + \int_\varsigma^\nu Y_{\mathfrak{q}}(\sigma,\omega)d\omega\right], \\ &= \left[1+4\mathfrak{q}, \tfrac{8-5\sqrt{2}}{3}(1-\mathfrak{q}) + \tfrac{9+2\sqrt{2}}{3}\mathfrak{q} + \tfrac{6-2\sqrt{2}}{3}\right] \end{aligned}$$

$$\frac{Y_{\mathfrak{q}}(\mu,\varsigma)+Y_{\mathfrak{q}}(\sigma,\varsigma)+Y_{\mathfrak{q}}(\mu,\nu)+Y_{\mathfrak{q}}(\sigma,\nu)}{4} = \left[1+4\mathfrak{q}, \frac{(1-\mathfrak{q})\left(2-\sqrt{2}\right)^2 + 4(1-\mathfrak{q})\left(2-\sqrt{2}\right) + 4(1-\mathfrak{q}) + 20\mathfrak{q}}{4}\right]$$

That is

$$[1+4\mathfrak{q}, 9-4\mathfrak{q}] \supseteq_I \left[1+4\mathfrak{q}, \frac{1}{3}\left(\left(9+2\sqrt{2}\right)\mathfrak{q} - 2\sqrt{2}+6\right)\right]$$

$$\supseteq_I \left[1+4\mathfrak{q}, \frac{1}{9}\left(\left(1+24\sqrt{2}\right)\mathfrak{q} - 24\sqrt{2}+44\right)\right] \supseteq_I \left[1+4\mathfrak{q}, \frac{8-5\sqrt{2}}{3}(1-\mathfrak{q}) + \frac{9+2\sqrt{2}}{3}\mathfrak{q} + \frac{6-2\sqrt{2}}{3}\right]$$

$$\supseteq_I \left[1+4\mathfrak{q}, \frac{(1-\mathfrak{q})\left(2-\sqrt{2}\right)^2 + 4(1-\mathfrak{q})\left(2-\sqrt{2}\right) + 4(1-\mathfrak{q}) + 20\mathfrak{q}}{4}\right]$$

Hence, Theorem 9 has been verified.

We will now obtain some HH inequalities to produce coordinated UD-convex FN-V-Ms. These inequalities are refinements of some Pachpatte-type inequalities on coordinates.

Theorem 10. *Let* $\widetilde{Y}, \widetilde{\mathfrak{S}} : \Delta = [\mu,\ \sigma] \times [\varsigma,\ \nu] \subset \mathbb{R}^2 \to \mathbb{E}_0$ *be two coordinated UD-convex FN-V-Ms on* Δ, *whose* $\mathfrak{q}$*-levels* $Y_{\mathfrak{q}}$, $\mathfrak{S}_{\mathfrak{q}} : [\mu,\ \sigma] \times [\varsigma,\ \nu] \to \mathbb{R}_I^+$ *are defined as* $Y_{\mathfrak{q}}(\sigma,\omega) = [Y_*((\sigma,\omega),\mathfrak{q}),\ Y^*((\sigma,\omega),\mathfrak{q})]$ *and* $\mathfrak{S}_{\mathfrak{q}}(\sigma,\omega) = [\mathfrak{S}_*((\sigma,\omega),\mathfrak{q}),\ \mathfrak{S}^*((\sigma,\omega),\mathfrak{q})]$ *for all* $(\sigma,\omega) \in \Delta$ *and for all* $\mathfrak{q} \in [0,\ 1]$. *Then, the following inequality holds:*

$$\begin{aligned} &\tfrac{1}{(\sigma-\mu)(\nu-\varsigma)} \odot \int_\mu^\sigma\int_\varsigma^\nu \widetilde{Y}(\sigma,\omega) \otimes \widetilde{\mathfrak{S}}(\sigma,\omega)d\omega d\sigma \\ &\supseteq_{\mathbb{F}} \tfrac{1}{9} \odot \widetilde{\mathcal{P}}(\mu,\sigma,\varsigma,\nu) \oplus \tfrac{1}{18} \odot \widetilde{\mathcal{M}}(\mu,\sigma,\varsigma,\nu) \oplus \tfrac{1}{36} \odot \widetilde{\mathcal{N}}(\mu,\sigma,\varsigma,\nu). \end{aligned} \tag{51}$$

where

$$\widetilde{\mathcal{P}}(\mu,\sigma,\varsigma,\nu) = \widetilde{Y}(\mu,\varsigma) \otimes \widetilde{\mathfrak{S}}(\mu,\varsigma) \oplus \widetilde{Y}(\mu,\nu) \otimes \widetilde{\mathfrak{S}}(\mu,\nu) \oplus \widetilde{Y}(\sigma,\varsigma) \otimes \widetilde{\mathfrak{S}}(\sigma,\varsigma) \oplus \widetilde{Y}(\sigma,\nu) \otimes \widetilde{\mathfrak{S}}(\sigma,\nu),$$

$$\widetilde{\mathcal{M}}(\mu,\sigma,\varsigma,\nu) = \widetilde{Y}(\mu,\varsigma) \otimes \widetilde{\mathfrak{S}}(\mu,\nu) \oplus \widetilde{Y}(\mu,\nu) \otimes \widetilde{\mathfrak{S}}(\mu,\varsigma) \oplus \widetilde{Y}(\sigma,\varsigma) \otimes \widetilde{\mathfrak{S}}(\sigma,\nu) \oplus \widetilde{Y}(\sigma,\nu) \otimes \widetilde{\mathfrak{S}}(\sigma,\varsigma),$$

$$\oplus(\mu,\varsigma) \otimes \widetilde{\mathfrak{S}}(\sigma,\varsigma) \oplus \widetilde{Y}(\sigma,\nu) \otimes \widetilde{\mathfrak{S}}(\mu,\nu) \oplus \widetilde{Y}(\sigma,\varsigma) \otimes \widetilde{\mathfrak{S}}(\mu,\varsigma) \oplus \widetilde{Y}(\mu,\nu) \otimes \widetilde{\mathfrak{S}}(\sigma,\nu)$$

$$\widetilde{\mathcal{N}}(\mu,\sigma,\varsigma,\nu) = \widetilde{Y}(\mu,\varsigma) \otimes \widetilde{\mathfrak{S}}(\sigma,\nu) \oplus \widetilde{Y}(\sigma,\varsigma) \otimes \widetilde{\mathfrak{S}}(\mu,\nu) \oplus \widetilde{Y}(\sigma,\nu) \otimes \widetilde{\mathfrak{S}}(\mu,\varsigma) \oplus \widetilde{Y}(\sigma,\varsigma) \otimes \widetilde{\mathfrak{S}}(\mu,\nu)$$

and for each $\mathfrak{q} \in [0,\ 1]$, $\widetilde{P}(\mu,\sigma,\varsigma,\nu)$, $\widetilde{\mathcal{M}}(\mu,\sigma,\varsigma,\nu)$, *and* $\widetilde{\mathcal{N}}(\mu,\sigma,\varsigma,\nu)$ *are defined as follows:*

$$P_{\mathfrak{q}}(\mu,\sigma,\varsigma,\nu) = [P_*((\mu,\sigma,\varsigma,\nu),\ \mathfrak{q}),\ P^*((\mu,\sigma,\varsigma,\nu),\ \mathfrak{q})]$$

$$\mathcal{M}_{\mathfrak{q}}(\mu,\sigma,\varsigma,\nu) = [\mathcal{M}_*((\mu,\sigma,\varsigma,\nu),\ \mathfrak{q}),\ \mathcal{M}^*((\mu,\sigma,\varsigma,\nu),\ \mathfrak{q})]$$

$$\mathcal{N}_{\mathfrak{q}}(\mu,\sigma,\varsigma,\nu) = [\mathcal{N}_*((\mu,\sigma,\varsigma,\nu),\ \mathfrak{q}),\ \mathcal{N}^*((\mu,\sigma,\varsigma,\nu),\ \mathfrak{q})].$$

Proof. Let $\widetilde{Y}$ and $\widetilde{\mathfrak{S}}$ be two coordinated UD-convex FN-V- Ms on $[\mu,\ \sigma] \times [\varsigma,\ \nu]$. Then,

$$\begin{gathered}\widetilde{Y}(\tau\mu + (1-\tau)\sigma,\ s\varsigma + (1-s)\nu) \\ \supseteq_{\mathbb{F}} \tau s \odot \widetilde{Y}(\mu,\varsigma) \oplus \tau(1-s) \odot \widetilde{Y}(\mu,\nu) \oplus (1-\tau)s \odot \widetilde{Y}(\sigma,\varsigma) \oplus (1-\tau)(1-s) \odot \widetilde{Y}(\sigma,\nu),\end{gathered}$$

and

$$\begin{gathered}\widetilde{\mathfrak{S}}(\tau\mu + (1-\tau)\sigma,\ s\varsigma + (1-s)\nu) \\ \supseteq_{\mathbb{F}} \tau s \odot \widetilde{\mathfrak{S}}(\mu,\varsigma) \oplus \tau(1-s) \odot \widetilde{\mathfrak{S}}(\mu,\nu) \oplus (1-\tau)s \odot \widetilde{\mathfrak{S}}(\sigma,\varsigma) \oplus (1-\tau)(1-s) \odot \widetilde{\mathfrak{S}}(\sigma,\nu).\end{gathered}$$

Since $\widetilde{Y}$ and $\widetilde{\mathfrak{S}}$ are both coordinated UD-convex FN-V-Ms, then via Lemma 1, the following exist:

$$\widetilde{Y}_{\sigma} : [\varsigma,\nu] \to \mathbb{E}_0,\ \widetilde{Y}_{\sigma}(\omega) = \widetilde{Y}(\sigma,\omega),\ \widetilde{\mathfrak{S}}_{\sigma} : [\varsigma,\nu] \to \mathbb{E}_0,\ \widetilde{\mathfrak{S}}_{\sigma}(\omega) = \widetilde{\mathfrak{S}}(\sigma,\omega),$$

and

$$\widetilde{Y}_{\omega} : [\mu,\sigma] \to \mathbb{E}_0,\ \widetilde{Y}_{\omega}(\sigma) = \widetilde{Y}(\sigma,\omega),\ \widetilde{\mathfrak{S}}_{\omega} : [\mu,\sigma] \to \mathbb{E}_0,\ \widetilde{\mathfrak{S}}_{\omega}(\sigma) = \widetilde{\mathfrak{S}}(\sigma,\omega).$$

Since $\widetilde{Y}_{\sigma}$, $\widetilde{\mathfrak{S}}_{\sigma}$, $\widetilde{Y}_{\omega}$ and $\widetilde{\mathfrak{S}}_{\omega}$ are FN-V-Ms, then via inequality Equation (13), we obtain

$$\begin{gathered}\frac{1}{\sigma-\mu} \odot \int_{\mu}^{\sigma} \widetilde{Y}_{\omega}(\sigma) \otimes \widetilde{\mathfrak{S}}_{\omega}(\sigma) d\sigma \\ \supseteq_{\mathbb{F}} \frac{1}{3} \odot \left[\widetilde{Y}_{\omega}(\mu) \otimes \widetilde{\mathfrak{S}}_{\omega}(\mu) \oplus \widetilde{Y}_{\omega}(\sigma) \otimes \widetilde{\mathfrak{S}}_{\omega}(\sigma)\right] \oplus \frac{1}{6}\left[\widetilde{Y}_{\omega}(\mu) \otimes \widetilde{\mathfrak{S}}_{\omega}(\sigma) \oplus \widetilde{Y}_{\omega}(\sigma) \otimes \widetilde{\mathfrak{S}}_{\omega}(\mu)\right],\end{gathered}$$

and

$$\begin{gathered}\frac{1}{\nu-\varsigma} \int_{\varsigma}^{\nu} \widetilde{Y}_{\sigma}(\omega) \otimes \widetilde{\mathfrak{S}}_{\sigma}(\omega) d\omega \\ \supseteq_{\mathbb{F}} \frac{1}{3} \odot \left[\widetilde{Y}_{\sigma}(\varsigma) \otimes \widetilde{\mathfrak{S}}_{\sigma}(\varsigma) \oplus \widetilde{Y}_{\sigma}(\nu) \otimes \widetilde{\mathfrak{S}}_{\sigma}(\nu)\right] \oplus \frac{1}{6}\left[\widetilde{Y}_{\sigma}(\varsigma) \otimes \widetilde{\mathfrak{S}}_{\sigma}(\nu) \oplus \widetilde{Y}_{\sigma}(\varsigma) \otimes \widetilde{\mathfrak{S}}_{\sigma}(\nu)\right].\end{gathered}$$

For each $\mathfrak{q} \in [0,\ 1]$, we obtain

$$\begin{gathered}\frac{1}{\sigma-\mu} \int_{\mu}^{\sigma} Y_{\mathfrak{q}_{\omega}}(\sigma) \times \mathfrak{S}_{\mathfrak{q}_{\omega}}(\sigma) d\sigma \\ \supseteq_I \frac{1}{3}\left[Y_{\mathfrak{q}_{\omega}}(\mu) \times \mathfrak{S}_{\mathfrak{q}_{\omega}}(\mu) + Y_{\mathfrak{q}_{\omega}}(\sigma) \times \mathfrak{S}_{\mathfrak{q}_{\omega}}(\sigma)\right] + \frac{1}{6}\left[Y_{\mathfrak{q}_{\omega}}(\mu) \times \mathfrak{S}_{\mathfrak{q}_{\omega}}(\sigma) + Y_{\mathfrak{q}_{\omega}}(\sigma) \times \mathfrak{S}_{\mathfrak{q}_{\omega}}(\mu)\right],\end{gathered}$$

and

$$\begin{gathered}\frac{1}{\nu-\varsigma} \int_{\varsigma}^{\nu} Y_{\mathfrak{q}\sigma}(\omega) \times \mathfrak{S}_{\mathfrak{q}\sigma}(\omega) d\omega \\ \supseteq_I \frac{1}{3}\left[Y_{\mathfrak{q}\sigma}(\varsigma) \times \mathfrak{S}_{\mathfrak{q}\sigma}(\varsigma) + Y_{\mathfrak{q}\sigma}(\nu) \times \mathfrak{S}_{\mathfrak{q}\sigma}(\nu)\right] + \frac{1}{6}\left[Y_{\mathfrak{q}\sigma}(\varsigma) \times \mathfrak{S}_{\mathfrak{q}\sigma}(\nu) + Y_{\mathfrak{q}\sigma}(\varsigma) \times \mathfrak{S}_{\mathfrak{q}\sigma}(\nu)\right].\end{gathered}$$

The above inequalities can be written as

$$\begin{aligned}\frac{1}{\sigma-\mu} \int_{\mu}^{\sigma} Y_{\mathfrak{q}}(\sigma,\omega) \times \mathfrak{S}_{\mathfrak{q}}(\sigma,\omega) d\sigma \supseteq_I & \frac{1}{3}[Y_{\mathfrak{q}}(\mu,\omega) \times \mathfrak{S}_{\mathfrak{q}}(\mu,\omega) + Y_{\mathfrak{q}}(\sigma,\omega) \times \mathfrak{S}_{\mathfrak{q}}(\sigma,\omega)] \\ & + \frac{1}{6}[Y_{\mathfrak{q}}(\mu,\omega) \times \mathfrak{S}_{\mathfrak{q}}(\sigma,\omega) + Y_{\mathfrak{q}}(\sigma,\omega) \times \mathfrak{S}_{\mathfrak{q}}(\mu,\omega)],\end{aligned} \tag{52}$$

and

$$\begin{aligned}\frac{1}{\nu-\varsigma} \int_{\varsigma}^{\nu} Y_{\mathfrak{q}}(\sigma,\omega) \times \mathfrak{S}_{\mathfrak{q}}(\sigma,\omega) d\omega \supseteq_I & \frac{1}{3}[Y_{\mathfrak{q}}(\sigma,\varsigma) \times \mathfrak{S}_{\mathfrak{q}}(\sigma,\varsigma) + Y_{\mathfrak{q}}(\sigma,\nu) \times \mathfrak{S}_{\mathfrak{q}}(\sigma,\nu)] \\ & + \frac{1}{6}[Y_{\mathfrak{q}}(\sigma,\varsigma) \times \mathfrak{S}_{\mathfrak{q}}(\sigma,\varsigma) + Y_{\mathfrak{q}}(\sigma,\nu) \times \mathfrak{S}_{\mathfrak{q}}(\sigma,\nu)].\end{aligned} \tag{53}$$

Firstly, we will solve inequality Equation (52). Integrating both sides of the inequality with respect to ω on the interval $[\varsigma,\ \nu]$ and dividing both sides by $\nu-\varsigma$, we obtain

$$\begin{aligned}&\frac{1}{(\sigma-\mu)(\nu-\varsigma)}\int_{\mu}^{\sigma}\int_{\varsigma}^{\nu}\Upsilon_{\mathfrak{q}}(\sigma,\omega)\times\mathfrak{S}_{\mathfrak{q}}(\sigma,\omega)d\omega d\sigma\\ \supseteq_I&\ \frac{1}{3(\nu-\varsigma)}\int_{\varsigma}^{\nu}[\Upsilon_{\mathfrak{q}}(\mu,\omega)\times\mathfrak{S}_{\mathfrak{q}}(\mu,\omega)+\Upsilon_{\mathfrak{q}}(\sigma,\omega)\times\mathfrak{S}_{\mathfrak{q}}(\sigma,\omega)]d\omega\\ &+\frac{1}{6(\nu-\varsigma)}\int_{\varsigma}^{\nu}[\Upsilon_{\mathfrak{q}}(\mu,\omega)\times\mathfrak{S}_{\mathfrak{q}}(\sigma,\omega)+\Upsilon_{\mathfrak{q}}(\sigma,\omega)\times\mathfrak{S}_{\mathfrak{q}}(\mu,\omega)]d\omega.\end{aligned}\tag{54}$$

Now, via inequality Equation (13), for each $\mathfrak{q}\in[0,\ 1]$, we obtain

$$\begin{aligned}\frac{1}{(\nu-\varsigma)}\int_{\varsigma}^{\nu}\Upsilon_{\mathfrak{q}}(\mu,\omega)\times\mathfrak{S}_{\mathfrak{q}}(\mu,\omega)d\omega\supseteq_I&\ \frac{1}{3}\int_{\varsigma}^{\nu}[\Upsilon_{\mathfrak{q}}(\mu,\varsigma)\times\mathfrak{S}_{\mathfrak{q}}(\mu,\varsigma)+\Upsilon_{\mathfrak{q}}(\mu,\nu)\times\mathfrak{S}_{\mathfrak{q}}(\mu,\nu)]d\omega\\ &+\frac{1}{6}\int_{\varsigma}^{\nu}[\Upsilon_{\mathfrak{q}}(\mu,\varsigma)\times\mathfrak{S}_{\mathfrak{q}}(\mu,\nu)+\Upsilon_{\mathfrak{q}}(\mu,\varsigma)\times\mathfrak{S}_{\mathfrak{q}}(\mu,\nu)]d\omega.\end{aligned}\tag{55}$$

$$\begin{aligned}\frac{1}{(\nu-\varsigma)}\int_{\varsigma}^{\nu}\Upsilon_{\mathfrak{q}}(\sigma,\omega)\times\mathfrak{S}_{\mathfrak{q}}(\sigma,\omega)d\omega\supseteq_I&\ \frac{1}{3}\int_{\varsigma}^{\nu}[\Upsilon_{\mathfrak{q}}(\sigma,\varsigma)\times\mathfrak{S}_{\mathfrak{q}}(\sigma,\varsigma)+\Upsilon_{\mathfrak{q}}(\sigma,\nu)\times\mathfrak{S}_{\mathfrak{q}}(\sigma,\nu)]d\omega\\ &+\frac{1}{6}\int_{\varsigma}^{\nu}[\Upsilon_{\mathfrak{q}}(\sigma,\varsigma)\times\mathfrak{S}_{\mathfrak{q}}(\sigma,\nu)+\Upsilon_{\mathfrak{q}}(\sigma,\varsigma)\times\mathfrak{S}_{\mathfrak{q}}(\mu,\nu)]d\omega\end{aligned}\tag{56}$$

$$\begin{aligned}\frac{1}{(\nu-\varsigma)}\int_{\varsigma}^{\nu}\Upsilon_{\mathfrak{q}}(\mu,\omega)\times\mathfrak{S}_{\mathfrak{q}}(\sigma,\omega)d\omega\supseteq_I&\ \frac{1}{3}\int_{\varsigma}^{\nu}[\Upsilon_{\mathfrak{q}}(\mu,\varsigma)\times\mathfrak{S}_{\mathfrak{q}}(\sigma,\varsigma)+\Upsilon_{\mathfrak{q}}(\mu,\nu)\times\mathfrak{S}_{\mathfrak{q}}(\sigma,\nu)]d\omega\\ &+\frac{1}{6}\int_{\varsigma}^{\nu}[\Upsilon_{\mathfrak{q}}(\mu,\varsigma)\times\mathfrak{S}_{\mathfrak{q}}(\sigma,\nu)+\Upsilon_{\mathfrak{q}}(\mu,\nu)\times\mathfrak{S}_{\mathfrak{q}}(\sigma,\varsigma)]d\omega.\end{aligned}\tag{57}$$

$$\begin{aligned}\frac{1}{(\nu-\varsigma)}\int_{\varsigma}^{\nu}\Upsilon_{\mathfrak{q}}(\sigma,\omega)\times\mathfrak{S}_{\mathfrak{q}}(\mu,\omega)d\omega\supseteq_I&\ \frac{1}{3}\int_{\varsigma}^{\nu}[\Upsilon_{\mathfrak{q}}(\sigma,\varsigma)\times\mathfrak{S}_{\mathfrak{q}}(\mu,\varsigma)+\Upsilon_{\mathfrak{q}}(\sigma,\nu)\times\mathfrak{S}_{\mathfrak{q}}(\mu,\nu)]d\omega\\ &+\frac{1}{6}\int_{\varsigma}^{\nu}[\Upsilon_{\mathfrak{q}}(\sigma,\varsigma)\times\mathfrak{S}_{\mathfrak{q}}(\mu,\nu)+\Upsilon_{\mathfrak{q}}(\sigma,\nu)\times\mathfrak{S}_{\mathfrak{q}}(\mu,\varsigma)]d\omega.\end{aligned}\tag{58}$$

From Equations (55)–(58) and inequality Equation (54), we obtain

$$\frac{1}{(\sigma-\mu)(\nu-\varsigma)}\int_{\mu}^{\sigma}\int_{\varsigma}^{\nu}\Upsilon_{\mathfrak{q}}(\sigma,\omega)\times\mathfrak{S}_{\mathfrak{q}}(\sigma,\omega)d\omega d\sigma\supseteq_I\frac{1}{9}P_{\mathfrak{q}}(\mu,\sigma,\varsigma,\nu)+\frac{1}{18}\mathcal{M}_{\mathfrak{q}}(\mu,\sigma,\varsigma,\nu)+\frac{1}{36}\mathcal{N}_{\mathfrak{q}}(\mu,\sigma,\varsigma,\nu).$$

That is,

$$\frac{1}{(\sigma-\mu)(\nu-\varsigma)}\odot\int_{\mu}^{\sigma}\int_{\varsigma}^{\nu}\widetilde{\Upsilon}(\sigma,\omega)\otimes\widetilde{\mathfrak{S}}(\sigma,\omega)d\omega d\sigma\supseteq_{\mathbb{F}}\frac{1}{9}\odot\widetilde{P}(\mu,\sigma,\varsigma,\nu)\oplus\frac{1}{18}\odot\widetilde{\mathcal{M}}(\mu,\sigma,\varsigma,\nu)\oplus\frac{1}{36}\odot\widetilde{\mathcal{N}}(\mu,\sigma,\varsigma,\nu).$$

Hence, this concludes the proof of the theorem. □

Theorem 11. *Let $\widetilde{\Upsilon},\widetilde{\mathfrak{S}}:\Delta=[\mu,\ \sigma]\times[\varsigma,\ \nu]\subset\mathbb{R}^2\to\mathbb{E}_0$ be two UD-convex FN-V-Ms. Then, from the q-levels, we obtain the collection of IVMs $\Upsilon_{\mathfrak{q}},\ \mathfrak{S}_{\mathfrak{q}}:\Delta\subset\mathbb{R}^2\to\mathbb{R}_I^+$ given as $\Upsilon_{\mathfrak{q}}(\sigma)=[\Upsilon_*((\sigma,\omega),\mathfrak{q}),\ \Upsilon^*((\sigma,\omega),\mathfrak{q})]$ and $\mathfrak{S}_{\mathfrak{q}}(\sigma)=[\mathfrak{S}_*((\sigma,\omega),\mathfrak{q}),\ \mathfrak{S}^*((\sigma,\omega),\mathfrak{q})]$ for all $(\sigma,\omega)\in\Delta$ and for all $\mathfrak{q}\in[0,\ 1]$. Then, the following inequality holds:*

$$\begin{aligned}&4\odot\widetilde{\Upsilon}\left(\tfrac{\mu+\sigma}{2},\tfrac{\varsigma+\nu}{2}\right)\otimes\widetilde{\mathfrak{S}}\left(\tfrac{\mu+\sigma}{2},\tfrac{\varsigma+\nu}{2}\right)\\ \supseteq_{\mathbb{F}}&\ \frac{1}{(\sigma-\mu)(\nu-\varsigma)}\odot\int_{\mu}^{\sigma}\int_{\varsigma}^{\nu}\widetilde{\Upsilon}(\sigma,\omega)\otimes\widetilde{\mathfrak{S}}(\sigma,\omega)d\omega d\sigma\oplus\tfrac{5}{36}\odot\widetilde{P}(\mu,\sigma,\varsigma,\nu)\oplus\tfrac{7}{36}\odot\widetilde{\mathcal{M}}(\mu,\sigma,\varsigma,\nu)\oplus\tfrac{2}{9}\odot\widetilde{\mathcal{N}}(\mu,\sigma,\varsigma,\nu).\end{aligned}\tag{59}$$

where $\widetilde{P}(\mu,\sigma,\varsigma,\nu)$, $\widetilde{\mathcal{M}}(\mu,\sigma,\varsigma,\nu)$, and $\widetilde{\mathcal{N}}(\mu,\sigma,\varsigma,\nu)$ are given in Theorem 10.

Proof. Since $\widetilde{\Upsilon},\widetilde{\mathfrak{S}}:\Delta\to\mathbb{E}_0$ are two UD-convex FN-V-Ms, then from inequality Equation (14) and for each $\mathfrak{q}\in[0,\ 1]$, we obtain

$$\begin{aligned}&2\Upsilon_{\mathfrak{q}}\left(\tfrac{\mu+\sigma}{2},\tfrac{\varsigma+\nu}{2}\right)\times\mathfrak{S}_{\mathfrak{q}}\left(\tfrac{\mu+\sigma}{2},\tfrac{\varsigma+\nu}{2}\right)\\ \supseteq_I&\ \frac{1}{\sigma-\mu}\int_{\mu}^{\sigma}\Upsilon_{\mathfrak{q}}\left(\sigma,\tfrac{\varsigma+\nu}{2}\right)\times\mathfrak{S}_{\mathfrak{q}}\left(\sigma,\tfrac{\varsigma+\nu}{2}\right)d\sigma+\tfrac{1}{6}\left[\Upsilon_{\mathfrak{q}}\left(\mu,\tfrac{\varsigma+\nu}{2}\right)\times\mathfrak{S}_{\mathfrak{q}}\left(\mu,\tfrac{\varsigma+\nu}{2}\right)+\Upsilon_{\mathfrak{q}}\left(\sigma,\tfrac{\varsigma+\nu}{2}\right)\times\mathfrak{S}_{\mathfrak{q}}\left(\sigma,\tfrac{\varsigma+\nu}{2}\right)\right]\\ &+\tfrac{1}{3}\left[\Upsilon_{\mathfrak{q}}\left(\mu,\tfrac{\varsigma+\nu}{2}\right)\times\mathfrak{S}_{\mathfrak{q}}\left(\sigma,\tfrac{\varsigma+\nu}{2}\right)+\Upsilon_{\mathfrak{q}}\left(\sigma,\tfrac{\varsigma+\nu}{2}\right)\times\mathfrak{S}_{\mathfrak{q}}\left(\mu,\tfrac{\varsigma+\nu}{2}\right)\right],\end{aligned}\tag{60}$$

and

$$\begin{aligned}2\Upsilon_{\mathfrak{q}}\left(\tfrac{\mu+\sigma}{2},\tfrac{\varsigma+\nu}{2}\right)\times\mathfrak{S}_{\mathfrak{q}}\left(\tfrac{\mu+\sigma}{2},\tfrac{\varsigma+\nu}{2}\right)\supseteq_I&\ \frac{1}{\nu-\varsigma}\int_{\varsigma}^{\nu}\Upsilon_{\mathfrak{q}}\left(\tfrac{\mu+\sigma}{2},\omega\right)\times\mathfrak{S}_{\mathfrak{q}}\left(\tfrac{\mu+\sigma}{2},\omega\right)d\omega\\ &+\tfrac{1}{6}\left[\Upsilon_{\mathfrak{q}}\left(\tfrac{\mu+\sigma}{2},\varsigma\right)\times\mathfrak{S}_{\mathfrak{q}}\left(\tfrac{\mu+\sigma}{2},\varsigma\right)+\Upsilon_{\mathfrak{q}}\left(\tfrac{\mu+\sigma}{2},\nu\right)\times\mathfrak{S}_{\mathfrak{q}}\left(\tfrac{\mu+\sigma}{2},\nu\right)\right]\\ &+\tfrac{1}{3}\left[\Upsilon_{\mathfrak{q}}\left(\tfrac{\mu+\sigma}{2},\varsigma\right)\times\mathfrak{S}_{\mathfrak{q}}\left(\tfrac{\mu+\sigma}{2},\nu\right)+\Upsilon_{\mathfrak{q}}\left(\tfrac{\mu+\sigma}{2},\nu\right)\times\mathfrak{S}_{\mathfrak{q}}\left(\tfrac{\mu+\sigma}{2},\varsigma\right)\right].\end{aligned}\tag{61}$$

Summing inequalities Equations (60) and (61) and then multiplying the result by 2, we obtain

$$\begin{aligned}
&8\Upsilon_q\left(\tfrac{\mu+\sigma}{2},\tfrac{\varsigma+\nu}{2}\right)\times\mathfrak{S}_q\left(\tfrac{\mu+\sigma}{2},\tfrac{\varsigma+\nu}{2}\right)\\
\supseteq_I\ &\tfrac{2}{\sigma-\mu}\int_\mu^\sigma\Upsilon_q\left(\sigma,\tfrac{\varsigma+\nu}{2}\right)\times\mathfrak{S}_q\left(\sigma,\tfrac{\varsigma+\nu}{2}\right)d\sigma+\tfrac{2}{\nu-\varsigma}\int_\varsigma^\nu\Upsilon_q\left(\tfrac{\mu+\sigma}{2},\omega\right)\times\mathfrak{S}_q\left(\tfrac{\mu+\sigma}{2},\omega\right)d\sigma\\
&+\tfrac{1}{6}\left[2\Upsilon_q\left(\mu,\tfrac{\varsigma+\nu}{2}\right)\times\mathfrak{S}_q\left(\mu,\tfrac{\varsigma+\nu}{2}\right)+2\Upsilon_q\left(\sigma,\tfrac{\varsigma+\nu}{2}\right)\times\mathfrak{S}_q\left(\sigma,\tfrac{\varsigma+\nu}{2}\right)\right]\\
&+\tfrac{1}{6}\left[2\Upsilon_q\left(\tfrac{\mu+\sigma}{2},\varsigma\right)\times\mathfrak{S}_q\left(\tfrac{\mu+\sigma}{2},\varsigma\right)+2\Upsilon_q\left(\tfrac{\mu+\sigma}{2},\nu\right)\times\mathfrak{S}_q\left(\tfrac{\mu+\sigma}{2},\nu\right)\right]\\
&+\tfrac{1}{3}\left[2\Upsilon_q\left(\mu,\tfrac{\varsigma+\nu}{2}\right)\times\mathfrak{S}_q\left(\sigma,\tfrac{\varsigma+\nu}{2}\right)+2\Upsilon_q\left(\sigma,\tfrac{\varsigma+\nu}{2}\right)\times\mathfrak{S}_q\left(\mu,\tfrac{\varsigma+\nu}{2}\right)\right]\\
&+\tfrac{1}{3}\left[2\Upsilon_q\left(\tfrac{\mu+\sigma}{2},\varsigma\right)\times\mathfrak{S}_q\left(\tfrac{\mu+\sigma}{2},\nu\right)+2\Upsilon_q\left(\tfrac{\mu+\sigma}{2},\nu\right)\times\mathfrak{S}_q\left(\tfrac{\mu+\sigma}{2},\varsigma\right)\right].
\end{aligned}\tag{62}$$

Now, with the help of integral inequality Equation (14), for each integral on the right-hand side of Equation (62), we obtain

$$\begin{aligned}
&2\Upsilon_q\left(\mu,\tfrac{\varsigma+\nu}{2}\right)\times\mathfrak{S}_q\left(\mu,\tfrac{\varsigma+\nu}{2}\right)\\
\supseteq_I\ &\tfrac{1}{\nu-\varsigma}\int_\varsigma^\nu\Upsilon_q(\mu,\omega)\times\mathfrak{S}_q(\mu,\omega)d\omega+\tfrac{1}{6}[\Upsilon_q(\mu,\varsigma)\times\mathfrak{S}_q(\mu,\varsigma)+\Upsilon_q(\mu,\nu)\times\mathfrak{S}_q(\mu,\nu)]\\
&+\tfrac{1}{3}[\Upsilon_q(\mu,\varsigma)\times\mathfrak{S}_q(\mu,\nu)+\Upsilon_q(\mu,\nu)\times\mathfrak{S}_q(\mu,\varsigma)]
\end{aligned}\tag{63}$$

$$\begin{aligned}
&2\Upsilon_q\left(\sigma,\tfrac{\varsigma+\nu}{2}\right)\times\mathfrak{S}_q\left(\sigma,\tfrac{\varsigma+\nu}{2}\right)\\
\supseteq_I\ &\tfrac{1}{\nu-\varsigma}\int_\varsigma^\nu\Upsilon_q(\sigma,\omega)\times\mathfrak{S}_q(\sigma,\omega)d\omega+\tfrac{1}{6}[\Upsilon_q(\sigma,\varsigma)\times\mathfrak{S}_q(\sigma,\varsigma)+\Upsilon_q(\sigma,\nu)\times\mathfrak{S}_q(\sigma,\nu)]\\
&+\tfrac{1}{3}[\Upsilon_q(\sigma,\varsigma)\times\mathfrak{S}_q(\sigma,\nu)+\Upsilon_q(\sigma,\nu)\times\mathfrak{S}_q(\sigma,\varsigma)]
\end{aligned}\tag{64}$$

$$\begin{aligned}
&2\Upsilon_q\left(\mu,\tfrac{\varsigma+\nu}{2}\right)\times\mathfrak{S}_q\left(\sigma,\tfrac{\varsigma+\nu}{2}\right)\\
\supseteq_I\ &\tfrac{1}{\nu-\varsigma}\int_\varsigma^\nu\Upsilon_q(\mu,\omega)\times\mathfrak{S}_q(\sigma,\omega)d\omega+\tfrac{1}{6}[\Upsilon_q(\mu,\varsigma)\times\mathfrak{S}_q(\sigma,\varsigma)+\Upsilon_q(\mu,\nu)\times\mathfrak{S}_q(\sigma,\nu)]\\
&+\tfrac{1}{3}[\Upsilon_q(\mu,\varsigma)\times\mathfrak{S}_q(\sigma,\nu)+\Upsilon_q(\mu,\nu)\times\mathfrak{S}_q(\sigma,\varsigma)].
\end{aligned}\tag{65}$$

$$\begin{aligned}
&2\Upsilon_q\left(\sigma,\tfrac{\varsigma+\nu}{2}\right)\times\mathfrak{S}_q\left(\mu,\tfrac{\varsigma+\nu}{2}\right)\\
\supseteq_I\ &\tfrac{1}{\nu-\varsigma}\int_\varsigma^\nu\Upsilon_q(\sigma,\omega)\times\mathfrak{S}_q(\mu,\omega)d\omega+\tfrac{1}{6}[\Upsilon_q(\sigma,\varsigma)\times\mathfrak{S}_q(\mu,\varsigma)+\Upsilon_q(\sigma,\nu)\times\mathfrak{S}_q(\mu,\nu)]\\
&+\tfrac{1}{3}[\Upsilon_q(\sigma,\varsigma)\times\mathfrak{S}_q(\mu,\nu)+\Upsilon_q(\sigma,\nu)\times\mathfrak{S}_q(\mu,\varsigma)].
\end{aligned}\tag{66}$$

$$\begin{aligned}
&2\Upsilon_q\left(\tfrac{\mu+\sigma}{2},\varsigma\right)\times\mathfrak{S}_q\left(\tfrac{\mu+\sigma}{2},\varsigma\right)\\
\supseteq_I\ &\tfrac{1}{\sigma-\mu}\int_\mu^\sigma\Upsilon_q(\sigma,\varsigma)\times\mathfrak{S}_q(\sigma,\varsigma)d\sigma+\tfrac{1}{6}[\Upsilon_q(\mu,\varsigma)\times\mathfrak{S}_q(\mu,\varsigma)+\Upsilon_q(\sigma,\varsigma)\times\mathfrak{S}_q(\sigma,\varsigma)]\\
&+\tfrac{1}{3}\left[\Upsilon_q\left(\tfrac{\mu+\sigma}{2},\varsigma\right)\times\mathfrak{S}_q\left(\tfrac{\mu+\sigma}{2},\varsigma\right)+\Upsilon_q\left(\tfrac{\mu+\sigma}{2},\varsigma\right)\times\mathfrak{S}_q\left(\tfrac{\mu+\sigma}{2},\varsigma\right)\right]
\end{aligned}\tag{67}$$

$$\begin{aligned}
&2\Upsilon_q\left(\tfrac{\mu+\sigma}{2},\nu\right)\times\mathfrak{S}_q\left(\tfrac{\mu+\sigma}{2},\nu\right)\\
\supseteq_I\ &\tfrac{1}{\sigma-\mu}\int_\mu^\sigma\Upsilon_q(\sigma,\nu)\times\mathfrak{S}_q(\sigma,\nu)d\sigma+\tfrac{1}{6}[\Upsilon_q(\mu,\nu)\times\mathfrak{S}_q(\mu,\nu)+\Upsilon_q(\sigma,\nu)\times\mathfrak{S}_q(\sigma,\nu)]\\
&+\tfrac{1}{3}\left[\Upsilon_q\left(\tfrac{\mu+\sigma}{2},\nu\right)\times\mathfrak{S}_q\left(\tfrac{\mu+\sigma}{2},\nu\right)+\Upsilon_q\left(\tfrac{\mu+\sigma}{2},\nu\right)\times\mathfrak{S}_q\left(\tfrac{\mu+\sigma}{2},\nu\right)\right]
\end{aligned}\tag{68}$$

$$\begin{aligned}
&2\Upsilon_q\left(\tfrac{\mu+\sigma}{2},\varsigma\right)\times\mathfrak{S}_q\left(\tfrac{\mu+\sigma}{2},\nu\right)\\
\supseteq_I\ &\tfrac{1}{\sigma-\mu}\int_\mu^\sigma\Upsilon_q(\sigma,\varsigma)\times\mathfrak{S}_q(\sigma,\nu)d\sigma+\tfrac{1}{6}[\Upsilon_q(\mu,\varsigma)\times\mathfrak{S}_q(\mu,\nu)+\Upsilon_q(\sigma,\varsigma)\times\mathfrak{S}_q(\sigma,\nu)]\\
&+\tfrac{1}{3}\left[\Upsilon_q\left(\tfrac{\mu+\sigma}{2},\varsigma\right)\times\mathfrak{S}_q\left(\tfrac{\mu+\sigma}{2},\nu\right)+\Upsilon_q\left(\tfrac{\mu+\sigma}{2},\varsigma\right)\times\mathfrak{S}_q\left(\tfrac{\mu+\sigma}{2},\nu\right)\right].
\end{aligned}\tag{69}$$

$$\begin{aligned}
&2\Upsilon_q\left(\tfrac{\mu+\sigma}{2},\nu\right)\times\mathfrak{S}_q\left(\tfrac{\mu+\sigma}{2},\varsigma\right)\\
\supseteq_I\ &\tfrac{1}{\sigma-\mu}\int_\mu^\sigma\Upsilon_q(\sigma,\nu)\times\mathfrak{S}_q(\sigma,\varsigma)d\sigma+\tfrac{1}{6}[\Upsilon_q(\mu,\nu)\times\mathfrak{S}_q(\mu,\varsigma)+\Upsilon_q(\sigma,\nu)\times\mathfrak{S}_q(\sigma,\varsigma)]\\
&+\tfrac{1}{3}\left[\Upsilon_q\left(\tfrac{\mu+\sigma}{2},\nu\right)\times\mathfrak{S}_q\left(\tfrac{\mu+\sigma}{2},\varsigma\right)+\Upsilon_q\left(\tfrac{\mu+\sigma}{2},\nu\right)\times\mathfrak{S}_q\left(\tfrac{\mu+\sigma}{2},\varsigma\right)\right].
\end{aligned}\tag{70}$$

From Equations (63)–(70), we obtain

$$\begin{aligned}
&8\Upsilon_q\left(\tfrac{\mu+\sigma}{2},\tfrac{\varsigma+\nu}{2}\right)\times\mathfrak{S}_q\left(\tfrac{\mu+\sigma}{2},\tfrac{\varsigma+\nu}{2}\right)\\
\supseteq_I\ &\tfrac{2}{\sigma-\mu}\int_\mu^\sigma\Upsilon_q\left(\sigma,\tfrac{\varsigma+\nu}{2}\right)\times\mathfrak{S}_q\left(\sigma,\tfrac{\varsigma+\nu}{2}\right)d\sigma+\tfrac{2}{\nu-\varsigma}\int_\varsigma^\nu\Upsilon_q\left(\tfrac{\mu+\sigma}{2},\omega\right)\times\mathfrak{S}_q\left(\tfrac{\mu+\sigma}{2},\omega\right)d\sigma\\
&+\tfrac{1}{6(\nu-\varsigma)}\int_\varsigma^\nu\Upsilon_q(\mu,\omega)\times\mathfrak{S}_q(\mu,\omega)d\omega+\tfrac{1}{6(\nu-\varsigma)}\int_\varsigma^\nu\Upsilon_q(\sigma,\omega)\times\mathfrak{S}_q(\sigma,\omega)d\omega\\
&+\tfrac{1}{6(\sigma-\mu)}\int_\mu^\sigma\Upsilon_q(\sigma,\varsigma)\times\mathfrak{S}_q(\sigma,\varsigma)d\sigma+\tfrac{1}{6(\sigma-\mu)}\int_\mu^\sigma\Upsilon_q(\sigma,\nu)\times\mathfrak{S}_q(\sigma,\nu)d\sigma\\
&+\tfrac{1}{3(\nu-\varsigma)}\int_\varsigma^\nu\Upsilon_q(\mu,\omega)\times\mathfrak{S}_q(\sigma,\omega)d\omega+\tfrac{1}{3(\nu-\varsigma)}\int_\varsigma^\nu\Upsilon_q(\sigma,\omega)\times\mathfrak{S}_q(\mu,\omega)d\omega\\
&+\tfrac{1}{3(\sigma-\mu)}\int_\mu^\sigma\Upsilon_q(\sigma,\varsigma)\times\mathfrak{S}_q(\sigma,\nu)d\sigma+\tfrac{1}{3(\sigma-\mu)}\int_\mu^\sigma\Upsilon_q(\sigma,\nu)\times\mathfrak{S}_q(\sigma,\varsigma)d\sigma\\
&+\tfrac{1}{18}P_q(\mu,\sigma,\varsigma,\nu)+\tfrac{1}{9}\mathcal{M}_q(\mu,\sigma,\varsigma,\nu)+\tfrac{2}{9}\mathcal{N}_q(\mu,\sigma,\varsigma,\nu).
\end{aligned}\tag{71}$$

Now, with the help of integral inequality Equation (14) for the first two integrals on the right-hand side of Equation (71), we obtain the following relation:

$$\begin{aligned}
&\frac{2}{\sigma-\mu}\int_{\mu}^{\sigma} \Upsilon_{q}\left(\sigma, \tfrac{\varsigma+\nu}{2}\right) \times \mathfrak{S}_{q}\left(\sigma, \tfrac{\varsigma+\nu}{2}\right) d\sigma \\
&\supseteq_{I} \frac{1}{(\sigma-\mu)(\nu-\varsigma)} \int_{\mu}^{\sigma}\int_{\varsigma}^{\nu} \Upsilon_{q}(\sigma,\omega) \times \mathfrak{S}_{q}(\sigma,\omega) d\omega d\sigma \\
&+\frac{1}{3(\sigma-\mu)}\int_{\mu}^{\sigma} [\Upsilon_{q}(\sigma,\varsigma) \times \mathfrak{S}_{q}(\sigma,\varsigma) + \Upsilon_{q}(\sigma,\nu) \times \mathfrak{S}_{q}(\sigma,\nu)] d\sigma \\
&+\frac{1}{6(\sigma-\mu)}\int_{\mu}^{\sigma} [\Upsilon_{q}(\varsigma,\sigma) \times \mathfrak{S}_{q}(\sigma,\nu) + \Upsilon_{q}(\sigma,\nu) \times \mathfrak{S}_{q}(\sigma,\varsigma)] d\sigma,
\end{aligned} \tag{72}$$

$$\begin{aligned}
&\frac{2}{\nu-\varsigma}\int_{\varsigma}^{\nu} \Upsilon_{q}\left(\tfrac{\mu+\sigma}{2}, \omega\right) \times \mathfrak{S}_{q}\left(\tfrac{\mu+\sigma}{2}, \omega\right) d\sigma \\
&\supseteq_{I} \frac{1}{(\sigma-\mu)(\nu-\varsigma)} \int_{\mu}^{\sigma}\int_{\varsigma}^{\nu} \Upsilon_{q}(\sigma,\omega) \times \mathfrak{S}_{q}(\sigma,\omega) d\omega d\sigma \\
&+\frac{1}{3(\nu-\varsigma)}\int_{\varsigma}^{\nu} [\Upsilon_{q}(\mu,\omega) \times \mathfrak{S}_{q}(\mu,\omega) + \Upsilon_{q}(\sigma,\omega) \times \mathfrak{S}_{q}(\sigma,\omega)] d\omega \\
&+\frac{1}{6(\nu-\varsigma)}\int_{\varsigma}^{\nu} [\Upsilon_{q}(\mu,\omega) \times \mathfrak{S}_{q}(\sigma,\omega) + \Upsilon_{q}(\sigma,\omega) \times \mathfrak{S}_{q}(\mu,\omega)] d\omega.
\end{aligned} \tag{73}$$

From Equations (72) and (73), we obtain

$$\begin{aligned}
&8\Upsilon_{q}\left(\tfrac{\mu+\sigma}{2}, \tfrac{\varsigma+\nu}{2}\right) \times \mathfrak{S}_{q}\left(\tfrac{\mu+\sigma}{2}, \tfrac{\varsigma+\nu}{2}\right) \\
&\supseteq_{I} \frac{1}{(\sigma-\mu)(\nu-\varsigma)} \int_{\mu}^{\sigma}\int_{\varsigma}^{\nu} \Upsilon_{q}(\sigma,\omega) \times \mathfrak{S}_{q}(\sigma,\omega) d\omega d\sigma \\
&+\frac{1}{3(\sigma-\mu)}\int_{\mu}^{\sigma} [\Upsilon_{q}(\sigma,\varsigma) \times \mathfrak{S}_{q}(\sigma,\varsigma) + \Upsilon_{q}(\sigma,\nu) \times \mathfrak{S}_{q}(\sigma,\nu)] d\sigma \\
&+\frac{1}{6(\sigma-\mu)}\int_{\mu}^{\sigma} [\Upsilon_{q}(\sigma,\varsigma) \times \mathfrak{S}_{q}(\sigma,\nu) + \Upsilon_{q}(\sigma,\nu) \times \mathfrak{S}_{q}(\sigma,\varsigma)] d\sigma \\
&+\frac{1}{(\sigma-\mu)(\nu-\varsigma)} \int_{\mu}^{\sigma}\int_{\varsigma}^{\nu} \Upsilon_{q}(\sigma,\omega) \times \mathfrak{S}_{q}(\sigma,\omega) d\omega d\sigma \\
&+\frac{1}{3(\nu-\varsigma)}\int_{\varsigma}^{\nu} [\Upsilon_{q}(\mu,\omega) \times \mathfrak{S}_{q}(\mu,\omega) + \Upsilon_{q}(\sigma,\omega) \times \mathfrak{S}_{q}(\sigma,\omega)] d\omega \\
&+\frac{1}{6(\nu-\varsigma)}\int_{\varsigma}^{\nu} [\Upsilon_{q}(\mu,\omega) \times \mathfrak{S}_{q}(\sigma,\omega) + \Upsilon_{q}(\sigma,\omega) \times \mathfrak{S}_{q}(\mu,\omega)] d\omega \\
&+\frac{1}{6(\nu-\varsigma)}\int_{\varsigma}^{\nu} \Upsilon_{q}(\mu,\omega) \times \mathfrak{S}_{q}(\mu,\omega) d\omega + \frac{1}{6(\nu-\varsigma)}\int_{\varsigma}^{\nu} \Upsilon_{q}(\sigma,\omega) \times \mathfrak{S}_{q}(\sigma,\omega) d\omega \\
&+\frac{1}{6(\sigma-\mu)}\int_{\mu}^{\sigma} \Upsilon_{q}(\sigma,\varsigma) \times \mathfrak{S}_{q}(\sigma,\varsigma) d\sigma + \frac{1}{6(\sigma-\mu)}\int_{\mu}^{\sigma} \Upsilon_{q}(\sigma,\nu) \times \mathfrak{S}_{q}(\sigma,\nu) d\sigma \\
&+\frac{1}{3(\nu-\varsigma)}\int_{\varsigma}^{\nu} \Upsilon_{q}(\mu,\omega) \times \mathfrak{S}_{q}(\sigma,\omega) d\omega + \frac{1}{3(\nu-\varsigma)}\int_{\varsigma}^{\nu} \Upsilon_{q}(\sigma,\omega) \times \mathfrak{S}_{q}(\mu,\omega) d\omega \\
&+\frac{1}{3(\sigma-\mu)}\int_{\mu}^{\sigma} \Upsilon_{q}(\sigma,\varsigma) \times \mathfrak{S}_{q}(\sigma,\nu) d\sigma + \frac{1}{3(\sigma-\mu)}\int_{\mu}^{\sigma} \Upsilon_{q}(\sigma,\nu) \times \mathfrak{S}_{q}(\sigma,\varsigma) d\sigma \\
&+\tfrac{1}{18}\mathcal{P}_{q}(\mu,\sigma,\varsigma,\nu) + \tfrac{1}{9}\mathcal{M}_{q}(\mu,\sigma,\varsigma,\nu) + \tfrac{2}{9}\mathcal{N}_{q}(\mu,\sigma,\varsigma,\nu).
\end{aligned}$$

It follows that

$$\begin{aligned}
&8\Upsilon_{q}\left(\tfrac{\mu+\sigma}{2}, \tfrac{\varsigma+\nu}{2}\right) \times \mathfrak{S}_{q}\left(\tfrac{\mu+\sigma}{2}, \tfrac{\varsigma+\nu}{2}\right) \\
&\supseteq_{I} \frac{2}{(\sigma-\mu)(\nu-\varsigma)} \int_{\mu}^{\sigma}\int_{\varsigma}^{\nu} \Upsilon_{q}(\sigma,\omega) \times \mathfrak{S}_{q}(\sigma,\omega) d\omega d\sigma \\
&+\frac{2}{3(\sigma-\mu)}\int_{\mu}^{\sigma} [\Upsilon_{q}(\sigma,\varsigma) \times \mathfrak{S}_{q}(\sigma,\varsigma) + \Upsilon_{q}(\sigma,\nu) \times \mathfrak{S}_{q}(\sigma,\nu)] d\sigma \\
&+\frac{1}{3(\sigma-\mu)}\int_{\mu}^{\sigma} [\Upsilon_{q}(\sigma,\varsigma) \times \mathfrak{S}_{q}(\sigma,\nu) + \Upsilon_{q}(\sigma,\nu) \times \mathfrak{S}_{q}(\sigma,\varsigma)] d\sigma \\
&+\frac{2}{3(\nu-\varsigma)}\int_{\varsigma}^{\nu} [\Upsilon_{q}(\mu,\omega) \times \mathfrak{S}_{q}(\mu,\omega) + \Upsilon_{q}(\sigma,\omega) \times \mathfrak{S}_{q}(\sigma,\omega)] d\omega \\
&+\frac{1}{3(\nu-\varsigma)}\int_{\varsigma}^{\nu} [\Upsilon_{q}(\mu,\omega) \times \mathfrak{S}_{q}(\sigma,\omega) + \Upsilon_{q}(\sigma,\omega) \times \mathfrak{S}_{q}(\mu,\omega)] d\omega \\
&+\tfrac{1}{18}\mathcal{P}_{q}(\mu,\sigma,\varsigma,\nu) + \tfrac{1}{9}\mathcal{M}_{q}(\mu,\sigma,\varsigma,\nu) + \tfrac{2}{9}\mathcal{N}_{q}(\mu,\sigma,\varsigma,\nu).
\end{aligned} \tag{74}$$

Now, using integral inequality Equation (13) for the integrals on the right-hand side of Equation (74), we obtain the following relation

$$\begin{aligned}
&\frac{1}{\sigma-\mu}\int_{\mu}^{\sigma} \Upsilon_{q}(\sigma,\varsigma) \times \mathfrak{S}_{q}(\sigma,\varsigma) d\sigma \\
&\supseteq_{I} \tfrac{1}{3}[\Upsilon_{q}(\mu,\varsigma) \times \mathfrak{S}_{q}(\mu,\varsigma) + \Upsilon_{q}(\sigma,\varsigma) \times \mathfrak{S}_{q}(\sigma,\varsigma)] + \tfrac{1}{6}[\Upsilon_{q}(\mu,\varsigma) \times \mathfrak{S}_{q}(\sigma,\varsigma) + \Upsilon_{q}(\sigma,\varsigma) \times \mathfrak{S}_{q}(\mu,\varsigma)],
\end{aligned} \tag{75}$$

$$\begin{aligned}
&\frac{1}{\sigma-\mu}\int_{\mu}^{\sigma} \Upsilon_{q}(\sigma,\nu) \times \mathfrak{S}_{q}(\sigma,\nu) d\sigma \\
&\supseteq_{I} \tfrac{1}{3}[\Upsilon_{q}(\mu,\nu) \times \mathfrak{S}_{q}(\mu,\nu) + \Upsilon_{q}(\sigma,\nu) \times \mathfrak{S}_{q}(\sigma,\nu)] + \tfrac{1}{6}[\Upsilon_{q}(\mu,\nu) \times \mathfrak{S}_{q}(\sigma,\nu) + \Upsilon_{q}(\sigma,\nu) \times \mathfrak{S}_{q}(\mu,\nu)]
\end{aligned} \tag{76}$$

$$\begin{aligned}
&\frac{1}{\sigma-\mu}\int_{\mu}^{\sigma} \Upsilon_{q}(\sigma,\varsigma) \times \mathfrak{S}_{q}(\sigma,\nu) d\sigma \\
&\supseteq_{I} \tfrac{1}{3}[\Upsilon_{q}(\mu,\varsigma) \times \mathfrak{S}_{q}(\mu,\nu) + \Upsilon_{q}(\sigma,\varsigma) \times \mathfrak{S}_{q}(\sigma,\nu)] + \tfrac{1}{6}[\Upsilon_{q}(\mu,\varsigma) \times \mathfrak{S}_{q}(\sigma,\nu) + \Upsilon_{q}(\sigma,\varsigma) \times \mathfrak{S}_{q}(\mu,\nu)],
\end{aligned} \tag{77}$$

$$\begin{aligned}
&\frac{1}{\sigma-\mu}\int_{\mu}^{\sigma} \Upsilon_{q}(\sigma,\nu) \times \mathfrak{S}_{q}(\sigma,\varsigma) d\sigma \\
&\supseteq_{I} \tfrac{1}{3}[\Upsilon_{q}(\mu,\nu) \times \mathfrak{S}_{q}(\mu,\varsigma) + \Upsilon_{q}(\sigma,\nu) \times \mathfrak{S}_{q}(\sigma,\varsigma)] + \tfrac{1}{6}[\Upsilon_{q}(\mu,\nu) \times \mathfrak{S}_{q}(\sigma,\varsigma) + \Upsilon_{q}(\sigma,\nu) \times \mathfrak{S}_{q}(\mu,\varsigma)],
\end{aligned} \tag{78}$$

$$\begin{aligned}
&\frac{1}{\nu-\varsigma}\int_{\varsigma}^{\nu} \Upsilon_{q}(\mu,\omega) \times \mathfrak{S}_{q}(\mu,\omega) d\omega \\
&\supseteq_{I} \tfrac{1}{3}[\Upsilon_{q}(\mu,\varsigma) \times \mathfrak{S}_{q}(\mu,\varsigma) + \Upsilon_{q}(\mu,\nu) \times \mathfrak{S}_{q}(\mu,\nu)] + \tfrac{1}{6}[\Upsilon_{q}(\mu,\varsigma) \times \mathfrak{S}_{q}(\mu,\nu) + \Upsilon_{q}(\mu,\nu) \times \mathfrak{S}_{q}(\mu,\varsigma)],
\end{aligned} \tag{79}$$

$$\begin{aligned}&\frac{1}{\nu-\varsigma}\int_{\varsigma}^{\nu}Y_{\mathfrak{q}}(\sigma,\omega)\times\mathfrak{S}_{\mathfrak{q}}(\sigma,\omega)d\omega\\ \supseteq_I\ &\tfrac{1}{3}[Y_{\mathfrak{q}}(\sigma,\varsigma)\times\mathfrak{S}_{\mathfrak{q}}(\sigma,\varsigma)+Y_{\mathfrak{q}}(\sigma,\nu)\times\mathfrak{S}_{\mathfrak{q}}(\sigma,\nu)]+\tfrac{1}{6}[Y_{\mathfrak{q}}(\sigma,\varsigma)\times\mathfrak{S}_{\mathfrak{q}}(\sigma,\nu)+Y_{\mathfrak{q}}(\sigma,\nu)\times\mathfrak{S}_{\mathfrak{q}}(\sigma,\varsigma)],\end{aligned}\tag{80}$$

$$\begin{aligned}&\frac{1}{\nu-\varsigma}\int_{\varsigma}^{\nu}Y_{\mathfrak{q}}(\mu,\omega)\times\mathfrak{S}_{\mathfrak{q}}(\sigma,\omega)d\omega\\ \supseteq_I\ &\tfrac{1}{3}[Y_{\mathfrak{q}}(\mu,\varsigma)\times\mathfrak{S}_{\mathfrak{q}}(\sigma,\varsigma)+Y_{\mathfrak{q}}(\mu,\nu)\times\mathfrak{S}_{\mathfrak{q}}(\sigma,\nu)]+\tfrac{1}{6}[Y_{\mathfrak{q}}(\mu,\varsigma)\times\mathfrak{S}_{\mathfrak{q}}(\sigma,\nu)+Y_{\mathfrak{q}}(\mu,\nu)\times\mathfrak{S}_{\mathfrak{q}}(\sigma,\varsigma)],\end{aligned}\tag{81}$$

$$\begin{aligned}&\frac{1}{\nu-\varsigma}\int_{\varsigma}^{\nu}Y_{\mathfrak{q}}(\sigma,\omega)\times\mathfrak{S}_{\mathfrak{q}}(\mu,\omega)d\omega\\ \supseteq_I\ &\tfrac{1}{3}[Y_{\mathfrak{q}}(\sigma,\varsigma)\times\mathfrak{S}_{\mathfrak{q}}(\mu,\varsigma)+Y_{\mathfrak{q}}(\sigma,\nu)\times\mathfrak{S}_{\mathfrak{q}}(\mu,\nu)]+\tfrac{1}{6}[Y_{\mathfrak{q}}(\sigma,\varsigma)\times\mathfrak{S}_{\mathfrak{q}}(\mu,\nu)+Y_{\mathfrak{q}}(\sigma,\nu)\times\mathfrak{S}_{\mathfrak{q}}(\mu,\varsigma)].\end{aligned}\tag{82}$$

From Equations (75)–(82) and inequality Equation (74), we obtain

$$\begin{aligned}&4Y_{\mathfrak{q}}\left(\tfrac{\mu+\sigma}{2},\tfrac{\varsigma+\nu}{2}\right)\times\mathfrak{S}_{\mathfrak{q}}\left(\tfrac{\mu+\sigma}{2},\tfrac{\varsigma+\nu}{2}\right)\\ \supseteq_I\ &\frac{1}{(\sigma-\mu)(\nu-\varsigma)}\int_{\mu}^{\sigma}\int_{\varsigma}^{\nu}Y_{\mathfrak{q}}(\sigma,\omega)\times\mathfrak{S}_{\mathfrak{q}}(\sigma,\omega)d\omega d\sigma+\tfrac{5}{36}P_{\mathfrak{q}}(\mu,\sigma,\varsigma,\nu)+\tfrac{7}{36}\mathcal{M}_{\mathfrak{q}}(\mu,\sigma,\varsigma,\nu)+\tfrac{2}{9}\mathcal{N}_{\mathfrak{q}}(\mu,\sigma,\varsigma,\nu)\end{aligned}$$

That is,

$$\begin{aligned}&4\widetilde{Y}\left(\tfrac{\mu+\sigma}{2},\tfrac{\varsigma+\nu}{2}\right)\otimes\widetilde{\mathfrak{S}}\left(\tfrac{\mu+\sigma}{2},\tfrac{\varsigma+\nu}{2}\right)\\ \supseteq_{\mathbb{F}}\ &\frac{1}{(\sigma-\mu)(\nu-\varsigma)}\odot\int_{\mu}^{\sigma}\int_{\varsigma}^{\nu}\widetilde{Y}(\sigma,\omega)\otimes\widetilde{\mathfrak{S}}(\sigma,\omega)d\omega d\sigma\oplus\tfrac{5}{36}\odot\widetilde{P}(\mu,\sigma,\varsigma,\nu)\oplus\tfrac{7}{36}\odot\widetilde{\mathcal{M}}(\mu,\sigma,\varsigma,\nu)\oplus\tfrac{2}{9}\odot\widetilde{\mathcal{N}}(\mu,\sigma,\varsigma,\nu).\end{aligned}$$

We will now obtain the HH–Fejér inequality for coordinated UD-convex FN-V-Ms by means of FOR in the following result. □

Theorem 12. *Let $\widetilde{Y}:\Delta=[\mu,\ \sigma]\times[\varsigma,\ \nu]\to\mathbb{E}_0$ be a coordinated UD-convex FN-V-M with $\mu<\sigma$ and $\varsigma<\nu$. Then, from the $\mathfrak{q}$-levels, we obtain the collection of IVMs $Y_{\mathfrak{q}}:\Delta\to\mathbb{R}_I^+$ given as $Y_{\mathfrak{q}}(\sigma,\omega)=[Y_*((\sigma,\omega),\mathfrak{q}),\ Y^*((\sigma,\omega),\mathfrak{q})]$ for all $(\sigma,\omega)\in\Delta$ and for all $\mathfrak{q}\in[0,\ 1]$. Let $\Omega:[\mu,\ \sigma]\to\mathbb{R}$ with $\Omega(\sigma)\geq 0$, $\int_{\mu}^{\sigma}\Omega(\sigma)d\sigma>0$, and $\mathcal{W}:[\varsigma,\ \nu]\to\mathbb{R}$ with $\mathcal{W}(\omega)\geq 0$, $\int_{\varsigma}^{\nu}\mathcal{W}(\omega)d\omega>0$, be two symmetric functions with respect to $\frac{\mu+\sigma}{2}$ and $\frac{\varsigma+\nu}{2}$, respectively. Then, the following inequality holds:*

$$\begin{aligned}\widetilde{Y}\left(\tfrac{\mu+\sigma}{2},\tfrac{\varsigma+\nu}{2}\right)&\supseteq_{\mathbb{F}}\tfrac{1}{2}\left[\frac{1}{\int_{\mu}^{\sigma}\Omega(\sigma)d\sigma}\odot\int_{\mu}^{\sigma}\widetilde{Y}\left(\sigma,\tfrac{\varsigma+\nu}{2}\right)\Omega(\sigma)d\sigma\oplus\frac{1}{\int_{\mu}^{\sigma}\mathcal{W}(\omega)d\omega}\odot\int_{\mu}^{\sigma}\widetilde{Y}\left(\tfrac{\mu+\sigma}{2},\omega\right)\mathcal{W}(\omega)d\omega\right]\\ &\supseteq_{\mathbb{F}}\frac{1}{\int_{\mu}^{\sigma}\Omega(\sigma)d\sigma\int_{\mu}^{\sigma}\mathcal{W}(\omega)d\omega}\odot\int_{\mu}^{\sigma}\int_{\varsigma}^{\nu}\widetilde{Y}(\sigma,\omega)\Omega(\sigma)\mathcal{W}(\omega)d\omega d\sigma\\ &\supseteq_{\mathbb{F}}\frac{1}{4\int_{\mu}^{\sigma}\Omega(\sigma)d\sigma}\odot\left[\int_{\mu}^{\sigma}\widetilde{Y}(\sigma,\varsigma)d\sigma\oplus\int_{\mu}^{\sigma}\widetilde{Y}(\sigma,\nu)d\sigma\right]\\ &\oplus\frac{1}{4\int_{\mu}^{\sigma}\mathcal{W}(\omega)d\omega}\odot\left[\int_{\varsigma}^{\nu}\widetilde{Y}(\mu,\omega)d\omega\oplus\int_{\varsigma}^{\nu}\widetilde{Y}(\sigma,\omega)d\omega\right]\\ &\supseteq_{\mathbb{F}}\frac{\widetilde{Y}(\mu,\varsigma)\oplus\widetilde{Y}(\sigma,\varsigma)\oplus\widetilde{Y}(\mu,\nu)\oplus\widetilde{Y}(\sigma,\nu)}{4}\end{aligned}\tag{83}$$

Proof. Since $\widetilde{Y}$ is a coordinated UD-convex FN-V-M on Δ, and it follows those functions, then via Lemma 1, the following exist:

$$\widetilde{Y}_{\sigma}:[\varsigma,\nu]\to\mathbb{E}_0,\ \widetilde{Y}_{\sigma}(\omega)=\widetilde{Y}(\sigma,\omega),\ \widetilde{Y}_{\omega}:[\mu,\sigma]\to\mathbb{E}_0,\ \widetilde{Y}_{\omega}(\sigma)=\widetilde{Y}(\sigma,\omega).$$

Thus, from inequality Equation (15), for each $\mathfrak{q}\in[0,\ 1]$, we obtain

$$Y_{\mathfrak{q}\sigma}\left(\frac{\varsigma+\nu}{2}\right)\supseteq_I\frac{1}{\int_{\varsigma}^{\nu}\mathcal{W}(\omega)d\omega}\int_{\varsigma}^{\nu}Y_{\mathfrak{q}\sigma}(\omega)\mathcal{W}(\omega)d\omega\supseteq_I\frac{Y_{\mathfrak{q}\sigma}(\varsigma)+Y_{\mathfrak{q}\sigma}(\nu)}{2},$$

and

$$Y_{\mathfrak{q}\omega}\left(\frac{\mu+\sigma}{2}\right)\supseteq_I\frac{1}{\int_{\mu}^{\sigma}\Omega(\sigma)d\sigma}\int_{\mu}^{\sigma}Y_{\mathfrak{q}\omega}(\sigma)\Omega(\sigma)d\sigma\supseteq_I\frac{Y_{\mathfrak{q}\omega}(\mu)+Y_{\mathfrak{q}\omega}(\sigma)}{2}$$

The above inequalities can be written as

$$Y_{\mathfrak{q}}\left(\sigma,\frac{\varsigma+\nu}{2}\right)\supseteq_I\frac{1}{\int_{\varsigma}^{\nu}\mathcal{W}(\omega)d\omega}\int_{\varsigma}^{\nu}Y_{\mathfrak{q}}(\sigma,\omega)\mathcal{W}(\omega)d\omega\supseteq_I\frac{Y_{\mathfrak{q}}(\sigma,\varsigma)+Y_{\mathfrak{q}}(\sigma,\nu)}{2},\tag{84}$$

and

$$\Upsilon_q\left(\frac{\mu+\sigma}{2},\omega\right) \supseteq_I \frac{1}{\int_\mu^\sigma \Omega(\sigma)d\sigma}\int_\mu^\sigma \Upsilon_q(\sigma,\omega)\Omega(\sigma)d\sigma \supseteq_I \frac{\Upsilon_q(\mu,\omega)+\Upsilon_q(\sigma,\omega)}{2}. \quad (85)$$

Multiplying Equation (84) by $\Omega(\sigma)$ and then integrating the result with respect to σ on $[\mu, \sigma]$, we obtain

$$\int_\mu^\sigma \Upsilon_q\left(\sigma,\frac{\varsigma+\nu}{2}\right)\Omega(\sigma)d\sigma \supseteq_I \frac{1}{\int_\varsigma^\nu \mathcal{W}(\omega)d\omega}\int_\mu^\sigma\int_\varsigma^\nu \Upsilon_q(\sigma,\omega)\Omega(\sigma)\mathcal{W}(\omega)d\omega d\sigma \supseteq_I \int_\mu^\sigma \frac{\Upsilon_q(\sigma,\varsigma)+\Upsilon_q(\sigma,\nu)}{2}\Omega(\sigma)d\sigma. \quad (86)$$

Now, multiplying Equation (85) by $\mathcal{W}(\omega)$ and then integrating the result with respect to ω on $[\varsigma, \nu]$, we obtain

$$\int_\varsigma^\nu \Upsilon_q\left(\frac{\mu+\sigma}{2},\omega\right)\mathcal{W}(\omega)d\omega \supseteq_I \frac{1}{\int_\mu^\sigma \Omega(\sigma)d\sigma}\int_\mu^\sigma\int_\varsigma^\nu \Upsilon_q(\sigma,\omega)\Omega(\sigma)\mathcal{W}(\omega)d\sigma d\omega \supseteq_I \int_\mu^\sigma \frac{\Upsilon_q(\mu,\omega)+\Upsilon_q(\sigma,\omega)}{2}\mathcal{W}(\omega)d\omega \quad (87)$$

Since $\int_\mu^\sigma \Omega(\sigma)d\sigma > 0$ and $\int_\mu^\sigma \mathcal{W}(\omega)d\omega > 0$, then by dividing Equations (86) and (87) by $\int_\mu^\sigma \Omega(\sigma)d\sigma > 0$ and $\int_\mu^\sigma \mathcal{W}(\omega)d\omega > 0$, respectively, we obtain

$$\begin{aligned}
&\frac{1}{2}\left[\frac{1}{\int_\mu^\sigma \Omega(\sigma)d\sigma}\int_\mu^\sigma \Upsilon_q\left(\sigma,\frac{\varsigma+\nu}{2}\right)\Omega(\sigma)d\sigma + \frac{1}{\int_\mu^\sigma \mathcal{W}(\omega)d\omega}\int_\mu^\sigma \Upsilon_q\left(\frac{\mu+\sigma}{2},\omega\right)\mathcal{W}(\omega)d\omega\right] \\
&\supseteq_I \frac{1}{\int_\mu^\sigma \Omega(\sigma)d\sigma\int_\mu^\sigma \mathcal{W}(\omega)d\omega}\int_\mu^\sigma\int_\varsigma^\nu \Upsilon_q(\sigma,\omega)\Omega(\sigma)\mathcal{W}(\omega)d\omega d\sigma \\
&\supseteq_I \left[\frac{1}{\int_\mu^\sigma \Omega(\sigma)d\sigma}\int_\mu^\sigma \frac{\Upsilon_q(\sigma,\varsigma)+\Upsilon_q(\sigma,\nu)}{4}\Omega(\sigma)d\sigma + \frac{1}{\int_\varsigma^\nu \mathcal{W}(\omega)d\omega}\int_\mu^\sigma \frac{\Upsilon_q(\mu,\omega)+\Upsilon_q(\sigma,\omega)}{4}\mathcal{W}(\omega)d\omega\right].
\end{aligned} \quad (88)$$

Now, from the left part of double inequalities Equations (84) and (85), we obtain

$$\Upsilon_q\left(\frac{\mu+\sigma}{2},\frac{\varsigma+\nu}{2}\right) \supseteq_I \frac{1}{\int_\varsigma^\nu \mathcal{W}(\omega)d\omega}\int_\varsigma^\nu \Upsilon_q\left(\frac{\mu+\sigma}{2},\omega\right)\mathcal{W}(\omega)d\omega, \quad (89)$$

and

$$\Upsilon_q\left(\frac{\mu+\sigma}{2},\frac{\varsigma+\nu}{2}\right) \supseteq_I \frac{1}{\int_\mu^\sigma \Omega(\sigma)d\sigma}\int_\mu^\sigma \Upsilon_q\left(\sigma,\frac{\varsigma+\nu}{2}\right)\Omega(\sigma)d\sigma \quad (90)$$

Summing inequalities Equations (89) and (90), we obtain

$$\Upsilon_q\left(\frac{\mu+\sigma}{2},\frac{\varsigma+\nu}{2}\right) \supseteq_I \frac{1}{2}\left[\frac{1}{\int_\mu^\sigma \Omega(\sigma)d\sigma}\int_\mu^\sigma \Upsilon_q\left(\sigma,\frac{\varsigma+\nu}{2}\right)\Omega(\sigma)d\sigma + \frac{1}{\int_\varsigma^\nu \mathcal{W}(\omega)d\omega}\int_\varsigma^\nu \Upsilon_q\left(\frac{\mu+\sigma}{2},\omega\right)\mathcal{W}(\omega)d\omega\right]. \quad (91)$$

Similarly, from the right part of Equations (84) and (85), we obtain

$$\frac{1}{\int_\varsigma^\nu \mathcal{W}(\omega)d\omega}\int_\varsigma^\nu \Upsilon_q(\mu,\omega)\mathcal{W}(\omega)d\omega \supseteq_I \frac{\Upsilon_q(\mu,\varsigma)+\Upsilon_q(\mu,\nu)}{2}, \quad (92)$$

$$\frac{1}{\int_\varsigma^\nu \mathcal{W}(\omega)d\omega}\int_\varsigma^\nu \Upsilon_q(\sigma,\omega)\mathcal{W}(\omega)d\omega \supseteq_I \frac{\Upsilon_q(\sigma,\varsigma)+\Upsilon_q(\sigma,\nu)}{2}, \quad (93)$$

and

$$\frac{1}{\int_\mu^\sigma \Omega(\sigma)d\sigma}\int_\mu^\sigma \Upsilon_q(\sigma,\varsigma)\Omega(\sigma)d\sigma \supseteq_I \frac{\Upsilon_q(\mu,\varsigma)+\Upsilon_q(\sigma,\varsigma)}{2}. \quad (94)$$

$$\frac{1}{\int_\mu^\sigma \Omega(\sigma)d\sigma}\int_\mu^\sigma \Upsilon_q(\sigma,\nu)\Omega(\sigma)d\sigma \supseteq_I \frac{\Upsilon_q(\mu,\nu)+\Upsilon_q(\sigma,\nu)}{2}. \quad (95)$$

Adding Equations (92)–(95) and dividing by 4, we obtain

$$\begin{aligned}
&\frac{1}{4\int_\varsigma^\nu \mathcal{W}(\omega)d\omega}\left[\int_\varsigma^\nu \Upsilon_q(\mu,\omega)\mathcal{W}(\omega)d\omega + \int_\varsigma^\nu \Upsilon_q(\sigma,\omega)\mathcal{W}(\omega)d\omega\right] + \frac{1}{4\int_\mu^\sigma \Omega(\sigma)d\sigma}\left[\int_\mu^\sigma \Upsilon_q(\sigma,\varsigma)\Omega(\sigma)d\sigma + \int_\mu^\sigma \Upsilon_q(\sigma,\nu)\Omega(\sigma)d\sigma\right] \\
&\supseteq_I \frac{\Upsilon_q(\mu,\varsigma)+\Upsilon_q(\mu,\nu)+\Upsilon_q(\sigma,\varsigma)+\Upsilon_q(\sigma,\nu)}{4}
\end{aligned} \quad (96)$$

Combining inequalities Equations (88), (91), and (96), we obtain

$$\begin{aligned}
\Upsilon_{\mathfrak{q}}\left(\tfrac{\mu+\sigma}{2}, \tfrac{\varsigma+\nu}{2}\right) &\supseteq_I \tfrac{1}{2}\left[\tfrac{1}{\int_\mu^\sigma \Omega(\sigma)d\sigma}\int_\mu^\sigma \Upsilon_{\mathfrak{q}}\left(\sigma, \tfrac{\varsigma+\nu}{2}\right)\Omega(\sigma)d\sigma + \tfrac{1}{\int_\varsigma^\nu \mathcal{W}(\omega)d\omega}\int_\varsigma^\nu \Upsilon_{\mathfrak{q}}\left(\tfrac{\mu+\sigma}{2}, \omega\right)\mathcal{W}(\omega)d\omega\right]. \\
&\supseteq_I \tfrac{1}{\int_\mu^\sigma \Omega(\sigma)d\sigma \int_\mu^\sigma \mathcal{W}(\omega)d\omega}\int_\mu^\sigma \int_\varsigma^\nu \Upsilon(\sigma,\omega)\Omega(\sigma)\mathcal{W}(\omega)d\omega d\sigma \\
&\supseteq_I \tfrac{1}{4\int_\varsigma^\nu \mathcal{W}(\omega)d\omega}\left[\int_\varsigma^\nu \Upsilon_{\mathfrak{q}}(\mu,\omega)\mathcal{W}(\omega)d\omega + \int_\varsigma^\nu \Upsilon_{\mathfrak{q}}(\sigma,\omega)\mathcal{W}(\omega)d\omega\right] \\
&+ \tfrac{1}{4\int_\mu^\sigma \Omega(\sigma)d\sigma}\left[\int_\mu^\sigma \Upsilon_{\mathfrak{q}}(\sigma,\varsigma)\Omega(\sigma)d\sigma + \int_\mu^\sigma \Upsilon_{\mathfrak{q}}(\sigma,\nu)\Omega(\sigma)d\sigma\right] \\
&\supseteq_I \tfrac{\Upsilon_{\mathfrak{q}}(\mu,\varsigma)+\Upsilon_{\mathfrak{q}}(\mu,\nu)}{2} + \tfrac{\Upsilon_{\mathfrak{q}}(\sigma,\varsigma)+\Upsilon_{\mathfrak{q}}(\sigma,\nu)}{2} + \tfrac{\Upsilon_{\mathfrak{q}}(\mu,\varsigma)+\Upsilon_{\mathfrak{q}}(\sigma,\varsigma)}{2} + \tfrac{\Upsilon_{\mathfrak{q}}(\mu,\nu)+\Upsilon_{\mathfrak{q}}(\sigma,\nu)}{2}.
\end{aligned}$$

That is,

$$\begin{aligned}
\widetilde{\Upsilon}\left(\tfrac{\mu+\sigma}{2}, \tfrac{\varsigma+\nu}{2}\right) &\supseteq_{\mathbb{F}} \tfrac{1}{2}\left[\tfrac{1}{\int_\mu^\sigma \Omega(\sigma)d\sigma} \odot \int_\mu^\sigma \widetilde{\Upsilon}\left(\sigma, \tfrac{\varsigma+\nu}{2}\right)\Omega(\sigma)d\sigma \oplus \tfrac{1}{\int_\mu^\sigma \mathcal{W}(\omega)d\omega} \odot \int_\mu^\sigma \widetilde{\Upsilon}\left(\tfrac{\mu+\sigma}{2}, \omega\right)\mathcal{W}(\omega)d\omega\right] \\
&\supseteq_{\mathbb{F}} \tfrac{1}{\int_\mu^\sigma \Omega(\sigma)d\sigma \int_\mu^\sigma \mathcal{W}(\omega)d\omega} \odot \int_\mu^\sigma \int_\varsigma^\nu \widetilde{\Upsilon}(\sigma,\omega)\Omega(\sigma)\mathcal{W}(\omega)d\omega d\sigma \\
&\supseteq_{\mathbb{F}} \tfrac{1}{4\int_\mu^\sigma \Omega(\sigma)d\sigma} \odot \left[\int_\mu^\sigma \widetilde{\Upsilon}(\sigma,\varsigma)d\sigma \oplus \int_\mu^\sigma \widetilde{\Upsilon}(\sigma,\nu)d\sigma\right] \\
&\oplus \tfrac{1}{4\int_\mu^\sigma \mathcal{W}(\omega)d\omega} \odot \left[\int_\varsigma^\nu \widetilde{\Upsilon}(\mu,\omega)d\omega \oplus \int_\varsigma^\nu \widetilde{\Upsilon}(\sigma,\omega)d\omega\right] \\
&\supseteq_{\mathbb{F}} \tfrac{\widetilde{\Upsilon}(\mu,\varsigma)\oplus\widetilde{\Upsilon}(\sigma,\varsigma)\oplus\widetilde{\Upsilon}(\mu,\nu)\oplus\widetilde{\Upsilon}(\sigma,\nu)}{4},
\end{aligned}$$

Hence, this concludes the proof. □

Remark 3. *From inequality Equation (56), the following exceptional results can be acquired:*

If $\mathcal{W}(\omega) = 1 = \Omega(\sigma)$, one can then obtain inequality Equation (36).

Let $\Upsilon_*((\sigma,\omega),\mathfrak{q}) \neq \Upsilon^*((\sigma,\omega),\mathfrak{q})$ with $\mathfrak{q} = 1$. Then, one can derive following inclusion [61]:

$$\begin{aligned}
\Upsilon\left(\tfrac{\mu+\sigma}{2}, \tfrac{\varsigma+\nu}{2}\right) &\supseteq \tfrac{1}{2}\left[\tfrac{1}{\int_\mu^\sigma \Omega(\sigma)d\sigma}\int_\mu^\sigma \Upsilon\left(\sigma, \tfrac{\varsigma+\nu}{2}\right)\Omega(\sigma)d\sigma + \tfrac{1}{\int_\mu^\sigma \mathcal{W}(\omega)d\omega}\int_\mu^\sigma \Upsilon\left(\tfrac{\mu+\sigma}{2}, \omega\right)\mathcal{W}(\omega)d\omega\right] \\
&\supseteq \tfrac{1}{\int_\mu^\sigma \Omega(\sigma)d\sigma \int_\mu^\sigma \mathcal{W}(\omega)d\omega}\int_\mu^\sigma \int_\varsigma^\nu \Upsilon(\sigma,\omega)\Omega(\sigma)\mathcal{W}(\omega)d\omega d\sigma \\
&\supseteq \tfrac{1}{4\int_\mu^\sigma \Omega(\sigma)d\sigma}\left[\int_\mu^\sigma \Upsilon(\sigma,\varsigma)d\sigma + \int_\mu^\sigma \Upsilon(\sigma,\nu)d\sigma\right] \\
&+ \tfrac{1}{4\int_\mu^\sigma \mathcal{W}(\omega)d\omega}\left[\int_\varsigma^\nu \Upsilon(\mu,\omega)d\omega + \int_\varsigma^\nu \Upsilon(\sigma,\omega)d\omega\right] \\
&\tfrac{\Upsilon(\mu,\varsigma)+\Upsilon(\sigma,\varsigma)+\Upsilon(\mu,\nu)+\Upsilon(\sigma,\nu)}{4}.
\end{aligned} \tag{97}$$

Let $\widetilde{\Upsilon}$ be a left coordinated UD-convex FN-V-M. Then, we can achieve the following outcome (see [91]*):*

$$\begin{aligned}
\widetilde{\Upsilon}\left(\tfrac{\mu+\sigma}{2}, \tfrac{\varsigma+\nu}{2}\right) &\leq_{\mathbb{F}} \tfrac{1}{2}\left[\tfrac{1}{\int_\mu^\sigma \Omega(\sigma)d\sigma} \odot \int_\mu^\sigma \widetilde{\Upsilon}\left(\sigma, \tfrac{\varsigma+\nu}{2}\right)\Omega(\sigma)d\sigma \oplus \tfrac{1}{\int_\mu^\sigma \mathcal{W}(\omega)d\omega} \odot \int_\mu^\sigma \widetilde{\Upsilon}\left(\tfrac{\mu+\sigma}{2}, \omega\right)\mathcal{W}(\omega)d\omega\right] \\
&\leq_{\mathbb{F}} \tfrac{1}{\int_\mu^\sigma \Omega(\sigma)d\sigma \int_\mu^\sigma \mathcal{W}(\omega)d\omega} \odot \int_\mu^\sigma \int_\varsigma^\nu \widetilde{\Upsilon}(\sigma,\omega)\Omega(\sigma)\mathcal{W}(\omega)d\omega d\sigma \\
&\leq_{\mathbb{F}} \tfrac{1}{4\int_\mu^\sigma \Omega(\sigma)d\sigma} \odot \left[\int_\mu^\sigma \widetilde{\Upsilon}(\sigma,\varsigma)d\sigma \oplus \int_\mu^\sigma \widetilde{\Upsilon}(\sigma,\nu)d\sigma\right] \\
&\oplus \tfrac{1}{4\int_\mu^\sigma \mathcal{W}(\omega)d\omega} \odot \left[\int_\varsigma^\nu \widetilde{\Upsilon}(\mu,\omega)d\omega \oplus \int_\varsigma^\nu \widetilde{\Upsilon}(\sigma,\omega)d\omega\right] \\
&\leq_{\mathbb{F}} \tfrac{\widetilde{\Upsilon}(\mu,\varsigma)\oplus\widetilde{\Upsilon}(\sigma,\varsigma)\oplus\widetilde{\Upsilon}(\mu,\nu)\oplus\widetilde{\Upsilon}(\sigma,\nu)}{4}.
\end{aligned} \tag{98}$$

Let $\widetilde{\Upsilon}$ be a left coordinated UD-convex FN-V-M and $\mathcal{W}(\omega) = 1 = \Omega(\sigma)$. Then, we can achieve the following outcome (see [91]*):*

$$\begin{aligned}
\widetilde{\Upsilon}\left(\tfrac{\mu+\sigma}{2}, \tfrac{\varsigma+\nu}{2}\right) &\leq_{\mathbb{F}} \tfrac{1}{2} \odot \left[\tfrac{1}{\sigma-\mu} \odot \int_\mu^\sigma \widetilde{\Upsilon}\left(\sigma, \tfrac{\varsigma+\nu}{2}\right)d\sigma \oplus \tfrac{1}{\nu-\varsigma} \odot \int_\varsigma^\nu \widetilde{\Upsilon}\left(\tfrac{\mu+\sigma}{2}, \omega\right)d\omega\right] \\
&\leq_{\mathbb{F}} \tfrac{1}{(\sigma-\mu)(\nu-\varsigma)} \odot \int_\mu^\sigma \int_\varsigma^\nu \widetilde{\Upsilon}(\sigma,\omega)d\omega d\sigma \\
&\leq_{\mathbb{F}} \tfrac{1}{4(\sigma-\mu)} \odot \left[\int_\mu^\sigma \widetilde{\Upsilon}(\sigma,\varsigma)d\sigma \oplus \int_\mu^\sigma \widetilde{\Upsilon}(\sigma,\nu)d\sigma\right] \oplus \tfrac{1}{4(\nu-\varsigma)} \odot \left[\int_\varsigma^\nu \widetilde{\Upsilon}(\mu,\omega)d\omega \oplus \int_\varsigma^\nu \widetilde{\Upsilon}(\sigma,\omega)d\omega\right] \\
&\leq_{\mathbb{F}} \tfrac{\widetilde{\Upsilon}(\mu,\varsigma)\oplus\widetilde{\Upsilon}(\sigma,\varsigma)\oplus\widetilde{\Upsilon}(\mu,\nu)\oplus\widetilde{\Upsilon}(\sigma,\nu)}{4}.
\end{aligned} \tag{99}$$

Let $\Upsilon_*((\sigma,\omega),\mathfrak{q}) \neq \Upsilon^*((\sigma,\omega),\mathfrak{q})$ *with* $\mathfrak{q}=1$ *and* $\mathcal{W}(\omega)=1=\Omega(\sigma)$*. Then, we acquire following inequality (see* [90]*):*

$$\begin{aligned}
\Upsilon\left(\tfrac{\mu+\sigma}{2},\tfrac{\varsigma+\nu}{2}\right) &\supseteq \tfrac{1}{2}\left[\tfrac{1}{\sigma-\mu}\int_\mu^\sigma \Upsilon\left(\sigma,\tfrac{\varsigma+\nu}{2}\right)d\sigma + \tfrac{1}{\nu-\varsigma}\int_\varsigma^\nu \Upsilon\left(\tfrac{\mu+\sigma}{2},\omega\right)d\omega\right] \\
&\supseteq \tfrac{1}{(\sigma-\mu)(\nu-\varsigma)}\int_\mu^\sigma\int_\varsigma^\nu \Upsilon(\sigma,\omega)d\omega d\sigma \\
&\supseteq \tfrac{1}{4(\sigma-\mu)}\left[\int_\mu^\sigma \Upsilon(\sigma,\varsigma)d\sigma + \int_\mu^\sigma \Upsilon(\sigma,\nu)d\sigma\right] + \tfrac{1}{4(\nu-\varsigma)}\left[\int_\varsigma^\nu \Upsilon(\mu,\omega)d\omega + \int_\varsigma^\nu \Upsilon(\sigma,\omega)d\omega\right] \\
&\supseteq \tfrac{\Upsilon(\mu,\varsigma)+\Upsilon(\sigma,\varsigma)+\Upsilon(\mu,\nu)+\Upsilon(\sigma,\nu)}{4}.
\end{aligned} \tag{100}$$

Let $\Upsilon_*((\sigma,\omega),\mathfrak{q}) = \Upsilon^*((\sigma,\omega),\mathfrak{q})$ *with* $\mathfrak{q}=1$*. Then, we can derive the following inclusion:*

$$\begin{aligned}
\Upsilon\left(\tfrac{\mu+\sigma}{2},\tfrac{\varsigma+\nu}{2}\right) &\leq \tfrac{1}{2}\left[\tfrac{1}{\int_\mu^\sigma \Omega(\sigma)d\sigma}\int_\mu^\sigma \Upsilon\left(\sigma,\tfrac{\varsigma+\nu}{2}\right)\Omega(\sigma)d\sigma + \tfrac{1}{\int_\mu^\sigma \mathcal{W}(\omega)d\omega}\int_\mu^\sigma \Upsilon\left(\tfrac{\mu+\sigma}{2},\omega\right)\mathcal{W}(\omega)d\omega\right] \\
&\leq \tfrac{1}{\int_\mu^\sigma \Omega(\sigma)d\sigma\int_\mu^\sigma \mathcal{W}(\omega)d\omega}\int_\mu^\sigma\int_\varsigma^\nu \Upsilon(\sigma,\omega)\Omega(\sigma)\mathcal{W}(\omega)d\omega d\sigma \\
&\leq \tfrac{1}{4\int_\mu^\sigma \Omega(\sigma)d\sigma}\left[\int_\mu^\sigma \Upsilon(\sigma,\varsigma)d\sigma + \int_\mu^\sigma \Upsilon(\sigma,\nu)d\sigma\right] \\
&+ \tfrac{1}{4\int_\mu^\sigma \mathcal{W}(\omega)d\omega}\left[\int_\varsigma^\nu \Upsilon(\mu,\omega)d\omega + \int_\varsigma^\nu \Upsilon(\sigma,\omega)d\omega\right] \\
&\leq \tfrac{\Upsilon(\mu,\varsigma)+\Upsilon(\sigma,\varsigma)+\Upsilon(\mu,\nu)+\Upsilon(\sigma,\nu)}{4}.
\end{aligned} \tag{101}$$

4. Conclusions

In this paper, we introduced and studied a new class of generalized convex fuzzy mappings on coordinates involving the up and down fuzzy relation, which are known as coordinated up and down convex fuzzy mappings. Several new versions of integral inequalities for this class of functions were obtained. It is interesting to note that most of the classes and other results are also exceptional cases of our defined class and main results, and these exceptional cases of our results are discussed as applications. For the validation of our main outcomes in this paper, some examples were also proved. In future, this concept will be explored in the field of quantum calculus.

Author Contributions: Conceptualization, M.B.K.; methodology, M.B.K.; validation, M.B.K. and M.S.S.; formal analysis, C.-T.L. and C.-C.L.; investigation, M.B.K.; resources, M.B.K. and C.-C.L.; data curation, M.B.K. and A.A.; writing—original draft preparation, M.B.K.; writing—review and editing, M.B.K.; visualization, M.S.S., C.-T.L., C.-C.L. and A.A.; supervision, M.B.K.; project administration, M.S.S.; funding acquisition, M.B.K. and C.-T.L. All authors have read and agreed to the published version of the manuscript.

Funding: This work was supported in part by the National Science and Technology Council in Taiwan under contract no. NSTC 110-2410-H-165-001-MY2. Also, the researchers also would like to acknowledge Deanship of Scientific Research, Taif University for funding this work.

Data Availability Statement: Not applicable.

Acknowledgments: The authors would like to thank the Rector of COMSATS University Islamabad, Islamabad, Pakistan, for providing excellent research. The researchers would like to acknowledge Deanship of Scientific Research, Taif University for funding this work.

Conflicts of Interest: The authors declare no conflict of interest.

References

1. Hille, E.; Phillips, R.S. *Functional Analysis and Semigroups*; American Mathematical Society: Providence, RI, USA, 1996; Volume 31.
2. Rosenbaum, R.A. Subadditive functions. *Duke Math. J.* **1950**, *17*, 227–247. [CrossRef]
3. Dannan, F.M. Submultiplicative and subadditive functions and integral inequalities of Bellman–Bihari type. *J. Math. Anal. Appl.* **1986**, *120*, 631–646. [CrossRef]
4. Zhao, T.H.; Castillo, O.; Jahanshahi, H.; Yusuf, A.; Alassafi, M.O.; Alsaadi, F.E.; Chu, Y.M. A fuzzy-based strategy to suppress the novel coronavirus (2019-NCOV) massive outbreak. *Appl. Comput. Math.* **2021**, *20*, 160–176.
5. Zhao, T.H.; Wang, M.K.; Chu, Y.M. On the bounds of the perimeter of an ellipse. *Acta Math. Sci.* **2022**, *42B*, 491–501. [CrossRef]
6. Zhao, T.H.; Wang, M.K.; Hai, G.J.; Chu, Y.M. Landen inequalities for Gaussian hypergeometric function. *RACSAM Rev. R Acad. A* **2022**, *116*, 53. [CrossRef]

7. Wang, M.K.; Hong, M.Y.; Xu, Y.F.; Shen, Z.H.; Chu, Y.M. Inequalities for generalized trigonometric and hyperbolic functions with one parameter. *J. Math. Inequal.* **2020**, *14*, 521–529. [CrossRef]
8. Zhao, T.H.; Qian, W.M.; Chu, Y.M. Sharp power mean bounds for the tangent and hyperbolic sine means. *J. Math. Inequal.* **2021**, *15*, 1459–1472. [CrossRef]
9. Chu, Y.M.; Wang, G.D.; Zhang, X.H. The Schur multiplicative and harmonic convexities of the complete symmetric function. *Math. Nachr.* **2011**, *284*, 53–663. [CrossRef]
10. Nwaeze, E.R.; Khan, M.A.; Chu, Y.M. Fractional inclusions of the Hermite-Hadamard type for m-polynomial convex interval-valued functions. *Adv. Differ. Equ.* **2020**, *2020*, 507. [CrossRef]
11. Zhao, T.H.; Bhayo, B.A.; Chu, Y.M. Inequalities for generalized Grötzsch ring function. *Comput. Meth Funct. Theory* **2022**, *22*, 559–574. [CrossRef]
12. Zhao, T.H.; He, Z.Y.; Chu, Y.M. Sharp bounds for the weighted Hölder mean of the zero-balanced generalized complete elliptic integrals. *Comput. Meth Funct. Thoery* **2021**, *21*, 413–426. [CrossRef]
13. Zhao, T.H.; Wang, M.K.; Chu, Y.M. Concavity and bounds involving generalized elliptic integral of the first kind. *J. Math. Inequal.* **2021**, *15*, 701–724. [CrossRef]
14. Zhao, T.H.; Wang, M.K.; Chu, Y.M. Monotonicity and convexity involving generalized elliptic integral of the first kind. *RACSAM Rev. R Acad. A* **2021**, *115*, 46. [CrossRef]
15. Chu, H.H.; Zhao, T.H.; Chu, Y.M. Sharp bounds for the Toader mean of order 3 in terms of arithmetic, quadratic and contra harmonic means. *Math. Slovaca* **2020**, *70*, 1097–1112. [CrossRef]
16. Zhao, T.H.; He, Z.Y.; Chu, Y.M. On some refinements for inequalities involving zero-balanced hyper geometric function. *AIMS Math.* **2020**, *5*, 6479–6495. [CrossRef]
17. Zhao, T.H.; Wang, M.K.; Chu, Y.M. A sharp double inequality involving generalized complete elliptic integral of the first kind. *AIMS Math.* **2020**, *5*, 4512–4528. [CrossRef]
18. Laatsch, R.G. Subadditive Functions of One Real Variable. Ph.D. Thesis, Oklahoma State University, Stillwater, OK, USA, 1962.
19. Matkowski, J. On subadditive functions and Φ-additive mappings. *Open. Math.* **2003**, *1*, 435–440.
20. Matkowski, J. Subadditive periodic functions. *Opusc. Math.* **2011**, *31*, 75–96. [CrossRef]
21. Matkowski, J.; Swiatkowski, T. On subadditive functions. *Proc. Am. Math. Soc.* **1993**, *119*, 187–197. [CrossRef]
22. Ali, M.A.; Sarikaya, M.Z.; Budak, H. Fractional Hermite–Hadamard type inequalities for subadditive functions. *Filomat* **2022**, *36*, 3715–3729. [CrossRef]
23. Botmart, T.; Sahoo, S.K.; Kodamasingh, B.; Latif, M.A.; Jarad, F.; Kashuri, A. Certain midpoint-type Fejér and Hermite–Hadamard inclusions involving fractional integrals with an exponential function in kernel. *AIMS Math.* **2023**, *8*, 5616–5638. [CrossRef]
24. Kadakal, M.; İşcan, İ. Exponential type convexity and some related inequalities. *J. Inequal. Appl.* **2020**, *1*, 82. [CrossRef]
25. Alomari, M.; Darus, M.; Kirmaci, U.S. Refinements of Hadamard-type inequalities for quasi-convex functions with applications to trapezoidal formula and to special means. *Comput. Math. Appl.* **2010**, *59*, 225–232. [CrossRef]
26. Zhang, X.M.; Chu, Y.M.; Zhang, X.H. The Hermite-Hadamard type inequality of *GA*-convex functions and its applications. *J. Inequal. Appl.* **2010**, *2010*, 507560. [CrossRef]
27. Dragomir, S.S.; Pećarič, J.; Persson, L.E. Some inequalities of Hadamard type. *Soochow J. Math.* **2001**, *21*, 335–341.
28. Guessab, A.; Schmeisser, G. Sharp integral inequalities of the Hermite–Hadamard type. *J. Approx. Theory* **2002**, *115*, 260–288. [CrossRef]
29. İşcan, İ.; Kunt, M. Hermite–Hadamard–Fejér type inequalities for quasi-geometrically convex functions via fractional integrals. *J. Math.* **2016**, *2016*, 6523041. [CrossRef]
30. Kashuri, A.; Liko, R. Some new Hermite–Hadamard type inequalities and their applications. *Stud. Sci. Math. Hung.* **2019**, *56*, 103–142. [CrossRef]
31. Xi, B.Y.; Qi, F. Some Hermite–Hadamard type inequalities for differentiable convex functions and applications. *Hacet. J. Math. Stat.* **2013**, *42*, 243–257.
32. Sarikaya, M.Z.; Saglam, A.; Yildirim, H. On some Hadamard-type inequalities for *h*-convex functions. *J. Math. Inequal.* **2008**, *2*, 335–341. [CrossRef]
33. Khan, M.B.; Noor, M.A.; Noor, K.I.; Chu, Y.M. New Hermite-Hadamard type inequalities for -convex fuzzy-interval-valued functions. *Adv. Differ. Equ.* **2021**, *2021*, 6–20. [CrossRef]
34. Moore, R.E. *Interval Analysis*; Prentice-Hall: Englewood Cliffs, NJ, USA, 1966.
35. Moore, R.E. *Methods and Applications of Interval Analysis*; SIAM: Philadelphia, PA, USA, 1979.
36. Bhurjee, A.K.; Panda, G. Multi-objective interval fractional programming problems: An approach for obtaining efficient solutions. *Opsearch* **2015**, *52*, 156–167. [CrossRef]
37. Zhang, J.; Liu, S.; Li, L.; Feng, Q. The KKT optimality conditions in a class of generalized convex optimization problems with an interval-valued objective function. *Optim. Lett.* **2014**, *8*, 607–631. [CrossRef]
38. Zhao, D.; An, T.; Ye, G.; Liu, W. Chebyshev type inequalities for interval-valued functions. *Fuzzy Sets Syst.* **2020**, *396*, 82–101. [CrossRef]
39. Guo, Y.; Ye, G.; Zhao, D.; Liu, W. *gH*-symmetrically derivative of interval-valued functions and applications in interval-valued optimization. *Symmetry* **2019**, *11*, 1203. [CrossRef]
40. Moore, R.E.; Kearfott, R.B.; Cloud, M.J. *Introduction to Interval Analysis*; SIAM: Philadelphia, PA, USA, 2009.

41. Rothwell, E.J.; Cloud, M.J. Automatic error analysis using intervals. *IEEE Trans. Educ.* **2011**, *55*, 9–15. [CrossRef]
42. Snyder, J.M. Interval analysis for computer graphics. In Proceedings of the 19th Annual Conference on Computer Graphics and Interactive Techniques, Chicago, IL, USA, 27–31 July 1992; pp. 121–130.
43. Chalco-Cano, Y.; Lodwick, W.A.; Condori-Equice, W. Ostrowski type inequalities and applications in numerical integration for interval-valued functions. *Soft Comput.* **2015**, *19*, 3293–3300. [CrossRef]
44. Zhao, D.; Chu, Y.M.; Siddiqui, M.K.; Ali, K.; Nasir, M.; Younas, M.T.; Cancan, M. On reverse degree based topological indices of polycyclic metal organic network, Polycyclic Aromatic Compounds. *Polycycl. Aromat. Compd.* **2022**, *42*, 4386–4403. [CrossRef]
45. Chu, Y.M.; Zhao, T.H. Concavity of the error function with respect to Hölder means. *Math. Inequal. Appl.* **2016**, *19*, 589–595. [CrossRef]
46. Zhao, T.H.; Shi, L.; Chu, Y.M. Convexity and concavity of the modified Bessel functions of the first kind with respect to Hölder means. *RACSAM Rev. R Acad. A* **2020**, *114*, 96. [CrossRef]
47. Zhao, T.H.; Zhou, B.C.; Wang, M.K.; Chu, Y.M. On approximating the quasi-arithmetic mean. *J. Inequal. Appl.* **2019**, *2019*, 42. [CrossRef]
48. Zhao, T.H.; Wang, M.K.; Zhang, W.; Chu, Y.M. Quadratic transformation inequalities for Gaussian hyper geometric function. *J. Inequal. Appl.* **2018**, *2018*, 251. [CrossRef]
49. Qian, W.M.; Chu, H.H.; Wang, M.K.; Chu, Y.M. Sharp inequalities for the Toader mean of order −1 in terms of other bivariate means. *J. Math. Inequal.* **2022**, *16*, 127–141. [CrossRef]
50. Zhao, T.H.; Chu, H.H.; Chu, Y.M. Optimal Lehmer mean bounds for the nth power-type Toader mean of n = −1, 1, 3. *J. Math. Inequal.* **2022**, *16*, 157–168. [CrossRef]
51. Ibrahim, M.; Saeed, T.; Hekmatifar, M.; Sabetvand, R.; Chu, Y.M.; Toghraie, D. Investigation of dynamical behavior of 3LPT protein-water molecules interactions in atomic structures using molecular dynamics simulation. *J. Mol. Liq.* **2021**, *329*, 115615. [CrossRef]
52. Xiong, P.Y.; Almarashi, A.; Dhahad, H.A.; Alawee, W.H.; Abusorrah, A.M.; Issakhov, A.; Abu-Hamhed, N.H.; Shafee, A.; Chu, Y.M. Nanomaterial transportation and exergy loss modeling incorporating CVFEM. *J. Mol. Liq.* **2021**, *330*, 115591. [CrossRef]
53. Wang, T.; Almarashi, A.; Al-Turki, Y.A.; Abu-Hamdeh, N.H.; Hajizadeh, M.R.; Chu, Y.M. Approaches for expedition of discharging of PCM involving nanoparticles and radial fins. *J. Mol. Liq.* **2021**, *329*, 115052. [CrossRef]
54. Xiong, P.Y.; Almarashi, A.; Dhahad, H.A.; Alawee, W.H.; Issakhov, A.; Chu, Y.M. Nanoparticles for phase change process of water utilizing FEM. *J. Mol. Liq.* **2021**, *334*, 116096. [CrossRef]
55. Chu, Y.M.; Abu-Hamdeh, N.H.; Ben-Beya, B.; Hajizadeh, M.R.; Li, Z.; Bach, Q.V. Nanoparticle enhanced PCM exergy loss and thermal behavior by means of FVM. *J. Mol. Liq.* **2020**, *320*, 114457. [CrossRef]
56. Chu, Y.M.; Xia, W.F.; Zhang, X.H. The Schur concavity, Schur multiplicative and harmonic convexities of the second dual form of the Hamy symmetric function with applications. *J. Multivar. Anal.* **2012**, *105*, 412–442. [CrossRef]
57. Hajiseyedazizi, S.N.; Samei, M.E.; Alzabut, J.; Chu, Y.M. On multi-step methods for singular fractional q-integro-differential equations. *Open. Math.* **2021**, *19*, 1378–1405. [CrossRef]
58. Jin, F.; Qian, Z.S.; Chu, Y.M.; Rahman, M. On nonlinear evolution model for drinking behavior under Caputo-Fabrizio derivative. *J. Appl. Anal. Comput.* **2022**, *12*, 790–806. [CrossRef]
59. Budak, H.; Tunç, T.; Sarikaya, M. Fractional Hermite-Hadamard type inequalities for interval-valued functions. *Proc. Amer. Math. Soc.* **2020**, *148*, 705–718. [CrossRef]
60. Sharma, N.; Singh, S.K.; Mishra, S.K.; Hamdi, A. Hermite-Hadamard type inequalities for interval-valued preinvex functions via Riemann–Liouville fractional integrals. *J. Inequal. Appl.* **2021**, *2021*, 98. [CrossRef]
61. Zhao, D.; Ali, M.A.; Murtaza, G.; Zhang, Z. On the Hermite-Hadamard inequalities for interval-valued coordinated convex functions. *Adv. Differ. Equ.* **2020**, *2020*, 570. [CrossRef]
62. Zhao, D.; Zhao, G.; Ye, G.; Liu, W.; Dragomir, S.S. On Hermite-Hadamard type inequalities for coordinated *h*-convex interval-valued functions. *Mathematics* **2021**, *9*, 2352. [CrossRef]
63. Budak, H.; Kara, H.; Ali, M.A.; Khan, S.; Chu, Y.M. Fractional Hermite-Hadamard-type inequalities for interval-valued coordinated convex functions. *Open. Math.* **2021**, *19*, 1081–1097. [CrossRef]
64. Kara, H.; Budak, H.; Ali, M.A.; Sarikaya, M.Z.; Chu, Y.M. Weighted Hermite–Hadamard type inclusions for products of coordinated convex interval-valued functions. *Adv. Differ. Equ.* **2021**, *2021*, 104. [CrossRef]
65. Kara, H.; Ali, M.A.; Budak, H. Hermite-Hadamard type inequalities for interval-valued coordinated convex functions involving generalized fractional integrals. *Math. Methods Appl. Sci.* **2021**, *44*, 104–123. [CrossRef]
66. Lai, K.K.; Bisht, J.; Sharma, N.; Mishra, S.K. Hermite-Hadamard type fractional inclusions for interval-valued preinvex functions. *Mathematics* **2022**, *10*, 264. [CrossRef]
67. Shi, F.; Ye, G.; Zhao, D.; Liu, W. Some fractional Hermite-Hadamard type inequalities for interval-valued coordinated functions. *Adv. Differ. Equ.* **2021**, *2021*, 32. [CrossRef]
68. Tariboon, J.; Ali, M.A.; Budak, H.; Ntouyas, S.K. Hermite-Hadamard inclusions for coordinated interval-valued functions via post-quantum calculus. *Symmetry* **2021**, *13*, 1216. [CrossRef]
69. Du, T.; Zhou, T. On the fractional double integral inclusion relations having exponential kernels via interval-valued coordinated convex mappings. *Chaos Solitons Fractals* **2022**, *156*, 111846. [CrossRef]

70. Khan, M.B.; Santos-García, G.; Zaini, H.G.; Treanţă, S.; Soliman, M.S. Some new concepts related to integral operators and inequalities on coordinates in fuzzy fractional calculus. *Mathematics* **2022**, *10*, 534. [CrossRef]
71. Ibrahim, M.; Saeed, T.; Alshehri, A.M.; Chu, Y.M. Using artificial neural networks to predict the rheological behavior of non-Newtonian grapheme-ethylene glycol nanofluid. *J. Therm. Anal. Calorim.* **2021**, *145*, 1925–1934. [CrossRef]
72. Wang, F.Z.; Khan, M.N.; Ahmad, I.; Ahmad, H.; Abu-Zinadah, H.; Chu, Y.M. Numerical solution of traveling waves in chemical kinetics: Time-fractional fisher's equations. *Fractals.* **2022**, *30*, 2240051. [CrossRef]
73. Chu, Y.M.; Siddiqui, M.K.; Nasir, M. On topological co-indices of polycyclic tetrathiafulvalene and polycyclic oragano silicon dendrimers. *Polycycl. Aromat. Compd.* **2022**, *42*, 2179–2197. [CrossRef]
74. Chu, Y.M.; Rauf, A.; Ishtiaq, M.; Siddiqui, M.K.; Muhammad, M.H. Topological properties of polycyclic aromatic nanostars dendrimers. *Polycycl. Aromat. Compd.* **2022**, *42*, 1891–1908. [CrossRef]
75. Chu, Y.M.; Numan, M.; Butt, S.I.; Siddiqui, M.K.; Ullah, R.; Cancan, M.; Ali, U. Degree-based topological aspects of polyphenylene nanostructures. *Polycycl. Aromat. Compd.* **2022**, *42*, 2591–2606. [CrossRef]
76. Chu, Y.M.; Muhammad, M.H.; Rauf, A.; Ishtiaq, M.; Siddiqui, M.K. Topological study of polycyclic graphite carbon nitride. *Polycycl. Aromat. Compd.* **2022**, *42*, 3203–3215. [CrossRef]
77. Anastassiou, G. *Fuzzy Mathematics: Approximation theory*; Springer: Berlin/Heidelberg, Germany, 2010; ISBN 978-3-642-11219-5.
78. Anastassiou, G.; Gal, S. On a fuzzy trigonometric Approximation theorem of Weierstrass-type. *J. Fuzzy Math.* **2001**, *9*, 701–708.
79. Gal, S. Approximation theory in fuzzy setting. In *Handbook of Analytic-Computational Methods in Applied Mathematics, Engineering and Technology*; Anastassiou, G., Ed.; Chapman&Hall/CRC: New York, NY, USA, 2000.
80. Khan, M.B.; Santos-García, G.; Noor, M.A.; Soliman, M.S. Some new concepts related to fuzzy fractional calculus for up and down convex fuzzy-number valued functions and inequalities. *Chaos Solitons Fractals* **2022**, *164*, 112692. [CrossRef]
81. Khan, M.B.; A. Othman, H.A.; Santos-García, G.; Saeed, T.; Soliman, M.S. On fuzzy fractional integral operators having exponential kernels and related certain inequalities for exponential trigonometric convex fuzzy-number valued mappings. *Chaos Solitons Fractals* **2023**, *169*, 113274. [CrossRef]
82. Goetschel, R.; Voxman, W. Elementery fuzzy calculus. *Fuzzy Sets Syst.* **1986**, *18*, 31–43. [CrossRef]
83. Gal, S. Linear continuous functionals on FN-type spaces. *J. Fuzzy Math.* **2009**, *17*, 535–553.
84. Wu, C.; Zengtai, G. On Henstock integral of fuzzy-number-valued functions part (I). *Fuzzy Sets Syst.* **2001**, *120*, 523–532. [CrossRef]
85. Khan, M.B.; Othman, H.A.; Voskoglou, M.G.; Abdullah, L.; Alzubaidi, A.M. Some Certain Fuzzy Aumann Integral Inequalities for Generalized Convexity via Fuzzy Number Valued Mappings. *Mathematics* **2023**, *11*, 550. [CrossRef]
86. Costa, T.M.; Roman-Flores, H. Some integral inequalities for fuzzy-interval-valued functions. *Inform. Sci.* **2017**, *420*, 110–125. [CrossRef]
87. Zhang, D.; Guo, C.; Chen, D.; Wang, G. Jensen's inequalities for set-valued and fuzzy set-valued functions. *Fuzzy Sets Syst.* **2020**, *2020*, 178–204. [CrossRef]
88. Kulish, U.; Miranker, W. *Computer Arithmetic in Theory and Practice*; Academic Press: New York, NY, USA, 2014.
89. Kaleva, O. Fuzzy differential equations. *Fuzzy Sets Syst.* **1987**, *24*, 301–317. [CrossRef]
90. Dragomir, S.S. On the Hadamard's inequlality for convex functions on the co-ordinates in a rectangle from the plane. *Taiwan. J. Math.* **2001**, *2001*, 775–788. [CrossRef]
91. Khan, M.B.; Mohammed, P.O.; Noor, M.A.; Abuahalnaja, K. Fuzzy Integral Inequalities on Coordinates of Convex Fuzzy Interval-Valued Functions. *Math. Biosci. Eng.* **2021**, *18*, 6552–6580. [CrossRef]
92. Khan, M.B.; Catas, A.; Aloraini, N.; Soliman, M.S. Some Certain Fuzzy Fractional Inequalities for Up and Down $\hbar$-Pre-Invex via Fuzzy-Number Valued Mappings. *Fractal Fract.* **2023**, *7*, 171. [CrossRef]
93. Khan, M.B.; Treanţă, S.; Soliman, M.S. Generalized Preinvex Interval-Valued Functions and Related Hermite–Hadamard Type Inequalities. *Symmetry* **2022**, *14*, 1901. [CrossRef]
94. Saeed, T.; Khan, M.B.; Treanţă, S.; Alsulami, H.H.; Alhodaly, M.S. Interval Fejér-Type Inequalities for Left and Right-λ-Preinvex Functions in Interval-Valued Settings. *Axioms* **2022**, *11*, 368. [CrossRef]
95. Khan, M.B.; Othman, H.A.; Santos-García, G.; Noor, M.A.; Soliman, M.S. Some new concepts in fuzzy calculus for up and down λ-convex fuzzy-number valued mappings and related inequalities. *AIMS Math.* **2023**, *8*, 6777–6803. [CrossRef]
96. Khan, M.B.; Santos-García, G.; Budak, H.; Treanţă, S. Soliman. M.S. Some new versions of Jensen, Schur and Hermite-Hadamard type inequalities for $(p, \mathfrak{J})$-convex fuzzy-interval-valued functions. *AIMS Math.* **2023**, *8*, 7437–7470. [CrossRef]
97. Khan, M.B.; Santos-García, G.; Treanţă, S.; Noor, M.A.; Soliman, M.S. Perturbed Mixed Variational-Like Inequalities and Auxiliary Principle Pertaining to a Fuzzy Environment. *Symmetry* **2022**, *14*, 2503. [CrossRef]

Disclaimer/Publisher's Note: The statements, opinions and data contained in all publications are solely those of the individual author(s) and contributor(s) and not of MDPI and/or the editor(s). MDPI and/or the editor(s) disclaim responsibility for any injury to people or property resulting from any ideas, methods, instructions or products referred to in the content.

mathematics

MDPI

Article

Epidemic Spreading on Weighted Co-Evolving Multiplex Networks

Bo Song [1], Huiming Wu [2], Yurong Song [2,*], Xu Wang [3] and Guoping Jiang [2]

1 School of Modern Posts, Nanjing University of Posts and Telecommunications, Nanjing 210023, China; songbo@njupt.edu.cn
2 College of Automation & College of Artificial Intelligence, Nanjing University of Posts and Telecommunications, Nanjing 210023, China; 1020051513@njupt.edu.cn (H.W.); jiangjp@njupt.edu.cn (G.J.)
3 GBDTC, University of Technology Sydney, Sydney, NSW 2007, Australia; xu.wang-1@uts.edu.au
* Correspondence: songyr@njupt.edu.cn; Tel.: +86-1395-1842-705

Abstract: The individual behaviors driven by information diffusion show an undeniable impact on the process of epidemic spreading and have been continuously evolving with the dynamic processes. In this paper, a novel weighted co-evolving multiplex network model is proposed to describe the interaction between information diffusion in online social networks and epidemic spreading in adaptive physical contact networks. Considering the difference in the connections between individuals, the heterogeneous rewiring rate, which is proportional to the strength of the connection, is introduced in our model. The simulation results show that the maximum infection scale decreases as the information acceptance probability grows, and the final infection decreases as the rewiring behaviors increase. Interestingly, an infection peak appears in our model due to the interaction between information diffusion and epidemic spread.

Keywords: co-evolving multiplex networks; epidemic spread; information diffusion; nonlinear differential systems

MSC: 65Q10

Citation: Song, B.; Wu, H.; Song, Y.; Wang, X.; Jiang, G. Epidemic Spreading on Weighted Co-Evolving Multiplex Networks. *Mathematics* **2023**, *11*, 3109. https://doi.org/10.3390/math11143109

Academic Editors: Lijuan Zha, Jian Liu, Jinliang Liu and Alfonso Niño

Received: 24 May 2023
Revised: 5 July 2023
Accepted: 12 July 2023
Published: 14 July 2023

Copyright: © 2023 by the authors. Licensee MDPI, Basel, Switzerland. This article is an open access article distributed under the terms and conditions of the Creative Commons Attribution (CC BY) license (https://creativecommons.org/licenses/by/4.0/).

1. Introduction

Information diffusion, i.e., positive information (e.g., authoritative information, news) and negative information (e.g., rumors and gossip) [1], is always accompanied by virus spreading on social networks or cascading failures on transportation networks, power grids, etc. To describe and analyze the coupling of information diffusion and virus spread/cascading failures, the study on multiplex networks becomes increasingly important as a result of the interactions among different real-world systems [2–5]. Both the difference in network structures of real-world systems and the interactions among different dynamic spread processes in real-world systems can be well described in the multiplex network model [6–10].

The impact of information diffusion on epidemic spread in multiplex networks has been widely studied in recent years [1,2]. The emergence and changing of information-related states enrich the whole epidemic spread process in social networks. First, the states of nodes have become more diversified since a single node owns two states at the same time; one is describing the physical state, and the other is describing the information-related state. And the increase in the node's states leads to the diversity of the propagation process. Furthermore, information diffusion leads to adaptive behavioral changes among individuals in response to epidemic outbreaks. When a public health event occurs on social networks, e.g., Coronavirus-2019 [11], people who had the awareness of prevention or received the relative information would actively take self-protective measures, such as wearing masks and washing their hands frequently. Then, a multiplex network with static network structures evolved into an adaptive multiplex network with a dynamic physical layer [12].

Although the interplay between information diffusion and biological infections has been extensively investigated within the framework of multiplex networks, there are still new challenges in the study of dynamic processes in multiplex networks. First, information diffusion affects not only the epidemic spread, but also the physical contact network structure. After accepting information, individuals are supposed to change their behavior to avoid infection; as a result, the physical network structure changes. Since the relationship between individuals is highly heterogeneous, individual behaviors are different in physical contact networks [13]. Moreover, most of the existing studies were focused on the impact of information diffusion on the epidemic spread, while epidemic spread also affects information diffusion, which is often ignored. As a matter of fact, information and epidemics are interacting and co-evolving. When the epidemic outbreaks, with the increasing number of patients, the epidemic itself receives more and more attention, and the relevant information spreads faster. That is to say, the probability of information diffusion changes as the virus spreads.

A weighted co-evolving multiplex network model with multiple time-varying parameters can be used to describe and analyze the challenges above. A two-layer multiplex network consisting of an information layer and a physical contact layer is introduced to describe the dynamic interaction between an online social (or communication) network and social contact network, where different dynamical processes can be supported. In online social networks, individuals exchange information related to disease, and a time-varying information acceptance rate is defined to describe the impact of the infection in social contact networks. While in a social physical network, actors also exchange biological elements that can carry on diseases. An aware and healthy individual can actively disconnect from infected neighbors and reconnect with healthy ones. The reconnecting rate between aware and unaware healthy nodes is time-varying due to the increase in aware ones. In addition, the heterogeneity of individual relationships in social contact networks cannot be ignored; therefore, both the infection rate and rewiring rate are closely related to the relationship, e.g., intimacy, social distance.

This paper presents a new mean-field model to describe the interaction between information dissemination and biological infections. Due to the new challenges, new nonlinear equations are necessary to extend the Susceptible–Infected–Susceptible (SIS) model and evaluate the impact of rewiring and weighted network links on the reliability of the adaptive weighted networks:

1. A novel weighted co-evolving multiplex network model is proposed to describe the interaction between information diffusion in online social networks and epidemic spreading in adaptive physical contact networks.
2. Two co-evolutionary processes have been considered in our model, the co-evolving of information diffusion and epidemic spreading between two layers and the co-evolving of epidemic spreading and network structure in the physical contact network.
3. Considering the difference in the connections between individuals, the heterogeneous rewiring rate, which is proportional to the strength of the connection, is introduced in our model.
4. Monte Carlo simulations in weighted co-evolving multiplex network models are carried out to describe and analyze the interaction between information diffusion and epidemic spreading.

The rest of this paper is organized as follows. In Section 2, the related works are reviewed. In Section 3, the structure of a weighted co-evolving multiplex network is described. Simulations have been conducted in different network structures to analyze and investigate the effect of network structure properties on propagation in weighted co-evolving multiplex networks in Section 4, followed by conclusions in Section 5.

2. Related Work

Many real-world systems are composed of multiple interacting subsystems, which can be described by multiplex networks, to provide an expressive model for modeling real-world complex networks [14], such as multi-layer social networks with multiple social platforms interacting, and multi-layer transportation networks with multiple transportation channels cooperating and coupling. Furthermore, the interplay or co-evolution of dynamics between networks with different structures was simulated and analyzed by multiplex network models [1–7]. Granell et al. [10] pioneered the analysis of the interrelation between two processes accounting for the spreading of an epidemic, and the information awareness to prevent its infection, on top of multiplex networks. Soriano-Paños et al. [8] proposed a two-layer multiplex network to study the interplay between information spreading and opinion formation in social systems. Velásquez-Rojas et al. [9] studied the dynamics of the voter model for opinion formation intertwined with that of the contact process for disease spreading in multiplex networks and found that the opinion dynamics has striking consequences on the statistical properties of disease spreading. Xia et al. [15–17] proposed a new coupled disease spreading model on a two-layered multiplex network, where one layer denotes the underlying topology for the epidemics and the other one represents the corresponding topology for the awareness spread and extended the multiplex network model of awareness disease dynamics to a susceptible–infected–recovered (SIR) epidemic process that results in permanent immunity after infection.

In recent years, the interaction between epidemic spreading and related information diffusion on multiplex networks has received widespread attention, as it can help model, predict, and control the spread of an epidemic. Clara et al. [10] presented an analysis of the interrelation between two processes accounting for the spread of an epidemic, and the information awareness to prevent its infection, on top of multiplex networks. Zhou et al. [18] developed a set of nonlinear differential equations that have a linearly growing state–space size to describe the epidemic spreading process in multilayer complex networks, including the spreading of viruses and information in computer networks and the spreading of multiple pathogens in a host population. Wang et al. [1] proposed a novel epidemic model based on two-layered multiplex networks to explore the influence of positive and negative preventive information on epidemic propagation. Wu et al. [19] proposed an aware–susceptible–infected model (ASI) to explore the effect of information literacy on the spreading process in multiplex networks by using the microscopic Markov chain method.

So far, however, most of the existing research assumed that information diffusion does not change the social network structure. In fact, as the information diffuses, some individuals who have risk awareness often change their behavior to avoid being infected, which leads to changes in the network structure. In single-layer networks, there has been extensive research on the collaborative evolution of network structure and propagation. Gross et al. [20] first proposed an adaptive network wherein susceptible nodes are able to avoid contact with the infected by rewiring their network connections, and they found that the interplay between dynamics and topology can have important consequences for the spreading of infectious diseases and related applications. Subsequently, more research has been conducted on adaptive networks. Adaptive (weighted) networks have become increasingly important, as a result of the proliferation of cloud computing [21,22], vehicular ad hoc networks (VANETs) [23], and social networks [24].

At present, based on the literature we have searched, there is relatively little research on the information and epidemic spreading in multiplex adaptive networks. Peng et al. [12] first developed a highly integrated effective degree approach to modeling epidemic and awareness-spreading processes on multiplex networks coupled with awareness-dependent adaptive rewiring. They derived a formula for the threshold condition of contagion outbreak and provided a lower bound for the threshold parameter to indicate the effect of adaptive rewiring. In this paper, based on the influence of information dissemination on both epidemic transmission and physical contact network structure, the influence of structural and propagation dynamics of physical contact networks on information dissemination is further introduced into the weighted co-evolving multiplex network model, based on the consideration of the influence of information dissemination on both epidemic transmission and physical contact network structure.

3. The Weighted Co-Evolving Multiplex Networks Model

Consider a two-layer network of N nodes connected by L_1 and L_2 links on each layer, respectively. The upper network describes the information diffusion network, and the lower network describes the individual contact network. Multiplex networks explicitly incorporate multiple channels of connectivity in a system, and they provide a natural description for systems in which entities have a different set of neighbors in each layer. Here, we use the two-layer network to describe and study the co-evolving of two different dynamical processes and the adaptive changing of the physical contact network structure.

3.1. Description of the Co-Evolving Processes in Multiplex Network

The coupling of multiplex networks brings rich co-evolutionary processes, as shown in Figure 1. The first co-evolution is the interaction between information diffusion and epidemic spreading. At the initial stage of epidemic spreading, the relevant information is very little and unconcerned. With the explosion of virus transmission, there is more and more information, from which people can obtain methods and strategies to address epidemics. In this process, the epidemic spreading process promotes information diffusion, which in turn can inhibit the epidemic spreading. The second co-evolution hidden inside the physical contact network is the network structure and the epidemic spreading, which is the so-called adaptive network in the single-layer network study. After accepting information, individuals who awaken the risk awareness change their own behavior to protect themselves, which means that the epidemic spread and network structure interact in the physical contact layer. We introduce the two co-evolution processes in detail, including the changing rules for the states of nodes and edges.

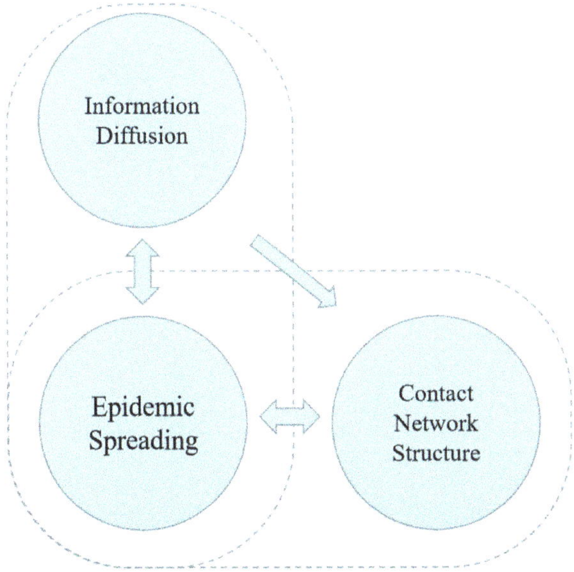

Figure 1. Interactions of inter-layer and inner-layer in multiplex network. Two co-evolutionary processes are shown in Figure 1: the first one is the interaction between information diffusion and epidemic spreading, and the second one hidden inside the physical contact network is the network structure and the epidemic spreading.

3.1.1. Co-Evolving of Information Diffusion and Epidemic Spreading between Two Layers

Consider a two-layer network of N nodes connected by L_1 and L_2 links on each layer, respectively. The upper information layer describes the online social (or communication) network, and the lower physical contact layer describes the social contact network, as shown in Figure 2. In the information diffusion layer, the Unaware–Aware (UA) model, where the node's state is unaware (U) or aware (A) of the existence of the epidemics and its prevention, is applied. In the UA model, U-state individuals do not have information about how to prevent infection, while A-state individuals reduce their risk to be infected. A U-state individual becomes aware with a probability α after communication with aware neighbors. Here, we assume that the A-state individual would remain aware of the infection due to the continuous spread of the epidemic.

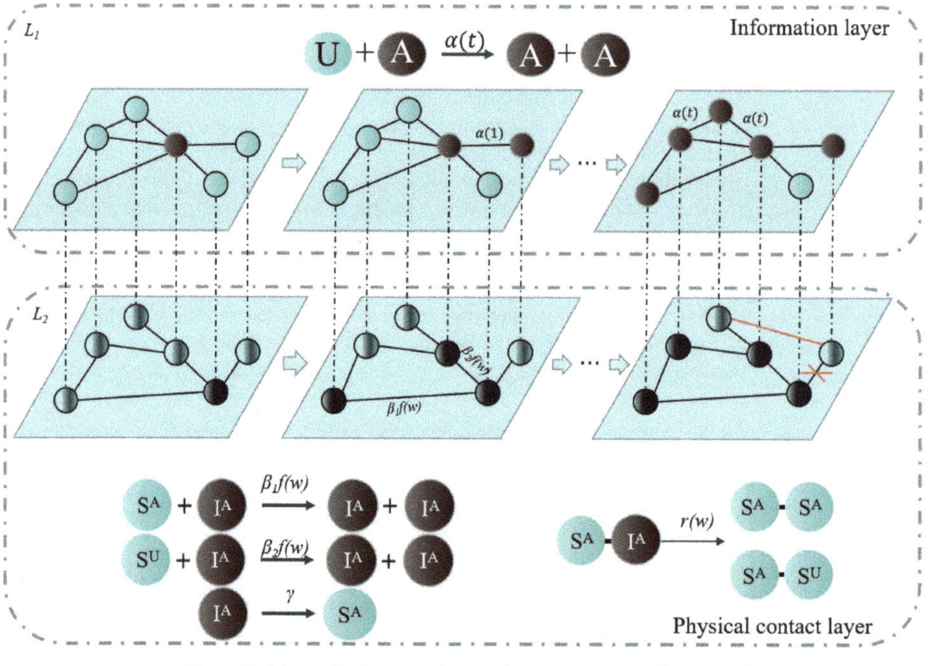

Figure 2. Schematic diagram of network state transition. The upper layer in the figure is the information layer (L_1), a U-state individual becomes aware with a probability $\alpha(t)$ after communication with an aware neighbor. The lower layer is the physical contact layer (L_2). In L_2, a healthy individual with risk awareness would disconnect the links with the infected person in a certain probability $r_w = r(w)$.

Different from the existing research, we take the impact of epidemic spreading on information diffusion into account. The probability of people acquiring information is not immutable, i.e., it is closely related to the spreading processes and the states of neighbors in the network. For example, when the scale of infected individuals becomes larger, people show stronger awareness and obtain information from more channels, which leads to faster information spreading. Therefore, we assume that a U-state individual becomes aware with a time-vary probability $\alpha(t)$, which is proportional to the infection density, i.e., $\alpha(t) \sim I(t)$.

3.1.2. Co-Evolving of Epidemic Spreading and Network Structure in the Physical Contact Network

Here, we use the SIS epidemic model in physical contact networks to simulate the epidemic spreading process [25–27]. There are three different states of node i: Susceptible with awareness (S^A), susceptible without awareness (S^U), and infected (I^A), who always have awareness. An S^A-state node can be infected with probability $\beta_1 f(w)$ by an I^A-state neighbor, while the probability is $\beta_2 f(w)$ if it is a S^U-state node. $f(w)$ is a function positively related to the weight of the link, and $\beta_1 < \beta_2$. I^A-state ones return to S^A-state with probability γ. The change in node states is shown in Figure 2.

The awareness can not only decrease the probability to be infected, but also make individual behaviors change to isolated from infected ones. A healthy individual with risk awareness would disconnect their links with the infected person in a certain probability r_w. The higher the link weight, the harder it is to disconnect, i.e., $r_w \sim 1/w$. In order to ensure the functional completion of the network, we assume that a healthy person in the network who disconnected an edge has to find a healthy person to connect, as shown in Figure 2. For example, healthy employees will transfer work tasks from infected employees to healthy ones. In this way, a weighted co-evolving multiplex model is built, where information and virus propagation interact.

Figure 3 presents the operations of a node in a weighted co-evolving multiplex network. A healthy node without awareness can obtain information from its neighbor with awareness. A healthy node is more likely to be infected by an infected neighbor it interacts with frequently, i.e., the one with a larger link-weight, than by one it interacts with infrequently. Once one of its neighbors is infected, the node can observe the misbehaviors of the neighbor and rewire its link to bypass the infected neighbor, thereby preventing the propagation of the attacks or failures. As a result, the topology of the network keeps changing in response to the infection, quarantining infected individuals and counteracting the vulnerability explorations.

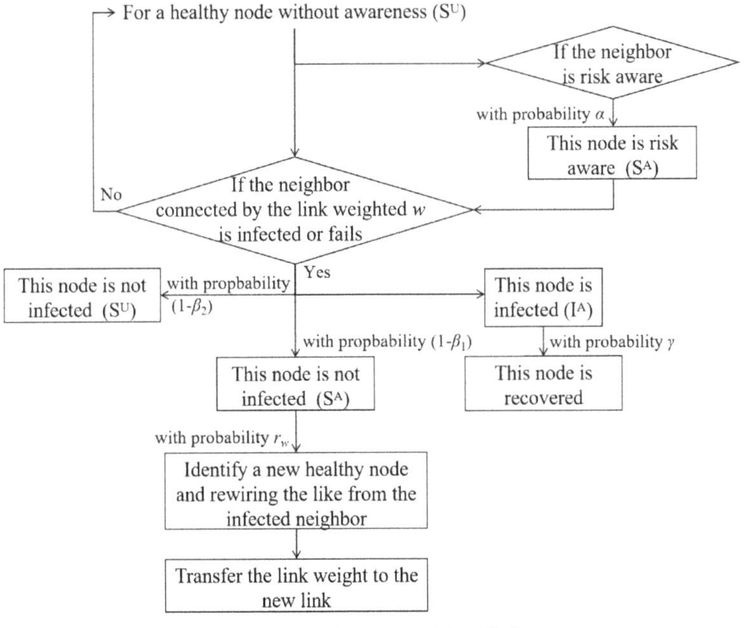

Figure 3. The flowchart of a node regarding a w-weighted link.

3.2. *Mathematical Description of the Weighted Co-Evolving Multiplex Networks Model*

Every node i has a certain probability of being in one of the three states at time t, denoted by $[S^A]$, $[S^U]$, and $[I^A]$, respectively. We provide the definition of the notations used in the model in Table 1, including node density, edge density in different states, and relevant parameters in the model.

Table 1. The notation used in the model formulation and analytical approximation.

Term	Definition
$[S^A]$	Fraction of aware susceptible nodes
$[S^U]$	Fraction of unaware susceptible nodes
$[I^A]$	Fraction of aware infected nodes
$[S^A I^A]_w$	Fraction of links between an aware susceptible node and an aware infected node with w-weight
$[S^U I^A]_w$	Fraction of links between an unaware susceptible node and an aware infected node with w-weight
$[S^A S^A]_w$	Fraction of links between two aware susceptible nodes with w-weight
$[S^U S^U]_w$	Fraction of links between two unaware susceptible nodes with w-weight
$[S^U S^A]_w$	Fraction of links between an unaware susceptible node and an aware susceptible node with w-weight
$[I^A I^A]_w$	Fraction of links between two aware infected nodes with w-weight
$\beta_1 f(w)$	Rate that an unaware susceptible node infected by an infected neighbor though a link with weight w
$\beta_2 f(w)$	Rate that an aware susceptible node infected by an infected neighbor though a link with weight w
α	The rate that an unaware node accepts the information and becomes aware
r_w	The rewiring rate that is proportional to the link weight w
br_w	The rate at which $[S^A I^A]_w$ link becomes $[S^A S^A]_w$ link due to the rewiring, and b is the scale parameter. Here, we set $b = \frac{[S^A]}{[S^A]+[S^U]}$. Then, the rate at which $S^A I^A$ link becomes $S^U S^A$ link due to the rewiring is $(1-b)r_w = \frac{[S^U]}{[S^A]+[S^U]} r_w$.

- Change the process of node state over time:

$$\frac{d[S^A]}{dt} = \gamma[I^A] - \sum_w \beta_1 f(w)[S^A I^A]_w + \alpha \sum_w ([S^U I^A]_w + [S^U S^A]_w) \tag{1}$$

$$\frac{d[S^U]}{dt} = -\sum_w \beta_2 f(w)[S^U I^A]_w - \alpha \sum_w ([S^U I^A]_w + [S^U S^A]_w) \tag{2}$$

$$\frac{d[I^A]}{dt} = -\gamma[I^A] + \sum_w \beta_1 f(w)[S^A I^A]_w + \sum_w \beta_2 f(w)[S^U I^A]_w \tag{3}$$

We call the system of Equations (1)–(3) the node-state changing model. On the right-hand side (RHS) of Equation (1), the first term accounts for the recovery of I^A-state node at rate γ. The second term indicates the infection process, where an S^A-state node is infected by an I^A-state neighbor through the w-weighted link at rate $\beta_1 f(w)$. The third term indicates the information transmission process, where the S^U-state individuals receive information from an A-state neighbor at rate α and change their state to S^A. Here, we assume that the probability of individuals accepting information and being aware of risks increases with the spread of infection $\alpha \sim p_1 I(t)$, where $p_1 \in [0,1]$ is an adjustment parameter and α is proportional to $I(t)$. On the RHS of Equation (2), the first term and second term are the infection process and information transmission process, respectively. A S^U-state node is infected by an I^A-state neighbor through the w-weighted link at rate $\beta_2 f(w)$, where $\beta_2 > \beta_1$ indicates that people without risk awareness are more likely to be infected. On the RHS of Equation (3), the first term is the recovery process and the second and third terms are the infection process.

- Change the process of link state over time:

$$\begin{aligned}\frac{d[S^A I^A]_w}{dt} = &-\beta_1 f(w)[S^A I^A]_w + \sum_{w'} f(w')(\beta_1 [S^A S^A I^A]_{ww'} + \beta_2 [S^A S^U I^A]_{ww'} \\ &- \beta_1 [I^A S^A I^A]_{w'w}) + 2\gamma[I^A I^A]_w - \gamma[S^A I^A]_w + \alpha[S^U I^A]_w - r_w [S^A I^A]_w\end{aligned} \tag{4}$$

$$\frac{d[S^U I^A]_w}{dt} = \sum_{w'} f(w')(\beta_1 [S^U S^A I^A]_{ww'} - \beta_2 [I^A S^U I^A]_{w'w} + \beta_2 [S^U S^U I^A]_{ww'}) \\ - \beta_2 f(w)[S^U I^A]_w - \gamma [S^U I^A]_w - \alpha [S^U I^A]_w \tag{5}$$

$$\frac{d[S^A S^A]_w}{dt} = -\beta_1 \sum_{w'} f(w')[S^A S^A I^A]_{ww'} + \gamma [S^A I^A]_w + \alpha [S^U S^A]_w + b r_w [S^A I^A]_w \tag{6}$$

$$\frac{d[S^U S^U]_w}{dt} = -\beta_2 \sum_{w'} f(w')[S^U S^U I^A]_{ww'} \tag{7}$$

$$\frac{d[S^U S^A]_w}{dt} = -\sum_{w'} f(w')(\beta_1 [S^U S^A I^A]_{ww'} + \beta_2 [I^A S^U S^A]_{w'w}) + \gamma [S^U I^A]_w \\ -\alpha [S^U S^A]_w + (1-b) r_w [S^A I^A]_w \tag{8}$$

$$\frac{d[I^A I^A]_w}{dt} = \sum_{w'} f(w')(\beta_1 [I^A S^A I^A]_{ww'} + \beta_2 [I^A S^U I^A]_{ww'}) + \beta_1 f(w)[S^A I^A]_w \\ +\beta_2 f(w)[S^U I^A]_w - 2\gamma [I^A I^A]_w \tag{9}$$

Equations (4)–(9) characterize the time-varying numbers of links weighted by different weights and connecting nodes in different states. The reasons for the changes in the states of the links can be broadly divided into three, the infection and recovery process associated with the physical contact layer, the information diffusion process associated with the dissemination of the information layer, and the rewiring process of the physical contact layer. For example, Equation (4) captures the time-changing number of the w-weighted links connecting an aware susceptible node and an aware infected node. The first term on the RHS of Equation (4) results from the infection of the susceptible ends of the links with the probability of $\beta_1 f(w)$. The second term is the number of previous w-weighted $S^A S^A / S^A S^U$ links which become $S^A S^A$ links due to the infection at one end of the links through a w' weighted link with the probability of $\beta_1 f(w')/\beta_2 f(w')$. $[ABC]_{ww'}$ denotes the number of triplets $A - B - C$, with edge AB weighted w and edge BC weighted w', $A, B, C \in \{S^U, S^A, I^A\}$. The third and fourth term on the RHS of Equation (4) results from the recovery of the infected ends of the links with the probability of γ. The fifth term on the RHS of Equation (4) results from the information diffusion with the probability of α, and the last term results from rewiring to bypass an infected node with the probability of r_w.
Specifically, in the stable state, due to information dissemination, all nodes eventually become risk-aware, so there are only two types of state left in the network, namely $[S^A]$ and $[I^A]$. In addition, all nodes and links in different states achieve dynamic stability, i.e., $(\frac{d[S^A]}{dt}, \frac{d[I^A]}{dt}, \frac{d[S^A I^A]}{dt}, \frac{d[S^A S^A]}{dt}, \frac{d[I^A I^A]}{dt}) = (0,0,0,0,0)$. The Equation of state in the stable state satisfies

$$\gamma [I^A] - \sum_w \beta_1 f(w)[S^A I^A]_w = 0 \tag{10}$$

$$\zeta \beta_1 \frac{[S^A S^A]_w - [S^A I^A]_w}{S^A} \sum_{w'} f(w')[S^A I^A]_{w'} - (\beta_1 f(w) + \gamma + r_w)[S^A I^A]_w + 2\gamma [I^A I^A]_w = 0 \tag{11}$$

$$-\zeta \beta_1 \frac{[S^A S^A]_w}{S^A} \sum_{w'} f(w') + (\gamma + b r_w)[S^A I^A]_w = 0 \tag{12}$$

$$\beta_1 f(w)[S^A I^A]_w - 2\gamma [I^A I^A]_w + \zeta \beta_1 \frac{[S^A I^A]_w}{S^A} \sum_{w'} f(w')[S^A I^A]_{w'} = 0 \tag{13}$$

Based on the approximation in [13], $[ABC]_{ww'} = \zeta \frac{[AB]_w [BC]_{w'}}{B}, A, B, C \in \{S^U, S^A, I^A\}$, $b = 1$.

An interesting result is shown in Equations (10)–(13). In a stable state, all nodes already have risk awareness, and we can see from the equations that the probability of information acceptance shows no impact on the final stable state of the network. That is, the result of our analysis is that the probability of information acceptance does not affect the final infection scale. Due to the isolation effect of the rewiring process on the infected nodes from susceptible ones, the rewiring rate shows an important impact on the final infection of the network.
We can see from the equations that information diffusion has changed the rules of epidemic spread and also changed the network structure. Conversely, the epidemic spreading affects the probability of information acceptance, i.e., the rules of information diffusion. Therefore, information diffusion, epidemic dynamics, and network structure interact with each other. In the next section, we conduct simulation experiments on the above processes through Monte Carlo methods to further explore the relationships among them.

4. Simulation Results

In this section, simulations are applied to analyze the propagation dynamics processes on the proposed multi-layer dynamic network model. Figures are plotted based on discrete-time Monte Carlo simulations of 100 iterations. Therefore, each data point in the figures is the average result of 100 independent runs. For each of the runs, a single infected node is randomly chosen at $t = 0$, as the initial point of infection.

Firstly, we constructed a two-layer network of size $N = 500$, where the information dissemination layer is a scale-free network [28], and the physical contact layer is a BBV-weighted scale-free network [29]. First, we establish a fully connected network with n initial nodes and assign each edge of the network the initial weight w_0. In our simulation, we set $n = 3$, $w_0 = 1$. In each time interval, add a new node with m edges, which are preferentially attached to existing nodes with a greater strength. Here, we set $m = 3$. The strength preference probability can be defined as $\prod_{new\to i} = \frac{s_i}{\sum_j s_j}$, where s_i represents the strength of node i, which can be expressed by $s_i = \sum_j w_{ij}$ with w_{ij} representing the weight of the edge between nodes i and j. When the new node j is linked to an existing node i, the weights of the edge between node i and its existed neighbors, such as node j, evolve as $w_{ij} \to w_{ij} + \Delta w_{ij}$, where $\Delta w_{ij} = \delta \frac{w_{ij}}{s_i}$ and δ is a constant. The average degree of both layers is $\langle k \rangle = 6$ and the average weight of the physical contact layer is $\langle w \rangle = 6$. The degree distribution, node strength distribution, and weight distribution of the BBV network all conform to the power-law distribution, and the degree and strength of the nodes have a positive correlation, as shown in Figure 4.

We aim to investigate the interplay between propagation processes on the multi-layer network. As described in the previous section, we use the UA model for information diffusion and the SIS model to describe the epidemic spread. The acceptance of positive epidemic-related information is closely related to the level of epidemic infection; here, the information acceptance probability of an unaware node from an aware neighbor is set as $\alpha(t) = p_1 I(t)$, $p_1 \in [0, 1]$. In the physical contact network, the rewiring rate is set to $r(w) = p_2 \frac{1}{w}$, $p_2 \in [0, 1]$. Both p_1 and p_2 are the adjustment parameters of $\alpha(t)$ and $r(w)$, respectively. And the larger p_1/p_2 is, the higher the information acceptance probability/rewiring rate. We explore the relationship between information dissemination and epidemic transmission processes through the changes in p_1 and p_2.

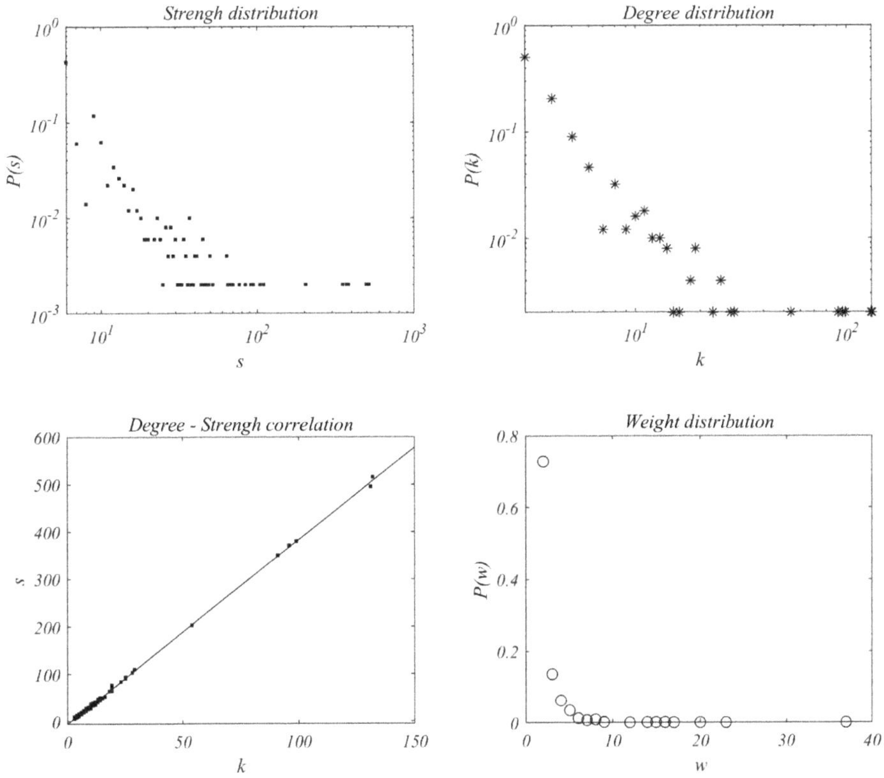

Figure 4. The distribution characteristics of the BBV network. The degree distribution, node strength distribution, and weight distribution of the BBV network all conform to the power-law distribution, and the degree and strength of the nodes have a positive correlation.

We first study the impact of information diffusion on the epidemic spread, as shown in Figure 5. The curves show the changes in the number of infected individuals $I(t)$ over time t under different p_1 in each subplot. We can see from each subplot that the maximum infection scale, i.e., peaks of the curves, decreases with the increase in p_1. When p_1 grows, the information acceptance probability becomes larger. Then, the number of S^A-state nodes that can be infected with a smaller probability increases, and infection velocity becomes slower. However, we can see from each of the subplots that the probability of information acceptance shows no impact on the final infection of the network, which is consistent with our theoretical analysis result in Section 3.

Interestingly, each curve in Figure 5 shows an infection peak due to the fact that all infected individuals are risk-aware, i.e., I^A-states, and the I^A-state nodes revert to the S^A-state with the recovery probability γ. Therefore, the S^A-state nodes in the network are increasing continuously, and the infection in the network is slowed down before reaching stability. When the recovering process disappears, i.e., $\gamma = 0$, the peak disappears, as shown in Figure 6 (the red curve).

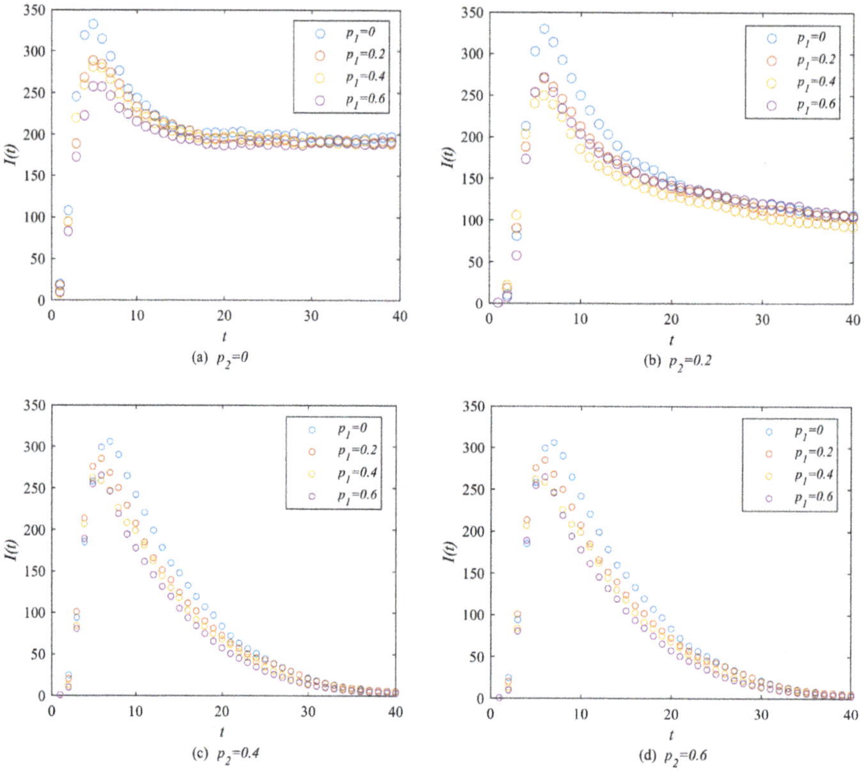

Figure 5. Theimpact of information diffusion on the epidemic spread under different parameter p_2 in rewiring rate r_w. Curves are the number of infected individuals $I(t)$ over time t as p_1 increases. In each subplot, we can see that the final infection ($I(t = 40)$) is almost the same, which means that the information diffusion has no impact on the final infection. But a high probability of receiving information can reduce the speed of epidemic spread.

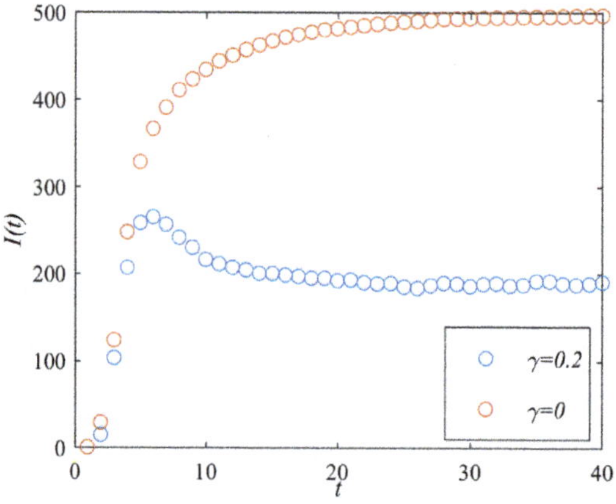

Figure 6. Comparison of infection processes with and without recovery process. Here, we set $p_1 = 0.8$, $p_2 = 0$.

We can also see from Figure 5 that, with the increase in the rewiring parameter p_2, the infection in the network has been greatly improved. We can see from Figure 5a–d that, as p_2 increases, the final infection ($I(t = 40)$) in the network significantly decreases. When $p_2 = 0$, the number of final infections is about 200; however, when $p_2 = 0.4/0.6$, the final infection disappears. Furthermore, we continue to study the impact of rewiring behaviors on the epidemic spread process. Figure 7 shows the impact of rewiring behaviors on the epidemic spread under different information acceptance parameters p_1. Curves are the number of infected individuals $I(t)$ over time t as p_2 increases. We can see from each subgraph that as p_2 increases, the scale of infections in the network decreases. The rewiring behavior has effectively inhibited the prevalence of the virus as it blocks the path of infection. Especially in the initial stage of infection, the higher the rewiring rate, the easier it is for the infection to eventually die out.

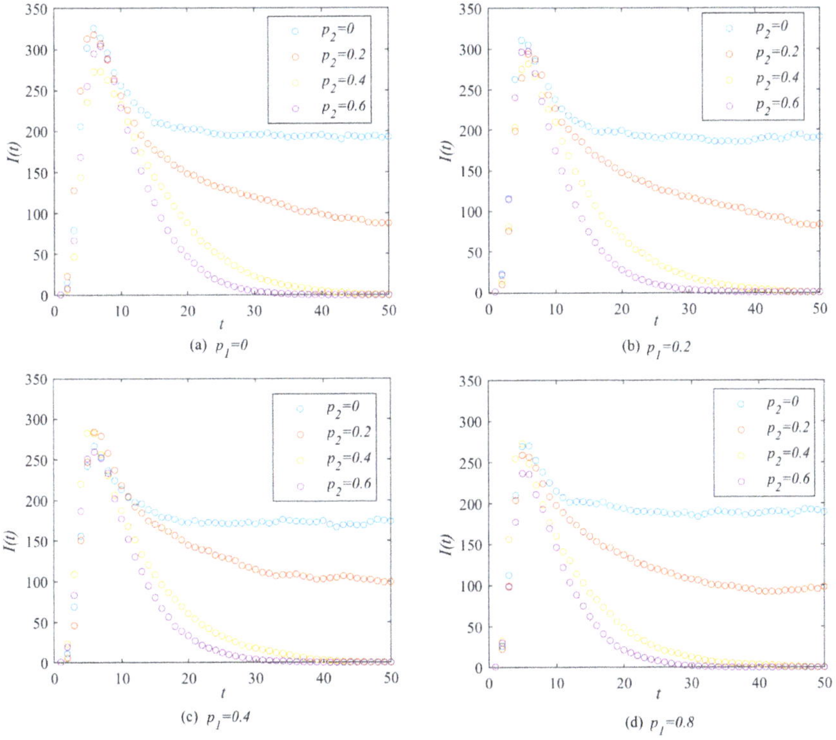

Figure 7. Theimpact of rewiring behaviors on the epidemic spread under different parameters p_1 in information acceptance rate. Curves are the number of infected individuals $I(t)$ over time t as p_2 increases. We can see from each subplot that the final infection was greatly inhibited with the increase in the rewiring parameter p_2.

Compared to the impact of information dissemination on the infection process, the rewiring behavior has a greater impact on the final infection scale, as shown in Figure 8. When we increase the rewiring parameter p_2, the final infection scale ($t = 100$) continuously decreases. As shown in Figure 8, when $p_2 > 0.32$, the final infection of the network approaches 0.

Another ongoing collaborative evolution is the structure of physical contact networks: both the degree distribution and weight distribution evolve along with the rewiring process. Adaptive rewiring of high-risk links leads to the breakdown of edges that connect a susceptible node with risk awareness and an infected one, and meanwhile, this gives rise to the formation of low-risk links connecting toward a randomly chosen susceptible node. As demonstrated in Figure 9, the degree distribution of the physical contact network exhibits time-varying scaling behaviors: In the initial stage without rewiring (Case of $t = 0$ in Figure 8), both the node degree and link weights follow a perfect power law, while as the rewiring process unfolds, the degree/weight values become closer to the average degree/weight, approximating a Poisson distribution.

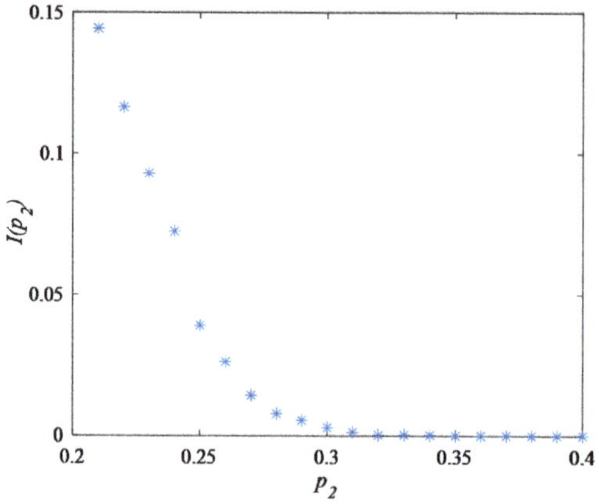

Figure 8. Thefinal infection $I(p_2)$ under different rewiring parameters p_2.

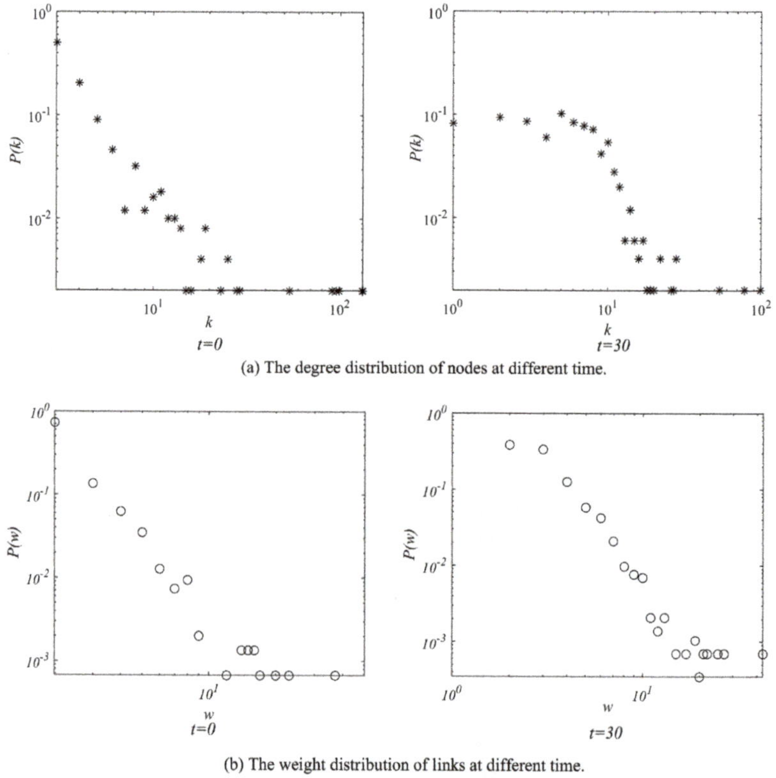

Figure 9. Theimpact of rewiring behaviors on network structure.

5. Conclusions

Information diffusion is an inevitable influencing factor in the process of epidemic spread, and in turn, epidemic spreading also affects information diffusion. This paper uses a two-layer network model to describe and analyze the interaction between information dissemination and epidemic transmission. Our model considers two co-evolutionary processes: the co-evolving of information diffusion and epidemic spreading between two layers and the co-evolving of epidemic spreading and network structure in the physical contact network. Considering the difference in the connections between individuals, the heterogeneous rewiring rate, which is proportional to the strength of the connection, is introduced in our model. Simulation results show that the epidemics spreading is closely related to the information diffusion and rewiring strategy. The maximum infection scale decreases as the information acceptance probability grows, and the final infection decreases as the rewiring behaviors increase. Interestingly, an infection peak appears in our model due to the interaction between information diffusion and epidemic spread.

The weighted co-evolving multiplex network model we propose is used to describe the dynamic interaction between information diffusion and epidemic spreading, which is more diverse in real life. Therefore, we hope to have a more realistic model based on our model to deepen the research on spreading dynamic interactions in real-world systems. In fact, besides social networks, a significant number of real-world systems, e.g., communication networks, transportation networks, and power networks, own multiplex network structures. For example, information diffusion can help drivers better understand road conditions and avoid traffic congestion in transportation networks. The information exchange in the communication network can help decision makers to appropriately load redistribution in a timely manner, thereby avoiding cascading failures in the power grid. The model we propose in this paper can be extended to more scenarios and will hopefully be used to study problems of multiplex network coexistence and cooperative evolution in these scenarios.

Author Contributions: Conceptualization, B.S. and X.W.; methodology, Y.S.; software, H.W.; formal analysis, B.S.; investigation, H.W.; data curation, Y.S.; writing—original draft preparation, B.S.; writing—review and editing, B.S.; supervision, G.J.; project administration, G.J. All authors have read and agreed to the published version of the manuscript.

Funding: This research was funded by National Natural Science Foundation (Grant Nos. 62203229, 61672298, 61873326 and 61802155), Philosophy and Social Sciences Research of Universities in Jiangsu Province (Grant No. 2018SJZDI142), Jiangsu Natural Science Foundation Youth Fund Project (Grant No. BK20200758), Qing Lan Project and the Science and Technology Project of Market Supervision Administration of Jiangsu Province (Grant No. KJ21125027).

Data Availability Statement: https://github.com/hm-harry/Epidemic-Spreading-on-Weighted-Co-evolving-Multiplex-Networks.

Conflicts of Interest: The authors declare no conflict of interest.

References

1. Wang, Z.; Xia, C.; Chen, Z.; Chen, G. Epidemic Propagation with Positive and Negative Preventive Information in Multiplex Networks. *IEEE Trans. Cybern.* **2021**, *51*, 1454–1462. [CrossRef] [PubMed]
2. Li, X.J.; Li, C.; Li, X. The impact of information dissemination on vaccination in multiplex networks. *Sci. China Inf. Sci.* **2022**, *65*, 172202. [CrossRef]
3. Chen, J.; Hu, M.B.; Li, M. Traffic-driven epidemic spreading in multiplex networks. *Phys. Rev. E* **2020**, *101*, 012301. [CrossRef]
4. Liu, H.; Yang, N.; Yang, Z.; Lin, J.; Zhang, Y. The impact of firm heterogeneity and awareness in modeling risk propagation on multiplex networks. *Phys. A* **2019**, *539*, 122919. [CrossRef]
5. Sanz, J.; Xia, C.Y.; Meloni, S.; Moreno, Y. Dynamics of interacting diseases. *Phys. Rev. X* **2014**, *4*, 041005. [CrossRef]
6. Danziger, M.M.; Bonamassa, I.; Boccaletti, S.; Havlin, S. Dynamic interdependence and competition in multilayer networks. *Nat. Phys.* **2019**, *15*, 178–185. [CrossRef]
7. Nicosia, V.; Skardal, P.S.; Arenas, A.; Latora, V. Collective phenomena emerging from the interactions between dynamical processes in multiplex networks. *Phys. Rev. Lett.* **2014**, *118*, 138302. [CrossRef] [PubMed]

8. Soriano-Paños, D.; Guo, Q.; Latora, V.; Gómez-Gardeñes, J. Explosive transitions induced by interdependent contagion-consensus dynamics in multiplex networks. *Phys. Rev. E* **2019**, *99*, 062311. [CrossRef]
9. Velásquez-Rojas, F.; Vazquez, F. Interacting opinion and disease dynamics in multiplex networks: Discontinuous phase transition and nonmonotonic consensus times. *Phys. Rev. E* **2017**, *95*, 052315. [CrossRef]
10. Granell, C.; Gómez, S.; Arenas, A. Dynamical interplay between awareness and epidemic spreading in multiplex networks. *Phys. Rev. Lett.* **2013**, *111*, 128701. [CrossRef]
11. Tizard, I.R. Vaccination against coronaviruses in domestic animals. *Vaccine* **2020**, *38*, 5123–5130. [CrossRef] [PubMed]
12. Peng, X.L.; Zhang, Y.D. Contagion dynamics on adaptive multiplex networks with awareness-dependent rewiring. *Chin. Phys. B* **2021**, *30*, 058901. [CrossRef]
13. Song, B.; Wang, X.; Ni, W.; Song, Y.; Liu, R.P.; Jiang, G.P.; Guo, Y.J. Reliability analysis of large-scale adaptive weighted networks. *IEEE Trans. Inf. Forensics Secur.* **2020**, *15*, 651–665. [CrossRef]
14. Mucha, P.J.; Richardson, T.; Macon, K.; Porter, M.A.; Onnela, J.P. Community structure in time-dependent, multiscale, and multiplex networks. *Science* **2010**, *329*, 876–878. [CrossRef]
15. Xia, C.; Wang, Z.; Zheng, C.; Guo, Q.; Shi, Y.; Dehmer, M.; Chen, Z. A new coupled disease-awareness spreading model with mass media on multiplex networks. *Inf. Sci.* **2019**, *471*, 185–200. [CrossRef]
16. Wang, Z.; Guo, Q.; Sun, S.; Xia, C. The impact of awareness diffusion on SIR-like epidemics in multiplex networks. *Appl. Math. Comput.* **2019**, *349*, 134–147. [CrossRef]
17. Zheng, C.; Wang, Z.; Xia, C.; Guo, Q.; Dehmer, M. Interplay between SIR-based disease spreading and awareness diffusion on multiplex networks. *J. Parallel Distrib. Comput.* **2018**, *115*, 20–28. [CrossRef]
18. Zhou, Y.; Zhou, J.; Chen, G.; Stanley, H.E. Effective degree theory for awareness and epidemic spreading on multiplex networks. *New J. Phys.* **2019**, *21*, 035002. [CrossRef]
19. Wu, J.; Zuo, R.; He, C.; Xiong, H.; Zhao, K.; Hu, Z. The effect of information literacy heterogeneity on epidemic spreading in information and epidemic coupled multiplex networks. *Phys. A* **2022**, *596*, 127119. [CrossRef]
20. Gross, T.; D'Lima, C.J.D.; Blasius, B. Epidemic dynamics on an adaptive network. *Phys. Rev. Lett.* **2006**, *96*, 208701. [CrossRef]
21. Alamer, A.; Deng, Y.; Wei, G.; Lin, X. Collaborative security in vehicular cloud computing: A game theoretic view. *IEEE Netw.* **2018**, *32*, 72–77.
22. Mijumbi, R.; Serrat, J.; Gorricho, J.L.; Bouten, N.; De Turck, F.; Boutaba, R. Network function virtualization: State-of-the-art and research challenges. *IEEE Commun. Surv. Tut.* **2017**, *18*, 236–262. [CrossRef]
23. Zha, X.; Ni, W.; Zheng, K.; Liu, R.P.; Niu, X. Collaborative authentication in decentralized dense mobile networks with key predistribution. *IEEE Trans. Inf. Forensics Secur.* **2017**, *12*, 2261–2275. [CrossRef]
24. Nadini, M.; Rizzo, A.; Porfiri, M. Epidemic spreading in temporal and adaptive networks with static backbone. *IEEE Trans. Netw. Sci. Eng.* **2018**, *7*, 549–561. [CrossRef]
25. Pastor-Satorras, R.; Castellano, C.; Van Mieghem, P. Epidemic processes in complex networks. *Rev Mod Phys.* **2015**, *87*, 925. [CrossRef]
26. Zhang, Y.Q.; Li, X. When susceptible-infectious-susceptible contagion meets time-varying networks with identical infectivity. *Eur. Lett.* **2014**, *108*, 28006. [CrossRef]
27. Li, C.; van de Bovenkamp, R.; Van Mieghem, P. Susceptible-infected-susceptible model: A comparison of N-intertwined and heterogeneous mean-field approximations. *Phys. Rev. E* **2012**, *86*, 026116. [CrossRef] [PubMed]
28. Barabási, A.L.; Albert, R. Emergence of scaling in random networks. *Science* **1999**, *286*, 509–512. [CrossRef] [PubMed]
29. Barrat, A.; Barthélemy, M.; Vespignani, A. Weighted evolving networks: Coupling topology and weight dynamics. *Phys. Rev. Lett.* **2004**, *92*, 228701. [CrossRef]

Disclaimer/Publisher's Note: The statements, opinions and data contained in all publications are solely those of the individual author(s) and contributor(s) and not of MDPI and/or the editor(s). MDPI and/or the editor(s) disclaim responsibility for any injury to people or property resulting from any ideas, methods, instructions or products referred to in the content.

mathematics

MDPI

Article

Weighted Fractional Hermite–Hadamard Integral Inequalities for up and down Ꭻ-Convex Fuzzy Mappings over Coordinates

Muhammad Bilal Khan [1,*], Eze R. Nwaeze [2], Cheng-Chi Lee [3,4,*], Hatim Ghazi Zaini [5], Der-Chyuan Lou [6,*] and Khalil Hadi Hakami [7]

1 Department of Mathematics and Computer Science, Transilvania University of Brasov, 29 Eroilor Boulevard, 500036 Brasov, Romania
2 Department of Mathematics and Computer Science, Alabama State University, Montgomery, AL 36101, USA; enwaeze@alasu.edu
3 Department of Library and Information Science, Fu Jen Catholic University, New Taipei City 24205, Taiwan
4 Department of Computer Science and Information Engineering, Fintech and Blockchain Research Center, Asia University, Taichung City 41354, Taiwan
5 Department of Computer Science, College of Computers and Information Technology, Taif University, P.O. Box 11099, Taif 21944, Saudi Arabia; h.zaini@tu.edu.sa
6 Department of Computer Science and Information Engineering, Chang Gung University, Stroke Center and Department of Neurology, Chang Gung Memorial Hospital at Linkou, Taoyuan 33302, Taiwan
7 Department of Mathematics, College of Science, Jazan University, P.O. Box. 114, Jazan 45142, Saudi Arabia; khakami@jazanu.edu.sa
* Correspondence: muhammad.bilal@unitbv.ro or bilal42742@gmail.com (M.B.K.); cclee@mail.fju.edu.tw (C.-C.L.); dclou@mail.cgu.edu.tw or dclouprof@gmail.com (D.-C.L.)

Abstract: Due to its significant influence on numerous areas of mathematics and practical sciences, the theory of integral inequality has attracted a lot of interest. Convexity has undergone several improvements, generalizations, and extensions over time in an effort to produce more accurate variations of known findings. This article's main goal is to introduce a new class of convexity as well as to prove several Hermite–Hadamard type interval-valued integral inequalities in the fractional domain. First, we put forth the new notion of generalized convexity mappings, which is defined as *UD*-Ꭻ-convexity on coordinates with regard to fuzzy-number-valued mappings and the up and down (*UD*) fuzzy relation. The generic qualities of this class make it novel. By taking into account different values for Ꭻ, we produce several known classes of convexity. Additionally, we create some new fractional variations of the Hermite–Hadamard (*HH*) and Pachpatte types of inequalities using the concepts of coordinated *UD*-Ꭻ-convexity and double Riemann–Liouville fractional operators. The results attained here are the most cohesive versions of previous findings. To demonstrate the importance of the key findings, we offer a number of concrete examples.

Keywords: fuzzy-number valued mappings; fractional integral; coordinated *UD*-Ꭻ-convexity; fractional Hermite–Hadamard inequalities

MSC: 26A33; 26A51; 26D10

Citation: Khan, M.B.; Nwaeze, E.R.; Lee, C.-C.; Zaini, H.G.; Lou, D.-C.; Hakami, K.H. Weighted Fractional Hermite–Hadamard Integral Inequalities for up and down Ꭻ-Convex Fuzzy Mappings over Coordinates. *Mathematics* **2023**, *11*, 4974. https://doi.org/10.3390/math11244974

Academic Editors: Lijuan Zha, Jian Liu and Jinliang Liu

Received: 17 November 2023
Revised: 6 December 2023
Accepted: 13 December 2023
Published: 16 December 2023

Copyright: © 2023 by the authors. Licensee MDPI, Basel, Switzerland. This article is an open access article distributed under the terms and conditions of the Creative Commons Attribution (CC BY) license (https://creativecommons.org/licenses/by/4.0/).

1. Introduction

The most fundamental area of mathematical analysis is known as convex analysis; see [1,2]. Due to its significant contribution to the advancement of both pure and applied mathematics, it has attracted considerable attention. A problem can be solved geometrically and analytically using convexity and its effects. Convexity plays a crucial role in topology, functional analysis, specifically separation axioms, fixed-point theory, engineering, and economics. First, by proposing the idea of convex mappings based on a convex set in 1905, Jensen greatly increased the appeal of the theory of convex functions. Since a positive second derivative denotes the convexity of functions, one would wish to describe it in terms of functions and their derivatives. It has a close relationship with optimization theory, particularly with linear programming. Convex mappings frequently offer distinctive minima and are used to derive a workable solution; see [3–5].

The theory of mathematical inequalities has various applications in many branches of physics and engineering. This theory is closely connected to fields such as approximation theory, probability theory, and information theory. The importance of this topic will increase in the future due to its impact on applied mathematics. The theory of inequalities has greatly benefited from the study of the theory of convex functions. By using the idea of convexity, it is possible to directly obtain many inequalities, like Jensen's inequality, the *HH* inequality, Young's inequality, etc. In this regard, we are reminded of the well-known inequality resulting from Hermite and Hadamard acting independently.

Theorem 1. *Assume that the convex mapping* $G : [\mathfrak{e}, \mathfrak{g}] \to \mathfrak{R}$. *Then, the following double-inequality holds:*

$$G\left(\frac{\mathfrak{e}+\mathfrak{g}}{2}\right) \leq \frac{1}{\mathfrak{g}-\mathfrak{e}}\int_{\mathfrak{e}}^{\mathfrak{g}} G(x)dx \leq \frac{G(\mathfrak{g})+G(\mathfrak{e})}{2}, \tag{1}$$

where $\mathfrak{R}$ *is set of real numbers.*

One can check the concavity of the mappings by using the aforementioned inequality. See [6,7] for further information about this. For more information, related to different inequalities, see [8–16] and the references therein.

With the help of new and creative ideas, particularly the use of weighted means, the concept of convexity has recently been improved and expanded. Examples include harmonic, geometric, and P-convexity, which are based on the weighted harmonic mean, the weighted geometric mean, and the generalized weighted p mean, respectively. In 2019, Wu et al. [17,18] used the quasi-arithmetic mean to investigate a new class of convexity.

We work with multi-valued functions in a set-valued analysis, and interval-valued (*IV*) analysis is a branch of this field. The initial method for calculating the error estimates of finite machines was an interval analysis. If we assign a single value to any variable, just like in everyday life operations, the likelihood of inaccuracy rises; to address this shortcoming, interval numbers are used in place of single numerical values. Moore authored some fascinating works on interval analysis that offered fresh approaches to putting this theory into practice and suggested some uses for it in computer programming and error analysis; see [19–21].

Since Moore's outstanding and useful work, several authors have expressed interest in the area and exploited it in various ways. Investigations into the dynamic systems of differential equations, fluid mechanics, combinatorics, neural networking, and inequalities are carried out using *IV* approaches (see [22]). Breckner [23] continued by advancing the concept of convexity from the standpoint of set-valued mappings.

By using the ordering relations and *IV* mappings defined over interval numbers, certain inequalities have recently been improved and extended; see [24–30]. Regarding this, Chalco Cano et al. [31,32] computed the well-known Ostrowski's integral inequality using *IV* mappings and Hukuhara derivatives and came to the conclusion that the primary results were useful in numerical analyses. In 2017, Costa et al. [33] applied the mappings established over fuzzy numbers to investigate fresh integral inequalities. In the follow-up, Flores et al. [34] calculated new integral inequality variations related to *IV* mappings. In [35], the authors looked into the preinvex-*IV*-mappings-related integral inequalities of *HH*. Jensen's and *HH*-type containments involving a general class of *IV* convexity, also known as the h-*IV* mapping and Chebyshev-type inequality, respectively, were established by Zhao et al. [36,37]. Extremely significant contributions to the growth of integral inequality have come from fractional calculus. The first successful attempt to build fractional equivalents of *HH*-type inequalities was carried out in 2012 by Sarikaya et al. [38], who essentially took integral fractional operators into consideration. Following this, other inequalities have been reduced utilizing fractional methods, and this area of study is still quite active. Mohammad et al. explored the novel tempered Hermite–Hadamard-like inequalities and offered several applications in [39–44], along with fractional mid-point-like inequalities within the framework of fractional calculus. In [45], Akdemir et al. used unified fractional operators to evaluate the Chebyshev-like inequality. Inequalities involving AB-fractional integral operators and the differentiability of convex mappings were the conclusions of Set et al.'s [46] work. Budak et al. [47] investigated the *HH*-type inequalities in 2020 by studying interval-valued fractional operators. In order to show several *HH*-type inequalities, Kara et al. [48] combined novel double-fractional operators with the idea of interval-valued coordinated convexity. In order to extract some novel fractional versions of the *HH*-type inequalities, Bin-Mohsin et al. [49] recently presented the concept of interval-valued coordinated, harmonically convex mappings and double-fractional operators using the modified Mittag-Leffler function introduced by Raina as a kernel. Trigonometric convex functions with exponential weights were investigated by Zhou et al. [50] to create some novel *HH*-like inequalities. A fuzzy order relation was used to execute their discussion of trigonometric convexity and related integral containment in [51]. *IV* convexity and (p, q) calculus were employed by Kalsoom et al. in [52] to establish some fresh refinements of previous findings. To create certain *HH*-like inequalities, the authors of [53] developed the idea of the fuzzy-interval-valued bi-convex function. For interval-coordinated convex functions and products of Hermite–Hadamard-type inequalities, the authors of [54,55], respectively, obtained fractional forms of these inequalities. They wrapped up this work in [56] with some fresh Hermite–Hadamard inequalities involving interval-valued convexity and generalized quantum calculus. See [33,57–66] for additional information and current developments.

The goal of the current study is to use AB-fractional notions to develop new generic inclusion relations of the *HH* type. First, we create a novel class of convexity based on the interval analysis bi-function and monotonically continuous function g. The uniqueness of this study is in the derivation of numerous new and existing fractional counterparts using various values. Additionally, we use numerical simulations to confirm the results of our theoretical work. To the best of our knowledge, these results are more helpful for obtaining variations of *IV HH*-type inequalities for some classes of convexity; see [55,59,67–74].

The work is divided into two sections. In the first half, we review some information about convexity and fractional calculus and discuss the problem's history. The newly proposed class of convexity is introduced in the second section, along with its implications and uses in integral inequalities. Concluding observations are included later.

2. Preliminaries

We will go through the fundamental terminologies and findings in this section, which aid in comprehending the ideas behind our fresh findings.

Definition 1 ([63,64]). *Let $\mathbb{F}_0$ be a fuzzy number space. Given $\widetilde{Đ} \in \mathbb{F}_0$, the level sets or cut sets are given by* $\left[\widetilde{Đ}\right]^{\gamma} = \left\{x \in \mathfrak{R} \middle| \widetilde{Đ}(x) > \gamma\right\} \forall \gamma \in [0,\ 1]$ *and by*

$$\left[\widetilde{Đ}\right]^{0} = \left\{x \in \mathfrak{R} \middle| \widetilde{Đ}(x) > 0\right\}. \tag{2}$$

These sets are known as γ-level sets or γ-cut sets of $\widetilde{Đ}$.

Proposition 1 ([33]). *Let $\widetilde{Đ}, \widetilde{\text{ⴖ}} \in \mathbb{F}_0$. Then, the relation " $\leq_{\mathbb{F}}$ " is given on $\mathbb{F}_0$ by $\widetilde{Đ} \leq_{\mathbb{F}} \widetilde{\text{ⴖ}}$ when and only when $\left[\widetilde{Đ}\right]^{\gamma} \leq_I \left[\widetilde{\text{ⴖ}}\right]^{\gamma}$ for every $\gamma \in [0,\ 1]$, which are left- and right-order relations or just order relations.*

Proposition 2 ([62]). *Let $\widetilde{Ð}, \widetilde{\text{m}} \in \mathbb{F}_0$. Then, the relation " $\supseteq_{\mathbb{F}}$ " is given on $\mathbb{F}_0$ by $\widetilde{Ð} \supseteq_{\mathbb{F}} \widetilde{\text{m}}$ when and only when $\left[\widetilde{Ð}\right]^{\gamma} \supseteq_I \left[\widetilde{\text{m}}\right]^{\gamma}$ for every $\gamma \in [0,\ 1]$, which is the UD−order relation on $\mathbb{F}_0$.*

Remember the approaching notions, which are offered in the literature. If $\widetilde{Ð}, \widetilde{\text{m}} \in \mathbb{F}_0$ and $t \in \mathfrak{R}$, then, for every $\gamma \in [0,\ 1]$, the arithmetic operations addition, "$\oplus$", multiplication, "$\otimes$", and scaler multiplication, "$\odot$", are defined by

$$\left[\widetilde{Ð} \oplus \widetilde{\text{m}}\right]^{\gamma} = \left[\widetilde{Ð}\right]^{\gamma} + \left[\widetilde{\text{m}}\right]^{\gamma}, \tag{3}$$

$$\left[\widetilde{Ð} \otimes \widetilde{\text{m}}\right]^{\gamma} = \left[\widetilde{Ð}\right]^{\gamma} \times \left[\widetilde{\text{m}}\right]^{\gamma}, \tag{4}$$

$$\left[t \odot \widetilde{Ð}\right]^{\gamma} = t\left[\widetilde{Ð}\right]^{\gamma}, \tag{5}$$

Equations (4) through to (6) have immediate consequences for these outcomes.

Theorem 2 ([33]). *The space $\mathbb{F}_0$ dealing with a supremum metric, i.e., for $\widetilde{Ð},\ \widetilde{\text{m}} \in \mathbb{F}_0$,*

$$d_\infty\left(\widetilde{Ð}, \widetilde{\text{m}}\right) = \sup_{0 \le \gamma \le 1} d_H\left(\left[\widetilde{Ð}\right]^{\gamma}, \left[\widetilde{\text{m}}\right]^{\gamma}\right), \tag{6}$$

is a complete metric space, where H indicates the well-known Hausdorff metric on the space of intervals.

Theorem 3 ([33]). *Let $\mathbb{R}_I$ be a set of inetervals and $\widetilde{G} : [\mathfrak{u}, \mathfrak{v}] \subset \mathfrak{R} \to \mathbb{F}_0$ be an FNVM; its IVMs are classified according to their γ-levels, $G_\gamma : [\mathfrak{u}, \mathfrak{v}] \subset \mathfrak{R} \to \mathbb{R}_I$ are given by $G_\gamma(x) = [G_*(x,\gamma), G^*(x,\gamma)] \forall x \in [\mathfrak{u}, \mathfrak{v}]$, and $\forall \gamma \in (0,\ 1]$. Then, $\widetilde{G}$ is FA-integrable over $[\mathfrak{u}, \mathfrak{v}]$ if and only if $G_*(x,\gamma)$ and $G^*(x,\gamma)$ are both A-integrable over $[\mathfrak{u}, \mathfrak{v}]$. Moreover, if $\widetilde{G}$ is FA-integrable over $[\mathfrak{u}, \mathfrak{v}]$, then*

$$\begin{aligned}\left[(FA)\int_{\mathfrak{u}}^{\mathfrak{v}} \widetilde{G}(x)dx\right]^{\gamma} = & \left[(A)\int_{\mathfrak{u}}^{\mathfrak{v}} G_*(x,\gamma)dx,\ (A)\int_{\mathfrak{u}}^{\mathfrak{v}} G^*(x,\gamma)dx\right] \\ & = (IA)\int_{\mathfrak{u}}^{\mathfrak{v}} G_\gamma(x)dx,\end{aligned} \tag{7}$$

$\forall\ \gamma \in (0,\ 1]$. $\forall\ \gamma \in (0,\ 1]$, $\mathcal{FA}_{([\mathfrak{u},\mathfrak{v}],\ \gamma)}$ denotes the collection of all FA-integrable FNVMs over $[\mathfrak{u}, \mathfrak{v}]$.

Definition 2. ([67]). Let $\mathbb{R}_I^+$ *be a set of positive intervals and $G : [\mathfrak{e}, \mathfrak{g}] \to \mathbb{R}_I^+$ be an IVM, where $G \in \mathcal{IR}_{[\mathfrak{e},\mathfrak{g}]}$. Then, interval Riemann–Liouville-type integrals of G are defined as*

$$\mathcal{I}_{\mathfrak{e}^+}^{\alpha} G(y) = \frac{1}{\Gamma(\alpha)} \int_{\mathfrak{e}}^{y} (y - \mathrm{t})^{\alpha-1} G(\mathrm{t}) d\mathrm{t} (y > \mathfrak{e}), \tag{8}$$

$$\mathcal{I}_{\mathfrak{g}^-}^{\alpha} G(y) = \frac{1}{\Gamma(\alpha)} \int_{y}^{\mathfrak{g}} (\mathrm{t} - y)^{\alpha-1} G(\mathrm{t}) d\mathrm{t} (y < \mathfrak{g}), \tag{9}$$

where $\alpha > 0$ and Γ is the gamma function.

Recently, Allahviranloo et al. [68] introduced the fuzzy version of this and defined fractional integrals, resulting in the following:

Definition 3. *Let $\alpha > 0$ and $L([\mathfrak{e}, \mathfrak{g}], \mathbb{F}_0)$ be the collection of all Lebesgue measurable FNVMs on $[\mathfrak{e}, \mathfrak{g}]$. Then, the fuzzy left and right Riemann–Liouville fractional integrals of $\widetilde{G} \in L([\mathfrak{e}, \mathfrak{g}], \mathbb{F}_0)$ with order $\alpha > 0$ are defined by*

$$\mathcal{I}^{\alpha}_{\mathfrak{e}^+} \widetilde{G}(y) = \frac{1}{\Gamma(\alpha)} \int_{\mathfrak{e}}^{y} (y - \mathrm{t})^{\alpha - 1} \widetilde{G}(\mathrm{t}) d\mathrm{t}, (y > \mathfrak{e}), \tag{10}$$

and

$$\mathcal{I}^{\alpha}_{\mathfrak{g}^-} \widetilde{G}(y) = \frac{1}{\Gamma(\alpha)} \int_{y}^{\mathfrak{g}} (\mathrm{t} - y)^{\alpha - 1} \widetilde{G}(\mathrm{t}) d\mathrm{t}, (y < \mathfrak{g}), \tag{11}$$

respectively, where $\Gamma(y) = \int_0^\infty \mathrm{t}^{y-1} e^{-\mathrm{t}} d\mathrm{t}$ is the Euler gamma function. The fuzzy left and right Riemann–Liouville fractional integral, y, based on the left and right endpoint functions, can be defined, that is

$$\begin{aligned} \left[\mathcal{I}^{\alpha}_{\mathfrak{e}^+} \widetilde{G}(y)\right]^{\gamma} &= \tfrac{1}{\Gamma(\alpha)} \int_{\mathfrak{e}}^{y} (y - \mathrm{t})^{\alpha - 1} G_{\gamma}(\mathrm{t}) d\mathrm{t} \\ &= \tfrac{1}{\Gamma(\alpha)} \int_{\mathfrak{e}}^{y} (y - \mathrm{t})^{\alpha - 1} [G_*(\mathrm{t}, \gamma), G^*(\mathrm{t}, \gamma)] d\mathrm{t}, (y > \mathfrak{e}), \end{aligned} \tag{12}$$

where

$$\mathcal{I}^{\alpha}_{\mathfrak{e}^+} G_*(y, \gamma) = \frac{1}{\Gamma(\alpha)} \int_{\mathfrak{e}}^{y} (y - \mathrm{t})^{\alpha - 1} G_*(\mathrm{t}, \gamma) d\mathrm{t}, (y > \mathfrak{e}), \tag{13}$$

and

$$\mathcal{I}^{\alpha}_{\mathfrak{e}^+} G^*(y, \gamma) = \frac{1}{\Gamma(\alpha)} \int_{\mathfrak{e}}^{y} (y - \mathrm{t})^{\alpha - 1} G^*(\mathrm{t}, \gamma) d\mathrm{t}, (y > \mathfrak{e}), \tag{14}$$

The right Riemann–Liouville fractional integral, denoted by $\left[\mathcal{I}^{\alpha}_{\mathfrak{g}^-} \widetilde{G}(y)\right]^{\gamma}$, can also be defined using the left and right endpoint functions.

Theorem 4. ([69]). *Let $\mathbb{F}_0^+$ be a set of positive fuzzy numbers, $\mathfrak{J} : [0, 1] \to \mathbb{R}^+$, and $\widetilde{G} : [\mathfrak{u}, \mathfrak{v}] \to \mathbb{F}_0^+$ be a UD-convex FNVM on $[\mathfrak{u}, \mathfrak{v}]$, whose γ-cuts set up the sequence of IVMs $G_{\gamma} : [\mathfrak{u}, \mathfrak{v}] \subset \mathbb{R} \to \mathbb{R}_C{}^+$, which is given by $G_{\gamma}(y) = [G_*(y, \gamma), G^*(y, \gamma)]$ for all $y \in [\mathfrak{u}, \mathfrak{v}]$ and for all $\gamma \in [0, 1]$. If $\widetilde{G} \in L([\mathfrak{u}, \mathfrak{v}], \mathbb{F}_0)$; then,*

$$\frac{1}{\alpha \mathfrak{J}\left(\frac{1}{2}\right)} \widetilde{G}\left(\frac{\mathfrak{u} + \mathfrak{v}}{2}\right) \supseteq_{\mathbb{F}} \frac{\Gamma(\alpha)}{(\mathfrak{v} - \mathfrak{u})^{\alpha}} \left[\mathcal{I}^{\alpha}_{\mathfrak{u}^+} \widetilde{G}(\mathfrak{v}) \oplus \mathcal{I}^{\alpha}_{\mathfrak{v}^-} \widetilde{G}(\mathfrak{u})\right] \supseteq_{\mathbb{F}} \left[\widetilde{G}(\mathfrak{u}) \oplus \widetilde{G}(\mathfrak{v})\right] \int_0^1 \tau^{\beta - 1} [\mathfrak{J}(\tau) + \mathfrak{J}(1 - \tau)] d\tau. \tag{15}$$

Interval and fuzzy Aumann's type integrals are defined as follows for the coordinated IVM $G(x, y)$ and the coordinated FNVM $\widetilde{G}(x, y)$:

Theorem 5. ([59]). *Let $\widetilde{G} : \Delta[\mathfrak{e}, \mathfrak{g}] \times [\mathfrak{u}, \mathfrak{v}] \subset \mathbb{R}^2 \to \mathbb{F}_0^+$ be an FNVM on coordinates, whose γ-cuts set up the sequence of IVMs $G_{\gamma} : \Delta \subset \mathbb{R}^2 \to \mathbb{R}_I$, which is given by $G_{\gamma}(x, y) = [G_*((x, y), \gamma), G^*((x, y), \gamma)]$ for all $(x, y) \in \Delta = [\mathfrak{e}, \mathfrak{g}] \times [\mathfrak{u}, \mathfrak{v}]$ and for all $\gamma \in [0, 1]$. Then, $\widetilde{G}$ is fuzzy double integrable (FD-integrable) over Δ if and only if $G_*(x, \gamma)$ and $G^*(x, \gamma)$ both are D-integrable over Δ. Moreover, if $\widetilde{G}$ is FD-integrable over Δ, then*

$$\begin{aligned} \left[(FD) \int_{\mathfrak{e}}^{\mathfrak{g}} \int_{\mathfrak{u}}^{\mathfrak{v}} \widetilde{G}(x, y) dy dx\right]^{\gamma} &= \left[(D) \int_{\mathfrak{e}}^{\mathfrak{g}} \int_{\mathfrak{u}}^{\mathfrak{v}} G_*((x, y), \gamma) dy dx,\ (D) \int_{\mathfrak{e}}^{\mathfrak{g}} \int_{\mathfrak{u}}^{\mathfrak{v}} G^*((x, y), \gamma) dy dx\right] \\ &= (ID) \int_{\mathfrak{e}}^{\mathfrak{g}} \int_{\mathfrak{u}}^{\mathfrak{v}} G_{\gamma}(x, y) dy dx, \end{aligned} \tag{16}$$

for all $\gamma \in [0, 1]$.

The families of all FD-integrable *FNVMs* over coordinates and D-integrable functions over coordinates are denoted by $\mathcal{FD}_{\Delta}$ and $\mathfrak{D}_{(\Delta, \gamma)}$ for all $\gamma \in [0, 1]$.

Here is the main definition of a fuzzy Riemann–Liouville fractional integral on the coordinates of the function $\widetilde{G}(x,y)$ by:

Definition 4 ([70]). *Let $\widetilde{G} : \Delta \to \mathbb{F}_0$ and $\widetilde{G} \in \mathcal{FD}_\Delta$. The double fuzzy interval Riemann–Liouville-type integrals $\mathcal{I}^{\alpha,\,\beta}_{\mathfrak{e}^+,\mathfrak{u}^+}$, $\mathcal{I}^{\alpha,\,\beta}_{\mathfrak{e}^+,\mathfrak{v}^-}$, $\mathcal{I}^{\alpha,\,\beta}_{\mathfrak{g}^-,\mathfrak{u}^+}$, $\mathcal{I}^{\alpha,\,\beta}_{\mathfrak{g}^-,\mathfrak{v}^-}$ of G of the order α, $\beta > 0$ are defined by:*

$$\mathcal{I}^{\alpha,\,\beta}_{\mathfrak{e}^+,\mathfrak{u}^+}\widetilde{G}(x,y) = \frac{1}{\Gamma(\alpha)\Gamma(\beta)}\int_{\mathfrak{e}}^{x}\int_{\mathfrak{u}}^{y}(x-\mathrm{t})^{\alpha-1}(y-\mathrm{s})^{\beta-1}\widetilde{G}(\mathrm{t},\mathrm{s})d\mathrm{s}d\mathrm{t}, \quad (x > \mathfrak{e}, y > \mathfrak{u}), \tag{17}$$

$$\mathcal{I}^{\alpha,\,\beta}_{\mathfrak{e}^+,\mathfrak{v}^-}\widetilde{G}(x,y) = \frac{1}{\Gamma(\alpha)\Gamma(\beta)}\int_{\mathfrak{e}}^{x}\int_{y}^{\mathfrak{v}}(x-\mathrm{t})^{\alpha-1}(\mathrm{s}-y)^{\beta-1}\widetilde{G}(\mathrm{t},\mathrm{s})d\mathrm{s}d\mathrm{t}, \quad (x > \mathfrak{e}, y < \mathfrak{v}), \tag{18}$$

$$\mathcal{I}^{\alpha,\,\beta}_{\mathfrak{g}^-,\mathfrak{u}^+}\widetilde{G}(x,y) = \frac{1}{\Gamma(\alpha)\Gamma(\beta)}\int_{x}^{\mathfrak{g}}\int_{\mathfrak{u}}^{y}(\mathrm{t}-x)^{\alpha-1}(y-\mathrm{s})^{\beta-1}\widetilde{G}(\mathrm{t},\mathrm{s})d\mathrm{s}d\mathrm{t}, \quad (x < \mathfrak{g}, y > \mathfrak{u}), \tag{19}$$

$$\mathcal{I}^{\alpha,\,\beta}_{\mathfrak{g}^-,\mathfrak{v}^-}\widetilde{G}(x,y) = \frac{1}{\Gamma(\alpha)\Gamma(\beta)}\int_{x}^{\mathfrak{g}}\int_{y}^{\mathfrak{v}}(\mathrm{t}-x)^{\alpha-1}(\mathrm{s}-y)^{\beta-1}\widetilde{G}(\mathrm{t},\mathrm{s})d\mathrm{s}d\mathrm{t}, \quad (x < \mathfrak{g}, y < \mathfrak{v}). \tag{20}$$

Here is the newly defined concept of coordinated *UD*-$\mathcal{J}$-convexity over fuzzy number space in the codomain via the *UD*-relation given by the following:

Definition 5. *The FNVM $\widetilde{G} : \Delta \to \mathbb{F}_0$ is referred to as a coordinated UD-$\mathcal{J}$-convex FNVM on Δ if*

$$\begin{aligned}&\widetilde{G}(\tau\mathfrak{e} + (1-\tau)\mathfrak{g}, \kappa\mathfrak{u} + (1-\kappa)\mathfrak{v}) \\ &\supseteq_{\mathbb{F}} \mathcal{J}(\tau)\mathcal{J}(\kappa)\widetilde{G}(\mathfrak{e},\mathfrak{u}) \oplus \mathcal{J}(\tau)\mathcal{J}(1-\kappa)\widetilde{G}(\mathfrak{e},\mathfrak{v}) \oplus \mathcal{J}(1-\tau)\mathcal{J}(\kappa)\widetilde{G}(\mathfrak{g},\mathfrak{u}) \oplus \mathcal{J}(1-\tau)\mathcal{J}(1-\kappa)\widetilde{G}(\mathfrak{g},\mathfrak{v}),\end{aligned} \tag{21}$$

for all $(\mathfrak{e},\mathfrak{g})$, $(\mathfrak{u},\mathfrak{v}) \in \Delta$ and $\tau,\kappa \in [0,\,1]$, where $\widetilde{G}(x) \geq_{\mathbb{F}} \widetilde{0}$. If inequality (21) is reversed, then $\widetilde{G}$ is referred to as a coordinate UD-$\mathcal{J}$-concave FNVM on Δ.

Lemma 1. *Let $\widetilde{G} : \Delta \to \mathbb{F}_0$ be a coordinated FNVM on Δ. Then, $\widetilde{G}$ is a coordinated UD-$\mathcal{J}$-convex FNVM on Δ if and only if there exist two coordinated UD-$\mathcal{J}$-convex FNVMs, $\widetilde{G}_x : [\mathfrak{u},\mathfrak{v}] \to \mathbb{F}_0$, $\widetilde{G}_x(w) = \widetilde{G}(x,w)$ and $\widetilde{G}_y : [\mathfrak{e},\mathfrak{g}] \to \mathbb{F}_0$, $\widetilde{G}_y(z) = \widetilde{G}(z,y)$.*

Theorem 6. *Let $\widetilde{G} : \Delta \to \mathbb{F}_0^+$ be an FNVM on Δ. Then, from γ-levels, we obtain the collection of IVMs $G_\gamma : \Delta \to \mathbb{R}_I^+ \subset \mathbb{R}_I$, which is given by*

$$G_\gamma(x,y) = [G_*((x,y),\gamma),\ G^*((x,y),\gamma)], \tag{22}$$

for all $(x,y) \in \Delta$ and for all $\gamma \in [0,\,1]$. Then, $\widetilde{G}$ is a coordinated UD-$\mathcal{J}$-convex FNVM on Δ if and only if for all $\gamma \in [0,\,1]$, $G_*((x,y),\,\gamma)$ and $G^*((x,y),\,\gamma)$ are coordinated $\mathcal{J}$-convex and $\mathcal{J}$-concave functions, respectively.

Proof. Assume that for each $\gamma \in [0, 1]$, $G_*(x, \gamma)$ and $G^*(x, \gamma)$ are coordinated $\mathcal{J}$-convex and $\mathcal{J}$-concave on Δ, respectively. Then, from Equation (21), for all $(\mathfrak{e}, \mathfrak{g})$, $(\mathfrak{u}, \mathfrak{v}) \in \Delta$, τ and $\kappa \in [0, 1]$, we have

$$G_*((\tau\mathfrak{e} + (1-\tau)\mathfrak{g}, \kappa\mathfrak{u} + (1-\kappa)\mathfrak{v}), \gamma)$$
$$\leq \mathcal{J}(\tau)\mathcal{J}(\kappa)G_*((\mathfrak{e}, \mathfrak{u}), \gamma) + \mathcal{J}(\tau)\mathcal{J}(1-\kappa)G_*((\mathfrak{e}, \mathfrak{v}), \gamma) + \mathcal{J}(\kappa)\mathcal{J}(1-\tau)G_*((\mathfrak{e}, \mathfrak{u}), \gamma) +$$
$$\mathcal{J}(1-\tau)\mathcal{J}(1-\kappa)G_*((\mathfrak{e}, \mathfrak{v}), \gamma),$$

and

$$G^*((\tau\mathfrak{e} + (1-\tau)\mathfrak{g}, \kappa\mathfrak{u} + (1-\kappa)\mathfrak{v}), \gamma)$$
$$\geq \mathcal{J}(\tau)\mathcal{J}(\kappa)G_*((\mathfrak{e}, \mathfrak{u}), \gamma) + \mathcal{J}(\tau)\mathcal{J}(1-\kappa)G^*((\mathfrak{e}, \mathfrak{v}), \gamma) + \mathcal{J}(\kappa)\mathcal{J}(1-\tau)G^*((\mathfrak{e}, \mathfrak{u}), \gamma) +$$
$$\mathcal{J}(1-\tau)\mathcal{J}(1-\kappa)G^*((\mathfrak{e}, \mathfrak{v}), \gamma),$$

Then, from Equations (3), (5), and (22), we obtain

$$G_\gamma((\tau\mathfrak{e} + (1-\tau)\mathfrak{g}, \kappa\mathfrak{u} + (1-\kappa)\mathfrak{v}))$$
$$= [G_*((\tau\mathfrak{e} + (1-\tau)\mathfrak{g}, \kappa\mathfrak{u} + (1-\kappa)\mathfrak{v}), \gamma),\ G^*((\tau\mathfrak{e} + (1-\tau)\mathfrak{g}, \kappa\mathfrak{u} + (1-\kappa)\mathfrak{v}), \gamma)]$$
$$\supseteq_I \mathcal{J}(\tau)\mathcal{J}(\kappa)[G_*((\mathfrak{e}, \mathfrak{u}), \gamma),\ G^*((\mathfrak{e}, \mathfrak{u}), \gamma)] + \mathcal{J}(\tau)\mathcal{J}(1-\kappa)[G_*((\mathfrak{e}, \mathfrak{v}), \gamma),\ G^*((\mathfrak{e}, \mathfrak{v}), \gamma)] +$$
$$\mathcal{J}(\kappa)\mathcal{J}(1-\tau)[G_*((\mathfrak{e}, \mathfrak{u}), \gamma),\ G^*((\mathfrak{e}, \mathfrak{u}), \gamma)] + \mathcal{J}(1-\tau)\mathcal{J}(1-\kappa)[G_*((\mathfrak{e}, \mathfrak{v}), \gamma),\ G^*((\mathfrak{e}, \mathfrak{v}), \gamma)]$$

That is

$$\widetilde{G}(\tau\mathfrak{e} + (1-\tau)\mathfrak{g}, \kappa\mathfrak{u} + (1-\kappa)\mathfrak{v})$$
$$\supseteq_{\mathbb{F}} \mathcal{J}(\tau)\mathcal{J}(\kappa)\widetilde{G}(\mathfrak{e}, \mathfrak{u}) \oplus \mathcal{J}(\tau)\mathcal{J}(1-\kappa)\widetilde{G}(\mathfrak{e}, \mathfrak{v}) \oplus \mathcal{J}(1-\tau)\mathcal{J}(1-\kappa)\widetilde{G}(\mathfrak{g}, \mathfrak{u}) \oplus$$
$$\mathcal{J}(1-\tau)\mathcal{J}(1-\kappa)\widetilde{G}(\mathfrak{g}, \mathfrak{v}),$$

and hence, $\widetilde{G}$ is a coordinated *UD*-$\mathcal{J}$-convex *FNVM* on Δ.

Conversely, let $\widetilde{G}$ be a coordinated *UD*-$\mathcal{J}$-convex *FNVM* on Δ. Then, for all $(\mathfrak{e}, \mathfrak{g})$, $(\mathfrak{u}, \mathfrak{v}) \in \Delta$, τ and $\kappa \in [0, 1]$, we have

$$\widetilde{G}(\tau\mathfrak{e} + (1-\tau)\mathfrak{g}, \kappa\mathfrak{u} + (1-\kappa)\mathfrak{v})$$
$$\supseteq_{\mathbb{F}} \mathcal{J}(\tau)\mathcal{J}(\kappa)\widetilde{G}(\mathfrak{e}, \mathfrak{u}) \oplus \mathcal{J}(\tau)\mathcal{J}(1-\kappa)\widetilde{G}(\mathfrak{e}, \mathfrak{v}) \oplus \mathcal{J}(1-\tau)\mathcal{J}(\kappa)\widetilde{G}(\mathfrak{g}, \mathfrak{u}) \oplus \mathcal{J}(1-\tau)\mathcal{J}(1-\kappa)\widetilde{G}(\mathfrak{g}, \mathfrak{v}).$$

Therefore, again from Equation (22), for each $\gamma \in [0, 1]$, we have

$$G_\gamma((\tau\mathfrak{e} + (1-\tau)\mathfrak{g}, \kappa\mathfrak{u} + (1-\kappa)\mathfrak{v}))$$
$$= [G_*((\tau\mathfrak{e} + (1-\tau)\mathfrak{g}, \kappa\mathfrak{u} + (1-\kappa)\mathfrak{v}), \gamma),\ G^*((\tau\mathfrak{e} + (1-\tau)\mathfrak{g}, \kappa\mathfrak{u} + (1-\kappa)\mathfrak{v}), \gamma)].$$

Again, from Equations (3) and (5), we obtain

$$\mathcal{J}(\tau)\mathcal{J}(\kappa)G_\gamma(\mathfrak{e}, \mathfrak{u}) + \mathcal{J}(\tau)\mathcal{J}(1-\kappa)G_\gamma(\mathfrak{e}, \mathfrak{v}) + \mathcal{J}(1-\tau)\mathcal{J}(\kappa)G_\gamma(\mathfrak{g}, \mathfrak{u}) + \mathcal{J}(1-\tau)\mathcal{J}(1-\kappa)G_\gamma(\mathfrak{g}, \mathfrak{v})$$
$$= \mathcal{J}(\tau)\mathcal{J}(\kappa)[G_*((\mathfrak{e}, \mathfrak{u}), \gamma),\ G^*((\mathfrak{e}, \mathfrak{u}), \gamma)] + \mathcal{J}(\tau)\mathcal{J}(1-\kappa)[G_*((\mathfrak{e}, \mathfrak{v}), \gamma),\ G^*((\mathfrak{e}, \mathfrak{v}), \gamma)]$$
$$+ \mathcal{J}(\kappa)\mathcal{J}(1-\tau)[G_*((\mathfrak{e}, \mathfrak{u}), \gamma),\ G^*((\mathfrak{e}, \mathfrak{u}), \gamma)] + \mathcal{J}(1-\tau)\mathcal{J}(1-\kappa)[G_*((\mathfrak{e}, \mathfrak{v}), \gamma),\ G^*((\mathfrak{e}, \mathfrak{v}), \gamma)],$$

for all $x, \omega \in \Delta$ and $\tau \in [0, 1]$. Then, through the coordinated *UD*-$\mathcal{J}$-convexity of $\widetilde{G}$, we have, for all $x, \omega \in \Delta$ and $\tau \in [0, 1]$, that

$$G_*((\tau\mathfrak{e}+(1-\tau)\mathfrak{g},\kappa\mathfrak{u}+(1-\kappa)\mathfrak{v}),\ \gamma)$$
$$\leq \mathcal{J}(\tau)\mathcal{J}(\kappa)G_*(\mathfrak{e},\mathfrak{u})+\mathcal{J}(\tau)\mathcal{J}(1-\kappa)G_*(\mathfrak{e},\mathfrak{v})+\mathcal{J}(1-\tau)\mathcal{J}(\kappa)G_*(\mathfrak{g},\mathfrak{u})+\mathcal{J}(1-\tau)\mathcal{J}(1-\kappa)G_*(\mathfrak{g},\mathfrak{v}),$$

and

$$G^*((\tau\mathfrak{e}+(1-\tau)\mathfrak{g},\kappa\mathfrak{u}+(1-\kappa)\mathfrak{v}),\ \gamma)$$
$$\geq \mathcal{J}(\tau)\mathcal{J}(\kappa)G^*(\mathfrak{e},\mathfrak{u})+\mathcal{J}(\tau)\mathcal{J}(1-\kappa)G^*(\mathfrak{e},\mathfrak{v})+\mathcal{J}(1-\tau)\mathcal{J}(\kappa)G^*(\mathfrak{g},\mathfrak{u})+\mathcal{J}(1-\tau)\mathcal{J}(1-\kappa)G^*(\mathfrak{g},\mathfrak{v}),$$

for each $\gamma \in [0,\ 1]$. Hence, the result follows. □

Example 1. *We consider the FNVM* $\widetilde{G} : [0,\ 1] \times [0,\ 1] \to \mathbb{F}_0$ *defined by*

$$G(x)(\sigma) = \begin{cases} \dfrac{\sigma - xy}{5 - xy},\ \sigma \in [xy,\ 5] \\ \dfrac{(6+e^x)(6+e^y)-\sigma}{(6+e^x)(6+e^y)-5},\ \sigma \in (5,\ (6+e^x)(6+e^y)] \\ 0\ ,\ otherwise, \end{cases} \tag{23}$$

Then, for each $\gamma \in [0,\ 1]$, *we have* $G_\gamma(x) = [(1-\gamma)xy + 5\gamma, (1-\gamma)(6+e^x)(6+e^y)+5\gamma]$. *Since the endpoint functions* $G_*((x,y),\gamma)$ *and* $G^*((x,y),\gamma)$ *are coordinate* $\mathcal{J}$*-concave functions for each* $\gamma \in [0,\ 1]$,$\widetilde{G}(x,y)$ *is a coordinate UD-*$\mathcal{J}$*-convex FNVM.*

From Lemma 1 and Example 1, we can easily note that each UD-$\mathcal{J}$*-convex FNVM is a coordinated UD-*$\mathcal{J}$*-convex FNVM. But the converse is not true.*

Remark 1. *If one assumes that* $\mathcal{J}(\tau) = \tau,\ \mathcal{J}(\kappa) = \kappa$ *and* $G_*((x,y),\gamma) = G^*((x,y),\gamma)$ *with* $\gamma = 1$, *then G is referred to as a coordinated convex function if G meets the stated inequality here:*

$$G(\tau\mathfrak{e}+(1-\tau)\mathfrak{g},\kappa\mathfrak{u}+(1-\kappa)\mathfrak{v}) \leq \tau\kappa G(\mathfrak{e},\mathfrak{u})+\tau(1-\kappa)G(\mathfrak{e},\mathfrak{v})+(1-\tau)\kappa G(\mathfrak{g},\mathfrak{u})+(1-\tau)(1-\kappa)G(\mathfrak{g},\mathfrak{v}). \tag{24}$$

Let one assume that $\mathcal{J}(\tau) = \tau,\ \mathcal{J}(\kappa) = \kappa$ *and* $G_*((x,y),\gamma) \neq G^*((x,y),\gamma)$ *with* $\gamma = 1$, $G_*((x,y),\gamma)$ *is an affine function, and* $G^*((x,y),\gamma)$ *is a concave function. Then, the stated inequality here, (see [68])*

$$G(\tau\mathfrak{e}+(1-\tau)\mathfrak{g},\kappa\mathfrak{u}+(1-\kappa)\mathfrak{v}) \supseteq \tau\kappa G(\mathfrak{e},\mathfrak{u})+\tau(1-\kappa)G(\mathfrak{e},\mathfrak{v})+(1-\tau)\kappa G(\mathfrak{g},\mathfrak{u})+(1-\tau)(1-\kappa)G(\mathfrak{g},\mathfrak{v}), \tag{25}$$

is true.

Definition 6. *Let* $\widetilde{G} : \Delta \to \mathbb{F}_0$ *be an FNVM on* Δ. *Then, from* γ*-levels, we obtain that the collection of IVMs* $G_\gamma : \Delta \to \mathbb{R}_I^+ \subset \mathbb{R}_I$ *is given by*

$$G_\gamma(x,y) = [G_*((x,y),\gamma),\ G^*((x,y),\gamma)], \tag{26}$$

for all $(x,y) \in \Delta$ *and for all* $\gamma \in [0,\ 1]$. *Then,* $\widetilde{G}$ *is a coordinated left-UD-*$\mathcal{J}$*-convex (concave) FNVM on* Δ *if and only if for all* $\gamma \in [0,\ 1]$, $G_*((x,y),\ \gamma)$ *and* $G^*((x,y),\ \gamma)$ *are coordinated* $\mathcal{J}$*-convex (concave) and affine functions on* Δ, *respectively.*

Definition 7. *Let $\widetilde{G} : \Delta \to \mathbb{F}_0$ be an FNVM on Δ. Then, from γ-levels, we obtain that the collection of IVMs $G_\gamma : \Delta \to \mathbb{R}_I^+ \subset \mathbb{R}_I$ is given by*

$$G_\gamma(x,y) = [G_*((x,y),\gamma),\ G^*((x,y),\gamma)],$$

for all $(x,y) \in \Delta$ and for all $\gamma \in [0,\ 1]$. Then, $\widetilde{G}$ is a coordinated right-UD-$\mathbb{J}$-convex (concave) FNVM on Δ if and only if for all $\gamma \in [0,\ 1]$, $G_*((x,y),\ \gamma)$ and $G^*((x,y),\ \gamma)$ are coordinated $\mathbb{J}$-affine and $\mathbb{J}$-convex (concave) functions on Δ, respectively.

Theorem 7. *Let Δ be a coordinated convex set, and let $\widetilde{G} : \Delta \to \mathbb{F}_0^+$ be an FNVM. Then, from γ-levels, we obtain that the collection of IVMs $G_\gamma : \Delta \to \mathbb{R}_I^+ \subset \mathbb{R}_I$ is given by*

$$G_\gamma(x,y) = [G_*((x,y),\gamma),\ G^*((x,y),\gamma)],$$

for all $(x,y) \in \Delta$ and for all $\gamma \in [0,\ 1]$. Then, $\widetilde{G}$ is a coordinated UD-$\mathbb{J}$-concave FNVM on Δ if and only if for all $\gamma \in [0,\ 1]$, $G_*((x,y),\ \gamma)$ and $G^*((x,y),\ \gamma)$ are coordinated $\mathbb{J}$-concave and $\mathbb{J}$-convex functions, respectively.

Proof. The demonstration of the proof of Theorem 7 is similar to the demonstration of the proof of Theorem 6. □

Example 2. *We consider the FNVMs $\widetilde{G} : [0,\ 1] \times [0,\ 1] \to \mathbb{F}_0^+$ defined by*

$$\widetilde{G}(x,y)(\sigma) = \begin{cases} \dfrac{\sigma - (6-e^x)(6-e^y)}{(6-e^x)(6-e^y) - 25}, & \sigma \in [(6-e^x)(6-e^y),\ 25] \\ \dfrac{35xy - \sigma}{35xy - 25}, & \sigma \in (25,\ 35xy] \\ 0, & otherwise. \end{cases} \quad (27)$$

Then, for each $\gamma \in [0,\ 1]$, we have $G_\gamma(x,y) = [(1-\gamma)(6-e^x)(6-e^y) + 25\gamma, 35(1-\gamma)xy + 25\gamma]$. Since the endpoint functions $G_*((x,y),\gamma)$ and $G^*((x,y),\gamma)$ are coordinated $\mathbb{J}$-concave and $\mathbb{J}$-convex functions for each $\gamma \in [0,\ 1]$, $\widetilde{G}(x,y)$ is a coordinated UD-$\mathbb{J}$-concave FNVM.

3. Main Results

Here is the first result of the coordinated integral inequalities of the Hermite–Hadamard type using fuzzy fractional operators via coordinated *UD*-$\mathbb{J}$-concave *FNVMs*.

Theorem 8. *Let $\widetilde{G} : \Delta \to \mathbb{F}_0^+$ be a coordinated UD-$\mathbb{J}$-convex FNVM on Δ, and let $\mathbb{J} : [0,\ 1] \to \mathbb{R}^+$. Then, from γ-cuts, we set up the sequence of IVMs $G_\gamma : \Delta \to \mathbb{R}_I^+$, which is given by $G_\gamma(x,y) = [G_*((x,y),\gamma),\ G^*((x,y),\gamma)]$ for all $(x,y) \in \Delta$ and for all $\gamma \in [0,\ 1]$. If $\widetilde{G} \in \mathcal{FO}_\Delta$, then the following inequalities hold:*

$$\begin{aligned}
&\frac{1}{\mathcal{J}^2\left(\frac{1}{2}\right)}\widetilde{G}\left(\frac{\mathfrak{e}+\mathfrak{g}}{2},\ \frac{\mathfrak{u}+\mathfrak{v}}{2}\right)\\
&\supseteq_{\mathbb{F}} \frac{\Gamma(\alpha+1)}{2\mathcal{J}\left(\frac{1}{2}\right)(\mathfrak{g}-\mathfrak{e})^{\alpha}}\left[\mathcal{I}^{\alpha}_{\mathfrak{e}^+}\widetilde{G}\left(\mathfrak{g},\frac{\mathfrak{u}+\mathfrak{v}}{2}\right)\oplus\mathcal{I}^{\alpha}_{\mathfrak{g}^-}\widetilde{G}\left(\mathfrak{e},\frac{\mathfrak{u}+\mathfrak{v}}{2}\right)\right]\oplus\frac{\Gamma(\beta+1)}{2\mathcal{J}\left(\frac{1}{2}\right)(\mathfrak{v}-\mathfrak{u})^{\beta}}\left[\mathcal{I}^{\beta}_{\mathfrak{u}^+}\widetilde{G}\left(\frac{\mathfrak{e}+\mathfrak{g}}{2},\mathfrak{v}\right)\oplus\mathcal{I}^{\beta}_{\mathfrak{v}^-}\widetilde{G}\left(\frac{\mathfrak{e}+\mathfrak{g}}{2},\mathfrak{u}\right)\right]\\
&\supseteq_{\mathbb{F}} \frac{\Gamma(\alpha+1)\Gamma(\beta+1)}{(\mathfrak{g}-\mathfrak{e})^{\alpha}(\mathfrak{v}-\mathfrak{u})^{\beta}}\left[\mathcal{I}^{\alpha,\beta}_{\mathfrak{e}^+,\mathfrak{u}^+}\widetilde{G}(\mathfrak{g},\mathfrak{v})\oplus\mathcal{I}^{\alpha,\beta}_{\mathfrak{e}^+,\mathfrak{v}^-}\widetilde{G}(\mathfrak{g},\mathfrak{u})\oplus\mathcal{I}^{\alpha,\beta}_{\mathfrak{g}^-,\mathfrak{u}^+}\widetilde{G}(\mathfrak{e},\mathfrak{v})\oplus\mathcal{I}^{\alpha,\beta}_{\mathfrak{g}^-,\mathfrak{v}^-}\widetilde{G}(\mathfrak{e},\mathfrak{u})\right]\\
&\supseteq_{\mathbb{F}} \frac{\beta\Gamma(\alpha+1)}{(\mathfrak{g}-\mathfrak{e})^{\alpha}}\left[\mathcal{I}^{\alpha}_{\mathfrak{e}^+}\widetilde{G}(\mathfrak{g},\mathfrak{u})\oplus\mathcal{I}^{\alpha}_{\mathfrak{e}^+}\widetilde{G}(\mathfrak{g},\mathfrak{v})\oplus\mathcal{I}^{\alpha}_{\mathfrak{g}^-}\widetilde{G}(\mathfrak{e},\mathfrak{u})\oplus\mathcal{I}^{\alpha}_{\mathfrak{g}^-}\widetilde{G}(\mathfrak{e},\mathfrak{v})\right]\times\int_0^1\kappa^{\beta-1}[\mathcal{J}(\kappa)+\mathcal{J}(1-\kappa)]d\kappa\\
&\oplus\frac{\alpha\Gamma(\beta+1)}{(\mathfrak{v}-\mathfrak{u})^{\beta}}\left[\mathcal{I}^{\beta}_{\mathfrak{u}^+}\widetilde{G}(\mathfrak{e},\mathfrak{v})\oplus\mathcal{I}^{\beta}_{\mathfrak{v}^-}\widetilde{G}(\mathfrak{g},\mathfrak{u})\oplus\mathcal{I}^{\beta}_{\mathfrak{u}^+}\widetilde{G}(\mathfrak{g},\mathfrak{v})\oplus\mathcal{I}^{\beta}_{\mathfrak{v}^-}\widetilde{G}(\mathfrak{g},\mathfrak{u})\right]\times\int_0^1\tau^{\alpha-1}\mathcal{J}(\tau)+\mathcal{J}(1-\tau)d\tau\\
&\supseteq_{\mathbb{F}} \alpha\beta\left[\widetilde{G}(\mathfrak{e},\mathfrak{u})\oplus\widetilde{G}(\mathfrak{g},\mathfrak{u})\oplus\widetilde{G}(\mathfrak{e},\mathfrak{v})\oplus\widetilde{G}(\mathfrak{g},\mathfrak{v})\right]\times\int_0^1\kappa^{\beta-1}[\mathcal{J}(\kappa)+\mathcal{J}(1-\kappa)]d\kappa\int_0^1\tau^{\alpha-1}[\mathcal{J}(\tau)+\mathcal{J}(1-\tau)]d\tau.
\end{aligned}\tag{28}$$

If $\widetilde{G}(x,y)$ is a coordinated *UD-*$\mathcal{J}$-concave *FNVM*, then

$$\begin{aligned}
&\frac{1}{\mathcal{J}^2\left(\frac{1}{2}\right)}\widetilde{G}\left(\frac{\mathfrak{e}+\mathfrak{g}}{2},\ \frac{\mathfrak{u}+\mathfrak{v}}{2}\right)\\
&\subseteq_{\mathbb{F}} \frac{\Gamma(\alpha+1)}{2\mathcal{J}\left(\frac{1}{2}\right)(\mathfrak{g}-\mathfrak{e})^{\alpha}}\left[\mathcal{I}^{\alpha}_{\mathfrak{e}^+}\widetilde{G}\left(\mathfrak{g},\frac{\mathfrak{u}+\mathfrak{v}}{2}\right)\oplus\mathcal{I}^{\alpha}_{\mathfrak{g}^-}\widetilde{G}\left(\mathfrak{e},\frac{\mathfrak{u}+\mathfrak{v}}{2}\right)\right]\oplus\frac{\Gamma(\beta+1)}{2\mathcal{J}\left(\frac{1}{2}\right)(\mathfrak{v}-\mathfrak{u})^{\beta}}\left[\mathcal{I}^{\beta}_{\mathfrak{u}^+}\widetilde{G}\left(\frac{\mathfrak{e}+\mathfrak{g}}{2},\mathfrak{v}\right)\oplus\mathcal{I}^{\beta}_{\mathfrak{v}^-}\widetilde{G}\left(\frac{\mathfrak{e}+\mathfrak{g}}{2},\mathfrak{u}\right)\right]\\
&\subseteq_{\mathbb{F}} \frac{\Gamma(\alpha+1)\Gamma(\beta+1)}{(\mathfrak{g}-\mathfrak{e})^{\alpha}(\mathfrak{v}-\mathfrak{u})^{\beta}}\left[\mathcal{I}^{\alpha,\beta}_{\mathfrak{e}^+,\mathfrak{u}^+}\widetilde{G}(\mathfrak{g},\mathfrak{v})\oplus\mathcal{I}^{\alpha,\beta}_{\mathfrak{e}^+,\mathfrak{v}^-}\widetilde{G}(\mathfrak{g},\mathfrak{u})\oplus\mathcal{I}^{\alpha,\beta}_{\mathfrak{g}^-,\mathfrak{u}^+}\widetilde{G}(\mathfrak{e},\mathfrak{v})\oplus\mathcal{I}^{\alpha,\beta}_{\mathfrak{g}^-,\mathfrak{v}^-}\widetilde{G}(\mathfrak{e},\mathfrak{u})\right]\\
&\subseteq_{\mathbb{F}} \frac{\beta\Gamma(\alpha+1)}{(\mathfrak{g}-\mathfrak{e})^{\alpha}}\left[\mathcal{I}^{\alpha}_{\mathfrak{e}^+}\widetilde{G}(\mathfrak{g},\mathfrak{u})\oplus\mathcal{I}^{\alpha}_{\mathfrak{e}^+}\widetilde{G}(\mathfrak{g},\mathfrak{v})\oplus\mathcal{I}^{\alpha}_{\mathfrak{g}^-}\widetilde{G}(\mathfrak{e},\mathfrak{u})\oplus\mathcal{I}^{\alpha}_{\mathfrak{g}^-}\widetilde{G}(\mathfrak{e},\mathfrak{v})\right]\times\int_0^1\kappa^{\beta-1}[\mathcal{J}(\kappa)+\mathcal{J}(1-\kappa)]d\kappa\\
&\oplus\frac{\alpha\Gamma(\beta+1)}{(\mathfrak{v}-\mathfrak{u})^{\beta}}\left[\mathcal{I}^{\beta}_{\mathfrak{u}^+}\widetilde{G}(\mathfrak{e},\mathfrak{v})\oplus\mathcal{I}^{\beta}_{\mathfrak{v}^-}\widetilde{G}(\mathfrak{g},\mathfrak{u})\oplus\mathcal{I}^{\beta}_{\mathfrak{u}^+}\widetilde{G}(\mathfrak{g},\mathfrak{v})\oplus\mathcal{I}^{\beta}_{\mathfrak{v}^-}\widetilde{G}(\mathfrak{g},\mathfrak{u})\right]\times\int_0^1\tau^{\alpha-1}[\mathcal{J}(\tau)+\mathcal{J}(1-\tau)]d\tau\\
&\subseteq_{\mathbb{F}} \alpha\beta\left[\widetilde{G}(\mathfrak{e},\mathfrak{u})\oplus\widetilde{G}(\mathfrak{g},\mathfrak{u})\oplus\widetilde{G}(\mathfrak{e},\mathfrak{v})\oplus\widetilde{G}(\mathfrak{g},\mathfrak{v})\right]\times\int_0^1\kappa^{\beta-1}[\mathcal{J}(\kappa)+\mathcal{J}(1-\kappa)]d\kappa\int_0^1\tau^{\alpha-1}[\mathcal{J}(\tau)+\mathcal{J}(1-\tau)]d\tau.
\end{aligned}\tag{29}$$

Proof. Let $\widetilde{G}:[\mathfrak{e},\mathfrak{g}]\to\mathbb{F}_0$ be a coordinated *UD-*$\mathcal{J}$-convex *FNVM*. Then, from our hypothesis, we have

$$\frac{1}{\mathcal{J}^2\left(\frac{1}{2}\right)}\widetilde{G}\left(\frac{\mathfrak{e}+\mathfrak{g}}{2},\frac{\mathfrak{u}+\mathfrak{v}}{2}\right)\supseteq_{\mathbb{F}}\widetilde{G}(\tau\mathfrak{e}+(1-\tau)\mathfrak{g},\tau\mathfrak{u}+(1-\tau)\mathfrak{v})\oplus\widetilde{G}((1-\tau)\mathfrak{e}+\tau\mathfrak{g},(1-\tau)\mathfrak{u}+\tau\mathfrak{v}).$$

By using Theorem 6, for every $\gamma\in[0,\ 1]$, we have

$$\begin{aligned}
&\frac{1}{\mathcal{J}^2\left(\frac{1}{2}\right)}G_*\left(\left(\frac{\mathfrak{e}+\mathfrak{g}}{2},\ \frac{\mathfrak{u}+\mathfrak{v}}{2}\right),\ \gamma\right)\\
&\le G_*((\tau\mathfrak{e}+(1-\tau)\mathfrak{g},\tau\mathfrak{u}+(1-\tau)\mathfrak{v}),\ \gamma)+G_*(((1-\tau)\mathfrak{e}+\tau\mathfrak{g},(1-\tau)\mathfrak{u}+\tau\mathfrak{v}),\ \gamma),\\
&\frac{1}{\mathcal{J}^2\left(\frac{1}{2}\right)}G^*\left(\left(\frac{\mathfrak{e}+\mathfrak{g}}{2},\ \frac{\mathfrak{u}+\mathfrak{v}}{2}\right),\ \gamma\right)\\
&\ge G^*((\tau\mathfrak{e}+(1-\tau)\mathfrak{g},\tau\mathfrak{u}+(1-\tau)\mathfrak{v}),\ \gamma)+G^*(((1-\tau)\mathfrak{e}+\tau\mathfrak{g},(1-\tau)\mathfrak{u}+\tau\mathfrak{v}),\gamma).
\end{aligned}$$

By using Lemma 1, we have

$$\begin{aligned}
&\frac{1}{\mathcal{J}\left(\frac{1}{2}\right)}G_*\left(\left(x,\ \frac{\mathfrak{u}+\mathfrak{v}}{2}\right),\ \gamma\right)\le G_*((x,\ \tau\mathfrak{u}+(1-\tau)\mathfrak{v}),\ \gamma)+G_*((x,\ (1-\tau)\mathfrak{u}+\tau\mathfrak{v}),\ \gamma),\\
&\frac{1}{\mathcal{J}\left(\frac{1}{2}\right)}G^*\left(\left(x,\ \frac{\mathfrak{u}+\mathfrak{v}}{2}\right),\ \gamma\right)\ge G^*((x,\ \tau\mathfrak{u}+(1-\tau)\mathfrak{v}),\ \gamma)+G^*((x,\ (1-\tau)\mathfrak{u}+\tau\mathfrak{v}),\gamma),
\end{aligned}\tag{30}$$

$$\begin{aligned}&\frac{1}{\text{ȷ}\left(\frac{1}{2}\right)}G_*\left(\left(\frac{\mathfrak{e}+\mathfrak{g}}{2},y\right),\ \gamma\right)\leq G_*((\tau\mathfrak{e}+(1-\tau)\mathfrak{g},y),\ \gamma)+G_*(((1-\tau)\mathfrak{e}+\tau\mathfrak{g},y),\ \gamma),\\&\frac{1}{\text{ȷ}\left(\frac{1}{2}\right)}G^*\left(\left(\frac{\mathfrak{e}+\mathfrak{g}}{2},y\right),\ \gamma\right)\geq G^*((\tau\mathfrak{e}+(1-\tau)\mathfrak{g},y),\ \gamma)+G^*(((1-\tau)\mathfrak{e}+\tau\mathfrak{g},y),\gamma).\end{aligned}\tag{31}$$

From (30) and (31), we have

$$\begin{aligned}&\frac{1}{\text{ȷ}\left(\frac{1}{2}\right)}\left[G_*\left(\left(x,\frac{\mathfrak{u}+\mathfrak{v}}{2}\right),\ \gamma\right),G^*\left(\left(x,\frac{\mathfrak{u}+\mathfrak{v}}{2}\right),\ \gamma\right)\right]\\&\supseteq_I[G_*((x,\ \tau\mathfrak{u}+(1-\tau)\mathfrak{v}),\ \gamma),G^*((x,\ \tau\mathfrak{u}+(1-\tau)\mathfrak{v}),\ \gamma)]\\&+[G_*((x,\ (1-\tau)\mathfrak{u}+\tau\mathfrak{v}),\ \gamma),G^*((x,\ (1-\tau)\mathfrak{u}+\tau\mathfrak{v}),\gamma)],\end{aligned}$$

and

$$\begin{aligned}&\frac{1}{\text{ȷ}\left(\frac{1}{2}\right)}\left[G_*\left(\left(\frac{\mathfrak{e}+\mathfrak{g}}{2},y\right),\ \gamma\right),G^*\left(\left(\frac{\mathfrak{e}+\mathfrak{g}}{2},y\right),\ \gamma\right)\right]\\&\supseteq_I[G_*((\tau\mathfrak{e}+(1-\tau)\mathfrak{g},y),\ \gamma),G^*((\tau\mathfrak{e}+(1-\tau)\mathfrak{g},y),\ \gamma)]\\&+[G_*((\tau\mathfrak{e}+(1-\tau)\mathfrak{g},y),\ \gamma),G^*((\tau\mathfrak{e}+(1-\tau)\mathfrak{g},y),\gamma)],\end{aligned}$$

It follows that

$$\frac{1}{\text{ȷ}\left(\frac{1}{2}\right)}G_\gamma\left(x,\frac{\mathfrak{u}+\mathfrak{v}}{2}\right)\supseteq_I G_\gamma(x,\ \tau\mathfrak{u}+(1-\tau)\mathfrak{v})+G_\gamma(x,\ (1-\tau)\mathfrak{u}+\tau\mathfrak{v}),\tag{32}$$

and

$$\frac{1}{\text{ȷ}\left(\frac{1}{2}\right)}G_\gamma\left(\frac{\mathfrak{e}+\mathfrak{g}}{2},y\right)\supseteq_I G_\gamma(\tau\mathfrak{e}+(1-\tau)\mathfrak{g},y)+G_\gamma(\tau\mathfrak{e}+(1-\tau)\mathfrak{g},y).\tag{33}$$

Since $G_\gamma(x,.)$ and $G_\gamma(.,y)$ are both coordinated *UD-ȷ*-convex-*IVM*s, then from inequality (15), for every $\gamma\in[0,\ 1]$, and from inequalities (32) and (43), we have

$$\begin{aligned}\frac{1}{\beta\text{ȷ}\left(\frac{1}{2}\right)}G_{\gamma_x}\left(\frac{\mathfrak{u}+\mathfrak{v}}{2}\right)&\supseteq_I\frac{\Gamma(\beta)}{(\mathfrak{v}-\mathfrak{u})^\beta}\left[\mathcal{I}^\beta_{\mathfrak{u}^+}G_{\gamma_x}(\mathfrak{v})+\mathcal{I}^\beta_{\mathfrak{v}^-}\ G_{\gamma_x}(\mathfrak{u})\right]\\&\supseteq_I\left[G_{\gamma_x}(\mathfrak{u})+G_{\gamma_x}(\mathfrak{v})\right]\int_0^1\kappa^{\beta-1}[\text{ȷ}(\kappa)+\text{ȷ}(1-\kappa)]d\kappa\end{aligned}\tag{34}$$

and

$$\begin{aligned}\frac{1}{\alpha\text{ȷ}\left(\frac{1}{2}\right)}G_{\gamma_y}\left(\frac{\mathfrak{e}+\mathfrak{g}}{2}\right)&\supseteq_I\frac{\Gamma(\alpha)}{(\mathfrak{g}-\mathfrak{e})^\alpha}\left[\mathcal{I}^\alpha_{\mathfrak{e}^+}G_{\gamma_y}(\mathfrak{g})+\mathcal{I}^\alpha_{\mathfrak{g}^-}G_{\gamma_y}(\mathfrak{e})\right]\\&\supseteq_I\left[G_{\gamma_y}(\mathfrak{e})+G_{\gamma_y}(\mathfrak{g})\right]\int_0^1\tau^{\alpha-1}\text{ȷ}(\tau)+\text{ȷ}(1-\tau)d\tau\end{aligned}\tag{35}$$

Since $G_{\gamma_x}(w)=G_\gamma(x,w)$, (34) can be written as

$$\begin{aligned}\frac{1}{\beta\text{ȷ}\left(\frac{1}{2}\right)}G_\gamma\left(x,\frac{\mathfrak{u}+\mathfrak{v}}{2}\right)&\supseteq_I\frac{\Gamma(\beta)}{(\mathfrak{v}-\mathfrak{u})^\beta}\left[\mathcal{I}^\alpha_{\mathfrak{u}^+}G_\gamma(x,\mathfrak{v})+\mathcal{I}^\alpha_{\mathfrak{v}^-}G_\gamma(x,\mathfrak{u})\right]\\&\supseteq_I[G_\gamma(x,\mathfrak{u})+G_\gamma(x,\mathfrak{v})]\int_0^1\kappa^{\beta-1}[\text{ȷ}(\kappa)+\text{ȷ}(1-\kappa)]d\kappa.\end{aligned}\tag{36}$$

That is

$$\begin{aligned}\frac{1}{\beta\text{ȷ}\left(\frac{1}{2}\right)}G_\gamma\left(x,\frac{\mathfrak{u}+\mathfrak{v}}{2}\right)&\supseteq_I\frac{1}{(\mathfrak{v}-\mathfrak{u})^\beta}\left[\int_\mathfrak{u}^\mathfrak{v}(\mathfrak{v}-\kappa)^{\beta-1}G_\gamma(x,\kappa)d\kappa+\int_\mathfrak{u}^\mathfrak{v}(\kappa-\mathfrak{u})^{\beta-1}G_\gamma(x,\kappa)d\kappa\right]\\&\supseteq_I[G_\gamma(x,\mathfrak{u})+G_\gamma(x,\mathfrak{v})]\int_0^1\kappa^{\beta-1}[\text{ȷ}(\kappa)+\text{ȷ}(1-\kappa)]d\kappa.\end{aligned}$$

Multiplying the double inequality of (36) by $\frac{(\mathfrak{g}-x)^{\alpha-1}}{(\mathfrak{g}-\mathfrak{e})^\alpha}$ and integrating with respect to x over $[\mathfrak{e},\mathfrak{g}]$, we have

$$\frac{1}{\beta(\mathfrak{g}-\mathfrak{e})^{\alpha}\mathcal{J}\left(\frac{1}{2}\right)}\int_{\mathfrak{e}}^{\mathfrak{g}} G_{\gamma}\left(x,\tfrac{\mathfrak{u}+\mathfrak{v}}{2}\right)(\mathfrak{g}-x)^{\alpha-1}dx$$
$$\supseteq_{I} \frac{1}{(\mathfrak{g}-\mathfrak{e})^{\alpha}(\mathfrak{v}-\mathfrak{u})^{\beta}}\int_{\mathfrak{e}}^{\mathfrak{g}}\int_{\mathfrak{u}}^{\mathfrak{v}} (\mathfrak{g}-x)^{\alpha-1}(\mathfrak{v}-\kappa)^{\beta-1}G_{\gamma}(x,\kappa)d\kappa dx+\int_{\mathfrak{e}}^{\mathfrak{g}}\int_{\mathfrak{u}}^{\mathfrak{v}} (\mathfrak{g}-x)^{\alpha-1}(\kappa-\mathfrak{u})^{\beta-1}G_{\gamma}(x,\kappa)d\kappa dx \quad (37)$$
$$\supseteq_{I} \frac{1}{(\mathfrak{g}-\mathfrak{e})^{\alpha}}\left[\int_{\mathfrak{e}}^{\mathfrak{g}} (\mathfrak{g}-x)^{\alpha-1}G_{\gamma}(x,\mathfrak{u})dx+\int_{\mathfrak{e}}^{\mathfrak{g}} (\mathfrak{g}-x)^{\alpha-1}G_{\gamma}(x,\mathfrak{v})dx\right]\int_{0}^{1}\kappa^{\beta-1}[\mathcal{J}(\kappa)+\mathcal{J}(1-\kappa)]d\kappa.$$

Again, multiplying the double inequality of (36) by $\frac{(x-\mathfrak{e})^{\alpha-1}}{(\mathfrak{g}-\mathfrak{e})^{\alpha}}$ and integrating with respect to x over $[\mathfrak{e},\mathfrak{g}]$, we have

$$\frac{1}{\beta(\mathfrak{g}-\mathfrak{e})^{\alpha}\mathcal{J}\left(\frac{1}{2}\right)}\int_{\mathfrak{e}}^{\mathfrak{g}} G_{\gamma}\left(x,\tfrac{\mathfrak{u}+\mathfrak{v}}{2}\right)(x-\mathfrak{e})^{\alpha-1}dx$$
$$\supseteq_{I} \frac{1}{(\mathfrak{g}-\mathfrak{e})^{\alpha}(\mathfrak{v}-\mathfrak{u})^{\beta}}\int_{\mathfrak{e}}^{\mathfrak{g}}\int_{\mathfrak{u}}^{\mathfrak{v}} (x-\mathfrak{e})^{\alpha-1}(\mathfrak{v}-\kappa)^{\beta-1}G_{\gamma}(x,\kappa)d\kappa dx$$
$$+\frac{1}{(\mathfrak{g}-\mathfrak{e})^{\alpha}(\mathfrak{v}-\mathfrak{u})^{\beta}}\int_{\mathfrak{e}}^{\mathfrak{g}}\int_{\mathfrak{u}}^{\mathfrak{v}} (x-\mathfrak{e})^{\alpha-1}(\kappa-\mathfrak{u})^{\beta-1}G_{\gamma}(x,\kappa)d\kappa dx \quad (38)$$
$$\supseteq_{I} \frac{1}{(\mathfrak{g}-\mathfrak{e})^{\alpha}}\left[\int_{\mathfrak{e}}^{\mathfrak{g}} (x-\mathfrak{e})^{\alpha-1}G_{\gamma}(x,\mathfrak{u})dx+\int_{\mathfrak{e}}^{\mathfrak{g}} (x-\mathfrak{e})^{\alpha-1}G_{\gamma}(x,\mathfrak{v})dx\right]\int_{0}^{1}\kappa^{\beta-1}[\mathcal{J}(\kappa)+\mathcal{J}(1-\kappa)]d\kappa.$$

From (37), we have

$$\frac{\Gamma(\alpha+1)}{2\mathcal{J}\left(\frac{1}{2}\right)(\mathfrak{g}-\mathfrak{e})^{\alpha}}\left[\mathcal{I}_{\mathfrak{e}^{+}}^{\alpha}G_{\gamma}\left(\mathfrak{g},\tfrac{\mathfrak{u}+\mathfrak{v}}{2}\right)\right]$$
$$\supseteq_{I} \frac{\Gamma(\alpha+1)\Gamma(\beta+1)}{(\mathfrak{g}-\mathfrak{e})^{\alpha}(\mathfrak{v}-\mathfrak{u})^{\beta}}\left[\mathcal{I}_{\mathfrak{e}^{+},\mathfrak{u}^{+}}^{\alpha,\,\beta}G_{\gamma}(\mathfrak{g},\mathfrak{v})+\mathcal{I}_{\mathfrak{g}^{-},\mathfrak{u}^{+}}^{\alpha,\,\beta}G_{\gamma}(\mathfrak{g},\mathfrak{u})\right] \quad (39)$$
$$\supseteq_{I} \frac{\beta\Gamma(\alpha+1)}{(\mathfrak{g}-\mathfrak{e})^{\alpha}}\left[\mathcal{I}_{\mathfrak{e}^{+}}^{\alpha}G_{\gamma}(\mathfrak{g},\mathfrak{u})+\mathcal{I}_{\mathfrak{e}^{+}}^{\alpha}G_{\gamma}(\mathfrak{g},\mathfrak{v})\right]\int_{0}^{1}\kappa^{\beta-1}[\mathcal{J}(\kappa)+\mathcal{J}(1-\kappa)]d\kappa.$$

From (38), we have

$$\frac{\Gamma(\alpha+1)}{2\mathcal{J}\left(\frac{1}{2}\right)(\mathfrak{g}-\mathfrak{e})^{\alpha}}\left[\mathcal{I}_{\mathfrak{g}^{-}}^{\alpha}G_{\gamma}\left(\mathfrak{e},\tfrac{\mathfrak{u}+\mathfrak{v}}{2}\right)\right]$$
$$\supseteq_{I} \frac{\Gamma(\alpha+1)\Gamma(\beta+1)}{(\mathfrak{g}-\mathfrak{e})^{\alpha}(\mathfrak{v}-\mathfrak{u})^{\beta}}\left[\mathcal{I}_{\mathfrak{g}^{-},\mathfrak{u}^{+}}^{\alpha,\,\beta}G_{\gamma}(\mathfrak{e},\mathfrak{v})+\mathcal{I}_{\mathfrak{g}^{-},\mathfrak{v}^{-}}^{\alpha,\,\beta}G_{\gamma}(\mathfrak{e},\mathfrak{u})\right] \quad (40)$$
$$\supseteq_{I} \frac{\beta\Gamma(\alpha+1)}{(\mathfrak{g}-\mathfrak{e})^{\alpha}}\left[\mathcal{I}_{\mathfrak{g}^{-}}^{\alpha}G_{\gamma}(\mathfrak{e},\mathfrak{u})+\mathcal{I}_{\mathfrak{g}^{-}}^{\alpha}G_{\gamma}(\mathfrak{e},\mathfrak{v})\right]\int_{0}^{1}\kappa^{\beta-1}[\mathcal{J}(\kappa)+\mathcal{J}(1-\kappa)]d\kappa.$$

Since, from γ-cuts, we obtain the collection of *IVMs* $G_{\gamma}:\Delta\to\mathbb{R}_{I}^{+}$, we have

$$\frac{\Gamma(\alpha+1)}{2\mathcal{J}\left(\frac{1}{2}\right)(\mathfrak{g}-\mathfrak{e})^{\alpha}}\left[\mathcal{I}_{\mathfrak{e}^{+}}^{\alpha}\widetilde{G}\left(\mathfrak{g},\tfrac{\mathfrak{u}+\mathfrak{v}}{2}\right)\right]$$
$$\supseteq_{\mathbb{F}} \frac{\Gamma(\alpha+1)\Gamma(\beta+1)}{(\mathfrak{g}-\mathfrak{e})^{\alpha}(\mathfrak{v}-\mathfrak{u})^{\beta}}\left[\mathcal{I}_{\mathfrak{e}^{+},\mathfrak{u}^{+}}^{\alpha,\,\beta}\widetilde{G}(\mathfrak{g},\mathfrak{v})\oplus\mathcal{I}_{\mathfrak{g}^{-},\mathfrak{u}^{+}}^{\alpha,\,\beta}\widetilde{G}(\mathfrak{g},\mathfrak{u})\right] \quad (41)$$
$$\supseteq_{\mathbb{F}} \frac{\beta\Gamma(\alpha+1)}{(\mathfrak{g}-\mathfrak{e})^{\alpha}}\left[\mathcal{I}_{\mathfrak{e}^{+}}^{\alpha}\widetilde{G}(\mathfrak{g},\mathfrak{u})\oplus\mathcal{I}_{\mathfrak{e}^{+}}^{\alpha}\widetilde{G}(\mathfrak{g},\mathfrak{v})\right]\int_{0}^{1}\kappa^{\beta-1}[\mathcal{J}(\kappa)+\mathcal{J}(1-\kappa)]d\kappa.$$

And

$$\frac{\Gamma(\alpha+1)}{2\mathcal{J}\left(\frac{1}{2}\right)(\mathfrak{g}-\mathfrak{e})^{\alpha}}\left[\mathcal{I}_{\mathfrak{g}^{-}}^{\alpha}\widetilde{G}\left(\mathfrak{e},\tfrac{\mathfrak{u}+\mathfrak{v}}{2}\right)\right]$$
$$\supseteq_{\mathbb{F}} \frac{\beta\Gamma(\alpha+1)\Gamma(\beta+1)}{(\mathfrak{g}-\mathfrak{e})^{\alpha}(\mathfrak{v}-\mathfrak{u})^{\beta}}\left[\mathcal{I}_{\mathfrak{g}^{-},\mathfrak{u}^{+}}^{\alpha,\,\beta}\widetilde{G}(\mathfrak{e},\mathfrak{v})\oplus\mathcal{I}_{\mathfrak{g}^{-},\mathfrak{v}^{-}}^{\alpha,\,\beta}\widetilde{G}(\mathfrak{e},\mathfrak{u})\right] \quad (42)$$
$$\supseteq_{\mathbb{F}} \frac{\beta\Gamma(\alpha+1)}{(\mathfrak{g}-\mathfrak{e})^{\alpha}}\left[\mathcal{I}_{\mathfrak{g}^{-}}^{\alpha}\widetilde{G}(\mathfrak{e},\mathfrak{u})\oplus\mathcal{I}_{\mathfrak{g}^{-}}^{\alpha}\widetilde{G}(\mathfrak{e},\mathfrak{v})\right]\int_{0}^{1}\kappa^{\beta-1}[\mathcal{J}(\kappa)+\mathcal{J}(1-\kappa)]d\kappa.$$

Similarly, since $\widetilde{G}_y(z) = \widetilde{G}(z, y)$, from (35), (41), and (42), we have

$$\begin{aligned} &\frac{\Gamma(\beta+1)}{2\mathcal{J}\left(\frac{1}{2}\right)(\mathfrak{v}-\mathfrak{u})^{\beta}}\left[\mathcal{I}^{\beta}_{\mathfrak{u}^+}\widetilde{G}\left(\tfrac{\mathfrak{e}+\mathfrak{g}}{2},\mathfrak{v}\right)\right] \\ &\supseteq_{\mathbb{F}} \frac{\Gamma(\alpha+1)\Gamma(\beta+1)}{(\mathfrak{g}-\mathfrak{e})^{\alpha}(\mathfrak{v}-\mathfrak{u})^{\beta}}\left[\mathcal{I}^{\alpha,\,\beta}_{\mathfrak{e}^+,\mathfrak{u}^+}\widetilde{G}(\mathfrak{g},\mathfrak{v}) \oplus \mathcal{I}^{\alpha,\,\beta}_{\mathfrak{g}^-,\mathfrak{u}^+}\widetilde{G}(\mathfrak{e},\mathfrak{v})\right] \\ &\supseteq_{\mathbb{F}} \frac{\alpha\Gamma(\beta+1)}{(\mathfrak{v}-\mathfrak{u})^{\beta}}\left[\mathcal{I}^{\beta}_{\mathfrak{u}^+}\widetilde{G}(\mathfrak{e},\mathfrak{v}) \oplus \mathcal{I}^{\beta}_{\mathfrak{u}^+}\widetilde{G}(\mathfrak{g},\mathfrak{v})\right]. \end{aligned} \tag{43}$$

And

$$\begin{aligned} &\frac{\Gamma(\beta+1)}{2\mathcal{J}\left(\frac{1}{2}\right)(\mathfrak{v}-\mathfrak{u})^{\alpha}}\left[\mathcal{I}^{\beta}_{\mathfrak{v}^-}\widetilde{G}\left(\tfrac{\mathfrak{e}+\mathfrak{g}}{2},\mathfrak{u}\right)\right] \\ &\supseteq_{\mathbb{F}} \frac{\Gamma(\alpha+1)\Gamma(\beta+1)}{(\mathfrak{g}-\mathfrak{e})^{\alpha}(\mathfrak{v}-\mathfrak{u})^{\beta}}\left[\mathcal{I}^{\alpha,\,\beta}_{\mathfrak{e}^+,\mathfrak{v}^-}\widetilde{G}(\mathfrak{g},\mathfrak{u}) \oplus \mathcal{I}^{\alpha,\,\beta}_{\mathfrak{g}^-,\mathfrak{v}^-}\widetilde{G}(\mathfrak{e},\mathfrak{u})\right] \\ &\supseteq_{\mathbb{F}} \frac{\alpha\Gamma(\beta+1)}{(\mathfrak{v}-\mathfrak{u})^{\beta}}\left[\mathcal{I}^{\beta}_{\mathfrak{v}^-}\widetilde{G}(\mathfrak{e},\mathfrak{u}) \oplus \mathcal{I}^{\beta}_{\mathfrak{v}^-}\widetilde{G}(\mathfrak{g},\mathfrak{u})\right]. \end{aligned} \tag{44}$$

The second, third, and fourth inequalities of (28) will be the consequence of adding the inequalities (41)–(44).

Now, for any $\gamma \in [0, 1]$, we have inequality (15)'s left side:

$$\frac{1}{\mathcal{J}^2\left(\frac{1}{2}\right)}G_\gamma\left(\frac{\mathfrak{e}+\mathfrak{g}}{2},\frac{\mathfrak{u}+\mathfrak{v}}{2}\right) \supseteq_I \frac{\Gamma(\beta+1)}{\mathcal{J}\left(\frac{1}{2}\right)(\mathfrak{v}-\mathfrak{u})^{\beta}}\left[\mathcal{I}^{\beta}_{\mathfrak{u}^+}G_\gamma\left(\frac{\mathfrak{e}+\mathfrak{g}}{2},\mathfrak{v}\right) + \mathcal{I}^{\beta}_{\mathfrak{v}^-}G_\gamma\left(\frac{\mathfrak{e}+\mathfrak{g}}{2},\mathfrak{u}\right)\right] \tag{45}$$

And

$$\frac{1}{\mathcal{J}^2\left(\frac{1}{2}\right)}G_\gamma\left(\frac{\mathfrak{e}+\mathfrak{g}}{2},\frac{\mathfrak{u}+\mathfrak{v}}{2}\right) \supseteq_I \frac{\Gamma(\alpha+1)}{\mathcal{J}\left(\frac{1}{2}\right)(\mathfrak{g}-\mathfrak{e})^{\alpha}}\left[\mathcal{I}^{\alpha}_{\mathfrak{e}^+}G_\gamma\left(\mathfrak{g},\frac{\mathfrak{u}+\mathfrak{v}}{2}\right) + \mathcal{I}^{\alpha}_{\mathfrak{g}^-}G_\gamma\left(\mathfrak{e},\frac{\mathfrak{u}+\mathfrak{v}}{2}\right)\right] \tag{46}$$

The following inequality is created by adding the two inequalities (45) and (46):

$$\begin{aligned} &\frac{1}{\mathcal{J}^2\left(\frac{1}{2}\right)}G_\gamma\left(\tfrac{\mathfrak{e}+\mathfrak{g}}{2},\tfrac{\mathfrak{u}+\mathfrak{v}}{2}\right) \supseteq_I \frac{\Gamma(\alpha+1)}{\mathcal{J}\left(\frac{1}{2}\right)(\mathfrak{g}-\mathfrak{e})^{\alpha}}\left[\mathcal{I}^{\alpha}_{\mathfrak{e}^+}G_\gamma\left(\mathfrak{g},\tfrac{\mathfrak{u}+\mathfrak{v}}{2}\right) + \mathcal{I}^{\alpha}_{\mathfrak{g}^-}G_\gamma\left(\mathfrak{e},\tfrac{\mathfrak{u}+\mathfrak{v}}{2}\right)\right] \\ &+\frac{\Gamma(\beta+1)}{\mathcal{J}\left(\frac{1}{2}\right)(\mathfrak{v}-\mathfrak{u})^{\beta}}\left[\mathcal{I}^{\beta}_{\mathfrak{u}^+}G_\gamma\left(\tfrac{\mathfrak{e}+\mathfrak{g}}{2},\mathfrak{v}\right) + \mathcal{I}^{\beta}_{\mathfrak{v}^-}G_\gamma\left(\tfrac{\mathfrak{e}+\mathfrak{g}}{2},\mathfrak{u}\right)\right]. \end{aligned}$$

Similarly, since we obtain the set of *IVMs* $G_\gamma : \Delta \to \mathbb{R}^+_I$ for $\gamma \in [0, 1]$, the inequality can be expressed as follows:

$$\begin{aligned} &\frac{1}{\mathcal{J}^2\left(\frac{1}{2}\right)}\widetilde{G}\left(\tfrac{\mathfrak{e}+\mathfrak{g}}{2},\tfrac{\mathfrak{u}+\mathfrak{v}}{2}\right) \\ &\supseteq_{\mathbb{F}} \frac{\Gamma(\alpha+1)}{\mathcal{J}\left(\frac{1}{2}\right)(\mathfrak{g}-\mathfrak{e})^{\alpha}}\left[\mathcal{I}^{\alpha}_{\mathfrak{e}^+}\widetilde{G}\left(\mathfrak{g},\tfrac{\mathfrak{u}+\mathfrak{v}}{2}\right) \oplus \mathcal{I}^{\alpha}_{\mathfrak{g}^-}\widetilde{G}\left(\mathfrak{e},\tfrac{\mathfrak{u}+\mathfrak{v}}{2}\right)\right] \oplus \frac{\Gamma(\beta+1)}{\mathcal{J}\left(\frac{1}{2}\right)(\mathfrak{v}-\mathfrak{u})^{\beta}}\left[\mathcal{I}^{\beta}_{\mathfrak{u}^+}\widetilde{G}\left(\tfrac{\mathfrak{e}+\mathfrak{g}}{2},\mathfrak{v}\right) \oplus \mathcal{I}^{\beta}_{\mathfrak{v}^-}\widetilde{G}\left(\tfrac{\mathfrak{e}+\mathfrak{g}}{2},\mathfrak{u}\right)\right]. \end{aligned} \tag{47}$$

The first inequality of (28) is this one.

Now, for any $\gamma \in [0, 1]$, we have inequality (15)'s right side:

$$\frac{\Gamma(\beta)}{(\mathfrak{v}-\mathfrak{u})^{\beta}}\left[\mathcal{I}^{\beta}_{\mathfrak{u}^+}G_\gamma(\mathfrak{e},\mathfrak{v}) + \mathcal{I}^{\beta}_{\mathfrak{v}^-}G_\gamma(\mathfrak{e},\mathfrak{u})\right] \supseteq_I [G_\gamma(\mathfrak{e},\mathfrak{u}) + G_\gamma(\mathfrak{e},\mathfrak{v})] \times \int_0^1 \kappa^{\beta-1}[\mathcal{J}(\kappa) + \mathcal{J}(1-\kappa)]d\kappa \tag{48}$$

$$\frac{\Gamma(\beta)}{(\mathfrak{v}-\mathfrak{u})^{\beta}}\left[\mathcal{I}^{\beta}_{\mathfrak{u}^+}G_\gamma(\mathfrak{g},\mathfrak{v}) + \mathcal{I}^{\beta}_{\mathfrak{v}^-}G_\gamma(\mathfrak{g},\mathfrak{u})\right] \supseteq_I [G_\gamma(\mathfrak{g},\mathfrak{u}) + G_\gamma(\mathfrak{g},\mathfrak{v})] \times \int_0^1 \kappa^{\beta-1}[\mathcal{J}(\kappa) + \mathcal{J}(1-\kappa)]d\kappa \tag{49}$$

$$\frac{\Gamma(\alpha)}{(\mathfrak{g}-\mathfrak{e})^{\alpha}}\left[\mathcal{I}^{\alpha}_{\mathfrak{e}^+}G_\gamma(\mathfrak{g},\mathfrak{u}) + \mathcal{I}^{\alpha}_{\mathfrak{g}^-}G_\gamma(\mathfrak{e},\mathfrak{u})\right] \supseteq_I [G_\gamma(\mathfrak{e},\mathfrak{u}) + G_\gamma(\mathfrak{g},\mathfrak{u})] \times \int_0^1 \tau^{\alpha-1}\mathcal{J}(\tau) + \mathcal{J}(1-\tau)d\tau \tag{50}$$

$$\frac{\Gamma(\alpha)}{(\mathfrak{g}-\mathfrak{e})^{\alpha}}\left[\mathcal{I}_{\mathfrak{e}^+}^{\alpha} G_\gamma(\mathfrak{g},\mathfrak{v}) + \mathcal{I}_{\mathfrak{g}^-}^{\alpha}\ G_\gamma(\mathfrak{e},\mathfrak{v})\right] \supseteq_I [G_\gamma(\mathfrak{e},\mathfrak{v}) + G_\gamma(\mathfrak{g},\mathfrak{v})] \times \int_0^1 \tau^{\alpha-1}\mathcal{J}(\tau) + \mathcal{J}(1-\tau)d\tau \tag{51}$$

Summing inequalities (48)–(51) and then taking the multiplication of the result with $\alpha\beta$, we have

$$\begin{aligned}
&\tfrac{\beta\Gamma(\alpha+1)}{(\mathfrak{g}-\mathfrak{e})^{\alpha}}\left[\mathcal{I}_{\mathfrak{e}^+}^{\alpha} G_\gamma(\mathfrak{g},\mathfrak{u}) + \mathcal{I}_{\mathfrak{g}^-}^{\alpha} G_\gamma(\mathfrak{e},\mathfrak{u}) + \mathcal{I}_{\mathfrak{e}^+}^{\alpha} G_\gamma(\mathfrak{g},\mathfrak{v}) + \mathcal{I}_{\mathfrak{g}^-}^{\alpha} G_\gamma(\mathfrak{e},\mathfrak{v})\right] \\
&+\tfrac{\alpha\Gamma(\beta+1)}{(\mathfrak{v}-\mathfrak{u})^{\beta}}\left[\mathcal{I}_{\mathfrak{u}^+}^{\beta} G_\gamma(\mathfrak{e},\mathfrak{v}) + \mathcal{I}_{\mathfrak{v}^-}^{\beta} G_\gamma(\mathfrak{e},\mathfrak{u}) + \mathcal{I}_{\mathfrak{u}^+}^{\beta} G_\gamma(\mathfrak{g},\mathfrak{v}) + \mathcal{I}_{\mathfrak{v}^-}^{\beta} G_\gamma(\mathfrak{g},\mathfrak{u})\right] \\
&\supseteq_I [G_\gamma(\mathfrak{e},\mathfrak{u}) + G_\gamma(\mathfrak{e},\mathfrak{v}) + G_\gamma(\mathfrak{g},\mathfrak{u}) + G_\gamma(\mathfrak{g},\mathfrak{v})] \times \textstyle\int_0^1 \kappa^{\beta-1}[\mathcal{J}(\kappa) + \mathcal{J}(1-\kappa)] \\
&d\kappa \textstyle\int_0^1 \tau^{\alpha-1}\mathcal{J}(\tau) + \mathcal{J}(1-\tau)d\tau.
\end{aligned}$$

Since we receive the collection of *IVMs* $G_\gamma : \Delta \to \mathbb{R}_I^+$ from γ-cuts, we have

$$\begin{aligned}
&\tfrac{\beta\Gamma(\alpha+1)}{(\mathfrak{g}-\mathfrak{e})^{\alpha}}\left[\mathcal{I}_{\mathfrak{e}^+}^{\alpha} \widetilde{G}(\mathfrak{g},\mathfrak{u}) \oplus \mathcal{I}_{\mathfrak{g}^-}^{\alpha} \widetilde{G}(\mathfrak{e},\mathfrak{u}) \oplus \mathcal{I}_{\mathfrak{e}^+}^{\alpha} \widetilde{G}(\mathfrak{g},\mathfrak{v}) \oplus \mathcal{I}_{\mathfrak{g}^-}^{\alpha} \widetilde{G}(\mathfrak{e},\mathfrak{v})\right] \\
&\oplus\tfrac{\alpha\Gamma(\beta+1)}{(\mathfrak{v}-\mathfrak{u})^{\beta}}\left[\mathcal{I}_{\mathfrak{u}^+}^{\beta} \widetilde{G}(\mathfrak{e},\mathfrak{v}) \oplus \mathcal{I}_{\mathfrak{v}^-}^{\beta} \widetilde{G}(\mathfrak{e},\mathfrak{u}) \oplus \mathcal{I}_{\mathfrak{u}^+}^{\beta} \widetilde{G}(\mathfrak{g},\mathfrak{v}) \oplus \mathcal{I}_{\mathfrak{v}^-}^{\beta} \widetilde{G}(\mathfrak{g},\mathfrak{u})\right] \\
&\supseteq_{\mathbb{F}} \left[\widetilde{G}(\mathfrak{e},\mathfrak{u}) \oplus \widetilde{G}(\mathfrak{e},\mathfrak{v}) \oplus \widetilde{G}(\mathfrak{g},\mathfrak{u}) \oplus \widetilde{G}(\mathfrak{g},\mathfrak{v})\right] \times \textstyle\int_0^1 \kappa^{\beta-1}[\mathcal{J}(\kappa) + \mathcal{J}(1-\kappa)] \\
&d\kappa \textstyle\int_0^1 \tau^{\alpha-1}\mathcal{J}(\tau) + \mathcal{J}(1-\tau)d\tau.
\end{aligned} \tag{52}$$

This is the final inequality of (28), and a conclusion has been established. □

Example 3. *We assume the FNVMs* $\widetilde{G} : [0,\ 2] \times [0,\ 2] \to \mathbb{F}_0$ *are defined by*

$$G(x,y)(\sigma) = \begin{cases} \frac{\sigma-(2-\sqrt{x})(2-\sqrt{y})}{4-(2-\sqrt{x})(2-\sqrt{y})}, & \sigma \in [(2-\sqrt{x})(2-\sqrt{y}),\ 4] \\ \frac{(2+\sqrt{x})(2+\sqrt{y})-\sigma}{(2+\sqrt{x})(2+\sqrt{y})-4}, & \sigma \in (4,\ (2+\sqrt{x})(2+\sqrt{y})] \\ 0, & otherwise, \end{cases} \tag{53}$$

and then, for each $\gamma \in [0,\ 1]$, *we have* $G_\gamma(x,y) = [(1-\gamma)(2-\sqrt{x})(2-\sqrt{y}) + 4\gamma, (1-\gamma)(2+\sqrt{x})(2+\sqrt{y}) + 4\gamma]$. *Since the endpoint functions* $G_*((x,y),\gamma)$ *and* $G^*((x,y),\gamma)$ *are co-*

ordinate $\mathcal{J}$*-convex and* $\mathcal{J}$*-concave functions for each* $\gamma \in [0, 1]$, $\widetilde{G}(x,y)$ *is a UD-*$\mathcal{J}$*-coordinate convex FNVM.*

$$G_\gamma\left(\tfrac{\mathfrak{e}+\mathfrak{g}}{2}, \tfrac{\mathfrak{u}+\mathfrak{v}}{2}\right) = [(1-\gamma)+4\gamma, 9(1-\gamma)+4\gamma],$$

$$\frac{\Gamma(\alpha+1)}{4(\mathfrak{g}-\mathfrak{e})^\alpha}\left[\mathcal{I}^\alpha_{\mathfrak{e}^+}\widetilde{G}\left(\mathfrak{g}, \tfrac{\mathfrak{u}+\mathfrak{v}}{2}\right) \oplus \mathcal{I}^\alpha_{\mathfrak{g}^-}\widetilde{G}\left(\mathfrak{e}, \tfrac{\mathfrak{u}+\mathfrak{v}}{2}\right)\right] \oplus \frac{\Gamma(\beta+1)}{4(\mathfrak{v}-\mathfrak{u})^\beta}\left[\mathcal{I}^\beta_{\mathfrak{u}^+}\widetilde{G}\left(\tfrac{\mathfrak{e}+\mathfrak{g}}{2}, \mathfrak{v}\right) \oplus \mathcal{I}^\beta_{\mathfrak{v}^-}\widetilde{G}\left(\tfrac{\mathfrak{e}+\mathfrak{g}}{2}, \mathfrak{u}\right)\right]$$

$$= \left[(1-\gamma)\left(2-\tfrac{\sqrt{2}}{4}-\tfrac{\sqrt{2}}{8}\pi\right)+4\gamma, (1-\gamma)\left(2+\tfrac{\sqrt{2}}{4}+\tfrac{\sqrt{2}}{8}\pi\right)+4\gamma\right]$$

$$\frac{\Gamma(\alpha+1)\Gamma(\beta+1)}{4(\mathfrak{g}-\mathfrak{e})^\alpha(\mathfrak{v}-\mathfrak{u})^\beta}\left[\mathcal{I}^{\alpha,\beta}_{\mathfrak{e}^+,\mathfrak{u}^+}G_\gamma(\mathfrak{g},\mathfrak{v}) \oplus \mathcal{I}^{\alpha,\beta}_{\mathfrak{e}^+,\mathfrak{v}^-}G_\gamma(\mathfrak{g},\mathfrak{u}) \oplus \mathcal{I}^{\alpha,\beta}_{\mathfrak{g}^-,\mathfrak{u}^+}G_\gamma(\mathfrak{e},\mathfrak{v}) \oplus \mathcal{I}^{\alpha,\beta}_{\mathfrak{g}^-,\mathfrak{v}^-}G_\gamma(\mathfrak{e},\mathfrak{u})\right]$$

$$= \left[(1-\gamma)\left(\tfrac{33}{8}-\sqrt{2}-\tfrac{\sqrt{2}}{2}\pi+\tfrac{\pi}{8}+\tfrac{\pi^2}{32}\right)+4\gamma, (1-\gamma)\left(\tfrac{33}{8}+\sqrt{2}+\tfrac{\sqrt{2}}{2}\pi+\tfrac{\pi}{8}+\tfrac{\pi^2}{32}\right)+4\gamma\right]$$

$$\frac{\Gamma(\alpha+1)}{8(\mathfrak{g}-\mathfrak{e})^\alpha}\left[\mathcal{I}^\alpha_{\mathfrak{e}^+}\widetilde{G}(\mathfrak{g},\mathfrak{u}) \oplus \mathcal{I}^\alpha_{\mathfrak{e}^+}\widetilde{G}(\mathfrak{g},\mathfrak{v}) \oplus \mathcal{I}^\alpha_{\mathfrak{g}^-}\widetilde{G}(\mathfrak{e},\mathfrak{u}) \oplus \mathcal{I}^\alpha_{\mathfrak{g}^-}\widetilde{G}(\mathfrak{e},\mathfrak{v})\right]$$

$$\oplus\frac{\Gamma(\beta+1)}{8(\mathfrak{v}-\mathfrak{u})^\beta}\left[\mathcal{I}^\beta_{\mathfrak{u}^+}\widetilde{G}(\mathfrak{e},\mathfrak{v}) \oplus \mathcal{I}^\beta_{\mathfrak{u}^+}\widetilde{G}(\mathfrak{g},\mathfrak{v}) \oplus \mathcal{I}^\beta_{\mathfrak{v}^-}\widetilde{G}(\mathfrak{e},\mathfrak{u}) \oplus \mathcal{I}^\beta_{\mathfrak{v}^-}\widetilde{G}(\mathfrak{g},\mathfrak{u})\right]$$

$$= \left[\frac{34\sqrt{2}+\left(\sqrt{2}-4\right)\pi-24}{8\sqrt{2}}(1-\gamma)+4\gamma, \frac{34\sqrt{2}+\left(\sqrt{2}+4\right)\pi+24}{8\sqrt{2}}(1-\gamma)+4\gamma\right]$$

$$\frac{G_\gamma(\mathfrak{u},\mathfrak{g})+G_\gamma(\sigma,\mathfrak{g})+G_\gamma(\mathfrak{u},\mathfrak{v})+G_\gamma(\sigma,\mathfrak{v})}{4} = \left[(1-\gamma)\left(\tfrac{9}{2}-2\sqrt{2}\right)+4\gamma, (1-\gamma)\left(\tfrac{9}{2}+2\sqrt{2}\right)+4\gamma\right].$$

That is,

$$[(1-\gamma)+4\gamma, 9(1-\gamma)+4\gamma] \supseteq_I \left[(1-\gamma)\left(2-\tfrac{\sqrt{2}}{4}-\tfrac{\sqrt{2}}{8}\pi\right)+4\gamma, (1-\gamma)\left(2+\tfrac{\sqrt{2}}{4}+\tfrac{\sqrt{2}}{8}\pi\right)+4\gamma\right]$$
$$\supseteq_I \left[(1-\gamma)\left(\tfrac{33}{8}-\sqrt{2}-\tfrac{\sqrt{2}}{2}\pi+\tfrac{\pi}{8}+\tfrac{\pi^2}{32}\right)+4\gamma, (1-\gamma)\left(\tfrac{33}{8}+\sqrt{2}+\tfrac{\sqrt{2}}{2}\pi+\tfrac{\pi}{8}+\tfrac{\pi^2}{32}\right)+4\gamma\right]$$
$$\supseteq_I \left[\frac{34\sqrt{2}+\left(\sqrt{2}-4\right)\pi-24}{8\sqrt{2}}(1-\gamma)+4\gamma, \frac{34\sqrt{2}+\left(\sqrt{2}+4\right)\pi+24}{8\sqrt{2}}(1-\gamma)+4\gamma\right]$$
$$\supseteq_I \frac{34\sqrt{2}+\left(\sqrt{2}-4\right)\pi-24}{8\sqrt{2}}(1-\gamma)+4\gamma.$$

Hence, Theorem 8 has been verified.

Remark 2. *If one assumes that* $\alpha = 1$, $\beta = 1$, *and* $\mathcal{J}(\tau) = \tau$, $\mathcal{J}(\kappa) = \kappa$, *then, from (28), as a result, there will be an inequality (see [70]):*

$$\begin{aligned}
&\widetilde{G}\left(\tfrac{\mathfrak{e}+\mathfrak{g}}{2}, \tfrac{\mathfrak{u}+\mathfrak{v}}{2}\right) \\
&\supseteq_{\mathbb{F}} \tfrac{1}{2}\left[\tfrac{1}{\mathfrak{g}-\mathfrak{e}}\int_{\mathfrak{e}}^{\mathfrak{g}}\widetilde{G}\left(x, \tfrac{\mathfrak{u}+\mathfrak{v}}{2}\right)dx \oplus \tfrac{1}{\mathfrak{v}-\mathfrak{u}}\int_{\mathfrak{u}}^{\mathfrak{v}}\widetilde{G}\left(\tfrac{\mathfrak{e}+\mathfrak{g}}{2}, y\right)dy\right] \supseteq_{\mathbb{F}} \tfrac{1}{(\mathfrak{g}-\mathfrak{e})(\mathfrak{v}-\mathfrak{u})}\int_{\mathfrak{e}}^{\mathfrak{g}}\int_{\mathfrak{u}}^{\mathfrak{v}}\widetilde{G}(x,y)dydx \\
&\supseteq_{\mathbb{F}} \tfrac{1}{4(\mathfrak{g}-\mathfrak{e})}\left[\int_{\mathfrak{e}}^{\mathfrak{g}}\widetilde{G}(x,\mathfrak{u})dx \oplus \int_{\mathfrak{e}}^{\mathfrak{g}}\widetilde{G}(x,\mathfrak{v})dx\right] \oplus \tfrac{1}{4(\mathfrak{v}-\mathfrak{u})}\left[\int_{\mathfrak{u}}^{\mathfrak{v}}\widetilde{G}(\mathfrak{e},y)dy \oplus \int_{\mathfrak{u}}^{\mathfrak{v}}\widetilde{G}(\mathfrak{g},y)dy\right] \\
&\supseteq_{\mathbb{F}} \tfrac{\widetilde{G}(\mathfrak{e},\mathfrak{u})\oplus\widetilde{G}(\mathfrak{g},\mathfrak{u})\oplus\widetilde{G}(\mathfrak{e},\mathfrak{v})\oplus\widetilde{G}(\mathfrak{g},\mathfrak{v})}{4}.
\end{aligned} \tag{54}$$

If one assumes that $\alpha = 1$, $\beta = 1$, $\mathcal{J}(\tau) = \tau$, $\mathcal{J}(\kappa) = \kappa$, *and* $\widetilde{G}$ *is a coordinated left-UD-*$\mathcal{J}$*-convex, then, from (28), as a result, there will be an inequality (see [59]):*

$$\begin{aligned}
&\widetilde{G}\left(\tfrac{\mathfrak{e}+\mathfrak{g}}{2}, \tfrac{\mathfrak{u}+\mathfrak{v}}{2}\right) \\
&\leq_{\mathbb{F}} \tfrac{1}{2}\left[\tfrac{1}{\mathfrak{g}-\mathfrak{e}}\int_{\mathfrak{e}}^{\mathfrak{g}} \widetilde{G}\left(x, \tfrac{\mathfrak{u}+\mathfrak{v}}{2}\right)dx \oplus \tfrac{1}{\mathfrak{v}-\mathfrak{u}}\int_{\mathfrak{u}}^{\mathfrak{v}} \widetilde{G}\left(\tfrac{\mathfrak{e}+\mathfrak{g}}{2}, y\right)dy\right] \leq_{\mathbb{F}} \tfrac{1}{(\mathfrak{g}-\mathfrak{e})(\mathfrak{v}-\mathfrak{u})}\int_{\mathfrak{e}}^{\mathfrak{g}}\int_{\mathfrak{u}}^{\mathfrak{v}} \widetilde{G}(x,y)dydx \\
&\leq_{\mathbb{F}} \tfrac{1}{4(\mathfrak{g}-\mathfrak{e})}\left[\int_{\mathfrak{e}}^{\mathfrak{g}} \widetilde{G}(x,\mathfrak{u})dx \oplus \int_{\mathfrak{e}}^{\mathfrak{g}} \widetilde{G}(x,\mathfrak{v})dx\right] \oplus \tfrac{1}{4(\mathfrak{v}-\mathfrak{u})}\left[\int_{\mathfrak{u}}^{\mathfrak{v}} \widetilde{G}(\mathfrak{e},y)dy \oplus \int_{\mathfrak{u}}^{\mathfrak{v}} \widetilde{G}(\mathfrak{g},y)dy\right] \\
&\leq_{\mathbb{F}} \tfrac{\widetilde{G}(\mathfrak{e},\mathfrak{u})\oplus\widetilde{G}(\mathfrak{g},\mathfrak{u})\oplus\widetilde{G}(\mathfrak{e},\mathfrak{v})\oplus\widetilde{G}(\mathfrak{g},\mathfrak{v})}{4}.
\end{aligned} \tag{55}$$

If $\mathcal{J}(\tau) = \tau$, $\mathcal{J}(\kappa) = \kappa$, and $G_*((x,y),\ \gamma) \neq G^*((x,y),\ \gamma)$ with $\gamma = 1$, then, from (28), we succeed in bringing about the upcoming inequality (see [55]):

$$\begin{aligned}
&G\left(\tfrac{\mathfrak{e}+\mathfrak{g}}{2}, \tfrac{\mathfrak{u}+\mathfrak{v}}{2}\right) \\
&\supseteq \tfrac{\Gamma(\alpha+1)}{4(\mathfrak{g}-\mathfrak{e})^{\alpha}}\left[\mathcal{I}_{\mathfrak{e}^+}^{\alpha} G\left(\mathfrak{g}, \tfrac{\mathfrak{u}+\mathfrak{v}}{2}\right) + \mathcal{I}_{\mathfrak{g}^-}^{\alpha} G\left(\mathfrak{e}, \tfrac{\mathfrak{u}+\mathfrak{v}}{2}\right)\right] + \tfrac{\Gamma(\beta+1)}{4(\mathfrak{v}-\mathfrak{u})^{\beta}}\left[\mathcal{I}_{\mathfrak{u}^+}^{\beta} G\left(\tfrac{\mathfrak{e}+\mathfrak{g}}{2}, \mathfrak{v}\right) + \mathcal{I}_{\mathfrak{v}^-}^{\beta} G\left(\tfrac{\mathfrak{e}+\mathfrak{g}}{2}, \mathfrak{u}\right)\right] \\
&\supseteq \tfrac{\Gamma(\alpha+1)\Gamma(\beta+1)}{4(\mathfrak{g}-\mathfrak{e})^{\alpha}(\mathfrak{v}-\mathfrak{u})^{\beta}}\left[\mathcal{I}_{\mathfrak{e}^+,\mathfrak{u}^+}^{\alpha,\beta} G(\mathfrak{g},\mathfrak{v}) + \mathcal{I}_{\mathfrak{e}^+,\mathfrak{v}^-}^{\alpha,\beta} G(\mathfrak{g},\mathfrak{u}) + \mathcal{I}_{\mathfrak{g}^-,\mathfrak{u}^+}^{\alpha,\beta} G(\mathfrak{e},\mathfrak{v}) + \mathcal{I}_{\mathfrak{g}^-,\mathfrak{v}^-}^{\alpha,\beta} G(\mathfrak{e},\mathfrak{u})\right] \\
&\supseteq \tfrac{\Gamma(\alpha+1)}{8(\mathfrak{g}-\mathfrak{e})^{\alpha}}\left[\mathcal{I}_{\mathfrak{e}^+}^{\alpha} G(\mathfrak{g},\mathfrak{u}) + \mathcal{I}_{\mathfrak{e}^+}^{\alpha} G(\mathfrak{g},\mathfrak{v}) + \mathcal{I}_{\mathfrak{g}^-}^{\alpha} G(\mathfrak{e},\mathfrak{u}) + \mathcal{I}_{\mathfrak{g}^-}^{\alpha} G(\mathfrak{e},\mathfrak{v})\right] \\
&+ \tfrac{\Gamma(\beta+1)}{8(\mathfrak{v}-\mathfrak{u})^{\beta}}\left[\mathcal{I}_{\mathfrak{u}^+}^{\beta} G(\mathfrak{e},\mathfrak{v}) + \mathcal{I}_{\mathfrak{v}^-}^{\beta} G(\mathfrak{e},\mathfrak{u}) + \mathcal{I}_{\mathfrak{u}^+}^{\beta} G(\mathfrak{g},\mathfrak{v}) + \mathcal{I}_{\mathfrak{v}^-}^{\beta} G(\mathfrak{g},\mathfrak{u})\right] \\
&\supseteq \tfrac{G(\mathfrak{e},\mathfrak{u})+G(\mathfrak{g},\mathfrak{u})+G(\mathfrak{e},\mathfrak{v})+G(\mathfrak{g},\mathfrak{v})}{4}.
\end{aligned} \tag{56}$$

If $\mathcal{J}(\tau) = \tau$, $\mathcal{J}(\kappa) = \kappa$ and $G_*((x,y),\ \gamma) \neq G^*((x,y),\ \gamma)$ with $\gamma = 1$, then, from (28), we succeed in bringing about the upcoming inequality (see [68]):

$$\begin{aligned}
&G\left(\tfrac{\mathfrak{e}+\mathfrak{g}}{2}, \tfrac{\mathfrak{u}+\mathfrak{v}}{2}\right) \\
&\supseteq \tfrac{1}{2}\left[\tfrac{1}{\mathfrak{g}-\mathfrak{e}}\int_{\mathfrak{e}}^{\mathfrak{g}} G\left(x, \tfrac{\mathfrak{u}+\mathfrak{v}}{2}\right)dx + \tfrac{1}{\mathfrak{v}-\mathfrak{u}}\int_{\mathfrak{u}}^{\mathfrak{v}} G\left(\tfrac{\mathfrak{e}+\mathfrak{g}}{2}, y\right)dy\right] \subseteq \tfrac{1}{(\mathfrak{g}-\mathfrak{e})(\mathfrak{v}-\mathfrak{u})}\int_{\mathfrak{e}}^{\mathfrak{g}}\int_{\mathfrak{u}}^{\mathfrak{v}} G(x,y)dydx \\
&\supseteq \tfrac{1}{4(\mathfrak{g}-\mathfrak{e})}\left[\int_{\mathfrak{e}}^{\mathfrak{g}} G(x,\mathfrak{u})dx + \int_{\mathfrak{e}}^{\mathfrak{g}} G(x,\mathfrak{v})dx\right] + \tfrac{1}{4(\mathfrak{v}-\mathfrak{u})}\left[\int_{\mathfrak{u}}^{\mathfrak{v}} G(\mathfrak{e},y)dy + \int_{\mathfrak{u}}^{\mathfrak{v}} G(\mathfrak{g},y)dy\right] \\
&\supseteq \tfrac{G(\mathfrak{e},\mathfrak{u})+G(\mathfrak{g},\mathfrak{u})+G(\mathfrak{e},\mathfrak{v})+G(\mathfrak{g},\mathfrak{v})}{4}.
\end{aligned} \tag{57}$$

If $\widetilde{G}$ is a coordinated right-UD-$\mathcal{J}$-convex function with $\mathcal{J}(\tau) = \tau$, $\mathcal{J}(\kappa) = \kappa$ and $G_*((x,y),\ \gamma) = G^*((x,y),\ \gamma)$ with $\gamma = 1$, then, from (28), we succeed in bringing about the upcoming inequality (see [71]):

$$\begin{aligned}
&G\left(\tfrac{\mathfrak{e}+\mathfrak{g}}{2}, \tfrac{\mathfrak{u}+\mathfrak{v}}{2}\right) \\
&\leq \tfrac{\Gamma(\alpha+1)}{4(\mathfrak{g}-\mathfrak{e})^{\alpha}}\left[\mathcal{I}_{\mathfrak{e}^+}^{\alpha} G\left(\mathfrak{g}, \tfrac{\mathfrak{u}+\mathfrak{v}}{2}\right) + \mathcal{I}_{\mathfrak{g}^-}^{\alpha} G\left(\mathfrak{e}, \tfrac{\mathfrak{u}+\mathfrak{v}}{2}\right)\right] + \tfrac{\Gamma(\beta+1)}{4(\mathfrak{v}-\mathfrak{u})^{\beta}}\left[\mathcal{I}_{\mathfrak{u}^+}^{\beta} G\left(\tfrac{\mathfrak{e}+\mathfrak{g}}{2}, \mathfrak{v}\right) + \mathcal{I}_{\mathfrak{v}^-}^{\beta} G\left(\tfrac{\mathfrak{e}+\mathfrak{g}}{2}, \mathfrak{u}\right)\right] \\
&\leq \tfrac{\Gamma(\alpha+1)\Gamma(\beta+1)}{4(\mathfrak{g}-\mathfrak{e})^{\alpha}(\mathfrak{v}-\mathfrak{u})^{\beta}}\left[\mathcal{I}_{\mathfrak{e}^+,\mathfrak{u}^+}^{\alpha,\beta} G(\mathfrak{g},\mathfrak{v}) + \mathcal{I}_{\mathfrak{e}^+,\mathfrak{v}^-}^{\alpha,\beta} G(\mathfrak{g},\mathfrak{u}) + \mathcal{I}_{\mathfrak{g}^-,\mathfrak{u}^+}^{\alpha,\beta} G(\mathfrak{e},\mathfrak{v}) + \mathcal{I}_{\mathfrak{g}^-,\mathfrak{v}^-}^{\alpha,\beta} G(\mathfrak{e},\mathfrak{u})\right] \\
&\leq \tfrac{\Gamma(\alpha+1)}{8(\mathfrak{g}-\mathfrak{e})^{\alpha}}\left[\mathcal{I}_{\mathfrak{e}^+}^{\alpha} G(\mathfrak{g},\mathfrak{u}) G \mathcal{I}_{\mathfrak{e}^+}^{\alpha} G(\mathfrak{g},\mathfrak{v}) + \mathcal{I}_{\mathfrak{g}^-}^{\alpha} G(\mathfrak{e},\mathfrak{u}) + \mathcal{I}_{\mathfrak{g}^-}^{\alpha} G(\mathfrak{e},\mathfrak{v})\right]. \\
&+ \tfrac{\Gamma(\beta+1)}{8(\mathfrak{v}-\mathfrak{u})^{\beta}}\left[\mathcal{I}_{\mathfrak{u}^+}^{\beta} G(\mathfrak{e},\mathfrak{v}) \widetilde{+} \mathcal{I}_{\mathfrak{v}^-}^{\beta} G(\mathfrak{e},\mathfrak{u}) + \mathcal{I}_{\mathfrak{u}^+}^{\beta} G(\mathfrak{g},\mathfrak{v}) + \mathcal{I}_{\mathfrak{v}^-}^{\beta} G(\mathfrak{g},\mathfrak{u})\right] \\
&\leq \tfrac{G(\mathfrak{e},\mathfrak{u})+G(\mathfrak{g},\mathfrak{u})+G(\mathfrak{e},\mathfrak{v})+G(\mathfrak{g},\mathfrak{v})}{4}.
\end{aligned} \tag{58}$$

In the next section, we are going to find very interesting outcomes that will be obtained over a product of two coordinate UD-$\mathcal{J}$-convex FNVMs. These inequalities are known as Pachpatte inequalities.

Theorem 9. *Let $\widetilde{G}$, $\widetilde{\mathcal{J}} : \Delta \to \mathbb{F}_0^+$ be two coordinated UD-$\mathcal{J}$-convex FNVMs on Δ, and let $\mathcal{J}_1, \mathcal{J}_2 : [0,\ 1] \to \mathbb{R}^+$. Then, from γ-cuts, we set up the sequence of IVMs $G_\gamma, \mathcal{J}_\gamma : \Delta \to \mathbb{R}_I^+$, which is given* *by* $G_\gamma(x,y) = [G_*((x,y),\gamma),\ G^*((x,y),\gamma)]$ *and* $\mathcal{J}_\gamma(x,y) = [\mathcal{J}_*((x,y),\gamma),\ \mathcal{J}^*((x,y),\gamma)]$ *for all* $(x,y) \in \Delta$ *and for all* $\gamma \in [0,\ 1]$. *If* $\widetilde{G} \otimes \widetilde{\mathcal{J}} \in \mathcal{FD}_\Delta$, *then the following inequalities hold:*

$$\begin{aligned}
&\frac{\Gamma(\alpha)\Gamma(\beta)}{(\mathfrak{g}-\mathfrak{e})^\alpha(\mathfrak{v}-\mathfrak{u})^\beta}\left[\mathcal{I}^{\alpha,\ \beta}_{\mathfrak{e}^+,\mathfrak{u}^+}\widetilde{G}(\mathfrak{g},\mathfrak{v}) \otimes \widetilde{\mathcal{J}}(\mathfrak{g},\mathfrak{v}) \oplus \mathcal{I}^{\alpha,\ \beta}_{\mathfrak{e}^+,\mathfrak{v}^-}\widetilde{G}(\mathfrak{g},\mathfrak{u}) \otimes \widetilde{\mathcal{J}}(\mathfrak{g},\mathfrak{u})\right]\\
&\oplus\frac{\Gamma(\alpha)\Gamma(\beta)}{(\mathfrak{g}-\mathfrak{e})^\alpha(\mathfrak{v}-\mathfrak{u})^\beta}\left[\mathcal{I}^{\alpha,\ \beta}_{\mathfrak{g}^-,\mathfrak{u}^+}\widetilde{G}(\mathfrak{e},\mathfrak{v}) \otimes \widetilde{\mathcal{J}}(\mathfrak{e},\mathfrak{v}) \oplus \mathcal{I}^{\alpha,\ \beta}_{\mathfrak{g}^-,\mathfrak{v}^-}\widetilde{G}(\mathfrak{e},\mathfrak{u}) \otimes \widetilde{\mathcal{J}}(\mathfrak{e},\mathfrak{u})\right]\\
&\supseteq_{\mathbb{F}} \widetilde{\mathcal{M}}(\mathfrak{e},\mathfrak{g},\mathfrak{u},\mathfrak{v}) \int_0^1 \tau^{\alpha-1}\kappa^{\beta-1}[Ɉ_1(1-\tau)Ɉ_2(1-\tau)Ɉ_1(1-\kappa)Ɉ_2(1-\kappa) + Ɉ_1(1-\tau)\\
&Ɉ_2(1-\tau)Ɉ_1(\kappa)Ɉ_2(\kappa) + Ɉ_1(\tau)Ɉ_2(\tau)Ɉ_1(1-\kappa)Ɉ_2(1-\kappa)+\\
&Ɉ_1(\tau)Ɉ_2(\tau)Ɉ_1(\kappa)Ɉ_2(\kappa)]d\tau d\kappa\\
&\oplus\widetilde{P}(\mathfrak{e},\mathfrak{g},\mathfrak{u},\mathfrak{v}) \int_0^1 \tau^{\alpha-1}\kappa^{\beta-1}[Ɉ_1(\tau)Ɉ_2(1-\tau)Ɉ_1(1-\kappa)Ɉ_2(1-\kappa) + Ɉ_1(1-\tau)\\
&Ɉ_2(\tau)Ɉ_1(1-\kappa)Ɉ_2(1-\kappa) + Ɉ_1(\tau)Ɉ_2(1-\tau)Ɉ_1(\kappa)Ɉ_2(\kappa) + Ɉ_1(1-\tau)\\
&Ɉ_2(\tau)Ɉ_1(\kappa)Ɉ_2(\kappa)]d\tau d\kappa\\
&\oplus\widetilde{\mathcal{N}}(\mathfrak{e},\mathfrak{g},\mathfrak{u},\mathfrak{v}) \int_0^1 \tau^{\alpha-1}\kappa^{\beta-1}[Ɉ_1(1-\tau)Ɉ_2(1-\tau)Ɉ_1(\kappa)Ɉ_2(1-\kappa) + Ɉ_1(1-\tau)Ɉ_2(1-\tau)\\
&Ɉ_1(1-\kappa)Ɉ_2(\kappa) + Ɉ_1(\tau)Ɉ_2(\tau)Ɉ_1(1-\kappa)Ɉ_2(\kappa) + Ɉ_1(\tau)Ɉ_2(\tau)Ɉ_1(\kappa)Ɉ_2(1-\kappa)]d\tau d\kappa\\
&\oplus\widetilde{Q}(\mathfrak{e},\mathfrak{g},\mathfrak{u},\mathfrak{v}) \int_0^1 \tau^{\alpha-1\beta-1}[Ɉ_1(\tau)Ɉ_2(1-\tau)Ɉ_1(\kappa)Ɉ_2(1-\kappa) + Ɉ_1(\tau)Ɉ_2(1-\tau)Ɉ_1(1-\kappa)\\
&Ɉ_2(\kappa) + Ɉ_1(1-\tau)Ɉ_2(\tau)Ɉ_1(\kappa)Ɉ_2(1-\kappa) + Ɉ_1(\tau)Ɉ_2(1-\tau)Ɉ_1(\kappa)Ɉ_2(1-\kappa)]d\tau d\kappa.
\end{aligned} \tag{59}$$

If $\widetilde{G}$ *and* $\widetilde{\mathcal{J}}$ *are both coordinated UD-Ɉ-concave FNVMs on* Δ, *then the inequality above can be expressed as follows:*

$$\begin{aligned}
&\frac{\Gamma(\alpha)\Gamma(\beta)}{(\mathfrak{g}-\mathfrak{e})^\alpha(\mathfrak{v}-\mathfrak{u})^\beta}\left[\mathcal{I}^{\alpha,\ \beta}_{\mathfrak{e}^+,\mathfrak{u}^+}\widetilde{G}(\mathfrak{g},\mathfrak{v}) \otimes \widetilde{\mathcal{J}}(\mathfrak{g},\mathfrak{v}) \oplus \mathcal{I}^{\alpha,\ \beta}_{\mathfrak{e}^+,\mathfrak{v}^-}\widetilde{G}(\mathfrak{g},\mathfrak{u}) \otimes \widetilde{\mathcal{J}}(\mathfrak{g},\mathfrak{u})\right]\\
&\oplus\frac{\Gamma(\alpha)\Gamma(\beta)}{(\mathfrak{g}-\mathfrak{e})^\alpha(\mathfrak{v}-\mathfrak{u})^\beta}\left[\mathcal{I}^{\alpha,\ \beta}_{\mathfrak{g}^-,\mathfrak{u}^+}\widetilde{G}(\mathfrak{e},\mathfrak{v}) \otimes \widetilde{\mathcal{J}}(\mathfrak{e},\mathfrak{v}) \oplus \mathcal{I}^{\alpha,\ \beta}_{\mathfrak{g}^-,\mathfrak{v}^-}\widetilde{G}(\mathfrak{e},\mathfrak{u}) \otimes \widetilde{\mathcal{J}}(\mathfrak{e},\mathfrak{u})\right]\\
&\subseteq_{\mathbb{F}} \widetilde{\mathcal{M}}(\mathfrak{e},\mathfrak{g},\mathfrak{u},\mathfrak{v}) \int_0^1 \tau^{\alpha-1}\kappa^{\beta-1}[Ɉ_1(1-\tau)Ɉ_2(1-\tau)Ɉ_1(1-\kappa)Ɉ_2(1-\kappa) + Ɉ_1(1-\tau)\\
&Ɉ_2(1-\tau)Ɉ_1(\kappa)Ɉ_2(\kappa) + Ɉ_1(\tau)Ɉ_2(\tau)Ɉ_1(1-\kappa)Ɉ_2(1-\kappa)+\\
&Ɉ_1(\tau)Ɉ_2(\tau)Ɉ_1(\kappa)Ɉ_2(\kappa)]d\tau d\kappa\\
&\oplus\widetilde{P}(\mathfrak{e},\mathfrak{g},\mathfrak{u},\mathfrak{v}) \int_0^1 \tau^{\alpha-1}\kappa^{\beta-1}[Ɉ_1(\tau)Ɉ_2(1-\tau)Ɉ_1(1-\kappa)Ɉ_2(1-\kappa)+\\
&Ɉ_1(1-\tau)Ɉ_2(\tau)Ɉ_1(1-\kappa)Ɉ_2(1-\kappa) + Ɉ_1(\tau)Ɉ_2(1-\tau)Ɉ_1(\kappa)Ɉ_2(\kappa) + Ɉ_1(1-\tau)\\
&Ɉ_2(\tau)Ɉ_1(\kappa)Ɉ_2(\kappa)]d\tau d\kappa\\
&\oplus\widetilde{\mathcal{N}}(\mathfrak{e},\mathfrak{g},\mathfrak{u},\mathfrak{v}) \int_0^1 \tau^{\alpha-1}\kappa^{\beta-1}[Ɉ_1(1-\tau)Ɉ_2(1-\tau)Ɉ_1(\kappa)Ɉ_2(1-\kappa) + Ɉ_1(1-\tau)Ɉ_2(1-\tau)\\
&Ɉ_1(1-\kappa)Ɉ_2(\kappa) + Ɉ_1(\tau)Ɉ_2(\tau)Ɉ_1(1-\kappa)Ɉ_2(\kappa) + Ɉ_1(\tau)Ɉ_2(\tau)Ɉ_1(\kappa)Ɉ_2(1-\kappa)]d\tau d\kappa\\
&\oplus\widetilde{Q}(\mathfrak{e},\mathfrak{g},\mathfrak{u},\mathfrak{v}) \int_0^1 \tau^{\alpha-1}\kappa^{\beta-1}[Ɉ_1(\tau)Ɉ_2(1-\tau)Ɉ_1(\kappa)Ɉ_2(1-\kappa) + Ɉ_1(\tau)Ɉ_2(1-\tau)Ɉ_1(1-\kappa)\\
&Ɉ_2(\kappa) + Ɉ_1(1-\tau)Ɉ_2(\tau)Ɉ_1(\kappa)Ɉ_2(1-\kappa) + Ɉ_1(\tau)Ɉ_2(1-\tau)Ɉ_1(\kappa)Ɉ_2(1-\kappa)]d\tau d\kappa
\end{aligned} \tag{60}$$

where

$$\widetilde{\mathcal{M}}(\mathfrak{e},\mathfrak{g},\mathfrak{u},\mathfrak{v}) = \widetilde{G}(\mathfrak{e},\mathfrak{u}) \otimes \widetilde{\mathcal{J}}(\mathfrak{e},\mathfrak{u}) \oplus \widetilde{G}(\mathfrak{g},\mathfrak{u}) \otimes \widetilde{\mathcal{J}}(\mathfrak{g},\mathfrak{u}) \oplus \widetilde{G}(\mathfrak{e},\mathfrak{v}) \otimes \widetilde{\mathcal{J}}(\mathfrak{e},\mathfrak{v}) \oplus \widetilde{G}(\mathfrak{g},\mathfrak{v}) \otimes \widetilde{\mathcal{J}}(\mathfrak{g},\mathfrak{v}),$$

$$\widetilde{P}(\mathfrak{e},\mathfrak{g},\mathfrak{u},\mathfrak{v}) = \widetilde{G}(\mathfrak{e},\mathfrak{u}) \otimes \widetilde{\mathcal{J}}(\mathfrak{g},\mathfrak{u}) \oplus \widetilde{G}(\mathfrak{g},\mathfrak{u}) \otimes \widetilde{\mathcal{J}}(\mathfrak{e},\mathfrak{u}) \oplus \widetilde{G}(\mathfrak{e},\mathfrak{v}) \otimes \widetilde{\mathcal{J}}(\mathfrak{g},\mathfrak{v}) \oplus \widetilde{G}(\mathfrak{g},\mathfrak{v}) \otimes \widetilde{\mathcal{J}}(\mathfrak{e},\mathfrak{v}),$$

$$\widetilde{\mathcal{N}}(\mathfrak{e},\mathfrak{g},\mathfrak{u},\mathfrak{v}) = \widetilde{G}(\mathfrak{e},\mathfrak{u}) \otimes \widetilde{\mathcal{J}}(\mathfrak{e},\mathfrak{v}) \oplus \widetilde{G}(\mathfrak{g},\mathfrak{u}) \otimes \widetilde{\mathcal{J}}(\mathfrak{g},\mathfrak{v}) \oplus \widetilde{G}(\mathfrak{e},\mathfrak{v}) \otimes \widetilde{\mathcal{J}}(\mathfrak{e},\mathfrak{u}) \oplus \widetilde{G}(\mathfrak{g},\mathfrak{v}) \otimes \widetilde{\mathcal{J}}(\mathfrak{g},\mathfrak{u}),$$

$$\widetilde{Q}(\mathfrak{e},\mathfrak{g},\mathfrak{u},\mathfrak{v}) = \widetilde{G}(\mathfrak{e},\mathfrak{u}) \otimes \widetilde{\mathcal{J}}(\mathfrak{g},\mathfrak{v}) \oplus \widetilde{G}(\mathfrak{g},\mathfrak{u}) \otimes \widetilde{\mathcal{J}}(\mathfrak{e},\mathfrak{v}) \oplus \widetilde{G}(\mathfrak{e},\mathfrak{v}) \otimes \widetilde{\mathcal{J}}(\mathfrak{g},\mathfrak{u}) \oplus \widetilde{G}(\mathfrak{g},\mathfrak{v}) \otimes \widetilde{\mathcal{J}}(\mathfrak{e},\mathfrak{u}),$$

and for each $\gamma \in [0,1]$, $\widetilde{\mathcal{M}}(\mathfrak{e},\mathfrak{g},\mathfrak{u},\mathfrak{v})$, $\widetilde{P}(\mathfrak{e},\mathfrak{g},\mathfrak{u},\mathfrak{v})$, $\widetilde{\mathcal{N}}(\mathfrak{e},\mathfrak{g},\mathfrak{u},\mathfrak{v})$, and $\widetilde{Q}(\mathfrak{e},\mathfrak{g},\mathfrak{u},\mathfrak{v})$ are defined as follows:

$$\mathcal{M}_\gamma(\mathfrak{e},\mathfrak{g},\mathfrak{u},\mathfrak{v}) = [\mathcal{M}_*((\mathfrak{e},\mathfrak{g},\mathfrak{u},\mathfrak{v}), \gamma), \mathcal{M}^*((\mathfrak{e},\mathfrak{g},\mathfrak{u},\mathfrak{v}), \gamma)],$$

$$P_\gamma(\mathfrak{e},\mathfrak{g},\mathfrak{u},\mathfrak{v}) = [P_*((\mathfrak{e},\mathfrak{g},\mathfrak{u},\mathfrak{v}), \gamma), P^*((\mathfrak{e},\mathfrak{g},\mathfrak{u},\mathfrak{v}), \gamma)],$$

$$\mathcal{N}_\gamma(\mathfrak{e},\mathfrak{g},\mathfrak{u},\mathfrak{v}) = [\mathcal{N}_*((\mathfrak{e},\mathfrak{g},\mathfrak{u},\mathfrak{v}), \gamma), \mathcal{N}^*((\mathfrak{e},\mathfrak{g},\mathfrak{u},\mathfrak{v}), \gamma)],$$

$$Q_\gamma(\mathfrak{e},\mathfrak{g},\mathfrak{u},\mathfrak{v}) = [Q_*((\mathfrak{e},\mathfrak{g},\mathfrak{u},\mathfrak{v}), \gamma), Q^*((\mathfrak{e},\mathfrak{g},\mathfrak{u},\mathfrak{v}), \gamma)].$$

Proof. Let $\widetilde{G}$ and $\widetilde{\mathcal{J}}$ be two coordinated *UD*-JJ_1 and JJ_2-convex *FNVM*s on $[\mathfrak{e},\mathfrak{g}] \times [\mathfrak{u},\mathfrak{v}]$, respectively. Then,

$$\widetilde{G}(\tau\mathfrak{e} + (1-\tau)\mathfrak{g}, \kappa\mathfrak{u} + (1-\kappa)\mathfrak{v})$$
$$\supseteq_\mathbb{F} JJ_1(\tau)JJ_1(\kappa)\widetilde{G}(\mathfrak{e},\mathfrak{u}) \oplus JJ_1(\tau)JJ_1(1-\kappa)\widetilde{G}(\mathfrak{e},\mathfrak{v}) \oplus JJ_1(1-\tau)JJ_1(\kappa)\widetilde{G}(\mathfrak{g},\mathfrak{u}) \oplus JJ_1(1-\tau)JJ_1(1-\kappa)\widetilde{G}(\mathfrak{g},\mathfrak{v}),$$

$$\widetilde{G}(\tau\mathfrak{e} + (1-\tau)\mathfrak{g}, (1-\kappa)\mathfrak{u} + \kappa\mathfrak{v})$$
$$\supseteq_\mathbb{F} JJ_1(\tau)JJ_1(1-\kappa)\widetilde{G}(\mathfrak{e},\mathfrak{u}) \oplus JJ_1(\tau)JJ_1(\kappa)\widetilde{G}(\mathfrak{e},\mathfrak{v}) \oplus JJ_1(1-\tau)JJ_1(1-\kappa)\widetilde{G}(\mathfrak{g},\mathfrak{u}) \oplus JJ_1(1-\tau)JJ_1(\kappa)\widetilde{G}(\mathfrak{g},\mathfrak{v}),$$

$$\widetilde{G}((1-\tau)\mathfrak{e} + \tau\mathfrak{g}, \kappa\mathfrak{u} + (1-\kappa)\mathfrak{v})$$
$$\supseteq_\mathbb{F} JJ_1(1-\tau)JJ_1(\kappa)\widetilde{G}(\mathfrak{e},\mathfrak{u}) \oplus JJ_1(1-\tau)JJ_1(1-\kappa)\widetilde{G}(\mathfrak{e},\mathfrak{v}) \oplus JJ_1(\tau)JJ_1(\kappa)\widetilde{G}(\mathfrak{g},\mathfrak{u}) \oplus JJ_1(\tau)JJ_1(1-\kappa)\widetilde{G}(\mathfrak{g},\mathfrak{v}),$$

$$\widetilde{G}((1-\tau)\mathfrak{e} + \tau\mathfrak{g}, (1-\kappa)\mathfrak{u} + \kappa\mathfrak{v})$$
$$\supseteq_\mathbb{F} JJ_1(1-\tau)JJ_1(1-\kappa)\widetilde{G}(\mathfrak{e},\mathfrak{u}) \oplus JJ_1(1-\tau)JJ_1(\kappa)\widetilde{G}(\mathfrak{e},\mathfrak{v}) \oplus JJ_1(\tau)JJ_1(1-\kappa)\widetilde{G}(\mathfrak{g},\mathfrak{u}) \oplus JJ_1(\tau)JJ_1(\kappa)\widetilde{G}(\mathfrak{g},\mathfrak{v}),$$

and

$$\widetilde{\mathcal{J}}(\tau\mathfrak{e}+(1-\tau)\mathfrak{g},\kappa\mathfrak{u}+(1-\kappa)\mathfrak{v})$$
$$\supseteq_{\mathbb{F}} J_2(\tau)J_2(\kappa)\widetilde{\mathcal{J}}(\mathfrak{e},\mathfrak{u})\oplus J_2(\tau)J_2(1-\kappa)\widetilde{\mathcal{J}}(\mathfrak{e},\mathfrak{v})\oplus J_2(1-\tau)J_2(\kappa)\widetilde{\mathcal{J}}(\mathfrak{g},\mathfrak{u})\oplus J_2(1-\tau)$$
$$J_2(1-\kappa)\widetilde{\mathcal{J}}(\mathfrak{g},\mathfrak{v}),$$
$$\widetilde{\mathcal{J}}(\tau\mathfrak{e}+(1-\tau)\mathfrak{g},(1-\kappa)\mathfrak{u}+\kappa\mathfrak{v})$$
$$\supseteq_{\mathbb{F}} J_2(\tau)J_2(1-\kappa)\widetilde{\mathcal{J}}(\mathfrak{e},\mathfrak{u})\oplus J_2(\tau)J_2(\kappa)\widetilde{\mathcal{J}}(\mathfrak{e},\mathfrak{v})\oplus J_2(1-\tau)J_2(1-\kappa)\widetilde{\mathcal{J}}(\mathfrak{g},\mathfrak{u})\oplus$$
$$J_2(1-\tau)J_2(\kappa)\widetilde{\mathcal{J}}(\mathfrak{g},\mathfrak{v}),$$

$$\widetilde{\mathcal{J}}((1-\tau)\mathfrak{e}+\tau\mathfrak{g},\kappa\mathfrak{u}+(1-\kappa)\mathfrak{v})$$
$$\supseteq_{\mathbb{F}} J_2(1-\tau)J_2(\kappa)\widetilde{\mathcal{J}}(\mathfrak{e},\mathfrak{u})\oplus J_2(1-\tau)J_2(1-\kappa)\widetilde{\mathcal{J}}(\mathfrak{e},\mathfrak{v})\oplus J_2(\tau)J_2(\kappa)\widetilde{\mathcal{J}}(\mathfrak{g},\mathfrak{u})\oplus$$
$$J_2(\tau)J_2(1-\kappa)\widetilde{\mathcal{J}}(\mathfrak{g},\mathfrak{v}),$$
$$\widetilde{\mathcal{J}}((1-\tau)\mathfrak{e}+\tau\mathfrak{g},(1-\kappa)\mathfrak{u}+\kappa\mathfrak{v})$$
$$\supseteq_{\mathbb{F}} J_2(1-\tau)J_2(1-\kappa)\widetilde{\mathcal{J}}(\mathfrak{e},\mathfrak{u})\oplus J_2(1-\tau)J_2(\kappa)\widetilde{\mathcal{J}}(\mathfrak{e},\mathfrak{v})\oplus J_2(\tau)J_2(1-\kappa)\widetilde{\mathcal{J}}(\mathfrak{g},\mathfrak{u})\oplus$$
$$J_2(\tau)J_2(\kappa)\widetilde{\mathcal{J}}(\mathfrak{g},\mathfrak{v}),$$

Since $\widetilde{G}$ and $\widetilde{\mathcal{J}}$ are both coordinated *UD*-J_1- and J_2-convex *FNVM*s on $[\mathfrak{e},\mathfrak{g}]\times[\mathfrak{u},\mathfrak{v}]$, respectively, then, for any $\gamma\in[0,\ 1]$, we have

$$G_\gamma(\tau\mathfrak{e}+(1-\tau)\mathfrak{g},\kappa\mathfrak{u}+(1-\kappa)\mathfrak{v})\times\mathcal{J}_\gamma(\tau\mathfrak{e}+(1-\tau)\mathfrak{g},\kappa\mathfrak{u}+(1-\kappa)\mathfrak{v})$$
$$+G_\gamma(\tau\mathfrak{e}+(1-\tau)\mathfrak{g},(1-\kappa)\mathfrak{u}+\kappa\mathfrak{v})\times\mathcal{J}_\gamma(\tau\mathfrak{e}+(1-\tau)\mathfrak{g},(1-\kappa)\mathfrak{u}+\kappa\mathfrak{v})$$
$$+G_\gamma((1-\tau)\mathfrak{e}+\tau\mathfrak{g},\kappa\mathfrak{u}+(1-\kappa)\mathfrak{v})\times\mathcal{J}_\gamma((1-\tau)\mathfrak{e}+\tau\mathfrak{g},\kappa\mathfrak{u}+(1-\kappa)\mathfrak{v})$$
$$+G_\gamma((1-\tau)\mathfrak{e}+\tau\mathfrak{g},(1-\kappa)\mathfrak{u}+\kappa\mathfrak{v})\times\mathcal{J}_\gamma((1-\tau)\mathfrak{e}+\tau\mathfrak{g},(1-\kappa)\mathfrak{u}+\kappa\mathfrak{v})$$
$$\supseteq_I \mathcal{M}_\gamma(\mathfrak{e},\mathfrak{g},\mathfrak{u},\mathfrak{v})[J_1(1-\tau)J_2(1-\tau)J_1(1-\kappa)J_2(1-\kappa)+J_1(1-\tau)J_2(1-\tau)$$
$$J_1(\kappa)J_2(\kappa)+J_1(\tau)J_2(\tau)J_1(1-\kappa)J_2(1-\kappa)+J_1(\tau)J_2(\tau)J_1(\kappa)J_2(\kappa)]$$
$$+P_\gamma(\mathfrak{e},\mathfrak{g},\mathfrak{u},\mathfrak{v})[J_1(\tau)J_2(1-\tau)J_1(1-\kappa)J_2(1-\kappa)+J_1(1-\tau)J_2(\tau)J_1(1-\kappa)J_2(1-\kappa)$$
$$+J_1(\tau)J_2(1-\tau)J_1(\kappa)J_2(\kappa)+J_1(1-\tau)J_2(\tau)J_1(\kappa)J_2(\kappa)]$$
$$+\mathcal{N}_\gamma(\mathfrak{e},\mathfrak{g},\mathfrak{u},\mathfrak{v})[J_1(1-\tau)J_2(1-\tau)J_1(\kappa)J_2(1-\kappa)+J_1(1-\tau)J_2(1-\tau)J_1(1-\kappa)$$
$$J_2(\kappa)+J_1(\tau)J_2(\tau)J_1(1-\kappa)J_2(\kappa)+J_1(\tau)J_2(\tau)J_1(\kappa)J_2(1-\kappa)]$$
$$+\mathcal{Q}_\gamma(\mathfrak{e},\mathfrak{g},\mathfrak{u},\mathfrak{v})[J_1(\tau)J_2(1-\tau)J_1(\kappa)J_2(1-\kappa)+J_1(\tau)J_2(1-\tau)J_1(1-\kappa)J_2(\kappa)+$$
$$J_1(1-\tau)J_2(\tau)J_1(\kappa)J_2(1-\kappa)+J_1(\tau)J_2(1-\tau)J_1(\kappa)J_2(1-\kappa)].$$

Taking the multiplication of the above fuzzy inclusion with $\tau^{\alpha-1}\kappa^{\beta-1}$ and then taking the double integration of the result over $[0,\ 1]\times[0,\ 1]$ with respect to $(\tau,\ \kappa)$ gives

$$
\begin{aligned}
&\int_0^1\int_0^1 \tau^{\alpha-1}\kappa^{\beta-1} G_\gamma(\tau\mathfrak{e}+(1-\tau)\mathfrak{g}, \kappa\mathfrak{u}+(1-\kappa)\mathfrak{v}) \times \mathcal{J}_\gamma(\tau\mathfrak{e}+(1-\tau)\mathfrak{g}, \kappa\mathfrak{u}+(1-\kappa)\mathfrak{v}) d\tau d\kappa \\
&+\int_0^1\int_0^1 \tau^{\alpha-1}\kappa^{\beta-1} G_\gamma(\tau\mathfrak{e}+(1-\tau)\mathfrak{g}, (1-\kappa)\mathfrak{u}+\kappa\mathfrak{v}) \times \mathcal{J}_\gamma(\tau\mathfrak{e}+(1-\tau)\mathfrak{g}, (1-\kappa)\mathfrak{u}+\kappa\mathfrak{v}) d\tau d\kappa \\
&+\int_0^1\int_0^1 \tau^{\alpha-1}\kappa^{\beta-1} G_\gamma((1-\tau)\mathfrak{e}+\tau\mathfrak{g}, \kappa\mathfrak{u}+(1-\kappa)\mathfrak{v}) \times \mathcal{J}_\gamma((1-\tau)\mathfrak{e}+\tau\mathfrak{g}, \kappa\mathfrak{u}+(1-\kappa)\mathfrak{v}) d\tau d\kappa \\
&+\int_0^1\int_0^1 \tau^{\alpha-1}\kappa^{\beta-1} G_\gamma((1-\tau)\mathfrak{e}+\tau\mathfrak{g}, (1-\kappa)\mathfrak{u}+\kappa\mathfrak{v}) \times \mathcal{J}_\gamma((1-\tau)\mathfrak{e}+\tau\mathfrak{g}, (1-\kappa)\mathfrak{u}+\kappa\mathfrak{v}) d\tau d\kappa \\
&\supseteq_I \mathcal{M}_\gamma(\mathfrak{e},\mathfrak{g},\mathfrak{u},\mathfrak{v}) \quad \int_0^1\int_0^1 \tau^{\alpha-1}\kappa^{\beta-1}[\text{Л}_1(1-\tau)\text{Л}_2(1-\tau)\text{Л}_1(1-\kappa)\text{Л}_2(1-\kappa) \\
&\qquad +\text{Л}_1(1-\tau)\text{Л}_2(1-\tau)\text{Л}_1(\kappa)\text{Л}_2(\kappa) + \text{Л}_1(\tau)\text{Л}_2(\tau)\text{Л}_1(1-\kappa)\text{Л}_2(1-\kappa) \\
&\qquad +\text{Л}_1(\tau)\text{Л}_2(\tau)\text{Л}_1(\kappa)\text{Л}_2(\kappa)] d\tau d\kappa \\
&+P_\gamma(\mathfrak{e},\mathfrak{g},\mathfrak{u},\mathfrak{v}) \quad \int_0^1\int_0^1 \tau^{\alpha-1}\kappa^{\beta-1}[\text{Л}_1(\tau)\text{Л}_2(1-\tau)\text{Л}_1(1-\kappa)\text{Л}_2(1-\kappa) \\
&\qquad +\text{Л}_1(1-\tau)\text{Л}_2(\tau)\text{Л}_1(1-\kappa)\text{Л}_2(1-\kappa) + \text{Л}_1(\tau)\text{Л}_2(1-\tau)\text{Л}_1(\kappa)\text{Л}_2(\kappa) \\
&\qquad +\text{Л}_1(1-\tau)\text{Л}_2(\tau)\text{Л}_1(\kappa)\text{Л}_2(\kappa)] d\tau d\kappa \\
&+\mathcal{N}_\gamma(\mathfrak{e},\mathfrak{g},\mathfrak{u},\mathfrak{v}) \quad \int_0^1\int_0^1 \tau^{\alpha-1}\kappa^{\beta-1}[\text{Л}_1(1-\tau)\text{Л}_2(1-\tau)\text{Л}_1(\kappa)\text{Л}_2(1-\kappa) \\
&\qquad +\text{Л}_1(1-\tau)\text{Л}_2(1-\tau)\text{Л}_1(1-\kappa)\text{Л}_2(\kappa) + \text{Л}_1(\tau)\text{Л}_2(\tau)\text{Л}_1(1-\kappa)\text{Л}_2(\kappa) \\
&\qquad +\text{Л}_1(\tau)\text{Л}_2(\tau)\text{Л}_1(\kappa)\text{Л}_2(1-\kappa)] d\tau d\kappa \\
&+Q_\gamma(\mathfrak{e},\mathfrak{g},\mathfrak{u},\mathfrak{v}) \quad \int_0^1\int_0^1 \tau^{\alpha-1}\kappa^{\beta-1}[\text{Л}_1(\tau)\text{Л}_2(1-\tau)\text{Л}_1(\kappa)\text{Л}_2(1-\kappa) \\
&\qquad +\text{Л}_1(\tau)\text{Л}_2(1-\tau)\text{Л}_1(1-\kappa)\text{Л}_2(\kappa) + \text{Л}_1(1-\tau)\text{Л}_2(\tau)\text{Л}_1(\kappa)\text{Л}_2(1-\kappa) \\
&\qquad +\text{Л}_1(\tau)\text{Л}_2(1-\tau)\text{Л}_1(\kappa)\text{Л}_2(1-\kappa)] d\tau d\kappa
\end{aligned} \tag{61}
$$

From the right-hand side of (61), we have

$$
\begin{aligned}
&\int_0^1\int_0^1 \tau^{\alpha-1}\kappa^{\beta-1} G_\gamma(\tau\mathfrak{e}+(1-\tau)\mathfrak{g}, \kappa\mathfrak{u}+(1-\kappa)\mathfrak{v}) \times \mathcal{J}_\gamma(\tau\mathfrak{e}+(1-\tau)\mathfrak{g}, \kappa\mathfrak{u}+(1-\kappa)\mathfrak{v}) d\tau d\kappa \\
&+\int_0^1\int_0^1 \tau^{\alpha-1}\kappa^{\beta-1} G_\gamma(\tau\mathfrak{e}+(1-\tau)\mathfrak{g}, (1-\kappa)\mathfrak{u}+\kappa\mathfrak{v}) \times \mathcal{J}_\gamma(\tau\mathfrak{e}+(1-\tau)\mathfrak{g}, (1-\kappa)\mathfrak{u}+\kappa\mathfrak{v}) d\tau d\kappa \\
&+\int_0^1\int_0^1 \tau^{\alpha-1}\kappa^{\beta-1} G_\gamma((1-\tau)\mathfrak{e}+\tau\mathfrak{g}, \kappa\mathfrak{u}+(1-\kappa)\mathfrak{v}) \times \mathcal{J}_\gamma((1-\tau)\mathfrak{e}+\tau\mathfrak{g}, \kappa\mathfrak{u}+(1-\kappa)\mathfrak{v}) d\tau d\kappa \\
&+\int_0^1\int_0^1 \tau^{\alpha-1}\kappa^{\beta-1} G_\gamma((1-\tau)\mathfrak{e}+\tau\mathfrak{g}, (1-\kappa)\mathfrak{u}+\kappa\mathfrak{v}) \times \mathcal{J}_\gamma((1-\tau)\mathfrak{e}+\tau\mathfrak{g}, (1-\kappa)\mathfrak{u}+\kappa\mathfrak{v}) d\tau d\kappa \\
&= \frac{\Gamma(\alpha)\Gamma(\beta)}{(\mathfrak{g}-\mathfrak{e})^\alpha(\mathfrak{v}-\mathfrak{u})^\beta}\left[\mathcal{I}^{\alpha,\,\beta}_{\mathfrak{e}^+,\mathfrak{u}^+} G_\gamma(\mathfrak{g},\mathfrak{v}) \times \mathcal{J}_\gamma(\mathfrak{g},\mathfrak{v}) + \mathcal{I}^{\alpha,\,\beta}_{\mathfrak{e}^+,\mathfrak{v}^-} G_\gamma(\mathfrak{g},\mathfrak{u}) \times \mathcal{J}_\gamma(\mathfrak{g},\mathfrak{u})\right]
\end{aligned} \tag{62}
$$

Combining (61) and (62), for each $\gamma \in [0,\ 1]$, we have

$$\frac{\Gamma(\alpha)\Gamma(\beta)}{(\mathfrak{g}-\mathfrak{e})^{\alpha}(\mathfrak{v}-\mathfrak{u})^{\beta}}\left[\mathcal{I}^{\alpha,\beta}_{\mathfrak{e}^{+},\mathfrak{u}^{+}}G_{\gamma}(\mathfrak{g},\mathfrak{v})\times\mathcal{J}_{\gamma}(\mathfrak{g},\mathfrak{v})+\mathcal{I}^{\alpha,\beta}_{\mathfrak{e}^{+},\mathfrak{v}^{-}}G_{\gamma}(\mathfrak{g},\mathfrak{u})\times\mathcal{J}_{\gamma}(\mathfrak{g},\mathfrak{u})\right]$$
$$\begin{aligned}\supseteq_{I} \mathcal{M}_{\gamma}(\mathfrak{e},\mathfrak{g},\mathfrak{u},\mathfrak{v}) \quad & \int_0^1\int_0^1 \tau^{\alpha-1}\kappa^{\beta-1}[\mathcal{J}_1(1-\tau)\mathcal{J}_2(1-\tau)\mathcal{J}_1(1-\kappa)\mathcal{J}_2(1-\kappa)\\ & +\mathcal{J}_1(1-\tau)\mathcal{J}_2(1-\tau)\mathcal{J}_1(\kappa)\mathcal{J}_2(\kappa)+\mathcal{J}_1(\tau)\mathcal{J}_2(\tau)\mathcal{J}_1(1-\kappa)\mathcal{J}_2(1-\kappa)\\ & +\mathcal{J}_1(\tau)\mathcal{J}_2(\tau)\mathcal{J}_1(\kappa)\mathcal{J}_2(\kappa)]d\tau d\kappa\\ +P_{\gamma}(\mathfrak{e},\mathfrak{g},\mathfrak{u},\mathfrak{v}) \quad & \int_0^1\int_0^1 \tau^{\alpha-1}\kappa^{\beta-1}[\mathcal{J}_1(\tau)\mathcal{J}_2(1-\tau)\mathcal{J}_1(1-\kappa)\mathcal{J}_2(1-\kappa)\\ & +\mathcal{J}_1(1-\tau)\mathcal{J}_2(\tau)\mathcal{J}_1(1-\kappa)\mathcal{J}_2(1-\kappa)+\mathcal{J}_1(\tau)\mathcal{J}_2(1-\tau)\mathcal{J}_1(\kappa)\mathcal{J}_2(\kappa)\\ & +\mathcal{J}_1(1-\tau)\mathcal{J}_2(\tau)\mathcal{J}_1(\kappa)\mathcal{J}_2(\kappa)]d\tau d\kappa\\ +\mathcal{N}_{\gamma}(\mathfrak{e},\mathfrak{g},\mathfrak{u},\mathfrak{v}) \quad & \int_0^1\int_0^1 \tau^{\alpha-1}\kappa^{\beta-1}[\mathcal{J}_1(1-\tau)\mathcal{J}_2(1-\tau)\mathcal{J}_1(\kappa)\mathcal{J}_2(1-\kappa)\\ & +\mathcal{J}_1(1-\tau)\mathcal{J}_2(1-\tau)\mathcal{J}_1(1-\kappa)\mathcal{J}_2(\kappa)+\mathcal{J}_1(\tau)\mathcal{J}_2(\tau)\mathcal{J}_1(1-\kappa)\mathcal{J}_2(\kappa)\\ & +\mathcal{J}_1(\tau)\mathcal{J}_2(\tau)\mathcal{J}_1(\kappa)\mathcal{J}_2(1-\kappa)]d\tau d\kappa\\ +Q_{\gamma}(\mathfrak{e},\mathfrak{g},\mathfrak{u},\mathfrak{v}) \quad & \int_0^1\int_0^1 \tau^{\alpha-1}\kappa^{\beta-1}[\mathcal{J}_1(\tau)\mathcal{J}_2(1-\tau)\mathcal{J}_1(\kappa)\mathcal{J}_2(1-\kappa)\\ & +\mathcal{J}_1(\tau)\mathcal{J}_2(1-\tau)\mathcal{J}_1(1-\kappa)\mathcal{J}_2(\kappa)+\mathcal{J}_1(1-\tau)\mathcal{J}_2(\tau)\mathcal{J}_1(\kappa)\mathcal{J}_2(1-\kappa)\\ & +\mathcal{J}_1(\tau)\mathcal{J}_2(1-\tau)\mathcal{J}_1(\kappa)\mathcal{J}_2(1-\kappa)]d\tau d\kappa.\end{aligned}$$

Moreover, we have

$$\frac{\Gamma(\alpha)\Gamma(\beta)}{(\mathfrak{g}-\mathfrak{e})^{\alpha}(\mathfrak{v}-\mathfrak{u})^{\beta}}\left[\mathcal{I}^{\alpha,\beta}_{\mathfrak{e}^{+},\mathfrak{u}^{+}}\widetilde{G}(\mathfrak{g},\mathfrak{v})\otimes\widetilde{\mathcal{J}}(\mathfrak{g},\mathfrak{v})\oplus\mathcal{I}^{\alpha,\beta}_{\mathfrak{e}^{+},\mathfrak{v}^{-}}\widetilde{G}(\mathfrak{g},\mathfrak{u})\otimes\widetilde{\mathcal{J}}(\mathfrak{g},\mathfrak{u})\right]$$
$$\oplus\frac{\Gamma(\alpha)\Gamma(\beta)}{(\mathfrak{g}-\mathfrak{e})^{\alpha}(\mathfrak{v}-\mathfrak{u})^{\beta}}\left[\mathcal{I}^{\alpha,\beta}_{\mathfrak{g}^{-},\mathfrak{u}^{+}}\widetilde{G}(\mathfrak{e},\mathfrak{v})\otimes\widetilde{\mathcal{J}}(\mathfrak{e},\mathfrak{v})\oplus\mathcal{I}^{\alpha,\beta}_{\mathfrak{g}^{-},\mathfrak{v}^{-}}\widetilde{G}(\mathfrak{e},\mathfrak{u})\otimes\widetilde{\mathcal{J}}(\mathfrak{e},\mathfrak{u})\right]$$
$$\begin{aligned}&\supseteq_{\mathbb{F}} \widetilde{\mathcal{M}}(\mathfrak{e},\mathfrak{g},\mathfrak{u},\mathfrak{v})\int_0^1 \tau^{\alpha-1}\kappa^{\beta-1}[\mathcal{J}_1(1-\tau)\mathcal{J}_2(1-\tau)\mathcal{J}_1(1-\kappa)\mathcal{J}_2(1-\kappa)+\mathcal{J}_1(1-\tau)\\ &\mathcal{J}_2(1-\tau)\mathcal{J}_1(\kappa)\mathcal{J}_2(\kappa)+\mathcal{J}_1(\tau)\mathcal{J}_2(\tau)\mathcal{J}_1(1-\kappa)\mathcal{J}_2(1-\kappa)+\\ &\mathcal{J}_1(\tau)\mathcal{J}_2(\tau)\mathcal{J}_1(\kappa)\mathcal{J}_2(\kappa)]d\tau d\kappa\\ &\oplus\widetilde{P}(\mathfrak{e},\mathfrak{g},\mathfrak{u},\mathfrak{v})\int_0^1 \tau^{\alpha-1}\kappa^{\beta-1}[\mathcal{J}_1(\tau)\mathcal{J}_2(1-\tau)\mathcal{J}_1(1-\kappa)\mathcal{J}_2(1-\kappa)+\mathcal{J}_1(1-\tau)\\ &\mathcal{J}_2(\tau)\mathcal{J}_1(1-\kappa)\mathcal{J}_2(1-\kappa)+\mathcal{J}_1(\tau)\mathcal{J}_2(1-\tau)\mathcal{J}_1(\kappa)\mathcal{J}_2(\kappa)+\mathcal{J}_1(1-\tau)\\ &\mathcal{J}_2(\tau)\mathcal{J}_1(\kappa)\mathcal{J}_2(\kappa)]d\tau d\kappa\\ &\oplus\widetilde{\mathcal{N}}(\mathfrak{e},\mathfrak{g},\mathfrak{u},\mathfrak{v})\int_0^1 \tau^{\alpha-1}\kappa^{\beta-1}[\mathcal{J}_1(1-\tau)\mathcal{J}_2(1-\tau)\mathcal{J}_1(\kappa)\mathcal{J}_2(1-\kappa)+\mathcal{J}_1(1-\tau)\mathcal{J}_2(1-\tau)\\ &\mathcal{J}_1(1-\kappa)\mathcal{J}_2(\kappa)+\mathcal{J}_1(\tau)\mathcal{J}_2(\tau)\mathcal{J}_1(1-\kappa)\mathcal{J}_2(\kappa)+\mathcal{J}_1(\tau)\mathcal{J}_2(\tau)\mathcal{J}_1(\kappa)\mathcal{J}_2(1-\kappa)]d\tau d\kappa\\ &\oplus\widetilde{Q}(\mathfrak{e},\mathfrak{g},\mathfrak{u},\mathfrak{v})\int_0^1 \tau^{\alpha-1}\kappa^{\beta-1}[\mathcal{J}_1(\tau)\mathcal{J}_2(1-\tau)\mathcal{J}_1(\kappa)\mathcal{J}_2(1-\kappa)+\mathcal{J}_1(\tau)\mathcal{J}_2(1-\tau)\mathcal{J}_1(1-\kappa)\\ &\mathcal{J}_2(\kappa)+\mathcal{J}_1(1-\tau)\mathcal{J}_2(\tau)\mathcal{J}_1(\kappa)\mathcal{J}_2(1-\kappa)+\mathcal{J}_1(\tau)\mathcal{J}_2(1-\tau)\mathcal{J}_1(\kappa)\mathcal{J}_2(1-\kappa)]d\tau d\kappa.\end{aligned}$$

Hence, we obtain the required result. □

Remark 3. *If one assumes that $\mathcal{J}(\tau)=\tau$, $\mathcal{J}(\kappa)=\kappa$, $\alpha=1$, and $\beta=1$, then, from (59), as a result, there will be an inequality (see [70]):*

$$\begin{aligned}&\frac{1}{(\mathfrak{g}-\mathfrak{e})(\mathfrak{v}-\mathfrak{u})}\int_{\mathfrak{e}}^{\mathfrak{g}}\int_{\mathfrak{u}}^{\mathfrak{v}}\widetilde{G}(x,y)\otimes\widetilde{\mathcal{J}}(x,y)dydx\\ &\supseteq_{\mathbb{F}}\frac{1}{9}\widetilde{\mathcal{M}}(\mathfrak{e},\mathfrak{g},\mathfrak{u},\mathfrak{v})\oplus\frac{1}{18}\left[\widetilde{P}(\mathfrak{e},\mathfrak{g},\mathfrak{u},\mathfrak{v})\oplus\widetilde{\mathcal{N}}(\mathfrak{e},\mathfrak{g},\mathfrak{u},\mathfrak{v})\right]\oplus\frac{1}{36}\widetilde{Q}(\mathfrak{e},\mathfrak{g},\mathfrak{u},\mathfrak{v}).\end{aligned} \tag{63}$$

If $\widetilde{G}$ is a coordinated left-UD-Ꭻ-convex function with $Ꭻ(\tau) = \tau$, $Ꭻ(\kappa) = \kappa$ and one assumes that $\alpha = 1$ and $\beta = 1$, then, from (59), as a result, there will be an inequality (see [59]):

$$\begin{aligned}&\frac{1}{(\mathfrak{g}-\mathfrak{e})(\mathfrak{v}-\mathfrak{u})}\int_{\mathfrak{e}}^{\mathfrak{g}}\int_{\mathfrak{u}}^{\mathfrak{v}}\widetilde{G}(x,y)\otimes\widetilde{\mathcal{J}}(x,y)dydx\\&\leq_{\mathbb{F}}\tfrac{1}{9}\widetilde{\mathcal{M}}(\mathfrak{e},\mathfrak{g},\mathfrak{u},\mathfrak{v})\oplus\tfrac{1}{18}\left[\widetilde{P}(\mathfrak{e},\mathfrak{g},\mathfrak{u},\mathfrak{v})\oplus\widetilde{\mathcal{N}}(\mathfrak{e},\mathfrak{g},\mathfrak{u},\mathfrak{v})\right]\oplus\tfrac{1}{36}\widetilde{Q}(\mathfrak{e},\mathfrak{g},\mathfrak{u},\mathfrak{v}).\end{aligned}\tag{64}$$

If $G_*((x,y),\gamma) \neq G^*((x,y),\gamma)$ with $\gamma = 1$ and $Ꭻ(\tau) = \tau$, $Ꭻ(\kappa) = \kappa$, then, from (59), we succeed in bringing about the upcoming inequality (see [55]):

$$\begin{aligned}&\frac{\Gamma(\alpha+1)\Gamma(\beta+1)}{4(\mathfrak{g}-\mathfrak{e})^{\alpha}(\mathfrak{v}-\mathfrak{u})^{\beta}}\left[\mathcal{I}^{\alpha,\beta}_{\mathfrak{e}^+,\mathfrak{u}^+}G(\mathfrak{g},\mathfrak{v})\times\mathcal{J}(\mathfrak{g},\mathfrak{v})+\mathcal{I}^{\alpha,\beta}_{\mathfrak{e}^+,\mathfrak{v}^-}G(\mathfrak{g},\mathfrak{u})\times\mathcal{J}(\mathfrak{g},\mathfrak{u})\right]\\&+\frac{\Gamma(\alpha+1)\Gamma(\beta+1)}{4(\mathfrak{g}-\mathfrak{e})^{\alpha}(\mathfrak{v}-\mathfrak{u})^{\beta}}\left[\mathcal{I}^{\alpha,\beta}_{\mathfrak{g}^-,\mathfrak{u}^+}G(\mathfrak{e},\mathfrak{v})\times\mathcal{J}(\mathfrak{e},\mathfrak{v})+\mathcal{I}^{\alpha,\beta}_{\mathfrak{g}^-,\mathfrak{v}^-}G(\mathfrak{e},\mathfrak{u})\times\mathcal{J}(\mathfrak{e},\mathfrak{u})\right]\\&\supseteq\left(\tfrac{1}{2}-\tfrac{\alpha}{(\alpha+1)(\alpha+2)}\right)\left(\tfrac{1}{2}-\tfrac{\beta}{(\beta+1)(\beta+2)}\right)\mathcal{M}(\mathfrak{e},\mathfrak{g},\mathfrak{u},\mathfrak{v})+\tfrac{\alpha}{(\alpha+1)(\alpha+2)}\left(\tfrac{1}{2}-\tfrac{\beta}{(\beta+1)(\beta+2)}\right)P(\mathfrak{e},\mathfrak{g},\mathfrak{u},\mathfrak{v})\\&+\left(\tfrac{1}{2}-\tfrac{\alpha}{(\alpha+1)(\alpha+2)}\right)\tfrac{\beta}{(\beta+1)(\beta+2)}\mathcal{N}(\mathfrak{e},\mathfrak{g},\mathfrak{u},\mathfrak{v})+\tfrac{\beta}{(\beta+1)(\beta+2)}\tfrac{\alpha}{(\alpha+1)(\alpha+2)}Q(\mathfrak{e},\mathfrak{g},\mathfrak{u},\mathfrak{v}).\end{aligned}\tag{65}$$

If $Ꭻ(\tau) = \tau$, $Ꭻ(\kappa) = \kappa$, and $G_*((x,y),\gamma) \neq G^*((x,y),\gamma)$ with $\gamma = 1$, then, from (59), we succeed in bringing about the upcoming inequality (see [68]):

$$\begin{aligned}&\frac{1}{(\mathfrak{g}-\mathfrak{e})(\mathfrak{v}-\mathfrak{u})}\int_{\mathfrak{e}}^{\mathfrak{g}}\int_{\mathfrak{u}}^{\mathfrak{v}}G(x,y)\times\mathcal{J}(x,y)dydx\\&\supseteq\frac{1}{9}\mathcal{M}(\mathfrak{e},\mathfrak{g},\mathfrak{u},\mathfrak{v})+\frac{1}{18}[P(\mathfrak{e},\mathfrak{g},\mathfrak{u},\mathfrak{v})+\mathcal{N}(\mathfrak{e},\mathfrak{g},\mathfrak{u},\mathfrak{v})]+\frac{1}{36}Q(\mathfrak{e},\mathfrak{g},\mathfrak{u},\mathfrak{v}).\end{aligned}\tag{66}$$

If $G_*((x,y),\gamma) = G^*((x,y),\gamma)$ and $\mathcal{J}_*((x,y),\gamma) = \mathcal{J}^*((x,y),\gamma)$ with $\gamma = 1$ and $Ꭻ(\tau) = \tau$, $Ꭻ(\kappa) = \kappa$, then, from (59), we succeed in bringing about the upcoming inequality (see [69]):

$$\begin{aligned}&\frac{\Gamma(\alpha+1)\Gamma(\beta+1)}{4(\mathfrak{g}-\mathfrak{e})^{\alpha}(\mathfrak{v}-\mathfrak{u})^{\beta}}\left[\mathcal{I}^{\alpha,\beta}_{\mathfrak{e}^+,\mathfrak{u}^+}G(\mathfrak{g},\mathfrak{v})\times\mathcal{J}(\mathfrak{g},\mathfrak{v})+\mathcal{I}^{\alpha,\beta}_{\mathfrak{e}^+,\mathfrak{v}^-}G(\mathfrak{g},\mathfrak{u})\times\mathcal{J}(\mathfrak{g},\mathfrak{u})\right]\\&+\frac{\Gamma(\alpha+1)\Gamma(\beta+1)}{4(\mathfrak{g}-\mathfrak{e})^{\alpha}(\mathfrak{v}-\mathfrak{u})^{\beta}}\left[+\mathcal{I}^{\alpha,\beta}_{\mathfrak{g}^-,\mathfrak{u}^+}G(\mathfrak{e},\mathfrak{v})\times\mathcal{J}(\mathfrak{e},\mathfrak{v})+\mathcal{I}^{\alpha,\beta}_{\mathfrak{g}^-,\mathfrak{v}^-}G(\mathfrak{e},\mathfrak{u})\times\mathcal{J}(\mathfrak{e},\mathfrak{u})\right]\\&\leq\left(\tfrac{1}{2}-\tfrac{\alpha}{(\alpha+1)(\alpha+2)}\right)\left(\tfrac{1}{2}-\tfrac{\beta}{(\beta+1)(\beta+2)}\right)\mathcal{M}(\mathfrak{e},\mathfrak{g},\mathfrak{u},\mathfrak{v})+\tfrac{\alpha}{(\alpha+1)(\alpha+2)}\left(\tfrac{1}{2}-\tfrac{\beta}{(\beta+1)(\beta+2)}\right)P(\mathfrak{e},\mathfrak{g},\mathfrak{u},\mathfrak{v})\\&+\left(\tfrac{1}{2}-\tfrac{\alpha}{(\alpha+1)(\alpha+2)}\right)\tfrac{\beta}{(\beta+1)(\beta+2)}\mathcal{N}(\mathfrak{e},\mathfrak{g},\mathfrak{u},\mathfrak{v})+\tfrac{\beta}{(\beta+1)(\beta+2)}\tfrac{\alpha}{(\alpha+1)(\alpha+2)}Q(\mathfrak{e},\mathfrak{g},\mathfrak{u},\mathfrak{v}).\end{aligned}\tag{67}$$

Theorem 10. *Let $\widetilde{G}, \widetilde{\mathcal{J}} : \Delta \to \mathbb{F}_0^+$ be a coordinated UD-Ꭻ-convex FNVM on Δ, and let $Ꭻ : [0, 1] \to \mathbb{R}^+$. Then, from γ-cuts, we set up the sequence of IVMs $G_\gamma, \mathcal{J}_\gamma : \Delta \to \mathbb{R}_I^+$, which is given by $G_\gamma(x,y) = [G_*((x,y),\gamma),\ G^*((x,y),\gamma)]$ and $\mathcal{J}_\gamma(x,y) = [\mathcal{J}_*((x,y),\gamma),\ \mathcal{J}^*((x,y),\gamma)]$ for all $(x,y) \in \Delta$ and for all $\gamma \in [0, 1]$. If $\widetilde{G} \otimes \widetilde{\mathcal{J}} \in \mathcal{FO}_\Delta$, then the following inequalities holds:*

$$\frac{1}{2\alpha\beta\mathcal{J}_1{}^2(\frac{1}{2})\mathcal{J}_2{}^2(\frac{1}{2})}\widetilde{G}(\tfrac{\mathfrak{e}+\mathfrak{g}}{2},\ \tfrac{\mathfrak{u}+\mathfrak{v}}{2})\otimes\widetilde{\mathcal{J}}(\tfrac{\mathfrak{e}+\mathfrak{g}}{2},\ \tfrac{\mathfrak{u}+\mathfrak{v}}{2})$$
$$\supseteq_{\mathbb{F}}\frac{\Gamma(\alpha)\Gamma(\beta)}{2(\mathfrak{g}-\mathfrak{e})^{\alpha}(\mathfrak{v}-\mathfrak{u})^{\beta}}\left[\mathcal{I}^{\alpha,\,\beta}_{\mathfrak{e}^+,\mathfrak{u}^+}\widetilde{G}(\mathfrak{g},\mathfrak{v})\otimes\widetilde{\mathcal{J}}(\mathfrak{g},\mathfrak{v})\oplus\mathcal{I}^{\alpha,\,\beta}_{\mathfrak{e}^+,\mathfrak{v}^-}\widetilde{G}(\mathfrak{g},\mathfrak{u})\otimes\widetilde{\mathcal{J}}(\mathfrak{g},\mathfrak{u})\right]$$
$$\oplus\frac{\Gamma(\alpha)\Gamma(\beta)}{2(\mathfrak{g}-\mathfrak{e})^{\alpha}(\mathfrak{v}-\mathfrak{u})^{\beta}}\left[\mathcal{I}^{\alpha,\,\beta}_{\mathfrak{g}^-,\mathfrak{u}^+}\widetilde{G}(\mathfrak{e},\mathfrak{v})\otimes\widetilde{\mathcal{J}}(\mathfrak{e},\mathfrak{v})\oplus\mathcal{I}^{\alpha,\,\beta}_{\mathfrak{g}^-,\mathfrak{v}^-}\widetilde{G}(\mathfrak{e},\mathfrak{u})\otimes\widetilde{\mathcal{J}}(\mathfrak{e},\mathfrak{u})\right]$$
$$\oplus\widetilde{\mathcal{M}}(\mathfrak{e},\mathfrak{g},\mathfrak{u},\mathfrak{v})\int_0^1\tau^{\alpha-1}\kappa^{\beta-1}[\mathcal{J}_1(\tau)\mathcal{J}_1(\kappa)[\mathcal{J}_2(\tau)\mathcal{J}_2(1-\kappa)+\mathcal{J}_2(1-\tau)\mathcal{J}_2(\kappa)+\mathcal{J}_2(1-\tau)$$
$$\mathcal{J}_2(1-\kappa)]+\mathcal{J}_1(\tau)\mathcal{J}_1(1-\kappa)[\mathcal{J}_2(\tau)\mathcal{J}_2(\kappa)+\mathcal{J}_2(1-\tau)\mathcal{J}_2(1-\kappa)+\mathcal{J}_2(1-\tau)\mathcal{J}_2(\kappa)]]d\tau d\kappa$$
$$\oplus\widetilde{P}(\mathfrak{e},\mathfrak{g},\mathfrak{u},\mathfrak{v})\int_0^1\tau^{\alpha-1}\kappa^{\beta-1}[\mathcal{J}_1(\tau)\mathcal{J}_1(\kappa)[\mathcal{J}_2(1-\tau)\mathcal{J}_2(1-\kappa)+\mathcal{J}_2(\tau)\mathcal{J}_2(\kappa)+\qquad(68)$$
$$\mathcal{J}_2(\tau)\mathcal{J}_2(1-\kappa)]+\mathcal{J}_1(\tau)\mathcal{J}_1(1-\kappa)[\mathcal{J}_2(1-\tau)\mathcal{J}_2(\kappa)+\mathcal{J}_2(\tau)\mathcal{J}_2(1-\kappa)+$$
$$\mathcal{J}_2(\tau)\mathcal{J}_2(\kappa)]d\tau d\kappa$$
$$\oplus\widetilde{\mathcal{N}}(\mathfrak{e},\mathfrak{g},\mathfrak{u},\mathfrak{v})\int_0^1\tau^{\alpha-1}\kappa^{\beta-1}[\mathcal{J}_1(\tau)\mathcal{J}_1(\kappa)[\mathcal{J}_2(\tau)\mathcal{J}_2(\kappa)+\mathcal{J}_2(1-\tau)\mathcal{J}_2(1-\kappa)+\mathcal{J}_2(1-\tau)$$
$$\mathcal{J}_2(\kappa)]+\mathcal{J}_1(\tau)\mathcal{J}_1(1-\kappa)[\mathcal{J}_2(\tau)\mathcal{J}_2(1-\kappa)+\mathcal{J}_2(1-\tau)\mathcal{J}_2(\kappa)+\mathcal{J}_2(1-\tau)\mathcal{J}_2(1-\kappa)]]d\tau d\kappa$$
$$\oplus\widetilde{Q}(\mathfrak{e},\mathfrak{g},\mathfrak{u},\mathfrak{v})\int_0^1\tau^{\alpha-1}\kappa^{\beta-1}[\mathcal{J}_1(\tau)\mathcal{J}_1(\kappa)[\mathcal{J}_2(1-\tau)\mathcal{J}_2(\kappa)+\mathcal{J}_2(\tau)\mathcal{J}_2(1-\kappa)+\mathcal{J}_2(\tau)\mathcal{J}_2(\kappa)]$$
$$+\mathcal{J}_1(\tau)\mathcal{J}_1(1-\kappa)[\mathcal{J}_2(1-\tau)\mathcal{J}_2(1-\kappa)+\mathcal{J}_2(\tau)\mathcal{J}_2(\kappa)+\mathcal{J}_2(\tau)\mathcal{J}_2(1-\kappa)]]d\tau d\kappa.$$

If $\widetilde{G}$ and $\widetilde{\mathcal{J}}$ are both coordinate UD-J-concave FNVMs on Δ, then the inequality above can be expressed as follows:

$$\frac{1}{2\alpha\beta\mathcal{J}_1{}^2(\frac{1}{2})\mathcal{J}_2{}^2(\frac{1}{2})}\widetilde{G}(\tfrac{\mathfrak{e}+\mathfrak{g}}{2},\ \tfrac{\mathfrak{u}+\mathfrak{v}}{2})\otimes\widetilde{\mathcal{J}}(\tfrac{\mathfrak{e}+\mathfrak{g}}{2},\ \tfrac{\mathfrak{u}+\mathfrak{v}}{2})$$
$$\subseteq_{\mathbb{F}}\frac{\Gamma(\alpha)\Gamma(\beta)}{2(\mathfrak{g}-\mathfrak{e})^{\alpha}(\mathfrak{v}-\mathfrak{u})^{\beta}}\left[\mathcal{I}^{\alpha,\,\beta}_{\mathfrak{e}^+,\mathfrak{u}^+}\widetilde{G}(\mathfrak{g},\mathfrak{v})\otimes\widetilde{\mathcal{J}}(\mathfrak{g},\mathfrak{v})\oplus\mathcal{I}^{\alpha,\,\beta}_{\mathfrak{e}^+,\mathfrak{v}^-}\widetilde{G}(\mathfrak{g},\mathfrak{u})\otimes\widetilde{\mathcal{J}}(\mathfrak{g},\mathfrak{u})\right]$$
$$\oplus\frac{\Gamma(\alpha)\Gamma(\beta)}{2(\mathfrak{g}-\mathfrak{e})^{\alpha}(\mathfrak{v}-\mathfrak{u})^{\beta}}\left[\mathcal{I}^{\alpha,\,\beta}_{\mathfrak{g}^-,\mathfrak{u}^+}\widetilde{G}(\mathfrak{e},\mathfrak{v})\otimes\widetilde{\mathcal{J}}(\mathfrak{e},\mathfrak{v})\oplus\mathcal{I}^{\alpha,\,\beta}_{\mathfrak{g}^-,\mathfrak{v}^-}\widetilde{G}(\mathfrak{e},\mathfrak{u})\otimes\widetilde{\mathcal{J}}(\mathfrak{e},\mathfrak{u})\right]$$
$$\oplus\widetilde{\mathcal{M}}(\mathfrak{e},\mathfrak{g},\mathfrak{u},\mathfrak{v})\int_0^1\tau^{\alpha-1}\kappa^{\beta-1}[\mathcal{J}_1(\tau)\mathcal{J}_1(\kappa)[\mathcal{J}_2(\tau)\mathcal{J}_2(1-\kappa)+\mathcal{J}_2(1-\tau)\mathcal{J}_2(\kappa)+\mathcal{J}_2(1-\tau)$$
$$\mathcal{J}_2(1-\kappa)]+\mathcal{J}_1(\tau)\mathcal{J}_1(1-\kappa)[\mathcal{J}_2(\tau)\mathcal{J}_2(\kappa)+\mathcal{J}_2(1-\tau)\mathcal{J}_2(1-\kappa)+\mathcal{J}_2(1-\tau)\mathcal{J}_2(\kappa)]]d\tau d\kappa$$
$$\oplus\widetilde{P}(\mathfrak{e},\mathfrak{g},\mathfrak{u},\mathfrak{v})\int_0^1\tau^{\alpha-1}\kappa^{\beta-1}[\mathcal{J}_1(\tau)\mathcal{J}_1(\kappa)[\mathcal{J}_2(1-\tau)\mathcal{J}_2(1-\kappa)+\mathcal{J}_2(\tau)\mathcal{J}_2(\kappa)+\qquad(69)$$
$$\mathcal{J}_2(\tau)\mathcal{J}_2(1-\kappa)]+\mathcal{J}_1(\tau)\mathcal{J}_1(1-\kappa)[\mathcal{J}_2(1-\tau)\mathcal{J}_2(\kappa)+\mathcal{J}_2(\tau)\mathcal{J}_2(1-\kappa)+$$
$$\mathcal{J}_2(\tau)\mathcal{J}_2(\kappa)]]d\tau d\kappa$$
$$\oplus\widetilde{\mathcal{N}}(\mathfrak{e},\mathfrak{g},\mathfrak{u},\mathfrak{v})\int_0^1\tau^{\alpha-1}\kappa^{\beta-1}[\mathcal{J}_1(\tau)\mathcal{J}_1(\kappa)[\mathcal{J}_2(\tau)\mathcal{J}_2(\kappa)+\mathcal{J}_2(1-\tau)\mathcal{J}_2(1-\kappa)+\mathcal{J}_2(1-\tau)\mathcal{J}_2(\kappa)]$$
$$+\mathcal{J}_1(\tau)\mathcal{J}_1(1-\kappa)[\mathcal{J}_2(\tau)\mathcal{J}_2(1-\kappa)+\mathcal{J}_2(1-\tau)\mathcal{J}_2(\kappa)+\mathcal{J}_2(1-\tau)\mathcal{J}_2(1-\kappa)]]d\tau d\kappa$$
$$\oplus\widetilde{Q}(\mathfrak{e},\mathfrak{g},\mathfrak{u},\mathfrak{v})\int_0^1\tau^{\alpha-1}\kappa^{\beta-1}[\mathcal{J}_1(\tau)\mathcal{J}_1(\kappa)[\mathcal{J}_2(1-\tau)\mathcal{J}_2(\kappa)+\mathcal{J}_2(\tau)\mathcal{J}_2(1-\kappa)+$$
$$\mathcal{J}_2(\tau)\mathcal{J}_2(\kappa)]+\mathcal{J}_1(\tau)\mathcal{J}_1(1-\kappa)[\mathcal{J}_2(1-\tau)\mathcal{J}_2(1-\kappa)+\mathcal{J}_2(\tau)\mathcal{J}_2(\kappa)+\mathcal{J}_2(\tau)\mathcal{J}_2(1-\kappa)]]d\tau d\kappa.$$

where $\widetilde{\mathcal{M}}(\mathfrak{e},\mathfrak{g},\mathfrak{u},\mathfrak{v})$, $\widetilde{P}(\mathfrak{e},\mathfrak{g},\mathfrak{u},\mathfrak{v})$, $\widetilde{\mathcal{N}}(\mathfrak{e},\mathfrak{g},\mathfrak{u},\mathfrak{v})$, and $\widetilde{Q}(\mathfrak{e},\mathfrak{g},\mathfrak{u},\mathfrak{v})$ are given in Theorem 9.

Proof. Since $\widetilde{G},\widetilde{\mathcal{J}}:\Delta\to\mathbb{F}_0$ are two *UD*-J-convex *FNVM*s, then, from inequality (17) and for each $\gamma\in[0,\ 1]$, we have

$$
\begin{aligned}
& G_\gamma\left(\tfrac{\mathfrak{e}+\mathfrak{g}}{2}, \tfrac{\mathfrak{u}+\mathfrak{v}}{2}\right) \times \mathcal{J}_\gamma\left(\tfrac{\mathfrak{e}+\mathfrak{g}}{2}, \tfrac{\mathfrak{u}+\mathfrak{v}}{2}\right) \\
&= G_\gamma\left(\frac{\tau\mathfrak{e}+(1-\tau)\mathfrak{g}}{2} + \frac{(1-\tau)\mathfrak{e}+\tau\mathfrak{g}}{2}, \frac{\kappa\mathfrak{u}+(1-\kappa)\mathfrak{v}}{2} + \frac{\mathfrak{u}+\mathfrak{v}}{2}\right) \times \mathcal{J}_\gamma\left(\frac{\tau\mathfrak{e}+(1-\tau)\mathfrak{g}}{2} + \frac{(1-\tau)\mathfrak{e}+\tau\mathfrak{g}}{2}, \frac{\kappa\mathfrak{u}+(1-\kappa)\mathfrak{v}}{2} + \frac{(1-\kappa)\mathfrak{u}+\kappa\mathfrak{v}}{2}\right) \\
&\supseteq_I \daleth_1{}^2\left(\tfrac{1}{2}\right)\daleth_2{}^2\left(\tfrac{1}{2}\right) \times \begin{bmatrix} G_\gamma(\tau\mathfrak{e}+(1-\tau)\mathfrak{g}, \kappa\mathfrak{u}+(1-\kappa)\mathfrak{v}) + G_\gamma((1-\tau)\mathfrak{e}+\tau\mathfrak{g}, \kappa\mathfrak{u}+(1-\kappa)\mathfrak{v}) \\ +G_\gamma(\tau\mathfrak{e}+(1-\tau)\mathfrak{g}, (1-\kappa)\mathfrak{u}+\kappa\mathfrak{v}) + G_\gamma((1-\tau)\mathfrak{e}+\tau\mathfrak{g}, (1-\kappa)\mathfrak{u}+\kappa\mathfrak{v}) \end{bmatrix} \\
&\quad \times \begin{bmatrix} \mathcal{J}_\gamma(\tau\mathfrak{e}+(1-\tau)\mathfrak{g}, \kappa\mathfrak{u}+(1-\kappa)\mathfrak{v}) + \mathcal{J}_\gamma((1-\tau)\mathfrak{e}+\tau\mathfrak{g}, \kappa\mathfrak{u}+(1-\kappa)\mathfrak{v}) \\ +\mathcal{J}_\gamma(\tau\mathfrak{e}+(1-\tau)\mathfrak{g}, (1-\kappa)\mathfrak{u}+\kappa\mathfrak{v}) + \mathcal{J}_\gamma((1-\tau)\mathfrak{e}+\tau\mathfrak{g}, (1-\kappa)\mathfrak{u}+\kappa\mathfrak{v}) \end{bmatrix} \\
&\supseteq_I \daleth_1{}^2\left(\tfrac{1}{2}\right)\daleth_2{}^2\left(\tfrac{1}{2}\right) \times \begin{bmatrix} G_\gamma(\tau\mathfrak{e}+(1-\tau)\mathfrak{g}, \kappa\mathfrak{u}+(1-\kappa)\mathfrak{v}) \times \mathcal{J}_\gamma(\tau\mathfrak{e}+(1-\tau)\mathfrak{g}, \kappa\mathfrak{u}+(1-\kappa)\mathfrak{v}) \\ +G_\gamma((1-\tau)\mathfrak{e}+\tau\mathfrak{g}, \kappa\mathfrak{u}+(1-\kappa)\mathfrak{v}) \times \mathcal{J}_\gamma((1-\tau)\mathfrak{e}+\tau\mathfrak{g}, \kappa\mathfrak{u}+(1-\kappa)\mathfrak{v}) \\ +G_\gamma(\tau\mathfrak{e}+(1-\tau)\mathfrak{g}, (1-\kappa)\mathfrak{u}+\kappa\mathfrak{v}) \times \mathcal{J}_\gamma(\tau\mathfrak{e}+(1-\tau)\mathfrak{g}, (1-\kappa)\mathfrak{u}+\kappa\mathfrak{v}) \\ +G_\gamma((1-\tau)\mathfrak{e}+\tau\mathfrak{g}, (1-\kappa)\mathfrak{u}+\kappa\mathfrak{v}) \times \mathcal{J}_\gamma((1-\tau)\mathfrak{e}+\tau\mathfrak{g}, (1-\kappa)\mathfrak{u}+\kappa\mathfrak{v}) \end{bmatrix} \\
&\quad +\daleth_1{}^2\left(\tfrac{1}{2}\right)\daleth_2{}^2\left(\tfrac{1}{2}\right) \times \\
&\begin{bmatrix} \daleth_1(\tau)\daleth_1(\kappa)[\daleth_2(\tau)\daleth_2(1-\kappa) + \daleth_2(1-\tau)\daleth_2(\kappa) + \daleth_2(1-\tau)\daleth_2(1-\kappa)] \\ +\daleth_1(\tau)\daleth_1(1-\kappa)[\daleth_2(\tau)\daleth_2(\kappa) + \daleth_2(1-\tau)\daleth_2(1-\kappa) + \daleth_2(1-\tau)\daleth_2(\kappa)] \\ +\daleth_1(1-\tau)\daleth_1(\kappa)[\daleth_2(1-\tau)\daleth_2(1-\kappa) + \daleth_2(\tau)\daleth_2(\kappa) + \daleth_2(\tau)\daleth_2(1-\kappa)] \\ +\daleth_1(1-\tau)\daleth_1(1-\kappa)[\daleth_2(\tau)\daleth_2(\kappa) + \daleth_2(1-\tau)\daleth_2(\kappa) + \daleth_2(\tau)\daleth_2(1-\kappa)] \end{bmatrix} \mathcal{M}_\gamma(\mathfrak{e}, \mathfrak{g}, \mathfrak{u}, \mathfrak{v}) \\
&\quad +\daleth_1{}^2\left(\tfrac{1}{2}\right)\daleth_2{}^2\left(\tfrac{1}{2}\right) \times \\
&\begin{bmatrix} \daleth_1(\tau)\daleth_1(\kappa)[\daleth_2(1-\tau)\daleth_2(1-\kappa) + \daleth_2(\tau)\daleth_2(\kappa) + \daleth_2(\tau)\daleth_2(1-\kappa)] \\ +\daleth_1(\tau)\daleth_1(1-\kappa)[\daleth_2(1-\tau)\daleth_2(\kappa) + \daleth_2(\tau)\daleth_2(1-\kappa) + \daleth_2(\tau)\daleth_2(\kappa)] \\ +\daleth_1(1-\tau)\daleth_1(\kappa)[\daleth_2(\tau)\daleth_2(1-\kappa) + \daleth_2(1-\tau)\daleth_2(\kappa) + \daleth_2(1-\tau)\daleth_2(1-\kappa)] \\ +\daleth_1(1-\tau)\daleth_1(1-\kappa)[\daleth_2(\tau)\daleth_2(\kappa) + \daleth_2(1-\tau)\daleth_2(1-\kappa) + \daleth_2(1-\tau)\daleth_2(\kappa)] \end{bmatrix} P_\gamma(\mathfrak{e}, \mathfrak{g}, \mathfrak{u}, \mathfrak{v}) \\
&\quad +\daleth_1{}^2\left(\tfrac{1}{2}\right)\daleth_2{}^2\left(\tfrac{1}{2}\right) \times \\
&\begin{bmatrix} \daleth_1(\tau)\daleth_1(\kappa)[\daleth_2(\tau)\daleth_2(\kappa) + \daleth_2(1-\tau)\daleth_2(1-\kappa) + \daleth_2(1-\tau)\daleth_2(\kappa)] \\ +\daleth_1(\tau)\daleth_1(1-\kappa)[\daleth_2(\tau)\daleth_2(1-\kappa) + \daleth_2(1-\tau)\daleth_2(\kappa) + \daleth_2(1-\tau)\daleth_2(1-\kappa)] \\ +\daleth_1(1-\tau)\daleth_1(\kappa)[\daleth_2(1-\tau)\daleth_2(\kappa) + \daleth_2(\tau)\daleth_2(1-\kappa) + \daleth_2(\tau)\daleth_2(\kappa)] \\ +\daleth_1(1-\tau)\daleth_1(1-\kappa)[\daleth_2(1-\tau)\daleth_2(1-\kappa) + \daleth_2(\tau)\daleth_2(\kappa) + \daleth_2(\tau)\daleth_2(1-\kappa)] \end{bmatrix} \mathcal{N}_\gamma(\mathfrak{e}, \mathfrak{g}, \mathfrak{u}, \mathfrak{v}) \\
&\quad +\daleth_1{}^2\left(\tfrac{1}{2}\right)\daleth_2{}^2\left(\tfrac{1}{2}\right) \times \\
&\begin{bmatrix} \daleth_1(\tau)\daleth_1(\kappa)[\daleth_2(1-\tau)\daleth_2(\kappa) + \daleth_2(\tau)\daleth_2(1-\kappa) + \daleth_2(\tau)\daleth_2(\kappa)] \\ +\daleth_1(\tau)\daleth_1(1-\kappa)[\daleth_2(1-\tau)\daleth_2(1-\kappa) + \daleth_2(\tau)\daleth_2(\kappa) + \daleth_2(\tau)\daleth_2(1-\kappa)] \\ +\daleth_1(1-\tau)\daleth_1(\kappa)[\daleth_2(\tau)\daleth_2(\kappa) + \daleth_2(1-\tau)\daleth_2(1-\kappa) + \daleth_2(1-\tau)\daleth_2(\kappa)] \\ +\daleth_1(\tau)\daleth_1(1-\kappa)[\daleth_2(\tau)\daleth_2(1-\kappa) + \daleth_2(1-\tau)\daleth_2(1-\kappa) + \daleth_2(1-\tau)\daleth_2(\kappa)] \end{bmatrix} \mathcal{Q}_\gamma(\mathfrak{e}, \mathfrak{g}, \mathfrak{u}, \mathfrak{v}).
\end{aligned}
$$

Taking the multiplication of the above fuzzy inclusion with $\tau^{\alpha-1}\kappa^{\beta-1}$ and then taking the double integration of the result over $[0, 1] \times [0, 1]$ with respect to (τ, κ), we have

$$
\begin{aligned}
&\int_0^1\int_0^1 \tau^{\alpha-1}\kappa^{\beta-1} G_\gamma\left(\tfrac{\mathfrak{e}+\mathfrak{g}}{2},\tfrac{\mathfrak{u}+\mathfrak{v}}{2}\right)\times\mathcal{J}_\gamma\left(\tfrac{\mathfrak{e}+\mathfrak{g}}{2},\tfrac{\mathfrak{u}+\mathfrak{v}}{2}\right)d\tau d\kappa \\
&\supseteq_I Ɉ_1{}^2\left(\tfrac{1}{2}\right)Ɉ_2{}^2\left(\tfrac{1}{2}\right) \\
&\times\int_0^1\int_0^1 \tau^{\alpha-1}\kappa^{\beta-1}\left[\begin{array}{c}
G_\gamma(\tau\mathfrak{e}+(1-\tau)\mathfrak{g},\kappa\mathfrak{u}+(1-\kappa)\mathfrak{v})\times\mathcal{J}_\gamma(\tau\mathfrak{e}+(1-\tau)\mathfrak{g},\kappa\mathfrak{u}+(1-\kappa)\mathfrak{v})\\
+G_\gamma((1-\tau)\mathfrak{e}+\tau\mathfrak{g},\kappa\mathfrak{u}+(1-\kappa)\mathfrak{v})\times\mathcal{J}_\gamma((1-\tau)\mathfrak{e}+\tau\mathfrak{g},\kappa\mathfrak{u}+(1-\kappa)\mathfrak{v})\\
+G_\gamma(\tau\mathfrak{e}+(1-\tau)\mathfrak{g},(1-\kappa)\mathfrak{u}+\kappa\mathfrak{v})\times\mathcal{J}_\gamma(\tau\mathfrak{e}+(1-\tau)\mathfrak{g},(1-\kappa)\mathfrak{u}+\kappa\mathfrak{v})\\
+G_\gamma((1-\tau)\mathfrak{e}+\tau\mathfrak{g},(1-\kappa)\mathfrak{u}+\kappa\mathfrak{v})\times\mathcal{J}_\gamma((1-\tau)\mathfrak{e}+\tau\mathfrak{g},(1-\kappa)\mathfrak{u}+\kappa\mathfrak{v})
\end{array}\right]d\tau d\kappa \\
&+Ɉ_1{}^2\left(\tfrac{1}{2}\right)Ɉ_2{}^2\left(\tfrac{1}{2}\right)\mathcal{M}_\gamma(\mathfrak{e},\mathfrak{g},\mathfrak{u},\mathfrak{v}) \\
&\times\int_0^1\int_0^1 \tau^{\alpha-1}\kappa^{\beta-1}\left[\begin{array}{c}
Ɉ_1(\tau)Ɉ_1(\kappa)[Ɉ_2(\tau)Ɉ_2(1-\kappa)+Ɉ_2(1-\tau)Ɉ_2(\kappa)+Ɉ_2(1-\tau)Ɉ_2(1-\kappa)]\\
+Ɉ_1(\tau)Ɉ_1(1-\kappa)[Ɉ_2(\tau)Ɉ_2(\kappa)+Ɉ_2(1-\tau)Ɉ_2(1-\kappa)+Ɉ_2(1-\tau)Ɉ_2(\kappa)]\\
+Ɉ_1(1-\tau)Ɉ_1(\kappa)[Ɉ_2(1-\tau)Ɉ_2(1-\kappa)+Ɉ_2(\tau)Ɉ_2(\kappa)+Ɉ_2(\tau)Ɉ_2(1-\kappa)]\\
+Ɉ_1(1-\tau)Ɉ_1(1-\kappa)[Ɉ_2(\tau)Ɉ_2(\kappa)+Ɉ_2(1-\tau)Ɉ_2(\kappa)+Ɉ_2(\tau)Ɉ_2(1-\kappa)]
\end{array}\right]d\tau d\kappa \\
&+Ɉ_1{}^2\left(\tfrac{1}{2}\right)Ɉ_2{}^2\left(\tfrac{1}{2}\right)P_\gamma(\mathfrak{e},\mathfrak{g},\mathfrak{u},\mathfrak{v}) \\
&\times\int_0^1\int_0^1 \tau^{\alpha-1}\kappa^{\beta-1}\left[\begin{array}{c}
Ɉ_1(\tau)Ɉ_1(\kappa)[Ɉ_2(1-\tau)Ɉ_2(1-\kappa)+Ɉ_2(\tau)Ɉ_2(\kappa)+Ɉ_2(\tau)Ɉ_2(1-\kappa)]\\
+Ɉ_1(\tau)Ɉ_1(1-\kappa)[Ɉ_2(1-\tau)Ɉ_2(\kappa)+Ɉ_2(\tau)Ɉ_2(1-\kappa)+Ɉ_2(\tau)Ɉ_2(\kappa)]\\
+Ɉ_1(1-\tau)Ɉ_1(\kappa)[Ɉ_2(\tau)Ɉ_2(1-\kappa)+Ɉ_2(1-\tau)Ɉ_2(\kappa)+Ɉ_2(1-\tau)Ɉ_2(1-\kappa)]\\
+Ɉ_1(1-\tau)Ɉ_1(1-\kappa)[Ɉ_2(\tau)Ɉ_2(\kappa)+Ɉ_2(1-\tau)Ɉ_2(1-\kappa)+Ɉ_2(1-\tau)Ɉ_2(\kappa)]
\end{array}\right]d\tau d\kappa \\
&+Ɉ_1{}^2\left(\tfrac{1}{2}\right)Ɉ_2{}^2\left(\tfrac{1}{2}\right)\mathcal{N}_\gamma(\mathfrak{e},\mathfrak{g},\mathfrak{u},\mathfrak{v}) \\
&\times\int_0^1\int_0^1 \tau^{\alpha-1}\kappa^{\beta-1}\left[\begin{array}{c}
Ɉ_1(\tau)Ɉ_1(\kappa)[Ɉ_2(\tau)Ɉ_2(\kappa)+Ɉ_2(1-\tau)Ɉ_2(1-\kappa)+Ɉ_2(1-\tau)Ɉ_2(\kappa)]\\
+Ɉ_1(\tau)Ɉ_1(1-\kappa)[Ɉ_2(\tau)Ɉ_2(1-\kappa)+Ɉ_2(1-\tau)Ɉ_2(\kappa)+Ɉ_2(1-\tau)Ɉ_2(1-\kappa)]\\
+Ɉ_1(1-\tau)Ɉ_1(\kappa)[Ɉ_2(1-\tau)Ɉ_2(\kappa)+Ɉ_2(\tau)Ɉ_2(1-\kappa)+Ɉ_2(\tau)Ɉ_2(\kappa)]\\
+Ɉ_1(1-\tau)Ɉ_1(1-\kappa)[Ɉ_2(1-\tau)Ɉ_2(1-\kappa)+Ɉ_2(\tau)Ɉ_2(\kappa)+Ɉ_2(\tau)Ɉ_2(1-\kappa)]
\end{array}\right]d\tau d\kappa \\
&+Ɉ_1{}^2\left(\tfrac{1}{2}\right)Ɉ_2{}^2\left(\tfrac{1}{2}\right)\mathcal{Q}_\gamma(\mathfrak{e},\mathfrak{g},\mathfrak{u},\mathfrak{v}) \\
&\times\int_0^1\int_0^1 \tau^{\alpha-1}\kappa^{\beta-1}\left[\begin{array}{c}
Ɉ_1(\tau)Ɉ_1(\kappa)[Ɉ_2(1-\tau)Ɉ_2(\kappa)+Ɉ_2(\tau)Ɉ_2(1-\kappa)+Ɉ_2(\tau)Ɉ_2(\kappa)]\\
+Ɉ_1(\tau)Ɉ_1(1-\kappa)[Ɉ_2(1-\tau)Ɉ_2(1-\kappa)+Ɉ_2(\tau)Ɉ_2(\kappa)+Ɉ_2(\tau)Ɉ_2(1-\kappa)]\\
+Ɉ_1(1-\tau)Ɉ_1(\kappa)[Ɉ_2(\tau)Ɉ_2(\kappa)+Ɉ_2(1-\tau)Ɉ_2(1-\kappa)+Ɉ_2(1-\tau)Ɉ_2(\kappa)]\\
+Ɉ_1(\tau)Ɉ_1(1-\kappa)[Ɉ_2(\tau)Ɉ_2(1-\kappa)+Ɉ_2(1-\tau)Ɉ_2(1-\kappa)+Ɉ_2(1-\tau)Ɉ_2(\kappa)]
\end{array}\right]
\end{aligned}
$$

which implies that

$$\frac{1}{\alpha\beta}G_\gamma\left(\frac{\mathfrak{e}+\mathfrak{g}}{2},\ \frac{\mathfrak{u}+\mathfrak{v}}{2}\right)\times\mathcal{J}_\gamma\left(\frac{\mathfrak{e}+\mathfrak{g}}{2},\ \frac{\mathfrak{u}+\mathfrak{v}}{2}\right)$$
$$\supseteq_{\mathbb{F}}\frac{\Gamma(\alpha)\Gamma(\beta)\mathcal{J}_1{}^2\left(\frac{1}{2}\right)\mathcal{J}_2{}^2\left(\frac{1}{2}\right)}{(\mathfrak{g}-\mathfrak{e})^\alpha(\mathfrak{v}-\mathfrak{u})^\beta}\left[\mathcal{I}^{\alpha,\,\beta}_{\mathfrak{e}^+,\mathfrak{u}^+}G_\gamma(\mathfrak{g},\mathfrak{v})\times\mathcal{J}_\gamma(\mathfrak{g},\mathfrak{v})+\mathcal{I}^{\alpha,\,\beta}_{\mathfrak{e}^+,\mathfrak{v}^-}G_\gamma(\mathfrak{g},\mathfrak{u})\times\mathcal{J}_\gamma(\mathfrak{g},\mathfrak{u})\right]$$
$$+\frac{\Gamma(\alpha)\Gamma(\beta)\mathcal{J}_1{}^2\left(\frac{1}{2}\right)\mathcal{J}_2{}^2\left(\frac{1}{2}\right)}{(\mathfrak{g}-\mathfrak{e})^\alpha(\mathfrak{v}-\mathfrak{u})^\beta}\left[\mathcal{I}^{\alpha,\,\beta}_{\mathfrak{g}^-,\mathfrak{u}^+}G_\gamma(\mathfrak{e},\mathfrak{v})\times\mathcal{J}_\gamma(\mathfrak{e},\mathfrak{v})+\mathcal{I}^{\alpha,\,\beta}_{\mathfrak{g}^-,\mathfrak{v}^-}G_\gamma(\mathfrak{e},\mathfrak{u})\times\mathcal{J}_\gamma(\mathfrak{e},\mathfrak{u})\right]$$
$$+2\mathcal{J}_1{}^2\left(\tfrac{1}{2}\right)\mathcal{J}_2{}^2\left(\tfrac{1}{2}\right)\mathcal{M}_\gamma(\mathfrak{e},\mathfrak{g},\mathfrak{u},\mathfrak{v})\int_0^1\tau^{\alpha-1}\kappa^{\beta-1}[\mathcal{J}_1(\tau)\mathcal{J}_1(\kappa)[\mathcal{J}_2(\tau)\mathcal{J}_2(1-\kappa)+\mathcal{J}_2(1-\tau)$$
$$\mathcal{J}_2(\kappa)+\mathcal{J}_2(1-\tau)\mathcal{J}_2(1-\kappa)]+\mathcal{J}_1(\tau)\mathcal{J}_1(1-\kappa)[\mathcal{J}_2(\tau)\mathcal{J}_2(\kappa)+\mathcal{J}_2(1-\tau)\mathcal{J}_2(1-\kappa)+$$
$$\mathcal{J}_2(1-\tau)\mathcal{J}_2(\kappa)]]d\tau d\kappa$$
$$+2\mathcal{J}_1{}^2\left(\tfrac{1}{2}\right)\mathcal{J}_2{}^2\left(\tfrac{1}{2}\right)P_\gamma(\mathfrak{e},\mathfrak{g},\mathfrak{u},\mathfrak{v})\int_0^1\tau^{\alpha-1}\kappa^{\beta-1}[\mathcal{J}_1(\tau)\mathcal{J}_1(\kappa)[\mathcal{J}_2(1-\tau)\mathcal{J}_2(1-\kappa)+$$
$$\mathcal{J}_2(\tau)\mathcal{J}_2(\kappa)+\mathcal{J}_2(\tau)\mathcal{J}_2(1-\kappa)]+\mathcal{J}_1(\tau)\mathcal{J}_1(1-\kappa)[\mathcal{J}_2(1-\tau)\mathcal{J}_2(\kappa)+\mathcal{J}_2(\tau)\mathcal{J}_2(1-\kappa)+$$
$$\mathcal{J}_2(\tau)\mathcal{J}_2(\kappa)]]d\tau d\kappa$$
$$+2\mathcal{J}_1{}^2\left(\tfrac{1}{2}\right)\mathcal{J}_2{}^2\left(\tfrac{1}{2}\right)\mathcal{N}_\gamma(\mathfrak{e},\mathfrak{g},\mathfrak{u},\mathfrak{v})\int_0^1\tau^{\alpha-1}\kappa^{\beta-1}[\mathcal{J}_1(\tau)\mathcal{J}_1(\kappa)[\mathcal{J}_2(\tau)\mathcal{J}_2(\kappa)+\mathcal{J}_2(1-\tau)$$
$$\mathcal{J}_2(1-\kappa)+\mathcal{J}_2(1-\tau)\mathcal{J}_2(\kappa)]+\mathcal{J}_1(\tau)\mathcal{J}_1(1-\kappa)[\mathcal{J}_2(\tau)\mathcal{J}_2(1-\kappa)+\mathcal{J}_2(1-\tau)\mathcal{J}_2(\kappa)+$$
$$\mathcal{J}_2(1-\tau)\mathcal{J}_2(1-\kappa)]]d\tau d\kappa$$
$$+2\mathcal{J}_1{}^2\left(\tfrac{1}{2}\right)\mathcal{J}_2{}^2\left(\tfrac{1}{2}\right)\mathcal{Q}_\gamma(\mathfrak{e},\mathfrak{g},\mathfrak{u},\mathfrak{v})\int_0^1\tau^{\alpha-1}\kappa^{\beta-1}[\mathcal{J}_1(\tau)\mathcal{J}_1(\kappa)[\mathcal{J}_2(1-\tau)\mathcal{J}_2(\kappa)+\mathcal{J}_2(\tau)\mathcal{J}_2(1-\kappa)+\mathcal{J}_2(\tau)\mathcal{J}_2(\kappa)]$$
$$+\mathcal{J}_1(\tau)\mathcal{J}_1(1-\kappa)[\mathcal{J}_2(1-\tau)\mathcal{J}_2(1-\kappa)+\mathcal{J}_2(\tau)\mathcal{J}_2(\kappa)+\mathcal{J}_2(\tau)\mathcal{J}_2(1-\kappa)]]d\tau d\kappa,$$

since $\gamma\in[0,\ 1]$, then, after simplification, we reach the required conclusion. □

Remark 4. *If one assumes that $\mathcal{J}(\tau)=\tau$, $\mathcal{J}(\kappa)=\kappa$, $\alpha=1$, and $\beta=1$, then, from (68), as a result, there will be an inequality (see [69]):*

$$\begin{aligned}&4\widetilde{G}\left(\tfrac{\mathfrak{e}+\mathfrak{g}}{2},\tfrac{\mathfrak{u}+\mathfrak{v}}{2}\right)\otimes\widetilde{\mathcal{J}}\left(\tfrac{\mathfrak{e}+\mathfrak{g}}{2},\tfrac{\mathfrak{u}+\mathfrak{v}}{2}\right)\\&\supseteq_{\mathbb{F}}\tfrac{1}{(\mathfrak{g}-\mathfrak{e})(\mathfrak{v}-\mathfrak{u})}\int_{\mathfrak{e}}^{\mathfrak{g}}\int_{\mathfrak{u}}^{\mathfrak{v}}\widetilde{G}(x,y)\otimes\widetilde{\mathcal{J}}(x,y)dydx\oplus\tfrac{5}{36}\widetilde{\mathcal{M}}(\mathfrak{e},\mathfrak{g},\mathfrak{u},\mathfrak{v})\\&\oplus\tfrac{7}{36}\left[\widetilde{P}(\mathfrak{e},\mathfrak{g},\mathfrak{u},\mathfrak{v})\widetilde{+}\widetilde{\mathcal{N}}(\mathfrak{e},\mathfrak{g},\mathfrak{u},\mathfrak{v})\right]\oplus\tfrac{2}{9}\widetilde{Q}(\mathfrak{e},\mathfrak{g},\mathfrak{u},\mathfrak{v}).\end{aligned}\quad(70)$$

If $\widetilde{G}$ is a coordinated left-UD-$\mathcal{J}$-convex function with $\mathcal{J}(\tau)=\tau$, $\mathcal{J}(\kappa)=\kappa$ and one assumes that $\alpha=1$ and $\beta=1$, then, from (68), as a result, there will be an inequality (see [59]):

$$\begin{aligned}&4\widetilde{G}\left(\tfrac{\mathfrak{e}+\mathfrak{g}}{2},\tfrac{\mathfrak{u}+\mathfrak{v}}{2}\right)\otimes\widetilde{\mathcal{J}}\left(\tfrac{\mathfrak{e}+\mathfrak{g}}{2},\tfrac{\mathfrak{u}+\mathfrak{v}}{2}\right)\\&\leq_{\mathbb{F}}\tfrac{1}{(\mathfrak{g}-\mathfrak{e})(\mathfrak{v}-\mathfrak{u})}\int_{\mathfrak{e}}^{\mathfrak{g}}\int_{\mathfrak{u}}^{\mathfrak{v}}\widetilde{G}(x,y)\otimes\widetilde{\mathcal{J}}(x,y)dydx\oplus\tfrac{5}{36}\widetilde{\mathcal{M}}(\mathfrak{e},\mathfrak{g},\mathfrak{u},\mathfrak{v})\\&\oplus\tfrac{7}{36}\left[\widetilde{P}(\mathfrak{e},\mathfrak{g},\mathfrak{u},\mathfrak{v})\widetilde{+}\widetilde{\mathcal{N}}(\mathfrak{e},\mathfrak{g},\mathfrak{u},\mathfrak{v})\right]\oplus\tfrac{2}{9}\widetilde{Q}(\mathfrak{e},\mathfrak{g},\mathfrak{u},\mathfrak{v}).\end{aligned}\quad(71)$$

If $G_*((x,y),\ \gamma)\neq G^*((x,y),\ \gamma)$ with $\mathcal{J}(\tau)=\tau$, $\mathcal{J}(\kappa)=\kappa$ and $\gamma=1$, then, from (68), we succeed in bringing about the upcoming inequality (see [55]):

$$\begin{aligned}&4\,G\left(\tfrac{\mathfrak{e}+\mathfrak{g}}{2},\tfrac{\mathfrak{u}+\mathfrak{v}}{2}\right)\times\mathcal{J}\left(\tfrac{\mathfrak{e}+\mathfrak{g}}{2},\tfrac{\mathfrak{u}+\mathfrak{v}}{2}\right)\\&\supseteq\tfrac{1}{(\mathfrak{g}-\mathfrak{e})(\mathfrak{v}-\mathfrak{u})}\int_{\mathfrak{e}}^{\mathfrak{g}}\int_{\mathfrak{u}}^{\mathfrak{v}}G(x,y)\times\mathcal{J}(x,y)dydx+\tfrac{5}{36}\mathcal{M}(\mathfrak{e},\mathfrak{g},\mathfrak{u},\mathfrak{v})\\&+\tfrac{7}{36}[P(\mathfrak{e},\mathfrak{g},\mathfrak{u},\mathfrak{v})+\mathcal{N}(\mathfrak{e},\mathfrak{g},\mathfrak{u},\mathfrak{v})]+\tfrac{2}{9}Q(\mathfrak{e},\mathfrak{g},\mathfrak{u},\mathfrak{v}).\end{aligned}\quad(72)$$

If $G_*((x,y),\ \gamma) \neq G^*((x,y),\ \gamma)$ *with* $\gamma = 1$ *and* $\rrbracket(\tau) = \tau,\ \rrbracket(\kappa) = \kappa$, *then, from (68), we succeed in bringing about the upcoming inequality (see [71]):*

$$
\begin{aligned}
&4G\left(\tfrac{\mathfrak{e}+\mathfrak{g}}{2},\ \tfrac{\mathfrak{u}+\mathfrak{v}}{2}\right) \times \mathcal{J}\left(\tfrac{\mathfrak{e}+\mathfrak{g}}{2},\ \tfrac{\mathfrak{u}+\mathfrak{v}}{2}\right) \\
&\supseteq \tfrac{\Gamma(\alpha+1)\Gamma(\beta+1)}{4(\mathfrak{g}-\mathfrak{e})^{\alpha}(\mathfrak{v}-\mathfrak{u})^{\beta}} \begin{bmatrix} \mathcal{I}^{\alpha,\ \beta}_{\mathfrak{e}^+,\mathfrak{u}^+}\ G(\mathfrak{g},\mathfrak{v}) \times \mathcal{J}(\mathfrak{g},\mathfrak{v}) + \mathcal{I}^{\alpha,\ \beta}_{\mathfrak{e}^+,\mathfrak{v}^-}\ G(\mathfrak{g},\mathfrak{u}) \times \mathcal{J}(\mathfrak{g},\mathfrak{u}) \\ +\mathcal{I}^{\alpha,\ \beta}_{\mathfrak{g}^-,\mathfrak{u}^+}\ G(\mathfrak{e},\mathfrak{v}) \times \mathcal{J}(\mathfrak{e},\mathfrak{v}) + \mathcal{I}^{\alpha,\ \beta}_{\mathfrak{g}^-,\mathfrak{v}^-}\ G(\mathfrak{e},\mathfrak{u}) \times \mathcal{J}(\mathfrak{e},\mathfrak{u}) \end{bmatrix} \\
&+\left[\tfrac{\alpha}{2(\alpha+1)(\alpha+2)} + \tfrac{\beta}{(\beta+1)(\beta+2)}\left(\tfrac{1}{2} - \tfrac{\alpha}{(\alpha+1)(\alpha+2)}\right)\right]\mathcal{M}(\mathfrak{e},\mathfrak{g},\mathfrak{u},\mathfrak{v}) \\
&+\left[\tfrac{1}{2}\left(\tfrac{1}{2} - \tfrac{\alpha}{(\alpha+1)(\alpha+2)}\right) + \tfrac{\alpha}{(\alpha+1)(\alpha+2)}\tfrac{\beta}{(\beta+1)(\beta+2)}\right]P(\mathfrak{e},\mathfrak{g},\mathfrak{u},\mathfrak{v}) \\
&+\left[\tfrac{1}{2}\left(\tfrac{1}{2} - \tfrac{\beta}{(\beta+1)(\beta+2)}\right) + \tfrac{\alpha}{(\alpha+1)(\alpha+2)}\tfrac{\beta}{(\beta+1)(\beta+2)}\right]\mathcal{N}(\mathfrak{e},\mathfrak{g},\mathfrak{u},\mathfrak{v}) \\
&+\left[\tfrac{1}{4} - \tfrac{\alpha}{(\alpha+1)(\alpha+2)}\tfrac{\beta}{(\beta+1)(\beta+2)}\right]Q(\mathfrak{e},\mathfrak{g},\mathfrak{u},\mathfrak{v}).
\end{aligned} \tag{73}
$$

If $G_*((x,y),\ \gamma) = G^*((x,y),\ \gamma)$ *and* $\mathcal{J}_*((x,y),\ \gamma) = \mathcal{J}^*((x,y),\ \gamma)$ *with* $\gamma = 1$ *and* $\rrbracket(\tau) = \tau,\ \rrbracket(\kappa) = \kappa$, *then, from (68), we succeed in bringing about the upcoming inequality (see [69]):*

$$
\begin{aligned}
&4G\left(\tfrac{\mathfrak{e}+\mathfrak{g}}{2},\ \tfrac{\mathfrak{u}+\mathfrak{v}}{2}\right) \times \mathcal{J}\left(\tfrac{\mathfrak{e}+\mathfrak{g}}{2},\ \tfrac{\mathfrak{u}+\mathfrak{v}}{2}\right) \\
&\leq \tfrac{\Gamma(\alpha+1)\Gamma(\beta+1)}{4(\mathfrak{g}-\mathfrak{e})^{\alpha}(\mathfrak{v}-\mathfrak{u})^{\beta}} \begin{bmatrix} \mathcal{I}^{\alpha,\ \beta}_{\mathfrak{e}^+,\mathfrak{u}^+} G(\mathfrak{g},\mathfrak{v}) \times \mathcal{J}(\mathfrak{g},\mathfrak{v}) + \mathcal{I}^{\alpha,\ \beta}_{\mathfrak{e}^+,\mathfrak{v}^-} G(\mathfrak{g},\mathfrak{u}) \times \mathcal{J}(\mathfrak{g},\mathfrak{u}) \\ +\mathcal{I}^{\alpha,\ \beta}_{\mathfrak{g}^-,\mathfrak{u}^+} G(\mathfrak{e},\mathfrak{v}) \times \mathcal{J}(\mathfrak{e},\mathfrak{v}) + \mathcal{I}^{\alpha,\ \beta}_{\mathfrak{g}^-,\mathfrak{v}^-} G(\mathfrak{e},\mathfrak{u}) \times \mathcal{J}(\mathfrak{e},\mathfrak{u}) \end{bmatrix}. \\
&+\left[\tfrac{\alpha}{2(\alpha+1)(\alpha+2)} + \tfrac{\beta}{(\beta+1)(\beta+2)}\left(\tfrac{1}{2} - \tfrac{\alpha}{(\alpha+1)(\alpha+2)}\right)\right]\mathcal{M}(\mathfrak{e},\mathfrak{g},\mathfrak{u},\mathfrak{v}) \\
&+\left[\tfrac{1}{2}\left(\tfrac{1}{2} - \tfrac{\alpha}{(\alpha+1)(\alpha+2)}\right) + \tfrac{\alpha}{(\alpha+1)(\alpha+2)}\tfrac{\beta}{(\beta+1)(\beta+2)}\right]P(\mathfrak{e},\mathfrak{g},\mathfrak{u},\mathfrak{v}) \\
&+\left[\tfrac{1}{2}\left(\tfrac{1}{2} - \tfrac{\beta}{(\beta+1)(\beta+2)}\right) + \tfrac{\alpha}{(\alpha+1)(\alpha+2)}\tfrac{\beta}{(\beta+1)(\beta+2)}\right]\mathcal{N}(\mathfrak{e},\mathfrak{g},\mathfrak{u},\mathfrak{v}) \\
&+\left[\tfrac{1}{4} - \tfrac{\alpha}{(\alpha+1)(\alpha+2)}\tfrac{\beta}{(\beta+1)(\beta+2)}\right]Q(\mathfrak{e},\mathfrak{g},\mathfrak{u},\mathfrak{v}).
\end{aligned} \tag{74}
$$

4. Conclusions

This study makes use of fuzzy-number-valued fractional integrals to handle certain fractional integral inclusions involving the Hermite–Hadamard integral inequality via a newly defined class of coordinated *UD*-Ꞁ-convex *FNVMs*. We also look into other set inclusion connections related to the fractional Pachpatte integral inequality. Additionally, a few examples are provided to support the accuracy of the conclusions drawn in the research. We highlight the links between the results obtained here and those previously published in order to demonstrate the generic properties of the fuzzy set inclusion relations offered. Based on published works [59,68] and the bibliographies cited in them, we can confidently conclude that fuzzy-number-valued analyses are commonly used in applied analyses, particularly in the field of optimality analysis. In the integration with the fuzzy-number-valued fractional integral operators, the fuzzy *UD*-inclusion relations are somewhat interesting and need more investigation.

Author Contributions: Conceptualization, M.B.K.; validation, M.B.K.; formal analysis, E.R.N., K.H.H. and C.-C.L.; investigation, M.B.K.; resources, M.B.K., E.R.N., C.-C.L., D.-C.L. and K.H.H.; writing—original draft, M.B.K.; writing—review and editing, M.B.K., E.R.N., K.H.H., C.-C.L., D.-C.L. and H.G.Z.; visualization, M.B.K.; supervision, M.B.K. and H.G.Z.; project administration, H.G.Z. and D.-C.L. All authors have read and agreed to the published version of the manuscript.

Funding: This work was supported by the National Science and Technology Council of the Republic of China under Contract No. MOST 111-2221-E-182-048- and Chang Gung Memorial Hospital under the grant BMRPB30. The researchers also would like to acknowledge Deanship of Scientific Research, Taif University for funding this work.

Data Availability Statement: Data sharing is not applicable to this article.

Acknowledgments: The authors would like to thank Transilvania University of Brasov, Romania, for providing excellent research. The researchers also would like to acknowledge Deanship of Scientific Research, Taif University for funding this work.

Conflicts of Interest: The authors claim to have no conflicts of interest.

References

1. Chu, Y.-M.; Wang, G.-D.; Zhang, X.-H. The Schur multiplicative and harmonic convexities of the complete symmetric function. *Math. Nachr.* **2011**, *284*, 653–663. [CrossRef]
2. Chu, Y.-M.; Xia, W.-F.; Zhang, X.-H. The Schur concavity, Schur multiplicative and harmonic convexities of the second dual form of the Hamy symmetric function with applications. *J. Multivar. Anal.* **2012**, *105*, 412–421. [CrossRef]
3. Nwaeze, E.R.; Khan, M.A.; Chu, Y.M. Fractional inclusions of the Hermite-Hadamard type for m-polynomial convex interval valued functions. *Adv. Differ. Equ.* **2020**, *2020*, 507. [CrossRef]
4. Zhao, T.H.; He, Z.Y.; Chu, Y.M. On some refinements for inequalities involving zero-balanced hyper geometric function. *AIMS Math.* **2020**, *5*, 6479–6495. [CrossRef]
5. Zhao, T.H.; Wang, M.K.; Chu, Y.M. A sharp double inequality involving generalized complete elliptic integral of the first kind. *AIMS Math.* **2020**, *5*, 4512–4528. [CrossRef]
6. Dragomir, S.S.; Pearce, C.E.M. Selected topics on Hermite–Hadamard inequalities and applications. In *RGMIA*; Victoria University: Melbourne, VIC, Australia, 2000.
7. Peajcariaac, J.E.; Tong, Y.L. *Convex Functions, Partial Orderings, and Statistical Applications*; Academic Press: Cambridge, MA, USA, 1992.
8. Zhao, T.H.; Wang, M.K.; Hai, G.J.; Chu, Y.M. Landen inequalities for Gaussian hypergeometric function. *Racsam Rev. R. Acad. A* **2022**, *116*, 53. [CrossRef]
9. Wang, M.K.; Hong, M.Y.; Xu, Y.F.; Shen, Z.H.; Chu, Y.M. Inequalities for generalized trigonometric and hyperbolic functions with one parameter. *J. Math. Inequal.* **2020**, *14*, 1–21. [CrossRef]
10. Zhao, T.H.; Shi, L.; Chu, Y.M. Convexity and concavity of the modified Bessel functions of the first kind with respect to Hölder means. *Racsam Rev. R. Acad. A* **2020**, *114*, 96. [CrossRef]
11. Zhao, T.H.; Zhou, B.C.; Wang, M.K.; Chu, Y.M. On approximating the quasi-arithmetic mean. *J. Inequal. Appl.* **2019**, *2019*, 42. [CrossRef]
12. Zhao, T.H.; Wang, M.K.; Zhang, W.; Chu, Y.M. Quadratic transformation inequalities for Gaussian hyper geometric function. *J. Inequal. Appl.* **2018**, *2018*, 251. [CrossRef] [PubMed]
13. Qian, W.M.; Chu, H.H.; Wang, M.K.; Chu, Y.M. Sharp inequalities for the Toader mean of order −1 in terms of other bivariate means. *J. Math. Inequal.* **2022**, *16*, 127–141. [CrossRef]
14. Zhao, T.H.; Chu, H.H.; Chu, Y.M. Optimal Lehmer mean bounds for the nth power-type Toader mean of n = −1, 1, 3. *J. Math. Inequal.* **2022**, *16*, 157–168. [CrossRef]
15. Wang, M.-K.; Chu, Y.-M. Refinements of transformation inequalities for zero-balanced hypergeometric functions. *Acta Math. Sci.* **2017**, *37*, 607–622. [CrossRef]
16. Wang, M.-K.; Chu, Y.-M. Landen inequalities for a class of hypergeometric functions with applications. *Math. Inequal. Appl.* **2018**, *21*, 521–537. [CrossRef]
17. Wu, S.; Awan, M.U.; Noor, M.A.; Noor, K.I.; Iftikhar, S. On a new class of convex functions and integral inequalities. *J. Inequalities Appl.* **2019**, *2019*, 131. [CrossRef]
18. Kashuri, A.; Awan, M.U.; Talib, S.; Noor, M.A.; Noor, K.I. On Exponetially $-Preinvex Functions and Associated Trapezium Like Inequalities. *Appl. Anal. Discret. Math.* **2021**, *15*, 317–336. [CrossRef]
19. Wang, M.-K.; Chu, Y.-M.; Qiu, Y.-F.; Qiu, S.-L. An optimal power mean inequality for the complete elliptic integrals. *Appl. Math. Lett.* **2011**, *24*, 887–890. [CrossRef]
20. Wang, M.-K.; Chu, Y.-M.; Zhang, W. Monotonicity and inequalities involving zero-balanced hypergeometric function. *Math. Inequal. Appl.* **2019**, *22*, 601–617. [CrossRef]
21. Chu, Y.-M.; Wang, M.-K. Inequalities between arithmetic geometric, Gini, and Toader means. *Abstr. Appl. Anal.* **2012**, *2012*, 830585. [CrossRef]
22. Moore, R.E. *Interval Analysis*; Prentice-Hall: Englewood Cliffs, NJ, USA, 1966; Volume 4, pp. 8–13.
23. Breckner, W.W. Continuity of generalized convex and generalized concave set-valued functions. *Rev. D'Anal. Numer. Theor. L'Approx* **1993**, *22*, 39–51.

24. Kilbas, A.A.; Srivastava, H.M.; Trujillo, J.J. *Theory and Applications of Fractional Differential Equations*; Elsevier: Amsterdam, The Netherlands, 2006; Volume 204.
25. Hu, X.-M.; Tian, J.-F.; Chu, Y.-M.; Lu, Y.-X. On Cauchy–Schwarz inequality for N-tuple diamond-alpha integral. *J. Inequal. Appl.* **2020**, *2020*, 8. [CrossRef]
26. Zhao, T.-H.; Chu, Y.-M.; Wang, H. Logarithmically complete monotonicity properties relating to the gamma function. *Abstr. Appl. Anal.* **2011**, *2011*, 896483. [CrossRef]
27. Chu, Y.M.; Rauf, A.; Ishtiaq, M.; Siddiqui, M.K.; Muhammad, M.H. Topological properties of polycyclic aromatic nanostars dendrimers. *Polycycl. Aromat. Compd.* **2022**, *42*, 1891–1908. [CrossRef]
28. Ashpazzadeh, E.; Chu, Y.-M.; Hashemi, M.S.; Moharrami, M.; Inc, M. Hermite multiwavelets representation for the sparse solution of nonlinear Abel's integral equation. *Appl. Math. Comput.* **2022**, *427*, 127171. [CrossRef]
29. Chu, Y.-M.; Ullah, S.; Ali, M.; Tuzzahrah, G.F.; Munir, T. Numerical investigation of Volterra integral equations of second kind using optimal homotopy asymptotic methd. *Appl. Math. Comput.* **2022**, *430*, 127304.
30. Chu, Y.-M.; Inc, M.; Hashemi, M.S.; Eshaghi, S. Analytical treatment of regularized Prabhakar fractional differential equations by invariant subspaces. *Comput. Appl. Math.* **2022**, *41*, 271. [CrossRef]
31. Chalco-Cano, Y.; Flores-Franulic, A.; Roman-Flores, H. Ostrowski type inequalities for interval-valued functions using generalized Hukuhara derivative. *Comput. Appl. Math.* **2012**, *31*, 457–472.
32. Chalco-Cano, Y.; Lodwick, W.A.; Condori-Equice, W. Ostrowski type inequalities and applications in numerical integration for interval-valued functions. *Soft Comput.* **2015**, *19*, 3293–3300. [CrossRef]
33. Costa, T.M.; Román-Flores, H. Some integral inequalities for fuzzy-interval-valued functions. *Inf. Sci.* **2017**, *420*, 110–125. [CrossRef]
34. Roman-Flores, H.; Chalco-Cano, Y.; Lodwick, W. Some integral inequalities for interval-valued functions. *Comput. Appl. Math.* **2018**, *37*, 1306–1318. [CrossRef]
35. Sharma, N.; Singh, S.K.; Mishra, S.K.; Hamdi, A. Hermite-Hadamard-type inequalities for interval-valued preinvex functions via Riemann-Liouville fractional integrals. *J. Inequalities Appl.* **2021**, *2021*, 98. [CrossRef]
36. Zhao, D.; An, T.; Ye, G.; Liu, W. New Jensen and Hermite-Hadamard type inequalities for H-convex interval-valued functions. *J. Inequalities Appl.* **2018**, *2018*, 302. [CrossRef]
37. Zhao, D.; An, T.; Ye, G.; Liu, W. Chebyshev type inequalities for interval-valued functions. *Fuzzy Sets Syst.* **2020**, *396*, 82–101. [CrossRef]
38. Sarikaya, M.Z.; Set, E.; Yaldiz, H.; Basak, N. Hermite-Hadamard's inequalities for fractional integrals and related fractional inequalities. *Math. Comput. Model.* **2013**, *57*, 2403–2407. [CrossRef]
39. Mohammed, P.O.; Sarikaya, M.Z.; Baleanu, D. On the generalized Hermite-Hadamard inequalities via the tempered fractional integrals. *Symmetry* **2020**, *12*, 595. [CrossRef]
40. Mohammed, P.O.; Brevik, I. A new version of the Hermite-Hadamard inequality for Riemann-Liouville fractional integrals. *Symmetry* **2020**, *12*, 610. [CrossRef]
41. Saeed, T.; Cătaş, A.; Khan, M.B.; Alshehri, A.M. Some New Fractional Inequalities for Coordinated Convexity over Convex Set Pertaining to Fuzzy-Number-Valued Settings Governed by Fractional Integrals. *Fractal Fract.* **2023**, *7*, 856. [CrossRef]
42. Saeed, T.; Khan, M.B.; Treanţă, S.; Alsulami, H.H.; Alhodaly, M.S. Interval Fejér-Type Inequalities for Left and Right-λ-Preinvex Functions in Interval-Valued Settings. *Axioms* **2022**, *11*, 368. [CrossRef]
43. Khan, M.B.; Cătaş, A.; Saeed, T. Generalized fractional integral inequalities for p-convex fuzzy interval-valued mappings. *Fractal Fract.* **2022**, *6*, 324. [CrossRef]
44. Kórus, P.; Valdés, J.E.N.; Bayraktar, B. Weighted Hermite–Hadamard integral inequalities for general convex functions. *Math. Biosci. Eng.* **2023**, *20*, 19929–19940. [CrossRef]
45. Akdemir, A.O.; Butt, S.I.; Nadeem, M.; Ragusa, M.A. New general variants of Chebyshev type inequalities via generalized fractional integral operators. *Mathematics* **2021**, *9*, 122. [CrossRef]
46. Set, E.; Butt, S.I.; Akdemir, A.O.; Karaoglan, A.; Abdeljawad, T. New integral inequalities for differentiable convex functions via Atangana-Baleanu fractional integral operators. *Chaos Solitons Fractals* **2021**, *143*, 110554. [CrossRef]
47. Budak, H.; Tunc, T.; Sarikaya, M. Fractional Hermite-Hadamard-type inequalities for interval-valued functions. *Proc. Am. Math. Soc.* **2020**, *148*, 705–718. [CrossRef]
48. Kara, H.; Ali, M.A.; Budak, H. Hermite-Hadamard-type inequalities for interval-valued coordinated convex functions involving generalized fractional integrals. *Math. Methods Appl. Sci.* **2021**, *44*, 104–123. [CrossRef]
49. Mohsin, B.B.; Awan, M.U.; Javed, M.Z.; Budak, H.; Khan, A.G.; Noor, M.A. Inclusions Involving Interval-Valued Harmonically Co-Ordinated Convex Functions and Raina's Fractional Double Integrals. *J. Math.* **2022**, *2022*, 5815993. [CrossRef]
50. Zhou, T.; Du, T. Certain Fractional Integral Inclusions Pertaining to Interval-Valued Exponential Trigonometric Convex Functions. *J. Math. Inequalities* **2023**, *17*, 283–314. [CrossRef]
51. Khan, M.B.; Catas, A.; Aloraini, N.; Soliman, M.S. Some New Versions of Fractional Inequalities for Exponential Trigonometric Convex Mappings via Ordered Relation on Interval-Valued Settings. *Fractal Fract.* **2023**, *7*, 223. [CrossRef]
52. Kalsoom, H.; Ali, M.A.; Idrees, M.; Agarwal, P.; Arif, M. New post quantum analogues of Hermite-Hadamard type inequalities for interval-valued convex functions. *Math. Probl. Eng.* **2021**, *2021*, 5529650. [CrossRef]
53. Bin-Mohsin, B.; Rafique, S.; Cesarano, C.; Javed, M.Z.; Awan, M.U.; Kashuri, A.; Noor, M.A. Some General Fractional Integral Inequalities Involving LR-Bi-Convex Fuzzy Interval-Valued Functions. *Fractal Fract.* **2022**, *6*, 565. [CrossRef]

54. Kara, H.; Budak, H.; Ali, M.A.; Sarikaya, M.Z.; Chu, Y.M. Weighted Hermite-Hadamard type inclusions for products of coordinated convex interval-valued functions. *Adv. Differ. Eqs.* **2021**, *2021*, 104. [CrossRef]
55. Budak, H.; Kara, H.; Ali, M.A.; Khan, S.; Chu, Y. Fractional Hermite-Hadamard-type inequalities for interval-valued coordinated convex functions. *Open Math.* **2021**, *19*, 1081–1097. [CrossRef]
56. Ali, M.A.; Budak, H.; Murtaza, G.; Chu, Y.M. Post-quantum Hermite-Hadamard type inequalities for interval-valued convex functions. *J. Inequalities Appl.* **2021**, *2021*, 84. [CrossRef]
57. Du, T.; Zhou, T. On the fractional double integral inclusion relations having exponential kernels via interval-valued coordinated convex mappings. *Chaos Solitons Fractals* **2022**, *156*, 111846. [CrossRef]
58. Abdeljawad, T.; Rashid, S.; Khan, H.; Chu, Y.M. On new fractional integral inequalities for p-convexity within interval-valued functions. *Adv. Differ. Eqs.* **2020**, *2020*, 330. [CrossRef]
59. Khan, M.B.; Mohammed, P.O.; Noor, M.A.; Abualnaja, K.M. Fuzzy integral inequalities on coordinates of convex fuzzy interval-valued functions. *Math. Biosci. Eng.* **2021**, *18*, 6552–6580. [CrossRef]
60. Bin-Mohsin, B.; Awan, M.U.; Javed, M.Z.; Khan, A.G.; Budak, H.; Mihai, M.V.; Noor, M.A. Generalized AB-Fractional Operator Inclusions of Hermite-Hadamard's Type via Fractional Integration. *Symmetry* **2023**, *15*, 1012. [CrossRef]
61. Vivas-Cortez, M.; Ramzan, S.; Awan, M.U.; Javed, M.Z.; Khan, A.G.; Noor, M.A. IV-CR-γ-Convex Functions and Their Application in Fractional Hermite-Hadamard Inequalities. *Symmetry* **2023**, *15*, 1405. [CrossRef]
62. Khan, M.B.; Santos-García, G.; Noor, M.A.; Soliman, M.S. Some new concepts related to fuzzy fractional calculus for up and down convex fuzzy-number valued functions and inequalities. *Chaos Solitons Fractals* **2022**, *164*, 112692. [CrossRef]
63. Diamond, P.; Kloeden, P. *Metric Spaces of Fuzzy Sets: Theory and Applications*; World Scientific: Singapore, 1994.
64. Bede, B. *Mathematics of Fuzzy Sets and Fuzzy Logic, Volume 295 of Studies in Fuzziness and Soft Computing*; Springer: Berlin/Heidelberg, Germany, 2013.
65. Zhang, D.; Guo, C.; Chen, D.; Wang, G. Jensen's inequalities for set-valued and fuzzy set-valued functions. *Fuzzy Sets Syst.* **2020**, *404*, 178–204. [CrossRef]
66. Goetschel, R., Jr.; Voxman, W. Elementary fuzzy calculus. *Fuzzy Sets Syst.* **1986**, *18*, 31–43. [CrossRef]
67. Lupulescu, V. Fractional calculus for interval-valued functions. *Fuzzy Sets Syst.* **2015**, *265*, 63–85. [CrossRef]
68. Allahviranloo, T.; Salahshour, S.; Abbasbandy, S. Explicit solutions of fractional differential equations with uncertainty. *Soft Comput.* **2012**, *16*, 297–302. [CrossRef]
69. Khan, M.B.; Zaini, H.G.; Macías-Díaz, J.E.; Treanţă, S.; Soliman, M.S. Some Fuzzy Riemann–Liouville Fractional Integral Inequalities for Preinvex Fuzzy Interval-Valued Functions. *Symmetry* **2022**, *14*, 313. [CrossRef]
70. Khan, M.B.; Santos-García, G.; Zaini, H.G.; Treanţă, S.; Soliman, M.S. Some New Concepts Related to Integral Operators and Inequalities on Coordinates in Fuzzy Fractional Calculus. *Mathematics* **2022**, *10*, 534. [CrossRef]
71. Zhao, D.F.; Ali, M.A.; Murtaza, G. On the Hermite-Hadamard inequalities for interval-valued coordinated convex functions. *Ad. Differ. Equ.* **2020**, *2020*, 570. [CrossRef]
72. Budak, H.; Sarikaya, M.Z. Hermite-Hadamard type inequalities for products of two co-ordinated convex mappings via fractional integrals. *Int. J. Appl. Math. Stat.* **2019**, *58*, 11–30.
73. Khan, M.B.; Althobaiti, A.; Lee, C.-C.; Soliman, M.S.; Li, C.-T. Some New Properties of Convex Fuzzy-Number-Valued Mappings on Coordinates Using Up and Down Fuzzy Relations and Related Inequalities. *Mathematics* **2023**, *11*, 2851. [CrossRef]
74. Sarikaya, M.Z. On the Hermite-Hadamard-type inequalities for coordinated convex function via fractional integrals. Integral Transform. *Spec. Funct.* **2013**, *25*, 134–147.

Disclaimer/Publisher's Note: The statements, opinions and data contained in all publications are solely those of the individual author(s) and contributor(s) and not of MDPI and/or the editor(s). MDPI and/or the editor(s) disclaim responsibility for any injury to people or property resulting from any ideas, methods, instructions or products referred to in the content.

mathematics

Article

Dissipative Fuzzy Filtering for Nonlinear Networked Systems with Dynamic Quantization and Data Packet Dropouts

Shuxia Jing, Chengming Lu and Zhimin Li *

School of Electronic and Control Engineering, North China Institute of Aerospace Engineering, Langfang 065000, China; jsx01@nciae.edu.cn (S.J.); bhhtchengming@stumail.nciae.edu.cn (C.L.)
* Correspondence: lizhimin@nciae.edu.cn

Abstract: This paper discusses the dissipative filtering problem for discrete-time nonlinear networked systems with dynamic quantization and data packet dropouts. The Takagi–Sugeno (T–S) fuzzy model is employed to approximate the considered nonlinear plant. Both the measurement and performance outputs are assumed to be quantized by the dynamic quantizers before being transmitted. Moreover, the Bernoulli stochastic variables are utilized to characterize the effects of data packet dropouts on the measurement and performance outputs. The purpose of this paper is to design full- and reduced-order filters, such that the stochastic stability and dissipative filtering performance for the filtering error system can be guaranteed. The collaborative design conditions for the desired filter and the dynamic quantizers are expressed in the form of linear matrix inequalities. Finally, simulation results are used to illustrate the feasibility of the proposed filtering scheme.

Keywords: dissipative filtering; T–S fuzzy systems; dynamic quantization; data packet dropouts

MSC: 93C42

1. Introduction

In recent years, there has been a surge in academic interest in networked systems. The fundamental reason is that, due to their benefits of low cost, easy maintenance, and high reliability, networked systems are gradually replacing traditional control systems and taking center stage in the development of control systems [1]. Nowadays, networked systems are used in industries such as autonomous vehicles, industrial process control, smart homes, and others, with great success [2]. However, because of network restrictions, networked systems invariably generate some issues such as quantization, data packet dropouts, and so on [3]. These issues not only cause networked systems to run less efficiently, but they additionally possess the potential to cause instability. One of the primary sources of these issues is signal quantization inaccuracy and data packet dropouts. Among them, one of these causes of networked systems' poor operating efficiency and instability is quantization error. Therefore, it is crucial to deal with the analysis and design problems for networked systems subject to signal quantization and data packet dropouts. Over the past several years, a great number of achievements have been reported on these topics. The analysis and design problems for networked systems with quantization were addressed in [4–11]. The analysis and design problems for networked systems with data packet dropouts were studied in [8–12].

As is well known, nonlinearities exist in many practical physical systems [13]. Therefore, nonlinear control systems have attracted the attention of many scholars. As an effective means to deal with nonlinear systems, the Takagi–Sugeno (T–S) fuzzy model approach has received extensive attention from many international scholars and a series of important results have been published in the open literature (see, e.g., [14–16] and references therein). In recent years, based on the T–S fuzzy model approach, the study on networked systems has also attracted attention and some important results have been achieved (see, e.g., [17–20] and references therein). Particularly, based on the T–S fuzzy model approach, the control

Citation: Jing, S.; Lu, C.; Li, Z. Dissipative Fuzzy Filtering for Nonlinear Networked Systems with Dynamic Quantization and Data Packet Dropouts. *Mathematics* **2024**, *12*, 203. https://doi.org/10.3390/math12020203

Academic Editors: Lijuan Zha, Jian Liu and Jinliang Liu

Received: 4 December 2023
Revised: 4 January 2024
Accepted: 6 January 2024
Published: 8 January 2024

Copyright: © 2024 by the authors. Licensee MDPI, Basel, Switzerland. This article is an open access article distributed under the terms and conditions of the Creative Commons Attribution (CC BY) license (https://creativecommons.org/licenses/by/4.0/).

problem of nonlinear networked systems with quantization was studied in [21–26] and the control problem of nonlinear networked systems subject to data packet dropouts was addressed in [27–29].

In addition, the filtering problem is considered to be an important issue in the study of control theory because the state variables that can reflect the inside of the system are not always available in the vast majority of practical systems. Scholars at home and abroad have undertaken enormous research on the filtering problem and many significant results have been proposed. For linear networked systems, the filter design problem was researched in [30–32]. For nonlinear systems, the resilient mixed $\mathcal{H}_\infty$ and energy-to-peak filtering problem and the $\mathcal{H}_\infty$ filtering problem with D stability constraints were addressed based on the T–S fuzzy model approach in [33] and [34], respectively. For nonlinear networked systems, based on the T–S fuzzy model approach, the event-triggered $\mathcal{H}_\infty$ filtering problem was addressed with the effect of weighted try-once-discard protocol in [35]. Particularly, based on the T–S fuzzy model approach, the filtering problem for nonlinear networked systems with the effect of quantization was investigated in [36–41] and the filtering problem for nonlinear networked systems with the effects of data packet dropouts was considered in [39–43]. However, it should be noted that most of the above literature is about $\mathcal{H}_\infty$ filtering. As pointed out in [23,44], the dissipative performance is more general than the $\mathcal{H}_\infty$ performance. As a result, the study of the dissipative filtering problem is significant for nonlinear networked systems. As far as the author knows, there is no relevant research on the dissipative filtering problem for nonlinear discrete-time networked systems under the effects of dynamic quantization and data packet dropouts on the measurement output and the performance output, simultaneously, which motivated the current research.

This paper considered the quantized dissipative filtering problem of discrete-time nonlinear networked systems with data packet dropouts based on the T–S fuzzy model strategy. The primary contributions of this paper can be summarized as follows.

(1) According to the T–S fuzzy model approach, the dissipative filtering problem is investigated for discrete-time nonlinear networked systems subject to dynamic quantization and data packet dropouts.
(2) In this paper, both the effects of dynamic quantization and data packet dropouts on the measurement output and performance output are considered, simultaneously. Moreover, a more general adjusting strategy is proposed for the dynamic parameter of the dynamic quantizer.
(3) By introducing a dimension adjustment matrix, the design conditions for both the desired full- and reduced-order dissipative filters are proposed in the unified framework of linear matrix inequalities.

The rest of this paper is organized as follows. The filtering problem to be investigated is formulated in Section 2. In Section 3, the main results on the design of the dissipative filter with dynamic quantization and data packet dropouts are presented. In Section 4, an example is provided to demonstrate the effectiveness of the developed filtering strategy. Finally, the conclusion of this paper is provided in Section 5.

Notations: The notations used in this paper are standard. $\mathbf{R}^n$ and $\mathbf{R}^{m\times n}$ indicate the n-dimensional Euclidean space and the set of all real matrices of dimension $m \times n$, respectively. I is used to denote the identity matrix with compatible dimensions. $|\cdot|$ stands for Euclidean vector norm. The symbols $diag\{\cdots\}$ and $*$ are utilized to denote block-diagonal matrix and symmetric element in the matrix, respectively. A^T and A^{-1} represent the transpose matrix and inverse matrix of matrix A, respectively. $\lambda_{min}(A)$ stands for the smallest eigenvalue of the matrix A and $l_2[0, \infty)$ denotes the space of the square integrable vectors over $[0, \infty)$.

2. Problem Formulation

2.1. Nonlinear Plant

In this paper, a discrete-time T–S fuzzy model is used to approximate the nonlinear plant under consideration and ith is formulated as follows

Plant Rule i: IF $n_1(t)$ is M_{1i} and $n_2(t)$ is M_{2i} and ...and $n_p(t)$ is M_{pi}, THEN

$$\begin{aligned} x(t+1) &= A_i x(t) + B_i w(t) \\ y(t) &= C_i x(t) + D_i w(t) \\ z(t) &= E_i x(t) + F_i w(t) \end{aligned} \tag{1}$$

where $M_{\tau i}$ with $i = 1, 2, \ldots, s$ and $\tau = 1, 2, \ldots, p$ are the fuzzy sets, s stands for the number of fuzzy rules, and $n(t) = [n_1(t), n_2(t), \ldots, n_p(t)]$ stands for the premise variable. $x(t) \in \mathbf{R}^{n_x}$ and $y(t) \in \mathbf{R}^{n_y}$ stand for the system state and the measurement output, respectively, $z(t) \in \mathbf{R}^{n_z}$ stands for the performance output, and $w(t) \in \mathbf{R}^{n_w}$ stands for the noise signal belonging to $l_2[0, \infty)$. $A_i \in \mathbf{R}^{n_x \times n_x}$, $B_i \in \mathbf{R}^{n_x \times n_w}$, $C_i \in \mathbf{R}^{n_y \times n_x}$, $D_i \in \mathbf{R}^{n_y \times n_w}$, $E_i \in \mathbf{R}^{n_z \times n_x}$, and $F_i \in \mathbf{R}^{n_z \times n_w}$ are the system matrices.

Denote

$$b_i(n(t)) = \prod_{\tau=1}^{p} M_{\tau i}(n_\tau(t)),\ i = 1, 2, \ldots, s \tag{2}$$

where $M_{\tau i}(n_\tau(t))$ is the grade of membership of $n_\tau(t)$ in $M_{\tau i}$.

Throughout this paper, it is assumed that

$$b_i(n(t)) > 0,\ \sum_{i=1}^{s} b_i(n(t)) > 0,\ i = 1, 2, \ldots, s. \tag{3}$$

Let

$$p_i(n(t)) = \frac{b_i(n(t))}{\sum_{i=1}^{s} b_i(n(t))},\ i = 1, 2, \ldots, s. \tag{4}$$

Then

$$p_i(n(t)) \geq 0,\ \sum_{i=1}^{s} p_i(n(t)) = 1,\ i = 1, 2, \ldots, s. \tag{5}$$

Moreover, the T–S fuzzy model can be further represented as

$$\begin{aligned} x(t+1) &= A(p)x(t) + B(p)w(t) \\ y(t) &= C(p)x(t) + D(p)w(t) \\ z(t) &= E(p)x(t) + F(p)w(t) \end{aligned} \tag{6}$$

where

$$\begin{aligned} A(p) &= \sum_{i=1}^{s} p_i(n(t))A_i,\ B(p) = \sum_{i=1}^{s} p_i(n(t))B_i, \\ C(p) &= \sum_{i=1}^{s} p_i(n(t))C_i,\ D(p) = \sum_{i=1}^{s} p_i(n(t))D_i, \\ E(p) &= \sum_{i=1}^{s} p_i(n(t))E_i,\ F(p) = \sum_{i=1}^{s} p_i(n(t))F_i. \end{aligned}$$

2.2. Dynamic Quantizers and Data Dropouts

In order to reduce the frequency of information exchange and the burden of communication, the measurement output $y(t)$ and the performance output $z(t)$ will be quantized by the dynamic quantizer developed in [6], respectively. According to [6], the quantized measurement output and the quantized performance output can be formulated as

$$g_{\alpha_\varsigma(t)}(\varsigma(t)) = \alpha_\varsigma(t) g_\varsigma\left(\frac{\varsigma(t)}{\alpha_\varsigma(t)}\right),\ \varsigma = y, z. \tag{7}$$

In (7), $\alpha_\varsigma(t) > 0$ stands for the dynamic parameter of the quantizer and $g_\varsigma(\varsigma(t)/\alpha_\varsigma(t))$ stands for a static quantizer satisfying

$$\left| g_\varsigma\left(\frac{\varsigma(t)}{\alpha_\varsigma(t)}\right) - \frac{\varsigma(t)}{\alpha_\varsigma(t)} \right| \leq \Delta_\varsigma,\ \text{IF} \left| \frac{\varsigma(t)}{\alpha_\varsigma(t)} \right| \leq \mathcal{R}_\varsigma \tag{8}$$

$$\left|g_{\varsigma}\left(\frac{\varsigma(t)}{\alpha_{\varsigma}(t)}\right)-\frac{\varsigma(t)}{\alpha_{\varsigma}(t)}\right|>\Delta_{\varsigma},\ \text{IF}\left|\frac{\varsigma(t)}{\alpha_{\varsigma}(t)}\right|>\mathcal{R}_{\varsigma} \tag{9}$$

where $\mathcal{R}_{\varsigma}$ stands for the range of the quantizer and Δ_{ς} denotes the bound of the quantization error.

As an important challenge in networked systems, the effects of data packet dropouts will also be considered in this paper. Two independent Bernoulli stochastic variables ε and ρ will be employed to characterize the effects of data packet dropouts on the quantized measurement output and quantized performance output. In this way, the measurement output and performance output signals received by the filter can be indicated as

$$\bar{y}(t)=\varepsilon\alpha_{y}(t)g_{y}\left(\frac{y(t)}{\alpha_{y}(t)}\right),\ \ \alpha_{y}(t)>0 \tag{10}$$

$$\bar{z}(t)=\rho\alpha_{z}(t)g_{z}\left(\frac{z(t)}{\alpha_{z}(t)}\right),\ \ \alpha_{z}(t)>0. \tag{11}$$

This implies that the quantized measurement output (quantized performance output) is successfully transmitted when $\varepsilon=1$ ($\rho=1$), and that the quantized measurement output (quantized performance output) is unsuccessfully transmitted when $\varepsilon=0$ ($\rho=0$). Moreover, we assume that ε and ρ satisfy

$$\begin{aligned}&Prob\{\varepsilon=1\}=\mathbf{E}\{\varepsilon\}=\bar{\varepsilon}\\&Prob\{\varepsilon=0\}=1-\bar{\varepsilon}\\&Prob\{\rho=1\}=\mathbf{E}\{\rho\}=\bar{\rho}\\&Prob\{\rho=0\}=1-\bar{\rho}\end{aligned} \tag{12}$$

with known constants $0\leq\bar{\varepsilon}\leq1$ and $0\leq\bar{\rho}\leq1$.

Remark 1. *As claimed in [38,43], in the study of the filtering problem for networked systems, both the measurement and performance outputs should be transmitted by an unreliable communication network. Therefore, the effects of both the dynamic quantization and data packet dropouts on the measurement and performance outputs are considered in this paper. In contrast with the results in [38] where only the effects of quantization are considered, and the results in [43] where only the effects of data packet dropouts are considered, the problem studied in this paper is more general for networked systems.*

2.3. Filtering Error Systems

In this paper, the structure of the employed filter is provided as

$$\begin{aligned}x_{f}(t+1)&=\widehat{A}x_{f}(t)+\widehat{B}\bar{y}(t)\\z_{f}(t)&=\widehat{E}x_{f}(t)\end{aligned} \tag{13}$$

where $x_{f}(t)\in\mathbf{R}^{n_{\bar{x}}}$ denotes the state of the filter and $z_{f}(t)\in\mathbf{R}^{n_{z}}$ stands for the output of the filter. $\widehat{A}\in\mathbf{R}^{n_{\bar{x}}\times n_{\bar{x}}}$, $\widehat{B}\in\mathbf{R}^{n_{\bar{x}}\times n_{y}}$, and $\widehat{E}\in\mathbf{R}^{n_{z}\times n_{\bar{x}}}$ stand for the parameters of the designed filter. The structure of the filter in (13) is general, which can be utilized to investigate the full-order filtering problem with $n_{\bar{x}}=n_{x}$ and the reduced-order filtering problem with $1\leq n_{\bar{x}}<n_{x}$.

Then, we can express the filtering error system as

$$\begin{aligned}\phi(t+1)=&(A_{a}+\tilde{\varepsilon}A_{b})\phi(t)+(B_{a}+\tilde{\varepsilon}B_{b})w(t)\\&+(H_{a}+\tilde{\varepsilon}H_{b})r_{y}(t)\\e(t)=&(C_{a}+\tilde{\rho}C_{b})\phi(t)+(D_{a}+\tilde{\rho}D_{b})w(t)\\&+(\bar{\rho}+\tilde{\rho})r_{z}(t)\end{aligned} \tag{14}$$

where $\phi^T(t) = [x^T(t)\ x_f^T(t)]$, $e(t) = \bar{z}(t) - z_f(t)$, and

$$\begin{array}{l} A_a = \begin{bmatrix} A(p) & 0 \\ \bar{\varepsilon}\widehat{B}C(p) & \widehat{A} \end{bmatrix}, A_b = \begin{bmatrix} 0 & 0 \\ \widehat{B}C(p) & 0 \end{bmatrix}, \\ B_a = \begin{bmatrix} B(p) \\ \bar{\varepsilon}\widehat{B}D(p) \end{bmatrix}, B_b = \begin{bmatrix} 0 \\ \widehat{B}D(p) \end{bmatrix}, \\ H_a = \begin{bmatrix} 0 \\ \bar{\varepsilon}\widehat{B} \end{bmatrix}, H_b = \begin{bmatrix} 0 \\ \widehat{B} \end{bmatrix}, \\ C_a = \begin{bmatrix} \bar{\rho}E(p) & -\widehat{E} \end{bmatrix}, C_b = \begin{bmatrix} E(p) & 0 \end{bmatrix}, \\ D_a = \bar{\rho}F(p), D_b = F(p), \\ r_y(t) = \alpha_y(t)\left(g_y\left(\frac{y(t)}{\alpha_y(t)}\right) - \frac{y(t)}{\alpha_y(t)}\right), \\ r_z(t) = \alpha_z(t)\left(g_z\left(\frac{z(t)}{\alpha_z(t)}\right) - \frac{z(t)}{\alpha_z(t)}\right), \\ \tilde{\varepsilon} = \varepsilon - \bar{\varepsilon}, \tilde{\rho} = \rho - \bar{\rho}. \end{array}$$

Next, we will provide the definitions on the dissipativity and stochastic stability of the filtering error system (14), which will be needed in the process of dissipative filtering performance analysis.

Definition 1 ([27,37,43]). *For any initial condition $\phi(0)$, if there exists a matrix $Y > 0$ such that*

$$\mathbf{E}\left\{\sum_{t=0}^{\infty} |\phi(t)|^2 \Big| \phi(0)\right\} < \phi^T(0)Y\phi(0) \tag{15}$$

holds. Then, the filtering error system in (14) is stochastically stable with $w(t) = 0$.

Definition 2 ([44]). *For zero initial condition, the filtering error system in (14) is strictly dissipative with the dissipativity performance bound $\gamma > 0$, such that*

$$\begin{array}{l} \sum_{t=0}^{\varrho} \mathbf{E}\{(e^T(t)J_1e(t) + e^T(t)J_2w(t) + w^T(t) \\ \qquad \times J_2^Te(t) + w^T(t)(J_3 - \gamma I)w(t))\} \geq 0 \end{array} \tag{16}$$

holds with $\varrho \geq 0$. In (16), $J_1 = J_1^T \in \mathbf{R}^{n_z \times n_z} \leq 0$, $J_2 \in \mathbf{R}^{n_z \times n_w}$, and $J_3 = J_3^T \in \mathbf{R}^{n_w \times n_w}$ are known matrices and $-J_1 = J_{11}^TJ_{11}$ with $J_{11} \in \mathbf{R}^{n_z \times n_z} \geq 0$.

Finally, the purpose of this paper is to design the filter in the form of (13), such that the filtering error system in (14) is stochastically stable in the sense of Definition 1 and strictly dissipative in the sense of Definition 2.

3. Main Results

3.1. Filtering Performance Analysis

In this subsection, it is assumed that the filter (13) studied in this paper is known. Based on the Lyapunov approach, a significant dissipative filtering performance analysis criterion for the filtering error system (14) will be presented in the following theorem.

Theorem 1. *Suppose that the quantization ranges $\mathcal{R}_y$ and $\mathcal{R}_z$, the quantization error bounds Δ_y and Δ_z, and the constants $\bar{\rho}$, $\bar{\varepsilon}$, $\gamma > 0$, $0 < c_{1y} \leq c_{2y}$, $0 < d_{1y} \leq d_{2y}$, $0 < c_{1z} \leq c_{2z}$, $0 < d_{1z} \leq d_{2z}$, satisfying $c_{1y}d_{1y} \geq 1$ and $c_{1z}d_{1z} \geq 1$ are provided. The filtering error system in (14) is stochastically stable with the provided dissipative filtering performance γ, if there exist matrix $P > 0$, positive scalars o_y, o_z, ζ_y, and ζ_z satisfying*

$$\frac{c_{1\varsigma}}{\mathcal{R}_\varsigma} \leq o_\varsigma \leq \frac{c_{2\varsigma}}{\mathcal{R}_\varsigma},\ \varsigma = y,\ z \tag{17}$$

$$\begin{bmatrix} \Upsilon_{11} & * & * & * \\ \Upsilon_{21} & \Upsilon_{22} & * & * \\ \Upsilon_{31} & 0 & -I & * \\ \Upsilon_{41} & 0 & 0 & \Upsilon_{44} \end{bmatrix} < 0 \tag{18}$$

where

$$\Upsilon_{11} = \begin{bmatrix} -P & * & * & * \\ -J_2^T C_a & \Omega_{22} & * & * \\ 0 & 0 & -\zeta_y I & * \\ 0 & -\bar{\rho} J_2 & 0 & -\zeta_z I \end{bmatrix},$$
$$\Upsilon_{21} = \begin{bmatrix} A_a & B_a & H_a & 0 \\ \hat{\varepsilon} A_b & \hat{\varepsilon} B_b & \hat{\varepsilon} H_b & 0 \end{bmatrix},$$
$$\Upsilon_{31} = \begin{bmatrix} J_{11} C_a & J_{11} D_a & 0 & \bar{\rho} J_{11} \\ \hat{\rho} J_{11} C_b & \hat{\rho} J_{11} D_b & 0 & \hat{\rho} J_{11} \end{bmatrix},$$
$$\Upsilon_{41} = \begin{bmatrix} \sigma_y \overline{C} & \sigma_y \overline{D} & 0 & 0 \\ \sigma_z \overline{E} & \sigma_z \overline{F} & 0 & 0 \end{bmatrix},$$
$$\Omega_{22} = -J_2^T D_a - D_a^T J_2 - (J_3 - \gamma I),$$

$\Upsilon_{22} = -diag\{P^{-1}, P^{-1}\}$, $\Upsilon_{44} = -diag\{\zeta_y{}^{-1} I, \zeta_z{}^{-1} I\}$, $\hat{\varepsilon} = (\bar{\varepsilon}(1-\bar{\varepsilon}))^{1/2}$, $\hat{\rho} = (\bar{\rho}(1-\bar{\rho}))^{1/2}$, $\overline{C} = [C(p)\ 0]$, $\overline{D} = D(p)$, $\overline{E} = [E(p)\ 0]$, $\overline{F} = F(p)$, $\sigma_y = (c_{2y} d_{2y} \Delta_y)/\mathcal{R}_y$, $\sigma_z = (c_{2z} d_{2z} \Delta_z)/\mathcal{R}_z$, *and the adjusting strategy for the dynamic parameters* $\alpha_y(t)$ *and* $\alpha_z(t)$ *are provided as:*

$$d_{1\varsigma} o_\varsigma |\varsigma(t)| \le \alpha_\varsigma(t) \le d_{2\varsigma} o_\varsigma |\varsigma(t)|, \ \varsigma = y, z. \tag{19}$$

Proof. For the filtering error system (14), the Lyapunov function is established as

$$V(\phi(t)) = \phi^T(t) P \phi(t), \ P > 0. \tag{20}$$

Then, one can be obtain that

$$\begin{aligned}
&\mathbf{E}\{V(\phi(t+1))\} - V(\phi(t)) - \mathbf{E}\big\{(e^T(t) J_1 e(t) + e^T(t) \\
&\quad \times J_2 w(t) + w^T(t) J_2^T e(t) + w^T(t)(J_3 - \gamma I) w(t))\big\} \\
&= \mathbf{E}\{((A_a + \tilde{\varepsilon} A_b)\phi(t) + (B_a + \tilde{\varepsilon} B_b) w(t) \\
&+ (H_a + \tilde{\varepsilon} H_b) r_y(t))^T P((A_a + \tilde{\varepsilon} A_b)\phi(t) \\
&+ (B_a + \tilde{\varepsilon} B_b) w(t) + (H_a + \tilde{\varepsilon} H_b) r_y(t))\} \\
&- \phi^T(t) P \phi(t) - \mathbf{E}\{((C_a + \tilde{\rho} C_b)\phi(t) \\
&+ (D_a + \tilde{\rho} D_b) w(t) + (\tilde{\rho} + \bar{\rho}) r_z(t))^T J_1 \\
&((C_a + \tilde{\rho} C_b)\phi(t) + (D_a + \tilde{\rho} D_b) w(t) \\
&+ (\tilde{\rho} + \bar{\rho}) r_z(t)) + ((C_a + \tilde{\rho} C_b)\phi(t) \\
&+ (D_a + \tilde{\rho} D_b) w(t) + (\tilde{\rho} + \bar{\rho}) r_z(t))^T J_2 w(t) \\
&+ w^T(t) J_2^T ((C_a + \tilde{\rho} C_b)\phi(t) \\
&+ (D_a + \tilde{\rho} D_b) w(t) + (\tilde{\rho} + \bar{\rho}) r_z(t)) \\
&+ w^T(t)(J_3 - \gamma I) w(t)\} \\
&= \eta^T(t)\Big(\mathbf{E}\Big\{([\ A_a\ B_a\ H_a\ 0\ ] + \tilde{\varepsilon}[\ A_b\ B_b\ H_b\ 0\ ])^T \\
&P([\ A_a\ B_a\ H_a\ 0\ ] + \tilde{\varepsilon}[\ A_b\ B_b\ H_b\ 0\ ]) \\
&-([\ C_a\ D_a\ 0\ \bar{\rho} I\ ] + \tilde{\rho}[\ C_b\ D_b\ 0\ I\ ])^T J_1 \\
&([\ C_a\ D_a\ 0\ \bar{\rho} I\ ] + \tilde{\rho}[\ C_b\ D_b\ 0\ I\ ]) \\
&-([\ C_a\ D_a\ 0\ \bar{\rho} I\ ] + \tilde{\rho}[\ C_b\ D_b\ 0\ I\ ])^T \\
&J_2[\ 0\ I\ 0\ 0\ ] - [\ 0\ I\ 0\ 0\ ]^T J_2^T([\ C_a\ D_a\ 0\ \bar{\rho} I\ ] \\
&+ \tilde{\rho}[\ C_b\ D_b\ 0\ I\ ])\Big\} - diag\{P,\ J_3 - \gamma I,\ 0,\ 0\}\Big)\eta(t) \\
&= \eta^T(t) \Phi_0 \eta(t)
\end{aligned} \tag{21}$$

where $\eta^T(t) = [\,\phi^T(t)\; w^T(t)\; r_y^T(t)\; r_z^T(t)\,]$ and

$$\begin{aligned}\Phi_0 = & [\,A_a\; B_a\; H_a\; 0\,]^T P[\,A_a\; B_a\; H_a\; 0\,] \\ & + \hat{\varepsilon}^2[\,A_b\; B_b\; H_b\; 0\,]^T P[\,A_b\; B_b\; H_b\; 0\,] \\ & - [\,C_a\; D_a\; 0\; \bar{\rho}I\,]^T J_1[\,C_a\; D_a\; 0\; \bar{\rho}I\,] \\ & - \hat{\rho}^2[\,C_b\; D_b\; 0\; I\,]^T J_1[\,C_b\; D_b\; 0\; I\,] \\ & - [\,C_a\; D_a\; 0\; \bar{\rho}I\,]^T J_2[\,0\; I\; 0\; 0\,] \\ & - [\,0\; I\; 0\; 0\,]^T J_2^T[\,C_a\; D_a\; 0\; \bar{\rho}I\,] \\ & - diag\{P,\; J_3 - \gamma I,\; 0,\; 0\}.\end{aligned}$$

As in [4], based on the online adjusting strategy in (19) and the conditions in (8) and (17), we have

$$\begin{aligned} r_y^T(t)r_y(t) \le \sigma_y^2 y^T(t)y(t) \\ r_z^T(t)r_z(t) \le \sigma_z^2 z^T(t)z(t) \end{aligned} \tag{22}$$

which can be further expressed as

$$\begin{aligned} \eta^T(t)\Phi_1\eta(t) \ge 0 \\ \eta^T(t)\Phi_2\eta(t) \ge 0 \end{aligned} \tag{23}$$

with

$$\begin{aligned}\Phi_1 &= [\,\sigma_y\overline{C}\; \sigma_y\overline{D}\; 0\; 0\,]^T[\,\sigma_y\overline{C}\; \sigma_y\overline{D}\; 0\; 0\,] - diag\{0,\; 0,\; I,\; 0\}, \\ \Phi_2 &= [\,\sigma_z\overline{E}\; \sigma_z\overline{F}\; 0\; 0\,]^T[\,\sigma_z\overline{E}\; \sigma_z\overline{F}\; 0\; 0\,] - diag\{0,\; 0,\; 0,\; I\}.\end{aligned}$$

By utilizing the Schur complement to (18), we obtain

$$\Phi_0 + \zeta_y\Phi_1 + \zeta_z\Phi_2 < 0. \tag{24}$$

According to the S-Procedure in [6,36], we have that $\eta^T(t)\Phi_0\eta(t) < 0$ based on (21), (23), and (24), i.e.,

$$\begin{aligned} & \mathbf{E}\{V(\phi(t+1))\} - V(\phi(t)) - \mathbf{E}\{\,(e^T(t)J_1e(t) + e^T(t) \\ & \times J_2w(t) + w(t)^T J_2^T e(t) + w^T(t)(J_3 - \gamma I)w(t))\} < 0 \end{aligned} \tag{25}$$

Then, by summing up (25) from $t = 0$ to $t = \varrho$ with $\varrho \ge 1$, one can obtain

$$\begin{aligned} & \mathbf{E}\{V(\phi(\varrho+1))\} - V(\phi(0)) - \textstyle\sum_{t=0}^{\varrho} \mathbf{E}\{\,(e^T(t)J_1e(t) + e^T(t) \\ & \times J_2w(t) + w(t)^T J_2^T e(t) + w^T(t)(J_3 - \gamma I)w(t))\} < 0 \end{aligned} \tag{26}$$

By considering $\mathbf{E}\{V(\phi(\varrho+1))\} \ge 0$ and $V(\phi(0)) = 0$, we have

$$\begin{aligned} & \textstyle\sum_{t=0}^{\varrho} \mathbf{E}\{\,(e^T(t)J_1e(t) + e^T(t)J_2w(t) + w(t)^T \\ & \times J_2^T e(t) + w^T(t)(J_3 - \gamma I)w(t))\} \ge 0 \end{aligned} \tag{27}$$

Therefore, according to Definition 2, one can obtain that the given dissipative filtering performance bound $\gamma > 0$ of the filtering error system in (14) can be guaranteed.

Next, for $w(t) = 0$, the stochastic stability of the filtering error system in (14) will be discussed.

For $w(k) = 0$, the inequality in (25) reduces to

$$\mathbf{E}\{V(\phi(t+1))\} - V(\phi(t)) < \mathbf{E}\{e^T(t)J_1e(t)\}. \tag{28}$$

By considering the fact that $J_1 \le 0$, we have that

$$\mathbf{E}\{V(\phi(t+1))\} - V(\phi(t)) = \overline{\eta}^T(t)\widehat{\Phi}_0\overline{\eta}(t) < 0 \tag{29}$$

where $\overline{\eta}^T(t) = [\ \phi^T(t)\ r_y^T(t)\ r_z^T(t)\ ]$ and

$$\begin{aligned}\widehat{\Phi}_0 = {} & [\,A_a\ H_a\ 0\,]^T P[\,A_a\ H_a\ 0\,] + \bar{\varepsilon}^2[\,A_b\ H_b\ 0\,]^T \\ & \times P[\,A_b\ H_b\ 0\,] - [\,C_a\ 0\ \bar{\rho}I\,]^T J_1[\,C_a\ 0\ \bar{\rho}I\,] \\ & - \bar{\rho}^2[\,C_b\ 0\ I\,]^T J_1[\,C_b\ 0\ I\,] - diag\{P,\ 0,\ 0\}.\end{aligned}$$

Based on (29), it can be obtained that

$$\mathbf{E}\{V(\phi(t+1))\} - V(\phi(t)) \leq -\lambda_{\min}(-\widehat{\Phi}_0)\overline{\eta}^T(t)\overline{\eta}(t). \tag{30}$$

By calculating the mathematical expectation of (30) on both sides and summing up both sides of (30) from $t = 0$ to $t = \varrho$ with $\varrho \geq 1$, one can obtain that

$$\begin{aligned}& \mathbf{E}\{\phi^T(\varrho+1)P\phi(\varrho+1)\} - \phi^T(0)P\phi(0) \\ & \leq -\lambda_{\min}(-\widehat{\Phi}_0)\mathbf{E}\Big\{\textstyle\sum_{t=0}^{\varrho}|\overline{\eta}(t)|^2\Big\},\end{aligned} \tag{31}$$

which is equivalent to

$$\begin{aligned}& \mathbf{E}\Big\{\textstyle\sum_{t=0}^{\varrho}|\overline{\eta}(t)|^2\Big\} \\ & \leq (\lambda_{\min}(-\widehat{\Phi}_0))^{-1}(\phi^T(0)P\phi(0) - \mathbf{E}\{\phi^T(\varrho+1)P\phi(\varrho+1)\}).\end{aligned} \tag{32}$$

For $\varrho \longrightarrow \infty$, we have that $\mathbf{E}\{\phi^T(\infty)P\phi(\infty)\} \geq 0$ and $\mathbf{E}\{\sum_{t=0}^{\infty}|\overline{\eta}(t)|^2\} \geq \mathbf{E}\{\sum_{t=0}^{\infty}|\phi(t)|^2\}$. Then, based on inequality in (32), it can be obtained that

$$\begin{aligned}& \mathbf{E}\{\textstyle\sum_{t=0}^{\infty}|\phi(t)|^2\} \\ & \leq (\lambda_{\min}(-\widehat{\Phi}_0))^{-1}(\phi^T(0)P\phi(0)) \\ & = \phi^T(0)(\lambda_{\min}(-\widehat{\Phi}_0))^{-1}P\phi(0) = \phi^T(0)Y\phi(0)\end{aligned} \tag{33}$$

with $Y = (\lambda_{\min}(-\widehat{\Phi}_0))^{-1}P$.

According to $\overline{\eta}^T(t)\widehat{\Phi}_0\overline{\eta}(t) < 0$, it can be deduced that $\widehat{\Phi}_0 < 0$, which implies that $\lambda_{\min}(-\widehat{\Phi}_0) > 0$. Based on the above discussions, we have that $Y = (\lambda_{\min}(-\widehat{\Phi}_0))^{-1}P > 0$. Therefore, for $w(t) = 0$, one can obtain that the filtering error system in (14) is stochastically stable in accordance with Definition 1. □

Remark 2. *As pointed out in [4], the adjusting strategy for the dynamic parameters $\alpha_y(t)$ and $\alpha_z(t)$ proposed in (19) is more general than the one in [6,11,36] and the one in [21,37]. The adjusting strategy in [6,11,36] can be obtained from the one in (19) by choosing $d_{1\varsigma} = d_{2\varsigma}$ and the adjusting strategy in [21,37] can be obtained from the one in (19) by choosing $c_{1\varsigma} = 1$, $d_{1\varsigma} = 1$, and $d_{2\varsigma} = 2$. Moreover, another advantage of the adjusting strategy in (19) is that the constant o_ς is independent of the matrix inequality (18).*

3.2. Filter Design

Based on the results developed in Theorem 1, the design results characterized by linear matrix inequalities for the desired filter in (13) will be proposed in the following theorem.

Theorem 2. *Suppose that the quantization ranges $\mathcal{R}_y$ and $\mathcal{R}_z$, the quantization error bounds Δ_y and Δ_z, the dimension adjustment matrix K, and the constants $\bar{\rho}$, $\bar{\varepsilon}$, $\gamma > 0$, $0 < c_{1y} \leq c_{2y}$, $0 < d_{1y} \leq d_{2y}$, $0 < c_{1z} \leq c_{2z}$, $0 < d_{1z} \leq d_{2z}$, satisfying $c_{1y}d_{1y} \geq 1$ and $c_{1z}d_{1z} \geq 1$ are provided. In the presence of the adjusting strategy for the dynamic parameters $\alpha_y(t)$ and $\alpha_z(t)$ provided in (19) with the inequality in (17), the filtering error system in (14) is stochastically stable with the provided dissipative filtering performance γ, if there exist matrices $P_1 > 0$, P_2, $P_3 > 0$, G_1, G_2, $\widetilde{A}$, $\widetilde{B}$, $\widetilde{E}$, nonsingular matrix G_3, and positive scalars ζ_y, ζ_z satisfying*

$$\Psi_i < 0,\ i = 1, 2, \ldots, s. \tag{34}$$

where

$$\Psi_i = \begin{bmatrix} \Theta_{11_i} & * & * & * & * \\ \Theta_{21_i} & \Theta_{22} & * & * & * \\ \Theta_{31_i} & 0 & \Theta_{22} & * & * \\ \Theta_{41_i} & 0 & 0 & -I & 0 \\ \Theta_{51_i} & 0 & 0 & 0 & \Theta_{55} \end{bmatrix},$$

$$\Theta_{11_i} = \begin{bmatrix} -P_1 & * & * & * & * \\ -P_2 & -P_3 & * & * & * \\ -\bar{\rho} J_2^T E_i & J_2^T \widetilde{E} & \Lambda_{33} & * & * \\ 0 & 0 & 0 & -\zeta_y I & * \\ 0 & 0 & -\bar{\rho} J_2 & 0 & -\zeta_z I \end{bmatrix},$$

$$\Lambda_{33} = -\bar{\rho} F_i^T J_2 - \bar{\rho} J_2^T F_i - (J_3 - \gamma I),$$

$$\Theta_{21_i} = \begin{bmatrix} \Delta_{11} & K\widetilde{A} & \Delta_{13} & \bar{\varepsilon} K \widetilde{B} & 0 \\ \Delta_{21} & \widetilde{A} & \Delta_{23} & \bar{\varepsilon} \widetilde{B} & 0 \end{bmatrix},$$

$$\Theta_{31_i} = \begin{bmatrix} \hat{\varepsilon} K \widetilde{B} C_i & 0 & \hat{\varepsilon} K \widetilde{B} D_i & \hat{\varepsilon} K \widetilde{B} & 0 \\ \hat{\varepsilon} \widetilde{B} C_i & 0 & \hat{\varepsilon} \widetilde{B} D_i & \hat{\varepsilon} \widetilde{B} & 0 \end{bmatrix},$$

$$\Theta_{41_i} = \begin{bmatrix} \bar{\rho} J_{11} E_i & -J_{11} \widetilde{E} & \bar{\rho} J_{11} F_i & 0 & \bar{\rho} J_{11} \\ \hat{\rho} J_{11} E_i & 0 & \hat{\rho} J_{11} F_i & 0 & \hat{\rho} J_{11} \end{bmatrix},$$

$$\Theta_{51_i} = \begin{bmatrix} \zeta_y \sigma_y C_i & 0 & \zeta_y \sigma_y D_i & 0 & 0 \\ \zeta_z \sigma_z E_i & 0 & \zeta_z \sigma_z F_i & 0 & 0 \end{bmatrix},$$

$$\Theta_{22} = \begin{bmatrix} P_1 - G_1 - G_1^T & * \\ P_2 - G_2 - G_3^T K^T & P_3 - G_3 - G_3^T \end{bmatrix},$$

$$\Theta_{55} = -diag\{\zeta_y I, \ \zeta_z I\},$$

$$\Delta_{11} = G_1 A_i + \bar{\varepsilon} K \widetilde{B} C_i, \Delta_{21} = G_2 A_i + \bar{\varepsilon} \widetilde{B} C_i,$$

$$\Delta_{13} = G_1 B_i + \bar{\varepsilon} K \widetilde{B} D_i, \Delta_{23} = G_2 B_i + \bar{\varepsilon} \widetilde{B} D_i.$$

Moreover, the parameters for the filter (13) can be obtained by

$$\widehat{A} = G_3^{-1} \widetilde{A}, \ \widehat{B} = G_3^{-1} \widetilde{B}, \ \widehat{E} = \widetilde{E}. \tag{35}$$

Proof. For the nonsingular matrix G, based on $-(P-G)^T P^{-1} (P-G) \leq 0$ and $P > 0$, we have that

$$-G^T P^{-1} G \leq -G - G^T + P \tag{36}$$

By considering (36) and performing congruence transformation to (18) by $diag\{I, \ \widehat{G}^T, I, \ \widehat{\zeta}\}$ with $\widehat{G} = diag\{G, \ G\}$ and $\widehat{\zeta} = diag\{\zeta_y I, \ \zeta_z I\}$, it can be obtained that

$$\begin{bmatrix} \Upsilon_{11} & * & * & * \\ \overline{\Upsilon}_{21} & \overline{\Upsilon}_{22} & * & * \\ \Upsilon_{31} & 0 & -I & * \\ \overline{\Upsilon}_{41} & 0 & 0 & \overline{\Upsilon}_{44} \end{bmatrix} < 0 \tag{37}$$

where

$$\overline{\Upsilon}_{21} = \begin{bmatrix} G^T A_a & G^T B_a & G^T H_a & 0 \\ \hat{\varepsilon} G^T A_b & \hat{\varepsilon} G^T B_b & \hat{\varepsilon} G^T H_b & 0 \end{bmatrix},$$

$$\overline{\Upsilon}_{22} = diag\{ -G - G^T + P, -G - G^T + P\} \ ,$$

$$\overline{\Upsilon}_{41} = \begin{bmatrix} \zeta_y \sigma_y \overline{C} & \zeta_y \sigma_y \overline{D} & 0 & 0 \\ \zeta_z \sigma_z \overline{E} & \zeta_z \sigma_z \overline{F} & 0 & 0 \end{bmatrix},$$

$$\overline{\Upsilon}_{44} = -diag\{\zeta_y I, \ \zeta_z I\}.$$

We assume $P = \begin{bmatrix} P_1 & * \\ P_2 & P_3 \end{bmatrix}$, $G^T = \begin{bmatrix} G_1 & KG_3 \\ G_2 & G_3 \end{bmatrix}$ with G_3 is nonsingular and define $\widetilde{A} = G_3 \widehat{A}$, $\widetilde{B} = G_3 \widehat{B}$, and $\widetilde{E} = \widehat{E}$, the inequality in (37) can be expressed as

$$\sum_{i=1}^{s} p_i(n(t)) \Psi_i < 0 \tag{38}$$

Finally, by considering $p_i(n(t)) \geq 0$ stated in (5), one can deduce that if the inequality in (34) is satisfied, then the inequality in (38) holds, which completes the proof. □

Next, some discussions on the main results in this paper will be provided.

Remark 3. *In Theorem 2, for the provided dimension adjustment matrix* K*, both the full-order dissipative filter and the reduced-order dissipative filter design results are presented in a unified framework characterized by linear matrix inequalities, which can be effectively solved by the LMI toolbox. In general, the dimension adjustment matrix* K *can be chosen as* $\mathrm{K} = I_{n_x \times n_x}$ *for full-order dissipative filter and* $\mathrm{K} = \begin{bmatrix} I_{n_{\bar{x}} \times n_{\bar{x}}} & 0_{n_{\bar{x}} \times (n_x - n_{\bar{x}})} \end{bmatrix}^T$ *for reduced-order dissipative filter.*

Remark 4. *The deign results proposed in Theorem 2 on the dissipative filter for nonlinear networked systems with dynamic quantization and data packet dropouts are general. By selecting* $J_{11} = I$, $J_2 = 0$, *and* $J_3 = (\gamma^2 + \gamma)I$, *the deign results proposed in Theorem 2 can be utilized to design the* $\mathcal{H}_\infty$ *filter. By selecting* $J_{11} = 0$, $J_2 = I$, *and* $J_3 = 2\gamma I$, *the deign results proposed in Theorem 2 can be utilized to design the passive filter. By selecting* $J_{11} = \sqrt{\kappa} I$, $J_2 = (1-\kappa)I$, *and* $J_3 = (\kappa(\gamma^2 - \gamma) + 2\gamma)I$ *with* $0 \leq \kappa \leq 1$, *the deign results proposed in Theorem 2 can be utilized to design the mixed passive/*$\mathcal{H}_\infty$ *filter.*

Remark 5. *Based on the results in [8,21], we know that a feasible adjusting rule is necessary for the dynamic parameter* $\alpha_\varsigma(t)$ *due to the use of the unreliable transmission communication network. As in [4], the adjusting rule for the dynamic parameter* $\alpha_\varsigma(t)$ *in this paper is proposed as*

$$\alpha_\varsigma(t) = \mathit{floor}(d_{2\varsigma} o_\varsigma |\varsigma(t)| \times 10^{-\jmath})$$

where $\jmath = \min\{\jmath \in \mathcal{N}^+ | (d_{2\varsigma} o_\varsigma |\varsigma(t)| \times 10^{\jmath}) > 1\}$ *and the function* $\mathit{floor}(\hbar)$ *denotes the maximum integer that is not bigger than* $\hbar$.

Remark 6. *According to the conclusions in [23], we have that the numerical complexity of the design results proposed in Theorem 2 is closely related to the number of variables* V *and the number of rows* L*. Moreover, the deign conditions in Theorem 2 can be solved in polynomial time with complexity proportional to* $\mathrm{C} = \mathrm{V}^3\mathrm{L}$, *where* $\mathrm{V} = 2 + 2n_{\bar{x}}n_{\bar{x}} + 2n_{\bar{x}}n_x + \frac{1}{2}n_x(n_x+1) + \frac{1}{2}n_{\bar{x}}(n_{\bar{x}} + 1) + n_x n_x + n_{\bar{x}} n_y + n_{\bar{x}} n_z$ *and* $\mathrm{L} = (3n_x + 3n_{\bar{x}} + 2n_y + 4n_z + n_w)s$.

Remark 7. *In general,* $\mathcal{R}_y$, $\mathcal{R}_z$, Δ_y, Δ_z *are provided parameters for dynamic quantizers and* $\bar{\varepsilon}$, $\bar{\rho}$ *are provided parameters for data packet dropouts. However, how to deal with the dissipative filtering problem with the unknown parameters* $\mathcal{R}_y$, $\mathcal{R}_z$, Δ_y, Δ_z, $\bar{\varepsilon}$, *and* $\bar{\rho}$ *is still a open problem, which needs further study. Moreover, it should be noted that the conservatism of the results proposed in Theorem 2 can be further reduced by employing the fuzzy Lyapunov function strategy in [15] and introducing slack matrix variables via Lemma 4 in [45].*

4. Simulation Example

In this section, we will show that the proposed dissipative filtering strategy is effective via a practical example.

Consider the tunnel diode circuit depicted in Figure 1, which is also employed to study the l_2–l_∞ fuzzy filtering problem for nonlinear networked systems with dynamic quantization in [36]. As in [36], by choosing $x_1(t) = v_C(t)$, $x_2(t) = i_{L1}(t)$, and $x_3(t) = i_{L2}(t)$, state equations for the tunnel diode circuit can be represented as

$$\begin{aligned} \mathbb{C}\dot{x}_1(t) &= -\mathbb{W}x_1(t) - \mathbb{N}x_1^3(t) + x_2(t) + x_3(t) \\ \mathbb{L}_1\dot{x}_2(t) &= -x_1(t) - \mathbb{R}_1 x_2(t) + \mathbb{V}w(t) \\ \mathbb{L}_2\dot{x}_3(t) &= -x_1(t) - \mathbb{R}_2 x_3(t) \end{aligned} \tag{39}$$

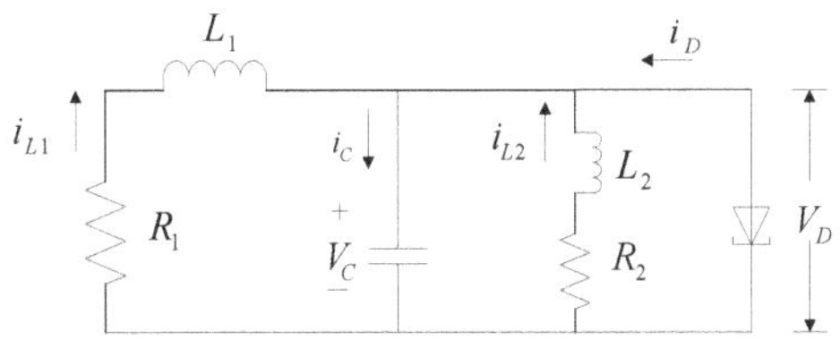

Figure 1. Tunnel diode circuit.

In this paper, we assume that $\mathbb{C} = 20\,\text{mF}$, $\mathbb{W} = 0.002\,\text{s}$, $\mathbb{N} = 0.01\,\text{s}$, $\mathbb{L}_1 = 1000\,\text{mH}$, $\mathbb{R}_1 = 10\,\Omega$, $\mathbb{V} = 1$, $\mathbb{L}_2 = 100\,\text{mH}$, $\mathbb{R}_2 = 1\,\Omega$, and $|x_1(t)| \leq 3$, i.e., $0 \leq x_1^2(t) \leq 9$. Then, the nonlinear tunnel diode circuit in (39) can be approximated by the following continuous-time T–S fuzzy model:

$$\begin{aligned} &\text{Plant Rule 1: IF } x_1^2(t) \text{ is } 0, \text{ THEN} \\ &\qquad \dot{x}(t) = A_1 x(t) + B_1 u(t) \\ &\text{Plant Rule 2: IF } x_1^2(t) \text{ is } 9, \text{ THEN} \\ &\qquad \dot{x}(t) = A_2 x(t) + B_2 u(t) \end{aligned} \tag{40}$$

where

$$A_1 = \begin{bmatrix} -0.1 & 50 & 50 \\ -1 & -10 & 0 \\ -10 & 0 & -10 \end{bmatrix}, \; B_1 = \begin{bmatrix} 0 \\ 1 \\ 0 \end{bmatrix},$$
$$A_2 = \begin{bmatrix} -4.6 & 50 & 50 \\ -1 & -10 & 0 \\ -10 & 0 & -10 \end{bmatrix}, \; B_2 = \begin{bmatrix} 0 \\ 1 \\ 0 \end{bmatrix}.$$

Moreover, the membership functions can be provided as

$$p_1(x_1(t)) = \begin{cases} 1 - \frac{x_1^2(t)}{9}, & -3 \leq x_1(t) \leq 3 \\ 0, & \text{otherwise} \end{cases}$$
$$p_2(x_1(t)) = 1 - p_1(x_1(t)).$$

By setting the sampling period $T = 0.02\,\text{s}$, we have that

$$A_1 = \begin{bmatrix} 0.8970 & 0.8726 & 0.8726 \\ -0.0175 & 0.8101 & -0.0086 \\ -0.1745 & -0.0859 & 0.7328 \end{bmatrix},$$
$$A_2 = \begin{bmatrix} 0.8170 & 0.8332 & 0.8332 \\ -0.0167 & 0.8104 & -0.0083 \\ -0.1666 & -0.0833 & 0.7354 \end{bmatrix},$$
$$B_1 = \begin{bmatrix} 0.0092 \\ 0.0181 \\ -0.0006 \end{bmatrix}, \; B_2 = \begin{bmatrix} 0.0089 \\ 0.0181 \\ -0.0006 \end{bmatrix},$$

and other relative matrices are supposed to be

$$C_1 = C_2 = \begin{bmatrix} 1 & 3 & 2 \end{bmatrix}, D_1 = D_2 = 0.4,$$
$$E_1 = E_2 = \begin{bmatrix} -2 & -2 & -4 \end{bmatrix}, F_1 = F_2 = 0.1.$$

By applying Theorem 2 with $K = I_{3\times3}$, $J_1 = -2$, $J_2 = 2$, $J_3 = 2$, $\mathcal{R}_y = \mathcal{R}_z = 50$, $\Delta_y = \Delta_z = 0.5$, $\bar{\rho} = \bar{\varepsilon} = 0.8$, $c_{1y} = c_{1z} = 1$, $d_{1y} = d_{1z} = 1$, $c_{2y} = c_{2z} = 2$, $d_{2y} = d_{2z} = 2$, and $\gamma = 0.55$, the related parameters for the desired full-order dissipative filter can be obtained as

$$\widehat{A} = \begin{bmatrix} 0.7820 & 0.4766 & 0.5534 \\ 0.0017 & 0.4906 & -0.0466 \\ -0.2126 & -0.0845 & 0.6139 \end{bmatrix}, \widehat{B} = \begin{bmatrix} -0.0809 \\ -0.0552 \\ -0.0111 \end{bmatrix},$$
$$\widehat{E} = \begin{bmatrix} 1.1356 & 6.0793 & 5.2254 \end{bmatrix}.$$

For the simulation, we assume that $x(0) = x_f(0) = [0\ \ 0\ \ 0]^T$ and $w(t) = 5\cos(0.25t)e^{-0.2t}$. The simulation results are presented in Figures 2–7, where the responses of $x(t)$ and $x_f(t)$ are indicated in Figure 2 and Figure 3, respectively, Figure 4 plots the responses of $z(t)$ and $z_f(t)$, Figure 5 shows the trajectory of $e(t)$, and the trajectories of the dynamic parameters $\alpha_y(t)$ and $\alpha_z(t)$ are shown in Figure 6 and Figure 7, respectively. The simulation results presented in Figures 2–7 demonstrate that the proposed dissipative filter design approach in this paper is effective.

Next, the tunnel diode circuit system (39) will be utilized to investigate the $\mathcal{H}_\infty$ filter design problem according to the results developed in Theorem 2, and the other parameters without detailed definition are same as the first case. Firstly, the effects of quantization error bound $\Delta_y(\Delta_z)$ and quantization range $\mathcal{R}_y(\mathcal{R}_z)$ on the optimized $\mathcal{H}_\infty$ filtering performance $\gamma_{\min}$ will be studied with $J_1 = -1$, $J_2 = 0$, and $J_3 = \gamma + \gamma^2$. The optimized $\mathcal{H}_\infty$ filtering performances $\gamma_{\min}$ computed by Theorem 2 with different quantization error bound $\Delta_y(\Delta_z)$ and quantization range $\mathcal{R}_y(\mathcal{R}_z)$ are shown in Figure 8 and Figure 9, respectively. As expected, one can observe that $\gamma_{\min}$ increases as the quantization range $\mathcal{R}_y(\mathcal{R}_z)$ decreases and $\gamma_{\min}$ increases as the quantization error bound $\Delta_y(\Delta_z)$ increases. Moreover, it is well known that a higher filter order $n_{\overline{x}}$ will lead to less design conservatism, i.e., a smaller optimized $\mathcal{H}_\infty$ filtering performance $\gamma_{\min}$. Then, we demonstrate this proposition. In the presence of different filter order $n_{\overline{x}}$, the optimized $\mathcal{H}_\infty$ filtering performances $\gamma_{\min}$ computed by Theorem 2 with different quantization error bounds and quantization ranges are shown in Tables 1 and 2, respectively.

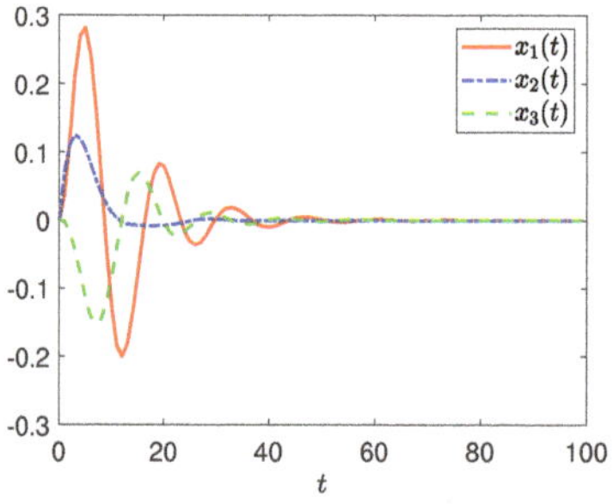

Figure 2. The response of $x(t)$.

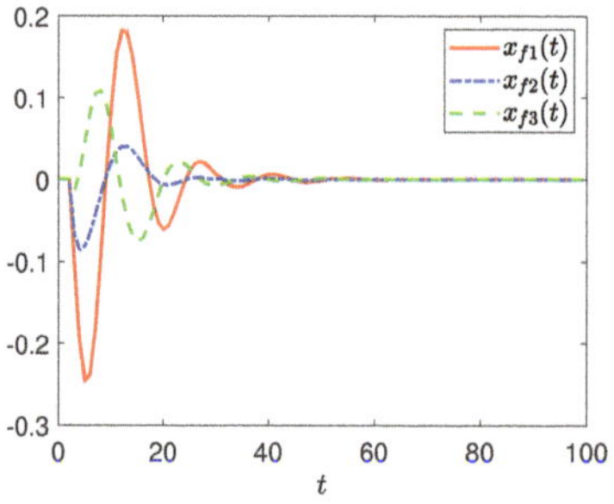

Figure 3. The response of $x_f(t)$.

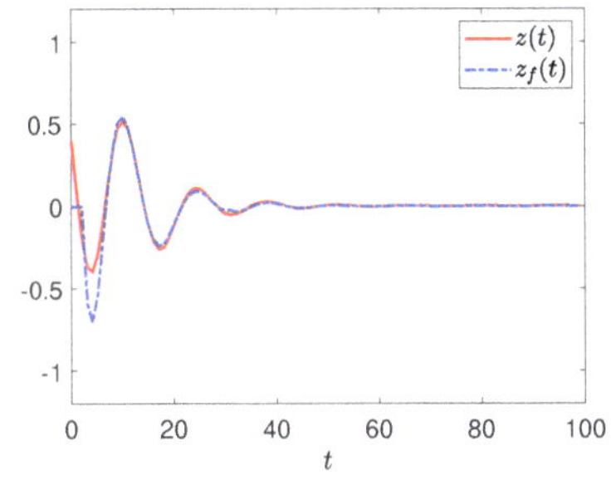

Figure 4. The responses of $z(t)$ and $z_f(t)$.

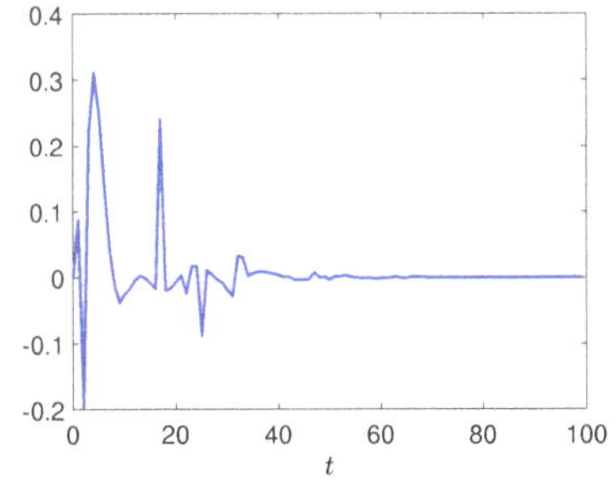

Figure 5. The trajectory of $e(t)$.

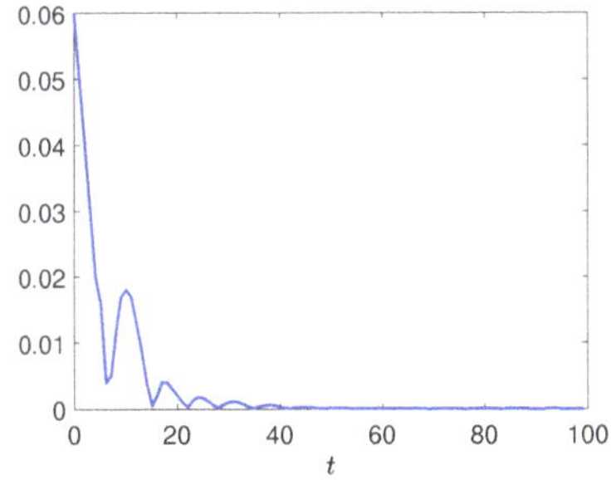

Figure 6. The trajectory of the dynamic parameter $\alpha_y(t)$.

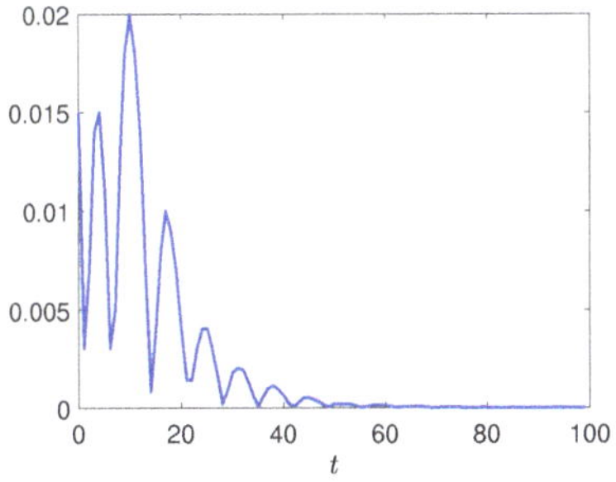

Figure 7. The trajectory of the dynamic parameter $\alpha_z(t)$.

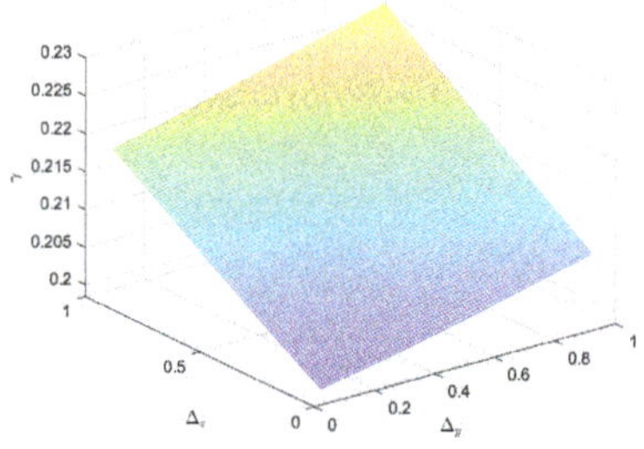

Figure 8. Optimized $\mathcal{H}_\infty$ filtering performance $\gamma_{\min}$ with different quantization error bound $\Delta_y(\Delta_z)$.

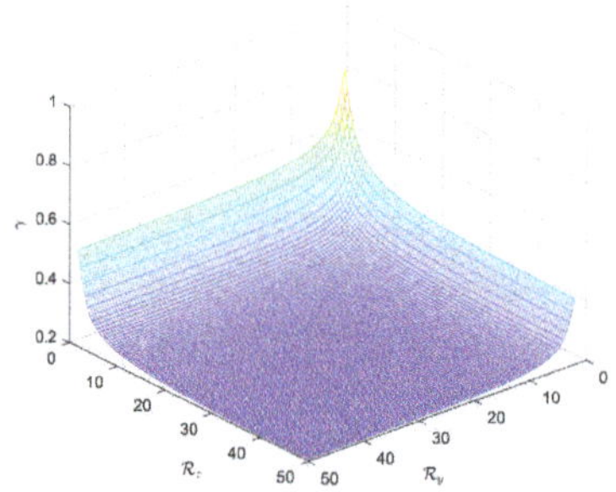

Figure 9. Optimized $\mathcal{H}_\infty$ filtering performance $\gamma_{\min}$ with different quantization error $\mathcal{R}_y(\mathcal{R}_z)$.

Table 1. Optimized $\mathcal{H}_\infty$ filtering performance $\gamma_{\min}$ with different quantization error bounds.

$\Delta_y = \Delta_z$	0.1	0.3	0.5	0.7	0.9
$\gamma_{\min}(n_{\overline{x}} = 3)$	0.1984	0.2040	0.2100	0.2163	0.2228
$\gamma_{\min}(n_{\overline{x}} = 2)$	0.3189	0.3257	0.3325	0.3393	0.3461
$\gamma_{\min}(n_{\overline{x}} = 1)$	0.3425	0.3504	0.3583	0.3664	0.3744

Table 2. Optimized $\mathcal{H}_\infty$ filtering performance $\gamma_{\min}$ with different quantization ranges.

$\mathcal{R}_y = \mathcal{R}_z$	10	30	50	70	90
$\gamma_{\min}(n_{\overline{x}} = 3)$	0.2850	0.2206	0.2100	0.2057	0.2034
$\gamma_{\min}(n_{\overline{x}} = 2)$	0.4021	0.3438	0.3325	0.3276	0.3249
$\gamma_{\min}(n_{\overline{x}} = 1)$	0.4405	0.3717	0.3583	0.3526	0.3495

Comparative Explanations: In this paper, the developed filtering strategy can effectively solve both the full- and reduced-order dissipative filtering problems for the nonlinear tunnel diode circuit system in (39) with the effects of dynamic quantization and data packet dropouts based on the T–S fuzzy model strategy. In contrast with the existing results, the main advantages of the proposed filtering strategy can be summarized in the following three aspects.

(1) The proposed dissipative filtering strategy in this paper is more general than the existing results on fuzzy $\mathcal{H}_\infty$ filtering for nonlinear networked systems in [34,35,37,39–42], because it can also be utilized to deal with several kinds of filtering problems, including passive, $\mathcal{H}_\infty$, and mixed passive/$\mathcal{H}_\infty$ filtering problems for the nonlinear tunnel diode circuit system (39). Particularly, both the effects of dynamic quantization and data packet dropouts on the measurement output and the performance output have been considered

simultaneously; it implies that the problem addressed in this paper is more in agreement with practical circumstances than the ones considered in [36,38,41–43].

(2) In contrast with the quantized filtering problem considered in [38,41], the dynamical quantization methodology employed herein is more general. This is mainly because the stochastic stability of the filtering error system can be ensured under a finite number of quantization levels. By choosing the relevant parameters, the online adjusting strategies in [36,39] can be obtained from the one developed in (17) and (19), which implies that the adjusting strategy for the dynamic parameters $\alpha_{\varsigma}(t)$ ($\varsigma = y, z$) provided in this paper is more general. Moreover, simulation results in Figure 6 and Figure 7 show that the adjustment of the dynamic parameters $\alpha_{\varsigma}(t)$ can be realized based on the online adjusting strategy developed in this paper.

(3) In contrast with the existing results of the filtering problem for networked systems where only full-order filtering problems [34,35,38,39,41] or reduced-order filtering problems [46] were considered, the developed filtering strategy can effectively solve both the full- and reduced-order filtering problems, which is more general. Moreover, different from the results in [36], this example illustrates that both full- and reduced-order filtering problems have been solved in the unified framework of linear matrix inequalities by introducing a dimension adjustment matrix K.

5. Conclusions

In this paper, the dissipative filtering problem has been addressed for discrete-time nonlinear networked systems with dynamic quantization and data packet dropouts based on the T–S fuzzy strategy. Both the effects of dynamic quantization and data packet dropouts have been taken into consideration in both communication channels from the plant to the filter and from the filter to the plant. The sufficient design conditions for both the desired full- and reduced-order dissipative filters have been established in the unified framework of linear matrix inequalities, which guarantees the stochastic stability and the predefined dissipative filtering performance for the filtering error system subject to dynamic quantization and data packet dropouts. In addition, a practical simulation example has been employed to show the effectiveness of the proposed dissipative filtering approach.

However, it is well known that communication delays and cyber attacks, as important challenges in networked systems, are also considered to be unavoidable in practical cases. In this paper, we have only addressed dynamic quantization and data packet dropouts, and the study of the dissipative fuzzy filtering problem for nonlinear networked systems with the simultaneous consideration of dynamic quantization, data packet dropouts, communication delays, and cyber attacks deserves further investigation.

Author Contributions: Conceptualization, S.J. and Z.L.; formal analysis, S.J. and Z.L.; methodology, S.J. and Z.L.; funding acquisition, Z.L.; investigation, writing—original draft preparation and editing, and writing—review and editing, S.J., C.L. and Z.L.; software, S.J. and C.L. All authors have read and agreed to the published version of the manuscript.

Funding: This work was supported in part by the National Natural Science Foundation of China under Grant 62003006, in part by the Science and Technology Project of Hebei Education Department under Grant BJK2022053, in part by the Langfang Youth Talent Support Program under Grant LFBJ202202, in part by the Graduate Innovation Support Program in Hebei Province (CXZ ZSS2024142), and in part by the Graduate Innovation Support Program in North China Institute of Aerospace Engineering under Grant YKY-2023-25.

Institutional Review Board Statement: Not applicable.

Informed Consent Statement: Not applicable.

Data Availability Statement: Data sharing not applicable.

Conflicts of Interest: The authors declare no conflicts of interest.

References

1. Liu, J.; Dong, Y.; Zha, L.; Tian, E.; Xie, X. Event-based security tracking control for networked control systems against stochastic cyber-attacks. *Inf. Sci.* **2022**, *612*, 306–321. [CrossRef]
2. Zha, L.; Liao, R.; Liu, J.; Xie, X.; Tian, E.; Cao, J. Dynamic event-triggered output feedback control for networked systems subject to multiple cyber attacks. *IEEE Trans. Cybern.* **2022**, *52*, 13800–13808. [CrossRef] [PubMed]
3. Zhang, X.M.; Han, Q.L.; Ge, X.; Ding, D.; Ding, L.; Yue, D.; Peng, C. Networked control systems: A survey of trends and techniques. *IEEE CAA J. Autom. Sin.* **2020**, *7*, 1–17. [CrossRef]
4. Xiong, J.; Chang, X.H.; Park, J.H.; Li, Z.M. Nonfragile fault-tolerant control of suspension systems subject to input quantization and actuator fault. *Int. J. Robust Nonlinear Control* **2020**, *30*, 6720–6743. [CrossRef]
5. Liberzon, D. Hybrid feedback stabilization of systems with quantized signals. *Automatica* **2003**, *39*, 1543–1554. [CrossRef]
6. Chang, X.H.; Xiong, J.; Li, Z.M.; Park, J.H. Quantized static output feedback control for discrete-time systems. *IEEE Trans. Industr. Inf.* **2018**, *14*, 3426–3435. [CrossRef]
7. Yu, K.; Chang, X.H. Quantized output feedback resilient control of uncertain systems under hybrid cyber attacks. *Int. J. Adapt. Control Signal Process.* **2022**, *36*, 2954–2970. [CrossRef]
8. Niu, Y.; Ho, D.W.C. Control strategy with adaptive quantizer's parameters under digital communication channels. *Automatica* **2014**, *50*, 2665–2671. [CrossRef]
9. Su, L.; Chesi, G. Robust stability of uncertain linear systems with input and output quantization and packet loss. *Automatica* **2018**, *87*, 267–273. [CrossRef]
10. Wu, C.; Zhao, X.; Xia, W.; Liu, J.; Başar, T. $\mathcal{L}_2$-gain analysis for dynamic event-triggered networked control systems with packet losses and quantization. *Automatica* **2021**, *129*, 109587. [CrossRef]
11. Li, Z.M.; Chang, X.H. Robust $\mathcal{H}_\infty$ control for networked control systems with randomly occurring uncertainties: Observer-based case. *ISA Trans.* **2018**, *83*, 13–24. [CrossRef] [PubMed]
12. Wang, Z.; Yang, F.; Ho, D.W.C.; Liu, X. Robust $\mathcal{H}_\infty$ control for networked systems with random packet losses. *IEEE Trans. Syst. Man Cybern. B Cybern.* **2007**, *37*, 916–924. [CrossRef] [PubMed]
13. Shen, H.; Hu, X.; Wang, J.; Cao, J.; Qian, W. Non-fragile $\mathcal{H}_\infty$ synchronization for Markov jump singularly perturbed coupled neural networks subject to double-layer switching regulation. *IEEE Trans. Neural Netw. Learn. Syst.* **2023**, *34*, 2682–2692. [CrossRef] [PubMed]
14. Nguyen, T.B.; Song, H.K. Further results on robust output-feedback dissipative control of Markovian jump fuzzy systems with model uncertainties. *Mathematics* **2022**, *10*, 3620. [CrossRef]
15. Tanaka, K.; Wang, H.O. *Fuzzy Control Systems Design and Analysis: A Linear Matrix Inequality Approach*; Wiley: New York, NY, USA, 2001.
16. Chang, X.H.; Jing, Y.W.; Gao, X.Y.; Liu, X.P. $\mathcal{H}_\infty$ tracking control design of T–S fuzzy systems. *Control Decis.* **2008**, *23*, 329–332. (In Chinese)
17. Liu, J.; Gong, E.; Zha, L.; Tian, E.; Xie, X. Observer-based security fuzzy control for nonlinear networked systems under weighted try-once-discard protocol. *IEEE Trans. Fuzzy Syst.* **2023**, *31*, 3853–3865. [CrossRef]
18. Yao, H.; Gao, F. Design of observer and dynamic output feedback control for fuzzy networked systems. *Mathematics* **2022**, *11*, 148. [CrossRef]
19. Liu, J.; Ke, J.; Liu, J.; Xie, X.; Tian, E. Secure event-triggered control for IT-2 fuzzy networked systems with stochastic communication protocol and FDI attacks. *IEEE Trans. Fuzzy Syst.* 2023, *in press*. Available online: https://ieeexplore.ieee.org/abstract/document/10265199 (accessed on 27 September 2023).
20. Qiu, J.; Gao, H.; Ding, S.X. Recent advances on fuzzy-model-based nonlinear networked control systems: A survey. *IEEE Trans. Ind. Electron.* **2016**, *63*, 1207–1217. [CrossRef]
21. Chang, X.H.; Yang, C.; Xiong, J. Quantized fuzzy output feedback $\mathcal{H}_\infty$ control for nonlinear systems with adjustment of dynamic parameters. *IEEE Trans. Syst. Man Cybern. Syst.* **2019**, *49*, 2005–2015. [CrossRef]
22. Zha, L.; Huang, T.; Liu, J.; Xie, X.; Tian, E. Outlier-resistant quantized control for T–S fuzzy systems under multi-channel-enabled round-robin protocol and deception attacks. *Int. J. Robust Nonlinear Control* **2023**, *33*, 10916–10931. [CrossRef]
23. Li, Z.M.; Park, J.H. Dissipative fuzzy tracking control for nonlinear networked systems with quantization. *IEEE Trans. Syst. Man Cybern. Syst.* **2020**, *50*, 5130–5141. [CrossRef]
24. Wang, J.; Yang, C.; Xia, J.; Wu, Z.G.; Shen, H. Observer-based sliding mode control for networked fuzzy singularly perturbed systems under weighted try-once-discard protocol. *IEEE Trans. Fuzzy Syst.* **2022**, *30*, 1889–1899. [CrossRef]
25. Liu, J.; Wei, L.; Xie, X.; Tian, E.; Fei, S. Quantized stabilization for T–S fuzzy systems with hybrid-triggered mechanism and stochastic cyber-attacks. *IEEE Trans. Fuzzy Syst.* **2018**, *26*, 3820–3834. [CrossRef]
26. Zheng, Q.; Xu, S.; Du, B. Quantized guaranteed cost output feedback control for nonlinear networked control systems and its applications. *IEEE Trans. Fuzzy Syst.* **2022**, *30*, 2402–2411. [CrossRef]
27. Gao, H.; Zhao, Y.; Chen, T. $\mathcal{H}_\infty$ fuzzy control of nonlinear systems under unreliable communication links. *IEEE Trans. Fuzzy Syst.* **2009**, *17*, 265–278.
28. Qiu, J.; Feng, G.; Gao, H. Fuzzy-model-based piecewise $\mathcal{H}_\infty$ static-output-feedback controller design for networked nonlinear systems. *IEEE Trans. Fuzzy Syst.* **2010**, *18*, 919–934. [CrossRef]

29. Li, H.; Wu, C.; Jing, X.; Wu, L. Fuzzy tracking control for nonlinear networked systems. *IEEE Trans. Cybern.* **2017**, *47*, 2020–2031. [CrossRef]
30. Liu, J.; Wang, Y.; Cao, J.; Yue, D.; Xie, X. Secure adaptive-event-triggered filter design with input constraint and hybrid cyber attack. *IEEE Trans. Cybern.* **2021**, *51*, 4000–4010. [CrossRef]
31. Gao, H.; Chen, T. $\mathcal{H}_\infty$ estimation for uncertain systems with limited communication capacity. *IEEE Trans. Autom. Control* **2007**, *52*, 2070–2084. [CrossRef]
32. Liu, J.; Gong, E.; Zha, L.; Xie, X.; Tian, E. Outlier-resistant recursive security filtering for multirate networked systems under fading measurements and round-robin protocol. *IEEE Trans. Control Netw. Syst.* 2023, *in press*. Available online: https://ieeexplore.ieee.org/abstract/document/10068263 (accessed on 13 March 2023).
33. Zheng, Q.; Xu, S.; Du, B. Asynchronous resilent state estimation of switched fuzzy systems with multiple state impulsive jumps. *IEEE Trans. Cybern.* **2023**, *53*, 7966–7979. [CrossRef]
34. Chang, X.H. $\mathcal{H}_\infty$ filter design for T–S fuzzy systems with *D* stability constraints. *Control. Decis.* **2011**, *26*, 1051–1055. (In Chinese)
35. Liu, J.; Zha, L.; Tian, E.; Xie, X. Interval type-2 fuzzy-model-based filtering for nonlinear systems with event-triggering weighted try-once-discard protocol and cyber-attacks. *IEEE Trans. Fuzzy Syst.* 2023, *in press*. Available online: https://ieeexplore.ieee.org/abstract/document/10221224 (accessed on 16 August 2023).
36. Chang, X.H.; Li, Z.M.; Park, J.H. Fuzzy generalized $\mathcal{H}_2$ filtering for nonlinear discrete-time systems with measurement quantization. *IEEE Trans. Syst. Man Cybern. Syst.* **2018**, *48*, 2419–2430. [CrossRef]
37. Li, Z.M.; Xiong, J. Event-triggered fuzzy filtering for nonlinear networked systems with dynamic quantization and stochastic cyber attacks. *ISA Trans.* **2022**, *121*, 53–62. [CrossRef] [PubMed]
38. Chang, X.H.; Wang, Y.M. Peak-to-peak filtering for networked nonlinear DC motor systems with quantization. *IEEE Trans. Ind. Inf.* **2018**, *14*, 5378–5388. [CrossRef]
39. Chang, X.H.; Liu, Y. Robust $\mathcal{H}_\infty$ filtering for vehicle sideslip angle with quantization and data dropouts. *IEEE Trans. Veh. Technol.* **2020**, *69*, 10435–10445. [CrossRef]
40. Zhao, X.Y.; Chang, X.H. $\mathcal{H}_\infty$ filtering for nonlinear discrete-time singular systems in encrypted state. *Neural Process. Lett.* **2023**, *55*, 2843–2866. [CrossRef]
41. Zhang, C.; Feng, G.; Gao, H.; Qiu, J. $\mathcal{H}_\infty$ filtering for nonlinear discrete-time systems subject to quantization and packet dropouts. *IEEE Trans. Fuzzy Syst.* **2011**, *19*, 353–365. [CrossRef]
42. Gao, H.; Zhao, Y.; Lam, J.; Chen, K.E. $\mathcal{H}_\infty$ fuzzy filtering of nonlinear systems with intermittent measurements. *IEEE Trans. Fuzzy Syst.* **2009**, *17*, 291–300.
43. Chang, X.H.; Liu, Q.; Wang, Y.M.; Xiong, J. Fuzzy peak-to-peak filtering for networked nonlinear systems with multipath data packet dropouts. *IEEE Trans. Fuzzy Syst.* **2018**, *27*, 436–446. [CrossRef]
44. Liu, Y.; Guo, B.Z.; Park, J.H.; Lee, S. Event-based reliable dissipative filtering for T–S fuzzy systems with asynchronous constraints. *IEEE Trans. Fuzzy Syst.* **2017**, *26*, 2089–2098. [CrossRef]
45. Chang, X.H.; Park, J.H.; Zhou, J. Robust static output feedback $\mathcal{H}_\infty$ control design for linear systems with polytopic uncertainties. *Syst. Control Lett.* **2015**, *85*, 23–32. [CrossRef]
46. Cai, L.J.; Chang, X.H. Reduced-order filtering for discrete-time singular systems under fading channels. *Int. J. Syst. Sci.* **2023**, *54*, 99–112. [CrossRef]

Disclaimer/Publisher's Note: The statements, opinions and data contained in all publications are solely those of the individual author(s) and contributor(s) and not of MDPI and/or the editor(s). MDPI and/or the editor(s) disclaim responsibility for any injury to people or property resulting from any ideas, methods, instructions or products referred to in the content.

mathematics

MDPI

Article

Key Vulnerable Nodes Discovery Based on Bayesian Attack Subgraphs and Improved Fuzzy C-Means Clustering

Yuhua Xu [1], Yang Liu [2], Zhixin Sun [3,4,*], Yucheng Xue [4], Weiliang Liao [4], Chenlei Liu [4] and Zhe Sun [4]

1 Engineering Research Center of Broadband Wireless Communication Technology of the Ministry of Education, Nanjing University of Posts and Telecommunications, Nanjing 210003, China; xuyh@njupt.edu.cn
2 School of Computer Science and Technology, Nanjing University of Posts and Telecommunications, Nanjing 210003, China; 1222045809@njupt.edu.cn
3 Engineering Research Center of Post Big Data Technology and Application of Jiangsu Province, Nanjing University of Posts and Telecommunications, Nanjing 210003, China
4 Research and Development Center of Post Industry Technology of the State Posts Bureau (Internet of Things Technology), Nanjing University of Posts and Telecommunications, Nanjing 210003, China; b21090431@njupt.edu.cn (Y.X.); b21090430@njupt.edu.cn (W.L.); 2019070270@njupt.edu.cn (C.L.); zhesunny@njupt.edu.cn (Z.S.)
* Correspondence: sunzx@njupt.edu.cn

Abstract: Aiming at the problem that the search efficiency of key vulnerable nodes in large-scale networks is not high and the consideration factors are not comprehensive enough, in order to improve the time and space efficiency of search and the accuracy of results, a key vulnerable node discovery method based on Bayesian attack subgraphs and improved fuzzy C-means clustering is proposed. Firstly, the attack graph is divided into Bayesian attack subgraphs, and the analysis results of the complete attack graph are quickly obtained by aggregating the information of the attack path analysis in the subgraph to improve the time and space efficiency. Then, the actual threat features of the vulnerability nodes are extracted from the analysis results, and the threat features of the vulnerability itself in the common vulnerability scoring standard are considered to form the clustering features together. Next, the optimal number of clusters is adaptively adjusted according to the variance idea, and fuzzy clustering is performed based on the extracted clustering features. Finally, the key vulnerable nodes are determined by setting the feature priority. Experiments show that the proposed method can optimize the time and space efficiency of analysis, and the fuzzy clustering considering multiple features can improve the accuracy of analysis results.

Keywords: Bayesian attack graphs; key vulnerability discovery; community division; fuzzy clustering

MSC: 93C42

Citation: Xu, Y.; Liu, Y.; Sun, Z.; Xue, Y.; Liao, W.; Liu, C.; Sun, Z. Key Vulnerable Nodes Discovery Based on Bayesian Attack Subgraphs and Improved Fuzzy C-Means Clustering. *Mathematics* **2024**, *12*, 1447. https://doi.org/10.3390/math12101447

Academic Editor: Hsien-Chung Wu

Received: 17 April 2024
Revised: 30 April 2024
Accepted: 4 May 2024
Published: 8 May 2024

Copyright: © 2024 by the authors. Licensee MDPI, Basel, Switzerland. This article is an open access article distributed under the terms and conditions of the Creative Commons Attribution (CC BY) license (https://creativecommons.org/licenses/by/4.0/).

1. Introduction

With the continuous progress of science and technology, the network has become an indispensable part of modern society. The development of the network has broken the restrictions of time and space and promoted the dissemination and sharing of information. Attackers penetrate and hijack data through device vulnerabilities, causing economic losses to individuals, institutions, large companies, and even countries [1]. Therefore, it is necessary to analyze the vulnerabilities in network systems and take corresponding defensive measures to prevent hacker attacks.

The large number and complex types of vulnerabilities in network systems always threaten the security and stability of the system. Many scholars have applied various methods to study system vulnerability analysis. Some methods evaluate the vulnerability threat in the network system by considering the threat characteristics of the vulnerability itself and the threat of its associated assets [2–5]. However, these methods only evaluate the stable vulnerability threat influencing factors, and do not take the actual changing network environment into account, so the factors considered are not comprehensive enough. In order to take various factors into account, some scholars use machine learning to evaluate the threat degree of vulnerabilities [6–10]. These studies combine various characteristic information of vulnerabilities and train various models to improve the effect of vulnerability detection. However, these methods only detect the vulnerability of a single device, and the correlation between the detection results and other vulnerabilities in the network and the whole attack process is not strong. The attack graph is a graphical security assessment technique that contains various network configurations and vulnerability information. It reveals all potential vulnerability combinations and their relationships and lists all potential attack paths from the perspective of the attacker to reflect the security state of the network, such as the number of attack paths, the length of the shortest attack path, and the key vulnerability. Multi-step attacks can be effectively prevented based on the attack graph [11,12]. To enhance the relevance between vulnerability assessment and network systems, many studies have conducted network vulnerability analysis based on attack graphs. They realized the association analysis of key vulnerabilities in network systems by studying attack graph construction techniques [13,14], node analysis techniques [15–17] and attack path analysis [18,19]. However, the attack graph does not have the ability of quantitative analysis. The Bayesian theory is a statistical method to deal with uncertainty through observation data. The key of Bayesian theory is to predict possible risks in advance by mathematical methods, and it does not focus on the random attack itself [20]. Many risk analysis methods based on attack graphs combine Bayesian theory to realize risk quantification and prediction analysis [21–23]. In the network attack graph with a large number of nodes, the existing studies have problems such as low efficiency and single consideration when searching for key vulnerable nodes. These problems coincide with the advantages of fuzzy C-means (FCM) clustering, which can integrate various characteristics of vulnerabilities and classify them spontaneously. Thus, a set of key vulnerable nodes with similar threat degrees can be effectively obtained.

To sum up, the temporal and spatial efficiency of attack graph analysis in large-scale networks needs to be improved, and the factors taken into account in searching key vulnerable nodes in network systems are not comprehensive enough. This paper uses the attack graph combined with the network division to divide the attack graph into multiple subgraphs for correlation analysis. Based on the analysis results, the actual threat features of vulnerability nodes are extracted. The actual threat features and inherent threat features of vulnerabilities are taken as FCM clustering indicators. The main contributions of this paper are as follows:

1. An analysis method based on Bayesian attack subgraphs is proposed. It divides the attack graph based on the idea of community division, quantifies the threat of nodes, constructs and analyzes Bayesian attack subgraphs to form the subgraph analysis information group, and aggregates information groups to quickly obtain the final analysis results of all paths so as to improve the spatiotemporal efficiency of the results;
2. A method based on improved FCM to discover key vulnerable nodes is proposed. It uses variance to design the total difference value between classes (TDVC) and determines the optimal number of FCM by maximizing the TDVC. Then, the actual threat features and inherent threat features of vulnerabilities are extracted based on the Common Vulnerability Scoring System (CVSS) and the analysis results of the attack graph. Next, FCM is used to cluster the vulnerability nodes based on the extracted features so as to improve the accuracy of the results. Finally, the feature priority is set, and the key vulnerability node cluster with the highest threat level is found according to the results.
3. The experimental scenario is designed and the data from the National Vulnerability Database (NVD) are collected for the experiment. The temporal and spatial effi-

ciency improvement of attack graph analysis and the accuracy improvement of key vulnerability nodes search results are verified by comparing with other methods.

2. Related Works

At present, there is much research on key vulnerability search. Hao et al. [24] and Tang et al. [25] train neural network models to identify key vulnerabilities on network devices using static analysis, but this method is only applicable to a single device and cannot be dynamically combined with other devices in the network. Li et al. [26] use the Kemeny constant as a global connectivity measure to identify network key connections and network decomposition is used to cut off connections to minimize global connectivity measures, thereby obtaining key vulnerabilities. However, this method is not intuitive enough and only considers a single influencing factor. Huang et al. [27] build an attack tree and conduct Bayesian inference to find key vulnerable nodes by tracing the attack path. However, the application scope of the attack tree is limited and vulnerabilities could not be associated.

To conduct association analysis of network nodes and make the analysis results more accurate and intuitive, many studies use the attack graph as the basic analysis method to search for key vulnerabilities. Yang et al. [28] quantify the asset value of the host through the attribute value and topology perspective on the attack graph and search for key vulnerable nodes in combination with attack probability. However, this method does not consider the influence of the location of the vulnerability in the attack path. Li et al. [29] use attack distance and atomic weight to optimize the complexity of the attack graph and improve the ant colony algorithm to solve the minimum key attack set through the pheromone adaptive update principle and local search strategy so as to obtain the key vulnerable nodes, but this method does not consider the threat characteristics of vulnerability nodes themselves. Qian et al. [30] optimize the attack graph with maximum hop count and reachability probability and quantify the reachability probability of vulnerable nodes. According to the vulnerability measurement value of nodes and paths, the key vulnerable nodes in the network are found, but this method only considers the attack path with the highest vulnerability measurement value. Xie et al. [31] use the Bayesian attack graph model to continuously carry out probabilistic correction learning according to the attack data, quantify the dynamic risk, and evaluate the risk value of key nodes according to the quantitative results. However, this method analyzes the complete attack graph and dynamically adjusts the attack graph model, which reduces the time efficiency of analysis. Li et al. [32] combine particle the swarm optimization algorithm and a grey wolf optimization algorithm to find the maximum weight spanning tree from the attack graph, evaluate the key nodes in the spanning tree based on interpretable structure modeling, and improve the simulated annealing algorithm. This method optimizes the time efficiency through heuristic ideas but reduces the accuracy of the result due to the pruning of part of the edges.

Previous studies have some problems when using the Bayesian attack graph to search for key vulnerable nodes. Many studies do not consider the threat characteristics of the vulnerability itself and the threat characteristics in the actual network at the same time, which leads to the accuracy of the search results of key vulnerable nodes needing to be improved. Some studies will lead to low search efficiency when they are applied to large-scale attack graphs, and large-scale attack graphs also need a lot of storage space. Therefore, this paper proposes a key vulnerable node discovery method based on Bayesian attack subgraphs and improved FCM. The large-scale network is divided by community division and the Bayesian attack subgraphs are constructed. The analysis result of the complete attack graph is formed by aggregating the attack path analysis information inside the attack subgraphs, and the threat characteristics of nodes are extracted from the result. Then, the TDVC is designed to adaptively determine the optimal number of clusters, and the FCM is used to cluster the nodes. Finally, the clustering results are analyzed based on the designed feature priority to obtain the key vulnerable nodes so as to improve the accuracy of results and the spatiotemporal efficiency of search analysis.

3. Key Nodes Discovery Model Based on Attack Subgraph Aggregation Search and Fuzzy C-Means Clustering

The key vulnerable nodes discovery model based on attack subgraph aggregation search and fuzzy C-means clustering is mainly divided into three steps: data preprocessing, attack path aggregation search based on Bayesian attack subgraph, and key vulnerable nodes discovery based on fuzzy C-means clustering. The overall process of the key node discovery model based on attack subgraph aggregation search and fuzzy C-means clustering is shown in Figure 1.

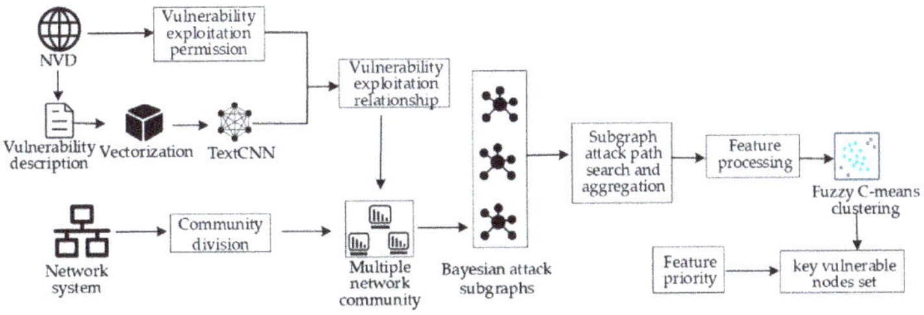

Figure 1. Key nodes discovery model based on attack subgraph aggregation search and fuzzy C-means clustering.

In the data preprocessing stage, the topology graph of the network system is constructed, and vulnerability scanning tools such as Nessus are used to obtain the vulnerability list existing on the device. At the same time, the vulnerability exploit relationship is analyzed for the subsequent construction of the attack graph. Since the current attack graph construction technology generally uses a manual analysis method to obtain the exploitation relationship between vulnerabilities, this method cannot be effectively implemented when there are a large number of vulnerabilities, and manual analysis has a strong subjective will. To make the construction of vulnerability exploitation relationships more accurate, the model in this paper uses the method based on Word2Vec and TextCNN in reference [33] to obtain the exploitation relationship between vulnerabilities. Firstly, the basic information such as permission requirements and description of vulnerabilities is obtained through the interface provided by the NVD, and then the description information is organized into a corpus to train the Word2Vec model. The output of the Word2Vec model is used as the input of TextCNN to train the text classification model. Finally, the permissions obtained after the vulnerability has been attacked are divided into three categories: other, user, and root through the text classification model, and the exploitation relationship between the vulnerabilities is obtained according to the comparison results of the permissions requirements of the vulnerability and the permissions obtained after the attack.

In the attack path aggregation search phase based on the Bayesian attack subgraph, the large-scale network is first divided into multiple communities with close internal connections by the community division algorithm. Then, the Bayesian attack subgraph is constructed in each community based on CVSS, network connection relationship, and vulnerability utilization relationship. Next, the attack path is searched in each subgraph, and the attack probability and other related information of each path are recorded for the aggregation of subsequent paths. Finally, the attack path and its information are aggregated based on the connection relationship between subgraphs to obtain the complete attack path information. Compared with the search of attack paths on the whole attack graph directly, the search of attack paths based on the subgraph can not only save the storage consumption of the attack graph but also improve the search efficiency of attack paths.

In the discovery stage of key vulnerable nodes based on fuzzy C-means clustering, the sample characteristics during clustering are determined first. Two inherent threat features and two actual threat features of the vulnerability are selected as sample features in this method. Inherent threat features include exploitability score and impact score, which can be directly obtained according to CVSS. The exploitability index of a vulnerability in CVSS reflects the difficulty of exploiting the vulnerability, and the impact index reflects the severity of the consequence of exploiting the vulnerability. Both of them are related to the severity of the vulnerability, but both of them are fixed characteristics of the vulnerability itself, so their applicability is weak. Therefore, this paper extracts two actual threat features of vulnerability attack probability and vulnerability occurrence frequency from the relevant information on attack paths. These two features can reflect the threat degree of vulnerabilities combined with specific attack paths in different networks and improve the accuracy of discovering key vulnerable nodes. Then, the optimal number of clusters is determined by maximizing the difference between the clustering results, and the fuzzy C-means clustering is realized by setting the membership degree, the maximum number of iterations, and other parameters. Finally, the feature priority is set to classify the clustering results so as to obtain the final set of key vulnerable nodes.

4. Attack Path Aggregation Search Based on Bayesian Attack Subgraph

At present, the attack graph analysis scheme involving the attack path is difficult to implement in large-scale network systems due to its space-time complexity. Therefore, an attack path aggregation search method based on a Bayesian attack subgraph is proposed in this paper to improve the spatiotemporal efficiency of this attack graph analysis. The information obtained based on this method will be used as the key features of subsequent clustering algorithms to find key vulnerable nodes. The process of the attack path aggregation search based on attack subgraphs is shown in Figure 2.

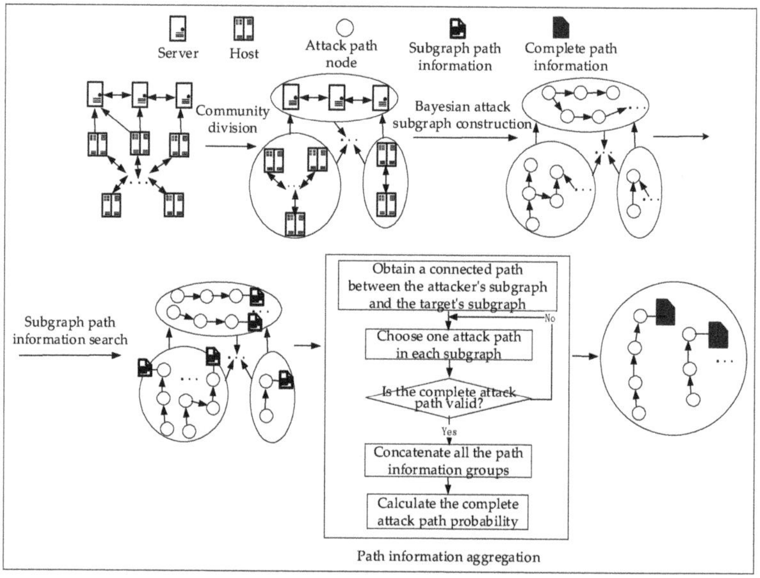

Figure 2. The process of the attack path aggregation search based on attack subgraphs.

In this method, the large-scale network is divided into multiple subnetworks using the network community partitioning algorithm, and the Bayesian attack subgraphs are constructed in the subnetworks first. All Bayesian attack subgraphs form the whole Bayesian attack graph. Then, the attack path is searched in each Bayesian attack subgraph, and the related information of the attack path is recorded. Finally, according to the attack paths in different attack subgraphs and the related information recorded, the attack paths and related information of the whole Bayesian attack graph are obtained.

4.1. Bayesian Attack Subgraph Construction

Definition 1 (The Bayesian attack graph BAG). *The BAG is a directed acyclic graph defined as a quintuple* $< N, E, R, P_a, P_s, P_c >$.

1. *N is the set of nodes.* $N = \left\{ N_{begin} \cup N_{middle} \cup N_{target} \right\}$. N_{begin} *is the set of nodes where the attacker is located in the Bayesian attack graph.* N_{target} *is the node set of the attack target.* N_{middle} *is the set of the remaining nodes. The value of* N_i *can be 0 or 1.* $N_i = 1$ *means that the node i has been compromised.* $N_i = 0$ *means that the node i is not compromised;*
2. *E is the set of directed edges between nodes.* $E = \{E_i | i = 1, 2 \ldots\}$. $E_k =< i, j >$ *means that an attacker at node i can attack node j after having sufficient privileges;*
3. *R is the set of parent–child node relationships in the attack graph.* $R = \left\{ r_{i,par(i)} \middle| i = 1, 2, \ldots \right\}$. $par(i)$ *is the set of parents of node i.* $r_{i,par(i)} = or$ *means that node i can be attacked when any of its parents has been compromised.* $r_{i,par(i)} = and$ *means that node i can only be attacked after all its parents have been compromised;*
4. P_a *is the set of node breach probabilities.* $P_a = \{P_a(i) | i = 1, 2 \ldots\}$. $P_a(i)$ *means the probability that node i is successfully attacked;*
5. P_s *is the set of node selection probabilities.* $P_s = \{P_s(i) | i = 1, 2 \ldots\}$. $P_s(i)$ *means the probability that node i is selected by the attacker as an attack target;*
6. P_c *is the set of conditional probabilities of nodes.* $P_c = \{P_c(i | Parent(i)) | i = 1, 2 \ldots\}$. $P_c(i | Parent(i))$ *means the conditional probability that the node i will be attacked after its parent is compromised.*

Aiming at the problem of efficiency caused by searching the attack path on the whole attack graph in traditional methods, this paper adopts the method of attack path analysis based on Bayesian attack subgraphs. The first step is to partition the network to form Bayesian attack subgraphs. The construction of Bayesian attack subgraphs includes three parts: network partition, attack subgraph construction, and node quantification.

Partitioning a large-scale network into multiple subnetworks is the basis for generating Bayesian attack subgraphs. In this paper, the Lovain algorithm based on modularity evaluation is used to divide the network. Modularity is used to evaluate the closeness of the community structure. The modularity gain reflects the comparison of the modularity of the whole graph when a node is merged from one community to another. The goal of Lovain algorithm partitioning is to maximize the modularity increment. The calculation formula of the modularity increment ΔQ is given in Equation (1).

$$\Delta Q = \frac{1}{2\varpi}(\kappa_{i,in} - \frac{\sum_{tot} \kappa_i}{\varpi}), \tag{1}$$

where $\kappa_{i,in}$ is the sum of edge weights between node i and all nodes in the merged target community. $\sum tot$ is the sum of edge weights related to nodes in the target community. κ_i is the sum of edge weights of node i. ϖ is the sum of all edge weights. In the directed unweighted graph, the weight of each edge can be regarded as one.

The attack subgraph is constructed based on subnetworks formed by community division. For each community network, the vulnerabilities of each host are obtained first. Then, it determines whether there is an exploitation relationship between any two vulnerabilities i and j on any two connected hosts; if there is, a directed edge $E_k =< i, j >$ is added between i and j to represent the attack relationship. After all the vulnerabilities are processed, the vulnerabilities in the subnetwork form N in the corresponding attack subgraph, and the attack relationship between the vulnerabilities form E.

To use Bayesian theory for analysis in attack subgraphs, vulnerability nodes in each attack subgraph need to be quantified to form a Bayesian attack subgraph. Each node i needs to quantify $P_a(i)$ and $P_s(i)$ based on CVSS. $P_a(i)$ is related to the difficulty of the node i being exploited, and the lower the difficulty, the easier it is to be compromised. $P_s(i)$ is related to the attack cost of the node i, and the lower the attack cost, the easier it is to be selected as an attack object. In CVSS, the attack vector score S_{AV} and the attack complexity score S_{AC} can measure the difficulty of exploiting the vulnerability, while the privileges required score S_{PR} and user interaction score S_{UI} can measure the exploitation cost of the vulnerability. Therefore, $P_a(i)$ and $P_s(i)$ are calculated by Equations (2) and (3), respectively.

$$P_a(i) = S_{AV} \times S_{AC}, \tag{2}$$

$$P_s(i) = S_{PR} \times S_{UI}, \tag{3}$$

According to the different relationship $r_{i,par(i)}$ between the node i and its parent node $par(i)$, the conditional probability $P_c(i|Par(i))$ will be quantized by different methods based on P_a and P_s. When $r_{i,par(i)} = and$, the conditional probability of node i is the probability that each parent node is compromised multiplied by the probability that node i is also compromised. When $r_{i,par(i)} = or$, the conditional probability of node i is the probability that any parent node is compromised multiplied by the probability that node i is also compromised. The calculation formulas of $P_c(i|Par(i))$ in the above two cases are shown as Equations (4) and (5), respectively. In particular, for the node j that has no parent node in the entire attack graph, its conditional probability is calculated as Equation (6).

$$P_c(i|Parent(i)) = \begin{cases} 0, \ N_k \in Parent(i), \ N_k = 0 \\ \prod P_a(Parent(i)) \times P_s(i) \times P_a(i)' \end{cases} \tag{4}$$

$$P_c(i|Parent(i)) = \begin{cases} 0, \ N_k \in Parent(i), \ N_k = 0 \\ \{1 - \prod[1 - P_a(Parent(i))]\} \times P_s(i) \times P_a(i)' \end{cases} \tag{5}$$

$$P_c(j|Parent(j)) = P_s(j) \times P_a(j), \tag{6}$$

4.2. Attack Subgraph Paths Search

Definition 2 (The basic attack path L)**.** *L is an attack path inside the Bayesian attack subgraph, which consists of nodes with an attack relationship. $L = (N_0, N_1, \ldots N_n)$. N_i is the node inside the Bayesian attack subgraph.*

Definition 3 (The attack path information group $\boldsymbol{I}$)**.** *$\boldsymbol{I}$ is the matrix used to record the node information that appears in the corresponding attack path. $\boldsymbol{I} = (\boldsymbol{i}_1, \ldots \boldsymbol{i}_n)$. $\boldsymbol{i}_k$ is a two-dimensional column vector where the first row is the node number and the second row is the depth of the node.*

Definition 4 (The path reachability probability P)**.** *P describes the possibility of an attacker attacking through a certain path.*

The second step of attack path analysis based on the Bayesian attack subgraph is to search the basic attack path and its corresponding attack path information group inside each attack subgraph, which will be used for subsequent path aggregation and then used as indicators for clustering. Since the analysis speed inside the attack subgraph is better than the analysis speed in the whole attack graph, and the storage space requirement of the attack subgraph is lower than that of the whole attack graph, the purpose of improving the time and space efficiency of the analysis can be achieved. This section will introduce how to search the attack path and record the attack path information inside the established Bayesian attack subgraph.

For each attack subgraph, firstly, the set of nodes whose out-degree value and in-degree value are both 0 are obtained, respectively. Then, the search starts from the node with in-degree 0 as the initial node, and the node connected to the current node is the next node on the attack path. The conditional probability of the nodes on the path is multiplied to calculate the reachability probability P of the basic attack path. After that, the search continues from the next node until the node with out-degree 0 is reached. Finally, a basic attack path is formed, and the information group $\boldsymbol{I}$ corresponding to the basic attack path is recorded during the search process for subsequent attack path aggregation. The formula for calculating P is shown as Equation (7).

$$P = \prod P_c(i|Parent(i)), \tag{7}$$

The attack subgraph path search algorithm is shown in Algorithm 1.

Algorithm 1: BasicPathSearch

Input: The Bayesian attack subgraph set *BAGs*
Output: The basic path set *Ls* in the Bayesian attack subgraph, the information group set *Is*, and the basic path reachability probability set *Probs*

```
FOR each attack subgraph BAG in BAGs
  The set N_out of nodes whose out-degree is 0 and the set N_in of nodes whose in- degree is 0
in BAG are counted
  FOR each node n in N_in
    Add n to L, store the information of n to I, Prob = P_c(n | Parent(n))
    FOR n's each neighbor node n'
      Add n' to L, store the information of n' to I, Prob = Pc(n' | Parent(n'))
      IF n' ∈ N_out
        Add L, I, Prob to the result sets Ls, Is, and Probs, respectively
      ELSE
        n = n'
```

4.3. Attack Paths and Its Information Aggregation

The reachability probability of the attack path in the Bayesian attack graph describes the possibility of the attacker attacking along the vulnerable nodes on the path. The larger the reachability probability is, the higher the threat degree of the nodes on the path is. Therefore, the reachability probability of the attack path is used as an evaluation index for the subsequent clustering algorithm. This method considers the influence of the node's position in the attack path on its threat degree and makes the search results of key vulnerable nodes more accurate. However, the attack probability is for the attack path, and cannot be used as the vulnerability node feature for clustering. It needs to combine the node depth information in the information group to convert it into the characteristics of the vulnerability node.

The attack path and its information group in the Bayesian attack graph are aggregated based on the basic attack path L in each attack subgraph, the corresponding path information group $\boldsymbol{I}$ and the basic path reachability probability P. Firstly, a directed path from the subgraph of the attacker to the subgraph of the attack target is selected according to the connectivity of attack subgraphs. Let the length of the path be $\mathcal{L}'$. Then, a basic path L_k is selected in each attack subgraph, and the path reachability probability vector $\widehat{\boldsymbol{P}}$ and the attack relation vector $\widehat{\boldsymbol{AR}}$ between paths are constructed based on these paths according to Equations (8) and (9).

$$\widehat{\boldsymbol{P}} = (P_{L_{k_1}}, P_{L_{k_2}}, \ldots, P_{L_{k_{\mathcal{L}'-1}}}, P_{L_{k_{\mathcal{L}'}}}), \tag{8}$$

$$\widehat{\boldsymbol{AR}} = \left(1, ar_{L_{k_1}L_{k_2}}, \ldots, ar_{L_{k_{\mathcal{L}'-1}}L_{k_{\mathcal{L}'}}}\right), ar_{L_{k_{\mathcal{L}'-1}}L_{k_{\mathcal{L}'}}} = 0 \; or \; 1, \tag{9}$$

where $P_{L_{k1}}$, $P_{L_{k2}}$ and so on are the reachability probabilities of the selected basic paths. $\mathcal{L}'$ is the number of subgraphs in the path between subgraphs. $ar_{L_{k_1}L_{k_2}} = 1$ indicates that the tail node of the basic path L_{k_1} can utilize the head node of the basic path L_{k_2}. $ar_{L_{k_1}L_{k_2}} = 0$ indicates that the tail node of the basic path L_{k_1} can not utilize the head node of the basic path L_{k_2}. ψ is the control variable of the attack path, which is used to control the effectiveness of the obtained attack path. When $\psi = 0$, it means that some selected basic paths are not connected, that is, the corresponding attack path is invalid. Only valid paths are taken into account. The calculation formula of ψ is given in Equation (10).

$$\psi = \prod \widehat{AR} = \prod_{i=0}^{\mathcal{L}'-1} ar_{L_{k_i} L_{k_{i+1}}}, \tag{10}$$

Finally, the reachability probability P' of the aggregated attack path is obtained through Equation (11), and the corresponding information group $\boldsymbol{I}'$ is obtained by merging the information groups of each basic path according to Equation (12).

$$P' = \widehat{\boldsymbol{P}} \times \widehat{\boldsymbol{AR}}^T, \tag{11}$$

$$\boldsymbol{I}' = \left[\boldsymbol{I}_{L_{k_1}}, \boldsymbol{I}_{L_{k_2}}, \ldots, \boldsymbol{I}_{L_{k_{\mathcal{L}'}}}\right], \tag{12}$$

The set of all effective attack paths, the set of corresponding attack path reachability probabilities, and the set of corresponding information groups of the whole attack graph formed by the aggregation will be used as the indicators of the subsequent clustering algorithm. The attack path aggregation algorithm based on the basic path and its information group is shown in Algorithm 2.

Algorithm 2: AttackPathAggregation

Input: The attack connection information C between subgraphs, the utilization relation U of nodes, the basic path reachability probability P, the basic path information group $\boldsymbol{I}$
Output: The aggregated reachability probability P' of the attack path and its corresponding information group $\boldsymbol{I}'$

1. Select an inter-subgraph path $SubBAGPath$ from the subgraph where the attacker is located to the subgraph where the attack target is located according to C.
2. $\widehat{\boldsymbol{AR}} = [1], \widehat{\boldsymbol{P}} = [], \psi = 1, \boldsymbol{I}' = []$
3. FOR each attack subgraph BAG' in $SubBAGPath$
4. Select a basic path L_k from BAG', whose tail node is *tail* and head node is *head*, and add P_{L_k} to $\widehat{\boldsymbol{P}}$
5. IF BAG' is not the attack subgraph where the attacker is located
6. IF $U(lastTail, head) = 1$
7. $ar_{L_{last} L_k} = 1$, update $\widehat{\boldsymbol{AR}}$ and ψ
8. ELSE
9. BREAK
10. ELSE
11. $L_{last} = L_k$
12. $lastTail = tail$, add I_{L_k} to $\boldsymbol{I}'$
13. $P' = \widehat{\boldsymbol{P}} * \widehat{\boldsymbol{AR}}^T$

5. Discovery of Key Vulnerable Nodes Based on Improved FCM

When the attack graph is used for security analysis, the threat degree of the vulnerability node is related to various factors, such as the exploitability score and impact score of the vulnerability node in CVSS, the position of the vulnerability node in the attack graph, and the occurrence times of the vulnerability node. Only one factor will lead to inaccurate search results for key vulnerability nodes. Therefore, this paper takes a variety of factors that affect the vulnerability threat degree as the characteristics of vulnerability nodes and uses FCM to cluster them. Then, the feature priority is set to find out the set of key vulnerability nodes with the highest priority. The discovery process of key vulnerable nodes based on improved FCM is shown in Figure 3.

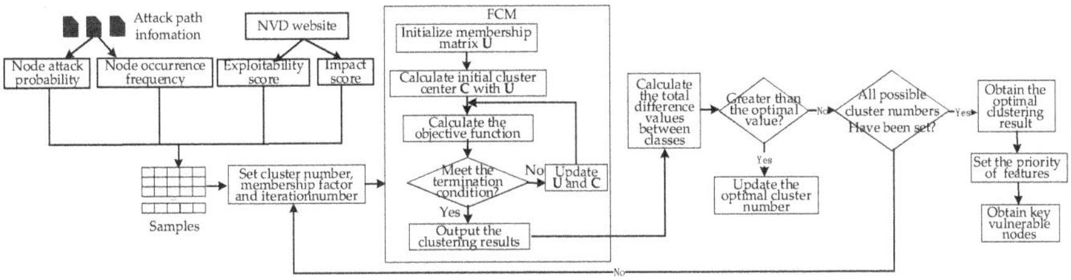

Figure 3. The discovery process of key vulnerable nodes based on improved FCM.

Firstly, it is necessary to determine the features of the participating clustering samples, which are considered from two aspects in this paper. The first is the inherent threat features of the vulnerability node, including the exploitability score and impact score. The inherent threat is the threat evaluation standard set by the National Vulnerability Database of the United States based on CVSS, combined with the damage degree of the vulnerability in various scenarios. It represents the comprehensive threat degree of the vulnerability. These two values do not change with the actual network environment of the vulnerability. The second is the actual threat features of the vulnerable nodes. Due to the vulnerability in different network environments, the threat degree is different. Its inherent threat cannot accurately reflect the threat of vulnerabilities in the actual situation. In this paper, an attack graph is constructed based on the actual network environment to realize the search for attack path information, which can reflect the actual threat situation of the vulnerability node in the current network environment. Therefore, this section will extract the actual threat features of the vulnerability node based on the attack path information, including the occurrence frequency and attack probability of the vulnerability node.

The occurrence frequency Ocr of the vulnerability node is the total number of occurrences of each node in all attack paths, which reflects the possibility that the attacker uses the node as the entry point to carry out the attack. It can be directly counted in the search process. The calculation formula of Ocr is shown in Equation (13).

$$Ocr_n = \sum_{p=1}^{tot} \sum_{i=0}^{N_p-1} \boldsymbol{I}^p_{0,i},\ \boldsymbol{I}^p_{0,i} = \begin{cases} 1, \boldsymbol{I}^p_{0,i} = n \\ 0, \boldsymbol{I}^p_{0,i} \neq n \end{cases}, \tag{13}$$

where Ocr_n is the occurrence frequency of node n, tot is the total number of attack paths, N_p is the total number of nodes in the p-th attack path, $\boldsymbol{I}^p_{0,i}$ is the value of row 0 and column i in the p-th attack path information group. The attack probability Pb of the vulnerable node reflects the probability that the node is compromised, which is obtained from the attack probability of its attack path and the corresponding information group. The calculation formula of Pb is shown in Equation (14).

$$Pb_n = \frac{\sum_p \frac{\boldsymbol{I}^p_{1,m} - d}{\boldsymbol{I}^p_{1,m}} \times P'_p}{number},\ (d = \boldsymbol{I}^p_{1,i}, \boldsymbol{I}^p_{0,i} = n)\ and\ (\forall p, \exists j, \boldsymbol{I}^p_{0,j} = n), \tag{14}$$

where Pb_n is the attack probability of node n, $\boldsymbol{I}^p_{1,m}$ is the maximum depth of the p-th attack path, d is the depth of n in the p-th attack path, P'_p is the attack probability of the p-th attack path, $number$ is the number of attack paths including n.

Secondly, the traditional FCM algorithm has no means to determine the optimal number of clusters, but determining the number of clusters only by subjective methods will reduce the accuracy of clustering results, making the difference between classes not obvious, and it is difficult to determine the key vulnerability nodes. To make the difference in the degree of clustering results obvious, combined with the demand characteristics of this method, this paper determines the optimal number of clusters based on the discrimination degree between clusters. For the current clustering results, this method first sets a cluster number, calculates the intra-class average vector $\boldsymbol{m}_j$ of each class, and obtains the total average vector $\boldsymbol{m}$ through the intra-class average vector. The calculation formula of $\boldsymbol{m}$ is shown in Equation (15).

$$\boldsymbol{m}_j = \frac{\sum_i \boldsymbol{F}_i}{d_j}, i = 1,2,\ldots,d_j, \ \boldsymbol{m} = \frac{\sum_{j=1}^{C} \boldsymbol{m}_j}{C}, \tag{15}$$

where $\boldsymbol{F}_i$ is the feature vector of the i-th sample in the j-th class, C is the total number of clusters, and d_j is the total number of samples of the j-th class. Then, the optimization objective is to maximize the sum of the squared Euclidean distance between the average vector within each class and the total average vector. This value is called the total difference value between classes (TDVC). Thus, the optimal number of clusters can be obtained. The optimization objective is shown in Equation (16).

$$maxf(c) = \frac{\sum_{j=1}^{c} (\boldsymbol{m}_j - \boldsymbol{m})^2}{c}, c \in [2, N], \tag{16}$$

where c is the number of clusters currently set, N is the total number of vulnerability nodes, and $f(c)$ is the TDVC corresponding to c.

Finally, FCM clustering is carried out after determining the sample features and the optimal number of clusters. FCM uses membership degree to assign uncertainty to classification. It allows a data point to belong to more than one class and assigns each sample to the class with the largest membership degree. This ability makes it better reflect the fuzziness and complexity of data in the real world. Therefore, the key of FCM is to determine the cluster center $\boldsymbol{V}$ and the membership degree matrix $\boldsymbol{U}$. The objective function of FCM is shown in Equation (17).

$$J_m = \sum_{i=1}^{D} \sum_{j=1}^{C} u_{ij}^{\alpha} \|x_i - v_j\|^2, \sum_{j=1}^{C} u_{ij} = 1, i = 1,2,\ldots D, \tag{17}$$

where α is the membership factor, i is the sample number, j is the class number, u_{ij} is the membership degree of sample i for class j, x_i is the i-th sample, C is the total cluster number, v_j is the j-th cluster center, and D is the total number of samples. FCM constantly updates $\boldsymbol{U}$ and $\boldsymbol{V}$ to minimize the objective function, thus completing the clustering. Constraints are added to the objective function by Lagrange multiplier method. Based on this formula, the partial derivatives of variables u and v are obtained, respectively. Then, the updated formula for $\boldsymbol{U}$ and $\boldsymbol{V}$ are obtained by setting the derivative to 0. These two formulas are shown in Equation (18).

$$u_{ij} = \frac{1}{\sum_{k=1}^{C} \left(\frac{\|x_i - v_j\|}{\|x_i - v_k\|}\right)^{\frac{2}{\alpha-1}}}, v_j = \frac{\sum_{i=1}^{D} u_{ij}^{\alpha} \cdot x_i}{\sum_{i=1}^{D} u_{ij}^{\alpha}}, \tag{18}$$

The vulnerability nodes clustering algorithm based on improved FCM is shown in Algorithm 3.

After the clustering is completed, the priority among features is set according to the feature characteristics. The clustering results are compared according to priority, and the nodes in the category ranked first are selected as the key vulnerable node set. Since the vulnerability impact score and exploitability score are authoritative indicators in CVSS, they should be considered first, and they have the same importance in CVSS calculation formula. For the node occurrence frequency and the node attack probability, the attack probability takes more factors into account, including the path location of the node and the attack path probability. It can divide the threat degree of the vulnerability node more fine-grained, so the attack probability is considered when the first three are close. To sum up, the order of feature priority is the impact score, exploitability score, occurrence frequency, and attack probability of the vulnerability.

Algorithm 3: VulnerabilityClusteringByImprovedFCM

Input: The vulnerability node samples $samples$, the total number of samples D
Output: The number of optimal clusters $number$, and the corresponding clustering result $result$

1. Initialize $number$, $result$, and the corresponding TDVC $value = 0$.
2. FOR $d = 1, 2, \ldots, D$
3. Initialize $\boldsymbol{U}$ and $\boldsymbol{V}$, set the membership factor α, set the number of clusters $C = d$, set the maximum number of iterations of the cluster to T
4. WHILE($T > 0$)
5. Update $\boldsymbol{U}$ and $\boldsymbol{V}$ by Equation (17)
6. $T = T - 1$
7. FOR $i = 1, 2, \ldots, D$
8. Set the class of sample i to the class to which the maximum membership degree of sample i belongs in $\boldsymbol{U}$
9. FOR $c = 1, 2, \ldots, C$
10. Calculate $\boldsymbol{m}_c$ by Equation (15)
11. Calculate $\boldsymbol{m}$ by Equation (15), and calculate the current TDVC f_C by Equation (16)
12. IF $f_C > value$
13. $value = f_C$, $number = C$, update $result$ to the current cluster result

---

6. Results

6.1. Experimental Scenario

This paper constructs an experimental scenario to verify the effectiveness of the proposed method. The experimental environment includes web servers, ftp servers, smtp servers, sql servers and multiple user devices. The vulnerabilities of each device can be obtained by using the vulnerability scanning tool. Information about vulnerabilities comes from NVD. Vulnerability quantification is based on CVSS. The attacker launched the attack from an external network, targeting important data on the SQL server. In addition, to obtain the utilization relationship between vulnerabilities, this paper uses Word2Vec combined with TextCNN to conduct a semantic analysis of vulnerability description to obtain the exploitation relationship. All code is written in Java and Python. Finally, in order to fully verify the effectiveness of the proposed method, this paper also verifies the effectiveness of the proposed method under different attack graph scales by extending the network.

6.2. Experimental Process

Firstly, the network topology of the experimental environment is abstracted. Use the vulnerability scanning tool to obtain vulnerabilities on each device to form a vulnerability set and prepare the information required for constructing Bayesian attack subgraphs. In order to obtain the unknown utilization relationship of vulnerabilities during the construction of the attack graph, the experiment uses NVD's official interface to obtain description information of common vulnerabilities and forms a corpus after word segmentation to train Word2Vec+TextCNN model to predict the utilization consequences of vulnerabilities. The basic score, impact score, exploitability score, and utilization conditions of each vulnerability in the vulnerability set are obtained from NVD. The utilization relationship is constructed according to the utilization conditions and the predicted utilization consequences. The vulnerability utilization relationship is shown in Equation (19).

$$\begin{cases} other \rightarrow NONE \\ user \rightarrow NONE, LOW \\ root \rightarrow NONE, LOW, HIGH \end{cases}, \tag{19}$$

where $con_1 \rightarrow con_2$ indicates that the vulnerability with utilization condition con_2 can be attacked after breaching the vulnerability with utilization consequence con_1. The vulnerability information and predicted exploitation consequences for some of the vulnerabilities in the vulnerability set are shown in Table 1.

Table 1. Information and predicted utilization consequences of partial vulnerabilities in the vulnerability set.

CVEID	Base Score	Exploitability Score	Impact Score	Utilization Condition	Utilization Consequence
CVE-2022-27502	7.8	5.9	1.8	LOW	user
CVE-2022-28704	7.2	5.9	1.2	HIGH	root
CVE-2022-29525	9.8	5.9	3.9	NONE	root
CVE-2022-29797	9.8	5.9	3.9	NONE	user
CVE-2022-20148	6.4	5.9	0.5	HIGH	user
CVE-2021-32546	8.8	5.9	2.8	LOW	other

The Louvain algorithm is used to divide the network into communities. The vulnerability on each device is abstracted as an attack graph node. In each community, an attack subgraph is constructed according to the attack graph nodes, network topology, and vulnerability utilization relationship. For each attack graph node, its node selection probability and breach probability are quantified to form multiple Bayesian attack subgraphs. In each community, the community connection relationship is constructed according to the network topology and vulnerability utilization relationship to quickly determine the connection between communities. The partial Bayesian attack subgraph structure is shown in Figure 4.

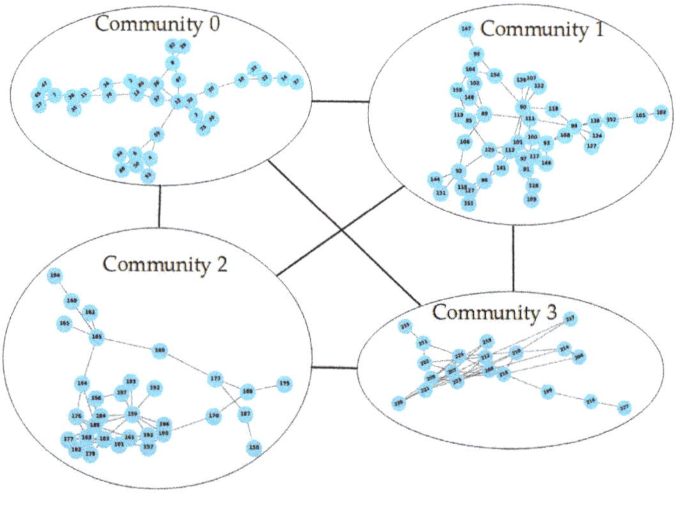

Figure 4. Partial Bayesian attack subgraphs.

Then, the method in Section 4 is used to search and aggregate the attack paths and their information groups in the constructed Bayesian attack subgraphs. The path search results in the attack subgraph and the aggregated complete path information are shown in Table 2.

Four features for FCM are extracted according to the aggregated complete attack paths and vulnerability information. The features of some samples are shown in Table 3.

Table 2. Part of the attack paths.

	Community	Attack Probability	Information Group
Attack subgraph paths	0	1.91×10^{-4}	$\begin{pmatrix} 1 & 23 & 49 & 18 & 29 & 52 & 36 \\ 1 & 2 & 3 & 4 & 5 & 6 & 7 \end{pmatrix}$
	1	2.36×10^{-2}	$\begin{pmatrix} 89 & 100 & 92 & 99 \\ 1 & 2 & 3 & 4 \end{pmatrix}$
	2	7.71×10^{-2}	$\begin{pmatrix} 155 & 188 & 162 \\ 1 & 2 & 3 \end{pmatrix}$
Aggregated paths	-	8.14×10^{-3}	$\begin{pmatrix} 226 & 215 & 198 & 217 & 37 & 189 \\ 1 & 2 & 3 & 4 & 5 & 6 \end{pmatrix}$
	-	3.34×10^{-4}	$\begin{pmatrix} 226 & 215 & 198 & 217 & 49 & 18 & 64 & 160 & 189 \\ 1 & 2 & 3 & 4 & 5 & 6 & 7 & 8 & 9 \end{pmatrix}$
	-	3.94×10^{-5}	$\begin{pmatrix} 226 & 215 & 198 & 217 & 127 & 71 & 5 & 58 & 189 \\ 1 & 2 & 3 & 4 & 5 & 6 & 7 & 8 & 9 \end{pmatrix}$

Table 3. Feature information of some samples.

Node Number	Exploitability Score	Impact Score	Occurrence Frequency	Attack Probability
1	5.9	1.0	2146	2.43×10^{-7}
18	2.7	2.8	27,762	3.39×10^{-7}
49	3.6	2.8	15,500	5.39×10^{-7}
160	3.6	2.8	15,186	4.46×10^{-7}
215	5.9	3.9	118,313	2.51×10^{-6}

Next, the improved FCM in Section 5 is used to determine the optimal number of clusters. According to the optimal cluster number, fuzzy C-means clustering is performed on the samples, and the result vulnerability set is obtained by analyzing the clustering results. The experimental results show that when the number of clusters is set to 14, the total value of the difference degree between classes reaches the maximum, that is, the optimal cluster number is 14. Some of the results of FCM clustering under the optimal number of clusters are shown in Table 4.

Table 4. Partial FCM clustering results under the optimal number of clusters.

Class Number	Node Number Contained in This Class
1	(141,189,215,217)
2	(1,2,3,8,11,26,51,71,74,121,136)
7	(4,14,28,52,55,63,116,117,120,124,140,182,183,192)
11	(6,9,12,21,30,32,72,78,80,83,87,185)
14	(18,29,39,46,47,155)

Finally, the average value of each feature in each class is calculated, and the clustering results are compared according to the set feature priority. Firstly, the exploitability score and the impact score are compared, and the comparison results are shown in Figure 5. It can be seen that the set of class numbers for which both features take the maximum mean value at the same time is (1,5,8,13).

After that, the node occurrence frequency and the node attack probability of these four types of nodes are compared. The comparison results are shown in Figure 6a,b, respectively. It can be seen from the comparison results that the mean value of each feature of Category 1 is the maximum value, so the key vulnerable node set obtained is (141,189,215,217).

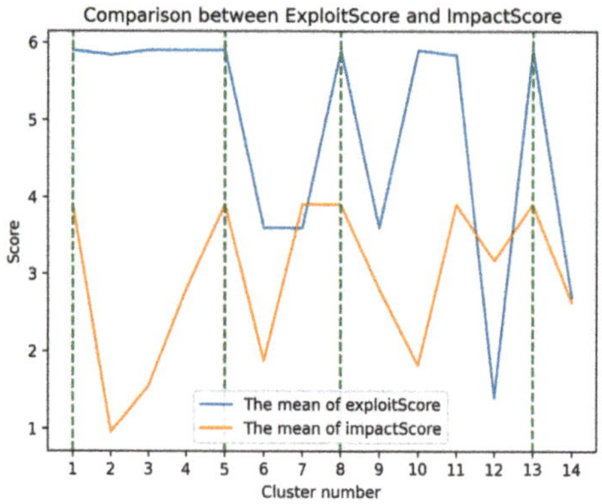

Figure 5. Comparison of the mean values of the exploitability score and the impact score.

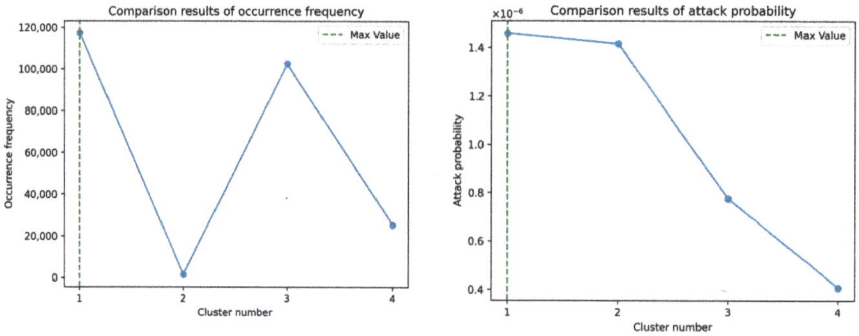

(**a**) (**b**)

Figure 6. Comparison of the mean values of the node occurrence frequency and the node attack probability: (**a**) comparison results of the node occurrence frequency; (**b**) comparison results of the node attack probability.

6.3. Experiment Results Analysis

Firstly, in order to verify the effectiveness of the optimization time efficiency of the attack path aggregation search method based on Bayesian attack subgraphs in this paper, this section makes an analysis with reference [34] from both theoretical and practical aspects. Reference [34] uses the method of searching and storing the complete attack graph. Since we cannot determine the attack graph storage strategy and search strategy of refs. [35,36], we can not check their time/space consumption.

Suppose that breadth-first search is selected as the basic search algorithm, the graph structure is stored by the adjacency matrix, and the number of nodes in the attack graph is $\mathbb{N}$. When the method of reference [34] is used to search, in the worst case, each node and its neighbors need to be traversed, and the time consumption is $\mathbb{N}^2$. When the method in this paper is used, it is assumed that the attack graph is evenly divided into m subgraphs, and each subgraph has $\mathbb{N}/m$ nodes. Then, the path search efficiency in the subgraph is $(\mathbb{N}/m)^2$. The number of paths in each subgraph is no more than $\mathbb{N}/m$ and the aggregation times of each complete path are no more than m. In the worst case, the number of traversal times to obtain all complete paths is $\mathbb{N}$, and the total time is $(\mathbb{N}/m)^2 + \mathbb{N}$. Since $m^2 > \mathbb{N}/(\mathbb{N}-1) > 1$, $\mathbb{N}/m^2 < \mathbb{N} - 1$, that is $(\mathbb{N}/m)^2 + \mathbb{N} < \mathbb{N}^2$. Therefore, the efficiency of the search method proposed in this paper is theoretically better than the efficiency of the search on the complete attack graph. Figure 7a,b show the effect of different $\mathbb{N}$ on the search efficiency of the two methods in theory and experiment, respectively.

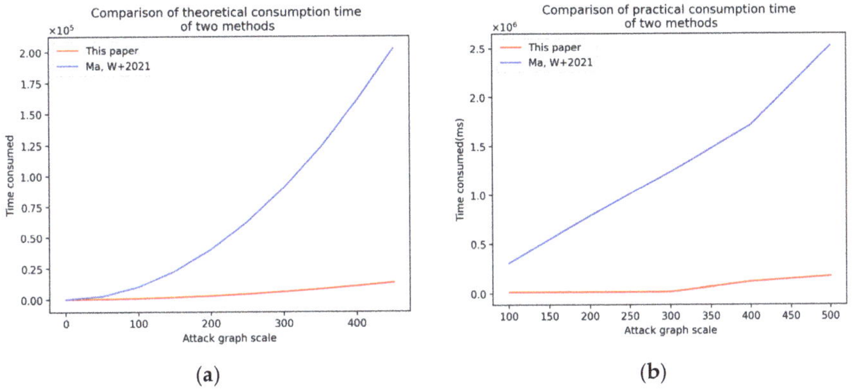

Figure 7. Comparison of search time consumption between the method in this paper and the method in reference [34]: (**a**) comparison of theoretical consumption time of two methods; (**b**) comparison of practical consumption time of two methods.

Because the attack graph is divided into four subgraphs in the experiment, $m = 4$ is taken. It can be seen from Figure 7 that with the increase in the graph scale, the time consumed by the proposed method increases slightly both in theory and experiment, which can optimize the search time. The optimization effect of the proposed method on time efficiency becomes more and more obvious with the increase in the graph scale.

Then, from the perspective of space efficiency, this paper adopts the method of storing the attack graph based on subgraphs rather than the complete attack graph. Suppose that the total number of nodes in the attack graph is $\mathbb{N}$, and it is evenly divided into m attack subgraphs, each subgraph contains $\mathbb{N}/m$ nodes. Theoretically, the space consumption of storing the complete attack graph using the adjacency matrix is $\mathbb{N}^2$, and the storage method based on subgraphs consumes $(\mathbb{N}/m)^2 \times m$. Since $m > 1$, obviously $(\mathbb{N}/m)^2 \times m < \mathbb{N}^2$. Figure 8 shows the comparison of the space consumed by the two methods under different attack graph scales in the experiment.

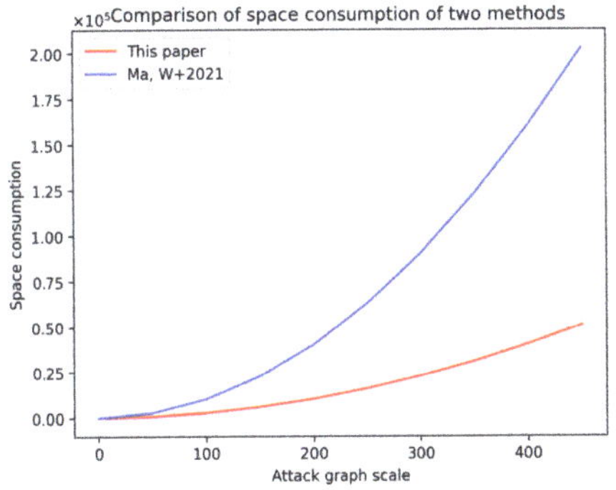

Figure 8. Comparison of the space consumed by the two methods under different attack graph scales [34].

It can be seen from Figure 8 that when the attack graph scale is small, the space consumption of the two methods is similar. However, with the increase in the graph scale, the storage method based on subgraphs has a more and more obvious effect on storage space optimization. When the attack graph has 500 nodes, the space optimization has reached 75%, so the latter can effectively improve the utilization efficiency of space.

After that, in order to verify the effectiveness of the method of determining the optimal cluster number in this paper and the superiority of improved FCM over other clustering methods, the clustering results of different clustering methods are analyzed. When only FCM is used for longitudinal analysis, the changes in the TDVC of different cluster numbers are shown in Figure 9.

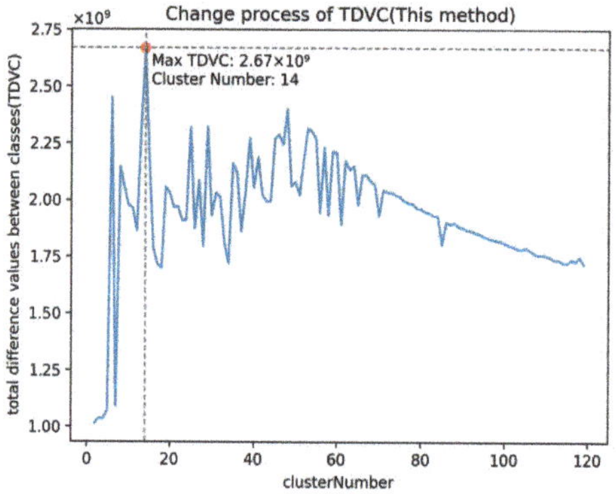

Figure 9. The change process of the TDVC of FCM.

It can be seen from Figure 9 that when the number of clusters is 14, the TDVC of clustering results is the largest. At this time, the difference between classes is the largest, and it is easy to distinguish the characteristics of various types, and the clustering effect is optimal.

Next, in the experiment, different clustering methods are selected for horizontal analysis, such as the common k-means clustering, hierarchical clustering and Density-Based Spatial Clustering of Applications with Noise (DBSCAN). The changes in TDVC for K-means clustering and hierarchical clustering are shown in Figure 10a,b, respectively.

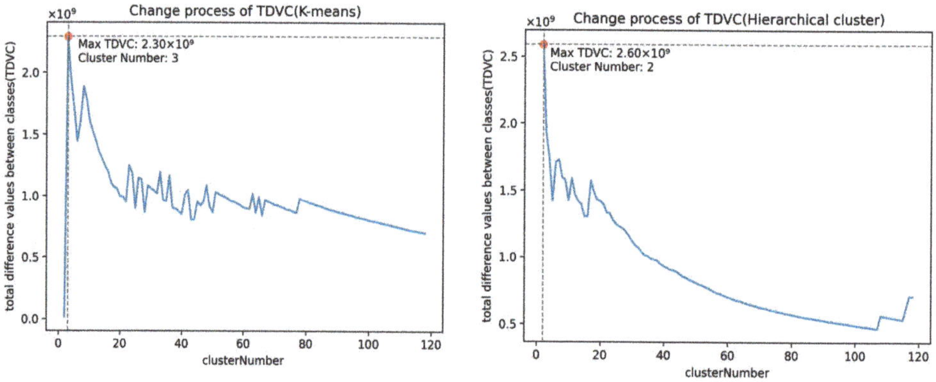

(**a**) (**b**)

Figure 10. The changes in TDVC for K-means clustering and hierarchical clustering: (**a**) the TDVC change process of K-means clustering; (**b**) the TDVC change process of hierarchical clustering.

DBSCAN, as a density clustering algorithm, does not need to specify the number of clusters in advance to complete clustering. The comparison results of the maximum TDVC of the three methods and the cluster number corresponding to the maximum TDVC are shown in Table 5.

Table 5. Comparison results of the maximum TDVC of the three methods.

Methods	FCM (This Method)	K-Means	Hierarchical Clustering	DBSCAN
Maximum TDVC	2.6692×10^9	2.2973×10^9	2.5907×10^9	5.3945×10^7
Corresponding cluster number	14	3	2	-

It can be seen from Table 5 that the maximum value of the TDVC obtained by the other clustering methods is lower than the maximum value of FCM. It shows that compared with other clustering results, the difference between the clusters in the clustering results of FCM is larger, which is more in line with the requirements of the proposed method. So using FCM as the clustering method is the optimal choice.

Finally, in order to verify the accuracy of the collection results of key vulnerability nodes in the proposed method, this experiment compares the results of this paper with the search results of [35–37], respectively. The search results of key vulnerable nodes, the reachability of target nodes, and the changes in the number of attack paths after repairing the four methods are shown in Table 6.

Table 6. Comparison of effectiveness of search results of four methods.

Methods	Key Vulnerability Node	Target Nodes Reachability	Number of Remaining Attack Paths
This paper	(92,141,152,189,215,217)	unreachable	0
[35]	(32,37,130,190,215)	reachable	79,983
[36]	(141,189,217)	reachable	635
[37]	(92,141,189,215,217)	reachable	13

Reference [35] only considers the CVSS score threat characteristics of vulnerabilities and takes the node with the highest score as the key vulnerable node. The attack probability of the attack path of nodes 32, 37, and 30 is only 3.1615×10^{-9}. In practice, it can be regarded as an impossible event that the attacker attacks along this path. Therefore, after repairing the nodes, the target node is still reachable, and the key vulnerable nodes are not accurately obtained. Reference [36] considers both the threat of vulnerability itself and the actual threat and removes part of the attack paths by pruning to improve the analysis efficiency in large-scale attack graphs. However, the removed attack paths affect the search accuracy of key vulnerable nodes, and there are 92,152,215 missing nodes. This results in that although the number of remaining attack paths is greatly reduced after repairing the key vulnerable nodes, the target nodes are still reachable. After analysis, the remaining 635 paths all contain one or more of the 92,152,215 nodes. Reference [37] adopts the current advanced neural network method. The results obtained in the set experimental environment are (92,141,189,215,217). However, like reference [36], partial pruning paths reduce the accuracy of search results. This results in a missing node 152 in the search results. After the key vulnerable nodes obtained by the proposed method are repaired, the target node is unreachable, which shows the accuracy and effectiveness of the search results. Because the method in this paper not only considers all attack paths but also considers the inherent and actual threat characteristics of the vulnerability. The characteristics of this paper compared with other reference methods are summarized in Table 7.

Table 7. Comparison of the characteristics of this paper with other references.

Methods	Time Optimization	Space Optimization	Consider Vulnerability Features	Consider Actual Features	Consider All Paths	Adaptive Adjustment of Cluster Number	Get Key Vulnerabilities
[19]	Yes	No	Yes	Yes	Yes	No	No
[29]	Yes	No	Yes	No	No	No	Yes
[31]	No	No	Yes	No	Yes	No	Yes
[35]	No	No	Yes	No	No	No	Yes
[36]	Yes	No	Yes	Yes	No	No	Yes
This paper	Yes	Yes	Yes	Yes	Yes	Yes	Yes

7. Conclusions

It is an important problem in network security analysis to obtain the key vulnerable nodes in large-scale networks quickly and accurately. In this paper, the large-scale network is divided into multiple subnetworks by the idea of community division, and the Bayesian attack subgraphs are constructed by quantifying the subgraph nodes. Then, the analysis results of the attack path information in the subgraph are aggregated to quickly obtain the analysis results of the complete attack graph. The experimental results show that under the attack graph scale of 500 nodes, the time consumption of the analysis method based on subgraphs is only 10% of that of the analysis method based on the complete attack graph, and the space consumption is only 25% of the latter, which has a great improvement in time and space efficiency. Next, the optimal number of clusters is adaptively determined by using the idea of variance, and the actual threat features of the vulnerability nodes in the network are extracted from the analysis results of the attack graph. The threat features of the vulnerability themselves proposed in CVSS are combined for fuzzy C-means clustering, and the key vulnerable nodes are obtained by setting feature priorities according to the clustering results. Fuzzy clustering can take into account a variety of features that affect the threat of vulnerabilities, and improve the accuracy of the search results of key vulnerable nodes. The experimental results confirm the effectiveness of the method in this paper. However, the method of quantifying the threat value of vulnerable nodes in this paper is relatively simple, and only CVSS is used as a single quantification standard. In addition, there is no pruning method in the aggregation process of attack subgraph paths, and the amount of attack path information in the aggregation process is small, so the accuracy of the results needs to be improved. In the future, the quantization scheme of node attack probability will be optimized by Bayesian theory, and the accuracy of key node search results will be improved by increasing the amount of information in path aggregation. For the obtained key vulnerable nodes, game theory can also be used to lay out the node defense scheme.

Author Contributions: Conceptualization, Y.X. (Yuhua Xu) and Y.L.; methodology, Y.X. (Yuhua Xu) and Y.L.; writing—review and editing, Y.X. (Yuhua Xu) and Y.L.; investigation, Y.X. (Yucheng Xue), W.L., C.L. and Z.S. (Zhe Sun); software, Y.X. (Yucheng Xue), W.L., C.L. and Z.S. (Zhe Sun); writing—original draft preparation, Y.X. (Yucheng Xue), W.L., C.L. and Z.S. (Zhe Sun); validation: Y.X. (Yuhua Xu) and Y.L.; supervision: Y.X. (Yuhua Xu) and Z.S. (Zhixin Sun). All authors have read and agreed to the published version of the manuscript.

Funding: This work is supported by the National Natural Science Foundation of China under Grant 62272239; Jiangsu Agriculture Science and Technology Innovation Fund (JASTIF) CX(22)1007; the Natural Science Foundation of the Jiangsu Higher Education Institutions of China Grant 22KJB520027; Natural Science Research Start-up Foundation of Recruiting Talents of Nanjing University of Posts and Telecommunications Grant NY222029; Guizhou Provincial Key Technology R&D Program [2023]272; the Postgraduate Research & Innovation Plan of Jiangsu Province under Grant KYCX20_0761.

Data Availability Statement: The dataset supporting this study is available through the official interface provided at https://nvd.nist.gov, accessed on 20 February 2024.

Conflicts of Interest: The authors of this study declare that no conflict of interest could influence the study of this paper.

References

1. Aslan, Ö.; Aktuğ, S.S.; Ozkan-Okay, M.; Yilmaz, A.A.; Akin, E. A comprehensive review of cyber security vulnerabilities, threats, attacks, and solutions. *Electronics* **2023**, *12*, 1333. [CrossRef]
2. Ferrara, P.; Mandal, A.K.; Cortesi, A.; Spoto, F. Static analysis for discovering IoT vulnerabilities. *Int. J. Softw. Tools Technol. Transf.* **2021**, *23*, 71–88. [CrossRef]
3. Vallabhaneni, R.; Vaddadi, S.; Maroju, A.; Dontu, S. Analysis on Security Vulnerabilities of the Modern Internet of Things (IOT) Systems. *Int. J. Recent Innov. Trends Comput. Commun.* **2024**, *11*, 9.
4. Jbair, M.; Ahmad, B.; Maple, C.; Harrison, R. Threat modelling for industrial cyber physical systems in the era of smart manufacturing. *Comput. Ind.* **2022**, *137*, 103611. [CrossRef]
5. Xiong, W.; Legrand, E.; Åberg, O.; Lagerström, R. Cyber security threat modeling based on the MITRE Enterprise ATT&CK Matrix. *Softw. Syst. Model.* **2022**, *21*, 157–177.
6. Cao, S.; Sun, X.; Bo, L.; Wei, Y.; Li, B. Bgnn4vd: Constructing bidirectional graph neural-network for vulnerability detection. *Inf. Softw. Technol.* **2021**, *136*, 106576. [CrossRef]
7. Liu, Z.; Qian, P.; Wang, X.; Zhuang, Y.; Qiu, L. Combining graph neural networks with expert knowledge for smart contract vulnerability detection. *IEEE Trans. Knowl. Data Eng.* **2021**, *35*, 1296–1310. [CrossRef]
8. Zheng, Y.; Pujar, S.; Lewis, B.; Buratti, L.; Epstein, E.; Yang, B.; Su, Z. D2a: A dataset built for ai-based vulnerability detection methods using differential analysis. In Proceedings of the 2021 IEEE/ACM 43rd International Conference on Software Engineering: Software Engineering in Practice (ICSE-SEIP), Madrid, Spain, 25–28 May 2021; pp. 111–120.
9. Chakraborty, S.; Krishna, R.; Ding, Y.; Ray, B. Deep learning based vulnerability detection: Are we there yet? *IEEE Trans. Softw. Eng.* **2021**, *48*, 3280–3296. [CrossRef]
10. Steenhoek, B.; Rahman, M.M.; Jiles, R.; Le, W. An empirical study of deep learning models for vulnerability detection. In Proceedings of the 2023 IEEE/ACM 45th International Conference on Software Engineering (ICSE), Melbourne, Australia, 14–20 May 2023; pp. 2237–2248.
11. Almazrouei, O.S.M.B.H.; Magalingam, P.; Hasan, M.K.; Hasan, M.K.; Shanmugam, M. A review on attack graph analysis for iot vulnerability assessment: Challenges, open issues, and future directions. *IEEE Access* **2023**, *11*, 44350–44376. [CrossRef]
12. Zenitani, K. Attack graph analysis: An explanatory guide. *Comput. Secur.* **2023**, *126*, 103081. [CrossRef]
13. Hankin, C.; Malacaria, P. Attack dynamics: An automatic attack graph generation framework based on system topology, CAPEC, CWE, and CVE databases. *Comput. Secur.* **2022**, *123*, 102938.
14. Mohammadzad, M.; Karimpour, J.; Mahan, F. MAGD: Minimal Attack Graph Generation Dynamically in Cyber Security. *Comput. Netw.* **2023**, *236*, 110004. [CrossRef]
15. Presekal, A.; Ştefanov, A.; Rajkumar, V.S.; Palensky, P. Attack graph model for cyber-physical power systems using hybrid deep learning. *IEEE Trans. Smart Grid* **2023**, *14*, 4007–4020. [CrossRef]
16. Shin, G.Y.; Hong, S.S.; Lee, J.S.; Han, I.-S.; Kim, H.-K.; Oh, H.-R. Network security node-edge scoring system using attack graph based on vulnerability correlation. *Appl. Sci.* **2022**, *12*, 6852. [CrossRef]
17. Al-Araji, Z.J.; Ahmad, S.S.S.; Abdullah, R.S. Propose vulnerability metrics to measure network secure using attack graph. *Int. J. Adv. Comput. Sci. Appl.* **2021**, *12*, 51–58. [CrossRef]
18. Al-Araji, Z.; Syed Ahmad, S.S.; Abdullah, R.S. Attack prediction to enhance attack path discovery using improved attack graph. *Karbala Int. J. Mod. Sci.* **2022**, *8*, 313–329. [CrossRef]
19. Kholidy, H.A. Multi-layer attack graph analysis in the 5G edge network using a dynamic hexagonal fuzzy method. *Sensors* **2021**, *22*, 9. [CrossRef] [PubMed]
20. Saravanakumar, T.; Lee, T.H. Hybrid-driven-based resilient control for networked T-S fuzzy systems with time-delay and cyber-attacks. *Int. J. Robust Nonlinear Control* **2023**, *33*, 7869–7891. [CrossRef]
21. Jiang, S.; Yang, L.; Cheng, G.; Gao, X.; Feng, T.; Zhou, Y. A quantitative framework for network resilience evaluation using Dynamic Bayesian Network. *Comput. Commun.* **2022**, *194*, 387–398. [CrossRef]
22. Xie, J.; Zhang, S.; Wang, H.; Chen, M. Multiobjective network security dynamic assessment method based on Bayesian network attack graph. *Int. J. Intell. Comput. Cybern.* **2024**, *17*, 38–60. [CrossRef]
23. Luo, Z.; Xu, R.; Wang, J.; Zhu, W. A Dynamic Risk Assessment Method Based on Bayesian Attack Graph. *Int. J. Netw. Secur* **2022**, *24*, 787–796.
24. Hao, J.; Luo, S.; Pan, L. A novel vulnerability severity assessment method for source code based on a graph neural network. *Inf. Softw. Technol.* **2023**, *161*, 107247. [CrossRef]
25. Tang, G.; Yang, L.; Zhang, L.; Cao, W.; Meng, L.; He, H.; Kuang, H.; Yang, F.; Wang, H. An attention-based automatic vulnerability detection approach with GGNN. *Int. J. Mach. Learn. Cybern.* **2023**, *14*, 3113–3127. [CrossRef]
26. Li, H.J.; Wang, L.; Bu, Z.; Cao, J.; Shi, Y. Measuring the network vulnerability based on markov criticality. *ACM Trans. Knowl. Discov. Data (TKDD)* **2021**, *16*, 1–24. [CrossRef]
27. Huang, B.; Liu, Y. A network vulnerability assessment method using general attack tree. In Proceedings of the 2022 5th International Conference on Data Science and Information Technology (DSIT), Shanghai, China, 22–24 July 2022; pp. 1–4.

28. Yang, H.; Yuan, H.; Zhang, L. Risk assessment method of IoT host based on attack graph. *Mob. Netw. Appl.* **2023**, 1–10. [CrossRef]
29. Li, Y.; Li, X. Reseasrch on multi-target network security assessment with attack graph expert system model. *Sci. Program.* **2021**, *2021*, 9921731.
30. Qian, K.; Jin, M.; Zhang, D.; Huang, H.C. Research on Evaluation Method of Network Vulnerability in Power Monitoring System. In *Advances in Intelligent Information Hiding and Multimedia Signal Processing: Proceeding of the IIH-MSP 2021 & FITAT 2021*; Springer: Singapore; Kaohsiung, Taiwan, 2022; Volume 2, pp. 113–123.
31. Xie, J.; Keda, S.; Xubing, L. Risk assessment method of power plant industrial control information security based on Bayesian attack graph. *J. Electr. Syst.* **2021**, *17*, 529.
32. Li, Z.; Liu, H.; Wu, C. Computer network security evaluation method based on improved attack graph. *J. Cyber Secur. Technol.* **2022**, *6*, 201–215. [CrossRef]
33. Ying, Y. *Research and Implementation of Network Security Measurement Technology Based on Attack Path Threat Analysis*; Beijing University of Posts and Telecommunications: Beijing, China, 2021.
34. Ma, W. Research on network vulnerability assessment based on attack graph and security metrics. *J. Phys. Conf. Ser. IOP Publ.* **2021**, *1774*, 012070. [CrossRef]
35. Vasilyev, V.; Kirillova, A.; Vulfin, A.; Nikonov, A. Cybersecurity risk assessment based on cognitive attack vector modeling with CVSS Score. In Proceedings of the 2021 International Conference on Information Technology and Nanotechnology (ITNT), Samara, Russia, 20–24 September 2021; IEEE: Piscataway, NJ, USA, 2021; pp. 1–6.
36. Kalogeraki, E.M.; Papastergiou, S.; Panayiotopoulos, T. An attack simulation and evidence chains generation model for critical information infrastructures. *Electronics* **2022**, *11*, 404. [CrossRef]
37. Fan, W.; Xu, H.; Jin, W.; Liu, X.; Tang, X.; Wang, S.; Li, Q.; Tang, J.; Wang, J.; Aggarwal, C. Jointly attacking graph neural network and its explanations. In Proceedings of the 2023 IEEE 39th International Conference on Data Engineering (ICDE), Anaheim, CA, USA, 1 April 2023; pp. 654–667.

Disclaimer/Publisher's Note: The statements, opinions and data contained in all publications are solely those of the individual author(s) and contributor(s) and not of MDPI and/or the editor(s). MDPI and/or the editor(s) disclaim responsibility for any injury to people or property resulting from any ideas, methods, instructions or products referred to in the content.

mathematics

Article

A Multi-Agent Reinforcement Learning-Based Task-Offloading Strategy in a Blockchain-Enabled Edge Computing Network

Chenlei Liu [1,2,3,†] and Zhixin Sun [1,2,3,*,†]

[1] Key Laboratory of Broadband Wireless Communication and Sensor Network Technology (Ministry of Education), Nanjing University of Posts and Telecommunications, New Mofan Road No. 66, Nanjing 210003, China; 2019070270@njupt.edu.cn
[2] Post Big Data Technology and Application Engineering Research Center of Jiangsu Province, Nanjing University of Posts and Telecommunications, New Mofan Road No. 66, Nanjing 210003, China
[3] Post Industry Technology Research and Development Center of the State Posts Bureau (Internet of Things Technology), Nanjing University of Posts and Telecommunications, New Mofan Road No. 66, Nanjing 210003, China
* Correspondence: sunzx@njupt.edu.cn
† These authors contributed equally to this work.

Abstract: In recent years, many mobile edge computing network solutions have enhanced data privacy and security and built a trusted network mechanism by introducing blockchain technology. However, this also complicates the task-offloading problem of blockchain-enabled mobile edge computing, and traditional evolutionary learning and single-agent reinforcement learning algorithms are difficult to solve effectively. In this paper, we propose a blockchain-enabled mobile edge computing task-offloading strategy based on multi-agent reinforcement learning. First, we innovatively propose a blockchain-enabled mobile edge computing task-offloading model by comprehensively considering optimization objectives such as task execution energy consumption, processing delay, user privacy metrics, and blockchain incentive rewards. Then, we propose a deep reinforcement learning algorithm based on multiple agents sharing a global memory pool using the actor–critic architecture, which enables each agent to acquire the experience of another agent during the training process to enhance the collaborative capability among agents and overall performance. In addition, we adopt attenuatable Gaussian noise into the action space selection process in the actor network to avoid falling into the local optimum. Finally, experiments show that this scheme's comprehensive cost calculation performance is enhanced by more than 10% compared with other multi-agent reinforcement learning algorithms. In addition, Gaussian random noise-based action space selection and a global memory pool improve the performance by 38.36% and 43.59%, respectively.

Keywords: blockchain; mobile edge computing; task offloading; multi-agent reinforcement learning

MSC: 68T07

check for updates

Citation: Liu, C.; Sun, Z. A Multi-Agent Reinforcement Learning-Based Task-Offloading Strategy in a Blockchain-Enabled Edge Computing Network. *Mathematics* **2024**, *12*, 2264. https://doi.org/10.3390/math12142264

Academic Editor: Florin Leon

Received: 21 June 2024
Revised: 13 July 2024
Accepted: 15 July 2024
Published: 19 July 2024

Copyright: © 2024 by the authors. Licensee MDPI, Basel, Switzerland. This article is an open access article distributed under the terms and conditions of the Creative Commons Attribution (CC BY) license (https://creativecommons.org/licenses/by/4.0/).

1. Introduction

Mobile Edge Computing (MEC) is an emerging computing paradigm that deploys computing resources at the edge of the network to provide low-latency, high-bandwidth, and customizable services that can deliver computing and storage capabilities at the edge of the network, close to the data source. In addition, MEC can improve the performance, efficiency, and security of various applications that require low latency, high bandwidth, and data privacy, such as augmented reality, smart cities, and autonomous driving. However, because the mobile edge computing network environment has the characteristics of openness and dynamics, the network is vulnerable to the threat of malicious node invasion and data attacks. Such attacks can cause problems such as shared data leakage, task execution interference, and resource allocation anomalies within the network, seriously affecting the security of MEC. Therefore, ensuring the safe sharing of data and trustworthy collaboration of nodes is an important issue that needs to be solved in MEC [1,2].

Blockchain, known as a distributed, tamper-proof, decentralized data storage technology, was first proposed by Nakamoto in the context of Bitcoin, which enables secure, transparent, and immutable transactions and transfer of data records between multiple parties without relying on a trusted third party [3]. Blockchain has been widely used in various fields, such as digital asset management, supply chain finance, and intelligent manufacturing. Blockchain-based MEC (BMEC) is a new type of architecture that applies blockchain technology to MEC systems and can solve many challenges, such as data security, privacy protection, incentive mechanisms, resource management, etc. [4]. The in-depth integration of blockchain and MEC has been widely discussed [5]. In telematics and intelligent transportation systems, blockchain can provide collaborative management of service resources [6], data security sharing management [7], and collaborative node identity authentication [8]. In the smart grid, blockchain-based MEC is mainly applied to system architecture design [9], energy transaction pricing [10], and transaction security [11]. In addition, benefiting from the advantages of blockchain-based MEC, intelligent health care [12] and artificial intelligence [13] are also beginning to be applied.

Although the blockchain-based MEC system has excellent application prospects and research value, it also faces some important problems, including task offloading. MEC task offloading refers to the technology of offloading computing tasks from user devices to edge nodes or clouds for execution in order to solve the deficiencies of user devices in terms of resource storage, computational performance, and energy efficiency. For the problem of task offloading in blockchain-based MEC systems, there are still some limitations in the current research, mainly with respect to the following aspects: (1) most existing works only consider the quality of service indicators of traditional mobile edge computing task offloading, such as task processing latency and energy consumption, but ignore blockchain mechanisms and user privacy leakage, which makes the problem modeling insufficient [14–16], and (2) task offloading algorithms are often based on heuristic learning methods or single-agent reinforcement learning algorithms [17–19]. The analytical performance and solution efficiency need to be more satisfactory for dynamically changing, high-dimensional, non-convex task-offloading problems. In this paper, blockchain-based mobile edge computing task-offloading modeling and a multi-agent reinforcement learning method are investigated, and the main innovative contributions are summarized as follows:

- We propose a novel task-offloading model for blockchain-based MEC networks that comprehensively considers the blockchain-specific incentive mechanism and consensus mechanism. It also takes the user privacy metric as the optimization objective, together with the task service quality as the joint optimization objective, which makes the modeling of the optimization problem more in line with the practical environment;
- We propose a reinforcement learning algorithm based on a multi-agent global memory pool. Agents can enhance the overall collaborative ability among the agents by sharing parameters;
- We adopt attenuatable Gaussian random noise in the action space selection process in the actor network to enhance the search capability and avoid falling into local optimum;
- We conduct several sets of comparative experiments to validate the performance of the proposed algorithm in dealing with the task-offloading problem.

This paper is structured as follows. Section 2 investigates state-of-the-art research related to the research content of this paper. Section 3 presents the proposed blockchain MEC network task-offloading optimization model to be solved in this paper. Section 4 describes the principle and process of the reinforcement learning algorithm used in this paper. Section 5 conducts simulation experiments to evaluate the performance and effectiveness of the proposed algorithm. Section 6 summarizes the full paper.

2. Related Works

Blockchain-based MEC networks constitute an emerging research field combining the decentralization, high security, and tamper-proof features of blockchain and the low-latency, high-bandwidth, and real-time advantages of MEC to provide ideas for solving a series of challenges faced by the MEC network structure, such as security, privacy protection, resource management, and so on. This combination is crucial for building the next-generation of intelligent, secure, and efficient network environments. It has attracted many scholars to research its architecture and operation mechanism in depth. Le et al. [20] established a unified six-layer architecture with high efficiency, security, compatibility, and flexibility for blockchain-based resource sharing and transactions in mobile access networks. The proposes architecture contains many new features, such as an enhanced blockchain structure, secure interaction methods, efficient service mechanisms, and scalable transaction models. Salim et al. [21] proposed a latency tolerance-based cybertwin-assisted task-scheduling scheme, where cybertwins using logger functionality and digital asset functionality exchange smart contracts with cloud operators using digital assets to ensure maximum computational resources for efficient job allocation to edge clouds. Sun et al. [22] considered incentive and cross-server resource allocation in blockchain-driven MEC, where the blockchain prevents malicious edge servers from tampering with player information by maintaining a continuous, tamper-proof ledger database. In addition, they proposed two double auction mechanisms, namely the break even-based double auction mechanism (DAMB) and the more efficient break-even free double auction mechanism (BFDA), in which users request multitasking services with declared bids and edge servers cooperate to serve the users. Ding et al. [23] proposed a new noma-based MEC wireless blockchain network that minimizes system energy consumption through task offloading decision optimization, user clustering, computational resources, and transmission power allocation. Zhang et al. [24] proposed a reliable and efficient system based on edge computing and blockchain and designed a new group agent strategy based on trust computing that ensures the edge devices in the process of interaction to ensure reliability and improve transmission efficiency.

Task offloading is an important computing strategy that allows mobile devices to shift computationally intensive tasks to be executed on more powerful remote servers or edge computing nodes to reduce the computational burden and energy pressure on mobile devices while increasing task processing speed and efficiency, which is particularly important in MEC environments. This is because MEC enables low-latency, high-bandwidth services by bringing computing resources and storage capacity to the edge of the network, i.e., close to users and data sources. However, some challenges are still associated with introducing blockchain technology into MEC networks. The resource allocation process of MEC involves parameters such as latency, resource utilization, service provider profit, service user satisfaction, and energy. Blockchain parameters such as throughput, block size, block time, and block reward also need to be considered while designing blockchain-based resource allocation systems. Blockchain ensures decentralization, transparency, and invariance but also introduces computational and communication overheads and increases latency. Therefore, joint optimization of MEC resource allocation and blockchain parameters is an open challenge [25]. In addition, data sharing and knowledge discovery are essential requirements for the integration of blockchain and edge computing systems in many application scenarios, e.g., the need to comprehensively analyze a large number of patient medical records in smart health care and the need for vehicles to share GPS positioning data in the Internet of Vehicles (IoV) in order to correct errors in assisted autonomous driving. However, as the number of devices increases and device-generated data become more decentralized, an explosive increase in network nodes drives a huge demand for data sharing due to the large amount of sensitive information and private data stored in the system. Therefore, protecting data privacy and security is an important challenge for blockchain-based MEC [26]. Therefore, exploring the effective combination of blockchain technology and MEC for a secure, efficient, and scalable task-offloading mechanism remains an active and challenging research area [27]. For example, Guo et al. [28] used the Stackelberg game to model the interactions between edge cloud operators and different collaborative mining networks to obtain the optimal resource prices and device resource requirements when offloading tasks to the edge cloud. Lin et al. [14] proposed an efficient Device-to-Device (D2D) network authorization blockchain framework and designed an elastic resource allocation scheme using Lyapunov optimization theory to achieve high throughput with limited resources. Zhang et al. [15] proposed an efficient and improved closed-ended quadratic bidding game for allocating communication and computation resources under the quality-of-service (QoS) constraints of smart terminals in response to the optimization problem of joint communication and computation resource allocation, thus creating an edge cloud resource-sharing model based on blockchain technology and an auction game. Devi et al. [29] developed a system model to solve the task-offloading algorithm to minimize the data center's completion time and energy consumption. In addition, blockchain-based, energy-aware task scheduling for data centers was proposed to provide the best solution for minimizing completion time and energy consumption. These works have investigated blockchain-based task offloading for MEC at the level of heuristic algorithms and mathematical computational methods such as game theory. However, these schemes have also become increasingly difficult to apply due to the random mobility of user terminals in the edge computing network, task uncertainty, and the complexity of the optimization problem, requiring the consideration of task offloading with multiple optimization objectives.

In recent years, due to the random mobility of user terminals in edge computing networks, the uncertainty of tasks, and the complexity of optimization problems, the task-offloading problem, which needs to consider multiple optimization objectives, has become increasingly challenging to be solved by traditional heuristics and game-theoretic methods. Deep reinforcement learning-based methods have gradually been widely applied to research with the aim of solving the traditional edge computing network task-offloading problem [30–33] and gradually extended and applied to research on task offloading for blockchain-based MEC networks. Yang et al. [34] integrated MEC (MEC) into a blockchain-based industrial IoT system to improve the computational power of industrial IoT devices with a comprehensive consideration of weighted system cost, including energy consumption and computational overheads, and formulated the posed problem as a Markov Decision Process (MDP), introducing Deep Reinforcement Learning (DRL) to solve the formal problem. Although the study demonstrated the effectiveness of the method in small-scale networks, further validation is needed for scalability and practical deployment in large-scale networks. Nguyen et al. [35] proposed a new distributed deep reinforcement learning-based approach employing a multi-agent deep deterministic policy gradient algorithm. Based on this, a game-theoretic solution was built to model the offloading and mining competition between edge devices as a potential game and prove the existence of a pure Nash equilibrium. However, the experimental scenarios and parameter settings in the study may not fully reflect the complexity of practical applications, and further verification of its generalization ability in different environments is needed. Yao et al. [36] proposed a blockchain-empowered collaborative task-offloading scheme for cloud-edge-device (CE-device) computation by modifying the blockchain consensus process to enable participants to reach a formulaic agreement by solving the task-offloading problem. To this end, each participant can apply a reinforcement learning-based approach to solve the task-offloading problem and compete for the block output right by comparing the performance of the offloading strategies and accepting the best strategy as the offloading solution for the next period. However, the scenario does not discuss the impact of operations in the blockchain on the task-offloading strategy. Nguyen et al. [19] proposed a reinforcement learning-based multi-user task-offloading algorithm to obtain a dynamic blockchain network with MEC using the optimal offloading strategy. The scheme formulates task offloading and privacy protection as a joint optimization problem and employs a reinforcement learning-based Q-network algorithm to learn the offloading strategy, which minimizes the total system cost in terms of combined computational latency and energy consumption while guaranteeing optimal user privacy and mining reward performance. However, the study adopted a single-agent reinforcement learning scheme, which is questionable for the computational efficiency of task offloading in complex network environments. Wang et al. [37] proposed a deep reinforcement learning (DRL)-based support scheme for blockchain-based IoT resource orchestration in which IoT edge servers and end users can reach a consensus on network resource allocation based on blockchain theory. In addition, agents relying on a policy network can be trained with these resource attributes to fully perceive changes in the network state and, thus, make dynamic resource allocation decisions. However, the study only considered the performance metrics of mobile edge computation tasks under a single user, and the user's mobile characteristics need to be fully considered. In summary, these works enrich the research on blockchain–MEC task offloading based on reinforcement learning but still have certain defects that need to be improved in subsequent research.

This paper investigates a blockchain-based task-offloading model for MEC networks that takes the incentive mechanism and consensus mechanism of blockchain into account in the task-offloading problem model and, at the same time, takes the user privacy metric and the task service quality as the joint optimization objectives so that the optimization problem is more in line with the practical environment. In addition, an actor–critic reinforcement learning algorithm based on a shared global memory pool of multiple agents is proposed to improve the robustness and stability of the performance by sharing parameters. An action space selection process based on Gaussian noise is added to increase the algorithm's spatial search ability to avoid falling into a local optimum.

3. Model

In this section, we propose a blockchain-based MEC system architecture, then provide a system overview and describe the operational flow and the blockchain consensus process.

3.1. System Model

In this paper, we propose a blockchain mobile edge network task-offloading model. The specific architecture of this model is shown in Figure 1. The network model mainly contains a blockchain layer, an edge server layer, and a device layer. The device layer contains a collection of devices, and different user devices interact with the MEC network environment, send task offload requests to the edge service node, and receive the offload policy feedback from the edge service node to complete task offloading. The edge server layer contains a collection of edge nodes; each node has certain task processing resources, receiving task-offloading requests sent by users and completing the task-offloading requests of the devices through cooperation between nodes. The edge service nodes also have the role of blockchain nodes, which can participate in network consensus and reward allocation in the blockchain layer and jointly maintain the blockchain that stores network information, ensuring the security of the network and incentivizing the participation of nodes.

The edge network of this model has a device set ($U = \{u_1, u_2, \ldots, u_n\}$) consisting of n user devices and an edge node set ($E = \{e_1, e_2, \ldots, e_m\}$) consisting of m edge nodes. For any user device, $u_i = (pw_{li}, f_{li}, enc_i^{max}, tk_i^t, loc_{li}^t = (x_{li}^t, y_{li}^t))$ can move along the irregular trajectory within the time slot and initiate a task-offloading request to the edge server, where pw_{li} is the total transmission power of the device, f_{li} is the processing speed (the number of processing cycles per second), enc_i^{max} is the upper energy limit of the device, tk_i^t is the task initiated by the user in time slot t, loc_{li}^t is the device localization, and x_{li}^t and y_{li}^t are the position coordinates.

In addition, the task (tk_i^t) of any user device can be expressed as an array (($d_i^t, D_i^t, Td_{i,max}^t$), where d_i^t(bit) is the size of the task, D_i^t is the number of computation cycles required for the computation task (500 CPU computation cycles are required to process the data of a 1 bit task in this paper), and $Td_{i,max}^t$ is the maximum tolerable delay of the task). Due to the limitation of energy consumption and computational capability of the device, these tasks cannot all be computed locally at the same time and need to be partially offloaded to the edge node by using $tk_i^{t,l}$ and $tk_{ij}^{t,o}$ to denote the local computation of the task (tk_i^t) and its offloading part to the node (e_j), respectively. The sizes of the corresponding offloading task and computational task cycle are denoted as $d_i^{t,l}$, $D_i^{t,l}$, $d_{ij}^{t,o}$, and $D_{ij}^{t,o}$, respectively.

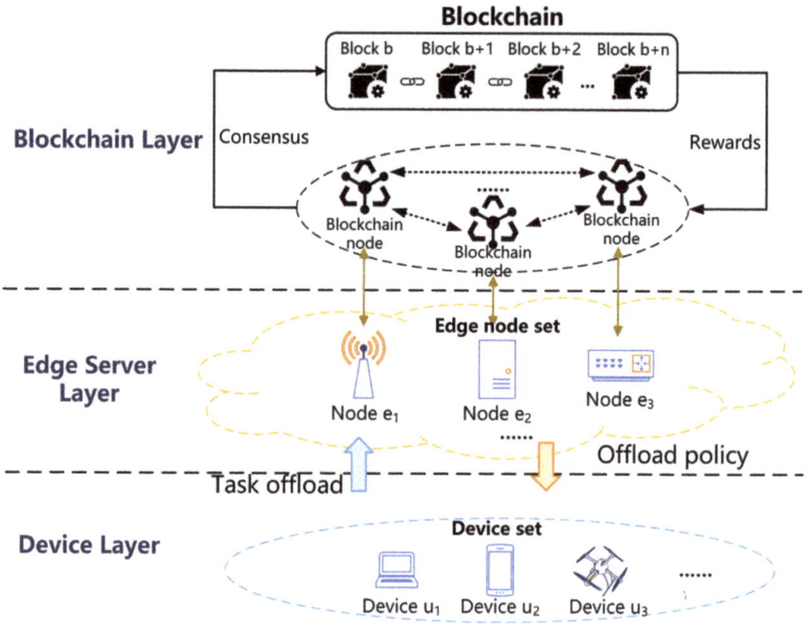

Figure 1. Blockchain-based edge computing network model.

For any edge node, $e_j = (k_j, pw_{ej}, f_{ej}, loc_{ej} = (x_{ej}, y_{ej}))$ can receive the task data offloaded by the device and process the task using its computational resources, then return the result to the smart device after task processing is completed. k_j^t denotes the number of tokens held by the block node corresponding to the edge node, pw_{ej} denotes the transmission power of the edge node, f_{ej} denotes the processing speed of the edge node, loc_{ej} denotes the fixed location of the server, and x_{ej} and y_{ej} are the location coordinates.

In the blockchain of this model, all the mobile edge network nodes also have the role of blockchain nodes, sharing parameters and recording proof of workload through the blockchain. The consortium blockchain uses a Proof of Stake (PoS)-based consensus method to validate the workload of the computing nodes and distribute incentive rewards to each of the individual nodes involved in the computation of the offloading task.

3.2. Consensus Model

The consensus mechanism in blockchain is the core method to ensure that all participating nodes agree on the state of the blockchain. Currently, there are two main consensus mechanisms in mainstream blockchain systems, namely Proof of Work (PoW) and proof of stake (PoS). In PoW, all entities compete to solve a mathematical puzzle to generate blocks and receive a reward. However, the process of PoW is very computationally intensive and only applies to mobile edge network scenarios. PoS is proposed to address the limitations of PoW, and unlike PoW, the probability of an entity getting the right to publish a block depends on its equity, i.e., the number of tokens owned by the entity [38]. A comparison of the two consensus mechanisms is shown in Table 1.

Table 1. Consensus mechanism comparison.

Characteristic	Proof of Work (PoW)	Proof of Stake (PoS)
Energy consumption	High; requires large amounts of power	Low; does not require large amounts of computing resources
Hardware requirements	Requires high-performance hardware	No high-performance hardware required
Attack cost	High; needs to control 50% of computing power of the whole network	High; needs to control 50% of the tokens of the whole network
Reward mechanism	Mining rewards (blockchain currency)	Token rewards
Block generation speed	Usually slow; affected by computational difficulty	Usually slow; affected by computational difficulty
Degree of decentralization	High but tends to be concentrated in mining pools	High; coin holders are more widely distributed

In this paper, the PoS-based consensus mechanism is used to implement the workload consensus checking of computing nodes. Its execution process is as follows:

(1) Packing node selection: The system selects a negative blockchain node [39] to construct a new block by periodically selecting the block creation node ($e_g \in E$) among all the nodes with equity based on the number of tokens held by the verifier;

(2) New block creation: The block creation node packages all blockchain network transactions in the system during time slot t into a new block, assuming that the block consists of the following two parts: the task (tk_i^t) offloading data (d_b^t) and the block-fixing data (d_0) contained in block b_i. The size of the task transaction data is calculated from the original size conversion of the task, noting the conversion rate as s. Then, the block size $d_{b_i}^t$ can be expressed as

$$d_{b_i}^t = d_b^t + d_0 = s\Sigma_{e_j \in E} d_{ij}^{t,o} + d_0 \tag{1}$$

(3) Block validation: The coalition chain calculates the selection probability of the edge nodes according to the number of tokens owned by the nodes using a Poisson distribution with parameter λ. The first v nodes according to the order of probability constitute the set of validation nodes (E^V), in which the probability distribution of the edge node (e_j) being selected as a validation node is

$$p_j^v = P(K = k_j) = \frac{\lambda^K}{K!} e^{-\lambda} \tag{2}$$

(4) Block addition: Once a new block is recognized by all the validation nodes, it is added to the blockchain;

(5) Incentive distribution: Based on the incentive mechanism, a certain reward is provided to the network nodes that participate in the task to compute and verify the new block.

The workflow of the blockchain-based MEC task-offloading system described in this section is shown in Figure 2.

3.3. Quality of Service Model

In this section, the blockchain-based MEC task-offloading quality of service model proposed in this paper is described in detail, in addition to description of the design methodology for quality of service models reported in existing MEC task-offloading research [15,29,33], to simulate a blockchain–mobile edge network within each time slot The delay and energy consumption generated by user task computation, task offloading communication, block verification, etc., are investigated to construct a blockchain-based network quality of service-oriented communication model and a computation model.

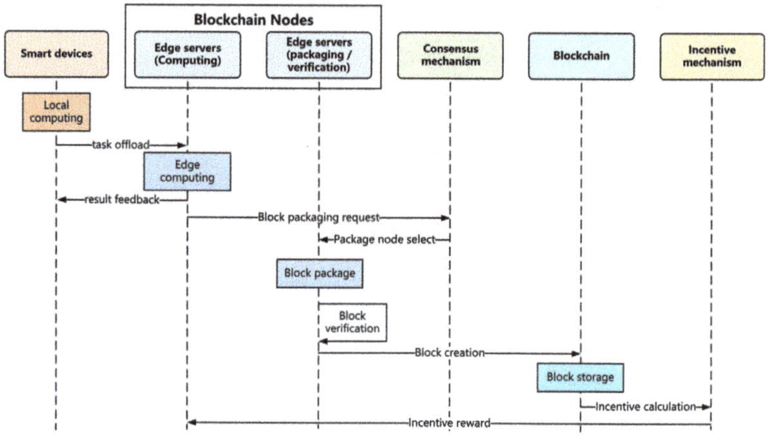

Figure 2. BMEC data process.

3.3.1. Communication Model

In this paper, it is assumed that the size of the task calculation result is much smaller than the task itself and that the communication overhead required to transmit the result is negligible. Therefore, this paper mainly considers the two data communication scenarios of user device task offloading and block verification and calculates the energy consumption and transmission delay in the communication process.

In this system model, the device and the MEC server are linked through a wireless network, and the transmission rate between them is affected by the transmission environment, communication resources, and transmission distance. In this paper, we refer to [40,41] and calculate the channel gain (h_{ij}^t) from any device (u_i) to edge node e_j in time slot t using the following formula:

$$h_{ij}^t = \frac{h_0}{dist_{ij}^{t\ \frac{\varphi}{2}}} \tag{3}$$

where h_0 denotes the initial gain of the channel, φ is the path loss exponent, and $dist_{ij}^t = \sqrt{(x_{li}^t - x_{ej})^2 + (y_{li}^t - y_{ej})^2}$ denotes the distance from device u_i to edge node e_j at time slot t.

The signal-to-interference-plus-noise ratio ($SINR_{i,j}^t$) from device u_i to edge node e_j is

$$SINR_{i,j}^t = \frac{pw_{ij}^t \left|h_{ij}^t\right|^2}{\Sigma_{e_j' \in E \setminus \{e_j\}} pw_{ij'}^t \left|h_{ij'}^t\right|^2 + N_0} \tag{4}$$

where pw_{ij}^t, N_0, and B denote the transmission power from device u_i to edge node e_j in time slot t, the Gaussian noise in the channel, and the channel communication bandwidth, respectively. $pw_{li} = \Sigma_{e_j \in E} pw_{ij}^t$, and the data transmission rate from device u_i to edge node e_j in time slot t is

$$R_{ij}^t = B \cdot log_2(1 + SINR_{i,j}^t) \tag{5}$$

Therefore, in the task-offloading communication scenario, the communication delay ($Td_{ij,comm}^{t,o}$) and energy consumption ($En_{ij,comm}^{t,o}$) of the user device (u_i) transmitting the task offloading to the edge node (e_j) during the time slot t is expressed as follows:

$$Td_{ij,comm}^{t,o} = \frac{d_{ij}^{t,o}}{R_{ij}^t} \tag{6}$$

$$En_{ij,comm}^{t,o} = pw_{ij}^{t} Td_{ij,comm}^{t,o} = pw_{ij}^{t} \frac{d_{ij}^{t,o}}{R_{ij}^{t}} \tag{7}$$

During the block consensus process, the block generation node transmits the block to the validation node for verification. Assuming that the block generation node (e_g) and v validation nodes have a fixed network transmission speed (R) between them, the consensus verification communication delay ($Td_{iv,comm}^{t,v}$) and energy consumption ($En_{iv,comm}^{t,v}$) between the block generation node (e_g) and the validation node (e_v) for block b are

$$Td_{iv,comm}^{t,v} = \frac{d_{b_i}^{t}}{R} \tag{8}$$

$$En_{iv,comm}^{t,v} = pw_{eg} v Td_{iv,comm}^{t,v} = pw_{eg} \frac{d_{b_i}^{t}}{R} \tag{9}$$

3.3.2. Computing Model

In this paper, we mainly consider three kinds of computing scenarios, namely local task computing, task-offloading computing, and block verification computing. The computing model must determine the processing delay and energy consumption according to the computing process. It is assumed that the blockchain selects block generation nodes according to the number of tokens owned by the nodes, and the calculation volume of generation node selection is ignored in this model.

In the task computation scenario locally executed by the user device, the energy consumption coefficient of the user device is assumed to be $\varepsilon^{l} = 10^{-11}$ [42] in this paper. The delay ($Td_{i,comp}^{t,l}$) and energy consumption ($En_{i,comp}^{t,l}$) of device u_i for local task processing are

$$Td_{i,comp}^{t,l} = \frac{D_{i}^{t,l}}{f_{li}} \tag{10}$$

$$En_{i,comp}^{t,l} = \varepsilon^{l} D_{i}^{t,l} (f_{li})^{2} \tag{11}$$

In the offloading task scenario executed by edge nodes, this paper assumes that the edge node provides a separate CPU computing core for each offloading task, i.e., tasks offloaded on the same edge node have the same task-computing speed, and the number of offloading tasks that the edge node can host at the same time is related to the number of CPU cores. The energy consumption factor of the edge node is defined as $\varepsilon^{o} = 10^{-27}$ [34]. The delay ($Td_{ij,comp}^{t,o}$) and energy consumption ($En_{ij,comp}^{t,o}$) of the edge node (e_j) in computing the offloading task (t_i^{o}) are

$$Td_{ij,comp}^{t,o} = \frac{D_{ij}^{t,o}}{f_{ej}} \tag{12}$$

$$En_{ij,comp}^{t,o} = \varepsilon^{o} D_{ij}^{t,o} (f_{ej})^{2} \tag{13}$$

In the block consensus verification scenario, the delay and energy consumption generated by block generation are not calculated in this paper because the overall overhead of block creation is small compared to that of block verification, where there is a large number of validation links, which has a low impact on the overall performance of the system. When the edge node performs block validation, assuming that the validation computation period of block b_i is $D_{b_i}^{t}$, the validation delay ($Td_{iv,comp}^{t,v}$) and energy consumption ($En_{iv,comp}^{t,v}$) of the blockchain validation node (e_v) are

$$Td_{iv,comp}^{t,v} = \frac{D_{b_i}^{t}}{f_{ev}} \tag{14}$$

$$En_{iv,comp}^{t,v} = \varepsilon^{o} D_{b_i}^{t} (f_{ev})^2 \tag{15}$$

3.3.3. Comprehensive Model

In this paper, we comprehensively calculate the delay and energy cost of the blockchain-based MEC task-offloading model by combining the designed communication and computation models.

(1) Latency Cost

The time delay in the quality of service model designed in this paper contains two links, namely task processing and block verification links. When calculating the time delay of the task processing link, it is assumed that all users start a local task and offload task processing from the same moment, i.e., local task computation and task offload transmission are carried out at the same time, so the actual time delay of task processing is the maximum value of the time delay of local computation and offload processing. The task-offloading delay consists of the communication delay ($Td_{ij,comm}^{t,o}$) of the user offloading the task to the edge node and the computation delay ($Td_{ij,comp}^{t,o}$) of the task on the edge node. If the user offloads the task to more than one edge node, the task-offloading delay is only computed for the longest processing delay; then, the task offloading delay ($Td_i^{t,o}$) of user u_i is denoted as

$$Td_i^{t,o} = \max\left(Td_{i1,comm}^{t,o} + Td_{i1,comp}^{t,o}, \ldots, Td_{im,comm}^{t,o} + Td_{im,comp}^{t,o}\right) \tag{16}$$

Furthermore, the task processing delay (Td'^{t}_i) of user u_i is denoted as

$$Td'^{t}_i = \max(Td_{i,comp}^{t,l}, Td_i^{t,o}) \tag{17}$$

Similarly, when calculating the delay of the block verification link, since the packing node sends the block to each verification node for block verification at the same time, the block verification delay ($Td_i^{t,v}$) is the maximum delay processed by each verification node and is denoted as

$$Td_i^{t,v} = \max\left(Td_{i1,comm}^{t,v} + Td_{i1,comp}^{t,v}, \ldots, Td_{im,comm}^{t,v} + Td_{im,comp}^{t,v}\right) \tag{18}$$

In summary, the delay (Td_i^t) of the quality of service model for user device u_i in time slot t is

$$Td_i^t = Td'^{t}_i + Td_i^{t,v} \tag{19}$$

(2) Energy Cost

In the energy consumption calculation process, the energy consumption of the communication model and the computation model are obtained by summing the processing energy consumption of each task.

Then, the communication and computation energy of user device u_i in time slot t are

$$En_i^{t,comm} = \Sigma_{e_j \in E} En_{ij,comm}^{t,o} + \Sigma_{e_v \in E^V} En_{iv,comm}^{t,v} \tag{20}$$

$$En_i^{t,comp} = En_{i,comp}^{t,l} + \Sigma_{e_j \in E} En_{ij,comp}^{t,o} + \Sigma_{e_v \in E^V} En_{iv,comp}^{t,v} \tag{21}$$

In summary, the energy consumption (En_i^t) of the quality of service model for user device u_i in time slot t is

$$En_i^t = En_i^{t,comm} + En_i^{t,comp} \tag{22}$$

3.4. *Incentive Reward Model*

Previous research [22,43–45] has integrated the incentive mechanism of blockchain into the study of task pricing and resource allocation of MEC, balancing the allocation of edge service resources and value gains by considering game theory and auction theory. In this paper, the design of the incentive mechanism is simplified, and only the edge nodes participating in task-offloading computation and block verification are considered to be provided with incentive tokens in equal proportions according to energy consumption. Hence, the incentive model favors edge nodes obtaining more incentive tokens to gain more benefits. In the incentive model, the blockchain uses the β ratio of the unit of energy converted into obtainable tokens based on the energy consumption of the edge nodes; then, the tokens generated by agent u_i are calculated as

$$I_i^t = \begin{cases} \beta \sum_{e_j \in E} \left(En_{ij,comp}^{t,o} + En_{ij,comp}^{t,v} \right), e_j \in E^V \\ \beta \sum_{e_j \in E} En_{ij}^{comp,o}, e_j \notin E^V \end{cases} \tag{23}$$

3.5. Privacy Model

In this section, we mainly consider that in the process of MEC task offloading, if we consider the energy consumption and delay factors of task communication and computation, user terminals often tend to offload a large number of tasks to edge nodes that are closer to them and have higher levels of resources. However, such a task-offloading method potentially risks data privacy leakage because MEC tasks usually contain sensitive private data such as the physical location of the device, identity characteristics, task data, etc. Suppose that many tasks containing private information are offloaded to an edge node. In that case, the edge node, out of its curiosity or due to being hijacked by an adversary, may collect and infer the user's location and business characteristics based on the user's offloading preferences. More seriously, the edge node may predict the user's private information based on these data characteristics, resulting in user privacy leakage [46]. Therefore, it is necessary to design a privacy metric model to evaluate the degree of privacy leakage that may be caused by the user in the process of task offloading.

Information entropy is a concept that measures the uncertainty or amount of information. Privacy computing models can be utilized to assess and reduce privacy risks. The information entropy-based privacy measure is advantageous in the task of measuring the privacy leakage of user data and has been applied in research on MEC task offloading [41,47]. Therefore, this paper uses the privacy metric based on information entropy to measure the MEC task offloading privacy protection effect.

We define user u_i's task-offloading preference (P_i) and measure the probability that user u_i's data are exposed to edge nodes by calculating the ratio of user u_i's offloaded task data volume to the total task data volume (P_i), which is calculated as follows:

$$P_i^t = \frac{d_i^{t,o}}{d_i^t} = \frac{\sum_{e_j \in E} d_{ij}^{t,o}}{d_i^t} \tag{24}$$

Based on the user's task-offloading preference, the concept of privacy entropy is further adopted to describe the amount of privacy information carried by the offloading strategy of user u_i H_i^t. When there is no task offloading on the user's terminal, i.e., $P_i^t = 0$, the edge node cannot infer the user's task information. The privacy entropy is at the maximum value (H_{max}), and in this paper, we set the value of maximum entropy to 10. The privacy entropy of user u_i is calculated as

$$H_i^t = \begin{cases} -P_i^t log_2 P_i^t, 0 < P_i^t < 1 \\ H_{max}, P_i^t = 0 \end{cases} \tag{25}$$

4. Problem Description

This paper's optimization objectives for task offloading in mobile blockchain edge networks focus on privacy preservation, quality of service, and incentive reward. Privacy protection requires maximization of the privacy entropy of the privacy-preserving model to prevent users from offloading too much private data to the edge servers, leading to user privacy leakage. Quality user experience requires minimization of the latency and energy consumption of offloading user tasks. Incentive rewards require maximization of the workload of nodes in the blockchain edge network and improvement of the workload and efficiency of nodes. In this paper, by comprehensively considering offloading privacy, quality of service, and incentive reward factors, the optimization problem can be formulated as the maximum value of the comprehensive optimization objective for user device u_i and edge servers within time slot t under the satisfaction of multiple constraints. The specific optimization objective function and constraints are expressed as follows:

$$P : \max C_i^t = \omega_1 * H_i^t + \omega_2 * I_i^t - \omega_3 * Td_i^t - \omega_4 * En_i^t \tag{26}$$

$$s.t. Td_i^t \leq Td_{i,max}^t \tag{27}$$

$$0 \leq pw_{ij}^t \leq pw_i^l \tag{28}$$

$$0 < P_i^t \leq 1 \tag{29}$$

$$H_i^t \leq H_{max} \tag{30}$$

where ω_1, ω_2, ω_3, and ω_4 are the weights of the indicators, which are used to specify the level of importance of different indicators. Equation (27) means the total task delay is constrained by the maximum tolerable delay of the task. Equation (28) means the device-to-node transmission power receives the constraint of the total transmission power. Equation (29) means the amount of offloaded task data of any user device does not exceed the constraint of the total task data. Equation (30) means the user's privacy entropy is subject to the constraint of the maximum entropy value.

It is not difficult to find that the optimization problem presented in this paper is a mixed-integer linear programming problem, which are usually NP-hard and, therefore, difficult to solve with a globally optimal solution. The decision-making process for such problems occurs in a dynamic environment of long-term optimization, which makes it difficult for traditional convex optimization algorithms to adapt to unknown environments and perform adaptive optimization.

5. Algorithm

To address the environmental complexity and multi-objective competitiveness possessed by the above optimization problem description, this section first proposes an actor–critic deep reinforcement learning algorithm based on multiple agents sharing a global memory pool to improve the robustness and stability of performance. Secondly, the optimization problem is reformulated as a Markov process (MDP) by constructing each agent's state space, action space, immediate rewards, and state transitions, and the algorithmic framework structure is described in detail.

5.1. Construction of the Markov Decision Process

In the blockchain mobile edge network task-offloading environment designed in this paper, each user device acts as a reinforcement learning agent, adopting a decentralized execution and centralized training model, which enables the agent to make independent decisions based on its observed and learned strategies. Multiple edge servers form a federated blockchain, sharing network parameters to jointly hold global information about the entire system. At the beginning of each time slot, user devices can initiate task processing requests, sending task and localization information to edge servers. After the edge server obtains the global network state information through blockchain sharing, it conducts centralized training. After training, each agent makes distributed local decisions based on its observations.

In order to solve the above optimization problem, it needs to be converted to the standard form of the Markov decision process (MDP) when using reinforcement learning algorithms. The key components of this transformation include defining the state space, action space, reward space, and state space transitions for each agent.

(1) State Space

The state space (s_i^t) of an agent (i) in time slot t consists of the localization ($loc_{li}^t = (x_{li}^t, y_{li}^t)$) of its corresponding user device (u_i) and the amount of requested task data (d_i^t), i.e., $s_i^t = (l_{li}^t, d_i^t)$. Therefore, the state space (s^t) of the reinforcement learning algorithm as a whole is denoted as $s^t = (s_1^t, \ldots, s_n^t)$.

(2) Action space

The action space (a_i^t) of agent i in time slot t represents the distribution of request data processing and channel power allocation of user device u_i in the current network state, i.e., $a_i^t = (d_i^{t,l}, d_{i1}^{t,o}, \ldots, d_{im}^{t,o}, pw_{i1}^t, \ldots, pw_{im}^t)$.

(3) Reward function

The reward function of the blockchain mobile edge network task-offloading model aims to maximize the optimization objective function (C_i^t) of each agent, i.e., maximize the privacy entropy of the user device to safeguard the privacy of user data, as well as the blockchain rewards computed by completing the offloaded tasks, and, at the same time, minimize the task processing latency and energy consumption of the user device in order to provide the user with a higher quality of service. The reward function at time slot t is expressed as follows:

$$r_i^t = \begin{cases} \omega_1 * H_i^t + \omega_2 * I_i^t - \omega_3 * Td_i^t - \omega_4 * En_i^t, \text{Equations (27)–(30)} \\ r_0, other \end{cases} \tag{31}$$

where r_0 is a constant much smaller than 0 that represents the value of the algorithmic base reward given by the environment if the current policy does not satisfy the constraints of Equations (27)–(30).

5.2. Algorithmic Framework

The framework of the algorithm proposed in this paper is shown in Figure 3. The algorithm sets a corresponding agent for each user device, including an actor network, a critic network, and a random sampler. The actor network and critic network adopt a dual neural network structure. The current network is responsible for constructing the actor's policy network (π_i) and the critic's value network (Q_i). The Q value of the critic network represents the expected reward for taking a particular action in a given state. The target network is softly updated using the current network parameters (θ_i^π and θ_i^Q), thus guaranteeing the stability of network learning.

We assume that the sample value function for the critic target network to compute time slot t is $Q_i(s_i^t, a_i^t|\theta_i^{Q'})$; then, the target Q value can be calculated as

$$q_i = r_i^t + \gamma Q_i(s^{t+1}, a_i^{t+1}|\theta_i^{Q'}), \tag{32}$$

where γ denotes the discount factor.

To update the critic's current network parameter (θ_i^Q), the loss values of the parameters are computed using a mean-square error function. The mean-square error function can help the critic network accurately predict the value of a state or state–action pair.

$$Loss(Q_i) = E[(Q_i(s^t, a_i^t|\theta_i^Q) - q_i)^2] = \frac{1}{n}\sum_{i=1}^{n}(Q_i(s^t, a_i^t|\theta_i^Q) - q_i)^2 \tag{33}$$

We minimize $Loss(\theta_i^Q)$ by gradient descent, and the update method for the θ_i^Q parameter is denoted by

$$\theta_i^Q \leftarrow \theta_i^Q + \alpha \nabla_{\theta_i^Q} Loss(Q_i), \tag{34}$$

where α is the learning rate of the critic's current network parameter (θ_i^Q).

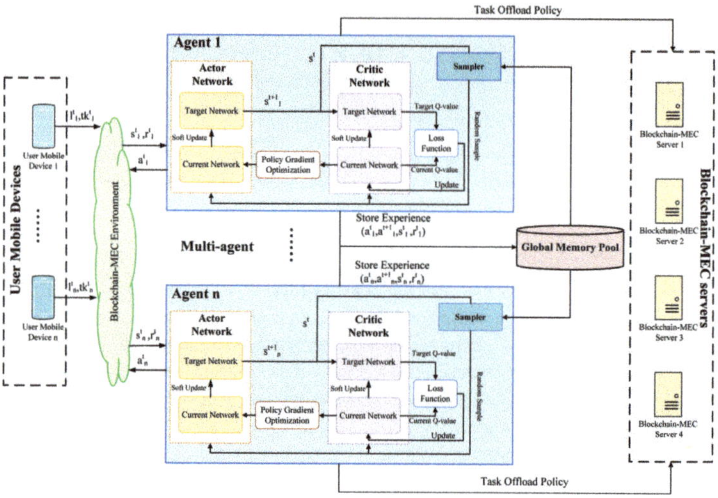

Figure 3. Algorithm structure.

The actor network constructs the action policy (π_i) based on the state space (s_i^t) of the reinforcement learning agent in time slot t and the reward function (r_i^t) and generates the action (a_i^t) in the time slot, which can be represented as

$$a_i^t = \pi_i(s_i^t|\theta_i^\pi) \tag{35}$$

However, using the output of the strategy network directly does not allow the agent to discover more strategies, so an exploration strategy needs to be constructed by adding noise.

$$a_i^t = \pi_i(s_i^t|\theta_i^\pi) + \tau N_t \tag{36}$$

where τ denotes the attenuation factor of the noise, which gradually decreases with the number of iterations of the algorithm to guarantee the stability of network training and N_t is Gaussian noise obeying a normal random distribution.

The policy objective function of the actor network is

$$J(\pi_i) = E[Q_i(s^t, a_i^t|\theta_i^Q)] \tag{37}$$

Then, the gradient of the objective function of the strategy is expressed as

$$\nabla_{\theta_i^\pi} J(\pi_i) = E[\nabla_{a_i^\pi} Q_i(s^t, a_i^t|\theta_i^Q) \nabla_{\theta_i^\pi} \pi(s^t|\theta_i^\pi)] \tag{38}$$

Then, the update method for the θ_i^π parameter is expressed as

$$\theta_i^\pi \leftarrow \theta_i^\pi + \beta \nabla_{\theta_i^\pi} J(\pi_i) \tag{39}$$

where β is the learning rate of the actor network's θ_i^π parameter.

In addition, the soft update method for the actor and critic target network parameters ($\theta_i^{\pi'}$ and $\theta_i^{Q'}$) can be represented as

$$\theta_i^{\pi'} \leftarrow \sigma\theta_i^{\pi} + (1-\sigma)\theta_i^{\pi'} \tag{40}$$

$$\theta_i^{Q'} \leftarrow \sigma\theta_i^{Q} + (1-\sigma)\theta_i^{Q'} \tag{41}$$

where $\sigma \in (0,1)$ is the soft update weight.

In order to reduce environmental changes due to policy learning by other agents, this paper adopts a global memory pool to store the experience samples $(s_i^t, s_i^{t+1}, a_i^t, r_i^t)$ of each agent and uses it to train the neural network of the agents. The global memory pool can be constructed by using the blockchain to realize the sharing of information among agents in the actual application process.

In order to better understand the idea and process of this paper, the pseudo-code of the algorithm is shown in Algorithm 1.

Algorithm 1: Actor–Critic Algorithm for Blockchain–MEC Task Offloading

Data: Blockchain-MEC environment parameters, user mobile device states
Result: Task offloading strategies for each user mobile device
for *agent* $i \in [1, N]$ **do**
    // initialize algorithm parameters
    initialize actor current network π_i with θ_i^{π}
    initialize critic current network Q_i with θ_i^{Q}
    initialize actor and critic target parameter $\theta_i'^{\pi} \leftarrow \theta_i^{\pi}$ and $\theta_i'^{Q} \leftarrow \theta_i^{Q}$
    clear global memory pool
end
for *iteration* $\in [1, max\_iter]$ **do**
    each agent initializes initial state space s_i^0
    for $t \in [1, T]$ **do**
        for *agent* $i \in [1, N]$ **do**
            // select action space
            get $a_i^t \leftarrow \pi_i(s_i^t|\theta_i^{\pi})$ by action current network
            // get state space
            get $(s_i^{t+1}, r_i^t) \leftarrow env(a_i^t)$ by environment
            // update global memory pool
            push $(s_i^t, s_i^{t+1}, a_i^t, r_i^t)$ in the memory pool
            // update state space
            $s_i^t \leftarrow s_i^{t+1}$
            get M samples from memory pool
            compute $y_i = r_i^t + \gamma Q_i(s^{t+1}, a_i^{t+1}|\theta_i^{Q'})$
            // calculate parameter gradient and update parameters
            $\theta_i^{Q} \leftarrow \theta_i^{Q} + \alpha\nabla_{\theta_i^{Q}} Loss(Q_i)$
            $\theta_i^{\pi} \leftarrow \theta_i^{\pi} + \beta\nabla_{\theta_i^{\pi}} J(\pi_i)$
            // soft update Actor and Critic network parameters
            $\theta_i^{Q'} \leftarrow \delta\theta_i^{Q} + (1-\delta)\theta_i^{Q'}$
            $\theta_i^{\pi'} \leftarrow \delta\theta_i^{\pi} + (1-\delta)\theta_i^{\pi'}$
        end
    end
end
return each device's optimal migration strategy a_i^* and the minimum total target cost C^*

5.3. Complexity Analysis

In this paper, the computational complexity of the proposed algorithm is mainly considered to be the sum of the training time overhead of all the agents. We assume that n is the number of agents, L_a is the number of neural network layers of the actor network, L_c is the number of neural network layers of the critic network, S is the number of samples of each agent from the global memory pool, I is the number of algorithmic iterations, d_s is the state-space dimension, and d_a is the action-space dimension. Then, the computational complexity of the algorithm can be calculated as $O(nSI(L_a + L_c)(d_s + d_a)^2)$.

6. Experiment and Discussion

In this section, our proposed algorithm is evaluated and analyzed through simulation experiments.

6.1. Experimental Environment

The hardware and software specifications of the experimental environment described in this paper are shown in Table 2.

Table 2. Hardware and software specifications.

	Designation	Specification Version
Hardware	CPU	AMD Ryzen 7-5800
	GPU	Nvidia RTX3060
	Memory	80 GB RAM
Software	Operation system	Windows11
	Language	python3.7.16
	Deep learning framework	torch1.10.0
	Library function	numpy1.21.6

6.2. Parameter Design

In order to realize the simulation of the network model, this paper simulates the mobile user task-offloading environment in real scenarios in a 1000×1000 area (Figure 4) that contains four blockchain–MEC servers at fixed locations and user mobile devices moving along the path of black arrows. The servers receive task offload requests from user mobile devices and specify the user offload policy for the devices through collaborative planning using multiple servers. The user's mobile device moves along the non-random irregular black arrow path with a fixed step size in each time slot. It generates a random amount of task data, which are offloaded to one or more servers for processing according to the task-offloading policy.

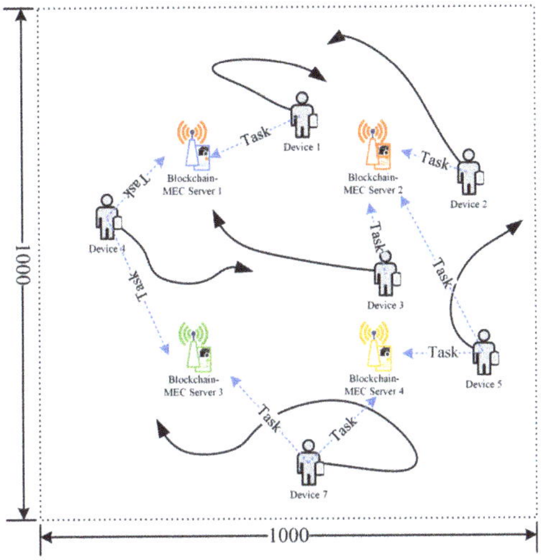

Figure 4. Network environment simulation.

The parameters of the reinforcement learning algorithm and blockchain edge network environment are shown in the following Table 3.

Table 3. Experimental parameter settings.

Parameter Kind	Parameter Symbol	Description	Value
Model parameters	d_s	State-space dimension	3
	d_a	Action-space dimension	10
	δ	Soft update weights	0.01
	α	Critic update parameters	0.99
	β	Actor update parameters	0.95
	$[\omega_1, \omega_2, \omega_3, \omega_4]$	Reward function weights	[0.8, 0.09, 0.09, 0.02]
Environmental parameters	$[loc_{e1}, loc_{e2}, loc_{e3}, loc_{e4}]$	Edge node location	(333, 333), (333, 666), (666, 333), (666, 666)
	pw_{li}	User terminal transmission power	1.5
	pw_{ej}	Edge node transmission power	3
	f_{li}	User terminal processing frequency	10×10^8
	f_{ej}	Edge node processing frequency	$4 \times 10 \times 10^9$
	d_0	Block header size	2
	N_0	Wireless channel noise	10×10^{-7}
	B	Wireless communication bandwidth	$3 \times 10 \times 10^9$
	R	Server wired communication rate	10

6.3. Experimental Analysis

6.3.1. Contrasted Algorithms

In this paper, the following algorithms are selected to be analyzed and compared:

- JODRL-PP [33]: The JODRL-PP (Joint Optimal Deep Reinforcement Learning with Privacy Preservation) algorithm is a stochastic game-theoretically based task-offloading problem for multi-access point environments proposed for multi-agent deep reinforcement learning algorithms. The algorithm uses a trusted third party for centralized training. It achieves distributed execution to improve the quality of the results while considering the dynamic changes in a multi-user environment and dealing with the complexity of multiple users and access points through stochastic game theory.

- IQL [48]: IQL (Independent Q-Learning) is a reinforcement learning algorithm applied in multi-agent systems. In a multi-agent system, each agent learns its own Q-value function independently without considering the actions and strategies of other agents and uses only its own state and action information in the learning process. In the IQL-based task-offloading algorithm, if an agent does not cache the corresponding requested service, the agent migrates the task to be executed to another agent that has cached the service based on the service cache information shared among the agents at the beginning of each time slot.
- QMIX [49]: QMIX (Q-value Mixing Network) is a value-based multi-agent reinforcement learning algorithm that can be used to train decentralized policies in a centralized end-to-end manner. In addition, QMIX's network estimates joint action values as complex nonlinear combinations of per-agent values conditional only on local observations. It requires that the joint action values for each agent be monotonic. This maximizes the joint action values that can be handled in non-strategy learning and ensures consistency between centralized and decentralized strategies.
- VDN [50]: The VDN (Value-Decomposition Network) is a value decomposition method for multi-agent systems that decomposes the global value function into local value functions. Each agent learns only the local value function associated with it. This network architecture learns to decompose the team value function into the value functions of agents. It solves the problem of collaborative reinforcement learning of multiple agents with a single joint reward signal. The VDN algorithm does not consider the spatial relationship of the type of service request and the state of the wireless network among agents, and it directly decomposes the joint action value function into the sum of the local action value functions of all agents.

6.3.2. Results

(1) Experiment 1: Performance Comparison

We set up ten random mobile users in the experimental simulation environment by recording the reward function during 1000 iterations of the reinforcement learning algorithm, the result of which is shown in Figure 5. From the figure, we can find that compared with other schemes, the proposed algorithm's curve of the final stabilization reward function value is significantly higher than that of other algorithms, and the fluctuation amplitude after stabilization is smaller.

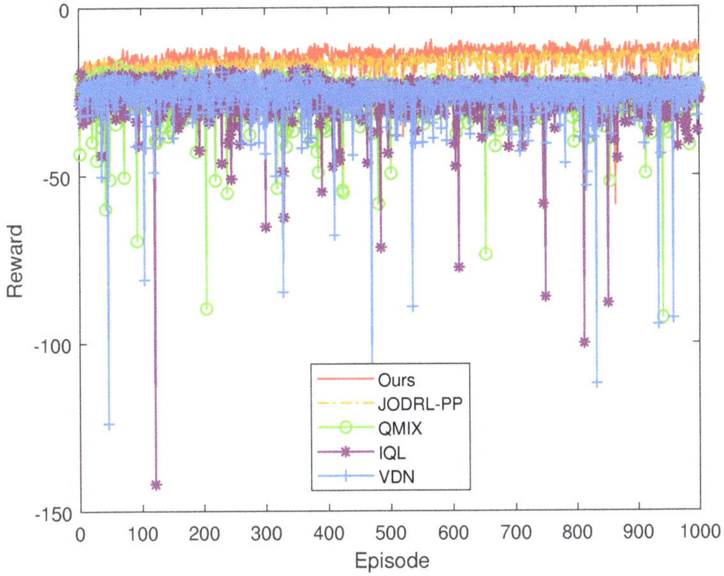

Figure 5. Reward function value iteration.

In order to minimize the impact of single-experiment error on the results, we conducted five repetitive experiments. We recorded the average reward function values for different algorithm configurations for all training cycles, and the comparison results are shown in Figure 6. From the figure, we can find that the proposed algorithm improves by more than 40% in performance compared to QMIX, IQL, and VDN and outperforms JODRL-PP, indicating that the proposed algorithm can obtain a better solution to the problem set in this paper.

In our experiments, we also recorded the average costs of task processing energy consumption, task processing latency, user privacy metrics, and blockchain incentive rewards in the reward function, and the comparison graphs are shown in Figure 7. Through the comparison, we can find that the proposed algorithm significantly outperforms QMIX, IQL, and VDN in all costs except blockchain incentive rewards, except that the proposed algorithm reduces the energy cost by 44.38% and improves the blockchain incentive rewards by 13.27% compared to the JODRL-PP algorithm. However, the proposed algorithm is inferior in terms of task processing latency and user privacy metrics.

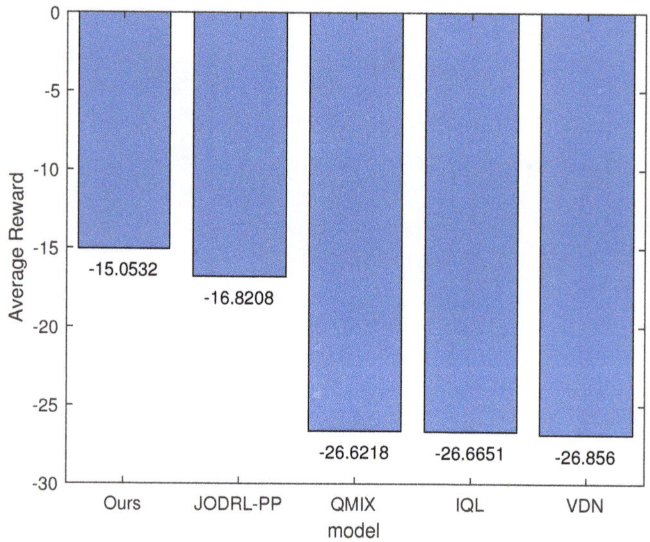

Figure 6. Average reward function value comparison.

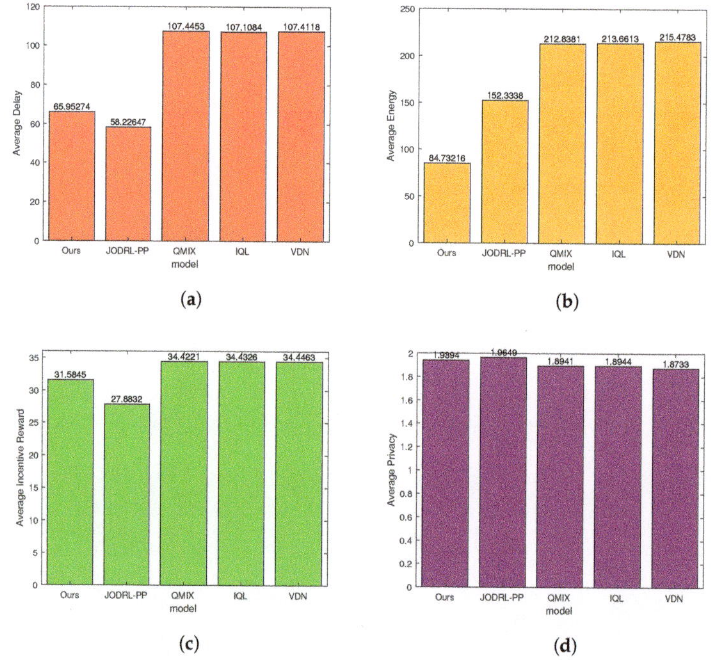

Figure 7. (**a**) Average processing delay comparison; (**b**) average energy consumption comparison; (**c**) average incentive reward comparison; (**d**) average privacy metric comparison.

(2) Experiment 2: Performance Comparison under Different User Scales

In order to test the changes of the algorithms in the optimization problem proposed in this paper under different user sizes, we set the user sizes to 10, 15, 20, 25, and 30 and recorded the average reward function values of the algorithms under different user sizes in five groups of repeated experiments. The results are shown in Figure 8. From the figure, we can find that with increasing user size, the average reward function value of all models decreases; this is because with the increase in users, the corresponding amount of user tasks is also raised. The delay and energy consumption required to process the task increase due to the existence of an upper limit of the user's privacy metric, and the blockchain network incentive rewards are subject to the limitation of the amount of nodes to receive the task. Hence, a decrease in the value of the reward function is a normal phenomenon. The proposed algorithm still has an optimal average reward function value based on different agent scales.

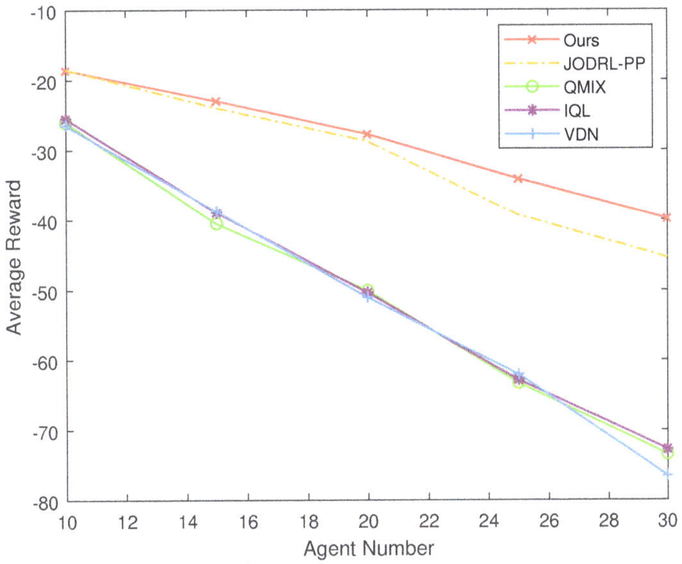

Figure 8. Reward function value iteration for different user scales.

The experimental comparison graphs of the average cost of task processing energy consumption, task processing delay, user privacy metrics, and blockchain incentive rewards are shown in Figure 9. The proposed algorithm has advantages in some single cost metrics in growing user size, and the experimental results are similar to those of Experiment 1.

(3) Experiment 3: Ablation Experiment

In this paper, we design ablation experiments to investigate the effects of Gaussian noise-based action-space search in the proposed algorithm and the global memory pool of agents on the performance of the algorithm. As in Experiment 1, we set up 10 random mobile users in the experimental simulation environment by recording the reward function value during 1000 iterations of the reinforcement learning algorithm, and the result is shown in Figure 10. From the figure, we can find that the curve of the proposed algorithm reaches a stabilization level faster than that of the other two configurations. It exhibits less fluctuation of the state after stabilization. In addition, the algorithm's final stabilization reward function value is significantly higher than that of the other two configurations, which indicates that the algorithm's overall performance has been improved.

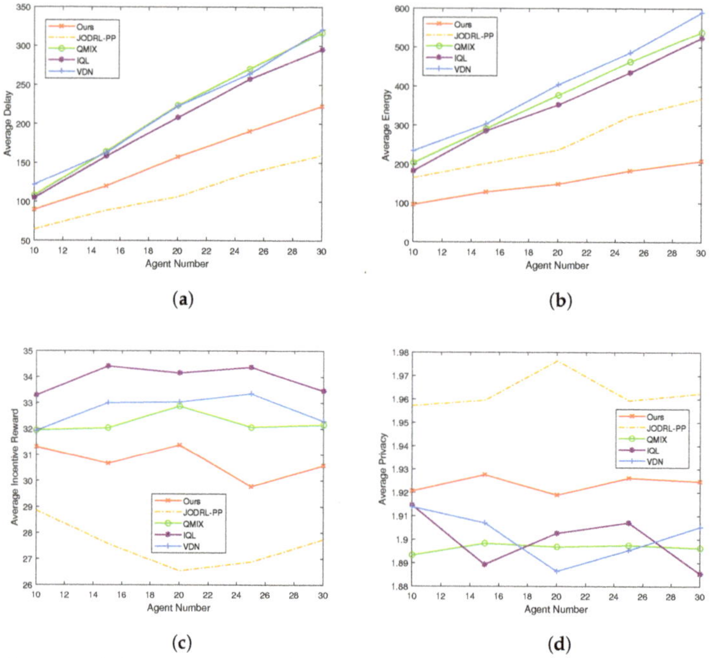

Figure 9. (**a**) Average processing delay comparison; (**b**) average energy consumption comparison; (**c**) average incentive reward comparison; (**d**) average privacy metric comparison for different agent scales.

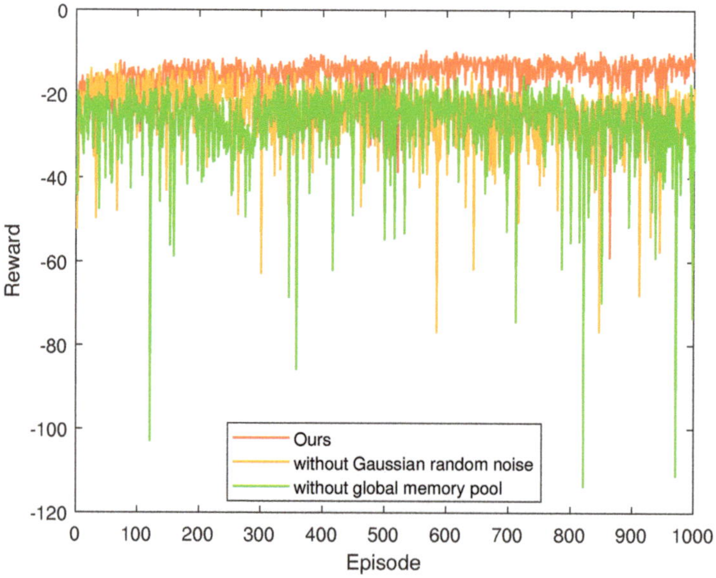

Figure 10. Reward function value iteration.

In addition, we compared the average rewards of different algorithm configurations through five repetitions of the experiment, as shown in Figure 11. From the figure, it can be seen that the average reward function value of the proposed algorithm possesses a significant advantage throughout the training cycle. The performance is improved by 38.36% and 43.59% compared to the schemes lacking Gaussian process action-space selection noise and global memory pool, respectively.

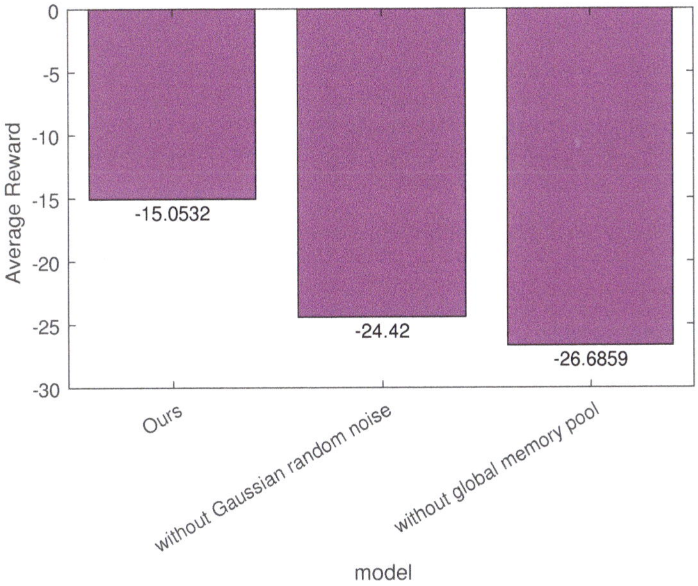

Figure 11. Average reward function value comparison.

According to the results of the ablation experiments, the introduction of Gaussian noise-based action-space search and global shared memeory pool significantly improved the algorithm's performance. These two improvements enhance the algorithm's ability to explore and utilize historical information, thus improving the learning efficiency and quality of the policy in the long run. This enhancement is significant in complex and dynamic environments, requiring the algorithm to adapt and discover new and better strategies quickly.

In summary, the proposed algorithm was analyzed and validated through many comparative experiments, and we demonstrated the advantages of the proposed algorithm over comparative algorithms in terms of global optimization objectives. Through ablation experiments, we analyzed the important role of Gaussian noise-based action-space search and global shared memory pooling. However, the proposed algorithm still has a disadvantage in calculating task processing delay cost.

7. Conclusions and Future Works

In this paper, we propose a blockchain-based MEC task offloading strategy based on multi-agent reinforcement learning that utilizes a global memory pool to enable each agent to acquire the experience of other agents during the training process in order to enhance the collaborative ability among agents and the overall performance of the system. Moreover, the algorithm introduces a search strategy based on decayable Gaussian random noise action space, improving the agents' search state space to avoid falling into the local optimum. In terms of the optimization objective function, this paper comprehensively considers cost factors such as task execution energy consumption, processing delay, user privacy metrics, and blockchain incentive rewards and innovatively proposes a blockchain-based MEC task-offloading model. The experimental results show that compared with other algorithms, the proposed algorithm improves the performance of the global optimization objective by more than 10% and has obvious advantages in energy consumption and blockchain incentive rewards. In addition, the ablation experiments show that the Gaussian process action-space selection noise and the global memory pool improve the performance by 38.36% and 43.59%, respectively.

However, this paper is subject to limitation in terms of problem modeling and algorithm design. Firstly, we only used the existing consensus mechanism and simplified incentive mechanism to simulate the execution process of blockchain on MEC, which still has a large deviation from the actual scenario. Secondly, we must consider more security elements of MEC task offloading in the model design. Thirdly, we still need to improve the algorithm's execution efficiency. Therefore, further research and optimization of problem modeling and algorithm design for blockchain-based MEC task offloading are important research directions for us in the future.

Author Contributions: C.L. developed the idea, performed research and analyses, and wrote the manuscript. Z.S. verified and revised the manuscript. All authors have read and agreed to the published version of the manuscript.

Funding: This work was funded by the National Natural Science Foundation of China (No. 62272239), the Postgraduate Research & Innovation Plan of Jiangsu Province (No. KYCX20_0761), and the Jiangsu Agriculture Science and Technology Innovation Fund (No. CX(22)1007).

Data Availability Statement: Data are contained within the article.

Acknowledgments: We wish to thank all code providers. We also wish to thank all colleagues, reviewers, and editors who provided valuable suggestions.

Conflicts of Interest: The authors declare no conflicts of interest.

References

1. Mao, Y.; You, C.; Zhang, J.; Huang, K.; Letaief, K.B. A Survey on Mobile Edge Computing: The Communication Perspective. *IEEE Commun. Surv. Tutor.* **2017**, *19*, 2322–2358. [CrossRef]
2. Qiu, H.; Zhu, K.; Luong, N.C.; Yi, C.; Niyato, D.; Kim, D.I. Applications of Auction and Mechanism Design in Edge Computing: A Survey. *IEEE Trans. Cogn. Commun. Netw.* **2022**, *8*, 1034–1058. [CrossRef]
3. Nakamoto, S. Bitcoin: A peer-to-peer electronic cash system. *Decentralized Bus. Rev.* **2008**, 21260. Available online: https://bitcoin.org/bitcoin.pdf (accessed on 14 July 2024).
4. Yu, R.; Oguti, A.M.; Obaidat, M.S.; Li, S.; Wang, P.; Hsiao, K.F. Blockchain-based solutions for mobile crowdsensing: A comprehensive survey. *Comput. Sci. Rev.* **2023**, *50*, 100589. [CrossRef]
5. Yang, R.; Yu, F.R.; Si, P.; Yang, Z.; Zhang, Y. Integrated Blockchain and Edge Computing Systems: A Survey, Some Research Issues and Challenges. *IEEE Commun. Surv. Tutor.* **2019**, *21*, 1508–1532. [CrossRef]
6. Wang, S.; Ye, D.; Huang, X.; Yu, R.; Wang, Y.; Zhang, Y. Consortium Blockchain for Secure Resource Sharing in Vehicular Edge Computing: A Contract-Based Approach. *IEEE Trans. Netw. Sci. Eng.* **2021**, *8*, 1189–1201. [CrossRef]
7. Aujla, G.S.; Singh, A.; Singh, M.; Sharma, S.; Kumar, N.; Choo, K.K.R. BloCkEd: Blockchain-Based Secure Data Processing Framework in Edge Envisioned V2X Environment. *IEEE Trans. Veh. Technol.* **2020**, *69*, 5850–5863. [CrossRef]
8. Liu, H.; Zhang, P.; Pu, G.; Yang, T.; Maharjan, S.; Zhang, Y. Blockchain Empowered Cooperative Authentication with Data Traceability in Vehicular Edge Computing. *IEEE Trans. Veh. Technol.* **2020**, *69*, 4221–4232. [CrossRef]
9. Lu, Y.; Tang, X.; Liu, L.; Yu, F.R.; Dustdar, S. Speeding at the Edge: An Efficient and Secure Redactable Blockchain for IoT-Based Smart Grid Systems. *IEEE Internet Things J.* **2023**, *10*, 12886–12897. [CrossRef]
10. Bao, Z.; Tang, C.; Lin, F.; Zheng, Z.; Yu, X. Rating-protocol optimization for blockchain-enabled hybrid energy trading in smart grids. *Sci. China Inf. Sci.* **2023**, *66*, 159205. [CrossRef]
11. Guan, Z.; Zhou, X.; Liu, P.; Wu, L.; Yang, W. A Blockchain-Based Dual-Side Privacy-Preserving Multiparty Computation Scheme for Edge-Enabled Smart Grid. *IEEE Internet Things J.* **2022**, *9*, 14287–14299. [CrossRef]
12. Li, Z.; Zhang, J.; Zhang, J.; Zheng, Y.; Zong, X. Integrated Edge Computing and Blockchain: A General Medical Data Sharing Framework. *IEEE Trans. Emerg. Top. Comput.* **2023**, 1–14. [CrossRef]
13. Sharma, D.; Kumar, R.; Jung, K.H. A bibliometric analysis of convergence of artificial intelligence and blockchain for edge of things. *J. Grid Comput.* **2023**, *21*, 79. [CrossRef]
14. Lin, Y.; Kang, J.; Niyato, D.; Gao, Z.; Wang, Q. Efficient Consensus and Elastic Resource Allocation Empowered Blockchain for Vehicular Networks. *IEEE Trans. Veh. Technol.* **2023**, *72*, 5513–5517. [CrossRef]
15. Zhang, X.; Zhu, X.; Chikuvanyanga, M.; Chen, M. Resource sharing of mobile edge computing networks based on auction game and blockchain. *EURASIP J. Adv. Signal Process.* **2021**, *2021*, 26. [CrossRef]
16. Xu, S.; Liao, B.; Yang, C.; Guo, S.; Hu, B.; Zhao, J.; Jin, L. Deep reinforcement learning assisted edge-terminal collaborative offloading algorithm of blockchain computing tasks for energy Internet. *Int. J. Electr. Power Energy Syst.* **2021**, *131*, 107022. [CrossRef]

17. Moghaddasi, K.; Rajabi, S.; Gharehchopogh, F.S. Multi-Objective Secure Task Offloading Strategy for Blockchain-Enabled IoV-MEC Systems: A Double Deep Q-Network Approach. *IEEE Access* **2024**, *12*, 3437–3463. [CrossRef]
18. Wu, H.; Wolter, K.; Jiao, P.; Deng, Y.; Zhao, Y.; Xu, M. EEDTO: An Energy-Efficient Dynamic Task Offloading Algorithm for Blockchain-Enabled IoT-Edge-Cloud Orchestrated Computing. *IEEE Internet Things J.* **2021**, *8*, 2163–2176. [CrossRef]
19. Nguyen, D.C.; Pathirana, P.N.; Ding, M.; Seneviratne, A. Privacy-Preserved Task Offloading in Mobile Blockchain with Deep Reinforcement Learning. *IEEE Trans. Netw. Serv. Manag.* **2020**, *17*, 2536–2549. [CrossRef]
20. Le, Y.; Ling, X.; Wang, J.; Guo, R.; Huang, Y.; Wang, C.X.; You, X. Resource Sharing and Trading of Blockchain Radio Access Networks: Architecture and Prototype Design. *IEEE Internet Things J.* **2023**, *10*, 12025–12043. [CrossRef]
21. Salim, M.M.; Pan, Y.; Park, J.H. Energy-efficient resource allocation in blockchain-based Cybertwin-driven 6G. *J. Ambient. Intell. Humaniz. Comput.* **2024**, *15*, 103–114. [CrossRef]
22. Sun, W.; Liu, J.; Yue, Y.; Wang, P. Joint Resource Allocation and Incentive Design for Blockchain-Based Mobile Edge Computing. *IEEE Trans. Wirel. Commun.* **2020**, *19*, 6050–6064. [CrossRef]
23. Ding, J.; Han, L.; Li, J.; Zhang, D. Resource allocation strategy for blockchain-enabled NOMA-based MEC networks. *J. Cloud Comput.* **2023**, *12*, 142. [CrossRef]
24. Zhang, L.; Zou, Y.; Wang, W.; Jin, Z.; Su, Y.; Chen, H. Resource allocation and trust computing for blockchain-enabled edge computing system. *Comput. Secur.* **2021**, *105*, 102249. [CrossRef]
25. Baranwal, G.; Kumar, D.; Vidyarthi, D.P. Blockchain based resource allocation in cloud and distributed edge computing: A survey. *Comput. Commun.* **2023**, *209*, 469–498. [CrossRef]
26. Xue, H.; Chen, D.; Zhang, N.; Dai, H.N.; Yu, K. Integration of blockchain and edge computing in internet of things: A survey. *Future Gener. Comput. Syst.* **2023**, *144*, 307–326. [CrossRef]
27. Liu, X. Towards blockchain-based resource allocation models for cloud-edge computing in IoT applications. *Wirel. Pers. Commun.* **2021**, *135*, 2483. [CrossRef]
28. Guo, S.; Dai, Y.; Guo, S.; Qiu, X.; Qi, F. Blockchain Meets Edge Computing: Stackelberg Game and Double Auction Based Task Offloading for Mobile Blockchain. *IEEE Trans. Veh. Technol.* **2020**, *69*, 5549–5561. [CrossRef]
29. Devi, I.; Karpagam, G.R. Energy-Aware Scheduling for Tasks with Target-Time in Blockchain based Data Centres. *Comput. Syst. Sci. Eng.* **2022**, *40*, 405–419. [CrossRef]
30. Xiong, J.; Guo, P.; Wang, Y.; Meng, X.; Zhang, J.; Qian, L.; Yu, Z. Multi-agent deep reinforcement learning for task offloading in group distributed manufacturing systems. *Eng. Appl. Artif. Intell.* **2023**, *118*, 105710. [CrossRef]
31. Lu, K.; Li, R.D.; Li, M.C.; Xu, G.R. MADDPG-based joint optimization of task partitioning and computation resource allocation in mobile edge computing. *Neural Comput. Appl.* **2023**, *35*, 16559–16576. [CrossRef]
32. Li, K.; Wang, X.; He, Q.; Yang, M.; Huang, M.; Dustdar, S. Task Computation Offloading for Multi-Access Edge Computing via Attention Communication Deep Reinforcement Learning. *IEEE Trans. Serv. Comput.* **2023**, *16*, 2985–2999. [CrossRef]
33. Wu, G.; Chen, X.; Gao, Z.; Zhang, H.; Yu, S.; Shen, S. Privacy-preserving offloading scheme in multi-access mobile edge computing based on MADRL. *J. Parallel Distrib. Comput.* **2024**, *183*, 104775. [CrossRef]
34. Yang, L.; Li, M.; Si, P.; Yang, R.; Sun, E.; Zhang, Y. Energy-Efficient Resource Allocation for Blockchain-Enabled Industrial Internet of Things with Deep Reinforcement Learning. *IEEE Internet Things J.* **2021**, *8*, 2318–2329. [CrossRef]
35. Nguyen, D.C.; Ding, M.; Pathirana, P.N.; Seneviratne, A.; Li, J.; Poor, H.V. Cooperative Task Offloading and Block Mining in Blockchain-Based Edge Computing with Multi-Agent Deep Reinforcement Learning. *IEEE Trans. Mob. Comput.* **2023**, *22*, 2021–2037. [CrossRef]
36. Yao, S.; Wang, M.; Qu, Q.; Zhang, Z.; Zhang, Y.F.; Xu, K.; Xu, M. Blockchain-Empowered Collaborative Task Offloading for Cloud-Edge-Device Computing. *IEEE J. Sel. Areas Commun.* **2022**, *40*, 3485–3500. [CrossRef]
37. Wang, C.; Jiang, C.; Wang, J.; Shen, S.; Guo, S.; Zhang, P. Blockchain-Aided Network Resource Orchestration in Intelligent Internet of Things. *IEEE Internet Things J.* **2023**, *10*, 6151–6163. [CrossRef]
38. Du, Y.; Wang, Z.; Li, J.; Shi, L.; Jayakody, D.N.K.; Chen, Q.; Chen, W.; Han, Z. Blockchain-Aided Edge Computing Market: Smart Contract and Consensus Mechanisms. *IEEE Trans. Mob. Comput.* **2023**, *22*, 3193–3208. [CrossRef]
39. Kaur, M.; Khan, M.Z.; Gupta, S.; Noorwali, A.; Chakraborty, C.; Pani, S.K. MBCP: Performance Analysis of Large Scale Mainstream Blockchain Consensus Protocols. *IEEE Access* **2021**, *9*, 80931–80944. [CrossRef]
40. Liang, L.; Kim, J.; Jha, S.C.; Sivanesan, K.; Li, G.Y. Spectrum and Power Allocation for Vehicular Communications with Delayed CSI Feedback. *IEEE Wirel. Commun. Lett.* **2017**, *6*, 458–461. [CrossRef]
41. Xu, X.; Liu, X.; Yin, X.; Wang, S.; Qi, Q.; Qi, L. Privacy-aware offloading for training tasks of generative adversarial network in edge computing. *Inf. Sci.* **2020**, *532*, 1–15. [CrossRef]
42. Chen, X. Decentralized Computation Offloading Game for Mobile Cloud Computing. *IEEE Trans. Parallel Distrib. Syst.* **2015**, *26*, 974–983. [CrossRef]
43. Huang, X.; Zhang, B.; Li, C. Incentive Mechanisms for Mobile Edge Computing: Present and Future Directions. *IEEE Netw.* **2022**, *36*, 199–205. [CrossRef]
44. Xu, Y.; Zhang, H.; Li, X.; Yu, F.R.; Ji, H.; Leung, V.C.M. Blockchain-Based Edge Collaboration with Incentive Mechanism for MEC-Enabled VR Systems. *IEEE Trans. Wirel. Commun.* **2024**, *23*, 3706–3720. [CrossRef]
45. Gao, Q.; Xiao, J.; Cao, Y.; Deng, S.; Ouyang, C.; Feng, Z. Blockchain-based collaborative edge computing: Efficiency, incentive and trust. *J. Cloud Comput.* **2023**, *12*, 72. [CrossRef]

46. Li, X.; Liu, S.; Wu, F.; Kumari, S.; Rodrigues, J.J.P.C. Privacy Preserving Data Aggregation Scheme for Mobile Edge Computing Assisted IoT Applications. *IEEE Internet Things J.* **2019**, *6*, 4755–4763. [CrossRef]
47. Xu, X.; He, C.; Xu, Z.; Qi, L.; Wan, S.; Bhuiyan, M.Z.A. Joint Optimization of Offloading Utility and Privacy for Edge Computing Enabled IoT. *IEEE Internet Things J.* **2020**, *7*, 2622–2629. [CrossRef]
48. Tampuu, A.; Matiisen, T.; Kodelja, D.; Kuzovkin, I.; Korjus, K.; Aru, J.; Aru, J.; Vicente, R. Multiagent cooperation and competition with deep reinforcement learning. *PLoS ONE* **2017**, *12*, e0172395. [CrossRef]
49. Rashid, T.; Samvelyan, M.; de Witt, C.S.; Farquhar, G.; Foerster, J.; Whiteson, S. Monotonic Value Function Factorisation for Deep Multi-Agent Reinforcement Learning. *J. Mach. Learn. Res.* **2020**, *21*, 1–51.
50. Sunehag, P.; Lever, G.; Gruslys, A.; Czarnecki, W.M.; Zambaldi, V.F.; Jaderberg, M.; Lanctot, M.; Sonnerat, N.; Leibo, J.Z.; Tuyls, K.; et al. Value-Decomposition Networks For Cooperative Multi-Agent Learning. *arXiv* **2017**, arXiv:1706.05296.

Disclaimer/Publisher's Note: The statements, opinions and data contained in all publications are solely those of the individual author(s) and contributor(s) and not of MDPI and/or the editor(s). MDPI and/or the editor(s) disclaim responsibility for any injury to people or property resulting from any ideas, methods, instructions or products referred to in the content.

MDPI AG
Grosspeteranlage 5
4052 Basel
Switzerland
Tel.: +41 61 683 77 34

Mathematics Editorial Office
E-mail: mathematics@mdpi.com
www.mdpi.com/journal/mathematics

Disclaimer/Publisher's Note: The statements, opinions and data contained in all publications are solely those of the individual author(s) and contributor(s) and not of MDPI and/or the editor(s). MDPI and/or the editor(s) disclaim responsibility for any injury to people or property resulting from any ideas, methods, instructions or products referred to in the content.